EDUCATION

IN THESE
UNITED STATES

EDUCATION

IN THESE

UNITED STATES

Ellis Ford HARTFORD

The Macmillan Company, New York
Collier-Macmillan Limited, London

First Printing

Library of Congress catalog card number:
64-14036

The Macmillan Company, New York
Collier-Macmillan Canada, Ltd., Toronto, Ontario

Printed in the United States of America

PREFACE

Every American who expects to live into the Space Age as a free self–realizing person, needs to make better use of the educational opportunity afforded by this great nation for all its people. This requires an understanding of American education—its character, its distinctive contributions to individual development and to national well–being, and to its vital role in our scientific and technological progress. It is clear that all Americans are now coming to rely upon education as the key to opportunity much as our forefathers valued free land somewhere to the west. Education, especially that of common schools, is vitally related to the lives of everyone—students, parents, taxpayers, office–holders, teachers, administrators, and professors. Popular understanding of this aspect of American life —basic component of both our historic past and of our potential future—must be improved in breadth and in depth. This suggests that a study of education in American society should become a part of the general education of all who expect to become adult participants in our democracy.

Education in These United States has been written to serve the needs of those who undertake that study early in their college experience. It is designed as a textbook for use in general education and in the pre–professional courses provided by most institutions that offer teacher education programs. The content is prin-cipally from the areas known as foundations of education and the organization has been planned to facilitate the integration of materials from the component fields into profound understandings of their significance and meaning. Those who will be the parents of the next generation may find here a background for appreciation of and interest in the educational enterprise upon which our institutions and values depend. Among these groups of students will be those who will choose to become teachers of the children from future American homes. All future adults, who will be parents and teachers, cannot begin too early to learn to share insights into and appreciations of the educational enterprise in these United States.

The future community leader should have a working definition of what education is, a clear concept of how it is related to our society, and an appreciation of the diverse agencies and influences that are concerned with education. All this is clearly preamble to any adequate conception of the role of the school in this democratic society of ours.

Appreciations of the story of education in American democracy, the varied development of the common school, the organization and support of public school systems, and current trends in democratic education are further significant insights and understandings for those who would teach our children. A clear concept of learning outcomes and how people really

v

learn should be a normative aspect of the preparation for those who will have the tasks of aiding and guiding learners in our culture. Future parents and teachers should develop a philosophy of education that is constructively and consistently related to our democratic society and to the values of our way of life. Understanding of and ability to work with people, especially the acceptance of children, is an indispensable prerequisite for those who will be parents, teachers, or school administrators.

Those who want to be career teachers will learn the nature of the teachers' responsibilities in the company of those who will work later with them in PTA and community activities. Future teachers and parents will find help in looking at the opportunities and challenges of teaching, choice of career, and planning one's program of education. Students are challenged to take control of their own educational progress and to use every form of experience for maximum benefits and returns. Students should gain from this study clearer purposes and goals to be pursued and achieved in such future related courses as cultural anthropology, cultural history, human growth and development, educational psychology, educational sociology, philosophy, social psychology.

This introductory textbook is significant only to the extent that it measures up to an occasion and deals with content of grave significance in American education. That occasion is the chronic inadequacy of support for our schools and colleges. The area of need is indicated by the continuing shortage in the supply of educated medical, scientific, techno-logical, and teaching personnel required by our institutions during the Space Age Sixties and the Seventies when our very way of life will be tried as never before in our history.

The orientation of a great many capable future leaders has never been more important than now. Education has proved to be strategically important to our democracy in a disordered postwar world in which America has performed an unprecedented role in contributions and leadership. Distinctive developments in the scientific and technological fields leading to peacetime uses of nuclear energy, various international recovery and aid programs, and the Peace Corps all reflect the strategic importance of high-quality education and research in today's world. Leadership in America's communities and at the fifty states' levels is just as important to the development of the full potential of all our people for significant living and achievement in the age that already has several unprecedented labels (Atomic, Nuclear, Space, Tranquilizers). This is the occasion and the setting for which a significant and high-quality general education should be made available for college youth who will be the parents and the specialized experts and the teachers of tomorrow. So much, then, for the timeliness and possible significance of a book designed for the purpose of assisting future leaders to basic understandings of American education as it relates to individual development and national wellbeing in our time.

The merits and worth of a textbook devoted to the orientation of future leaders must certainly be evaluated in terms of the purposes and philosophy upon which it is based. These may be briefly presented. The whole progress of one's education for teaching depends upon the person—what he is, does, experiences, and learns. The student is the answer, and the key whether he knows it now or discovers it in some later experience of his life. This book and the companion guide have been designed to help each student to work out his own *orientation* to education.

Students who use this book will find useful the companion volume, entitled *Education in Your Future*. This is an individual guidebook arranged in units to fit the six parts of *Education in These United States*. It provides an abundant choice of instructional materials, activities, and suggestions for instructors and students. Each unit includes bibliographies, glossaries, suggestions for individual study and for group projects, questions for discussion and thought, space for a variety of notes, miscellaneous materials and self–evaluation exercises. The student will be able to develop and keep his own book upon American education during the course, choosing and using from among the wide variety of materials in the guidebook. Instructors will find the guide a great convenience in teaching the course, particularly in efforts to serve the interests and needs of individual students. All will recognize the importance of the student's own activity and participation in terms of his achievement and growth from the experience served by these two books.

Much emphasis has been placed upon activity; students really learn by having experiences, by doing something, and noting the result. The ability to be conscious, to see and know what goes on, to evaluate or judge results, and to use the benefits or findings of that experience in later and better experiences are what make each of us a human being. The degree and quality of the meanings which one derives from experience indicate much about the kind of person one has become. This means that students who have aptitude and who go about it seriously, can make themselves effective and capable participants in a specialized field of competence and in community life as well as an interesting, responsible person. We may consider this as a desirable outcome of general education, one devoutly to be desired.

NOTE TO INSTRUCTORS

Lack of experience of students presents one of the fundamental problems faced by the teacher of the course in orientation to education. Beginning students frequently do not have the experiences and background to appreciate the kind of textbook materials usually provided for their use. It is difficult for them to visualize in terms of a parent's concerns or of the teacher's work the sort of questions which are often discussed in the class sessions. They need to have enough experiences of sufficient variety to enable them to understand what is meant or involved in the school situations, the examples cited, and by the terminology used in educational literature.

It is suggested that the orientation course be developed to meet this fundamental need of the students. Many activities and experiences should be provided from and through which the students will gain the needed background to understand the material which is presented in the subject matter of this course. In this book numerous suggestions have been made for this purpose.

Much help may be derived from extensive additional reading by the students as they acquire the proper background to give it meaning. Numerous suggestions for reading and use of current materials have been made in bibliographies for the chapters. It may be a good idea to assemble a reference shelf. The class and/ or the campus SNEA chapter could benefit from a project devoted to the assembling and arranging of such a worksheet.

Pertinent audio-visual materials appropriate for use with various chapters have been listed in the follow up material for each of the six parts of the book. Instructors and class groups will find ample opportunity for individuals to choose topics for research or further study and for committees and groups to select different problems and projects for investigation and reporting. Use of the companion guidebook, *Education in Your Future,* will provide a convenient means of focusing both individual and group work upon the content of the course.

ACKNOWLEDGMENTS

Grateful acknowledgment is made to all who have made contributions to the work of the author. The many publishers who have courteously granted permission to quote from publications have been credited in appropriate footnotes. Picture credits have been noted as they appear in the various chapters. Sincere thanks are due to those professionals who give generous aid in the matter of procuring pictures of actual schools in operation, particularly Miss Vera C. Freid, Cincinnati Public Schools; Mr. Don E. Matthews, Dallas Independent School District; Mr. Thomas O. Sinks, Principal, Nichols Junior High School, Evanston Community Consolidated Schools, District #65, Cook County, Evanston, Illinois; Dr. Lloyd S. Michael, Superintendent and Principal, Evanston Township High School; Mr. B. L. Lovenstein, Superintendent, Kanawha County Public Schools, Charleston, West Virginia; Dr. John E. Ridgway, Superintendent, Lexington (Kentucky) Public Schools; Dr. Paul Sparks, Assistant Superintendent, Louisville Public Schools, and Mr. John Wredling, Superintendent, St. Charles (Illinois) Schools, District #303. Officials of the National Aeronautics and Space Administration (Office of Public Information) and of the Peace Corps rendered valuable assistance in supplying recent photographs and informational materials. Mrs. William Hume deserves an especial note of gratitude for executing preliminary sketches from which most of the drawings were made. A grateful acknowledgment of faithful help is due Mrs. Lurid Gulley who carried most of the burden of typing the manuscript. The help of the many friends, former students and professional colleagues who have inadvertently or deliberately rendered assistance through discussion of ideas, encouraging words, and constructive criticism is gratefully acknowledged. The encouragement of my family through a long period of concentrated work has sustained and supported my efforts beyond the telling.

ELLIS FORD HARTFORD
Lexington, Kentucky

CONTENTS

II. PATTERN · Of Unity and Diversity

III. PROGRAM · A Ladder of Opportunity

IV. PEOPLE · All the Children of All the·People

V. PROFESSION · The Cause of Education

VI. PROSPECT

CHARTS

TABLES

Introduction

Education in an Age
of Challenge

Challenges and responses are a fundamental aspect of life. The course of life has been characterized as a series of challenges and responses of great number and variety. Individual lives exhibit this phenomenon in the form of major threats and of opportunities to be met and realized respectively through appropriate efforts. The history of civilizations yields evidence of this phenomenon, a succession of challenges and efforts to cope with them fills the records of mankind.

A book upon any serious subject that has relevance to the times and people should take into account the challenges that are faced. Any treatment of education in our times should begin with an orientation to the concerns and aspirations of the people, the compelling problems and potentials of their societies, and the imperatives that relate to their future. This generation of Americans and the peoples of every continent are confronted by unprecedented challenges, which should permeate the content of education and be given top priority in educational plans and programs.

A catalog of crises

This generation of mankind must learn to appreciate the nature of the age in which it lives and strives to achieve its destiny. The primary understanding must be that men live in the very shadow of catastrophe. The word *crisis* is too commonplace, and *challenge* is too polite. Nothing short of letters of living fire such as Moses envisioned on Mount Sinai could fully delineate the major lessons that whole nations must learn quickly. There is no adequate word for the ambivalent crisis-situation that encompasses the human race even as it enters the first stages of the Space Age.

History records many crises and catastrophes, some of which marked the end of their civilizations, but it has no precedents for the contemporary standoff, or cold war, now precariously maintained because of mutual certainty of annihilation. Indeed history counts twenty-odd major civilizations that developed, flourished, and disappeared for lack of capacity to respond to challenges that occurred and recurred in various forms. The recorded efforts of civilizations and peoples to cope with famine, flood, pestilence, aggression, treachery, witchcraft, slavery, tyranny, bigotry, crime and novel weapons of warfare clearly yield no answers for the tense world leadership of the Space Age Sixties.

What of this unprecedented era of perils and promise that gives perceptive

1

men the shivers of mixed anticipation and dread? Mankind has lived nearly two decades with the knowledge of the destructive atomic bomb as well as nuclear fission, which is a potential source of energy for peacetime uses. More than half of that time people have contemplated the graver horrors of the thermonuclear bomb made graphic and real by the Geiger-counted residues from fallout following atmospheric testing of weapons of unprecedented power. Added to these have been reports and rumors of such further refinements of the arts and sciences of destruction as germ warfare, nerve gas, "clean" bombs, and a potential cobalt bomb deadly beyond imagination. Human capacities for concern are overloaded and overwhelmed. Diplomats expended years of effort before the limited test-ban treaty could be negotiated. A series of prolonged conferences on disarmament have been disappointing. Meanwhile, the cheerless cold war continues. This is but one aspect of the threat to the future of humanity. There are others of baleful significance, grave threats to human dignity and freedom, but the "Big Bang" takes precedence in its impact upon the aspirations and plans of men.

In the divided world situation there are no sound grounds for efforts to minimize the threats of annihilation, but this is not the only major concern that all intelligent persons should recognize. The catalog of prospects calculated to cause nightmares must be extended to include others less immediate but no less disastrous in consequences for human life and civilization. A leading candidate for our major long-range threat is the spectre of overpopulation. Overpopulation is already the basic problem in many areas of the globe; the resulting pressures even now complicate the economic problems and international relationships of a tense world community of nations. There are difficult problems to be solved and hard lessons to be learned by the peoples of the world about overpopulation, while the time for this educational experience grows short.

A modern Cassandra would be needed to descry the major threats to the future of humankind that must be anticipated by sound education and policy-making. Ability to appreciate some of these depends upon adequate scientific knowledge. A number of scientists recognize the basic problems that follow from the prospective depletion of certain irreplaceable resources. Equally significant portents of disaster can be discerned in the destruction of nature's balance among life forms in various environments. Chains of consequences that follow destruction of wild life can lead to disaster. Those who have read the book, *Silent Spring,* have an example to contemplate, as the destruction of birds by insecticides used indiscriminately leads to increased ravages by insects. The prospect of an insect-riddled globe with no green leaf or blade remaining is the ultimate end of that chain of consequences. Destruction of nature's balance in fresh-water systems of lakes and streams brings other perils as do problems of pollution of coastal areas and waters. Grave problems have been caused by the denudation of the natural cover of lands, by lowering of the water table in many areas of the country and by unsound practice of land use that threaten the long-time growth of the nation. The catalog of problems reported from reputable scientific and scholarly sources is longer. It is time that the content of education gave adequate space and attention to these challenges.

The contemporary troubled world scene poses further threats to the freedoms of men that must be recognized for what they are, the end of opportunity for individual aspirations and purpose. Inherent in the cold war alignment is the conflict between two ways of life based on different concepts of people: one a society of free self-realizing individuals who can and will cooperate for the common good while each is regarded as worthy and unique, *versus* the view that human beings are units in and of the state, valuable insofar as they further the ends and decisions of the social order that controls all aspects of living. This is an old struggle. Many manifestations of this tension show in history. Conflicts between different totalitarian powers have also taken much space in the histories of mankind. Those who recognize the significance of *1984* will have some insight into a potential threat that should be known and dreaded by all who wish to remain free men. The police state complete with programs for rewriting history to support the opportunistic policies of those in power, close surveillance of individual behavior through modern detection devices, use of indoctrination techniques like brainwashing and double think are not fantasies in the mind of a perceptive novelist. Most of these techniques have already been utilized in some form and degree in most totalitarian regimes.

Some potentials for progress

Dire predictions and prospects of doom are not final although the margin of escape is narrow. There is another side to the crisis-situation that can be exam-ined and interpreted to support a more optimistic prospect for humankind in the years ahead. Potentials for increased productivity, better living, international peace, scientific progress, and human happiness are substantial enough to appear entrancing if there is opportunity for their realization.

It is possible to identify some of the unrealized potentials for constructive growth and harmonious human relationships in the next century. Atomic energy can be devoted to myriad peacetime uses for power, transportation, industry, research and testing, medical therapy and scores of applications yet to be discovered. A mere start has been made upon the possibilities for constructive use of nuclear fission in the service of mankind. Other fabulous discoveries such as laser may prove to have uses that make possible still other developments and applications. The industries of the civilized world are being remade by automatic processes and equipment undreamed of a few decades back; changes that have lightened the labor of millions of workers. Although the potentials for a reduced working force and labor-saving have materialized to a large degree, the opportunity for wise utilization of leisure time and qualitative living has rarely been realized. Extensive automatized and computing installations are revolutionizing office, warehouse, shipping, and many routine operations in business and commerce. Giant computers have become necessities for major concerns, government agencies, universities, and research institutions, all of which have grown tremendously in recent years. Homemaking has been materially changed thanks to modern equipment, air conditioning and other developments. All of which spells new freedoms for people—from backbreaking labor, from harsh working conditions, from sweat and physical fatigue, and the like. The question is whether there has been a complementary freeing of the human spirit, the direction of human energies and interests into constructive and productive channels. This is one of the largely unrealized potentialities of the Age of Automation now upon us.

The ageless spectre of scarcity, ever a part of human tradition, has been supplanted in certain economies by the fantastic phenomenon of overproduction and a promise of potential plenty. Large-scale shifts and changes must be expected in family patterns and personal living with the advent of surplus foods, abundance of consumer goods, and the controlled production of many commodities and products. This phenomenon appears on a modest sized globe that presents vast pictures of human misery and want, a fact that strongly supports educational efforts and emphases upon policies of population control, improved living standards, and the use of resources for human needs rather than armaments. The age of plenty will not dawn suddenly upon all human beings around the world, its achievement will depend upon comprehensive programs of reforms, education, and hard work. The problems are complicated by the existence of many vested interests, including certain religious sanctions, and the extreme conservatism of peoples held back by illiteracy and ignorance. The time must soon come when the need for intelligent communication will be possible among all the people of the world through the printed as well as the spoken word. The potential positive force now lost through the low living standards of illiterate millions could make a great difference in achieving the goals related to building a peaceful world.

The recognition of human rights in the United Nations *Declaration* was a great step forward; it will take supreme efforts to implement their achievement, but there is no alternative. "Fundamental education" as developed and tried out by UNESCO represents a promising idea and a mere beginning. Methods of mass attack upon illiteracy have been demonstrated but the big job of carrying out massive programs is yet to be undertaken.

In recent decades the conquest of many diseases and health hazards has been rapid and spectacular. One of the brightest pages in modern history records the efforts to find causes and controls for the major diseases and afflictions that threaten human life. Many accomplishments and developments give support to the faith that research will find ways to cope with the killer diseases and to prolong active life. These desirable developments will usher in further problems of how and of how well people will use their added years of living.

All societies experience growing pains during periods of marked expansion and different problems related to the loss of opportunity when physical growth ends and pressures begin to build up. The disappearance of the physical frontier in America marked the emergence of many economic and social changes. The lack of free land, so prominent in a century and more of American history, required adjustments and changes in many aspects of the culture.

In recent decades new frontiers have been discovered and pioneers have found the zest and thrills of discovery in laboratories, research programs, inventions, creative work of many kinds, and in cooperating with significant movements in other countries. The Fifties marked the start of the greatest of the new frontiers. Researches of the Atomic Energy Commission, the National Science Foundation, and the National Institutes of Health brought investigators into new posts devoted to discovery and development. The National Aeronautics and Space Administration was established to develop and conduct America's programs for the exploration of space. This has resulted in a remarkable series of achievements culminating in "Project Mercury" during 1962 and 1963 with orbital flights by the new heroes of the American people—the original astronauts. Other projects designed to effect exploration of the moon, the planets, and into deep space will follow. The prospect defies description; to live in such an age should be a privilege. This promise of participation in an age of new discoveries and developments should be included in the challenges presented through educational programs for our times.

Some barriers to action

Although thoughtful students of human affairs have raised questions and urged action upon most of the critical situations that threaten civilization their solution is nowhere in sight. Evidence of this is unmistakable; one can buy books about most of the crisis-situations at any adequate bookstore. Clearly something more than the warning words of the scientists and scholars is necessary to the development of policies and action such as will be required.

We know something of the conservatism of people who find old ways best,

who dread the prospect of facing the unknown and the unfamiliar prospect, especially if sustained thinking is involved. It is evident that the vested interests are willing to take the short-term view for the sake of profits, the desire for an expanding economy, promise of steady employment, or some other economic benefit. This is the limited perspective of the strip miner, the crude "cut-and-slash" lumberman and other irresponsible users of the resources base that must support most of our economy. A great many people abhor change of any kind for reasons of emotional security. Traditional religious and cultural forces resist innovations and changes that run counter to the dogmas and practices that have come to be traditional and revered. History suggests that the masses of people will go to great lengths to avoid thinking. This reluctance leaves the "thinking-through" function to the leaders who may use the opportunity to make decisions without adequate study and rational thought upon policy. The opportunity to select leaders may be ill-used by the electorate, frequently being decided upon bases little beyond a popularity contest or a response to the performance of an entertainer. In other instances and places, leadership is attained through such practices as privilege, pull, party power struggle, and even by forceful means. Mankind continues to pay a dear price for the privilege of refusing to think through the imperative problems and sound policies for their solution. Were this the last word there would be little use to finish this book or to take further time to discuss the apparent dilemma.

The current occasion may be different; perhaps the fact that this crisis is novel in the history of mankind will make a difference in the response of modern civilizations and of people in general. This time the crisis is evident and the stakes are survival. In atomic warfare no one can expect a victory; all peoples can expect incalculable losses including most of what we call civilization. Should there be time and intelligent study there is the chance that people can learn to see and understand the threat of annihilation. This is the one chance that men and civilizations have to avoid catastrophe.

Potentials for growth and action

Consideration of the crisis-situation of the times must lead to review of the alternative courses of action that must be considered. One obvious policy is that of assigning greater responsibility to education to teach the realities and alternatives related to the crises we face. An appropriate intermediate step might consider the potential strengths and abilities that have not been fully utilized and realized. There are some possibilities for more effective educational policies and performance if ways to develop and use certain positive abilities and practices can be found.

Man is an educable being. Under normal circumstances, people can learn what is needed and what is interesting to them. Most people do not approach the achievement of their potential for learning and reasoning. The typical person does not utilize more than a fraction of his brainpower. An educational policy and program adequate to the imperative needs of the Space Age could be planned and implemented if human beings could be challenged to realize a greater use of their potential for learning and thinking.

An adequate educational program should foster and benefit from wider understanding and practice of techniques related to mental health. People can learn to understand themselves better, to develop an improved self-image, to make reasonable demands on themselves, to achieve a larger measure of self-direction, to appreciate others and their self-needs, to follow empathic insights, and to seek positive human relationships. The goal is personality growth and more responsible behavior in our social groups and relations.

Education for the times must teach the processes, and emphasize the practice, of reflective thinking. A number of promising experiments and studies are available to parents and teachers who will concern themselves with the improvement of the educational experience of learners. There are possibilities for emphases upon "creativity" as an educational outcome of highest significance. The emphases upon reflective thinking and creativity deserve high priority and support by all who look for an educational effort adequate to meet contemporary challenges.

A potential source of strength inheres in the thinking and constructive leadership of certain perceptive individuals and groups who address themselves to the imperative issues and needs of the times. Examples would be the considered statements of an association of atomic scientists, the reflections of philosophical-minded scientists, for example, Julian Huxley, upon the future prospects of humankind, the demonstration of constructive diplomacy in the interest of peace-making by men such as Ralph Bunche, the popular response even across the iron curtain to the work of creative artists, the views of statesmen of great vision and perspective in widely separated nations, as demonstrated by U Nu, of Burma, David Ben-Gurion, of Israel, and Adlai Stevenson, of the United States, and the challenging pronouncements of many spiritual leaders, from the World Council of Churches to the provocative encyclical *Pacem in Terris* by the beloved Pope John XXIII. The challenging *Declaration of Human Rights* of the United Nations represents a clarion call to peoples everywhere. There have been notable constructive efforts to make ideas work in the service of humanity. The record shows exciting instances of voluntary assistance from people in one country to those in another, apart from official foreign-aid programs. Educational exchanges of students and scholars and the "fundamental education" approach as demonstrated by UNESCO offer encouragement to those who hope for peace and international good will. Efforts of various individuals and groups to devise and strengthen international agreements, and machinery designed to keep the peace on a global scale, must continue to elicit the support of thoughtful persons everywhere.

A compelling need of the times is: How can the moral and ethical imperatives of the past be restated and/or revised to serve the vital needs of people and human relationships today? This is a challenge of the profoundest nature and significance for the civilized leadership of mankind. An effort on the part of any significant portion of the world's leadership to address itself to this task-plus-opportunity would represent a source of potential strength of incalculable value. Deliberations upon questions of this nature and significance should have priority upon the agenda of international convocations and organizations from the East-West Conference on Philosophy to the United Nations Organization.

Evidences that the barriers of the cold-war alignment and the traditional dichotomies of Eastern and Western cultural traditions may be crossed or bridged are available in recent intellectual and scientific advances. The International Geophysical Year 1957–1958, in which scientists and scientific groups around the globe cooperated in unprecedented research and exploration programs and communicated their findings despite cultural, ideological, and national differences, represents a prime example. Apparently the top-ranking scientists of many fields are able to appreciate and accept the work of their colleagues without too much difficulty. For example, the mathematicians and scientists behind the iron curtain can verify and utilize the concepts, formulas, and theories of the great Albert Einstein and communicate with their colleagues on an international scale. Cooperation of this nature, involving concepts and ideas that can be universally accepted as true, can be the means of building a tradition of international communication about other related matters and issues to the mutual benefit of all peoples. It seems reasonable to expect that scientists who universally accept and use the formula $E = mc^2$ can discover the need to share their research findings and concern about radioactive fallout hazards and other problems that threaten humankind. The probability that the governments and councils of men may come to respect the findings and warnings of the scientific and scholarly groups is more than a vain hope. By some such means, there might come to pass an era of international relationships characterized by greater reliance upon rational

PROJECT MERCURY

John H. Glenn, Jr.
3 orbits, Feb. 20, 1962
4 hrs. 55 mins. in space

L. Gordon Cooper, Jr.
22 orbits, May 15-16, 1963
34 hrs. 20 mins. in space

M. Scott Carpenter
3 orbits, May 24, 1962
4 hrs. 56 mins. in space

Walter Schirra, Jr.
6 orbits, Oct. 3, 1962
9 hrs. 13 mins. in space

A step into the Space Age (photographs courtesy NASA).

policies developed in the light of universally accepted facts and concepts. There have been historical instances of traditional conflicts between Christians and Moslems, Catholics and Protestants, and groups with other differences that have been supplanted by other kinds of relationships, both continuing to exist with their differences in religion and cultural values. The chance that a pluralistic world community of nations could learn to cooperate upon matters of mutual concern without threat to their respective cultural values and commitments is a prospect that may depend upon the growth of a new tradition in communication and common understandings. The abstract ideas and concepts of mathematics and scientific fields may represent the content of that new development.

There is ground for encouragement from certain new developments that exemplify constructive contributions of education. Achievements of the National Aeronautics and Space Administration's Project Mercury and the unparalleled performance of the original astronauts indicate the potential that inheres in high-quality scientific and technological education. The personal lives, the nature and quality of the interests, and the ethical standards of the astronauts suggest that the intellectual and spiritual aspects of their educational experiences were both qualitative and effective. It is good fortune that the pioneers in space exploration have given young Americans a new set of heroes, worthy examples in all aspects of living.

Another heartening development has been the growing accomplishments of the Peace Corps since 1960. An idealistic venture calculated to appeal to youth will-

ing to give service in the interest of international understanding, good will, and peace, the Peace Corps has grown steadily and substantially. Calls for services in and through education have constituted the largest phase of the program. The full story of the Corps as it develops may offer challenge to the youth of today in form of the purposes and satisfactions people should realize in their lives.

These illustrations of some potential strengths and assets, as well as two examples of constructive developments, serve to underscore the significance of the part of education in efforts to meet the challenges of our times. Education, if it is sound and maximally effective, can make the difference in the choices that men and their civilizations make. The prophetic statement of the late H. G. Wells that characterized civilization as a race between education and catastrophe has added significance for the Space Age.

THE CRITICAL ROLE OF EDUCATION

The determining factor in the choice that mankind makes can be education, an education that deals with realities and alternatives. This brings into clear focus the role and function of education in the new ages in which we live. Unless we learn to choose constructive and sound policies for using resources, our scientific discoveries, and to develop ethical relationships with other human beings, we can expect the same end that has come to many civilizations, only one more final and terrible. But, there will be another difference: the chance of other civilizations arising upon the ruins of the old will be nil. Education for the complex of new ages in which we will live must help all

Peace Corps volunteers at work (photographs courtesy Peace Corps).

peoples to appreciate these facts and to face up to the difficult tasks of thinking about sound choices for the future.

Can education be expected to accomplish such a critical function? Can mankind be taught to think about complex problems, unrealized potentialities, reconstruction of human institutions, and reassessment of values? Have people the potential for learning that gives any assurance that this critical role for education can be fulfilled? This is the nature of the challenge to education and to all who have a stake in education. This is for the future parents and teachers of the next generation. A truly adequate educational policy and a vitalized content for the curriculums cannot be developed without widespread participation of thoughtful responsible citizens. This is fundamental to the development of up-to-date educational policy and program; it represents the best way to implement the kind of education we shall need; it offers the best guarantee of the sustained support that an effective education must have. Widespread concern about and participation in education is an imperative, if Americans are to meet the challenges of the times. As the United States Commissioner of Education Francis G. Keppel has said, "Educational policy is not a spectator sport."

"We agreed that popular education was essential to a free government and for individual human happiness."

"We wanted our children to have a better chance than we had to get ahead and to make the most of themselves."

"We worked to establish systems of common schools to serve all the people and our growing democracy."

I. PERSPECTIVE

An Everyman's
View of
American Education

INSTITUTIONS

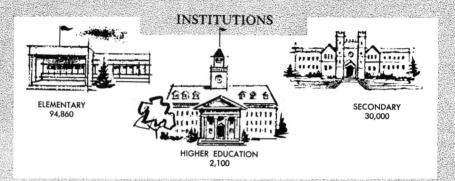

ELEMENTARY
94,860

HIGHER EDUCATION
2,100

SECONDARY
30,000

TEACHERS

PUBLIC ELEMENTARY
901,820

PUBLIC HIGH SCHOOL
607,460

HIGHER EDUCATION

Full-time campus faculty	312,900
Other	50,000

BOARD MEMBERS

Local	147,860
State	840
College and University	35,000

ADMINISTRATORS AND SUPERVISORS

Superintendents	13,130
Principal and Supervisors	6,540
College and University Presidents	2,100
Other College Staff	40,400

STUDENTS

ELEMENTARY

Public	29,400,000
Nonpublic	5,400,000
Other	200,000

SECONDARY

Public	10,700,000
Nonpublic	1,300,000
Other	100,000

HIGHER EDUCATION

Public	631,600
Private	1,754,400

Chapter 1

A Sketch of American Education

The American educational system has come nearest to achieving a classless school in the entire history of human society. Morally, this is its most glorious achievement.*

Introduction

All Americans take pride in their common school system and in the educational opportunity that democracy provides for all. But not many appreciate the factual and historical bases that complement these views. The truth is that education in the United States is an amazing but integral and indispensable aspect of the American way of life.

If asked by a foreign student on campus to give a brief explanation of the American public-school system, it might be difficult to explain how there is no single, centrally organized school system in America, as is the case in many foreign countries. Instead, one might say there are more than fifty school systems in these United States. The establishment and maintenance of education in our democ-

racy is a *state* function. This is generally accepted since state constitutions make the legislatures responsible for necessary school legislation. Moreover, the Tenth Amendment to the Constitution, which reserves for the states those powers not granted to the national government, confirms this principle.

Three other sets of facts might add to the confusion. The first refers to the division of authority for the administration and support of public schools. Local districts, towns, townships, cities, counties, and even larger areas are made the unit of school administration in the various states. People speak of this or that "school system," when they really mean a district or unit of the state system. Therefore, one needs to give careful attention to terminology and consistent use of terms.

Second, American education is also pluralistic in character. That is, other systems, not publicly controlled or supported,

* Sidney Hook, "Modern Education and Its Critics," *Seventh Yearbook*, American Association of Colleges for Teacher Education, 1954.

15

exist alongside public schools in most communities of the United States. These nonpublic school systems, and individual schools, comprise several systems of church-related or parochial schools and various others that we may call simply private schools. Nonpublic education also includes a large number of diverse institutions of higher education under various sources of control and support. Among these are some of the best and oldest universities in the United States.

The third major concept is that education in the United States, as in all cultures, is broader in scope than the general meaning attached to the notion of schools. Education and schools are often deemed to be synonymous, but the former is really far more comprehensive in meaning. It includes all the activities of the various agencies and institutions of a culture which help individuals to learn and finally to fit into that culture. We must include home, playgroups, neighborhood experiences, the religious educational institutions, work experiences, and the influence of comic books, movies, radio, television, the press, and many other agencies, when we think of education. The school plays a part, a distinctive and significant one, to be sure, in the total education of a person. All these terms and ideas would have to be cleared up before the foreign visitor could be given an adequate explanation of American education and the public school.

The Character of American Education

THE PUBLIC SYSTEMS OF SCHOOLS AND HIGHER EDUCATION

Public education in the United States comprises some thirty-two thousand systems of public schools—elementary or secondary or both—and the 721 institutions of higher education—junior colleges, colleges, and universities—supported by municipalities, districts, or states.[1] The aggregate is a huge comprehensive pattern characterized by much variety, flexibility, and complexity. It involves connections with all levels of government—local, state and federal—although it is clear that the primary responsibility originates in the state legislatures. This vast pattern of systems directly involves roughly one-fourth of the nation, more people than work in any other enterprise. The 1962–63 total public school enrollment of 40 millions marked the tenth straight year of an in-

crease of over a million pupils.[2] The age limits of its participants range from preschool children to adults of all classifications (there are even adult education classes for the aging). Public education costs over twenty billions of tax dollars each year and its effect upon our economy and the productivity of American free enterprise makes this expenditure an excellent investment. The vast majority of American parents look to the public schools and institutions of higher education as the avenue to better opportunity and accomplishment for their children. Those who lead in the formulation and execution of our national policies in both foreign and domestic affairs and in the

[1] Figures are for year 1962–63.

[2] Adapted from figures in "The Magnitude of the American Educational Establishment," *Saturday Review*, **XLVI**, No. 38 (September 21, 1963), p. 63; and NEA Research Report, *Estimates of School Statistics, 1962–63*. (Research Division, *NEA*, December 1962), p. 5.

direction of economic and public service establishments depend upon education to yield the educated manpower to do these major tasks. Through all of this, America's public schools and higher education stand out as indigenous institutions as American as the Fourth of July, hotdogs, and Huckleberry Finn.

Those who would understand American public education must be prepared to find some differences, much diversity, and many common features. Legislation for public education originates in state legislatures, under our Constitutional system of governments, but the statutory provisions for school are chiefly implemented by local school districts. The American people expect to keep education close to home and under their own control. This arrangement serves our democratic institutions well. It is unlikely that a pressure group can gain control of public education as long as the real decisions are made by local boards representing their own communities and fellow citizens who elected them.

Everyone who lives in the United States outside Federal reservations, lives in one or more school districts. School districts vary in size, shape, and purpose. There are still several thousand districts for one-teacher schools, although their number is decreasing annually;[3] at the opposite extreme are huge blocks of counties in Western states with consolidated centers and fleets of school buses and large city systems that maintain hundreds of schools with thousands of teachers and nonprofessional employees. School districts vary in geography, in population, in

economic wealth, and in all the other ways common to American culture. The pattern of school districts in some states is complex, having different districts for different levels of schools. In such cases, people live in more than one district, paying taxes to support elementary and high schools (even junior colleges) to different school systems. The scope of American public education is nationwide but the pattern of organization is a patchwork of local districts.

The total number of public school districts in the United States is approximately 32,000. During the past thirty years, the consolidation movement has increased the size but lowered the number of administrative districts to one-fourth of the former total.[4]

The scope of American public education has also been expressed in tangible fashion by the provision of school buildings and facilities for diverse programs and functions. Any modern school plant will serve as an illustration of this fact. Gone forever, save in museums and our cultural histories, is the nineteenth-century image of America's public school—the little red schoolhouse. Gone, too, is its successor, the boxlike graded school with median hallway and standard classrooms opening off either side. Visit a comprehensive school—whether elementary, junior high, or senior high school—and you find space and equipment designed for use by many age groups for many types of learning experience.

Public educational opportunity has been extended to more and more age groups among our total population. The

---

[3] In 1962 there were still about 15,000 one-teacher schools, many of which represented a separate school district. See *NEA Journal*, **LI**, No. 8 (November 1962), p. 5.

[4] In 1936, the total number of public school districts in U.S.A. was 127,649, in 1962 it was 32,891. See *NEA* Research Report, *Estimates of School Statistics, 1962–63* (Research Division, NEA, December 1962), p. 6.

kindergarten for 5-year-old groups of children are commonplace in the nation,[5] and there are even pre-school programs for younger children in scattered school systems here and there. The number and variety of educational programs for "out-of-school" youth have increased markedly in recent decades. Provision of educational opportunity at the junior college level has grown so rapidly since World War II as to become one of the stronger trends. Adult education has become an accepted feature of public education in several states; ten provide support from state public school appropriations. More than five million adults are currently enrolled in programs provided through public education.

These figures present further evidence of the broad dimensions or magnitude of the pattern of public education in the United States. It is truly an enterprise of great dimensions and diversity.

NONPUBLIC EDUCATION IN THE U.S.A.

There are a great many nonpublic schools and institutions of higher education in the United States. These comprise a wide variety of institutions that operate under various sponsors at all levels from preschool to graduate education. The term includes schools under many forms of control and for different purposes but it refers to educational programs supported by private funds and controlled by individuals, religious bodies, or nonpublic organizations. The great majority of nonpublic schools are parochial schools; that is, supported and controlled by a religious body —church, teaching order, congregation, synagogue, or society. Among the parochial systems of education, that of the Roman Catholic church is far larger than the combined total of all the others. Nonpublic schools and colleges, other than the parochial and church-related types, are fewer in number but they include some of the most influential and renowned institutions of the nation.

Enrollments in nonpublic schools

Data for nonpublic education is incomplete but available figures give most of the picture. The percentage of nonpublic school enrollments is increasing. In 1900 the figure was slightly over 8%; in 1930 about 9%; and in 1960, approximately 17%. The increase represents about one-half of the Catholic children of school age who attend schools controlled by that church.

The ratio of nonpublic to public school enrollments varies greatly among the states. The largest percentages are in eight states: three in New England— Rhode Island, New Hampshire and Massachusetts; three in eastern states—New York, New Jersey, and Pennsylvania; and two in the Midwest—Illinois and Wisconsin. At the other extreme, the percentage is negligible in several Southern states, Utah, and West Virginia.

The nonpublic school enrollment of the nation is principally comprised of parochial school populations. The Catholic parochial schools account for approximately 90% of the total, about 2% are in Lutheran parochial schools, 4% are

---

[5] In 1958 approximately 64% of the 5-year-olds were enrolled in kindergarten or in school; over 99% of the 6-to 13-year olds were enrolled; over 89% of the secondary school age group, between 14 and 17 years old, were enrolled. See *Progress of Public Education in the U.S.A., 1958–59,* U.S. Department of Health, Education, & Welfare, Office of Education (Washington: U.S. Government Printing Office, 1959), p. 11.

enrolled in nonsectarian private schools of various kinds.

Enrollments in nonpublic higher education

The percentage of enrollments in all nonpublic colleges and universities has dropped in recent decades and continues to decrease. In 1960 about 40% of all students in American higher education were in nonpublic institutions. It has been estimated that the percentage will drop to 30 by 1970. It should be understood that there has been no decreased enrollment in nonpublic institutions; actually there have been increases. The significant fact is that public higher education has increased at an unprecedented rate since World War II, a phenomenon expected to continue.

Extremes of high and low percentages are found among the states and regions. In New England not quite three-fourths of college enrollments are in nonpublic institutions; in California the situation is reversed.[6] In the District of Columbia there are no comprehensive public colleges, so enrollment in nonpublic institutions is predominant. Massachusetts, Rhode Island, New Jersey and Pennsylvania show relatively high enrollment in nonpublic institutions. On the other hand, there are no nonpublic colleges or universities in Nevada or Wyoming where enrollment in public higher education is 100%.

Policies and programs

Nonpublic educational schools and higher education exist alongside public educational systems in most communities of the nation. Their right to operate has

[6] Educational Policies Commission, *Higher Education in a Decade of Decision* (Washington: NEA, 1957), p. 17. See also "Higher Education" in *Saturday Review*, **XLIV**, No. 3 (January 21, 1961), p. 99.

been clearly recognized in the Fourteenth Amendment. In a celebrated case, the Oregon decision in 1925, the Supreme Court decided that the right to attend a nonpublic school is part of the personal liberty guaranteed by the Federal Constitution. This decision set aside an Oregon law that would require all children to attend public schools. The Supreme Court ruled that the law interfered with the right of parents to decide about education of their children. Further, the Court also held that the Oregon law would impair the value of the nonpublic school property. A significant phrase from the decision stated that children are not mere creatures of the State and that parents have the right (and duty) to direct their education. This has been a cornerstone of American educational policy along with the famous Dartmouth College Case of 1819, which held that a charter is a contract and states may make no law that violates agreements contained in contracts. This clearly established the right of private chartered colleges to operate in this country.

It is clearly a part of the American educational tradition to encourage freedom in education. The vast number and variety of charters granted by legislatures to colleges and schools and the liberality of American philanthropists and patrons which endowed and supported private schools are testimonials to this fact. In brief, this is a part of the vital American tradition, that man may freely serve his conscience in matters of religion and his state in matters of loyalty. This is a part of the indigenous American discovery, the separation of church and state.

Nonpublic schools and colleges may be established, operated, and supported by churches, organizations, and even individuals for various purposes. The right of parents to patronize nonpublic education is clear, so is the right of such institutions to own and control property. The states exempt property used for educational and religious purposes from public taxation.

Nonpublic education is subject to legal provisions that apply to educational programs generally. The Supreme Court has recognized the right of states to exercise reasonable regulation over all schools (Oregon decision). State legislation attempts to guarantee that children attending nonpublic schools will have an adequate education, that health and safety standards are met, that the attendance be regular, that teachers are prepared by training and character to teach, and that the curriculum contributes to good citizenship and the public welfare.

An important responsibility devolves upon the sponsors of nonpublic education, namely that of providing for its support. Most states have clear provisions in their constitutions or statutes or both that forbid the use of public funds for support of nonpublic schools. Tradition and court decisions in the several states have established and interpreted this principle as public policy over many decades.

In recent years there have been issues that raised questions about the interpretation of separation of church and state in matters that related to parochial schools. Benefits and services paid for by public funds have been sought (and in a few cases obtained) under an interpretation known as the child benefit theory. This view holds that services direct to a child and provided from public funds other than taxes levied for educational purposes are legitimate. Under this interpretation the child, not the church school, is considered the beneficiary of public support. Likewise, the funds used are usually not directly from the school taxes but from other tax levies and sources. Proponents hold that the aid to parochial schools under this plan is incidental and indirect, hence not in violation of constitutional and statutory provisions of various states and the Federal Constitution. The Supreme Court utilized this position in two cases: the Cochran Case, 1930, sustained a Louisiana law that provided free textbooks for pupils in parochial schools; the Everson Case, 1947, sustained New Jersey school authorities' use of public funds to provide free transportation of children to a parochial school, holding that it was the child who benefitted in each case rather than the church or school. However, in the latter decision the Supreme Court took the occasion to reiterate in strong terms the traditional constitutional principle of the separation of church and state. Various proposals for aid to parochial schools have been made in certain states in recent years, using the argument of the child benefit theory.

In a few places, children from Catholic schools have actually attended public schools part of the day for instruction in subjects not offered in their schools. An experiment has been started in certain schools of Allegheny County and Pittsburgh whereby Catholic pupils will go to public high schools for instruction in mathematics, foreign languages, industrial arts, commercial subjects, and physical education. They will spend the remaining time in the parochial school for courses in English, social studies, fine arts, and religion. This scheme has been called the "shared time" plan.[7] Educators will watch

[7] *Look* Magazine, **XXVI,** No. 18 (August 28, 1962), pp. 54–62.

these efforts with great interest to see if the practical problems and questions can be handled. The plan raises no major constitutional question unless there are public expenditures for transportation or some other purpose that benefits the parochial school. Most questions raised are the practical ones about the complications of crowding certain courses and facilities, scheduling, and the like.

Types of nonpublic schools

There are many types and distinctive characteristics among nonpublic schools in the United States. The simplest plan of classification would be to place them in two categories: (1) parochial schools which are those elementary and secondary schools controlled and supported by churches, synagogues, or other religious organizations; and (2) private schools, a variety of nonpublic schools maintained and controlled by secular or nonsectarian sponsors, sometimes called independent schools. A number of churches and some Jewish groups maintain parochial schools but those of the Roman Catholics account for over 90% of their enrollment. Private schools are usually single institutions designed to serve a particular clientele and to emphasize specific objectives. Some of the best known are college preparatory schools or academies that have long traditions of service and great reputations.

PAROCHIAL SCHOOLS

Catholic school systems

There are several types of Roman Catholic schools at both elementary and secondary levels. The commonest type is the parochial school maintained by the local parish. This may be an elementary school if the parish is small or include a high school if the church can support it. The policy of providing Catholic schools at the parish level began early in the nineteenth century and became mandatory after the Third Plenary Council in Baltimore in 1885. European immigrants had come to the United States in growing numbers and the church authorities deplored the influence of the public schools upon the children of Catholic families.

Under the policy established by the Catholic hierarchy at the Third Plenary Council in Baltimore in 1885, each parish must maintain a school. Catholic parents, who are responsible for the education of their children, are obliged to send them to parochial schools, if they are available, under pain of violation of Canon Law 1374.[8] Only the bishop of the diocese may grant exceptions to this obligation.

In effect, the parochial schools of a diocese constitute a system in that they are controlled by diocesan policy and supervised by the diocesan school board and school authorities. The bishop presides over the board of education, composed of selected clergy, which makes policy. In most dioceses, a priest trained in education is made superintendent to represent the bishop and direct the operation of schools. There are 136 archdioceses and dioceses in the United States.[9]

At the parish level, the priest is the titular head of the parochial school, especially in matters of finance and religion. The superior in charge of the teaching nuns (or brothers) is the actual principal of the parish school. The vast majority of teachers in parochial schools comprise

[8] *The 1958 National Catholic Almanac* (Paterson, N.J.: St. Anthony's Guild, 1957), p. 18.
[9] *Ibid.*, pp. 480–483.

TABLE 1–1. DATA FOR CATHOLIC SCHOOLS AND HIGHER EDUCATION, 1960*

| | Elementary Schools | | High Schools | | Higher Education | | | |
	Parochial	Private	Diocesan and Parochial	Private	Colleges and Univ.	Jr. Col.	Other	Teachers
Number	9,896	475	1,567	866	265	33	20	160,632
Enrollment	4,195,781	90,115	520,128	324,171	302,908			10,890 teaching priests
								4,778 teaching brothers
								98,471 teaching sisters
								45,506 lay teachers

* Adapted from information in Frank S. Mead, *Handbook of Denominations in the United States* (2nd rev. ed., New York: Abingdon, 1961).

members of teaching orders of nuns or brothers dedicated to educational service. There are a few lay teachers, particularly in certain subjects in types of Catholic high schools.

Curriculums of Catholic elementary and high schools usually include the subjects offered in the public schools but provide strong emphasis upon religious instruction. Textbooks in many subjects, especially in social studies, reflect this emphasis upon religion.

Protestant and other Christian church schools

Protestant churches generally favor public education but a few maintain a small number of schools, principally at the elementary level. A total of approximately 4,800 small schools enroll about 300,000 pupils.[10] Most of the Protestant parochial schools belong to the Missouri Synod Lutherans (1,430 schools), American Lutheran (90 schools), Reformed churches (approx. 60), the Mennonites (approx. 60), the Seventh Day Adven-

[10] *1962 Yearbook of American Churches* (New York: National Council of Churches of Christ in U.S.A., 1961), p. 279. Data is for 1959 and includes 1,350 kindergartens with 18,000 enrollment.

tists (approx. 1,000), the Episcopalians (180), and scattered Baptist churches. Incidentally, the Seventh Day Adventists have the highest percentage of their children in religious schools of any church in the U.S. but the total number is small.

In general, Protestant churches strongly support the public schools and supplement the secular curriculum therein, by providing extensive programs of religious education in Sunday schools, vacation Bible schools, and week-day Bible classes. In many communities over the nation the various churches cooperate with the public school authorities in a "released-time" program. This arrangement allows children, whose parents so desire, to leave school for a time one afternoon each week to go to a church or synagogue for religious instruction. This plan does not violate the principle of separation of church and state and it is practicable in some communities. In others it is wellnigh unworkable because of distances to some churches, traffic and safety hazards, the problems of absenteeism, and the "standstill" programs in the public school when most of the children are absent. The future success of the religious education programs of the churches and synagogues will require educated leadership, sound curriculum materials, and vigorous effort. This is a field of great challenge for many responsible parents who are willing to learn to teach and work with the children and youth of their church or synagogue.

Some churches make a conscientious effort to patronize public schools and simultaneously to provide effective religious instruction without infringing upon the school day. The policy of the Church of Jesus Christ of Latter-Day Saints (Mormon Church) accomplishes this dual objective by an ingenious arrangement. In certain western states, whole communities may be predominately Mormon in religion and their children attend a secular public school the full day. After school hours, the children cross the road or street and attend religious instruction in one of the 200 "seminaries" or institutes which the Mormon wards (congregations) have provided for this purpose. Afterwards, the children return home via bus or the usual means. This is an encouraging illustration of sincere devotion to their religion and respect for the constitutional principle of separation of church and state in the same church policy. Individual churches in various places follow comparable policies.

In the early periods of our history a number of Protestant churches established secondary schools and colleges, some of which represent strong institutions today. Their names would represent an extensive roll of distinguished colleges and universities, and a few outstanding secondary schools. Many more disappeared as public institutions came to the fore and the need for private schools declined. In recent decades, the principal growth in Protestant schools has been at the preschool level. Nursery schools have been operated in the religious education facilities of many churches for young children.

The most impressive figures about the educational activities of the Protestant and other Christian churches are those about their religious education programs. An abridged table of facts and figures will suffice to show the scope and significance of this aspect of education in the U.S.A.

Hebrew day and part-time schools

Most Jewish parents send their children to the public schools of their community and cooperate in efforts to strengthen their programs. The special needs of Jewish children in matters of religious instruction, the Hebrew language, and Jewish culture are served by attendance at a part-time school in late afternoon, or during the week end.

The traditional subjects taught in Jewish schools are Hebrew, Bible, history, customs and ceremonies, prayer, music, and arts and crafts. Pupils attend the Jewish Sunday School about 2½ hours per week; time spent in the week day afternoon classes ranges from 5 to 7½ hours weekly.[11] The vast majority of Jewish children have a public school experience plus part-time participation in a Hebrew school for several years. Fewer than 10 per cent of the children who attend any Jewish school at all attend a Jewish day school. The average number of years Jewish children attend Jewish schools is 2 to 3 and 5 to 6 respectively for week day and Sunday schools. Only

[11] *American Jewish Year Book, 1962* (New York and Philadelphia: American Jewish Committee and Jewish Publication Society of America, 1962), pp. 214, 220.

TABLE 1–2. LARGEST RELIGIOUS EDUCATION PROGRAMS, U.S.A.*

Church	Number of Sunday or Sabbath Schools	Officers and Teachers Enrolled	Total Enrollment (includes officers and teachers)
Assemblies of God	8,460	119,955	974,823
American Baptist Convention	6,317	101,708	1,003,419
National Baptist Convention of America	17,374	——	2,500,000
National Baptist Convention, U.S.A.	22,040	143,079 (1950)	2,407,348 (1958)
Southern Baptist Convention	31,762	784,742 (1954)	7,382,550
Christian Churches	7,911	66,577 (1954)	1,108,835
Church of the Nazarene	4,372	56,584	671,174
Congregational Christian Churches	4,762	70,395 (1936)	737,546
Evangelical and Reformed Church	2,650	95,910 (1958)	548,295
Evangelical and United Brethren Church	4,355	68,891	732,827
Church of Jesus Christ of Latter Day Saints	3,437	81,717	1,413,045
Lutheran Church Missouri Synod	5,115	89,390	869,781
American Lutheran Church	4,655	88,155	812,577
United Lutheran Church in America	4,350	110,882	1,045,009
The Methodist Church	38,076	637,529	7,132,422
Presbyterian Church in the United States	3,975	75,749	750,793
The United Presbyterian Church in the U.S.A.	9,000	195,567	2,045,910
Protestant Episcopal Church	5,619 (1951)	105,087	979,637
Roman Catholic Church	13,961	168,694	2,558,483

* Adapted from "Religious Education Statistics 1960 or 1961" in 1962 Yearbook of American Churches. See current edition for more recent data.

7% of Jewish children go to Jewish schools above the elementary level; the *bar mitzvah* is terminal for most. The Hebrew schools are usually maintained and supported by individual synagogues. There are a number of Jewish community centers in larger cities in which a varied educational, recreational, and cultural program is maintained by several congregations. This pattern of religious and cultural instruction has served well both the Jewish families and the communities where they live.

Another type of Hebrew school is found chiefly in larger cities. This is the Hebrew day school, elementary and secondary. About 200 day schools enroll some 40,000 pupils. These are individual schools maintained by local congregations and supported entirely by Hebrew parents. The curriculum is the same as that of the public schools with added instruction in religion and Hebrew studies. Some active work in curriculum development has been done in recent years; an example may be cited in the new Los Angeles Jewish curriculum which is reported as outstanding.

PRIVATE SCHOOLS

Most private schools are single units under management of their respective boards of control. The term *independent schools* is often used to refer to this group, particularly to the college preparatory type.

Academies and preparatory schools

Academies represent America's second type of secondary school, beginning with Benjamin Franklin's famous Pennsylvania Academy in 1751. A goodly number of fine old academies still exist from the vast number that were chartered and established during the eighteenth and nineteenth centuries. Nearly everyone has heard of Phillips Andover and Phillips Exeter, in Massachusetts and New Hampshire respectively, the two oldest but many other excellent schools of this general type can be found by study of the directory of independent schools. Most of these are in New England and the Atlantic states but they can be found in many states of the Union.

The term *independent schools* is preferred by some private schools and their patrons. These vary as to types of control, purposes, curriculum, and basis of support. Some are endowed, have charters from the legislature, and select their students carefully. Others depend chiefly upon parents' tuition and cater to their ambitions for their children. Some are coeducational, but segregation by sex is fairly common. Many activities are provided, there is choice of several curriculum patterns, while students receive counseling service and individual atten-

tion. This is possible because many private schools have great prestige, waiting lists for admission, and their income from tuition can support excellent faculties and staffs.

Other private schools

Private secondary schools comprise several types, such as military schools for boys, select finishing schools for girls, coed schools for boarding and day students, the country day schools of suburban areas, and the laboratory or demonstration schools attached to teacher education institutions. There is also a miscellany of private-school enterprises including some that offer vocational training programs—business courses, commercial art, drafting, beauty culture, trade, industrial, and auto-mechanics. Certain industrial concerns maintain schools at secondary level for the benefit of employees. There is no complete data for all types of schools in this category.

Private schools at the elementary level include several types. There are a good many private-enterprise day nurseries, kindergartens, and nursery schools for preschool children, supported by tuition payments from parents. Some states have established certain minimum legal standards for preschool education through licensing procedure and/or supervision by state school authorities. Some private elementary school programs are provided in connection with country day schools, in junior school departments of military and other boarding schools, and in the laboratory or demonstration schools of teacher education institutions. There are some types of private elementary schools for exceptional children—handicapped, mentally retarded, and emotionally disturbed. There are even a few private schools that cater to the interests and needs of gifted children.

Private higher education institutions

Nonpublic institutions of higher education dominated the field until relatively recent times. Colleges established before the American Revolution started as or became private institutions with one exception, Rutgers. A number of state universities were established late in the eighteenth and in the nineteenth centuries, but they lacked the prestige and influence of the older church-related and independent institutions of the Eastern seaboard. The coming of the land-grant institutions under the provisions of the Morrill Act (1862) started the popularization of higher education that resulted in the magnificent galaxy of great state universities now serving the nation. Therefore, the great and older private universities no longer dominate the field of higher education at the graduate and professional levels.

Comparison of numbers is difficult; for the term *university* is used loosely. Sometimes it refers to an institution of college grade. Authorities now count slightly more public than private universities, 70 and 62 respectively, with attendance at the latter including approximately 40% of the total university enrollment. Male students outnumber female by approximately 3 to 1. Enrollment in the private universities has increased slightly but its percentage of the total for higher education is declining gradually due to sharply climbing growth of public higher education.

A number of private universities continue to hold their position of leadership in various fields of higher education. Har-vard, the oldest university in the nation, continues to hold first rank in many respects—libraries, faculty, and resources —its prestige and influence are undiminished. A small number of private universities, long recognized centers of excellence, have made invaluable contribution to many strategic programs of research and development sponsored by federal agencies. It is impossible to conceive of the incredible scientific progress through research and development without the contributions of Harvard, M. I. T., Yale, Columbia, Cornell, Princeton, Johns Hopkins, Pennsylvania, Chicago, Northwestern, Cal Tech, Stanford, to name only a dozen. There are other notable contributions of private universities to our national life. Many faculty scholars and experts are called to government service, for consulting by industry, communications media, business, and by international agencies under the United Nations Organization. The independent status of great private universities often enables their leadership to take a stand upon issues that threaten academic freedom or civil liberties. It is not mere coincidence that some of our greatest private universities are frequently counted in leading positions to challenge and to defend policies and developments in the interest of truth and freedom. It is important to the nation's interest that private universities continue to find financial support and command the respect of the American people, who are also paying taxes for public higher education.

Private colleges

The popular "image" of college that many Americans have is the small liberal arts institution. Its tree-shaded, pleasant campus, academic halls, covered with ivy, a leisurely pace of social life, October leaves, exhilarating football afternoons, and a host of other nostalgic recollections compose this picture. This was the picture of higher education in many areas as the liberal arts college held sway as the typical institution, until recent decades. The small private liberal arts college still outnumbers public institutions of comparable functions and size. Nearly 650 accredited institutions of this type continue to provide higher education to approximately 650,000 students in the U.S.A.[12] Many of these have some form of relationship to a church organization but cannot be compared to parochial institutions. Many more are Christian but nonsectarian in matters of religion. A great many are secular but in no sense negative toward religion. All are independent of public control or systems of any kind, each having its own board of trustees. Tradition plays a great part in the operation and place of the private college and they have made invaluable contribution to the national welfare by providing able leaders in all walks of life. Americans in general should appreciate and support private colleges as an intelligent investment in our future.

Other private institutions

There are more than sixty private technological institutes in the nation, including the most distinguished names in this field—M. I. T., Cal Tech, Carnegie Tech, Case, Illinois Tech, Rensselaer Poly, to use the popular titles of a few.

[12] *Education Directory, 1961–62*, Part 3, "Higher Education," Office of Education, U.S. Dept. of Health, Education, & Welfare (Washington: Govt. Printing Office, 1962), p. 13.

Some of the best known schools of music and of fine arts are private institutions. There are other private institutions in architecture, business, and other specialized professions, at both undergraduate and graduate levels. There are approximately 90 accredited seminaries or graduate schools of theology that serve the major denominations in this country.

SIGNIFICANCE OF NONPUBLIC EDUCATION

The nonpublic schools and higher education represent important components of the total educational enterprise in the United States. Their magnitude alone would be impressive compared to the educational systems of many countries. The fact that nonpublic schools and colleges have provided educational service for a good fraction of our population can be regarded as a tangible contribution to the national welfare, one that has eased the burden upon public school systems and institutions.

It is in other respects, however, that nonpublic education has made distinctive contributions to American culture. The very fact of the existence of parochial and private schools and colleges is eloquent testimonial to the realities of the American way of life. Who can doubt that the freedom of choice is a part of the liberty American parents have and exercise in the education of their children? The existence of nonpublic and public agencies of education in most American communities is living proof of the pluralistic nature of American democracy.

Nonpublic educational institutions have made some special contribution in form of experimentation and tryout of new practices and programs. This is not universally true of nonpublic education which has its full quota of static programs, but there are private schools and colleges that have made distinctive contributions in the form of new programs and improved practices. The fact that nearly half of the "Thirty Schools" that participated in the "Eight-Year Study," a curriculum study project in cooperation with many colleges, were private secondary schools is an illustration of this point.

It is important that all Americans have an understanding of the whole educational enterprise—public and nonpublic—in this country. Parents make choices regarding the education of their children and they should do this in light of full knowledge of the merits and strengths of the respective programs. They should appreciate the freedom of educational choice in this pluralistic culture of ours and the fact that democracy guarantees all the right to choose religious schools or private schools instead of the secular public school. But they must also see the responsibility that this choice entails, namely that of paying for the nonpublic education of their children. The public school is open to all but it cannot play favorite in matters of religion or any other basic freedom of Americans; it can only try to teach loyalty to that basic freedom so critically important to all free Americans, the right to differ, to choose, and to live as neighbors with one's fellow "different" citizens. This kind of appreciation and loyalty to all our schools and colleges—public and nonpublic—it should endeavor to teach. American democracy would not be true to its tradition or worthy of the name if it were to become monolithic and uniform in any important aspect of its life. That goes double strength for its educational enterprise.

Characteristics of American Education

AMERICAN EDUCATION IS A VAST ENTERPRISE

One of the first impressions the student of education in these United States recognizes is that of its hugeness, the tremendous size of this great public and nonpublic pattern of schools and higher education. Judged by many standpoints, the figures are impressive. The number of persons directly affected by education in America is tremendous. The total enrollment of all schools and of all institutions of higher education for 1963–64 was nearly 51,500,000. Studies of America's educational enterprise show that nearly 30% of Americans, old and young, are engaged in education on a full-time basis as students, teachers, administrators, supervisors, or board members.[13] Approximately 27%, or well over one-quarter of the population of these United States, is enrolled as full-time students in our schools and colleges. More than one-fifth of our total population is enrolled as students in our public schools and higher education. A total of approximately five million adults is currently

[13] The total and percentage would be materially increased if we should add those who serve education as custodians, school bus drivers, lunchroom workers, clerks, and secretaries.

enrolled in public programs of adult education. It becomes clear that education in the United States directly involves a large proportion of the whole population; it is a vast enterprise from the standpoint of participants.

The number of teachers, administrators, and supervisors engaged in American education is well over the two million mark. This impressive total for the teaching profession clearly outnumbers any other professional group, as is shown on the chart following.

The manpower needs of American education offer another illustration of the vastness of our educational enterprise.

The citizens elected or appointed to serve as policy-makers for our schools and colleges comprise a sizable group of leaders in community life and public affairs. The total number of members of our school boards and boards of control of higher education is approximately 184,000. This group represents the most strategically important factor in framing policies and planning improvements in American education.

Other important groups of leaders and citizens have important relationships to American education. Each of the fifty state legislatures has committees that consider and report on bills and matters related to education; the total number of members would run into the hundreds. The staff members of the fifty state departments of education and of the U.S. Office of Education in the Department of Health, Education, and Welfare comprise a professional group of leaders and specialists of several thousand persons. In the various states and in Washington, D.C., the staffs of the professional organizations represent a comparable leadership group in American education. A large number

APPROXIMATE NUMBER OF PERSONS IN SELECTED PROFESSIONS, 1960

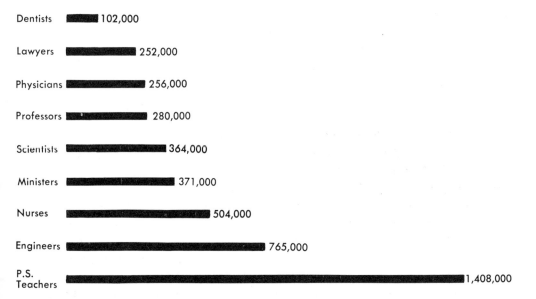

Dentists	102,000
Lawyers	252,000
Physicians	256,000
Professors	280,000
Scientists	364,000
Ministers	371,000
Nurses	504,000
Engineers	765,000
P.S. Teachers	1,408,000

Sources: NEA Research Division; *Statistical Abstract of the United States; Yearbook of American Churches.*

of scholarly bodies and professional organizations associated with higher education maintain headquarters and staffs in Washington, D.C. or some other center. The constituent members of the American Council of Learned Societies, the American Council on Education, the National Research Council, and other organizations represent a major force in American education. Colleges and universities have alumni organizations and offices that are concerned with many aspects of American education, representing a large total membership.

Much strength and support for American education comes from the influential and active patterns or organizations known as the PTA movement. The National Congress of Parents and Teachers comprises fifty state and 47,000 local chapters with over 12,000,000 parents and teachers. Since World War II, there have been literally thousands of "citizens study groups"—two estimates at different times totalled 6,000 and 20,000—formed in communities across the nation to work at educational problems and planning. These interested groups represent a vast army of active supporters of American education and a tremendous force of public opinion and support for the educational enterprise. In terms of the people involved, education in these United States can justly be considered an enterprise of great magnitude; vastness is the word for the American educational establishment.

Another index would be the number of organizational units or branches which comprises the American educational enterprise. It is an impressive total, nearly 127,000. The nation's educational enterprise includes 94,860 elementary schools, 30,000 secondary schools and 2,100 institutes of higher education (universities and colleges and junior colleges), a grand total of 126,960. Truly this is a far-flung enterprise, one that dwarfs even big business or the military establishment. In terms of the number and size of units of the different types of institutions involved, American education is a vast enterprise.

Another index to the vast size of American education is the matter of expenditures. The grand total for public school expenditures has increased steadily since World War II. In 1955–56 the grand total was ten billion, seven hundred million dollars. In 1961–62 this was over eighteen billion dollars, and for the school year, 1962–63, the estimated total was above nineteen and one-half billion. In capital investment for public school buildings, the total would run well beyond the twenty billion mark even at a conservative estimate. In this respect, public education would rank seventh after manufacturing, agriculture, railroads, oil, electric power, and lumber. This figure is another index to the vastness of American education.

AMERICAN EDUCATION IS A VARIED ENTERPRISE

The American educational enterprise is not only vast in scale or scope; it is characterized by great *variety* in types of administrative units and in its patterns of organization. The complexity of education in the United States can be further appreciated when we observe that the vast systems of public schools and of higher education exist alongside a number of nonpublic systems and patterns of schools and colleges. These nonpublic systems and patterns of education include the parochial systems of several denominations and a large number and variety of types of private schools, including some of commercial character.

Another clue to the variety of American education can be found in the figures for nonpublic institutions. For example, there are more than 5,400,000 pupils in nonpublic elementary schools, the parochial and private types. There is also a modest number of 200,000 pupils who attend other schools, such as those on government reservations, military establishments, special schools for demonstration purposes, and the like. In secondary schools, there is a total of 1,300,-000 students in nonpublic institutions, both parochial and private. There are also 100,000 in the secondary schools of the "other" label. At the college level, there is a grand total of 1,750,000 students, full and part-time, enrolled for degree programs in nonpublic institutions, that is, private, church-related and other nonpublic institutions. Serving the nonpublic schools at the elementary and secondary level are 190,000 teachers. This data gives tangible evidence of the variety that characterizes the educational enterprise in these United States.

A practical way to test our understanding of this major point would be to name as many different types of schools as possible. Begin with nursery schools (mostly under private sponsorship), kindergartens (which are both public and private), elementary schools of six grades (mostly public), and of eight grades (public, parochial, and private), and a few other categories. Go on to the junior high schools, and to senior high schools (each three-year types and mostly public) and to the four-year high schools, both public and private (since parochial high schools are usually the four-year type). There are also a few military schools, some private academies and "prep" schools for both boys and girls, and a few that are proprietary, owned and managed as commercial enterprises. Among the senior high schools are various trade, industrial and vocational schools, usually under public control and support.

There is also a variety of junior colleges, sponsored and controlled in various ways. Some of these are maintained by a district, comparable to a school district, others are supported by the state, and still others by a local city government. There are many junior colleges under church ownership and control and some that are independent, privately controlled by their own boards of trustees.

The final level of American education comprehends the great number of colleges, colleges for many different purposes and emphases under a great variety of sponsorship and control. The first colleges were controlled by churches and private sponsors and these still comprise a large number. There are also public colleges sponsored by states and by municipal governments. There are a very few that are proprietary, that is, managed for profit, but this type has largely disappeared. There are universities, the multi-purpose type of institution, sponsored in the same variety of ways, both public and private. There are technical schools, schools of engineering and other special fields, both public and private, and there are many types of graduate schools, apart from the universities, including theological seminaries, and schools of fine arts.

There are also various miscellaneous types of institutions like the business college, which is usually a private enterprise.

There is abundant evidence and support for the thesis that education on a formal, organized basis in this nation, is characterized by amazing variety.

AMERICAN EDUCATION IS A VIABLE ENTERPRISE

A third important characteristic of American education is viability, that is, it is live and growing. Evidence of this may be seen in the fact that new types of institutions have been developed throughout our educational history. Early in this century, for example, two distinctly American types of institutions were born, namely, the junior high school and the junior college. In the last fifty years, these new types of institutions have come into use throughout the nation under various kinds of sponsorship.

Another indication of the live and growing character of American education is found in the marked growth of the curriculum offered in schools and colleges. A review of the history of school textbooks, for example, will serve to illustrate this point. A survey of older and current courses of study used in the schools will give some idea of the growth of curriculums. A comparison of the catalogues of any good college for different periods of its history may serve as an illustration.

Further evidence for the viability of the nation's educational enterprise may be found in the degree and kind of financial support it has elicited over the years. Public support is increasing at all levels. The sources of nonpublic support are also on the increase. Leading American corporations make annual donations to private colleges and universities. The great private philanthropic foundations represent an important group of agencies with substantial commitments to both public and nonpublic education in this country. In 1960 there were sixty-four of these which had assets of $20,000,000 or more. The largest, the Ford Foundation, counts its total assets in ten figures. Nine others range from approximately $650,000,000 to $110,000,000.[14] All of these have made substantial contributions to education, for research, instruction, scholarships and fellowships, new programs, and publications.

The era of World War I, the decade of the 1930's, and the period since World War II, probably offer the best testimony to the viability of the educational program. Some recent developments provide significant examples of this growth. Since World War II, there have been impressive and extensive studies by scholarly groups and committees of teachers for the development of new and revised courses in the various fields of science and mathematics for American schools. For the first time, these efforts have engaged the services of leading scientists and mathematicians who are endeavoring to modernize the vast amount of new knowledge and material that should provide valuable content for the courses and subjects of instruction of our schools. Experimental textbooks are now available in the major science fields and in mathematics. Several different series are already in print and forward looking teachers across the nation have begun to experiment with their use. In other words, a great revolution is under way in

[14] See *The Economic Almanac, 1962* (New York: National Industrial Conference Board, 1962), p. 413. Data quoted from *Congressional Record* (May 8, 1961).

the science and mathematics classrooms of the alert teachers of the nation.

Another type of development has been the perfection of a number of instructional devices and aids, popularly called teaching machines. This type of aid to instruction may be used in various ways to supplement and strengthen teachers' efforts to teach many kinds of factual material, and to drill on fundamentals. This type of approach to effective teaching involves the preparation of course material in programs of learning, material being organized in steps that can be mastered readily by the student. There is considerable controversy over this approach to teaching as many teachers have reservations and questions about their indiscriminate use. Nevertheless, teaching machines undoubtedly represent a real contribution to the work of the perceptive teacher and a growing number are making use of these aids.

A third important new development gives further indication of the flexibility and vitality of American education. It may be seen in the extensive experiments designed to make the most effective use of teachers' aptitudes and of instruction time. These experiments have most frequently been labeled team teaching. This pattern varies in detail but will involve three major emphases: (a) instruction in large groups using the teacher with best preparation and background to make the presentation, (b) the small group for discussion and follow-up using teachers as consultants, and (c) study projects of students on an individual basis according to interest, needs and ability. This tripartite pattern was developed by a study group of American educators working in close cooperation with a number of secondary schools willing to experiment with new ideas.

Education in the 1960's makes increasing use of educational television, which actually got under way in the 1950's. In 1962, after 10 years of operation, 67 ETV stations were telecasting part of the curriculum for approximately four million students. About one-half of the states were making some use of ETV and others were planning networks and stations. This was the second year of operation by the Midwest Program of Airborne Television Instruction, "MPATI" for short. Programs were beamed to schools in 6 states (Illinois, Indiana, Kentucky, Michigan, Ohio, and Wisconsin) from a specially-designed plane flying aloft over a village in north central Indiana. The curriculum offerings included 28 different courses.

A 1962 study by the National Association of Educational Broadcasters for the U.S. Office of Education indicated that complete coverage of the nation would require more than 1,100 ETV channels, a threefold increase over the number already allocated (309).[15]

About one-third of our ETV stations are operated by each of the following agencies: by public school boards or state agencies, by universities, and by nonprofit educational broadcasting associations. The total cost of ETV operation for 1962 was $15,000,000. TV magazines report there is no such thing as a typical ETV station; each reflects the needs and character of its community. Some of the better known ETV stations are Miami's

[15] *TV Guide,* **X,** No. 43 (October 27, 1962).

WTHS (channel 2), KQED in San Francisco (channel 9), and Chicago's WTTW (channel 11). Adult education courses, and even a complete junior college curriculum have been offered by WTTW. ETV has grown from nothing but an idea to an impressive enterprise in a decade.

Other evidences of the dynamism and capacity for growth and change in American education may be found in reports of new developments from year to year. The National Education Association makes studies and reports findings on curriculum developments and improvements from time to time. These reports are lengthy and include a variety of programs and approaches. One of the most exciting types of current experimentation is under way in universities and certain schools in several midwestern states. The projects have undertaken to discover better ways to foster and develop creativity on the part of pupils.[16] More will be heard of projects of this kind as the research becomes better known. Experimentation with the introduction of various foreign languages in elementary schools is increasing. Schools have successfully introduced science material, especially astronomy, in the intermediate grades, others have tried geometry in the elementary school and the like. The list of experimental programs and innovations could be extended to great lengths.

A review of the current educational scene with attention to capacity for evaluation, for experimentation, for adaptability to societal needs and demands, and the motivation for improvement should provide evidence of the vitality that characterizes American education.

AMERICAN EDUCATION IS A VITAL ENTERPRISE

Another way to characterize American education would recognize its vital connection with the well-being of our economy, and to the very survival of our way of life. Every study of the place of education in America's future tends to reemphasize this vital relationship. All tend to agree that the vital importance of education has never been more evident and the need for quality education for our new frontiers and problems more imperative than right now. One illustration will suffice to make the point. Everyone who reads and understands would acknowledge that science and technology will continue to have an instrumental role in the changing economy of the United States; in the emerging era of space exploration these are positively indispensable. Some challenging studies have recently been made that show clearly the vital role of scientific and technological education upon the survival potential of our way of life. Every serious student of the contemporary scene should understand the findings and the significance of the critical reports by the Rockefeller Brothers Fund Panel, the Gardner Committee, and the President's Commission on National Goals. These place in sharp relief some of the imperative challenges that result from the continued cold war period of intensive rivalry for dominance in nuclear weapons, in development of ballistic missiles, in space exploration, and

[16] See the special feature "Creativity" in *NEA Journal,* **L,** No. 3 (March 1961) pp. 17–18. See also Harold H. Anderson, "Creativity and Education" in *College and University Bulletin,* **XIII,** No. 14 (May 1, 1961).

research achievements that exceed the wildest dreams of good scientists of past generations. Challenges for the constructive use of new scientific knowledge, developments, and techniques in medicine, engineering, power for industry, transportation, and many other fields have been voiced by leading scientists and spokesmen of humanity's conscience. Through all this runs the imperative need to develop further the machinery, for effective handling of problems of international relations, tensions, and preserving peace by the United Nations and its several bodies and agencies.

In the domestic scene, the American people have unprecedented challenges that must enlist the efforts of their best manpower and leadership potential. A number of noteworthy studies have brought these problems into the limelight of public attention. Dr. Conant, the great friend and constructive critic of American public education, has clearly shown the dangerous potential in the chronic situations existing in slum areas of our cities. Clearly, the emerging metropolitan centers have encountered many critical problems, including educational crises that demand programs better and unlike anything that we have ever known. "Megalopolis" is the term used to refer to a vast complex of urban centers that stretch from Virginia to Boston and extend into parts of ten states. Areas along the Gulf Coast, around Chicago and southern end of Lake Michigan and the Pacific Coast are already in the midst of unprecedented social change and chaos. These megalopolitan centers include one-tenth of all Americans and represent a new frontier of human relationships, housing, city planning, transportation, in-and-out migration, interstate governmental relationships, educational facilities and programs.[17] Who can doubt that the parents and teachers of the next generation must be able to cope with unprecedented social change?

The American people will need to utilize all their best problem-solving ability in the years ahead, as well as their creative and inventive talents. This means optimum utilization of education, with emphasis upon research, new knowledge of many areas and fields, and crash programs of development. These are necessary merely to keep up in the race for survival.

One clear indication is that every study available clearly indicates the growth of demands for scientists and engineers in the next decade or two. A recent study by the Bureau of Labor Statistics for the National Science Foundation showed that a 90% increase would be needed over 1955–59 levels, something over two million (550,000 scientists and 1,485,000 engineers.), by 1970.[18] It is reasonable to expect this educated manpower will be provided through the good offices of America's schools and technological institutions.

Another large area of increased demand for professional personnel is in the area of health. It is estimated that in spite of the one-half million nurses we have, America's hospitals now have 20,000 vacancies. In spite of the increased number

[17] See B. J. Chandler, Lindley J. Stiles, and John J. Kitsuse, *Education in Urban Society* (New York: Dodd, Mead & Co.), 1962.

[18] Selma T. Mushkin (ed.), *Economics of Higher Education*, Office of Education Bulletin 1962, 5, U.S. Department of Health, Education, and Welfare (Washington: U.S. Government Printing Office, 1962), p. 64.

of nursing school graduates during the 1950's the need for more nurses persists. In like manner, in spite of a slight increase in numbers of dentists, the number per 100,000 population decreased from 59 to 56 during the past three decades. At the present inadequate rate of preparation, the number of new dentists needed to maintain current ratio to the general population will reach nearly 120,000 by 1975. If we are to meet the need, the number of dentists graduated annually would have to be doubled.

Similar demands for physicians are evident. Although the number of doctors has increased in recent decades, the growth has not kept pace with the population increase. The number of physicians per 100,000 population is 142. America would need 335,000 more physicians by 1975 in order to maintain the present ratio of doctors to population. This would not allow for increasing use of doctors in research and medical groups. Studies show that to meet the future need we would have to have an increase of medical graduates to 11,000 annually, a jump of nearly 50%. Here again, to provide trained health personnel in numbers sufficient to maintain present levels of supply in relation to population for the next decade will require vigorous action.[19] Clearly, the proper functioning of our educational programs at school, college, and graduate levels is imperative. Studies of the need for other categories of skilled personnel tell the same story. Our future national requirements will demand huge increases in the number of educational levels of many kinds of skilled and professional workers. All resources of the nation's educational establishment will have to be utilized fully to educate the manpower needed to meet our national requirements in the next two decades. American education has a vital relationship to the survival of the democratic way of life.

[19] *Ibid.,* pp. 47–57.

Selected Bibliography

Bereday, George F., and Volpicelli, Luigi. *Public Education in America.* New York: Harper & Row, 1958.

Brimm, R. P. *The Junior High School.* Washington, D.C.: The Center of Applied Research in Education, 1963. See Ch. 1.

Broudy, Harry S. "Teaching Machines: Threats and Promise." *Educational Theory,* **XII** (July 1962), pp. 151–156. Reprinted in *Education Digest,* **XXVIII,** No. 3 (November 1962), pp. 1–4.

Cox, Philip W. L., and Mercer, Blaine E. *Education in Democracy: The Social Foundations of Education.* New York: McGraw-Hill 1961.

Digest of Educational Statistics, 1963 Edition, Office of Education, U.S. Department of Health, Education & Welfare. Washington: U.S. Government Printing Office, 1963.

Editors of Education, U.S.A. *The Shape of Education* for 1962–63. A Handbook on Current Educational Affairs, Washington: National Education Association, 1962.

"Education," *Building America,* **XIII,** No. 3 (March 1948).

"Education," *Time,* **LXXIV,** No. 11 (September 14, 1959), pp. 70–79.

Educational Policies Commission. *Public Education and the Future of America,* Washington, NEA, 1954.

————. *The Contemporary Challenge to American Education.* Washington: NEA, 1958.

ETV, *A Ford Foundation Pictorial Report.* New York: Ford Foundation, 1961.

Fleming, Thomas J. "The Crisis in Catholic Schools," *The Saturday Evening Post,* **CCXXXVI,** No. 37 (October 26, 1963), pp. 19–24.

Givens, Willard E., and Farley, Belmont M. *Our Public Schools.* Washington: The Supreme Council, 33°, Ancient and Accepted Scottish Rite of Freemasonry, Southern Jurisdiction, U.S.A., 1959.

Grafton, Samuel. "Educational Television: Boon or Boondoggle." *TV Guide,* **X,** No. 43, (October 27, 1962). See also issues for November 3rd and 10th for other installments.

Graham, Grace. *The Public School in the American Community.* New York: Harper & Row, 1963.

Gross, Calvin E. "Team Teaching at Pittsburgh," in 1959 annual report for superintendent of schools, *Pupils, Patterns, and Possibilities,* pp. 9–27. Reprinted in *Education Digest,* **XXVII** (November 1962), pp. 12–15.

The Handbook of Private Schools. Boston: Porter Sargent, 1963. See current edition.

Harris, Raymond P. *American Education–Facts, Fancies, Folklore.* New York: Random House, Inc., 1962.

King, Edmund J. *Other Schools and Ours,* Rev. ed., New York: Holt, Rinehart & Winston, Inc., 1963, pp. 1–9, 113–157.

Kneller, George F. *Foundations of Education.* New York: John Wiley & Sons, 1963.

Lambert, Hazel M. *Elementary Education.* Washington, D.C.: The Center for Applied Research in Education, 1963, pp. 1–16.

Leonard, George B. "Revolution in Education." *Look* Magazine (June 5, 1962), pp. 58–70.

"The Magnitude of the American Education Establishment." *Saturday Review,* **XLVI,** No. 38 (September 21, 1963), p. 63.

McMurrin, Sterling M. "A Crisis of Conscience." *Saturday Review,* **XLIV,** No. 37 (September 16, 1961), pp. 58–59, 77–78.

Markle, Susan Mayer. "Inside the Teaching Machine." *Saturday Review,* **XLIV,** No. 46 (November 18, 1961), pp. 55, 66–68.

Maurois, Andre. "A Frenchman Appraises U.S. Schools." *Saturday Review,* **XLIV,** No. 15 (April 15, 1961), pp. 54–55, 74.

Michalak, Joseph. "The Machines That Teach." *New York Herald Tribune,* Sunday, November 4, 1962, Section 2, p. 10.

Morse, Arthur D. *Schools of Tomorrow–Today,* A Report on Educational Experiments, Garden City, New York: Doubleday & Co., Inc., 1960, p. 191.

NEA Research Division, *Estimates of School Statistics.* 1962–63, Research Report 1962–R13, Washington: NEA. (December 1962.)

————. *Research Bulletin.* **XLI,** No. 1, NEA (February 1963).

————. *Status and Trends: Vital Statistics, Education, and Public Finance,* Research Report 1959–R13, Washington: NEA (August 1959).

Newton, Willoughby. "Protestant Parochial Schools," *Saturday Review,* **XLV,** No. 3 (January 20, 1962), pp. 49–50.

Peters, Herman J., Burnett, Collins W., and Farwell, Gail. *Introduction to Teaching.* New York: The Macmillan Company, 1963, pp. 1–30.

Progress of Public Education in the United States of America, 1962–63. Summary report of the Office of Education, U.S. Department of Health, Education and Welfare to the Twenty-sixth International Conference on Public Education, Geneva, Switzerland, July 1–12, 1963, jointly sponsored by the United Nations Educational, Scientific and Cultural Organization and the International Bureau of Education. Washington: U.S. Government Printing Office, 1963.

Review of the American Educational System. Hearings before the subcommittee of the Committee on Appropriations, Hous of Rpresntativs, 86th Congress, Second session, Washington: U.S. Government Printing Office, 1960.

Riccio, Anthony C., and Cyphert, Frederick R. *Teaching in America.* Columbus: Charles E. Merrill Books, Inc., 1962.

Sharkey, Don. *These Young Lives,* A Review of Catholic Education in the United States. New York: William H. Sadlier, Inc., 1950, p. 85.

Williams, Charl Ormond (Ed.). *Schools for Democracy.* Chicago: National Congress of Parents and Teachers, 1939.

Chapter 2

The Setting of American Education

> . . . the school has to give special consideration to the demands of the environment, to the culture into which the child is born and develops. Personality does not develop and does not operate apart from a social context; self does not exist apart from society. At birth the child begins the long and arduous task of adjusting himself to his culture; to the intricate and often baffling patterns of human relationships, to the morals and values of his own particular family, to the institutions basic to civilized life generally, and to the institutional forms and arrangements of his own society. It is the task of the school to develop the intelligence of the child; it is also its task to weave the strands of the core values of the culture into the structure of his personality. Experiences need to be provided that will develop in the individual the motivation, the desires, the attitudes, the sensitivities, the initiative, and the creative interests that will best enable him to adjust to his world of social reality. The school of the future will be called upon to give more attention to the development of the individual who possesses emotional stability even in the face of novel and difficult situations and who has initiative and versatility.*

Introduction

An understanding of American education must be grounded in adequate conceptions of what education is: of its role in society, and its relation to personality development. One must begin *with* or, more properly, *in* society only to find that our society, like all societies, has pro-

vided for education as a principal means of maintaining and perpetuating itself. It appears that education in a free society has the further opportunity to help change and improve that society. Varied patterns of institutions are developed and utilized to accomplish these societal purposes. These educative agencies range all the way from the family and other primary groups at the neighborhood level to organizations such as UNESCO on an international

* Newton Edwards and Herman G. Richey, *The School in the American Social Order* (Boston: Houghton Mifflin, 1947), pp. 850–851. Used by permission.

scale. These functions and agencies serve society and individuals simultaneously; they preserve, maintain and improve the society while enabling the individual to reach his potentialities in the culture. It is through this process of social interaction that the individual becomes the person. Education takes place as individuals interact with other individuals and groups and in the total environment, thus learning to participate fully and constructively in society. When one can visualize this comprehensive process in which a number of varied agencies are concerned, one begins

to see why so many definitions of the word *education* were formulated.

One could say that education is both an individual and societal process; it comprehends both a number of functions and a pattern of agencies which must be viewed together. It is essential to the ongoing processes of society; it is instrumental in the development of individual personality. The further one carries this study, the more certain he becomes of this conclusion: "Look at any society, always to find education." In a word, education is universal.

The Cultural Setting of Education

SOCIETY, EDUCATION,
AND SCHOOLS

In any society we find education; in modern societies we find schools. Schools are by no means coextensive with education; they are a relatively recent type of institution. Schools arose in society when other older agencies could no longer be depended upon to transmit the cultural heritage. Or as societies changed and grew in complexity, schools became necessary. When the knowledge and skills within the culture became so diversified and specialized that the typical adult could no longer be the adequate teacher, the school had to be provided. The school and the teacher became necessary when existing agencies could no longer carry out their primary functions and handle the tasks of education as well. The cultural heritage had become too extensive, too complex, and the task of transmitting it too heavy to be accomplished by incidental means.

The explanation of how schools developed within complex cultures utilizes

some concepts and understandings that may be developed through study of cultural anthropology and sociology.[1] One learns that all cultures grow and change; certainly they do not remain static. Gradually the changes within and the growth of the culture accumulate what we call the "social heritage," which must be passed on to all participants as a means of social control. All young people must

[1] The subject matter of this section hardly requires documentation, as some of the references will show. Appropriate references for the beginning student are: (a) Florence Greenhoe Robbins, *Educational Sociology* (New York: Henry Holt, 1953), chapters 2 and 4; (b) Myles W. Rodeheaver, William B. Axtell, and Richard E. Gross, *The Sociology of the School* (New York: Thomas Y. Crowell Co., 1957), chapters 1, 2, 8, and 12; and (c) Robert J. Havighurst and Bernice C. Neugarten, *Society and Education*, 2nd edition (Boston: Allyn and Bacon, Inc., 1962), pp. 227–248. More advanced students may prefer George D. Spindler, *et al.*, *Education and Culture, Anthropological Approaches* (New York: Holt, Rinehart, and Winston, 1963), see pp. 132–172, 302–399.

learn the social heritage well enough to fit into the culture and perform satisfactorily if that society is to be maintained and preserved. When the youth were adjudged ready to take a full part in the life of the group-class, tribe, or community—they participated in an initiation ceremony. The informal, incidental education of the young was then completed and the youth took on the role of adults in the culture.

It should be understood that this incidental provision for education worked well in many cultures over long periods of time. In modern societies as long as much of education can be done in the home—as an outcome of play, through day-by-day activities and contacts within the neighborhood, in the course of work experiences, and to some degree by participation in religious practices—these primary societal agencies continue to serve this need of society.

A brief essay into the history of education will show that the cultural transition which resulted in the development of schools, began early in Western history. This could only be considered recent from the standpoint of society as a whole and from the viewpoint of the anthropologist. Students become familiar with schools as a part of the civilizations of the Hebrews, the Greeks and the Romans—with various schools of the medieval and Renaissance periods in Western Europe—and with the great increase of schools in many modern nations. There is further evidence of the cultural transition to schools in the findings of anthropologists, historians, sociologists and archaeologists who study cultural history. The explanation of this development is supported by some recent instances of the transition to the school which are available from the cultures of the Acomas and the Navahos in our Southwest. Other illustrations may be found in certain references and authoritative works in anthropology and sociology.[2]

Schools are society's agents

The school has developed in most societies around the world today. It seems necessary to note that in various cultures there are many schools of widely different types.[3] There are several obvious ways of classifying schools for purposes of study. Our present needs may be served best by the use of some convenient categories for schools—schools for young (or even pre-school children), elementary schools (often termed primary in other lands), secondary schools, and various miscellaneous types including continuation, vocational, and other schools. Schools can be divided into public and nonpublic or private schools. The latter category often includes significant parochial (church-sponsored) systems of schools. Major functions of certain types of schools also suggest means of classifying certain groups as college preparatory, general, technical, vocational, or trade. Although these groupings are largely superficial, they may serve to point out the complex pattern of institutions which the schools of various cultures now present. One caution must be noted: such terms as *public* and *primary* do not necessarily have the same meaning when used in connection with schools of another nation. For example, the British use these terms in meanings altogether different from those which are familiar to us. There

[2] See Spindler, *op. cit.*, Chapters 20–25 for pertinent examples.

[3] See Edmund J. King, *Other Schools and Ours*, rev. ed. (New York: Holt, 1963), for brief treatment of several national systems of education.

is a great diversity to be found in the schools of a complex culture and among those of the various societies around the globe.

Although schools differ widely, there are some important common characteristics. In all countries we find that schools are society's agents; that schools always serve the principal purpose of *education*. In this respect the school differs from other educative agencies. Education for other agencies of society is secondary, may even be an incidental or a concomitant function, but for the schools it is *the* function.

Society delegates to its agent, the school, the task of formal instruction of its younger members in order to prepare them for full participation in adult life. The school emphasizes the goals of full fellowship in the adult society, and readiness to accept the duties and responsibilities of citizenship in the instruction of youth.

Students may not expect either the role or the organization of schools to be uniform or static in various societies. In many countries, for example, France, entire national systems of schools are organized and managed from a central authority. There are certain practices whereby both public and nonpublic schools receive public support as at present in the province of Quebec, Canada, and in Holland. In a few countries public schools may be less important and even inferior in quality to parochial schools. In the United States and various other democracies there are public schools open to all and nonpublic schools for those who prefer to maintain them. It becomes evident that societies can and do set up schools to serve their needs for specialized and consistent attention to education.

Democracy uses common schools

In our democratic society one educative agency seems to stand out as distinctive and significant.[4] It is the public school, universally regarded as a cultural force of major significance. It is true that the United States permits nonpublic schools, even whole systems of parochial schools, but this is part of a socio-political system which gives recognition and respect to minorities and to the principle of diversity. It is the provision for and faith in public education on the part of the American people that distinguishes their educational history. The common schools have been hailed as the most distinctive institution of the Republic.

Public education is that part of the pattern of societal institutions and functions which is provided and controlled by the public *in the common interest*. The public school is the principal agency through which the deliberate educational needs of the general public are served. It is society's only agency whose sole purpose is education. To serve "all the children of all the people" is its ideal and purpose. The public school must conceive of its task in the light of the comprehensive functions, agencies, and processes of democratic society. Its policies and practices should reflect both sympathetic *understanding of* and cooperative *attitudes toward* all other educative agencies for

[4] This observation is well-documented by many authorities and works. For a brief discussion of the major point made in this section, see Ellis F. Hartford, *Moral Values in Public Education* (New York: Harper & Row, 1958), pp. 42–46.

the wellbeing of democracy and for the wholesome growth of human personalities. However, the public school must be vigorously alert to recognize and serve the educational functions and needs of the whole society.

There was relatively general agreement upon schools when they were first established in the colonial American communities of New England. Time passed, conditions and needs changed, but the school largely kept its traditional character. This process of a lag between society's needs and its traditional institutions illustrates the necessity for continuous attention to schools and other societal agencies. Truly, "new occasions teach new duties," for schools as well as other educative agencies.

Schools in our democracy must undertake to prepare youth for intelligent, responsible and voluntary participation in this complex free society of ours. This function involves the education of young people for full responsibility as citizens, consumers, producers, marriage partners, and the like. This versatile task also involves primary concern about the fullest possible all-round development or optimum self-realization of individuals. In democracy, this accords with the basic societal needs, and is in sharp contrast to the situation in regimented societies. Our society delegates this responsibility to the public schools which accept and carry it out with a maximum of freedom and latitude for details of local policy, program content, and procedures. This same freedom of inquiry and action for our educational leadership enables public education to make constructive contributions to the development of public policy.

Public schools serve the whole society

Public education must be viewed in terms of its cultural setting, and as a part of the comprehensive pattern of functions and agencies which serve our democratic society. Education is a principal means by which all societies are maintained and perpetuated; in democracy it may foster social change and improvement. Education accounts for much of the societal process itself—social interaction—through which the culture provides for its own needs and for the development of individual personality. Education in our society is both pervasive and continuous; in terms of the individual it is co-terminous with life.

Much that has been said in general about education-in-society can be applied to American education. One distinctive characteristic needs to be recognized and appreciated, namely, the peculiar role of the public school in our society. The public school—one of the truly distinctive American social inventions—differs from other educative agencies in its responsibility to the whole of society. No segment of society, nor vested interest can provide the education that would be required to fully prepare the young for full participation in this complex, plural society of ours. Only a free system of education, open to all, and operated in the public interest can be adequate to serve a dynamic and diversified democracy.

Most citizens accept the statement that public education is an indispensable part of American culture and essential to our democratic way of life. It is necessary that future leaders in the communities and educational institutions of this great nation have a clear working knowledge of public education, of the nature and functions of education in our distinctive way of life, of the many educative agencies in our communities and of the meaning of these for each of us. We can begin to approach this set of concepts by starting with ourselves.

The Community Setting of Schools

WE ARE CULTURAL PRODUCTS

Each and every one of us is a product of the comprehensive and continuous process which is provided in and by the culture. There is nothing extraordinary about this. Every functionally normal person is the product of this process. Education, in its broadest or societal sense, applies to everyone who learns to participate in society. It is principally through the educative experiences in the total culture that an individual becomes the person that he is. This means that many informal, even casual experiences are *educative* in nature; it means that a great many institutions of the culture are to be regarded as educative agencies.[5]

American culture utilizes many educative agencies

Our society develops and uses an increasing number and variety of institutions which perform educational functions.[6] Educative agencies increase and change because society itself changes and grows in complexity. Some traditional institutions may disappear as their functions are outgrown by society. There are in-

stances of change in the functions of an old institution to accord more nearly with the needs of society as in the case of some types of schools. Upon other occasions when new needs have been discovered, the responsibility for dealing with them has been delegated to an institution already in existence. In most cases the appearance of new problems is the signal for the development of new agencies to deal with them. The resulting diverse pattern of institutions serves a multitude of functions, many of which are educative in nature. All prospective citizens need to appreciate the diversified pattern of educative agencies which is an important characteristic of contemporary American culture.

The variety and number of these educative agencies suggests the need for some means of classifying them for study purposes. At least three large groupings may be warranted.[7] First, there are several *institutions*, which have been *established by society as educational agencies and designed to serve one or more major functions in education*. These provide as their primary function organized and deliberate programs of education: schools, colleges and universities, religious edu-

---

[5] For further reading consult such references as Robbins, *op. cit.*, pp. 79–147, 173–240; Havighurst and Neugarten, *op. cit.*, pp. 93–148, 173–204, and Spindler, *op. cit.*, pp. 268–283.

[6] See works cited above and also Bernard N. Meltzer, Harry R. Doby, and Philip M. Smith, *Education in Society* (New York: Thomas Y. Crowell Co., 1958), pp. 140–151.

[7] Most educational sociology texts should deal with this general topic. For one classification of four groups see Francis J. Brown, *Educational Sociology,* 3rd edition (New York: Prentice-Hall, Inc., 1954), p. 207.

cation programs of churches and synagogues, libraries, museums, municipal playgrounds, school camps, educational radio and TV stations, and others, depending upon circumstances. Many people stop right there in their conception of what constitutes education in our culture.

A second category of great significance are those *primary groups which serve basic societal needs including some effective educational functions.* Among these the greatest is the oldest—the family. The important role of the play group makes it one of the most influential agencies in the early development of human personality. In the teenage years the adolescent peer group, be it "gang" or "country club set," qualifies as one of the strongest influences in the educative experiences of youth. The neighborhood influences the education of young members of society and the wider community is often an important educative agency that belongs in this category. These agencies exist for a number of purposes and serve societal needs other than education but that very fact may indicate why these groups are effective educative agencies. Education is related to the performance and/or accomplishment of other societal functions.

In the third group there are *numerous commercial and voluntary establishments and organizations that appeal to various interests of people but serve some incidental educational purposes.* Many such well established agencies as the press, theatre, the movies, and the radio have been joined by a newcomer, television. Other illustrations may be recognized in the great diversity of workers' education groups, promotional programs of professional organizations, public relations offices and campaigns, certain advertising, a variety of schools of the armed services, and a host of others. A quick check can be made by a survey of the advertisements in popular slick magazines.

All of these and many not mentioned operate with some effect upon the processes of social adjustment and social control in our culture. Other cultures have patterns of comparable significance. This should suggest to future parents and teachers that instruction in the school is but a major part in a vast and complicated set of educative institutions. This perception may serve to correct the notion that the school is the most effective of all educative agencies. It may be futile to use time in pointless effort to determine which are the most important or effective of these agencies. Instead, we might better ponder the opportunity, even the responsibility, before us, namely that of intelligently relating the school programs of the future to that large societal process of education which goes on in American culture all the time.

The home as first educative agency

The home has many functions besides education, but it is generally conceded to be the most effective educational agency in society.[8] Much is heard about the decline of the home, the serious consequences of changing patterns of family living. While it is true that many patterns of home life are changing, these changes are not necessarily bad and many have proved constructive and preferable to the patterns they supplanted. Changes in the home correspond to changes elsewhere in

[8] See in Florence Greenhoe Robbins, *op. cit.,* pp. 114–147 and Havighurst and Neugarten, *op. cit.,* pp. 93–122; for useful discussions of the social interaction in the home.

the culture. Some are good; some are bad. Many are indifferent. In the midst of varied changes, the home or family pattern of living normally represents the strongest educative influence in the culture.

Anyone can make a simple check on this fact by reviewing the normative educative experiences of people:

Where and how do we learn to talk, learn the names of things, or "use" vocabulary, mannerisms of speech and expression? When and where do people learn to pick up their clothes and care for their belongings? Where do most of us first learn to respond to other people and to play with children, have our first experiences in getting and giving affection, receive recognition for trying to accomplish a task? Where do some learn fears which may continue throughout life? What is the origin of most beliefs and feelings about God, the purpose of life? How and where do communicants learn to prefer a given church or synagogue? What is the source of habits which have been learned and practiced consistently? How do they accept what they most deeply believe, how to decide what they most enjoy doing?

An attempt to think about some of these questions will provide an indication of the importance of the home as an educative agency. These learnings have persisted, and have contributed to our growth as personalities. These learnings have helped to make us the persons that we are.

Many differences of opinion about the family's role in education may be found, but practically all will agree that the home provides the child's first social relationships among many other *firsts* in his education. The famous study by G. Stanley Hall, *The Contents of Children's Minds on Entering School*, that appeared late in the last century, helped teachers and parents to see that children's personalities are relatively well-developed when they enter school. Many habits, attitudes, standards of judgment, speech patterns, ways of social behavior, and even values are well established when five-year-olds enter kindergarten.

Teachers with experience in cooperating with parents, are able to appreciate the educative influence of the home. Alert teachers in good schools are ever watchful for opportunities to improve school-home cooperation to the end of better educative experiences for children. Some of the practices which have proved to be worthwhile may be observed in visits to schools—a feature of teacher education programs. The preschool child is helped by intelligent cooperation between school and parents in the form of conferences, health examinations, and care. Teachers visit homes to take the school census, to learn firsthand of the child's home situation and his early educative experiences. Parents and teachers cooperate in PTA work, and in many joint group efforts and studies. They have conferences about the progress of pupils, and take intelligent action to strengthen the efforts of each other in order to foster optimum child growth and development. The teacher sends full accounts of pupil progress to the parent, perhaps in the form of a letter plus needed enclosures. Parents are free to discuss problems with teachers. The teachers request helpful information from parents for the cumulative file they keep for each child. The good school and the adequate home may be tied together by intelligent concern for the effective all-round education of the children.

Many school systems utilize the services of *visiting teachers* who work with parents and homes which need help to solve problems concerning the education of the children. The visiting teacher is professionally trained in both social work and education. Classroom teachers often find their help indispensable in solving some problems of children. Most large school systems use the services of trained nurses, school psychologists, sociologists and other specialists whose assistance enables the teacher to do a better job of understanding and meeting pupil needs.

Schools which try to go all the way to cooperate with the home often offer study opportunities for parents in various areas related to family problems, and specific courses for prospective parents. It is important for the alert school to try to do something to improve the family of the future by providing a program of education for family living for high school youth. Such a school makes a worthy contribution to the improvement of society.

Membership in play groups is educational

We often recognize the play group which comes next to the family, in point of time, as an important educative agency.[9] This primary group may perform many functions as it serves needs for play of young children. Here personality must be developed in sterner, realistic, often less sympathetic environs than those found at home. Learning how to relate to others may come either hard or naturally, but much of it comes typically through experiences with an activity group.

[9] For other references see Florence Greenhoe Robbins, *op. cit.,* pp. 173–176 and Havighurst and Neugarten, pp. 125–135.

A few illustrations will suggest the significance of the play group in the personality development of children. Teachers can quickly identify those children who have not had the opportunities to learn which come through participation in activities of the play group. Many can remember the immaculate child whose parents refused to let him mix with the "noisy, dirty kids" of the neighborhood. Parents report that language never used in the home may be heard from the lips of children of tender age. The sources from which many children get their first information about who really performs those functions ascribed to Santa Claus represent another example. In like fashion, children get early information, however accurate or garbled, about sex. Many parents have been puzzled to know where Junior or Suzie picked up a stereotype expression and the attitude which might accompany it. Elders have noted that irrational fears and superstitions have been quickly learned by children from members of the play group. It has been shown that feelings of belonging, of having a place in the group, may stem from early experience. Such important life patterns as being dominant or submissive, having self-confidence or self-consciousness, and various defense mechanisms develop from truly educative experiences in early life. Most sociologists would agree that the role of the play group may be an extremely important one in the development of individual personality.

What does this mean for the parent and teacher? Can they help what is learned from experiences within the play group? There are no simple or even uniform answers to such questions although one point is clear. What has gone before the child's school experiences has to be understood and accepted before the teacher can effectively provide for better or additional necessary learnings. It may be possible, early in the school term, to recognize the children in the class that lack the social skills which come from play group participation and to arrange for richer experiences along this line. An alert teacher may tactfully suggest that parents of preschool children arrange for play experiences for those who need more opportunity. When this kind of experience and the play group as an educative agency are understood by the teacher, the school program can be planned to take account of these early learnings of the child.

Churches and synagogues provide education

No uniform conclusion can be stated concerning the role of the church and synagogue as an educative agency in our culture, as both forms and functions have varied in terms of factors of time and place.[10] In a number of Western cultures, and particularly in medieval times, the church played a dominant role in formal education. The synagogue and religious instruction have played a consistent part in the preservation of Hebrew culture through centuries of history in many lands. In colonial America the initiative of various Protestant church groups was responsible for establishing early schools and colleges. The amazing growth of America—growth in complexity, in diversity, in democracy—led inevitably to

both a multiplication and a variety of educative agencies. Democratic America found it necessary to erect a wall between church and state and to develop the public school to serve the secular needs of society. Consequently the role of the church as an educative agency has changed.

The present day influence of the church as an educative agency depends upon several factors. In the first place, there are many denominations represented in the churches of America with widely varying policies and views toward education. Some have been preoccupied with other major functions. Certain denominational groups maintain that education should belong to the church, usually meaning their own. A great many churches and synagogues would view education as a broad function of the community and in society and hold that the church bears a part of the responsibility along with other agencies. Still another view holds that certain aspects of education belong to the church and/or to the family. Other factors which affect the role of the church in education include the need for leadership and the limitations of resources.

Community organization and the performance of other educative agencies affect the work of the religious education programs. Our modern communities differ in numerous ways and church membership is a widely varying factor. Although it is still possible to find localities where nearly everyone belongs to one church, there are far more localities where church affiliation is widely divided and heterogeneous. In homogeneous communities, the church may exert a strong and uniform role in education through parochial

[10] See Robbins, *op. cit.,* pp. 194–215; see also Havighurst and Neugarten, *op. cit.,* pp. 173–191.

schools, Sunday schools, weekday and vacation Bible schools, youth groups, and through its intimate relationships to family life. The heterogeneous communities will present a varied pattern of ethnic groups, types of religious education programs, and successes and failures. Other cultural patterns of the community affect the opportunity of the church. Some towns are known as church going towns; others exhibit different patterns of participation. The educational activities of churches will vary widely in different communities. Churches and synagogues are not uniformly effective, but they represent a major educative force.

How does all of this relate to the work of the teacher and the task of the school? One aspect of the answer is that teachers should respect the churches and synagogues and attempt to understand how their activities may contribute to the development of personality. Teachers who are interested should cooperate with the churches by helping to provide better church school opportunities for children. As individuals, teachers along with other educated parents should seek better church programs for children and youth.

The school can find intelligent ways of relating its program so as to avoid imposing undue hardships and problems for the churches of the community. The school authorities can ascertain the need for free evenings or other out-of-school time for educational activities of the churches and arrange the school activities calendar accordingly. It should be possible to schedule athletic contests, concerts, dramatic events and other programs without preempting too much of the time of children and youth after school hours. The

success of many Jewish synagogues in providing religious instruction after the close of the secular school week indicates that this is possible for other religious education programs.

The public school cannot, and should not, engage in religious instruction. This is the responsibility of the churches. In any event, our historic policy of separate church and state has worked too well to justify any effort to modify it. Evidence upon this point can be had by checking on church membership and attendance in America as compared with nations which have established churches. Although the public school may not give religious instruction, it bears a heavy responsibility for emphasizing moral and spiritual values.[11] Moral and spiritual values which are necessary for the survival of highly organized society are acceptable to all religious groups. Responsibility for the realization of these values through education is shared by home, church, school, and possibly other agencies. School administrations and teachers should be aware of this mutual responsibility of our most influential educative agencies.

Youth learns the peer culture

The complex society in which we learn to participate as we become the persons we are, has several other active agencies which perform educational func-

[11] See recent reports of practicable programs that have been developed in many school situations: (1) Educational Policies Commission, *Moral and Spiritual Values in Public Schools* (Washington: NEA, 1951); (2) William Clayton Bower, *Moral and Spiritual Values in Education* (Lexington: University of Kentucky Press, 1951); (3) Ellis F. Hartford, *Moral Values in Public Education* (New York: Harper & Row, 1958).

tions.[12] Some of the most effective of these are the peer groups which play significant roles in the growth and development of the young. Studies of the gang and its functions confirm our observations of the potent role of peer groups among adolescent youth. Parents and teachers who can recall their own participation in the youth groups of high school days and their activities, have background for appreciating the peer culture. It is doubtful if anyone thought of the after-school chocolate soda sessions and informal get-togethers as educative. Probably these were some of the most effective educative experiences the youth ever had.

Membership in the peer group is so important that wise teachers and able group leaders of youth have utilized its force in worthwhile organizations and activities. Good illustrations are cited in "Teen Taverns" and certain youth groups sponsored by churches and synagogues. Even more pertinent is the fact that many of the student activities both in and after the regular school hours, appeal strongly to youth for much the same reasons as these informal peer groups do.

The potent influence of youth groups points up their significance as educative agencies and their nature and purpose become matters of societal concern. Groups can be utilized by selfish and

[12] Much insight into the teen-age culture can be gained from recent studies. See, for example, Hollingshead's *Elmtown's Youth* for helpful information about informal educative experiences and values. See also Robt. J. Havighurst, *et al.*, *Growing Up in River City*, a recent comprehensive study (New York: John Wiley & Sons, 1962). Florence Greenhoe Robbins, *op. cit.*, has a brief treatment, pp. 175–191. The classic study of this subject was by Frederic M. Thrasher, *The Gang* (Chicago: University of Chicago Press, 1936).

even vicious leaders, especially in those communities which neglect youth. The informal cliques and groups which frequent places of amusement such as the pool hall, the juke joint, and the drive-in establishments serve to show how youth learn some of the things they do learn. Some establishments operated primarily for commercial gain and subject to only nominal controls are not always recognized as educative agencies, but teachers and parents would be wrong to ignore them. The leisure time and recreational patterns of behavior comprise an important aspect of the total education of youth. No parent or teacher can afford to ignore the fact that much behavior is learned in these situations. Neither can the conscientious teacher forget the wholesome opportunity which the school has, through an adequate student activities program, to help pupils to develop hobbies as well as social skills and poise which will carry over into adult life.

The school may find means of making constructive use of desirable youth groups. Good teachers have advised parents that participation in this or that youth activity group would be a desirable part of educational experience. The wise teacher considers the experiences that youthful students have in scouting, Hi-Y clubs, 4-H clubs, the FFA and FHA, and other recognized organizations in planning the instructional program of school.

Finally the school in any community must be concerned with the problems of coordination of the activities and functions of the numerous youth groups. The farseeing teacher and school welcome the opportunity to work with other active educative agencies. School programs can hardly be sound or realistic if developed apart from the total community pattern of education. This would indicate that the school leadership should actively seek ways and means of cooperating with other educative agencies. Every school should attempt to be community-minded. When schools understand the functions and the effects of other educative agencies they are in position to make intelligent responses to them. Often this means cooperation. Occasionally it might involve some means of substituting more desirable activities. It is necessary for the school to relate its program to the total educative experiences of youth in the community.

Activity groups of children and other peer groups among teenagers are needed to fill gaps left by the decline in primary group functions of the family and neighborhood. How well this area of need is filled depends upon the adequacy of the planned services which are provided for youth. Schools which do not serve the basic needs of youth leave a vacuum which may be partially filled by vicious peer groups. The school must never assume that it can exist and do its work in isolation from other educative agencies of the culture.

Schools and communities which ignore these principles will find that much of the educative experiences of youth are acquired outside the school. The same child who fills a role in a teen-age peer group or even a gang comes to school for about six hours a day. Since the school has educated leadership, it is reasonable to expect it to take the lead in trying to understand and provide for the best possible educational growth of the young. Common sense and the evidence from

history alike serve to indicate what society does to an agency when it fails to meet the needs it was created to serve. Educative agencies may come and go, but the functional school should be continued for its distinctive role among other effective groups and institutions of society.

Passive agencies figure in education

There are other agencies not primarily concerned with education which nevertheless exert strong influence upon what people learn, act, and do. They are really educative agencies affecting adult and child alike—the press, the radio, the movies, and television. Although each has specific responsibilities in our society these agencies perform significant educative functions.[13]

Some teachers have failed to recognize the fact that many societal agencies have strong influence upon the education of people—young and old. Consider the problem of the teacher whose concern about the usage of English is aggravated by the colorful speech of radio comedians, disc jockeys, sports announcers, and TV shows. Many teachers find evidence of need for further teaching when they see the so-called funny papers and examine some of the comic books on newsstands.[14] These are deliberate examples, but we should note that much of the incidental

[13] See Havighurst and Neugarten, *op. cit.,* pp. 198–204.

[14] A good number of research studies on the problems and effects of comic books are available from the early Fifties. Evidence indicates that the comic books peak sales in 1952 have not been equalled in recent years. See article in NEA *Journal,* December, 1955, p. 532. The aroused public opinion of the early Fifties and the self-regulation of the comic book industry by most firms brought significant improvement.

education which results from society's passive agencies is constructive and good. Teachers have the problem of utilizing and making intelligent use of these educative influences.[15] Shall the situation be left to chance or should there be more concern about the nature and quality of these influences? What should be their function? To sell beer? Or long playing records? Or dog biscuits? To teach the habit of using facilities for chest X rays? To show how to rob a bank? To popularize catchy slang expressions? To learn some of what is in certain great books? To flout the common rules of grammar? To spread half-truths or other devices used by the propagandist? To provide a forum for the best thinkers on public affairs? Whose business is this? Parents and teachers of the future will have to make decisions about questions like these.

The press has long performed a prominent role in our society. The historic contribution of a free press to the development of our democracy and the continuing influence of newspapers and journals upon public policy should be understood by teachers. Most students of democracy recognize the intimate relationship of a free press and other media for spreading information for the proper growth and functioning of a free society. The contributions of a truly free press to public information and attitudes of the people indicate significant educative functions and responsibilities. This topic and its implications for teaching deserves more elaborate consideration than can be given

[15] There is a good discussion of the roles of mass media in Florence Greenhoe Robbins, *op. cit.*, pp. 216–239.

here. Teachers should, at least, point out the role of the press and teach children to read and evaluate the papers and journals which provide so much of their information. All teachers should be sensitive to the critical need for a free press and they should be concerned about the problems which relate to this basic institution of our democracy.

The significance of a free press in a democratic society applies with equal force to the radio and television media as channels of public information. Many studies show the effectiveness of programs designed to present information about live public questions. The experience of a number of school systems and universities with educational broadcasting opens up opportunities for schools and adult education programs. American schools have lagged behind those of some countries in their use of educational broadcasting. How to realize this opportunity and to find the means of using television for educational purposes are pertinent problems of educational policy today. The classroom teacher not concerned with issues of policy still has some practical problems related to radio and television. Many ask whether school children spend too much time viewing television. Some are concerned about the possible adoption of slangy speech patterns of radio and TV comedians by children and youth. Others wonder whether the people will be able to keep a proper perspective upon issues, problems, and topics which are presented by vested interests. Parents and teachers question current emphases on advertising of many products not suitable for use by children. These and many other practical questions arise from the programs and influence of the mass media agencies which affect education both directly and indirectly. This promises to be a continuing concern for parents' and teachers' groups that will study ways and means to utilize these programs and facilities in constructive fashion.[16]

A great deal of this general point-of-view might well be applied to the movies and the theatre. There is evidence that shows the effectiveness of these media for presenting ideas and influencing attitudes of people. Studies have shown that one movie has materially changed the opinions of people about a given subject. America's cultural history records some influential stage plays as *Uncle Tom's Cabin*. Implications for education are simply tremendous but adequate treatment of this subject might require entire books.[17] Students may recall instances of effective use of current films by teachers and think of other occasions when the teacher should have corrected some points of fact or misinformation from a historical movie. The educational potentialities of such media as newsreels, short subjects, travelogues, and documentary films are tremendous to say nothing of the vast field of teaching films. Again it appears that teachers must accept more responsibility including: make effective use of educational films, teach children to detect propaganda, to evaluate visual materials, and to be constructively critical of commercial media which affect education.

Certain other passive and incidental agencies that affect education in our society include numerous organizations which try to carry on education programs. One whose name gets on various mailing lists or who writes for free literature soon comes to realize the number and activity of these organizations. Parents and teachers may become concerned about printed matter sometimes available at the corner drug store or a newsstand or when comic books are circulating in the school. Granted that many of these are harmless, teachers should try to learn what the children get from them. Sometimes they may provide ideas or beginning points for the work of the instructor. These are but some examples of the many agencies and organizations in communities which affect education either directly or indirectly. Future parents and teachers will be wiser and more effective if they know about these forces and take their functions into account in teaching and guiding their children.

Social class affects education in the community

All cultures exhibit various forms and patterns of social organization which change, as indeed does the culture itself. Cultures often exhibit some kind of class system; the social organization of non-literate peoples has exhibited a class structure. Many American Indian tribes had a class organization. Anthropologists find class systems in studies of certain cultures in parts of the world today. This is another aspect of culture that may have an important relation to education.

Modern mid-twentieth century U.S.A. has discovered that more people recognize a social class structure in our

[16] See Havighurst and Neugarten, *op. cit.,* pp. 192–197.

[17] See Edgar Dale, *Audiovisual Methods in Teaching,* revised edition (New York: Dryden Press, 1954).

communities.[18] This discovery comes as a shock to some who have never questioned the American tradition of an open-class system. Our long tradition has meant that one's membership in social organization depended not on birth and special privilege but upon initiative, effort, and merit. In the terms of the sociologists, the American people have depended on *attained status* rather than *ascribed status* for acceptance and membership in social groups and in the community generally. Generations of poor but hard-working, honest youth made this tradition real.[19] This fitted neatly into the larger pattern of educational opportunity for all: the chance to get ahead, the possibility of moving up to a better station in life, social mobility, and the American dream that one's children would be in a better position at the start than their parents.

While this has not altogether disappeared it is no longer the pervasive pattern of the last century and American culture today exhibits some social stratification. The passing of the physical frontier just prior to the end of the nineteenth century with the unprecedented growth and complexity of modern industrial enterprise, and the accompanying social changes altered the nature of oppor-

tunity for American youth. Gradually the urban communities of America have come to show a social class structure—one that has no legal basis, but is no less real. Many Americans find this hard to accept or believe, but the evidence before us cannot be ignored. It behooves those who will become parents and teachers to gain an understanding of this facet of modern American life that they may intelligently relate to it.

Our first concern should be to understand it. Available are many readable studies that describe the social class structure of American communities, big city, suburbia, small town, and rural area. An early but comprehensive study of social class was that by the famed Yankee City research team of social scientists that identified six classes in a New England city—upper-upper, upper-lower, middle-upper, middle-lower, lower-upper, and lower-lower. Many studies that followed this general approach after World War II published varied findings of social class structure in "Brasstown," "Elmtown," "Plainville U.S.A.," "Southerntown," and other equally intriguing names. These studies will be available to you in certain social science courses and cultural anthropology and sociology.

Our second concern should be to recognize that social class structure has important implications for the education of children and youth of a given community. It is not enough to know that pupils live in a certain community, it is also important for teachers to know the neighborhood and the class orientation of their homes and families. You will see this point when you learn that a given youth lives in a neighborhood that has long been called a slum area, one that

---

[18] See William Lloyd Warner, *Social Class in America* (Chicago: Science Research Associates, Inc., 1949). Brief treatment may be found in Robbins, *op. cit.*, pp. 89–110; Meltzer, Doby, and Smith, *op. cit.*, pp. 334–365; Rodeheaver, Axtell and Gross, *op. cit.*, pp. 86–104.

[19] Grandparents of this college generation will recall the extended series of Horatio Alger books that expressed this theme. The ideals and values of this tradition were taught to American school children for decades through the medium of the William Holmes McGuffey readers, probably the most successful series of textbooks ever published.

is now scheduled to be razed in an urban renewal program. Immediately, you realize that the environment and the growing-up experiences of this youth have been radically different from others who live in family-owned modest but neat houses on Midland Avenue. When you think of the differences in the manner of living between both of these and that of a small number who live in an exclusive suburban setting adjacent to golf club, country day school, and yacht basin you will further appreciate the educational implications of social class.

Differences in family patterns of living are marked. A great variety in attitudes toward school, discipline, work experiences, family aspirations for their children, and values have been found in different social classes. Many of these pose problems of absenteeism, dropouts, aggressive behavior, and discipline for the school.

There have been some provocative studies of social class structures and education in communities—especially the impact upon teen-agers. Students should come to know Elmtown's youth, those of River City and Wabash and to see how the class system may affect the overall educational experience of children and youth.

One should take care to avoid hasty generalizations about this; it would be wrong to conclude that social class and neighborhoods are deterministic in their effect upon all youth. Some do overcome the lack of opportunity and the relatively poor chance to get ahead in an inferior environment but it is not easy.

An implication of especial interest to future teachers is that many studies have determined that persons entering the profession tend to come from the so-called middle class. One of the most obvious results is the tendency of teachers to emphasize the values and patterns characteristic of their own class orientation and experience. In past decades this has not been a critical problem in smaller communities. It becomes increasingly important for teachers to gain insight into this aspect of our culture and to understand the cultural and individual differences that will be found in school groups of metropolitan communities.[20]

Parents and teachers must understand the informal social structure of the community in order to plan to meet the problems and to effect the improved experiences that may be called for if the community is to do its best for all its children.

EVERY COMMUNITY HAS A PATTERN

A community is certain to have a number and variety of educative agencies. This is true of our society as a whole; it has been true of societies in general. Community leaders should understand this universal pattern if the schools are to view their tasks intelligently. How else can the school relate its program to the functions and activities of other agencies?

It is possible to view the local neighborhood and even the wider community as educative agencies. All communities do depend upon education, but it is hard to separate this overall process from that which results from the work of all the

[20] See David G. Ryans, *Characteristics of Teachers* (Washington: American Council on Education, 1960); see also Robbins, *op. cit.,* pp. 340–346; see also Havighurst and Neugarten, *op. cit.,* pp. 459–479.

agencies we have noted. All these agencies do compose some sort of a pattern.

The teachers, administrators, and supporters of public schools should understand this provision of society and respect the functions of other essential agencies. They should be on the alert to utilize the educational programs of other community agencies, and there should be effective cooperation among all educative agencies to the end of better provision for the needs of people and society.

The Regional Pattern and Education

All of us are good Americans, products of the American way of life, graduates of the culture, so to speak. At the same time we can be identified as New England Yankees, Easterners, Southerners; also, representatives of the Corn Belt, the Prairies, the Pacific coast or some other region. This can be recognized in the speech of Americans from "Down East" in Maine to the Golden Gate, from the Great Lakes to the Gulf. Most students could identify the regional setting of a given scene by studying the picture for regional variations. This is probably enough to identify the concept of the cultural regions of the United States, areas that represent distinctive subcultures of the national culture. The regional pattern of America is partly geographical, but it is the blending of many economic, historical, social, and psychological factors that comprise its real nature.[21]

This facet of American life has something to do with education, i.e., the total education of a person. When we consider all that people learn, we can think of many examples of this fact. People of a given region share distinctive speech patterns, learn some common folklore, learn attitudes and values that stem from the traditions of their forbears. It is clear that education bears a regional stamp in addition to the shaping received from community and home living patterns.

Pupils can and do move from the schools of one region to those of another and find themselves able to fit into and continue their grade level. But it is not always easy. Sometimes the subtle differences in the regional experiences affect the adjustment to different ways of behaving and believing. It will not be necessary to look far for an illustration in these days of mobility, desegregation, migration of workers, and extensive travel.

The regional pattern has affected education in various ways. One important relation has been noted in the economic factors that are common to states of certain regions. Much of the argument for Federal aid to education has been based on the need of Southern states (mostly) for additional resources to support educational opportunity for their children. It is easy to see how the complex of problems that affect a region may relate to education. Indices of functional illiteracy, low health standards, lack of skilled workers, low income, and high birth rate

[21] An excellent treatment may be found in Howard Odum and H. E. Moore, *American Regionalism* (New York: Holt, Rinehart & Winston, 1938). A brief discussion may be found in Robbins, *op. cit.*, pp. 86–89.

that mark a state or region pose problems for the schools. Regional organizations to promote cooperation in higher education have been established in the South, New England, the West. The accrediting associations of colleges and secondary schools are regional in scope.[22] Education may differ somewhat in terms of the regional orientation in which it is identified and studied.

The Changing American Culture and Education

American education is the distinctive product of the democratic society that surrounds and supports it and whose agent it is. The public educational systems bear the hallmarks of democracy; their role and functions stem from the nature and goals of the environing culture. No people have been so well served by a set of institutions developed to serve them and their aspirations. Common schools have served and helped to extend democracy even while, as institutions, they have been expanded into complete systems of free education, extending from the kindergarten through the halls of graduate and professional study. These are the people's schools and it is imperative that those who must support them and depend upon them should understand them, especially their vital relationship to the continued growth and success of democratic institutions.

Those who would understand American culture and its public educational systems must be prepared to study a culture that is on the move—changing, growing, reconstructing at a rapid rate. The distinctive way of life that we call American is now characterized by change, new forms, and different patterns—most of it at an unprecedented rate. That same American culture that developed and used for generations "the little red schoolhouse" and the "old blue-backed speller" has now produced schools that occupy skyscrapers and curriculums that require textbooks stacked eight feet high. Educational opportunity for all who can take advantage of it is still the ideal of America's parents and teachers. What would Horace Mann or James G. Carter or Charles Brooks think of social change if they could visit the best-planned modern school and learn of its program for youth and adults? Appreciation of social change and the relationship of the common schools *in* and *to* that changing culture is necessary if we are to continue to provide educational opportunity for all in a changing future.

Any attempt to achieve an understanding of American public education must consider the national cultural setting with its characteristic social changes and trends. Many studies are available on this general subject, but a complete catalog of their findings would fill a good-sized book.[23] Representative trends and movements in contemporary American culture serve to illustrate the significance of the changes and to suggest implications for

[22] These are six in number: New England, Middle States, North Central, Southern, Northwest, and Western.

[23] A sample of what is available may be found in Havighurst and Neugarten, *op. cit.,* pp. 3–68, 227–248; Rodeheaver, Axtell, and Gross, *op. cit.,* pp. 16–30.

the work of the public educational systems of these United States.

A SURVEY OF AMERICAN LIFE

Change itself, the unchanging characteristic of life and human cultures, appears to be changing. At least, the rate of change is; it is speeding up and moving faster. That's what the social scientists find about life in the United States. The American way of life is undergoing significant changes as patterns of living are being reshaped across the nation.[24] The nation's earnings mount, and consumer spending rises to new heights. High priced luxury items are popular choices but spending for services increases more slowly. Investing and saving habits are becoming more cautious and conservative. Marriages are on the increase as the teens and twenties age-groups increase fastest of any in the total population. The trend toward larger families of World War II and post-war years appears to be dropping. Nevertheless the U.S. population will reach 210,000,000 by 1970 if present trends continue.[25]

Women workers in the economy have doubled since the start of World War II. The efficiency of the economy is shown by the fact that fewer than one-half of American workers are required in production. It is clear that the great growth of employment comes in the area of services. The prospect of earlier retirement appeals to more workers. The two-

car family has been followed by many two-homes-families, one being used for week end retreats. Apartment living is returning to favor. High property taxes in suburbs and the crab-grass war continue. Eating and dining practices have changed radically with increased use of pre-packaged foods and much dining out by families. Outdoor living practices of all kinds increase in popularity. Active sports grow in popularity and new activities increase. Hunting and fishing licenses have doubled in the past decade. Vacation trips increase in length and foreign travel rises in popularity. Nearly two million Americans go abroad annually.

Many people do not realize that a cultural revolution has begun in the United States. More Americans are engaging in more cultural pursuits with attendance at art galleries, concerts, and museums reaching new heights. Attendance at American museums and art galleries far exceed those for European centers. Average expenditures for education and reading almost doubled between 1950 and 1960. Aspirations of American parents for a college education for their children have reached an all-time high.

This brief sketch shows clearly the dynamic character of the American way of life.[26] Much of it appears incredible to persons accustomed to think in terms of an economy of scarcity. So effective are the means of production that present-day farms and factories use fewer workers

---

[24] See "How Life in U.S. is Changing," *U.S. News and World Report,* **LIII,** No. 23 (December 3, 1962), pp. 68–73.

[25] Hoke S. Simpson (ed.), *The Changing American Population,* A Report of the Arden House Conference (New York: Institute of Life Insurance, 1962).

[26] An excellent recent reference for this general topic is Solon T. Kimball and James L. McClellan, *Education and the New America* (New York: Random House, Inc., 1962). See also Havighurst and Neugarten, *op. cit.,* pp. 322–432; Meltzer, Doby and Smith, *op. cit.,* pp. 93–138; and Spindler, *op. cit.,* pp. 132–172 for useful chapters.

and have to devise ways to limit their output. Who can doubt that the schools must take social change into account as they serve our society?

Another study after the 1970 census will undoubtedly reveal more changes and new developments. The implication for education seems unmistakably clear.

SOME ASPECTS OF SOCIAL CHANGE

Population changes

The most obvious change is that of the sharply increased rate of population growth since 1940. It now seems strange to recall that school boards and superintendents of former decades believed that available school plants would care for elementary enrollments indefinitely.

The growth of urban population is continuing at an increased rate. Migration of families has become common, 20% move yearly for jobs, climate, health, or other reasons. The population changes in composition; it is now growing at both ends of the life span with the number of young people increasing rapidly and the percentage of people over 65 also rising.[27]

All of these changes and shifts in population have clear implications for school policy and programs. School boards and superintendents in many districts have encountered problems that stem directly from the changing population of our society. A few illustrations will suffice. You are a principal and your school building is already full. An important crop begins to mature and several score of migrant workers' families move

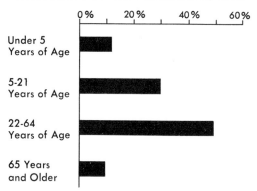

DISTRIBUTION OF THE POPULATION, 1960

Source: NEA Research Division.

into the crude camps and quarters provided by farmers. They bring a bevy of children of school age and many understand so little English that they cannot follow the instruction. Before you get the problem in hand, working with your superintendent, faculty, and board, along comes another influx.

Another time the problem is brought in by a small group of community leaders, retired or approaching retirement age, who want the school system to provide educational, recreational and avocational activities and classes for the aging citizens of the school district who still pay taxes to your district. When you go to discuss this with your superintendent, he wants a listener for his new headache. Farmer Jones, whose children have graduated and moved to the city, has sold his fine farm to a promoter and moved to the city to be near his grandchildren. Now a trailer camp is to occupy the field fronting the highway about two miles from the school. Mr. Jones paid school taxes promptly on a large valuable piece of property and had only 2 children to be educated. Now, there will be two or three dozen families with a large number of children to be

[27] See N.E.A. Research Division, *Rankings of the States*, 1963, Report, 1963–R1, (January 1963), for figures and tables, pp. 7–16.

hauled to school, and educated at the expense of the district. The taxes on this former farmland will now provide only a small fraction of the cost involved in the education of the children of families that move frequently, that have no roots in a community. This kind of development is a normal consequence of the changing character of our population in our dynamic and dazzling culture.

An urban culture

City dwellers first outnumbered rural population in the Census of 1920 with 51.2% of the total. In 1930 and 1940 the percentage of urban population was 56.2 and 56.5 respectively, by 1950 it was 59 and in 1960 up to 64.7. Nearly two-thirds of Americans lived in a city; only 35.3% of the 1960 total were rural population and these were divided between rural nonfarm and rural farm dwellers. The proportion of nonfarm rural inhabitants who commute to urban jobs is increasing. Every population expert expects that fewer people will be engaged in agricultural pursuits, that cities will grow as our population reaches an estimated 260,000,000 well before the end of the twentieth century.

America has already become an urban culture, irrevocably committed to the ways of the crowd, the machine, and the marketplace. A great metropolitan cluster of cities stretches across state lines and geography from New Hampshire into Virginia. This unbroken chain of urban centers and congestion may ultimately extend as far south as Charleston. This is what geographers call Megalopolis. Others are consolidating all around Chicago and the Lake Michigan area, along

the Gulf Coast, and in the coastal areas of California.

The educational problems and implications of the new urban society have begun to attract attention of national leaders in various fields as well as educators. A department for urban affairs has been proposed for the cabinet. Provocative books and studies upon the educational problems of urbanized American communities have begun to appear.[28]

Changes in family and home life

The new conditions and changes in American life have left their mark upon the family and the patterns of home life. There are many significant changes in the American family. The family is not as well integrated as formerly. Many mothers work outside the home. Community and social activities take much time of certain parents. Members of formerly closely-knit families are scattered over the United States and abroad. Parents have less influence on the character and education of their children. Marriages come early; divorce is easy. Broken homes provide the community agencies with myriad problems. The competent teacher knows all too well the problems and the educational handicaps of anxiety, emotional instability, hostility, and tension the school children bring from poor home environments.

No college youth of today needs to have the changing patterns of home living spelled out; he has lived *in* or *through* it.

[28] See B. J. Chandler, Lindley J. Stiles, and John I. Kitsuse, *Education in our Urban Society* (New York: Dodd, Mead & Co., 1962). A good chapter may be found in Havighurst and Neugarten, *op. cit.*, pp. 322–348.

Consider the educational implications of the use of time involved in TV viewing. The annual family vacation trip is another recent development, and has worthwhile educational possibilities. Most important of all is the kind of influence upon and its contribution to the total personality development that takes place in the home and in the family pattern of living.

The scientific and technological revolutions

References to the profound changes in American life due to scientific discoveries and technological developments have become commonplace. Everyone has heard this kind of expression and talks about it but it is unlikely that we will overemphasize its meaning and significance. Industry has been the principal basis of modern economy for many decades since the Industrial Revolution was accomplished. The industrialization (and urbanization) of American society has continued with new developments in sources of power, more complicated installations, and efficient operation. The transition to cheap electric power facilitated the technological revolution. This was made practicable by application of basic physical sciences to industrial production. The whole new field of electronics and its many applications was a result. The newer revolutions had hardly been achieved when the principle of nuclear fission was discovered with the possibility of atomic power for practical use. Applications of this principle to the production of power, to propulsion of ocean vessels and certain industrial uses are currently in progress. A concomitant of the new developments in electronics and modern technology was the growing use of automation. The vast trends that pervaded our economy that tended to separate persons further and further away from the sources of raw materials and the production process were accentuated. Older science fiction predictions have already become outmoded by the performance of many automatized plants.

Students of the contemporary social scene will recognize important educational implications. There are challenging responsibilities for preparing workers for the new world of work. Whether this can or should be done in schools are vexing questions. Certainly older conceptions of educating persons for a particular trade are inadequate. Workers change jobs for various reasons; the nature of jobs change frequently; industrial processes and plants are shifted and moved on short notice, and personnel policies reflect these changes. Much retraining is necessary in a modern industry and community. What represents the best preparation for vocational efficiency is an important question for all who have a stake in education. The answer has to be formulated in terms of the important factors of time and place and occasion. One point seems clear for our philosophy of vocational preparation: education of persons adaptable to changes and new situations is an important start upon any kind of program.

The continuing job of interpreting the complexity and the functioning of the economy including the productive enterprise to the general population must be taken seriously by schools and colleges. This should include the whole matter of *resource use* or conservation of natural resources, the basis of all productive enterprise. Despite the vast and profound revolutions in our economy there is still a dependence upon raw materials, resources, many of which are scarce or irreplaceable. Man cannot expect to flout principles of wise use of resources and get away with it indefinitely.

Another continuing task of economic education is that of interpreting the nature of the private enterprise system or economy to those who have benefitted from its operations and to the peoples of our good neighbor nations who visit us.

Some problem areas and groups

History shows that adults have always tended to view the oncoming generation with alarm and trepidation. Inscriptions to this effect can be found in earliest written languages, and the writings of ancient, medieval and modern authors repeat the theme. In other words, ours is neither the first civilization nor the first century to be plagued with juvenile delinquency. Perhaps the most disturbing fact is the rapid increase of juvenile delinquency since the late days of the Second World War. This phenomenon of the war was not temporary; its continuation gives concern to teachers, youth leaders, clergymen, social workers, and civil authorities. Part of this general problem is environmental; it is a concomitant of the blight that overcomes neighborhoods in our major cities. Dr. Conant treated this problem in one of his recent noteworthy studies of American education.[29] The "social dynamite" of the slums presents the schools with a complex and baffling set of problems. Slum clearance programs and urban renewal projects do not always solve the problem; they simply move the people with problems.

Another problem of serious proportions is the perennial loss of teenagers from school—the dropout problem. A complex of factors and conditions relate to this problem and each community may need to study its own situation for clues to the solution. As the nation gets well into the Sixties this problem of the disadvantaged has become the concern of leaders from the national to community level and noteworthy studies have been undertaken.[30] The conditions and problems that contribute to the dropout phenomenon now seem to be matched by another complex of results and consequences that follow from the educational shortages it brings. The nation and many communities have come to see that the outlook for the dropout in future decades is bleak due to the lack of opportunity for the individual, and added costs of public welfare and other services to society.

Delinquency and dropouts are not confined to slum areas and metropolitan cities. This amazing urbanized, automated, and mobile civilization, based on machines and capable of production miracles year after year, has some of its problems built into its very structure. The truth is that contemporary American culture provides only one big responsibility for teenagers—going to school. Earlier and simpler cultures that could require many definite tasks and functions on the part of adolescents had less delinquency.

[29] James B. Conant, *Slums and Suburbs: A Commentary on Schools in Metropolitan Areas* (New York: McGraw-Hill, 1961).

[30] Havighurst and Neugarten, *op. cit.*, pp. 231–237; see also Percy V. Williams, "School Dropouts," *NEA Journal,* **LII,** No. 2 (February 1963), pp. 10–12; and the new publication by the Educational Policies Commission, *Education and the Disadvantaged American* (Washington: NEA, 1962).

How the culture and the culture's schools can solve these and other knotty problems is an imperative challenge.

The explosion of knowledge

The history of mankind numbers many great intellectual achievements and advances. Certain periods of history are clearly marked by extraordinary developments and movements in intellectual history. The Golden Age of Athens, the Alexandrian center of learning, the flowering of Moslem culture in Granada and in Bagdad, the Renaissance, and the Age of Enlightenment could come to mind. Cultural and intellectual historians of the future will need to account for the incredible advances in human knowledge during the twentieth century. New developments in scientific and technological fields, in certain social sciences, in modern art forms, and whole new areas of study have amounted to an explosion of knowledge.

The educational implications are immediately obvious. This new knowledge is important, it is dangerous to be misinformed or even uninformed, hence the need for educators to keep abreast of human intellectual advances. Teachers and all who try to be students must ever keep alert and intent upon the quest for knowledge and understanding. This quest, continued throughout life, is a worthwhile and gratifying motive or incentive to achievement. Pursuit of that elusive question mark which the inquiring mind keeps projecting forward is a distinctive characteristic of man in one of his best performances.

A practical question for educators at all levels must be faced: how to reorganize the curriculums to make possible the teaching of the most significant knowledge. Few pupils can begin to master a great deal of the available subject matter, old and new. The vast majority will be able to comprehend only a part of the most essential fields of study. This brings up the perennial question raised by Aristotle nearly twenty-four hundred years ago: how to decide what should be taught to boys and girls.

There is also an encouraging facet to this important development. The explosion of knowledge includes a good deal more about learners, what they are, how they behave and why, and their perceptions and learning. Teachers and parents of the later twentieth century should be more skillful and effective as guides of the learning activities of children.

Cultural trends and problems

Contemporary American life is marked by unprecedented social change and the problems of readjustment that follow inevitably. Social scientists of the Fifties and the Sixties have observed many trends that reflect profound changes in our culture. The total findings of all major studies from the time of the Committee on Social Trends would fill an encyclopedia.[31] Some of the most significant recent changes and trends will illustrate their significance for the educational systems and the work of schools in our dynamic democratic culture.

Evaluations differ about the effects of many changes in the ways Americans live but all agree that the changes are many and varied. Most observers recog-

[31] A renowned landmark study by a national committee of social scientists. See *Report of the President's Research Committee on Social Trends* (New York: McGraw-Hill Book Co., 1932).

nize change in the traditional American idealism which has given way to emphasis upon material success and status symbols. So far has change taken Americans from the days of Horatio Alger and the Mc-Guffey readers that practice of such virtues as modesty, simplicity, and thrift has all but disappeared. Instead, the display of status symbols—big cars, imported cars, mink coats, suburban homes in the latest mode, swimming pools, right country club membership, art objects, exclusive private schools—these have come to indicate favored social and economic position. The thing to do is to give the impression of charm, achievement, sophistication, poise, wealth, whether one has a genuine claim to them or not. This will sound like harsh criticism and a one-sided view. When you recall some of the movies that give people overseas such distorted notions about the American people and our way of life, you may understand how rash judgments get started.

Certain cultural trends become even more significant when changes in our society bring conditions that accentuate their importance. A prime example is the decreasing workweek for workers in most major industries. The other side of this phenomenon is increased leisure time, at least the promise of opportunity to exercise free choice of activities, to follow one's interests. Whether the outcome is socially desirable or not depends in large part upon education. Does increased leisure time bring enriched experiences? Or, does it merely mean more of the same low-level uncritical type of existence that passes for life by too many people?

Closely related to the shorter work week and increased leisure time complex is what has been called the trend toward softer living. Most of the hard physical labor has been eliminated from housekeeping and upkeep of the household by automatic appliances and machinery. Chores are no longer available for character building experiences for youth, even parttime employment of any kind is growing scarce. Coupled with the lack of strenuous activity in the household and chores is the growing popularity of sedentary activities for amusement. In a few decades, American life has changed materially in this respect. Observers see cause for concern about the lack of physical fitness among the school population which may be attributed to softer living of American families. Merely getting by in studies, election of soft courses and efforts to get good marks instead of achievement of scholarship are frequently cited as manifestations of this same trend in the field of education.

Most studies of social changes and trends include increased influence of mass media of communication. All media— television, radio, movies, and the press— continue to gain or hold strong positions of influence in the recreational interests of the population. Television gains viewers and more of the viewers' time, but there is also more reading of books, magazines, and newspapers. It would appear that this is where some of that increased leisure time has been going. There are many problems related to the use of mass media for advertising and for indoctrination purposes that suggest some important tasks for education. The great potential for educational use of most mass media has only been explored. The realization is yet to come.

National Organizations and American Education

THE FEDERAL GOVERNMENT AND EDUCATION

Education is an increasingly important concern in the national capital not withstanding the fact that education is the responsibility of the several states. As your study of American education continues, you will find that the Federal Government has long had specific interests in education and has made important contributions to the state public educational systems upon various occasions. All this will be examined in our consideration of the history and the organizational pattern of American public education.

The Federal Government has several specific areas of responsibility and concern about education, all of which lie outside the jurisdiction of the states. These provide the starting point for many of the activities of the federal agencies that relate to education:

1. Educational opportunity for people who reside on Federal Government reservations and districts that lie outside the legal jurisdiction of a state.
2. Education of the people of the territories and other outlying possessions.
3. Educational programs for the native Indian populations who reside under the American flag.
4. Educational and training programs for persons in the armed forces and other services of the federal government.
5. Assistance to the states through the collection and dissemination of statistical and other information about education.
6. Scientific research and development related to national defense and other federal functions.
7. Provision of educational leadership and other assistance as part of international cooperation and development programs for underdeveloped nations.
8. Cooperation with international agencies concerned with educational and intellectual programs.

It does not take long to find that a number of federal departments and agencies are concerned with one or more of these functions.[32] Every cabinet department finds it necessary to provide educational or training programs for its employees as do many other agencies and offices. The Department of State has primary responsibility for the educational relationships of the United States with international agencies (e.g., UNESCO and the International Bureau of Education), and for educational assistance to other nations under the Agency for International Development programs. It also cooperates with the Department of Health. Education and Welfare in programs of educational exchange with other countries. The Treasury Department maintains the Coast Guard Academy and a number of training schools for various groups of employees. The Department of Justice with its special schools for FBI agents and the Department of Agriculture's graduate school for specialized personnel in

[32] A list of Federal programs for education requires an entire page in *Statistical Abstract of the United States*, 1962, Eighty-third edition (Washington, D.C., 1962), p. 143. See also *The Federal Government and Education*. House Document No. 159, 88th Congress, 1st Session (Washington: Government Printing Office, 1963).

many fields are good illustrations of the various needs of federal agencies in education.

The Department of Defense maintains numerous schools and training programs for officers and enlisted men in all branches of the armed service. The Military Academy at West Point, New York, the Naval Academy at Annapolis, Maryland, and the Air Force Academy at Colorado Springs, Colorado, are well-known in their function of preparing officer personnel for their respective services. Schools for children of service men on overseas duty are maintained by the Army, the Navy and the Air Force. All services of the armed forces maintain many types of schools, postgraduate schools, and U.S.A.F.I.—a correspondence school programs for both officers and enlisted men.

There are many other types of programs. The Veterans Administration has administered literally billions of dollars of educational benefits to millions of veterans of World War II and the Korean War. The Department of Interior maintains schools on the Indian reservations through its Bureau of Indian Affairs. The Department of Agriculture is concerned with adult education through the land-grant colleges and agricultural extension and with the 4-H clubs for the youth of the nation. There are literally scores of federal educational programs.

Even the Congress is in the educational field. Not only does it deal with legislative measures but it actually provides a school for its pages during off-duty hours at the Capitol. The Supreme Court of the United States has been brought into education in many instances as cases involving interpretation of school law have been carried to the highest court in the land. Some of the major decisions of the Court have related to education from the celebrated Dartmouth College Case (1819) to the decision banning an officially prescribed prayer in public schools, *Engel vs Vitale* (1962). Justice Jackson once remarked that the Supreme Court was being made the "super-school board" for the nation.

Many federal activities and programs related to education have some relationship to or with the Office of Education and the Department of Health, Education, and Welfare. The Office was established shortly after the Civil War and has experienced several reorganizations during its history. Its original functions—collecting and disseminating statistics and other information on education among the several states—have been augmented substantially in recent decades. It has been designated to administer appropriations of federal funds to assist the states with vocational education, special education, and school lunch programs. It also handles administrative details for assistance to school districts that are affected by federal projects located in their general area. Certain grants for educational research are administered by the Office. Since 1958 it has had responsibility for various programs under the National Defense Education Act which provide assistance to the states in improving instruction in sciences, mathematics, modern languages, in strengthening guidance and counseling services, and funds for loans and fellowships for college and graduate students. For many years, the Office has assisted territorial governments in programs of education and performed useful services to other federal agencies and state institutions in educational matters. The Office of Education has become an important but not preeminent agency for educational affairs and functions in the federal government and at the national level.

There are, however, many other official bodies and formal organizations concerned with education at the national level. Among official bodies the Congress is of primary importance, every piece of proposed legislation on education and every dollar of federal money spent for this purpose must be approved and appropriated by both houses. This is not the whole story. Congress is composed of 537 members—100 senators and 437 representatives—all with a full quota of individual differences. These differences comprehend widely divergent views and attitudes toward public and nonpublic education, varying philosophies of government's role in education and spending of the people's money. Most of them are experienced and skillful politicians, adept at discerning and supporting the popular choice, and quick to sense issues and positions that will alienate blocs and groups of voters. Unofficial rules and courtesy among members of congress discourage actions and statements that tend to put one's colleague(s) on the spot. Finally, there are many interests and favorite projects among the members of both houses for which they work very hard. This often involves trading or dealing with colleagues to support their respective favorite pieces of legislation. The discriminating student can begin to see how complex and how difficult is the gauntlet which a bill for federal aid to public education has to run.

Each House of Congress uses the committee system to study, screen, and recommend action upon the thousands of bills and other proposals for legislation that each session brings. Chairmen and members of the committees derive their places from a traditional system of seniority. In each House, there are committees with high prestige on which members naturally prefer to serve. Those on Foreign Relations and Appropriations tend to rate high in Senate and House respectively. You can begin to see how this affects the performance of the legislative branch of our national government.

The Committees that consider bills relating to education are the Committee on Labor and Public Welfare in the Senate and the Committee on Education and Labor in the House. Each of these committees forms subcommittees to give first consideration to bills relating to education. Thus, the official course of an education bill through the Congress would involve these steps: assuming introduction in the House of Representatives the bill would have to be approved by the House subcommittee on Education, and the full House Committee on Education and Labor, be passed by the House, sent to the Senate, where it would have to gain approval of similar subcommittees and committee and be passed by the Senate, hence to the President for signature. Only then would the bill actually become law.

The steps outlined represent only the formal and visible procedure; the unofficial but actual process involves many actions, maneuvers, agreements, countermeasures, attempts to exert pressure, use of propaganda pro and con by groups and individuals, many compromises, over a long period, much of it on a private, even confidential basis. Sophisticated students of government are prepared to understand that this actual operation of the lawmaking process is not fully explained in textbooks.

The role of the Executive branch in lawmaking is important, particularly when the President chooses to exercise it. Until recent administrations the chief executive showed little interest in federal legislation on education. Since World II every president has taken a position upon proposals for federal aid to education. It is manifest that the President is normally in position to wield strong influence in Congress either for or against legislation in which he is interested. Sometimes the chief executive may delegate to or encourage a cabinet member or other official to work closely with Congressional leaders upon educational legislation. In some instances this role may be performed by an aide or even an adviser without official position.

The highest-ranking federal office in education is that of the Commissioner of Education, who heads the United States Office of Education, a part of the Department of Health, Education, and Welfare. The Commissioner of Education reports to the Secretary of the Department. The roles played by these officials varies in terms of the administration in office, its policies and personnel, because the top educational leaders themselves are individuals, and because of the relationships between and among all these and the influential leaders in Congress.[33]

In recent years, the burgeoning expenditures of Federal agencies and departments concerned with programs of research and development have become a significant force in education at the national level, particularly in higher education. Grants and contractual programs to higher education institutions comprise a major source of income for many universities of the country. The appropriations distributed by the Atomic Energy Commission, National Science Foundation, National Institutes of Health, the Department of Defense, National Aeronautics and Space Administration and others assume astronomical proportions compared to normal figures related to education.

NATIONAL PROFESSIONAL GROUPS AND EDUCATION

Education has long been an important concern in the national capital and this interest is on the increase. At the national level, there are some highly important and powerful organizations and groups that represent educational interests.

The National Education Association of the United States is the professional organization of the public school personnel of the nation, and it also includes some teachers from nonpublic systems. Its membership totals approximately 860,000 dues-paying members.[34] All state education associations are affiliates of NEA with an aggregate membership of over 1½ million teachers. The NEA has influential departmental organizations for superintendents (AASA), supervisors (ASCD), secondary school principals (NASSP), and elementary school principals (DESP), and for all departments of

[33] See article on the role of the Commissioner of Education, Francis G. Keppel, in *Education, U.S.A.* (May 2, 1963).

[34] *NEA News,* **XVII,** No. 11 (April 3, 1963).

teaching. It maintains an effective research division and public relations department and publishes numerous reports, studies, and teaching aids. The Educational Policies Committee, jointly representative of the NEA and AASA, prepares important policy statements for the teaching profession of the nation. The National Council of Chief State School Officers maintains an active headquarters staff in Washington.

The only rival organization of any strength is the American Federation of Teachers—not large—but having affiliation with the American Federation of Labor—Congress of Industrial Organizations. Its membership of 70,000 (1962) in 433 locals and 38 states is found chiefly in states with large cities. Illinois, Michigan, New York, Minnesota, California and Ohio account for more than half its membership. The division in the organization ranks of the teaching profession has become more serious in recent years with increased efforts by the labor union leadership to offset declining membership in certain unions by recruiting other groups and to strengthen the American Federation of Teachers organization.

Another strong and influential organization on the Washington scene is the American Council on Education organized in 1918. The Council is composed of several classes of members: colleges and universities, organizations in the field of higher education, school systems, and affiliated groups. Its chief function is that of representing higher education at the national level. It carries on various studies and performs miscellaneous services.

Certain other national organizations of scientists and scholars exert great influence in Washington and the nation generally because of the competency of their membership. The American Association for the Advancement of Science, with a total membership of over 60,000 (1960) is composed of 18 sections related to branches of science. The American Association of University Professors, the principal group to represent the interests of teachers in higher education institutions, has membership of over 42,000 (1960). The American Council of Learned Societies, composed of 30 constituent societies of scholars, maintains national headquarters in Washington for coordination and other services to its total membership of 77,000 (1960). Other organizations include the National Research Council, the National Council on Accreditation, National Association of State Universities, the Association of Land-Grant Colleges and State Universities, the Association of American Colleges, and the Association of American Universities. There are various other smaller professional organizations and bodies represented in the nation's capital.

It is obvious that education has many spokesmen and representative groups in the national capital. The genius for organization is a typical American characteristic. A great deal of diversity and versatility is required to represent the many fields and interests comprehended in the American educational enterprise. Obviously, no single modest organization would be adequate. On the other hand, the great number of professional organizations, few of which represent their entire professional group, sometimes leads to confusion, duplication, and even controversy.

There is a power structure in the

organizational patterns of education at the national level. Those who know the structure and its functioning can observe cooperation or competition or both in a given situation.

The "Big Three" among all the agencies, organizations, and groups representing American education in Washington has been the Office of Education (Department of Health, Education, and Welfare), the NEA, and the American Council on Education. Upon occasions each has had vigorous leadership and exercised initiative to represent American education at the national level. Today it appears to be a shared kind of function that provides each with work to do. There are occasions when the Washington leaders and groups do not agree upon policy or a position to be taken upon proposed legislation. This may disconcert some people but we should remember that the American way permits dissent, encourages discussion and debate, and guarantees minority rights. Should not educational groups be expected to fully exercise the basic privileges of all democratic citizens and groups—especially when principles are involved?

OTHER INFLUENTIAL GROUPS AND ORGANIZATIONS

There are some important groups and organizations in American education that are located outside of Washington, D.C. The largest and most consistent supporter of public education is the National Congress of Parents and Teachers which maintains headquarters in Chicago. Its total membership exceeds 12,100,000 with state organization and approximately 47,-000 local chapters in most school systems

of the nation.[35] Its chief purpose is to promote mutual understanding among all concerned with the education of children. It works to improve schools generally and to support needed legislation for child welfare and education. The National School Boards Association, which represents the state organizations of school board members, maintains headquarters in Evanston, Illinois. Various other associations and groups could be named in a complete catalog.

Among the most influential types of organizations in American education are certain philanthropic foundations. There are perhaps a thousand funds or foundations of all descriptions, large and small, in the nation. At least sixty-four have assets of $20,000,000 or more; the largest —the Ford Foundation—manages assets valued at over $3,000,000,000. At least half of these have exhibited interest in education by grants of funds and other assistance for experimentation, research studies, and new developments.

Certain funds are well-known for their particular emphasis upon specific objectives. The W. K. Kellogg Fund financed the Cooperative Program in Educational Administration. The former General Education Board underwrote programs to improve southern education as did the George Peabody Fund and the Rosenwald Fund. The Carnegie Foundation for the Advancement of Teaching stimulated teacher retirement programs. The Ford Foundation has underwritten various experiments and tryouts of ideas designed to improve American education —ETV, teacher aides, team teaching, new

[35] See current issue of the *PTA Magazine* for recent data.

patterns of teacher education and the like. The influence of the funds becomes apparent when the roll of recent changes and innovations in American education is examined. This is a strategically important and powerful force in and upon American education.

Considerable time could be spent in an exhaustive study of all the organizations that relate to American education. There are many groups of voluntary nature that work for certain specific objectives and goals in education. An example would be the Council on Basic Education which advocates a conservative emphasis in all phases of education. There is a large number and great variety of organizations—mostly small—that seek to influence American education.

The nonpublic educational enterprise comprehends some important organizations. The National Council of Independent Schools represents the well-established private preparatory schools. Many churches maintain national boards and offices that are concerned with educational institutions and programs. The National Catholic Educational Association represents the religious and day instructional corps of parochial and other Roman Catholic institutions. An important policy-making body is the National Catholic Welfare Conference with a Department of Education headquarters in Washington, D.C. Standard reference works provide a convenient source of information for further study. The conscientious student will learn to use these tools of research.

The International Relationships of American Education

Long treatises would be required to deal with the many aspects of the international relations of the U.S.A.[36] At the present rate of social change, an article would be out-of-date by the time it could be published. Parents and teachers who would understand our involvement in the currents of global affairs must read widely and with discrimination.

America has had world leadership responsibility since World War II. Her orientation must recognize the policies of several major international organizations, various groupings of nations, and the United Nations Organization. The United States of America is the leader of the Free World, an elder brother within the Or-

ganization of American States; a senior partner in the North Atlantic Treaty Organization, SEATO, various multilateral pacts; and is obligated by a number of lesser commitments and voluntary associations. It must continually keep informed about and in defensive stance toward the communist bloc of nations, and be sympathetically patient toward the large number of uncommitted nations of Africa and Asia. Policies of arms for friendly nations for strengthening their defense potential, and aid to underdeveloped countries have to be formulated in light of many conflicting factors and sets of conditions, some merely domestic political considerations.

All this has had to proceed while much time and resources have been ex-

[36] See Havighurst and Neugarten, *op. cit.*, pp. 433–455.

pended in long-drawn-out parleys upon proposals for disarmament, a ban on nuclear testing, and other strategic programs. The programs and policies of numerous departments and other federal agencies must be geared to the international scene and especially to our perception of it. Major programs under the Agency for International Development involve education at various levels. Prime examples are contractual arrangements for American universities to direct in building and strengthening universities in underdeveloped nations. The New Peace Corps has many projects that require teachers to go abroad.

American education is actively involved in most educational programs and organizations on the international level today. American educators and diplomats took leading roles in the formation of the UNO specialized agency for education—the United Nations Educational, Scientific, and Cultural Organization. Its third director-general was the former Librarian of Congress, Luther Evans. The United States National Commission for UNESCO holds biennial conferences to discuss the policies, programs and problems with representative groups of American citizens and leaders. The contributions and cooperation of this country have been a large factor in the successful start of this new international organization.

The United States cooperates with the International Bureau of Education (Geneva, Switzerland) in various activities including participation in the International Conferences on Public Education, and in publications. Various other programs for exchange of students and teachers include fellowships for study abroad and cultural exchange, cooperation in matters of copyrights, and participation in conferences of scholarly groups and societies. More students from abroad study in the United States each year, over 64,-000 in 1962–63 and 13,000 American students studied overseas in the same year.[37] About 8,000 persons representing over 100 nations were exchanged for teaching, study, and research programs under programs conducted by the Department of State in 1962. Over two thousand American teachers and professors taught abroad under provisions of the Fulbright-Hays Act the same year.

The teachers of the United States have representation and participation in international educational movements through the World Confederation of Organizations of the Teaching Profession. The NEA took the initiative shortly after World War II ended in reorganizing the WOTP, an international body of national teachers groups. In 1952 this organization was reorganized and enlarged to become the WCOTP.

Education has the task of teaching awareness of and concern about the international relations and America's commitments to the future. This involves the education of an army of potential diplomats, international minded representatives for business and government agencies, and experts in many fields. One specific emphasis for curriculums for today's world is the emphasis upon foreign languages.

[37] *Newsweek,* **LXI,** No. 6 (April 22, 1963), pp. 59–66; see also Herbert Mazo, "American Students Abroad: A Proposal for Standards," *The Modern Language Journal,* **XLVII,** No. 1 (Jan. 1963), p. 4.

The Context of Education

Education in these United States is a vast enterprise, dynamic and varied, vital to the survival and future well-being of our democratic way of life. The American educational establishment is genuinely dedicated to the purposes and principles of a free society. Its organization and control, the means of support, and its major features reflect the wishes and will of the people. Truly, our educational systems present an amazing and inspiring example to the free world.

Education is everywhere directly related to and connected with the culture it serves. It is never apart or autonomous; it is in and of the environing society. We may study any society and find education. If it is a literate culture, we will find organized schools. In many modern ones we find public education. Any culture, anywhere, has a set of institutions that does the educational tasks that must be done for its maintenance and preservation. This means that students of education must learn to look beyond the formally organized schools and other institutions to find the informal but actual agencies that perform educational functions. The whole culture must be understood if we are to really appreciate the nature of education in any society.

American education is an extremely complicated and fascinating pattern of formal and informal institutions and agencies. This would be true if our culture would remain static long enough for us to study it thoroughly. It is on the move, however, and the student of American society must be prepared to take this dynamism and growth into account. American education is broader than its schools and colleges and its organized programs. It is deeper reaching from the school to the home and neighborhood. It has a new global dimension inasmuch as American education is represented in United Nations Educational, Scientific, and Cultural Organization, Agency for International Development, the Peace Corps, exchange of teachers and of students, to name a few. If we are to understand and work intelligently as citizens we must see how and why our culture functions as it does and utilizes all its educative agencies to this end. We should start at the neighborhood level and examine the concentric layers of cultural organization and function to the United Nations Organization.

Selected Bibliography

Ambrose, Edna, and Miel, Alice. *Children's Social Learnings*. Washington: Association for Supervision and Curriculum Development, 1958.

Bossard, James H. S., and Bell, Eleanor Stoker. *The Sociology of Child Development*. New York: Harper & Row, 1960. See chapters 2–7.

Chandler, B. J., Stiles, Lindley J., and Kitsuse, John I. *Education in Our Urban Society*. New York: Dodd, Mead & Co., 1962.

Conant, James B. *Slums and Suburbs: A Commentary on Schools in Metropolitan Areas*. New York: McGraw-Hill 1961.

Davis, Allison. *Social-Class Influence on Learning*. Cambridge: Harvard University Press, 1948.

Digest of Educational Statistics, 1963 Edition, Office of Education, U.S. Department of Health, Education & Welfare. Washington: Government Printing Office, 1963.

"Education and the Disadvantaged American," *NEA Journal*, **LI**, No. 4 (April 1961), pp. 9–12.

Educational Policies Commission, *Education and the Disadvantaged American*. Washington: NEA, 1962.

The Federal Government and Education. Committee on Education and Labor, House of Representatives, 88th Congress, 1st Session. Washington: U.S. Government Printing Office, June 1963.

Flack, Michael J. *International Educational Activities*. Washington: American Council on Education, 1958.

Frank, Josette. *Comics, Radio, Movies and Children*. Public Affairs Pamphlet, No. 148, New York Public Affairs Committee, 1949.

Goodman, Paul. *Growing Up Absurd*. Problems of Youth in Organized Society. New York: Random House, First Vintage edition, 1963.

Gordon, C. Wayne. *The Social System of the High School*. Glencoe, Ill.: The Free Press, 1957.

Grafton, Samuel. "The Tense Generation," *Look*, **XVII**, No. 17 (August 27, 1963), pp. 17–23.

Graham, Grace. *The Public School in the American Community*. New York: Harper & Row, 1963.

Havighurst, Robert J., and Neugarten, Bernice. *Society and Education*. Boston: Allyn & Bacon, 1957, see chapters 1–2, 5, 16.

Havighurst, Robert J., *et al. Growing up in River City*. New York: John Wiley & Sons, 1962.

Hodgkinson, Harold L. *Education in Social and Cultural Perspectives*. Englewood Cliffs, N.J.: Prentice-Hall, Inc., 1962, chapters 2–4.

Hollingshead, A. B. *Elmtown's Youth*. New York: John Wiley & Sons, 1949.

"How Life in U. S. is Changing," *U.S. News and World Report*, **LIII**, No. 23 (December 3, 1962), pp. 68–73.

Kimball, Solon T., and McClellan, James L. *Education and the New America*. New York: Random House, 1962.

King, Edmund J. *Other Schools and Ours* (Rev. ed.). New York: Holt, Rinehart & Winston, 1963.

Lerner, Max. *America as a Civilization*. New York: Simon & Schuster, 1957, chapter 7.

Odum, Howard W., and Moore, H. E. *American Regionalism*. New York: Holt, Rinehart & Winston, 1938.

Peters, Herman J., *et al. Introduction to Teaching*. New York: The Macmillan Company, 1963, pp. 101–121, 148–171.

Pounds, Ralph L., and Bryner, James R. *The School in American Society*. New York: Macmillan 1959.

Quattlebaum, C. K. *Federal Educational Policies, Programs, & Proposals, A Survey and Handbook*. Committee on Education and Labor, House of Representatives, 86th Congress, 2nd session. Washington: U.S. Government Printing Office, 1960.

Remmers, H. H., and Radler, D. H. "Teenage Attitudes," *Scientific American*, **CXCVIII**, No. 6 (June 1958), pp. 25–26.

Report of the President's Research Committee on Social Trends. New York: McGraw-Hill, 1932.

Robbins, Florence C. *Educational Sociology*. New York: Holt, Rinehart & Winston, 1953, see chapters 4–7, 12–14.

Ryans, David G. *Characteristics of Teachers*. Washington: American Council on Education, 1960.

Scanlon, John. "Strikes, Sanctions, and the Schools," *Saturday Review,* **XLVI,** No. 42 (October 19, 1963), pp. 51–54, 70–74.

Simpson, Hoke S. (Ed.) *The Changing American Population*. A Report of the Arden House Conference. New York: Institute of Life Insurance, 1962.

Spindler, George D. *Education and Culture, Anthropological Approaches*. New York: Holt, Rinehart & Winston, Inc., 1913, pp. 132–172, 302–399.

Thayer, V. T. "The Family and the School," *The Role of the School in American Society*. New York: Dodd, Mead & Co., 1960, pp. 136–155.

Thrasher, Frederic M. *The Gang*. Chicago: University of Chicago Press, 1936.

Warner, W. Lloyd, Meeker, M., and Ells, K. *Social Class in America*. Chicago: Science Research Associates Inc., 1949.

"The Way People Live Today," *U.S. News and World Report,* **LV,** No. 20 (November 11, 1963), pp. 56–61.

Williams, Percy V. "School Dropouts," *NEA Journal,* **LII,** No. 2 (February 1963), pp. 10–12.

Chapter 3

The Story of Common Schools

Their (the American people) primary concern was to design a universal, free, public school that would promote free institutions and free citizenship. For the first one hundred years of the Republic, the need for creating the common bonds and loyalties of a free community was paramount.*

Introduction

Graduates of our schools have studied a good deal of American history during their student days, but it is unlikely that they have heard enough of the interesting history of public education, an aspect of our national history that has fundamental significance and importance. Any well-informed citizen and leader in the community should achieve real understanding of the history of our public schools—the cornerstone of our free society. This understanding should ever be an inspiration and foundation for a deep faith *in* and a philosophy *of* democratic education.

A thoughtful student can hardly escape the conclusion that American public education is central in our democratic culture and society. Nowhere has a people dreamed about, worked for, invested in,

and expected more of education; in no culture has the ideal of educational opportunity for all been so nearly achieved. Education in the United States has been called the road to culture and a search for freedom. A noted European scholar, Dennis W. Brogan, termed the faith in education as ". . . the national religion of America." This is a democracy and people have more chance to achieve their potentialities and aspirations in such a social order. The interesting fact is that so many Americans have sought their opportunity to improve through education. The amazing growth, development, and extension of American education have made it our largest public enterprise, characterized by its diversity and dynamic strengths. These very facts make it as recognizably American as apple pie.

Since public education is a unique and central institution of our democracy, its growth and development is part and

* R. Freeman Butts, "A Search for Freedom," in *NEA Journal,* **XLIX,** No. 3 (March 1960), p. 38. Used by permission.

parcel of our cultural history. The story of American public schools is a story of dreams and ideas, of battles and struggles, of setbacks and losses, but of achievements and victories as well. Horace Mann viewed the common school as the greatest discovery that man ever made.

A SYNOPSIS OF THE STORY

All of this vast institution which we know as American education did not develop overnight. Concern about and regard for education came to America with many of the colonists, who brought with them their institutions, ideas, and values. Their experience with education was reflected in the earliest schools and colleges which were largely based upon European models. We must remember also that the colonists came from widely differing backgrounds. Religious differences were great, and many groups came to America in order to have more freedom in this respect. There were several different languages besides English; Dutch, Swedish, French, and German were used by certain minorities, chiefly in the middle and in some southern colonies. This great diversity of cultural backgrounds made possible a variety of ways of living, and various local institutions served the purposes, needs, values, of the several groups in the different colonies. As the economies and types of local government developed in different forms in the English colonies, several types of schools also developed. From the beginning American education was not limited to a single type of school or a single standardized program. Our educational systems have continued to grow to meet the varied needs and conditions in the different states. With its dif-

ferences, American education has developed remarkable common features and strengths. "Alike but different" is one way to put it, alike in essentials, but flexible and varied as necessary to fit needs and conditions which differ.

The great history of public education reflects several major trends or developments. First was the period of varied beginnings marked by emphases upon religious and civil education in colonies where church and state interests were common because of cultural and ethnic homogeneity. Public schools had their beginning in America. Private (church related) schools and colleges of New England and New Netherlands did much to originate what became the common publicly-supported schools. Second, the amazing growth of the colonies toward cultural diversity and ethnic heterogeneity with religious pressures led to establishment of state control of public common schools early in the national period. The need for emphasis upon political knowledge and citizenship participation along with other factors influenced the curriculum from this period. Third, the severe sectarian strife and rivalry for the control of schools and for state funds was largely responsible for the relatively early removal of religious content from the curriculum. In other words, the new state school systems had or changed to a secular curriculum. Finally, this gradual process which resulted in a free, publicly-supported, common, and secular school was accompanied by the adaptation and development of effective religious educational agencies and institutions by and for the growing American denominational bodies. The Protestant churches found an adaptable and useful agency in the Sunday school which served them well for many decades. Other church groups relied more upon types of parochial schools. The Jewish parents tended to use the common schools supplemented by afternoon classes for religious instruction. The supplementary arrangement has been a functional part of American education for decades and served our people well. Only recently with growth of social, ideological, religious, and ethnic tensions has there been resurgence of demands for religion in the public schools and for public support of parochial schools. By and large, the American people know how much they owe to their free, open, publicly-supported, common schools. The well-informed citizen should know the full story and thus be prepared to evaluate the bouquets and the brickbats that are directed at the common schools of this great democracy. It is a story of a people's search for freedom.

The American People Achieved Nationality, Democracy, and Common Schools

COLONIAL SCHOOLS REFLECTED RELIGIOUS AND SOCIAL DIFFERENCES

The diversity of American education showed early as the settlers in New England, the Middle Colonies, and the South established their first schools and colleges. Some historians have noted that these early schools in the colonies could be characterized as "democratic," "religious," and "aristocratic" for New England, Middle, and Southern Colonies respectively. This is true in a general sense, but we must not conclude too much from such labels. The distinctions were not as clear-cut as these terms might indicate. For example, there was a strong religious motivation for schools among the people of the colonies generally.

Schools came early in New England. Old records show that some form of school existed in different towns shortly after first settlement. Some of these were of the famous "Dame school" type and others were kept by the minister. What grew into the public school began in New England towns by 1635. That year also marked the opening of the Boston Latin Grammar School for Boys; others soon followed in nearby towns. In 1636 the first college, Harvard, was established chiefly for the purpose of providing an educated ministry to replace learned clergymen who came from the English universities. In 1642 the colony of Massachusetts Bay enacted legislation requiring parents to provide for their children to be taught to read. In 1647 came the famous "Old Deluder Satan Act" which required towns of fifty or more families to maintain an elementary school and towns of one hundred or more families to provide both elementary and secondary schools.[1] Connecticut passed similar laws by 1650 and Plymouth followed some earlier legislation with laws of this type in 1671. Before the end of the 17th century nearly all of New England legally provided for schools. Not

[1] The Law of 1642 specified that children be taught reading, religion, the capital laws of the province, and some orthodox catechism. The School Law of 1647 required reading and writing in all schools, and a grammar school in larger towns. These set forth the objectives of the earliest English schools on the continent.

too many of the towns followed these provisions faithfully; some seemed to choose payment of the fines instead of maintaining schools. It is true that here the idea of public school and that of local self-government seemed to grow up together. New England was largely settled by groups of similar religious persuasion, and there were few extremes of wealth. Church and state were not separate and the local town and the congregation were practically synonymous. There was a good working agreement upon the values and ideas which should be fostered in government and through education. Overwhelmingly Puritan in religion, the people had little reason to be fearful of the influence of the church in public affairs. All this made it easy for the people to agree upon the kind of education they wanted. The compact settlements made the "town" a feasible unit of political action and the first type of school district. It was possible for church and state responsibility for education to be gradually separated as the colonies grew into stronger political units. By this time they had the beginnings of a public school system, open to all children, and the benefit of some experience in providing public support.

An interest in education came to the middle colonies with the first Dutch settlers of New Amsterdam. These were strong Protestants, who wanted language and religious instruction for their children. They had a parish school as early as 1642 and possibly by 1638. Control of the first school was shared by the church and the local government, in this case the Dutch West India Company. Later, other elementary schools and some Latin grammar schools were established in the colony. After the English took control of the colony, and renamed it New York

(1664), the schools were largely controlled by the church, although funds were collected for their support by consent of the government. Other schools were sponsored by charitable organizations and even by private patrons. New York grew rapidly and many faiths, nationalities and languages were soon represented. This brought the establishment of parochial schools by Anglicans and other congregations. The stage was set for the development of a varied pattern of education, in matters of control, support, and sponsorship.

Patterns of education in other middle colonies tended to be diversified in the hands of sectarian, charitable, and private interests. William Penn's original plans for the colony of Pennsylvania included provision for public schools. An early law (1683) required parents to provide for instruction in reading, writing, and a trade for each of their children. Neither of these was to prove influential in setting the pattern of education in the colony. The large religious groups—Quakers, Moravians, Mennonites, German Lutherans, Scotch-Irish Presbyterians, Anglicans, and others—tended to set up their own parochial schools. The Quakers in particular, founded some early Latin grammar schools. Support for these parochial schools was derived through fees from prosperous parents, gifts, assessments, public subscription, and charity. Here, as in New York, early education grew chiefly under the sponsorship of sectarian and philanthropic interests.

Although the Southern colonies included the first English settlements they were not to lead in the development of schools for most of the children. Indeed there were no families in Virginia during the first perilous years. As Virginia developed economically, great extremes of wealth and social position emerged. The landed class could afford to employ tutors for their children and to send them to England to complete an education. Labor on the plantations was performed by bond servants and Negro slaves, neither of whom could take an interest in education. A great middle class of people simply did not exist to need and to demand schools. The economic system, the great distances between settled towns and plantations, and the social class system discouraged the growth of local government patterns and community action such as developed in New England. The Church of England was strong. All of these conditions tended to perpetuate the typical English view toward education, namely, it is the parent's responsibility to provide education for his children. The wealthy planters hired tutors for their own and neighboring families. The churches often maintained schools for the pauper children for the parish. In Maryland, first settled by English Catholics, parochial schools were developed under church control. These patterns of education were more-or-less followed in the other Southern colonies. Sometimes, wealthy sponsors maintained neighborhood and "old field" schools. It may be seen that education in the Southern colonies was mainly at the elementary level except for the tutorial instruction for the children of the wealthy. The first college in the South was William and Mary, established in 1693.

The growth of schools throughout the colonial period was neither uniform nor consistent. Elementary schools were usually poor in quality and offered meager curriculums. Latin grammar schools were established in cities and towns of most colonies. This type of school never reached enough of the people to fill the need for secondary education. Its curriculum was narrow (strictly college preparatory) and designed for boys who would become clergymen, lawyers, and for sons of the wealthy. Toward the end of the colonial period, an indigenous secondary school, the academy appeared. Benjamin Franklin was instrumental in the establishment of the first academy in Philadelphia in 1751. This type of school expanded during the next hundred years in the colonies and states of the Union. Its curriculum was broader and included some of the useful as well as the ornamental subjects as Franklin termed it. The academy tended to do more for the education of girls than had been provided through the Latin grammar school. Patterns of control and support for the academy varied in the different sections of the country.

The eighteenth century witnessed the establishment of more colleges. Between 1700 and the Revolution seven appeared: Yale (1701), Princeton, (1746), Pennsylvania (1753–55), Kings, now Columbia (1754), Brown (1764), Rutgers (1766) (now a state university), and Dartmouth (1769). Although we now think of all except one of these as private institutions, it should be remembered that most had instances or periods of public control and support. Most of these reflected the strong Protestant religious motivation of the period in matters of education.

Colonial schools, schoolmasters and scholars

Colonial schools were small and usually taught in crude one-room buildings, heated by fireplace or a stove in the middle of the floor, poorly ventilated if at all, and furnished with rude benches. At times there were no floors, only the ground. Books were non-existent save those brought from home by the children and those of the schoolmaster.

The pupils ranged from young children, three and four years of age, who accompanied older pupils, to young men and women in their late teens.[2] Terms were short, only a few weeks per year, and the curriculum was confined to the simplest elements of the four *R*'s—reading, 'ritin', 'rithmetic, and religion. Bibles brought from home were used as texts as were the *Bay Psalm Book* and *The New England Primer*. The latter came into universal use, except where the Anglican Church was established and continued until after the Revolution, going through many editions for a total of 3,000,000 copies. The *Primer* provided instruction in the elements of reading and religious doctrine simultaneously. It was said of this small crude book of 88 pages that it taught millions to read and not one to sin. In the later editions objections to the emphasis upon Calvinistic dogma led to revisions that stressed "manners and morals." A catechism was included along with prayers to be recited.

The methods of teaching were described by the term "keeping school." Children learned chiefly by memorizing and the master's role was chiefly that of hearing individual recitations. Instruction was largely individualized in colonial schools as grades and graded schools were yet to be invented. The master had a second major role, discipline with a strict capital "D." The ability to keep order and to elicit hard work at study from the scholars were the prime qualifications for colonial schoolmasters. Discipline was deemed necessary and good for the waywardness and foolishness of children, and correction was a religious necessity for their spiritual wellbeing.

Schoolmasters of colonial schools represented a variety of background and education, especially outside New England.[3] Many New England towns were fortunate to have early schoolmasters with college degrees but it is to be remembered that the Puritan settlers included an extraordinary group from an intellectual and cultural standpoint. Perhaps the most famous and respected schoolmaster of New England was Ezekiel Cheever of New Haven who taught 38 years in Boston. Another great teacher was Elijah Corlett, head of the Cambridge Latin School for 43 years. In many towns the minister served as schoolmaster when no other was available. The older type of "dame school," kept by a housewife for a few beginners around the kitchen hearth, taught only the merest rudiments. Typical qualifications of these teachers were low. Masters in the Boston and other Latin grammar schools were college graduates but their number was never large.

The schoolmasters of other colonies, especially in the South, were principally itinerants, serving as teachers in a school when an opening was available, and as tutor for a planter's family on other occasions. Some were indentured servants whose services were provided by contract. A number of schoolmasters maintained their own schools and charged tuition. Some achieved considerable fame and

[2] See for example H. G. Good, *A History of American Education,* Second edition (New York: Macmillan, 1962), pp. 19–45, for a good account of schooling of colonial children.

[3] Willard S. Elsbree, *The American Teacher* (New York: American Book Co., 1939). He is one of the authorities on the subject. The book is readable and thorough.

recognition as in the case of Christopher Dock, the noted Mennonite master of Pennsylvania, who wrote the first book on pedagogy in America.

Schoolmasters were usually assigned other duties in connection with the church and town affairs such as sexton, gravedigger, and clerk. There is evidence that a great many engaged in various sidelines. Some were able to invest in lands or a business, others studied law and held public office. The use of teaching as the stepping-stone to another professional opportunity was an early American tradition.

Pay of colonial teachers varied widely among the colonies and, to some degree, according to the time. The schoolmasters of Boston and New York were the envy of teachers in smaller communities. In early New England twenty pounds per annum was an approximate minimum rate, although records show that outstanding masters rose to the incredible rate of sixty pounds. Salaries in the middle and southern colonies ranged widely. Records of the time also show that complaints about schoolmasters' salaries were frequent, both by teachers for inadequacy, and by citizens as extravagant.

Masters often received a portion of pay in services and commodities—skins, corn, wheat, livestock, tobacco, and wampum. Sometimes a dwelling and use of land were included in the contract. Another inducement was to grant the schoolmaster the right to make and sell ink, quill pens, copy books, and to use the school for private tutoring. The common practice of "boarding round" was another way of payment in kind in lieu of money.

The status of teachers varied greatly among cities and colonies. In general, those of larger towns, especially in New England, enjoyed greater prestige. A number of sources accorded schoolmasters respect next to the minister but this was probably not typical of all colonies.

Scholars ranged in age from preschool years to adulthood. Both boys and girls attended most schools although there were some misgivings about the education of girls. Many children received little or no schooling and in Southern colonies the number was large. All were expected to have some kind of education to fit them to make a living. Usually this meant apprenticeship to a shopkeeper, miller, artisan, or farmer to learn the business, a form of education that is older than the Pyramids. Orphans were provided for in this fashion by the parish wardens in the South or town officials in New England. Sometimes elementary instruction was provided for orphans and children of paupers in parish schools.

Students from wealthy families could expect to attend the Latin grammar school or have a tutor in Latin, Greek, mathematics, ancient history, and literature. A small number of planter families and affluent folk in cities sent their children to England to complete their schooling. Especially in earlier decades, there were social distinctions among pupils and college students in terms of the rank of their families. The roster of Harvard College listed names by family rank in the early period.

The colonial contribution to American education

The educational experiences of the colonists continued as problems were encountered and solved. In New England, the district plan of organization developed as the increasing population and the factor of distance made the central town school inaccessible to all the children. Thus appeared the district school, with its trustees, as a subdivision of the town. Now the one-room school, popularly known as the "Deestrict" or the little red schoolhouse, became a famous landmark in our history. Students may well recall Whittier's "In Schooldays," a classic narrative with its vivid image of that long-vanished institution. When the nation was young and the tide of settlement ran westward, the ideas and practices of New England were carried over a broad area of the midwestern states.

Most of our attention has been given to the development of schools in our early history. This should not obscure the fact that other strong educative agencies were at work in the total task of preparing the young for adulthood in society. Much of the education of anyone takes place in the home; in colonial days this was more true than for present times. Children learned to work, received religious instruction, played together, and were prepared for most of life's responsibilities in the home and family circle. The church was almost everywhere an important educational institution, not only because of its charity or parochial schools, but also through the teaching-preaching-visiting activities of clergymen and its cooperation with parents. Vocational education was an activity of the home, but apprenticeship systems were common in most places. In colonial America, people learned much from life and daily living because schooling was meager, books and periodicals were scarce, and most of our modern media of transmitting information were undreamed of by anyone.

Looking back, it is clear that the early experiences of the American people in developing schools were to prove invaluable. In the various sections of the English colonies, many types of schools were tried, different forms of control were developed, and patterns of school support were evolved. Semi-public and, later, public schools, parochial and neighborhood types, missionary and charity efforts, private and tutorial systems, all were used under various conditions. Both town and district organizations were developed and several patterns of support were tried out in the various colonies. Ideas of state control and of noninterference by the state were given extensive tryouts in different sections of the new country. The colonial period served the coming nation well as a proving ground for education and as a step in the growth toward democratic institutions. The idea of the public school was developed; many kinds of private schools gained footholds, and there was some indication that both could be permitted to exist in a free land.

Colonial education certainly exhibited diversity, but it also was characterized by a strong common feature in the *religious motive*. As these early communities and colonies gained political experience and developed institutions to fit their varied conditions and realities, it was inevitable that other motives would appear in American education.

AMERICAN NATIONALITY BROUGHT POLITICAL DEMANDS AND CHANGES

Although some public schools started early in America the present extensive state systems of public education were not developed until after long and bitter struggle. The dominant purposes or functions of education have differed and have been changed in the course of our national history. Every citizen should have a clear understanding of the great faith which the American people have demonstrated in education. This became more pronounced in our early national history than during colonial days.

The vigorous growth of American nationality and democratic patterns of government were early reflected in demands for more education. Many of the Founding Fathers saw clearly the need for a better educated citizenry able to handle the affairs and concerns of government and citizenship. This has been called the *political motive*, and its influence was clearly marked from the Revolution until after the establishment of the Constitution. It is true that the Federal Constitution contained not a single word about education. But the Congress under the Articles of Confederation had included legislative provisions for education in the Northwest Territory in the Ordinance of 1787. Education had earlier become a concern of the new state governments. Jefferson advocated a comprehensive program of education for the state of Virginia as early as 1779, and maintained a lifelong interest in public schools. He wrote:

A system of general instruction which will reach every description of our citizens from the richest to the poorest, as it was my earliest, so it will be the latest of all public concern in which I shall permit myself to take an interest.

Other leading statesmen such as James Madison strongly advocated popular education so that citizens would be informed and able to vote intelligently. All of the presidents of the United States have expressed strong interest in education. As John Adams saw it:

The whole people must take upon themselves the education of the whole people and must be willing to bear the expense of it.

A long struggle for a full, free system of schools began in the various states. Some early state constitutions provided for education. Slowly, more schools were opened, supported chiefly by local funds. Free school societies in the larger cities urged and received partial state support for a few schools. There were objections by those who abhorred the idea of being taxed to pay for the schooling of other folks' children. This battle raged through the first half of the nineteenth century, waxing particularly strong during the period historians call "Jacksonian democracy."[4] New York took early steps in the direction of a state system of common schools. It reversed its stand and then returned to establish one of the early state boards and school support.

In 1837, the first permanent State Board of Education was established by the Commonwealth of Massachusetts. Its first secretary, Horace Mann, became one of the greatest figures in American education. Leaving a promising career as a lawyer and public figure, he did prodigious labor to place public education upon an adequate basis of support and acceptance. Mann urged, as did Thomas Jefferson, John Adams, James Madison, DeWitt Clinton, and many others, the necessity for an enlightened populace as the best guarantee that our free institutions would work. The evils and problems of his day

[4] All histories of American education treat of this phase of our history. A brief readable account may be found in Elwood P. Cubberley, *Public Education in the United States* (Boston: Houghton Mifflin). Another excellent reference is Lawrence A. Cremin and Merle L. Borrowman, *Public Schools in Our Democracy* (New York: Macmillan, 1956), pp. 71–86.

were seen as faulty performances to be corrected and not as indictment of the political and economic systems themselves. Mann was more successful than many other leaders in convincing the wealthy that their best interests lay in supporting public education. Largely by his efforts in behalf of education, Massachusetts achieved a notable system of public schools before the turn of the century. He was also instrumental in having public institutions for the education of teachers established in Massachusetts; the first one opened in Lexington in 1839. Mann's broad vision and energetic leadership earned him recognition as our first great "educational statesman." His influence extended to many other states and was felt in several foreign countries, notably in South America.

Other great leaders took up the fight in various states. Leaders in New York and Pennsylvania struggled successfully to set up common schools about the same time as in Massachusetts. Henry Barnard in Connecticut and Rhode Island, Calvin Wiley in North Carolina, Calvin Stowe in Ohio, Benjamin O. Peers and Robert J. Breckenridge in Kentucky, Caleb Mills in Indiana, Ninian Edwards in Illinois, and John Swett in California, were particularly effective and able leaders in the fight for free, tax-supported schools. Gradually, the early domination of education by private and church schools was replaced by state systems. By 1870, practically all of the existing states had established an eight-year program of public education for all children. Efforts to make attendance compulsory and to lengthen the term of rural schools were next in order, efforts which continued well into the twentieth century.

The struggles to establish the common schools varied greatly among the states. Many forces and factors figured in the opposition—economics, weight of tradition, apathy, the opposition of private schools, and influence of religious groups were prominent. The friendly forces were many and varied in different states. Influence of leaders, the growing democratic spirit, parental aspirations for children, sectarian rivalry, changed conditions on the frontier were among these influences. In the fight for free public schools in all states was the ideal of the common school and its vital relation to democratic institutions. The strong appeal of this idea may be seen in the following statement of an influential figure of the time:

The Common School is *common,* not as inferior, not as a school for poor men's children, but as the light and air are common.[5]

This view appealed to people who had aspirations for a better life for their children. Most of them wished to avoid the stigma of free schooling provided only for paupers. It was also argued that monitorial schools could provide economical instruction. The major churches of the time were actively establishing and promoting the Sunday school as a chief means of religious instruction. All of these and perhaps others were factors in the development of our common school systems, but the strongest appeal was the idea of common schools as the kind of education fit for the people's children in a democratic society. A noted educational historian sums it up as follows:

It is important to realize how strongly positive was this idea of "common schooling" in the minds of those early leaders.

[5] Bishop George Doane, "Address to the People of New Jersey," 1838.

Assuming that association of children would engender mutual respect and friendship, these men hoped that the common school would not only be *open*, to all, but eventually voluntarily *used* by all. The children of many nationalities, religions, and economic levels would then have an opportunity to mix together in the same schoolroom. It was argued that after such warm association in childhood, different groups in the community would have common memories, values, and respect on which to build a harmonious national society.[6]

Other notable struggles for public education followed. Massachusetts removed religious instruction from her schools by law in 1827; other states followed suit until the principle of the nonsectarian curriculum was generally adopted. Likewise, the states usually prohibited use of public funds for private schools by constitution or statute. Increasing immigration of Roman Catholic groups and resulting pressures upon the public schools of certain metropolitan centers led to even more stringent moves toward a secular curriculum. By the end of the third quarter of the 19th century, America had a common free secular elementary school and had begun to require compulsory attendance.

Another great battle was fought and won for the establishment and support of public secondary schools. The older secondary schools, such as the Latin grammar school and the academy, had catered chiefly to the needs of pupils who were preparing for college. New demands for vocational education, the desires of people to have their children get ahead and to improve their station in life resulted in popular support for greater

educational opportunity at the secondary level. The first public high school, an English school for boys, was started in Boston in 1821. One for girls followed in 1826, and a year later the Massachusetts legislature enacted a law requiring districts with 500 families or more to support high schools. The new high school idea spread over the country by the end of the century.

The battle for the publicly-supported free high school was won more quickly than the preceding one for elementary schools. In 1870, only 70,000 youth were enrolled in high schools in the entire nation; by 1900 the enrollment was 10 per cent of pupils of high school age; after 1900 the growth of the high school was phenomenal. In this battle, the critical issue was settled in the famous Kalamazoo Case in Michigan (1872)[7] and by similar decisions in other states. Once the principle was established that all the people could be taxed to support public high schools, secondary education developed rapidly. At long last the American people had developed an institution to fill the gap between the elementary school and the college.

Life in the common schools

As the young nation grew and its economy expanded, life became more settled and opportunities more varied. True there was the rampaging frontier, but it continued to recede westward. The town and country folk of most communities were freed of many of the harsher realities that had characterized life in the settlements. The long arduous effort in the eastern and northern states that resulted in the establishment of systems of free

---

[6] L. A. Cremin, *Public Education and the Future of America* (Washington: NEA, 1955), p. 18. (Used by permission.)

[7] *Stuart vs. School District No. 1 of the Village of Kalamazoo*, 30 Michigan, 69.

publicly-supported schools was a phase of this growth which was partly economic, social, intellectual, political, and educational. The schools reflected many characteristics and features of this era of national growth.[8]

Schools showed this in many ways. There were far more children and more of them went to school. In many communities the need to organize schools for efficiency and economy led to new plans of organizing classes and instruction. For a time there was a great stir and trials of the monitorial school, a system that utilized older pupils to instruct those next below them in their studies. This was largely supplanted later in the century by the graded school developed at Quincy, Massachusetts, that has continued to be a feature of elementary schools. Individualized instruction and recitations were too numerous and too brief, and schoolmasters had to learn new ways.

The little red (or unpainted) schoolhouse by the road remained the typical school for children of the 19th century. It was not as crude and uncomfortable as those of colonial days. There were windows, a better stove, blackboards on the wall, and rough but serviceable desks or tables for writing. Framed mottoes of scripture verses, proverbs, and maxims hung on the walls. The teacher had a desk and there were long recitation benches up front for classes. The high

stool and the dunce cap had not disappeared, nor had the paddle and switches. Teachers or an older boy still came early to build fires, boys carried drinking water from springs or wells, and all came to school wet or cold in inclement weather. Life in the 19th century one-room school was no picnic, but it was less hazardous than in earlier times.

Teachers in the new states were a diverse lot in matters of education and qualifications for teaching children. As the states enacted school laws and established school systems, requirements for the education and licensing of teachers were adopted. The normal school idea took hold in other states soon after Massachusetts opened the first public institution at Lexington in 1839 (later moved to Bridgewater). Gradually, the practice of issuing certificates to teach to almost anyone of nominally good character who could answer a few questions put by a school committeeman (or the minister, or by a politically-appointed school commissioner) gave way to a system of examinations. "Institutes" were held to instruct teachers in the theory and practice of teaching and in the subject matter they would teach. These patterns of teacher preparation continued throughout the country for most of the century. The early colonial schools probably had a larger proportion of college graduates for teachers than did the typical state system during most of the 19th century. The economic and social growth of the nation shows why; there were too many children and schools and not enough college graduates to go around. Moreover, there were other bright, beckoning opportunities for the well-educated young man of the early 19th century.

[8] One of the best places to get insight into the life and thought of the early periods of American education is to use a "source book" such as: Elwood P. Cubberley, *Readings in Public Education in the United States* (Boston: Houghton Mifflin, 1934), and Edgar W. Knight and Clifton L. Hall, *Readings in American Educational History* (New York: Appleton-Century-Crofts, 1951).

By the time of the Civil War there was a trend to employ women teachers, especially in the New England states. There was appealing evidence that women teachers could be employed for lower salaries, a matter not to be overlooked by school committees and officials. The coming of the graded school opened classes of younger children easier to manage, giving more women the chance to teach. Horace Mann and others encouraged girls to enter the normal schools. The Civil War called most young men teachers to the colors and many never returned. The three-quarter mark of the century found that women teachers outnumbered men in the elementary schools for the first time in our history.

Discipline was still the number one problem and parents expected teachers to control the pupils or get out. Discipline by whipping continued until late in the century. Horace Mann and the Boston schoolmasters engaged in a sharp controversy over the policy of strict corporal punishment. Reports of scores of thrashings on a typical school day were common.

Teachers were expected to teach more than the rudiments of reading, writing, and ciphering. Several new subjects and textbooks had been added beginning with Noah Webster's famous "blue-backed speller" about the time the Revolution was concluded by the Treaty of Paris. Older texts brought from England like Dilworth's *Grammar* gave way to books written and published in America: Greenwood's *Arithmetic*, Lindley Murray's *English Reader*, Samuel Goodrich's *History*, Morse's *Geography*, and others. In 1836 there began to appear the fabulously-successful McGuffey's *Readers*,

a series of texts that was to go through five major revisions, to last for generations and sell a grand total of 122 million copies.[9] More significantly the moral tone and the literary content of McGuffey's text were to leave an imprint upon the American character, speech, and thought patterns that has never been equalled by any publication save the King James version of the Bible. Teachers were expected to teach more subjects and more pupils. They were to be models in dress and deportment in the community. Early 19th century teachers' contracts make interesting reading for youth of today.

Some idea of the teacher's life in most states at the middle of the 19th century can be gained from knowing the conditions and pay for their work. Teachers' pay has been a perennial problem for those who believe in common schools.[10] Prior to the Civil War period, men teachers predominated in the profession with average salaries per month that ranged from about $18.45 to $41.45 in the New England states. The average monthly pay of women teachers was $7.79 to $17.96. In addition, they got board, usually a matter of "boarding 'round," one week at a time in homes of the patrons of the school. Since eight of every ten teachers in the 1850's taught rural schools, they had no problem of getting acquainted with the parents. Usually teachers walked to the schoolhouse early enough to start

[9] William E. Drake, *The American School in Transition* (New York: Prentice-Hall, Inc., 1955), p. 350; see also Henry Steele Commager, "McGuffey and His Readers," *Newsweek*, XLV, No. 24 (July 16, 1962), pp. 50–51, 69–70.

[10] Illustrative figures taken from Henry Barnard (ed.), *American Journal of Education, 1856*, II (Hartford, Connecticut: Brownell, 1956), pp. 472–544.

the fire before the "scholars" arrived. Annual school terms ranged from four to seven and one-half months. Teachers often attempted to arrange a "subscription" school, by collecting weekly tuition from parents, to supplement the public school program and their own pocketbooks. Teachers' diaries and contemporary accounts all report the difficulties and hardships endured by the intrepid and responsible schoolmasters and school marms who taught our forefathers to read, write, and cipher to the "rule of three."

Children had more fun at schools of the last century than their predecessors ever had in colonial days. They walked, often great distances, to school after doing chores around the home or farm and knew none of the conveniences and amusements so commonplace today. Nevertheless, there were recess periods and the "dinner hour" for games with much running and shouting. Friday afternoons were often devoted to spelling matches, a ciphering contest, or a "literary exercise" during which the girls would recite "pieces" and the boys declaim "Spartacus' Address to the Gladiators" or "Marco Bozzaris"—both great favorites of schoolboys for generations. There were opportunities for shy meetings and friendship among the adolescent pupils as immortalized by the verse of John Greenleaf Whittier.[11]

Going to school was a busy, "no-nonsense" responsibility but it was for many more pleasant and easy than the rough work of the farm and factory.

[11] See "In Schooldays" in any collection of Whittier's poems or an anthology. Another poem by Whittier provides an interesting description of the country schoolmaster who was domiciled with the family in "Snowbound."

There were still crude schoolhouses and harsh schoolmasters in frontier areas where conditions were much like those of earlier schools. The stories of Edward Eggleston and others reflect this circumstance. Most parents saw that education was the key to getting somewhere and wanted that opportunity for their children. This motive had the power to produce schools open to all pupils and to impress many young people with the necessary purpose to make the opportunity good. Much of the growth and great strength of American life of the past century came from the nature and quality of the school experiences of the great-grandparents of many of our people.

Ideas and institutions of public education

The early national period of our history saw great growth and development in education. The so-called *political motive* gained the support of leaders and citizens who saw a clear relationship between an informed electorate and democratic government. As the new Federal government demonstrated its worth, there appeared need to overcome strong sectional barriers and to avoid the divisive influence of competing sectarian and private educational systems. The idea of full, free, publicly-supported state systems of public schools required a half-century of vigorous effort. The result was the achievement of common schools for all the children of all the people. This battle was hardly won before the school leadership and the people found it necessary to seek better secondary schools to meet growing needs for more education in more fields for more young people. The outcome of these efforts is that universal feature of American communities today —the high school—now part of the common school system. This period also marked the establishment of state universities in Georgia, North Carolina, Ohio, Virginia, Michigan, Indiana and other states. Pioneer efforts for the establishment of colleges for women were successful in the first half of the 19th century through the work of Mary Lyon, Catherine Ward Beecher, and other pioneers in this field. From today's vantage point it is difficult for us to visualize the significance of the realities and accomplishments of this period from mere reading of our histories of education.

NATIONAL GROWTH INVOLVED PRACTICAL DEMANDS

American education has changed and grown in many directions and respects during the past 80 years. By 1870, there were unmistakable evidences of profound changes and major developments in our national life and economy. The nation had passed its severest test in civil war, democracy had been extended, marked expansion of industry had materialized, transcontinental transportation by rail had been accomplished, and vast frontier areas were in process of occupation. Since then, the frontier has long since disappeared; industrialization and urbanization have become normative characteristics of our way of life; big business, big government, and big labor have appeared on the scene; and technology has changed the scale and manner of living to marked degree. The everyday life of the typical American changed so radically during this time that it cannot be compared with any preceding period of comparable length. In every

respect, the economy, the world of work and business, the financial structure, and the legal-social controls became complex beyond comparison. And abroad, the strong growing nation quickly came into more intimate contacts and relationships as time and distance were telescoped by modern media of communication and transportation and world trade grew apace. "America as a world power" came to be a textbook phrase by 1900; two world wars and numerous international commitments and responsibilities now make that term appear somewhat naive. Throughout this period, the institutions of our culture were responding, changing, and growing as strong impacts and new demands were encountered. Family life, modes of recreation, the churches, and other institutions were profoundly affected; whole new agencies and institutions appeared. In all of this the public school received its share of new demands and needs. New motives appeared to which some authorities have given the label of "practical"; the *utilitarian motive* became a strong characteristic of American education between 1870–1920.

Only general characteristics and developments can be suggested here as massive portions of history of education textbooks might properly be devoted to this period alone in American education. During this time the various public schools and institutions of higher education were gradually encompassed into whole systems of education under state control. All of the states established universities and/or land grant colleges as capstones for their systems of educational opportunity for the people. One of the great success stories of America's educational history begins with the important role of the Federal Government in the establishment of land-grant colleges through the Morrill Act (1862). The U.S. Office of Education was established by Act of Congress (1867) as a Department. It was changed to a bureau in 1870 and remained in the Department of the Interior until 1939 when it was placed in the Federal Security Agency. In 1953 the office became one component of the new Department of Health, Education, and Welfare.

In the early 20th century, there came other significant Federal legislation which provided funds for certain kinds of vocational education. It was also during this time that strong programs of professional education developed at both undergraduate and the graduate levels.

Elsewhere in the educational systems of the nation appeared new types of schools which catered to the need for "practical" education. A look into the histories of education would show that this period witnessed the growth of the manual training movement, the trade schools, business colleges, technical schools of many kinds, Smith-Hughes vocational schools, and others which have become commonplace.

This era marked tremendous changes in the curriculum of public schools, both elementary and secondary. An effort to investigate subjects, textbooks, and additions to the high school curriculum during this time will pay big dividends in terms of understanding the changing public school program. It will be seen that the elementary school was largely transformed by several important movements. Some were imported from abroad, but many of these were developed in our own schools. The strong influence of the normal schools

was beginning to be felt as better educated teachers entered the profession. The NEA was organized (1857) to serve the needs of the teaching profession. The kindergarten was added to many public school systems, chiefly in cities, and the municipal college became commonplace.

Education had come a long way in America by 1920. The public school had emerged as the people's instrument for education. School attendance through elementary grades had become *universal* and high school enrollments had grown rapidly. The principles of public education had been extended to include preschool children and college students (even graduate students) in an open system of education. More and more American schools had grown to meet demands for practical education along with other functions. The utilitarian demands seemed to grow from the needs of a nation which had suddenly become vast, industrialized, and complex. Children could no longer participate in all of the important kinds of experience needed for the understanding of life and their times.

The school was challenged to do more about this through broader curriculums and more effective learning experiences. Certain educational deficiencies and health problems among the general population were disclosed by the gigantic effort to build a citizen's army by the use of the selective service principle. The grave problems of illiteracy and lack of physical fitness were challenges to the educational and civic leadership of the nation. Intensive programs to eradicate illiteracy followed—the famed "moonlight schools" movement headed by Cora Wilson Stewart, received most attention. State departments of education and school authorities prepared new curriculums to strengthen the health and physical education programs. Several states developed, with foundation support, entire new courses of study for the 12 grade statewide system. The General Education Board, the Rosenwald Fund, W. K. Kellogg Fund, the Sloan Foundation, and other philanthropic organizations gave material aid in educational research and developments.

Schools for all the children of all the people

After the nation returned to peacetime status following the Civil War there were many educational deficiencies and needs to be met. Progress toward the development of a state system of common schools continued to a successful conclusion almost everywhere by the 1870's. Extension of educational opportunity to the children of the "freedmen" represented a tremendous undertaking and most Southern states needed assistance. Many philanthropic groups and individuals made notable contributions to the education of Negro children in the South during the decades after the war. Many of the schools for both white and Negro children were crude and the programs meager but the effort was the beginning of another larger phase in the provision of educational opportunity for all.

In the states that had successful systems of common elementary schools, efforts to extend the educational opportunity for youth by providing a public high school were under way. The high school launched in Boston (1821) was the model for this new public secondary school which stressed a broader range of subjects than the traditional academy and early Latin grammar school. Massachusetts led the way by setting up public high schools in 1827 and the idea caught on in cities in various states. Opposition to the extension of public education and tax support came to a head in the celebrated Kalamazoo Case in 1872. The decision of Justice Cooley supported the school district trustees and this precedent paved the way for rapid growth of public high schools. Boys and girls in their teens who were not bound for college were served by educational offerings deemed to have functional values in their adult responsibilities.

The same period brought another extension of educational opportunity in the form of the kindergarten for children under school age. This European innovation introduced by American visitors to Germany and German immigrants had several beginnings in Boston, Milwaukee, and St. Louis. The ideas and educational program advanced by the great German innovator, Froebel, were modified and adapted to fit conditions and needs of American communities. The names of Elizabeth Peabody, Mrs. Carl Schurz, Susan Blow, and Patty Hill became recognized leaders in this new movement. The first publicly-supported kindergarten in St. Louis was the inspiration for a considerable growth of the idea in cities and towns before the turn of the century. Later came the beginnings of the nursery school for younger preschool children. The junior high school appeared in the first decade of the 20th century.

The development of new types of schools for children of all the families required a great deal of specialized preparation for teachers. Kindergarten teachers had to have special preparation for work with younger children. The high school program of broadened course offerings necessitated more teacher preparation in a great many subject fields.

It was during this period that women teachers came to outnumber the men and have since dominated the elementary schools of the nation. All of this resulted in demands which the normal schools were not prepared to meet and the four year teacher's college came into the higher education picture. A look at the course offerings of any school system at intervals from 1850 to 1960 will provide a good illustration of the continuing growth of the school curriculum.

In this period schools were organized on a more extensive basis with separate elementary and secondary schools or departments, principals, and corps of teachers. The graded school plan, started at Quincy, Massachusetts, in 1848, became the standard pattern in larger schools and systems. Equipment for laboratories, libraries, playgrounds, and gymnasia became necessities. School costs rose as new programs required teachers, books, materials, and equipment and the problem of school finance became commonplace. Other developments followed as social and economic changes were reflected in public education policies and programs. States followed the lead of Massachusetts again in enactment of compulsory attendance laws, and the long contest between truants and truant officers became a legal matter.

By the end of the first decade of the new century, the American people had the model of a public educational system to accommodate the children at every level from early preschool years through the public college or state university. This included nursery schools (in a few places), kindergarten, elementary schools (6 or 8 years), junior high school, senior high school, and state universities (or public colleges under state or municipal control). The phrase frequently quoted was not without foundation: "schools for the children of all the people."

Practical education for a diversified nation and people

Social change was reflected in some practical developments in public education. Many new types of schools and curriculums were added to make good on democracy's commitment of educational opportunity for all. The school consolidation movement to eliminate several one-teacher schools in favor of a central school and broader curriculum gained headway. Transportation of public school pupils by horse-drawn vehicles quickly gave way to motor buses as the states built modern roads. Public schools reflected the increasingly urbanized, industrial society about them.

American education had made good upon some of the commitments people understood. Schools had helped to induct millions of immigrants into the American way of life. Elementary education had come to be universal and high school enrollment was growing by leaps and bounds. The NEA Committee on Reorganization of Secondary Education framed the "Seven Cardinal Principles" and promoted the junior high school movement. The public junior college took hold in several states. More and more states raised the requirements for teacher education and certification and enacted compulsory attendance laws. There were "alarms" and concerns about fundamentals in strategic areas of the curriculum. State legislatures, concerned about threats and pressures of the first World War period, had emphasized concern about citizenship education, Bible reading in public schools, physical education and health instruction, and loyalty to "Americanism." The NEA established joint committees with the American Legion and the American Medical Association to study matters of mutual interest. Public education had become a major enterprise in a nation and a period that was used to "bigness." Since most Americans had long since expected to have "the biggest and best," much of the growth was commonplace.

The new America of proven industrial might and of world power harkened to the clamor and demands that attended its amazing material growth and responded in the form of institutions and programs that served the *utilitarian* motive. American education had taken a strong practical turn. This gave educators a talking point of great appeal.

Modern America Met New Problems and Global Responsibilities

EMBATTLED DEMOCRACY EXTENDED EDUCATIONAL OPPORTUNITY

Twentieth century America, a world power with problems

As the American people reviewed their way of life after the first World War they encountered new challenges, threats, and even conflicts. There was a new social invention, the League of Nations, designed to preserve the peace among the nations even at the cost of a fraction of national "sovereignty." The holocaust of the great war horrified millions and made the wish to return to an uncomplicated isolated status very strong. The demand for reduced armaments was felt in all allied nations as a way to peace. Many problems and conflicts were evident in the fields of labor relations and economic policies affecting farm prices, the tariff, cost of living, and monopolies. There were periods of inflation and of sharp business reverses. In other areas of living there were marked changes, as in use of automobiles, new labor-saving devices, in other transportation, in the coming of air mail and radio broadcasting, and in growing popularity of spectacular entertainment in movies, theater, and the press. The "Roaring Twenties" were on the stage of history.

The period between the two world wars was characterized by severe economic crises and changes, by "booms and busts." The great bull market of the late "Twenties" ended in the stockmarket crash of 1929, and the American people were soon involved in the longest, hardest "depression" ever known. Political changes brought new policies under the "New Deal" that profoundly changed the traditional economic practices and values of many Americans.

The growth of American schools and colleges was pronounced in many respects during this period. Buildings, equipment, school buses, and other facilities transformed the image of the public school in the public mind. Curriculum changes reflected several new concerns and demands. Emphasis on character education, citizenship, "Americanism," and orthodoxy were reflected in laws for Bible reading, as well as in the anti-evolution bills in legislature, loyalty oaths for teachers, and laws providing for instruction in American and state history (and constitutions). This was also a period of growth in athletic competition in both schools and colleges. Many practical demands and concerns contributed to the increased development of vocational education (aided by the Smith-Hughes Act of 1917), plans for greater use of school facilities such as the "Platoon School," a new approach to curriculum-making based on "activity analysis," and in consolidation of schools and of school districts. Teacher education received new impetus as normal schools were raised to four year college status and departments of education flourished in public universities.

The Federal government came upon the educational scene through many of the relief and emergency programs of the depression years. Many communities got help on new school buildings by grants through public work programs. Unemployed out-of-school youth received useful education and wholesome outdoors experience in the Civilian Conservation Corps. Others benefitted from National Youth Authority work projects that provided enough income to help them stay in school or college. Added funds for vocational education made available by the George-Dean Act in 1936, stimulated trade and industrial education and in the distributive trades. Other programs provided nursery schools, literacy education, and school lunches during part of this period.

One major issue pervaded educational circles during this period; namely, Federal aid to education. The NEA made this its principal objective and proposed legislation for this end was introduced into each congress. This was a time of marked growth in state teachers' organizations and of steady increase in strength by the NEA.

Another controversial development was the "Progressive Education" movement that received much attention in America and abroad. The P.E.A. was started at the end of World War I and became part of the New Education Fellowship with branches in Western Europe, Australia, and elsewhere. The movement was led by a smaller number of able educators and exerted more influence than did many larger groups. Its objectives, which were seven in number, first stated in 1924, were mild and modest viewed in retrospect. Nevertheless, there have been few movements in the history of education that have excited more controversy or have been as poorly understood. The organization, the P.E.A., disbanded in 1954 with the pronouncement that its chief objectives had been incorporated into American education.

One interesting bit of educational history during the depression decade makes interesting reading today. In this period, a slower rate of population growth and a decreased birthrate led to predictions of a stabilized population. School superintendents and school boards read the projections to mean that the big growth in elementary schools was ended, that school plant problems would be largely in secondary schools.

In this era the growth of large comprehensive high schools began. A number of school districts took the added step of providing for 13th and 14th years of instruction through a junior college. Adult education programs in various centers progressed to the point that a "movement" was organized.

Despite extensive curriculum growth as new courses were added to meet societal demands upon elementary and secondary schools, there were many features that perceptive educators wished to change. American schools had accepted many innovations and ideas from abroad (especially from Europe) such as the kindergarten of Froebel, the ideas of Herbart including the "doctrine" of interest, and certain Pestalozzian practices like "object teaching" and the developmental concept. Some modifications were made by American educators, notably Patty Hill, in the kindergarten movement in this country. On the other hand, certain of these had tended to become oversimplified and poorly interpreted in practice. For example, the Herbartian Theory had become the "Five Formal Steps" to teaching and some "object lessons" had become artificial routine procedures of little value. New courses and subjects had led to mountainous requirements of memory work, more drills, and more imitation. Reformers in various fields, humanitarians, and philanthropists led drives for educational reforms. Out of this climate of opinion, the ideas and practices of able educational thinkers gained support. A principal innovator who had a great influence upon education in the 20th century was John Dewey, whose experimental school at Chicago pioneered a new approach to education of children.

American education, like many aspects of the culture, was subjected to many stresses and strains during the two decades between the world wars. Econ-

omy drives, criticisms from those who feared that social change would be fostered by the schools and by those who wished the schools to preserve the status quo, the renewed controversies over progressive education, the pressures of groups favoring tax support for nonpublic schools, the discouraging battle to gain Federal aid to equalize educational opportunity among the states, the challenge of labor union type of organization to represent teachers, and the looming threats to academic freedom that stemmed from the totalitarian menace overseas—all marked the educational scene.

The decade of the Thirties brought forth some of the best statements of educational aims and objectives and studies of curriculum that have been produced. Examples may be seen in *The Purposes of Education in American Democracy,* and in references to the celebrated "Eight Year Study" by thirty secondary schools in cooperation with many colleges.[12]

A second phase of universal education

Throughout the period there appeared a discernible theme—the *mass education motive*—that characterized education in these United States. In these decades, secondary education became well-nigh universal for the teenage group of the population, graduation from high school became the normative goal for youth and the key to the door of employment opportunity. This was the second great wave of universal public education. There were important gains made in adult

[12] References are Educational Policies Commission, Washington, NEA, 1938, and Wilfred M. Aikin, *The Story of the Eight Year Study* (New York: Harper & Row, 1942), respectively.

education programs. College enrollments increased as the proportion of high school graduates entering higher education rose steadily. Education, on a democratic basis, *as much as people could take,* was the pervasive view. In many respects, this phase of America's educational history could be characterized by an emphasis upon *quantity.*

AMERICAN EDUCATION AND THE PURSUIT OF EXCELLENCE

The postwar period brought new challenges and demands upon school systems and higher education both of which had been working under severe hardships and deficiencies during World War II. Science equipment was obsolete, science teachers lost to industry and the war effort never returned, shortages of supplies and building materials limited school plant construction, even teaching materials were in short supply due to wartime shortages of paper and printing. The teacher shortage, evident throughout the war, became chronic, as did the classroom shortage. America's school leaders warned and worked to solve the reconstruction problems, but the needed nationwide response was not forthcoming.

At the same time, the birthrate of the war period had produced ever-increasing classes of beginning pupils for the schools each year. The result of all these factors was a decade of critical shortages of everything save pupils.

American education was the target of a growing volume of criticism and controversy about many topics—aims, discipline, methods of teaching reading (and all the 3 "R's"), and the curriculum. Certain aspects of public education were savagely attacked: e.g., progressive education, the new movement termed "life adjustment" education, soft discipline, easy courses, the secular curriculum, and the control of schools by the educationists. "McCarthyism" found its reflection in efforts to prescribe loyalty oaths for teachers and professors and in some cases of intimidation of certain liberal educators. The NEA was forced to investigate both charges of reactionary policies by school boards and leaders and of unwarranted attacks upon school systems. The Pasadena, California, case was the most celebrated instance of the latter.

One of the most significant events of the Fifties was the reversal of the "separate but equal" policy for schools for Negro children in the South and border states. After a lengthy series of court battles to insure full status for Negroes as students in public institutions of higher education, the crucial case of *Brown vs. Board of Education* came to the Supreme Court.[13] This was linked with a number of similar test cases in other states. On May 17, 1954, the Supreme Court handed down its decision. Segregation was to go, states were to make all deliberate speed to integrate the public schools. The old policy established by *Plessy vs. Ferguson* (1896)[14] was officially dead. Most border states took relatively early action to carry out the Court's decision. The beginnings in some Southern states were slow, but there was progress. Violence at Clinton, Tennessee, and Little Rock, Arkansas, were counterbalanced by smooth transitions in Louisville, Kentucky, and Atlanta,

[13] *Brown vs. Board of Education of Topeka,* 349 U.S. 483 (1954).
[14] *Plessy vs. Ferguson,* 163 U.S. 537 (1896).

Georgia. By 1962 only three states had made little or no effort to integrate the public schools.

A sharp controversy ensued when a bill for Federal aid (1946) under strong sponsorship passed the U.S. Senate only to be killed in the House of Representatives. Hopes of the NEA and of public education groups for the end they had sought since the 1920's were dimmed when troublesome questions of racial and religious relationships prevented affirmative action by Congress. Despite presidential endorsement on several occasions and strong support by the National Congress of Parents and Teachers, the perennial question was still unrealized in the 1960's. After nearly a century of Congressional debate over the inequalities of opportunity and of resources among the states, particularly those of the South, there was no evidence that the three types of obstructions to Federal aid would be soon removed. The traditional objection on grounds of economy was still heard by conservative political groups and economic organizations, notably the National Association of Manufacturers and United States Chamber of Commerce. The old racial bias still had some influence among die-hard states righters who resisted school integration with every device they could muster, even when it was clearly a hopeless struggle. To these were added the long dormant objection by many Roman Catholic churchmen and politicians who made determined efforts to block Federal aid unless parochial schools and schools of higher education were included. Despite approval of all post-war presidents these forces prevented further participation of the Federal government in promoting equality of educational opportunity for Americans everywhere.

Federal funds had been used for broader educational purposes after World War II. The "GI Bill of Rights" (1944) provided funds for higher education of millions of veterans of World War II and of the Korean conflict. This was clearly a noteworthy success story in American higher education. After a hectic period of sharp controversy and debate over Russia's successful launching of Sputnik in October, 1957, the Congress passed the National Defense Education Act (1958) to strengthen educational programs in foreign languages, mathematics, the sciences, guidance services, audio-visual instructional aids, and for student loans and fellowships.

A strong theme of reform pervaded many movements within and pressures upon public education in the 1950's and 1960's. Sometimes these were quite inconsistent; often the criticisms voiced the very shortcomings educational leaders had warned about in the 1940's, but the clamor showed that public education was deemed important. Despite the bitterness, even injustice occasioned by criticisms and reactionary movements, there were some notable gains and contributions. The pressures by certain groups to gain a place for religious instruction in public schools gave impetus to efforts of school leaders and professional groups to emphasize the teaching of moral and spiritual values, which was a slight trend of the Fifties.[15] The Supreme Court ruled that religious

[15] Educational Policies Commission. See *Moral and Spiritual Values in the Public Schools* (Washington: NEA, 1951); John Dewey Society, *Spiritual Values and Public Schools* (New York: Macmillan, 1947); or Ellis F. Hartford, *Moral Values in Public Education* (New York: Harper & Row, 1958).

instruction, even on released time, could not be given in public schools and involve use of public funds (McCollum Decision, 1948),[16] but that released time programs outside the public schools were constitutional (Zorach Decision, 1952).[17] Increasing tensions growing out of certain religious practices in public schools of various states led to notable court cases and policy decisions in the early 1960's. Two significant decisions by the Supreme Court upon three cases have established firmly the principle that public schools may not prescribe or provide religious exercises. In 1962 the Court declared unconstitutional the recitation of a prayer composed by the New York State Board of Regents (*Engel vs. Vitale*). In June 1963 the Court's decision on Bible reading and recitation of the Lord's Prayer in public schools held that both as required practices were unconstitutional (*School District of Abingdon Township, Pennsylvania vs. Schempp, et al.,* and *Murray vs. Curlett*). These decisions have implications for school practices in many districts over the nation. Parents and teachers should understand the basis for the Court's decision which strengthens the basic freedoms of all Americans.[18]

Reactionary and destructive critics of public education lost most of their following as school leaders made serious

[16] *McCollum vs. Champaign (Illinois) Board of Education,* 333 U.S. 203 (1948).

[17] *Zorach vs. Clauson,* 343 U.S. 306 (1952).

[18] A brief report may be found in "Supreme Court Decision on Bible Reading and Prayer Recitation," *NEA Journal,* **LII,** No. 6 (September 1963), pp. 55–56. The citations are as follows: *Engel v. Vitale,* 370 U.S. 421 (1962); *School District of Abingdon Township, Pennsylvania v. Schempp, et al.,* and *Murray v. Curlett,* 374 U.S. 203 (1963).

efforts to provide a better educational opportunity for more and more children. A generation of young parents with war babies had to take a stand for support of adequate facilities for school opportunity. Teachers' salaries increased markedly after 1950 although the rising cost of living tended to minimize the actual gain in purchasing power.

Some significant constructive developments occurred during the hectic decade of the Fifties. The National Citizen Commission for the Public Schools spearheaded the organization of literally thousands of local citizens' study groups over the nation, creating a favorable climate of opinion for political action. Another type of new development was the series of studies of different levels of public education under the direction of Dr. James Bryant Conant, onetime president of Harvard, later ambassador to Germany, and constructive critic of education. The studies of senior high schools, junior high schools, elementary schools, and teacher education disclosed little new to abler leaders but did arouse substantial response and popular backing for the nation's schoolboards who were charged with leadership responsibility.

Reports of studies by outstanding groups of distinguished American leaders in many fields included education and its relation to national goals and the survival of the American way of life. Among these were the Report of the President's Committee on National Goals (1960), the Rockefeller Panel Reports 1958–1960.

In other areas there were some innovations and experiments that promised to strengthen and improve the curriculums and instructional programs of the schools. A number of study groups, composed of noted authorities from higher education and public schools, worked to revitalize and reform the subject matter content of the mathematics and science curriculums. Several learned societies were represented in these groups, by active participants on the working committees which included noted physicists, mathematicians, chemists, biologists, and other authorities. A rollcall of this large class of study groups would list alphabetical titles reminiscent of "alphabet soup" days of emergency governmental agencies of the 1930's.

In the same general period, what were termed "teaching machines" were developed by B. F. Skinner, Harvard psychologist, and others. These new auto-instruction devices, designed to simplify certain aspects of teaching, led quickly to the formulation of whole courses of "programmed learning," some planned for home use, others for individual study in the classroom. Automation had come into public education.

Significant efforts to devise new approaches to teaching were made in a number of places by various groups. The most fruitful of these, sponsored by the National Association of Secondary School Principals, headed by Dr. Lloyd R. Trump, University of Illinois, developed what came to be called the "team teaching" plan.

Higher education experienced tremendous growth and changes during the postwar era. The old image of the liberal arts college was replaced by impressions of multi-purpose institutions with emphasis upon research and service functions in addition to teaching. Clear evidence of the national dependence upon higher education could be seen in the story of the developments of wartime research. These were followed by studies on the uses of atomic energy and by huge investments in university research programs under contract with various federal agencies. New patterns of organization had emerged at the state and regional levels. California had a tri-partite arrangement of its university (with 8 branches), 15 state colleges and over 70 junior colleges; New York had a vast system of diverse units under a state university organization and several states set up junior college networks. Regional organizations for co-operation of various states in use of higher education facilities and programs began with the Southern Regional Education Board in 1950. Others followed shortly in New England and in the Rocky Mountain area. All aspects of higher education were involved in new patterns of change and growth.

A number of significant experimental studies and research projects made educational history in the two postwar periods. After World War II the Ford Foundation established the Fund for the Advancement of Education, the Fund for the Republic, and a center for the study of democratic institutions. The Ford Foundation supported many experimental programs in use of educational television, the use of "teacher aides" in schools, and new patterns of teacher education. It also studied various phases of American education, published numerous reports, and aided various other activities. The General Education Board and the Rockefeller Foundation made an invaluable contribution to education in the South during the first half of this century. The W. K. Kellogg Fund supported the Cooperative Project in Educational Administration and underwrote three continuing education centers in universities. Carnegie libraries dotted the campuses over the nation as did Peabody education buildings in Southern universities. The Sloan and the Lilly funds have paid for important research projects in a variety of fields. Many foundations have aided college endowments, building plans, salary and retirement programs, and other projects across the nation. Similarly, many state curriculum programs and significant experiments in public education have been conducted on foundation grants.

The quest for quality education

As the American people prepared to enter the sixties there was much discussion of plans to celebrate or commemorate the Civil War in communities and all the states of the nation. Had there been comparable interest in reviewing our educational history and in assessing the progress Americans have witnessed in public education there would have been some exciting findings. The public high school was to be found in but few communities in 1860. By 1870 it enrolled 70,000 students; by 1900, a half million; and in 1960 there were approximately 8 million in America's public secondary schools. Data for expenditures per pupil are not available for the Civil War period but the per pupil figures for average daily attendance in 1900 was $16.88, in 1960, $375. Total school expenditures in 1900 were $220,000,000; in 1960 it approximated $15 billion. Enrollments in higher education rose from less than 250,000 in 1900, to somewhat under 4 million in 1960. The total income for all higher education was about $41 million in 1900; in 1960 it was slightly under $6 billion. Clearly, higher education had begun a period of unprecedented growth much as had secondary education only a few decades

earlier. A third great wave of growth was under way, possibly to universalize education beyond the high school.

A prominent historian offered this resume of the educational progress of the U.S.A. in this troubled century of ours:

The great ideas and practical achievements of the twentieth century included progressive education, educational measurements, school surveys, intelligence tests, the junior high school, the rebirth of the senior high school, the junior college, federal aid, and the great effort to provide equal and not separate education for the proud descendants of the pioneers, and founders, and the Negro, the Mexican, the Puerto Rican, and the stranger within our gates. Equal opportunity and the full development of every talent through the cooperation of the community, state, and nation is a worthy goal, not yet attained.[19]

Students have been universally impressed with the incredibly rapid increase of the rate of social change in our recent history. The tempo of changes that affect education and in education has become faster in recent decades. A backward look at the twenty-odd years since the start of World War II reveals many significant developments and events that have a place in any assessment or evaluation. One impression of the postwar era is that of hugeness, vastness, in short the magnitude of the entire educational enterprise of the American people. It appears that the quantitative growth and extension of other levels of American education have now appeared in higher education.

An exciting and significant characteristic of American education of the Fifties and the Sixties is the pervasive *theme* that might be called "The Quest for

[19] H. G. Good, *A History of American Education* (2nd ed., New York: Macmillan, 1962), pp. 594–595.

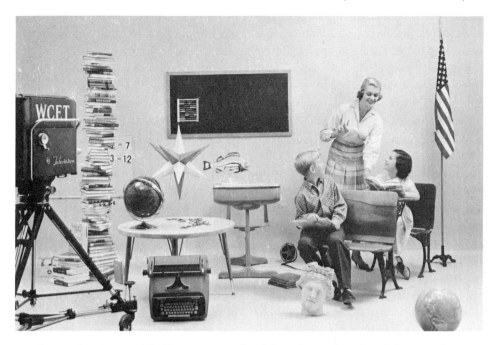

Instructional materials illustrate growth of American education (photograph, courtesy Cincinnati Public Schools).

Quality Education." Nothing less will be adequate for a nation and a way of life with their great potential, nor sound from the standpoint of survival in a divided world. This generation of college youth should be willing to settle for nothing short of a quality education for themselves and their children in the new Space Age.

The American Faith in Democracy and Education

Historians have frequently spoken of the traditional faith of the American people in public education. They have pointed out that no people anywhere at any time have built so extensive and elaborate programs of education nor gone further in conceiving of education as the birthright of all. Undoubtedly, that faith shows clearly through our history of over three hundred years. Expressed and manifested variously by times and places this common theme has been maintained and shows perhaps even more clearly now than ever before.

Cubberley has summed up our progress in public education in terms of seven great battles for: compulsory education, tax-supported schools, state control of schools, elimination of sectarianism, extension of the school system, the development of the high school, and increased state support for schools.[20] In recent decades a battle in American education has been in progress over the issue of federal aid for public education; even now it may

[20] Elwood P. Cubberley, *Public Education in the United States* (Boston: Houghton Mifflin, 1919), pp. 118–212.

be renewed. Looking back upon these episodes in the history of our culture, it is almost impossible for us to appreciate the gravity and magnitude of these great struggles and efforts in behalf of education. Few Americans today have any adequate conception of the real achievements and contributions in a half-dozen states of such men as Horace Mann, Henry Barnard, Caleb Wiley, Robert J. Breckenridge, and Calvin Stowe. Associated with them were many other notable figures and a host of plain folk, who shall ever be nameless in the history books, who wished the birthright of education for their children. Counts has spoken of this faith of our people in the school as ". . . the American road to culture." His tories of education properly give prominent place to this finding. The considered judgment of a leading historian upon this point follows:

> Few Americans who today enjoy the benefits of public education are aware of the arguments, struggles, and tremendous personal sacrifices that went into the battle to obtain public schools. The chapter in American history which relates to these struggles and sacrifices gives proof that public schools would never have come to be had it not been the clear decision of the American people to build them.[21]

This faith is reflected in the public utterances and writings of numerous leaders and statesmen whose leadership was accepted by our people. Almost without exception, our presidents have given strong expressions of their belief and faith in public education. No less convincing and clear are the resolutions and official state-

[21] L. A. Cremin, *Public Education and the Future of America* (Washington: NEA, 1955), p. 26.

ments of organizations and groups of people down through the years—working men's associations, trade unions, town meetings, political groups, the press, and more recently, PTA's, chambers of commerce, and many others which express the American dream and faith in education. The great documents of our educational history are a source of inspiration and pride. Every student of education should know of the "Old Deluder Satan Act," or "Article Third" in the Ordinance of 1787, of Judge Cooley's decision in the famous "Kalamazoo Case," the decision in the "Asheville Case," and the ringing affirmations of the principles of public education by the Supreme Court of the United States in recent years. It is regrettable that high school and college courses in American history usually leave untouched most of this great phase of our national cultural history. It seems reasonable to expect that Horace Mann should be as well known as Davy Crockett, Buffalo Bill or even Jesse James. The parents and teachers of America should be concerned about the inclusion of significant content in the public school curriculum.

AMERICANS KEEP FAITH WITH COMMON SCHOOLS

The historic faith of the American people must have appeared dim and weak upon many occasions. No doubt Thomas Jefferson, Mary Lyon, and Horace Mann must have felt at times that their dreams were in vain. It was a long period of nearly 200 years between the first school laws in Massachusetts and the start of Mann's labors as head of the schools of that state. Since then, we have gained another century of experience in the conduct of public schools. In retrospect, therefore, that faith appears to have been vigorous and strong; moreover, it continues.

American education shows no sign of an old, decadent institution. It exhibits possibilities for even greater growth and improvement. Growth is indicated at both the terminal and beginning points of our educational ladder. Publicly-owned and supported junior colleges are increasing in many states and everywhere there is discussion of the need for additional opportunity for youth beyond the 12th grade. Beyond that are the statements of challenge to the American people to provide for greatly increased college enrollments through public aid and scholarships to potential leaders. The demonstrations of the privately-sponsored preschool programs, together with federal aid during wartime at the nursery school level have induced intelligent demands for public education for young children. This, too, is a development which we may expect in our time. One should become informed upon such developments and issues in one's state and be ready to assist in the efforts which must come in future years.

American education, too, exhibits strength and vigor in its capacity for evaluation and improvement. Educators have developed many agencies and groups for careful, systematic study of their fields and activities. A vast outpouring of reports, surveys, research studies is one result. More significant is the evidence that much has happened as the result of the recent reports of the Educational Policies Commission—the "conscience" of the public education profession in the U.S.A.—destined to challenge and influence the thinking of a generation of students and teachers.[22] Back of these great documents may be found a series of studies and reports covering more than fifty years of work by leading educators. The study of some of these landmarks in educational thought, beginning with the Committee of Ten of the Gay Nineties down to the present time when no less than a half-dozen groups of nationwide significance are at work upon educational policy, would be rewarding. This capacity for study and self-criticism is indicative of the vigor and strength of American education and its leadership. It is one good sign that American education is still on the way to greater things.

One of America's great historians, Henry Steele Commager, believed that Americans have demanded more of their schools and been better served by them than any other people. He expressed strong faith in the performance of American education in the future:

> For a century and a half American schools have served and strengthened the commonwealth. They provided a citizenry as enlightened as any on earth. They justified and vindicated democracy's promise. If society clearly defines the new duties it wishes the schools to fulfill and if it steadfastly supports them not only with money but also with faith, they will surely justify that faith as they have in the past.[23]

[22] Reference is made to such noteworthy commission publications as: *Purposes of Education in American Democracy* (1938), *Education for All American Youth* (1944), *Education for All American Children* (1948), *Moral and Spiritual Values in the Public Schools* (1951), *The Contemporary Challenge to American Education* (1958), *An Essay on Quality in Public Education* (1959), and *The Central Purpose of American Education* (1961).

[23] Henry Steele Commager, "Our Schools Have Kept Us Free," *Life Magazine,* Special Issue, **XXIX**, No. 16 (October 16, 1950), pp. 46–47. Courtesy *Life* magazine, © 1950 Time, Inc.

There should be exciting and challenging frontiers ahead for Americans and their children. The study of our history should help to uncover new meanings in the story of our great common school system. During the decades when the frontier nation grew to maturity the public school systems were established. By the time of World War I, an elementary school education had become the norm for American citizens. This was the first *universal* school in these United States. The years between the two world wars marked a period of unprecedented growth of the secondary school population. High schools flourished in every community, enrollments rose to include the great majority of teenagers, and graduation became a *commonplace*. The second "universal" school—the public high school—became a substantial reality before 1940. The third great wave of unprecedented growth of educational opportunity has followed World War II. Millions of veterans thronged colleges and universities, using their benefits under the GI Bill. There had never been such an educational revolution in all the history of higher education. Another great influx followed the Korean conflict in the Fifties. Meanwhile, vast technological development and social change have brought new demands and aspirations for higher education. Every survey of parental attitudes and plans has reflected this. The percentage of high school graduates who enter college has continued to rise steadily through the Fifties and Sixties. Clearly, the third great wave of growth in educational opportunity has arrived.

The scholarly Santayana once observed that those who cannot remember their history are compelled to repeat it. Perceptive young collegians of this generation should read the history of their democratic institutions, including the common school, with enthusiasm and insight, to the ends of greater appreciation and wiser utilization.

Selected Bibliography

Bagley, William C. *A Century of the Universal School.* New York: Macmillan, 1937.

Benedict, Agnes E. *Progress to Freedom.* New York: G. P. Putnam's Sons, 1942.

Blake, Raymond J. *A History of Education Through Time Lines.* Palo Alto, California: National Press Publications, 1962.

Butts, R. Freeman. "A Search for Freedom," *NEA Journal,* **XLIX,** No. 3 (March 1960).

Butts, R. Freeman, and Cremin, Lawrence A. *History of Education in American Culture.* New York: Holt, Rinehart & Winston, 1953.

Caswell, Hollis P. "Achievement and Challenge," *NEA Journal,* **XLVI,** No. 3 (March 1957), pp. 139–143.

Commager, Henry Steele. "Our Schools Have Kept Us Free," *Life,* Special Issue, **XXIX,** No. 16 (October 16, 1950) pp. 46–47.

————. "McGuffey and His Readers," *Saturday Review,* **XLV,** No. 24 (June 16, 1962), pp. 50–51, 69–70.

Cremin, Lawrence A., and Borrowman, Merle L. *Public Schools in Our Democracy.* New York: Macmillan, 1950.

Cubberley, Elwood P. *Public Education in the United States,* Rev. ed. Boston: Houghton Mifflin, 1934.

————. *Readings in Public Education in the United States.* Boston: Houghton Mifflin, 1934.

Drake, William E. *The American School in Transition.* New York: Prentice-Hall, 1955.

Earle, Alice M. *Childlife in Colonial Days.* New York: Macmillan, 1953.

"Education" Issue, *Building America,* **XIII,** No. 3 (March 1948), pp. 258–267.

Educational Policies Commission, *Public Education and the Future of America.* Washington: NEA, 1955.

Eggleston, Edward. *The Hoosier School-boy.* New York: Charles Scribner's Sons, 1871.

————. *The Hoosier Schoolmaster.* New York: Charles Scribner's Sons, 1871.

Elsbree, Willard S. *The American Teacher.* New York: American Book Co., 1939.

Federal Security Agency. *Expressions on Education by Builders of American Democracy.* U.S. Office of Education, Bulletin 1940, No. 10. Washington: U.S. Government Printing Office, 1941.

Fenner, Mildred, and Fishburn, Eleanor C. *Pioneer American Educators.* Washington: NEA, 1944.

Good, Harry G. *A History of American Education.* 2nd ed. New York: Macmillan, 1962.

Johnson, Clifton. *The Country School.* New York: Thomas Y. Crowell, 1907.

————. *Old-time Schools and School-books.* New York: Peter Smith, 1935.

Jorgenson, Lloyd P. "The Birth of a Tradition," *Phi Delta Kappan,* **XLIV,** No. 9 (June 1963), pp. 407–414.

Knight, Edgar W. *Education in the United States.* Boston: Ginn & Company, 1951.

————, and Hall, Clifton W. *Readings in American Educational History.* New York: Appleton-Century-Crofts, Inc., 1951.

Marshall, Robert A. *The Story of Our Schools.* Washington: National Council for the Social Studies, 1962.

Meyer, Adolphe E. *An Educational History of the American People.* New York: McGraw-Hill, 1957.

Minnich, Harvey C. *Old Favorites from the McGuffey Readers.* New York: American Book Company, 1936.

National Citizens Commission for the Public Schools. *How Have Our Schools Developed?* New York: The Commission, 1954.

Noble, Stuart G. *A History of American Education.* Rev. ed. New York: Holt, Rinehart & Winston, 1954.

"Supreme Court Decision on Bible Reading and Prayer Recitation," *NEA Journal,* **LII,** No. 6 (September 1963), pp. 55–56.

Washington, Booker T. *Up from Slavery.* Garden City, New York: Doubleday & Co., 1927.

Williams, Charl Ormond. (Ed.) *Schools for Democracy.* Chicago: National Congress of Parents and Teachers, 1939, pp. 26–46.

DISTINCTIVE FEATURES
OF AMERICAN EDUCATION

1. CENTRALIZED AUTHORITY AND DECENTRALIZED ADMINISTRATION.

2. PUBLIC SUPPORT FROM LARGER AND LARGER UNITS.

3. A SINGLE-TRACK SYSTEM OF PUBLIC EDUCATION OPEN TO ALL.

4. DEMOCRATIC METHODS OF CONTROL IN PUBLIC EDUCATION.

5. LARGE FREEDOM FOR PRIVATE AND RELIGIOUS EDUCATION.

6. A WIDENING TASK FOR THE EDUCATIONAL PROGRAM.

7. PROGRAMS REFLECT THE EXPANSION AND COMPLEXITY OF KNOWLEDGE.

8. HUMANE CONCEPTIONS OF HUMAN DEVELOPMENT AND OF EDUCATIONAL METHOD.

Chapter 4

The Significance of Public Education

The American system of free and universal elementary and secondary education is unique in world history and a distinguishing characteristic of our society. This system is the greatest safeguard of the freedom of our people. It is one of the best guarantees of their social and economic well-being. The education of our citizens in the ways of democracy is one of the most important responsibilities of each community, of each State and of the United States as the greatest nation in the world.*

Introduction

What is it all about anyway, all this talk about our schools? A great many American parents and taxpayers have become confused by so many contradictory and disturbing reports about public schools in the United States. A popular article that won nationwide acclaim for accuracy and fairness began by noting that people are told much about education that is disturbing and confusing, and some that cannot be true.[1] Some claim that Johnny can't read; others show evidence that he reads better than children of his age did in previous generations. Schools are poorer than those of the good old days; an editorial from the *New York Sun* in 1902 deplored the decline of schools since the editor's own schoolboy days. Classes are too large for good teaching, *but* there aren't enough qualified teachers now to go around! Teachers should have aides to do the nonprofessional tasks, say some; this is denounced by others as lowering the professional standards. There are too many "soft" courses, there should be different kinds of diplomas to show what course of study has been followed, and too many youth go through high school and try for college who have no business there anyway. This clashes with the comforting views that people have had of educational opportunity for all as one of the cornerstones of the American way of life. Talk of building needs, classroom shortages, and emergency teachers,

* National Council of Chief State School Officers, *Our System of Education* (Washington, D.C.: 1950), p. 5.
[1] George B. Leonard, "The Truth About the Teacher Crisis," *Look Magazine,* **XX**, No. 9 (February 21, 1956).

111

current ever since World War II, distracts attention from a worthy effort to interpret the school program to the people. Through it all like a theme runs the familiar note of *crisis* which has become almost normative.

In view of the controversies and debates concerning American education in this generation it appears uncommonly appropriate to give some thoughtful and serious study to the basic question about the real significance of public education. There are about 20,000 local citizens groups engaged in studying or working on school problems in the nation.[2] Members of these groups are actively engaged in exploring approaches to the answer to our basic question.

Students of American education who have surveyed its nature and scope, its cultural setting and relationships, and its thrilling history in our democracy have the right to begin asking questions. One that is certain to emerge has to do with the significance, the real meaning of education in these United States. The serious student will surely want to know "What difference does American education make?" It is a fair question and future community lead-

ers should have every opportunity to formulate a sound and intelligent answer. A sound approach involves consideration of the question from all viewpoints with accurate information upon each so that the resulting answer will have an informed basis.

The question and its answer is of interest to people generally, certainly to all responsible American citizens. Fred Hechinger, Education editor of *The New York Times,* noted that "Education became the greatest domestic concern of the American people in 1962," in a review of the accomplishments and events of the year.[3] Our approach must comprehend the evidence of the usefulness and value of education to people. Since democracy is the social system that places highest premium upon individuals, this type of education will be appropriate. American education is the agent of democratic society; it should be studied and evaluated from that standpoint. The answer to the basic question about the significance of American public education can be framed from the evidence about its meaning and contributions to the differing *individuals* and to the democratic *society* it serves.

Education and Individual Well-being

Education turns out to be important in the lives of individuals according to many studies made from different vantage points. Economic aspects of success and accomplishment have been studied from various approaches and all indicate that "Education pays off." This is not to say

that the dollars and cents evaluation of education is most significant—far from it. The findings of studies of this kind are easier to explain and present to people than some of the intangible returns and values that are of highest significance.

As a starting point, let us review some of the economic aspects of the gen-

[2] Grace Hechinger, "Good Schools Don't Just Happen," *Parents Magazine,* **XXXVI,** No. 2 (February 1961), p. 10.

[3] *The New York Times* News Service, January 1, 1963.

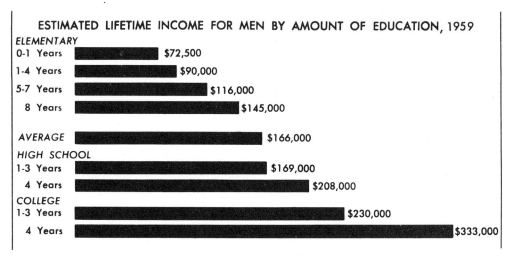

ESTIMATED LIFETIME INCOME FOR MEN BY AMOUNT OF EDUCATION, 1959

ELEMENTARY
0-1 Years $72,500
1-4 Years $90,000
5-7 Years $116,000
8 Years $145,000

AVERAGE $166,000

HIGH SCHOOL
1-3 Years $169,000
4 Years $208,000

COLLEGE
1-3 Years $230,000
4 Years $333,000

Source: Southern Regional Education Board, *Investing in People* (Atlanta, 1959).

eral thesis that "Education is related to individual progress."

EDUCATION IS IMPORTANT

An initial approach might be to review some of the economic aspects of the general thesis that education is an important factor in the economic progress of individuals.

Education and earnings

People in America and other countries are becoming aware of the significance of education as an *investment* in economic growth. More people now see that the effort, money, and time put into an education has a relationship to the standard of living that individuals may have. Many studies show the direct relationship between the educational level of individuals and their lifetime earnings. One based on studies of Census data showed that a college graduate could be

expected to earn $125,000 more during his lifetime than a schoolmate who only finished high school.

Studies reviewed in a recent publication of the Department of Health, Education, and Welfare show clearly the relationship between educational level and the lifetime income of male workers.[4] Moreover, there was a progressive increase in average amount of income associated with each level of schooling. In 1949 the differential in annual income between elementary school and high school graduates for white and nonwhite workers was $700 and $400 respectively.[5]

Other studies of education and lifetime earnings show similar findings. Male college graduates could have expected a lifetime earning of about $296,000 under 1949 conditions; the average estimate in

[4] Selma J. Mushkin (Ed.), *Economics of Higher Education* (U.S. Office of Education Bulletin, 1962, 50027, No. 5, U.S. Government Printing Office, 1962). See Chapter 9.

[5] *Ibid.,* p. 138.

1958 had risen to $435,000.[6] In 1958 the average expected lifetime earnings of high school graduates was $258,000; that of elementary school graduates was only $182,000—a differential of $76,000 or 42%.[7]

Another study found that men with college or high school educations earned 82% of all annual individual incomes of $10,000 or more in the United States. Conversely, the great majority (77%) of annual individual incomes under $500 were earned by men with inadequate elementary school education.

Yearly earnings would show equally interesting differentials between groups based on educational attainment of workers. The annual income of all workers (full time and part time) by education for both male and female exhibit marked differentials in favor of groups with high school and college preparation. Figures for 1961 provide a useful illustration.

Incomes of college graduates show greater differences between start and peak of their careers than for men with lower levels of educational attainment. In 1956, college graduates started careers with annual incomes that averaged about $5,400. College graduates in their productive "peak" years—late forties and early fifties —had an average annual income of about $9,100. This was an increase of 70% between average incomes at start and peak. The comparable figure was a 14% increase in the average annual incomes for both elementary and high school gradu-

ates.[8] This report stated that "education is one of the more important determinants of the amount of income received by individuals."

Estimates of average college costs and for the 12 years of public school have been published which afford opportunity for further comparisons of earnings of persons with high school and college education respectively. In 1961 the 19,000 public high schools graduated 1,700,000 youth. The total estimated cost in public funds of their twelve years of public education was $7,855,054,000.[9] The average cost of four years of college was estimated at $6,200 in 1961.[10] Very little arithmetic is needed to show that the public and the parental investments in high school and college education pays off in terms of increased earnings compared to workers with lower educational attainment.

Education and employment

The relationship between education and employment has been shown in many studies. Invariably, the unemployed groups include high proportions of persons whose educational level is low.

A recent study of the educational level among 215,000 unemployed men and women in a midwestern state revealed that two-thirds had not completed high

---

[6] Herman P. Miller, "Annual and Lifetime Income in Relation to Education: 1939–59," *American Economic Review*, **50** (December 1960), 962–986.

[7] John K. Norton, "Education as Investment," *NEA Journal*, **LII**, No. 1 (January 1963), p. 56.

[8] *Citizens Speak Out on School Costs*, pp. 18–19. Quoted report of U.S. Dept. of Commerce, Bureau of the Census, *Income of Families and Persons in the United States*, 1956 Current Population Reports—Consumer Income Series, p. 60, No. 27 (Washington: Bureau of the Census, April 1958), p. 10.

[9] See "Studies of High School Graduates," *NEA Research Bulletin*, **XL**, No. 2 (May 1962), p. 42.

[10] See "Education and Lifetime Earnings," *NEA Research Bulletin*, **XXXIX**, No. 2 (May 1961), pp. 58–60.

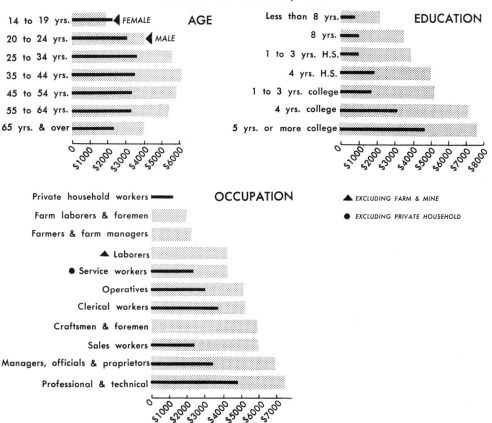

INCOME OF PERSONS, 1961

Source: *Road Maps of Industry*, No. 1399, October 19, 1962. Reproduced by permission of The Conference Board, New York.

school while only 1% of the group were college graduates.[11]

The amount of schooling a person has had shows a close relationship to employment opportunity and to security of the worker in his job. Figures for a sample month just before the last census illustrates how unemployment was related to the amount of education workers have had:

Workers	% unemployed
With elementary education	8.5
With high school education	4.8
With some college education	2.4

[11] *Education, U.S.A.* (October 18, 1962), p. 26.

In the labor force about one-fourth of male workers, in the 25–54 age group, have completed high school. Among those who have not completed high school, the long-term unemployment is *nearly three times as high* as for those who are high school graduates; their rate of involuntary part-time work is *three times* as great.

In 1900, nearly two-thirds of the entire U.S. labor force were unskilled workers; in 1960 hardly one job out of five could be filled by untrained labor.

The Rockefeller Fund Panel reported that it is precisely those fields of employment which require the highest competence and most extended preparation that exhibit the greatest increases in employment.[12]

Education and family income

The relationship between education and income is further substantiated by 1958 figures for family income according to amount of schooling of head of family.[13]

FAMILY INCOME REFLECTS EDUCATION

PER CENT DISTRIBUTION OF
FAMILIES BY MONEY INCOME

SCHOOLING OF
HEAD OF FAMILY

Elementary
8 yrs. only   59%   35%   6%

High School
Graduate   38%   52%   10%

College 4
or more yrs.   16%   52%   32%

0 10 20 30 40 50 60 70 80 90 100
PER CENT

under $5,000 ▇ $5,000-$9,999 ▨ $10,000 & over ☐

Source: NEA Research Division.

The data for 1958 also showed these median incomes:

For families headed by college graduates	$8,143
For families headed by high school graduates	$5,667
For families headed by persons with elementary schooling	$4,386
For *all* forty-four million families in U.S.A.	$5,087

Of these, nearly one-fourth of the families had incomes of less than $3,000 and nearly one-half of the families had incomes of less than $5,000. Almost 4 out of 10 families had incomes of $5,000 to $10,000 and 1 out of 10 families reported income over $10,000. The study of data for any recent year leads to similar findings.

The information about family income for a recent year substantiates the observation concerning the relationship between educational attainment and level of income. Figures for 1961 according to occupation of head of family show marked differentials in favor of professional and technical workers (whose education would include college and professional school) and of manager-proprietors and officials over other groups. Lowest family incomes were found among families headed by household workers, farm workers, and laborers, groups with low average educational attainment. The same groups held highest places in studies for 1955 and 1950 respectively. Median income of families of all employed civilians increased from $3,319 in 1950 to $5,620 in 1960 and $5,737 in 1961. Median income of families of professional and technical workers increased from $5,029 in 1950, to $6,447 in 1955, to $8,806 in 1961.

Education and occupation

The educational attainment of individuals has some relationship to occupational choices. In general, higher educational attainment (years of education completed) affords easier access to occupations that are recognized as economically and socially more desirable. In this respect it might be said that higher educational attainment and social mobility were related. The data for 1959 showed this relationship (see Table 4–1).

The occupational picture of our economy is one of those aspects of the culture that changes at an increased rate. In 1900 there was one engineer for every 250 workers; there is now about one in

[12] Rockefeller Panel Report, *The Pursuit of Excellence, Education and the Future of America*, 1958, p. 7.

[13] "It Pays to Go to School," *NEA Research Bulletin*, **XXXVIII**, No. 4 (December 1960), pp. 114–116.

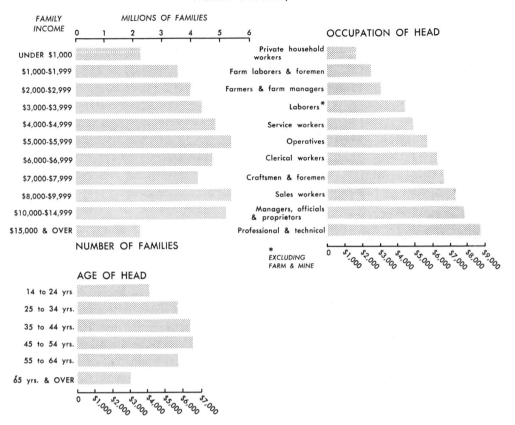

FAMILY INCOME, 1961

| FAMILY INCOME | MILLIONS OF FAMILIES | OCCUPATION OF HEAD |

UNDER $1,000
$1,000-$1,999
$2,000-$2,999
$3,000-$3,999
$4,000-$4,999
$5,000-$5,999
$6,000-$6,999
$7,000-$7,999
$8,000-$9,999
$10,000-$14,999
$15,000 & OVER

Private household workers
Farm laborers & foremen
Farmers & farm managers
Laborers*
Service workers
Operatives
Clerical workers
Craftsmen & foremen
Sales workers
Managers, officials & proprietors
Professional & technical

* EXCLUDING FARM & MINE

NUMBER OF FAMILIES

AGE OF HEAD

14 to 24 yrs
25 to 34 yrs.
35 to 44 yrs.
45 to 54 yrs.
55 to 64 yrs.
65 yrs. & OVER

Source: *Road Maps of Industry,* No. 1398, October 11, 1962. Reproduced by permission of The Conference Board, New York.

TABLE 4–1. AVERAGE FAMILY INCOME BY OCCUPATIONAL GROUP AND EDUCATION OF HEAD

Occupational Group	Years of Education Completed	Average Family Income
Professional and technical workers	16.2	$7,788
Proprietors and managers (excluding farmers)	12.4	$7,012
Clerical and sales workers	12.5	$5,692 (clerical) $6,268 (sales)
Skilled workers (craftsmen, foremen, etc.)	11.0	$6,018
Semi-skilled workers	9.9	$5,157
Unskilled workers	8.6	$4,089

Source: NEA Research Division. See: *NEA Research Bulletin,* XXXVIII, No. 4 (December 1960), p. 116.

50. An increase of 90 per cent has occurred in the number of electricians since the end of the First World War. Our needs for scientists in all fields will require a 75 per cent increase during the decade ending in 1970. Personnel employed in the various health services has increased five-fold in twenty years' time. All of these fields present clear illustrations of the key importance of education, at both professional and vocational levels.[14] A study of the occupational distribution of American

[14] See Ralph W. Tyler and Richard I. Miller, "Social Forces and Trends," *NEA Journal,* **LI,** No. 7 (September 1962), pp. 26–28.

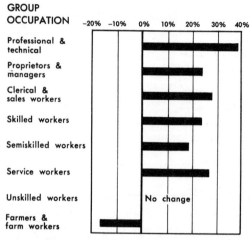

PER CENT CHANGE IN EMPLOYMENT
1960-1970

Source: Hoke S. Simpson (Ed.), *The Changing American Population* (New York: Institute of Life Insurance, 1962).

workers over a 75-year period showed the key importance of high level of educational attainment in the changing future employment picture.[15] The importance of education in future job opportunity has been studied (see figure).

EDUCATION IS A MEANS

Education and individual happiness

The evidence concerning the relationship between education and individual wellbeing from the economic standpoint should not obscure the more important concern about individual happiness. It should be remembered that economic factors and education are not ends in themselves; they are *means* for the accomplishment and fulfillment of individual

aspirations and purposes. Economic progress and education are important and significant to the degree to which they contribute to the achievement of optimum personal growth and human happiness. This concern for individual fulfillment has always been a prime consideration in the American tradition and democratic society. The Founding Fathers universally recognized human happiness as the goal of democratic institutions and expected that public education would make its major contribution to this end. Through the educational history of this Republic, there has been a consistent emphasis upon individual achievement, the realization of one's potential as the end product of education. This concern has continued to be recognized in the purposes and objectives of education in American democracy.

The Committee for the White House Conference on Education reported to the President in 1956 that one fundamental fact had emerged from its work, namely, that schools affect the welfare of the nation more now than ever before and that this new importance of education has been dangerously underestimated far too long. Continuing, the report noted a major reason for the growing importance of education was:

. . . The plain fact that the schools have become the direct instrument for keeping this nation the fabled land of opportunity it started out to be.[16]

The Committee further found that schools have taken the place of the fron-

[15] David L. Kaplan and M. Claire Casey, *Occupational Trends in the United States, 1900–1950*, Working Paper No. 5 (Washington, D.C.: Department of Commerce, Bureau of the Census, 1958), p. 7, includes projections to 1975.

[16] Committee for the White House Conference on Education, *A Report to the President* (Washington, D.C.: Superintendent of Documents, Government Printing Office, April 1956), p. 4.

tier in earlier American life. There the pioneer strength is renewed as schools give a fresh start to each generation. The schools' program should not be restricted to mental skills; it should put first things first, meaning to search out human talents, and help each to full development rather than to allow waste by neglect. Priorities are needed in education; an emphasis on quality should come first.

Education and people

In a very real sense our concern about education for better living and for democratic ideas and values was based upon their use by people. Human beings who use things and resources to live better and who accept ideas and values in the purpose and direction of their lives—these are the ends of education. One should really know and accept it as a philosophy if one is to reach the potential usefulness and purpose of one's role as an educated community leader.

There are many possible ways to consider education, and its relation to and effect upon people. One might start by making the assumption that "everybody is somebody," that everybody has worth and potentiality.[17] This is demonstrably true and it is the cornerstone of a democratic philosophy about education. You can see that persons have, or can have, purposes in terms of their needs, interests, aptitudes, capabilities, and problems. Since people were created different and develop in different fashions, all their talents and potentialities must have meaning and

worth. It is another cornerstone for a sound philosophy that education should begin with needs, interests, and problems of the different persons and should then help meet those needs and interests, thus helping people to grow, to become better persons, to realize their potentials. This is the high and lofty purpose of education that many people talk about but do not always understand. The principal problem is that of implementation, i.e., getting this concept carried out in actual practice. That implementation involves a clear understanding of these concepts by educators before they can hope to have the ideas put into practice by the people.

We could go on to discern how education would thus become functional and effective in leading to change and improvement. This ideal education would elicit the best efforts of the individuals because it would be on terms or purposes best known to the individual himself. The people would provide their own motivation to try and to learn because the purposes were so clearly their own. Education would thus be closely involved in helping people to understand themselves, their needs, interests, purposes, and to take increasing responsibility for realizing their own purposes. The motive power for learning activities and experiences would be found in the individual's attack upon the problem situation and the importance of the free learning environment in which to use the energy and effort expended in learning. We can begin to see the real relationship among better people, freedom, and functional education. This is what public education has contributed in large measure to the millions of American school population of each generation.

[17] One little fifth grade girl expressed it in this way after reading the little book *People Are Important,* "Remember that everybody is as special as you."

Education and National Well-being

EDUCATION AND ECONOMIC PROGRESS

There is a growing awareness of the relationship between the *investment* a people make in education and their economic progress. The standard of living is high in those national cultures where people invest their time, money, and efforts in education. This is no less true for nations than for individuals. Studies have been made at various times that point out this relationship between education and the economic progress of a people.

The head of one of America's leading industrial corporations judged that this country had made its greatest investment in its public school system.[18]

Education and national productivity

The relationship between education and national productivity can be shown in comparative studies of economies of different nations. The United States has the most productive economy of any nation. The 1961 per capita income for the U.S.A. was $2,265.[19] In 1959 the United States figure was more than twice that of any other major nation except Australia, Canada, New Zealand, Sweden, and Switzerland. It was more than four times the average for more than two-thirds of the

[18] *The Stake of Business in Public School Education,* An address by Frank W. Abrams, Chairman of the Board, Standard Oil Company (New Jersey) before the National Citizens Commission for the Public Schools, Cleveland, Ohio, January 12, 1951.

[19] See *Road Maps of Industry,* **1382** (June 22, 1962), The Conference Board, 460 Park Ave., New York 22, New York, for graphic data for U.S. and individual states.

75 nations for which comparable figures were available.[20] Some great nations, such as India, Pakistan and Thailand, had per capita incomes under $100 a year.

TABLE 4–2. NATURAL RESOURCES, EDUCATION AND INCOME

Nation	Natural Resources	Educational Development	Per Capita Income Average 1957–1959*
1	2	3	
Brazil	High	Low	$ 100– 199
Colombia	High	Low	$ 200– 299
Denmark	Low	High	$ 900– 999
Mexico	High	Low	$ 200– 299
New Zealand	High	High	$1,200–1,299
Switzerland	Low	High	$1,200–1,299
United States	High	High	$2,100–2,199

*In U.S. dollars at official rates of exchange.

Sources: Various reports of studies of education and economic growth have been made during and since World War II. See American Association of School Administrators, *Schools for a New World,* 25th Yearbook (Washington, D.C.: National Education Association, 1947), pp. 26–30; similar studies have been made, the latest by Harold M. Groves, *Education and Economic Growth* (Washington, D.C.: National Education Association, 1961). See summary "Education and Economic Growth" in *NEA Journal,* LI, No. 2 (February 1962), pp. 46–47. Data for column 4 used by permission of The National Industrial Conference Board from Gertrude Deutsch (ed.) *The Economic Almanac, 1962,* table, "Per Capita National Incomes of 75 Countries, Annual Average, 1957–59," p. 490.

What accounts for the wide range in per capita production of different countries and for the paramount position of the United States? A number of studies shed light on this question. In one series of studies seven countries have been compared on natural resources, educational development, and per capita income.

Both Brazil and the United States stand relatively high in natural resources. Educational development, both general and technical, until recently has been low in Brazil and high in the United States.

[20] Data adapted from *The Economic Almanac 1962,* New York, The National Industrial Conference Board, 1962, table, p. 490.

This in part accounts for the fact that productivity per person in the United States averaged over $2,100 during the years 1957–59, while that of Brazil was under $200 for the same period.

Postwar studies abroad have reported similar relationships between educational expenditure and the national income in highly industrial countries.[21] This same general thesis can be studied in these United States which afford comparisons in productivity and in educational expenditures. In general, states which have a good record of investing in good public schools by above-average support for years are found to have high per capita incomes. This relationship is found, although the pattern of natural resources may vary considerably. There are states with limited minerals and soil resources and short growing seasons that rank high on educational support and productivity. There are also some states with relatively rich resources that rank low in productivity as shown by per capita income. These have traditionally supported their public schools at low levels.[22]

Education and standards of living

It has long been established that the educational level of a people has a definite relationship to their living standards. The United States Chamber of Commerce has sponsored extensive studies of the relationships among the educational level of the people, the natural resources base, and the standard of living in various countries of the world. The findings are available in the form of popular publications with a film of the same title. The introductory statement clearly presents the theme of the study:

People who have a good education produce more goods, earn more money, buy and consume more goods, read more magazines and newspapers, are more active in civic and national affairs, enjoy a higher standard of living—and, in general, contribute more to the economy—than those who are not so well educated.[23]

This theme has been recognized by business and cultural interests. Publishers know well the relationship between educational levels of population and the cultural indices of living. The publisher of *Time,* commenting on the extraordinary growth of the magazine, noted that the number of high school and college graduates in the United States had increased respectively 12 and 8 times as fast as had the total population. Retailers of quality merchandise, professional men, bankers and investment brokers, insurance salesmen, booksellers, and proprietors of art shops and galleries know well this relationship.

Denmark and Mexico present an interesting contrast. Denmark a century ago had poor soil. It had little mineral wealth and a short growing season. During the past century, however, it developed a program of education which has become world famous. Mexico has abundant natural resources, but until recently provided relatively little education for its people. During the years of these studies,

[21] See *Citizens Speak Out on School Costs,* pp. 16–17 for a brief summary of a 1958 German study on this project.

[22] *Op. cit.,* p. 17.

[23] Chamber of Commerce of the United States, Education Department, see introduction, *Education—an Investment in People,* Revised edition. (Washington, D.C.: 1955). See also *Citizens Speak Out on School Costs* (NEA, 1959), for a summation of these studies. Used by permission.

Denmark's per capita income has been more than three times that of Mexico.

Colombia is a nation with rich natural resources, ranks extremely high in this respect, but stands at the bottom in wealth. Switzerland is an inspiring example of a country with few natural resources and a high per capita income. The differences in their educational efforts has had a great influence upon income and standard of living.

The foregoing examples can be duplicated many times. Rich natural resources do not necessarily result in high productivity, nor does their lack sentence a nation to poverty. The effective use of education can make the difference.

EDUCATION AND ECONOMIC GROWTH

Americans need to understand the implications for education and the educational program for national policy that follow from the question: "Will we grow fast enough to meet the economic needs of a free but threatened society?"[24] There is general appreciation of the nature of recent economic growth of this country; per capita income has doubled in a few decades, and people can recall specific instances in their standard of living. Furthermore, parents look forward to continued economic progress for the benefit of their children for whom they expect an even higher standard of living and economic security.

[24] This challenging question is implied in an editorial for educators by the chairman of the President's Council of Economic Advisers. See Walter W. Heller "Education and Economic Growth" in *NEA Journal*, L, No. 9 (October 1961), p. 9.

Economic progress that increases productivity, wages and salaries, and brings better living standards is good and desirable, but it is not the only important concern for the future. There are at least two or three other important ones for intelligent persons to consider. Economic growth should not be encouraged at the cost of unwise depletion of basic natural resources. Horrible examples of exploitation of an area by irresponsible interests may be found in many "strip-mined" landscapes ruined and abandoned for all practical purposes. A second concern is related to this, namely, economic growth should not be at the cost of human well-being. The result of poor economic growth can be seen in abandoned mining towns, deserted one-industry villages, in cut-over lands never suited for farming, and the like. Economic growth should be calculated to best serve the long-term needs and purposes of people. Narrow, selfish, and short-sighted policies designed to prevent outside competition and to restrict trade with other nations can only help an economy temporarily; then reprisals lead to decline. Economic growth should be in terms of wise use of resources, concern for effect upon people involved, and sound from the long-term best interests of the country. Our best investment in economic growth is that which returns benefits to ourselves and to those abroad who do business with us. One more pertinent point should be made. Economic growth should be directed and guided with a view to the best interests of the nation from the survival standpoint. Our investments abroad are really investments in the future. Gradually the educational, technical, and other aid will enable some

VALUE OF GOODS AND SERVICES PRODUCED, 1948-1970

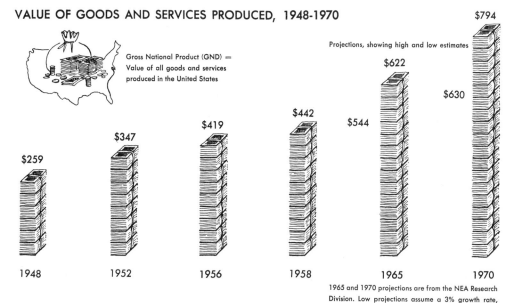

Gross National Product (GND) =
Value of all goods and services
produced in the United States

Projections, showing high and low estimates

$794

$622

$630

$544

$442

$419

$347

$259

1948   1952   1956   1958   1965   1970

1965 and 1970 projections are from the NEA Research Division. Low projections assume a 3% growth rate, high projections a 5% growth rate. All projections are in 1958 prices.

Source: NEA Committee on Educational Finance, *What Everyone Should Know about Financing Our Schools* (1960), p. 26.

peoples to assume more of their own support. Every time a "have-not" country develops toward the "have" status the more security for the well-developed economic nations.

Enough has been suggested to show how complex and strategically important that economic growth is to our future. It should also be clear that much of the responsibility and contributions to growth of the American economy depends upon educated people, especially a wise and prudent leadership. The better educated the great majority of people the more potential capability that can be called upon to work, lead and contribute and in more capacities. A policy of optimum educational opportunity for all seems to "pay off" in this respect. The provision for education of all people costs more, but their productivity is raised, and the taxes they begin to pay to governments

at all three levels show what a sound investment free public education has always been. An advanced and efficient economic system does not need the typical large group of unskilled labor with low educational levels and aspirations, cannot use a low quality labor force in fact.

Our past emphasis upon providing for as much educational opportunity for everybody as they would take has continued to pay off. The net result has been that the development of more capabilities of more people has always provided man power and a labor force unequalled in any quarter of the globe. The challenge is to keep educational opportunity for all open in this generation and to promote its optimum use in face of greater competition to our economy with its free labor, occupational mobility, chances for adult or worker's education and advancement. Problems of how to meet new competition in production from those nations whose new industrial plant we helped to build can be partially offset by the assistance they can give in maintaining the peace. The domestic problems of the economy may be perplexing but the free economy has more flexibility and potential for adjustment and solution. The best bet seems to be an emphasis upon educational progress that will insure better manpower, wiser leadership, and commitment to the extension of democracy as the key to survival.

The sharp competition of the Soviet Union in phases of industrial production and world markets presents some challenges to our educational institutions as well as to our major industries. Highly skilled manpower, engineers, scientists, and technicians in all fields are required in greater numbers than ever before. There is nothing basically wrong with a strong emphasis upon education of many specialists in these fields if their education is well-balanced and includes studies that contribute to the broader interests and human values of the free citizen. In other words, the scientists and engineers needed to keep American industry going and growing can be educated to be interesting, versatile, responsible persons that exemplify human values as well as the specialties for which they have aptitude. Here the challenge comes right down to the schools and colleges.

The chairman of the President's Council of Economic Advisers, Dr. Walter H. Heller, has stated that education, training, and research have accounted for about half the rise in output in this country during the past half century, approximately the period between World War I

and the start of the Space Age. Investment in a college yields a rate of return comparable to that for business investments in general; rates of returns upon investment in elementary and secondary education were even better.[25]

It might be fun to imagine how a publicity man for a large business enterprise or a local chamber of commerce would write up American education. It might read something like the following excerpt from an article in an education journal:

Education is the biggest business in the country—largest number of owners, most extensive plants, and most valuable product. This enterprise called *education* is a growing concern—never passed a dividend, or watered its stock, or sold any non-voting stock. Never had a boom or a depression. It has always paid a profit and never turned away an intellectual beggar. All the people are its stockholders, school boards its directors, teachers its technicians, students its "raw materials" and the community its laboratory. And its product has had the greatest influence on both America and the world.[26]

EDUCATION AND SCIENTIFIC PROGRESS

Many of those who have used the Russian successes with Sputnik I and the first manned space flights as occasions for irresponsible criticism of public schools have ignored some of the evidence that top flight scientists and engineers have been produced by those same institutions. An interesting point is that many of the

[25] *Education, U.S.A.* (October 18, 1962), p. 26.
[26] Eugene P. Bertin in *Pennsylvania School Journal*, **CXI**, No. 8 (November 1962), p. 95. Used by permission.

alleged weaknesses and problems of the schools had been publicized by educational and community leaders during and after the World War II period. This does not imply that there could be no criticizing public education either before or after the Russian successes; there were (and still are) grounds for improvement in many school systems. The important consideration is that the evaluation be fair, the reporting accurate, and the motive be clear.

There are many success stories for the public education systems of these United States before and after World War II. One of them could well report on the performance of scientists, engineers, and technical experts in many fields who aided in the war effort, and whose services have been indispensable in the tremendous success of American science in recent years.

One story you have never heard from certain well-publicized individuals and active organizations has to do with an outstanding group of young scientists who were at work when the comment about and criticism of public schools occurred after October 4, 1957 when the first "Sputnik" went into orbit about the earth.

Within a few months Explorer I, America's first satellite, was launched successfully, complete with many novel scientific instruments and devices. Little mention was made of the fact that fifteen of the sixteen young scientists (in their thirties) were graduates of public high schools, ten of them in California. Eight of the ten took degrees at California Tech.[27] The sixteen scientists worked at Huntsville, Alabama, in the Army Ballistic Missile Agency and at California Technology Institute in Pasadena.

This is a symbol of the best potential of public education in the U.S. and a kind of evidence, pertinent to the great controversy over public education, that received little notice.

The following summation of why American education is important in a scientific age by a group of outstanding leaders expresses it clearly and concisely:

The mounting importance of education in the United States, therefore, rests upon several basic considerations. It provides much of the specialized and advanced education to meet the mounting demand for highly trained manpower. It is a principal source of basic research which provides new knowledge, the very stuff of progress in a scientific age. Education is an essential ingredient of our increasingly productive economy upon which a high standard of living and national security depend. It is a principal source of an enlightened citizenry qualified to deal with a growing range of personal, domestic, and foreign affairs which constantly increase in difficulty. It is a primary means whereby the ideal of equality of opportunity is given reality in action.

In short, ours is the kind of civilization which requires a lot of education—more in amount and of better quality for a growing number and percentage of our people. Our material wellbeing, our national security, and the further fulfillment of our democratic ideals require more and better education. Such are the considerations which today underscore the great and mounting importance of education in the United States.[28]

[27] *California Teachers Association Journal* (March 1958).

[28] Committee on Tax Education and School Finance, *Citizens Speak Out on School Costs* (Washington, D.C.: National Education Association, 1959), p. 26. Used by permission.

EDUCATION AND
CULTURAL PROGRESS

The incredible transformation of American life which social change has wrought has transpired during the lifetime of many citizens. During this era, America and Americans have made impressive accomplishments in fields related to the arts and cultural pursuits. Many living persons can recall references to the "cultural wasteland," chronic complaints by managers of entertainment talent, the condescension of visiting artists, and the alleged inferiority of native American art and artists in many fields. Only a few decades ago, the dearth of American composers and conductors was common talk; American art galleries, museums, and concert halls featured publicity of visiting European attractions; aspiring students went abroad to study and to start their careers. Major orchestras were few in number and not a single symphony orchestra of any significance existed in the South. Music, painting, sculpture, and other arts media held minor places in the indigenous culture of the early 20th century.

A half-century has brought amazing developments and growth of the arts and cultural fields in American life. Some have termed this the "cultural explosion in our national life."[29] In 1920 there were less than a hundred symphony orchestras in the whole United States; in 1960 there were 1,142; and the nation had more than 35 million music lovers (concert goers). A whole galaxy of native American artists, composers, and conductors has brought new forms and content to the

[29] See *Reader's Digest* (February 1960), p. 96.

world of music. It may be significant that these have a great following among the school and college population.

The American theatre has survived many changes and kinds of competition during its long history. In the Sixties it exhibits remarkable vitality and a capacity for growth that equal anything in its history. Its traditions and expressions have become part of American culture. Stage personalities range freely among the entertainment fields and arts media to appear before audiences that artists of other decades would never have believed possible.

The growing popularity of our art galleries and museums would make an amazing success story if this were part of their tradition. Although they make fewer headlines than our sports arenas and ball parks, their attendance is larger. In 1960 the total attendance at the Metropolitan Museum of Art was nearly 4,000,000, over twice the number that saw the New York Yankees play at their Stadium. The long tradition of European supremacy in popular interest in art appears to be ending. Comparison of attendance figures for famous European and American museums support this observation. American museums outdraw those of European centers significantly as shown by 1960 figures:

The Louvre drew 1,671,000 visitors, less than one-half the total for the Metropolitan;

The British Museum drew 752,826, less than Detroit's Museum;

The Rijks Museum (Amsterdam) drew 490,426, less than the New York Museum of Modern Art;

The Hague Museum (Amsterdam) drew 148,145, less than Houston's Museum of Fine Arts.

In 1932 the United States had a total of 1,400 museums of all kinds and sizes; the 1960 total exceeded 2,500.

The data relating to the extensiveness and growth of the arts in America is impressive and convincing. Yet it is possible that the evidence for the quality and content of the American arts would be more significant. Whole movements in the various fields reveal new content, invention of new forms, rise of innovators, new developments that bring artists of different fields into collaboration, and the use of mass media to reach the general public which has made the whole nation a potential audience. Students of cultural history can find much of vitality and strength in the versatile dynamic fields of the arts in America of the Sixties.

The relationships between the educational cultural progress in American life hardly needs exposition. A student could trace the connection by a review of the cultural and educational history of his home community. Many persons have lived in and observed this transformation; some have written books and articles upon aspects of this growth. Journals and papers that are concerned with the intellectually and socially significant phases of our national life have recognized this relationship by diverse means. Education, at all levels, has participated significantly in the cultural revolution in American life.

EDUCATION AND
NATIONAL LEADERSHIP

The relationship between an educated citizenry and democratic governmental institutions has been so long recognized that many take it for granted. This concept has been shared and expressed variously by America's greatest leaders and the men in the streets and by-ways. As Jefferson saw it, a nation could never expect to be both ignorant and free; Madison thought a popular government without popular enlightenment was headed for disaster; and virtually all Founding Fathers from Benjamin Franklin to Andrew Jackson expressed faith in public education as the foundation of a free society. The common man was equally conscious of education, especially as the means of rising to a better station in life. Generations of farmers' sons and the youth of village homes were admonished to seek means of improving themselves and to look to their chances to accomplish something worthwhile by strict attention to duty and to study. This foundation of acceptance by national leaders and by the people made it possible for state public school systems to be established in a relatively brief time.

The product of that indigenous American institution—the common school —provided occupational and social mobility for the children of the people and yielded capable national leadership through the various periods of our history. The public educational system was extended into secondary and into higher education as the aspirations and desires of the people expanded in terms of new demands and opportunities. The products of the log cabin and the little red schoolhouse served the courts, legislatures, and governmental posts at all levels, filled the growing ranks of professional men in many fields, and contributed the inventors, enterprisers, thinkers, and writers that enriched the growing culture of the Republic. Through the decades, the increasing stream of American abilities and talents issuing from high schools and colleges provided the people with leaders in all areas of our national life.

The dependence upon public education for leadership has not lessened in recent decades. Americans need only to step back from the daily headlines and newscasts far enough to gain a perspective to test whether this is true. This observation has been made by responsible commentators upon various occasions. An interesting analysis of the contemporary scene in America's public schools included a sampling of leaders in diverse fields— banking, industry, education, federal government, literature, military, and religious —who were products of public schools.[30]

The Contribution of Public Education

PUBLIC SCHOOLS HAVE
SERVED AMERICA

Many scholarly critics and observers have credited the public schools with major contributions to the development and preservation of our democratic institutions. One of the able statements of this provides an excellent starting point for examination of this thesis:[31]

1. *The public schools helped develop unity in diversity among the American people*

America was settled and expanded by a great diversity of peoples representing many ethnic groups, languages, national origins, political beliefs, religions and social classes. The centuries of colonial experience and national expansion westward saw the rise of public education that helped to develop common loyalties to the promise of freedom and guaranteed rights for all. The new common school provided the cohesive integrating experiences needed for the children

of all groups to learn to accept each other (with their differences) and to develop a common loyalty to the over-arching institution that supported the freedom of all. Although the new nation experienced trying tests and crises, its educative agencies contributed to the finding of a larger unity among the diverse peoples and their values. This common loyalty with optimum freedom of choice and preferences depended upon the separation of church and state and the civil rights guaranteed everyone under the Constitution. No nation has ever had greater diversity of people, beliefs, creeds, and values than ours. No lands have been freer of religious interference and clericalism, economic or social class conflict, or irresponsible and divisive political alignments than this land of the free. Major political parties have had adherents from all groups and conditions of men—second-generation Americans, newly-arrived immigrants, various ethnic and religious groups, employers and employees, conservatives and liberals, rural and urban dwellers—and attempted to represent all the people. These evidences of a unity among the wholesome diversity that characterizes America represent the product of our his-

[30] See "Public School Products," *Time Magazine*, **LXXIV**, No. 11 (September 14, 1959), p. 71.

[31] See Educational Policies Commission, *Public Education and the Future of America* (Washington: NEA, 1955), pp. 67–76 for an able presentation of this viewpoint.

torical experience to a people. In all of this, the common school had a primary role and made its distinctive contribution.

2. *The public schools helped to induct immigrants into American culture*

As the new nation grew and prospered, more peoples from more lands came to the "Land of Opportunity." These numbered thirty million persons, first and last, and they brought every manner of difference among human beings: race, religion, custom, creed, dress, habits, languages, occupations, attitudes, appreciations, values, and ways of living. As the 19th century drew to a close the stream of immigrants from south and eastern Europe greatly outnumbered those from its northern and western nations. This meant greater differences and graver problems of adjustment and assimilation into American life for the immigrant families. This tremendous problem was largely handled by the public schools of New York and other ports of entry communities. Public schools held evening classes for language instruction, Americanization programs and the like. Millions of immigrants really "graduated" from an educational program when they were formally admitted to citizenship before a United States district court. The children of immigrant families attended the neighborhood public school and often helped their parents learn the English language and American customs. Amercanization worked and the nation received millions of fine people as citizens and good Americans. The public school took an active hand in this massive induction process.

3. *Public schools have emphasized ethical character development*

The public school has always been concerned with character education. In this it has recognized the educational responsibilities of home, church, and synagogue and has seen its task as one of partnership with the other great educative agencies. The public schools have found the peculiar function in this respect is to teach moral and spiritual values on a functional basis. The values common to all great religions and acceptable to all faith groups serve to raise the national level of morality but leave the individual free to pursue the religious dictates of his own conscience.

The common school cannot engage in religious instruction because we have long since ceased to be a homogeneous community in religion; there are over 260 different faiths and denominations in America, without considering other differences. The public school accepts children of all faiths (and those with none), shows no favoritism, respects their differences and teaches values on a functional basis. This means that the public school must teach values of "behaving and living," for unless they are used, values have not been taught; the exemplification of values in human relationships and conduct is the best evidence of effective teaching of character. The matter of interpreting values in terms of their origins and meanings in a given religion is properly left to the home, church, synagogue, or temple where it belongs.

Character education takes place in all aspects of the school program: in the daily-living-together of many persons in the school community; in the planned curriculum experiences (courses); through guidance and counselling situations; in the various student activities with voluntary participation; in the play life and recreation of the school; and by means of symbolic expression.

4. *Public education has implemented the ideal of equality of opportunity*

The door to opportunity has always been open in the public school and higher education institution. Through education millions of Americans opened doors to wider horizons and a fuller life. There are many thousands of persons in America today, successful and wholesome citizens, whose talents would have been neglected and wasted but for the chance the common school afforded them. Among them are professional men (doctors, dentists, and lawyers), engineers and scientists, artists, musicians and other creative persons, many kinds of skilled technical experts, and countless others who have made a useful and respected place for themselves in their communities. Public education has been the means of educational opportunity, occupational choice, and social mobility for many Americans.

5. *Public schools have contributed to the productivity of our economy*

It has been shown that the American economic system has accomplished miraculous advances and records in all areas of production. As a result, Americans enjoy a higher standard of living and a shorter average work week than any people in all of human history. So marvelous is the productivity record of American agriculture and industry that the people must develop new ways of thinking about and managing certain aspects of the economy. For example, it makes little sense to plan in terms of an economy of scarcity when America's farms and factories can produce more goods and products than consumers can use. Remember that fewer than half of America's workers are now engaged in production, and more are needed in services occupations.

The miracle of American production has been wrought in a nation which had several favorable factors: rich natural resources, a favorable geographical location, an energetic people, a genius for organization, and an emphasis upon education of all people in terms of their potential. Education has been closely related to all interests and needs of people, including the area of vocational choice and competence. Public education has been instrumental in developing the manpower that helped to effect the productivity of our economic system.

Public schools began to provide practical subjects, such as commerce, navigation, bookkeeping, and surveying in the nineteenth century. Later, the needs of business and labor were met in the development of new programs of vocational education. Factories and farms received millions of skilled workers from public schools, vocational schools and area trade schools. The science departments of universities, engineering colleges and technological institutes furnished personnel to lead in the development of industrial processes, machinery, and products. The land-grant colleges have led in the virtual revolution of the farms of the nation which has enabled fewer workers to feed Americans and millions overseas and still produce a surplus. Public education has helped increase much of our economic productivity.

6. *Public schools have promoted popular knowledge and understanding*

Public education has provided elementary schooling to practically all Americans, now affords a high school education to nearly ninety per cent of the teen age population, and offers college opportunity to an increasing stream of older youth. No nation has so nearly universalized twelve or more free years of schooling for its citizens with college for those who really choose to go. This is is an important clue to the significance of America's public schools.

This universal experience of its citizens has been the means of developing the two sets of skills that qualify people to manage their affairs through a democratic government. The skills of literacy, especially that of reading, provide the tools for finding out, for knowing. The ability to read is the means of making Thomas Jefferson and Abraham Lincoln one's acquaintances and it opens up communication with the ideas and inspiration of the past and with the wider present.

The skills of inquiry open approaches to understanding. The abilities and practices that enable one to find information, to examine, organize, and evaluate it, to think about it in terms of principles involved, and to reach logical conclusions, are the skills of inquiry. Good schools and teachers are merely beginning their tasks when the skills of literacy have developed. The skills of inquiry are peculiarly significant in a free society. Literacy is important, even essential, in democracy but there is more to it than that, there have been literate societies under dictators. The democratic citizen must be literate, but he must also be skilled in the arts and habits of inquiry. He must be able to understand if he is to keep his freedoms and to help extend the institutions of freedom. The public schools and higher education have been instrumental in the promotion of the popular knowledge and understanding basic to our free society.

7. *American schools have fostered loyalty to the American way of life*

Public schools have done much to realize and to extend the ideals of democracy through the spread of knowledge and understanding. They have done more by helping to inspire a respect *for* and loyalty *to* the principles of freedom, human rights, equality before the law, and democracy on the part of several generations of Americans. Public schools have taught the rights and responsibilities of citizenship to youth and to adult immigrants. Pupils have been encouraged to examine the issues of contemporary American life, to survey the background of our problems, to evaluate alternatives in terms of democratic values, and to decide for themselves. This brand of patriotism features a mature devotion to American values and skills in order to recognize propaganda and falseness, and have the moral courage to withstand challenges. The three strong points established for the support of democracy by the public schools can be labelled *literacy, inquiry,* and *loyalty.*

Something of the significance of the common schools has long been evident to Americans of various stations and walks of life. The common man expressed his faith in public education by voting for taxes, helping to build the first schools, and working to extend the system to provide further opportunity. Dedicated leaders voiced the aspirations and sentiments of the people for their schools on platforms across the several states of the Union in the early 19th century. A good illustration may be found in the conclusion of an official commission of a state legislature that reported a study of need for a state school system that expressed the concept of the common school. The Barry Commission (1821) expressed it to the General Assembly of Kentucky:

From the full consideration of all these systems, your commissioners have come to the conclusion that wherever it is practical common schools open and free to every description of children are the most consonant to the principles of our institutions and produce the most beneficial effect from the minds of the rising generation. It is a system of practical equality in which the children, the rich and the poor, meet upon a perfect level and the only superiority is that of the mind.[32]

Distinctive Features of American Public Education

The significance of American public education can be approached by various means. One important assessment should take into account its distinctive features. There are several uniquely American characteristics of our public educational systems that should be appreciated by the citizens of these United States. There are many possible items to be considered in this appraisal but certain selected features will serve the purpose.

1. *Centralized authority and decentralized administration*

The over-all authority for provision of public education and its control have been vested in the *States,* but direct administration of the schools has been largely delegated to local units (districts).

This genuinely creative social invention, designed to achieve a balance between the values to be achieved by centralized authority and those of flexibility, variety, and originality to be realized by decentralized management, contrasts sharply with the educational systems and patterns of other lands.

2. *A single-track system of public education open to all*

A ladder of opportunity is available in a single and common public system extending from preschool years upward into post-college years and even adult education, free to all as far as one's talents enable one to go. This contrasts sharply with dual (double-track) systems of Europe that provide "class" education. Free schooling is not uniquely American but the ideal of equality of educational opportunity is best served here.

3. *Public support from larger and larger units*

There is increasing dependence upon public tax support and increasing use of larger taxing units to provide more and more equality of educational opportunity. This involves countywide, then statewide, and probably nationwide tax support. The basic principle: "Tax where the wealth is, spend where the children are."

4. *Democratic methods of control in public education*

Those most concerned about public education—the people—have voice in the control of the common schools by election of local boards of education. Administrators and teachers share professional interests by action through organizations. The people's elected representatives at local, state, and federal levels bear fiscal and other rsponsibilities.

[32] Kentucky General Assembly, *House Journal,* 1822, pp. 235 ff.

5. *Large freedom for private and religious education*

There is no monopoly by public education in these United States. Religious groups are free to establish, maintain, and support their own schools. From the end of World War II to 1960, Roman Catholic parochial schools doubled their student bodies; other nonpublic schools grew from 200,000 to 1,200,000 in enrollment.[33] Private schools, even commercial venture schools, freely exist in this country. All nonpublic schools must comply with minimum statutory and regulatory provisions designed to insure that all educational opportunity shall be equivalent to that in public schools.

6. *A widening task for the educational program*

The curriculum has expanded beyond recognition by any colonial schoolmaster. The original 3 R's (and 4 R's) were supplemented by several 19th century additions (history, geography, physiology, civics, music, manual training, commercial subjects, modern languages, etc.); the 20th century brought a flood: sciences, more foreign languages, vocational education courses, technical courses, higher mathematics courses, family living, driver education, safety, etc., with new ones on the way. The program has been extended upward to comprehend adult education, downward to provide nursery and play schools.

7. *Programs reflect the expansion and complexity of knowledge*

A veritable explosion of knowledge has necessitated continuous curriculum revision and development of new pro-

[33] *Education Summary,* December 27, 1960.

grams of instruction. Sciences and social sciences have expanded beyond the comprehension of the best-educated scholars of early generations in the country; whole new sciences have developed within two or three decades. Many new sciences and technological fields are studied in secondary schools, junior colleges, colleges, universities, and professional graduate schools.

8. *Humane conception of human development and of educational method*

The understanding of and attitude toward children have changed drastically since colonial days; external discipline should be supplanted by developing self-controls; all students are worthy of acceptance in their own right; students' self-image and perceptions are regarded as important; all needs and capacities should be considered; curriculums must offer something for everyone; and the teacher is a guide.

9. *Growth of the teaching profession*

The development of a profession never dreamed of by Ichabod Crane roughly paralleled the development of state school systems. The NEA, established in 1857, is now the largest professional organization in U.S.A. (nearly 860,000 dues-paying members) with one and one-half million in affiliated organizations.

10. *Improvement of the professional preparation of teachers*

A concomitant of educational progress has been the rise of teacher education and its extension to college and graduate levels, followed by in-service programs for teachers. The first public normal school in Lexington, Massachusetts (1839) activated a movement that none of its supporters—Brooks, Carter, Mann, and Pierce—could have foreseen. The key to the continued quest for excellence in American education is a profession of men and women ever concerned with their own growth and improvement as guides for the learning experiences of American youth.

Some Evaluative Views

Evaluation of public education has been going on ever since the people built the first common schools. The practice has not diminished noticeably in recent years. The various approaches employ tests and questions that range from the practical and tangible to theoretical and intangible considerations. A sampling of these may serve as the conclusion of this appraisal.

A practical test of a society or a social institution is to determine how well it meets emergencies and crises. This is one which our democratic institutions have passed in various forms in recent decades, including world wars, depression, totalitarian threats to the free world, new international responsibilities, prolonged cold war, and numerous crises of many kinds. In all of these, public schools have served American democracy and the people marvelously well. On this point, the champion of public education and an altruistic leader, Mrs. Agnes E. Meyer, commented that World War II should have taught us that our public schools were the greatest stabilizing force in our national life. Americans of all complexions might well agree, particularly if they try to answer for themselves the question of how would America fare without her public education systems.

The best-known student of American public education, Dr. James Bryant Conant, once suggested that our citizens should adopt a general slogan that would express our reliance upon education in time of national danger. Education, he thought, must develop the potentialities of youth for their individual good and for the preservation of American freedom.

The strong and sincere expressions of faith in America's public education does not ignore the fact that we have problems and issues both on the national scale and in the educational systems. The people in our democratic society should be fully aware that a democracy is a society least able to hide and deny its problems, a point that we should appreciate. It is to the credit of our schools that so many problems are identified, studied, and acted on. There are some grave problems that are being met by energetic efforts. There are others that appear to be growing more acute, and there are still others that tend to recur. A brief catalog of some that have received attention in the Sixties will provide illustrations: (1) automation and its implications for education, (2) the dropout problem, (3) disadvantaged areas and groups (particularly in metropolitan centers), (4) the unmet educational and rehabilitation needs of handicapped groups, (5) the problems of policy involved in vocational education fields due to technological change, automation, and related factors, (6) the growing demand for specialized technicians in new and growing fields in programs at the junior college level (an average of seven technicians needed for every professional), (7) needs for educational opportunity for retired people and for effective programs for workers in preparation for future retirement, (8) demands and pressures upon educational institutions dictated by concern about status symbols on the part of parents: e.g., exclusive programs for children with high I.Q.'s, marks, discriminatory favors and recognition, (9) how to identify and provide challenging programs for the creative pupils, (10) how can American education end the wastage of human talent by providing excellent programs for the intellectually superior children and youth, (11) attracting an adequate number of capable youth into the teaching profession, and (12) finding democratic constitutional bases for solving problems of religious practices in public schools with simultaneous strengthening of religious educational efforts of churches and synagogues. This dozen could appropriately occupy the minds of school and lay leaders for a season. In this democracy of ours, people are free to undertake the solution of problems. That is part of the American way that functions within and is taught by the common school and its big brother institutions of public higher education.

Two outstanding groups of widely different character have reached favorable conclusions concerning the significance of American public schools. The report of the Gardner Committee, published by the Rockefeller Brothers Fund, voiced the concern that education be recognized as a nceessary condition for national survival:

Education has always been essential to achievement of our political and moral objectives. It has emerged as a necessary ingredient in our technological advancement. And now events have underscored its value in terms of sheer survival.[34]

The national organization representing the public school administrators and school-board members joined in a ringing affirmation of belief in public education.

We believe our schools are our one best hope for individual attainment and for national strength and welfare. Without appropriate education of children, youth, and adults, our values will be lost, our economy and productivity famished, and vision blurred, and the individual obscured.[35]

A fitting statement for the close of this appraisal comes from the strongest organization associated with public schools. The following salute to our schools appeared on the cover of the PTA magazine, *The National Parent Teacher,* for November 1960:

We give our schools awesome assignments. From the most diverse materials— malleable, refractory, explosive—we expect them to fashion uniformly superior products. We ask them to tame the rebellious, embolden the timid, spur the laggard, sharpen the dull, burnish the bright. We ask them to make every child good, healthy, competent, happy, and useful.

We ask our schools to be the nation's first line of defense, the cradle of democracy, the forge of national unity, the generator of economic productivity, the seedbed of talent, and every child's highway to self-realization and the good life.

[34] Rockefeller Brothers Fund, *The Pursuit of Excellence—Education and the Future of America,* Panel Report V of The Special Studies Project (Garden City, New York: Doubleday & Company, 1958), p. 38. Quoted by permission of Doubleday & Co., Inc.

[35] American Association of School Administrators, *This We Believe.* Joint statement by A.A.S.A. and the National School Board Association (Washington: NEA, 1958), p. 3. Used by permission.

What we ask of our schools, however audacious our demands, they try valiantly to do. Understaffed, underfinanced, overburdened, they have nevertheless written a record of impressive achievements. We salute them.

Our schools are the nation's pride and the nation's scapegoat. In the past decade they have been praised extravagantly, criticized mercilessly, blamed unreasonably. If we would strengthen our schools for the 60's, let us reassess their assignments, set reasonable expectations, and provide the resources they need. Let us praise our schools justly, and soberly appraise our own efforts to support them.

Americans can continue into the Sixties and the decades to come with an admixture of concern and confidence in their thinking and purposing. *Concern* on the part of intelligent, prudent men is the wisest and soundest approach to living and problem-solving. A nation that permits its people to use their diverse abilities and talents as freely as possible is building up the problem-solving potential and its chances of survival in face of the challenges that will be met. An education, free and open to all, designed to foster the development of individual capabilities, is the soundest kind of insurance a people can take out for their future wellbeing and the continued improvement of their society. Confidence is justifiable and sound when it is based upon concepts of democracy and democatic education held by a people willing to trust and defend them by their full utilization. Democratic education and the people it serves will continue to have problems—as we do in this good hour—and grave crises in future years but this has always been true of every society man has known upon this globe. The great philosopher-historian, Toynbee, has concluded that most of them ended for lack of continued ability to meet the recurring challenges that history brought into their course. This lesson is clear: it is normal to expect challenges and problems. No culture has ever survived indefinitely by exploiting and limiting its people and by neglecting the use of their abilities, all of which may be needed by that society. This lesson suggests that this people and nation would be wise to cherish and strengthen that system of free public education that places greatest premium and value upon optimum development of every person.

Selected Bibliography

American Association of School Administrators. *This We Believe*. Washington: NEA, 1958.

Bereday, George Z. F., and Volpicelli, Luigi. *Public Education in America,* a new Interpretation of Purposes and Practices. New York: Harper & Row, 1958.

Chamber of Commerce of the U.S., *Education–An Investment in People*. Rev. ed. Washington: the Chamber, 1955.

Cousins, Norman. "Why Would Anyone Ever Stop Learning?", *McCall's* Magazine, (February 1961).

———. "The Great Debate in American Education," *Saturday Review,* **XXXVII**, No. 36 (September 11, 1954), pp. 11–13, 47.

Educational Policies Commission. *Public Education and the Future of America*. Washington: NEA, 1955.

———. *The Contemporary Challenge to American Education.* Washington: NEA, 1958.

Graham, Grace. *The Public School in the American Community.* New York: Harper & Row, 1963, pp. 108–176, 214–248.

Groves, Harold M. *Education and Economic Growth.* Washington: National Education Association, 1961.

"Have Public Schools Had It?", *Cosmopolitan,* **CLV,** No. 3 (September 1963), pp. 42–47.

Heller, Walter W. "Education and Economic Growth," *NEA Journal,* **L,** No. 7 (October 1961), p. 9.

Kaplan, David L., and Casey, M. Claire. *Occupational Trends in the United States, 1900–1950,* Working paper No. 5. Washington: Department of Commerce, Bureau of Commerce, Bureau of the Census, 1958.

Kleeman, Richard P. "Five Years of Change," *Saturday Review,* **XLIII,** No. 11 (March 18, 1961), pp. 50–51, 63.

Kneller, George F. (Ed.) *Foundations of Education.* New York: John Wiley & Sons, Inc., 1963. See chapters 1 and 9.

Lear, John. "America Tomorrow: The Resources of Greatness," *Saturday Review* (September 2, 1961), pp. 35–38.

Lippmann, Walter. "The Shortage in Education," *Atlantic,* **CXCIII,** No. 5 (May 1954), pp. 35–38.

Manpower—Challenge of the 1960's, U.S. Department of Labor. Washington: Government Printing Office, 1960.

Mushkin, Selma J. (Ed.) *Economics of Higher Education.* U.S. Office of Education Bulletin 1962–50027, No. 5. Washington: U.S. Government Printing Office, 1962, see chapter 9.

National Council of Chief State School Officers, *Our System of Education.* Washington: The Council, 1950.

NEA Research Bulletin, Ten Criticisms of Public Education, **XXXV,** No. 4 (December 1957).

———. **XXXVIII,** No. 4 (December 1960), pp. 114–116.

———. **XL,** No. 2 (May 1962), pp. 42–60.

———. **XLI,** No. 1 (February 1963), pp. 3–9, 21–31.

National Industrial Conference Board, *Economic Almanac 1962.* New York: The Conference Board, 1962.

Norton, John K. *Citizens Speak Out on School Costs.* Washington: NEA, 1959.

Perkinson, Henry J. "American Education: Icons and Images," *Education Digest,* **XXVIII,** No. 8 (April 1963), pp. 1–5.

Research Division, *Estimates of School Statistics 1962–63,* Research Report 1962–R13. Washington: NEA (December 1962).

———. *Rankings of the States 1962,* Research Report 1962–R1. Washington: NEA (January 1962).

———. *Status & Trends: Vital Statistics, Education, and Public Finance,* Research Report 1959–R13. Washington: NEA (August 1959).

Rockefeller Brothers Fund, *The Pursuit of Excellence, Education, and the Future of America,* Panel Report V of the Special Studies Project. Garden City, N.Y.: Doubleday & Co., 1958.

"The Truth About Our Public Schools," *Changing Times,* **VIII,** No. 6 (June 1954), pp. 7–16.

Tead, Ordway. "The Roots of Teaching Power in the American Culture," *Seventh Yearbook,* American Association of Colleges for Teacher Education. Oneonta, N.Y.: A.A.C.T.E., 1954.

The Federal Government and Education, Committee on Education and Labor, House of Representatives, 88th Congress, 1st Session. Washington: U.S. Government Printing Office, 1963, pp. 113–165.

Willett, Henry I. "Public Schools Under Pressure," *Atlantic,* **CXCIV,** No. 4 (October 1954), pp. 131–139.

Aids for Part I

AUDIO-VISUAL MATERIALS

Figures in brackets refer to chapters.

FILMS

The Challenge, NEA (28 min., b & w). Summary of 1955 White House Conference on Education.   [1, 2]

A Desk for Billie, NEA (Feature length, 57 min., color, sound). Inspiring true story of educational opportunity in America and its significance.   [1, 4]

Dilemma of Thomas Jefferson, University of Michigan (29 min., b & w). Vision that led to establishment of our common school systems.   [1]

Education in America, The 17th and 18th Centuries, Coronet, (16 min., sound, color). Excellent historical background.   [3]

Education in America, the 19th Century, Coronet, (16 min., sound, color). Development of public education in American life.   [3]

Education in America, 20th Century Developments, Coronet, (16 min., sound, color). Brings history of American education up to date.   [3]

Education for All, Harmon Films (22 min., sound, color). Historical development of schools and colleges.   [3]

Education Is Good Business, General Pictures (10 min., sound, color). An excellent film for questions related to the subject.   [4]

Educational Opportunities for All the Children (2 reels, silent). (Available from Illinois Education Association, Springfield.)   [4]

Free Schools; The Hope of Democracy (2 reels, silent).   [1, 4]

Horace Mann, Encyclopedia Britannica Films (19 min., sound). Excellent for historical background.   [3]

How Good Are Our Schools? NEA (28 min., b & w). Presents highlights of the Conant Report.   [4]

Lessons in Living, Canadian Film Board (2 reels, sound). Useful comparison of schools.   [1, 4]

Near Home, International Film Bureau (27 min., b & w). English school children study their community.   [2]

New Schools for Old, Museum of Modern Art Film Library (10 min., sound). Vivid contrasts between old and modern schools.   [3, 4]

Right Angle, NEA (28 min., b & w). Findings of a newsman who investigated schools' performance in attempting to educate all children.   [1, 4]

School and the Community, McGraw-Hill Text Films (14 min., b & w).   [2]

Section Sixteen, Westinghouse (28 min., b & w). Good historical summary.   [3]

Secure the Blessings, NEA (27 min., b & w). Stresses the important role public schools have played in history of our democracy. [3, 4]

Social Class in America, McGraw-Hill (16 min.). Shows contrasts in life experiences of boys from different social backgrounds, school influence, and social mobility.

World Without End, UNESCO (45 min., b & w). Reviews programs of UNESCO in various parts of the globe and its functions as an international agency. [2]

FILMSTRIPS

Aim for Excellence, NEA (10 min.). How schools are undertaking to provide quality education. [1, 4]

Five Important Years—Then School, American Legion (15 min., sound). [2]

The School and the Community, McGraw-Hill (35 frames). [2]

RECORDINGS

Tomorrow Won't Wait, NEA (6½ min., 33⅓ rpm). The children of tomorrow cannot be educated in schools inadequate for today. [1, 4]

QUESTIONS FOR DISCUSSION

1. How does education in the U.S.A. compare with other major enterprises—public and private—in the nation? Discuss.
2. What are the major characteristics of American education? Explain.
3. Are size, costs, and numbers the most important features of American education? Why?
4. It has been noted that the American people have made greater effort than any other to provide free public education for all. Do you find agreement in the histories of American education?
5. What does the term *education* actually mean? Explain.
6. Do all cultures make some kind of provision for education? When do schools appear in a culture?
7. How did schools begin in America? Why did common schools develop in our democracy?
8. What agencies or "institutions" are included when you refer to educational institutions or programs in a community?
9. Is it possible to speak of an educational "ladder of opportunity" open to all in your state? Why?
10. Do you think tax-supported nursery schools should be provided for all pupils? Kindergarten? Junior College? Any other? Why?
11. Should adult education opportunity be provided at public expense in your state? Why?
12. Are there any facilities and opportunities for adult education in your community? Specify.
13. Why is the free public school designated a unique American institution? Explain.
14. What are the functions of private schools in our democracy? Explain.
15. What is meant by "Education is the function of the state"? Where is this principle stated?
16. Should American schools try to imitate those of any other nation? Why?
17. Is educational research important? Necessary in America? Why?

18. What would you identify as some of the big issues in American education today? Explain.
19. Does everyone have a stake in public education? What about public interest in nonpublic schools and colleges? How are these different?
20. Should the American people expect their teachers to appreciate the significance of common schools and to be loyal to public education in our democracy? Why?

IDEAS FOR INDIVIDUAL STUDY

1. Watch the newspaper files for one month during your study of Part I, and clip news features and editorials about American education. Mount and file these in your notes according to an appropriate scheme.
2. Devise a graphic chart, diagram, or outline to show the comprehensive nature and diversity of "Education in the U.S.A."
3. Make a brief study of the various meanings of the word *education*. Consult the *Dictionary of Education*, other standard reference works, and books in the various foundations of education fields. Group your findings into a logical classification if possible.
4. Follow the same procedure to find the various meanings of the term "culture."
5. Make a list of all the educative agencies you find in reading related to the four chapters in Part I. Use an asterisk (*) to show those types with which you have had some previous knowledge or experience.
6. Keep a list during your reading of all the different types of schools you find. Arrange these in logical classification. Use some means of identifying those terms that are synonymous; also those that have differing connotations in different cultures.
7. Choose some aspect of the history of American education (or education in your state) and do research to become well-informed about it. Write a concise but complete report.
8. Investigate the influences that education in England (or France or Germany, etc.) has had upon education in the United States and make a report.
9. Search out and choose the best statements or quotations you can find about the concept of the common school system, and its relationship to the development and growth of our democratic society. Better still, write yours after reading and thought.
10. Make a table of "firsts" in the history of education in your state or for the nation.
11. Undertake some research about schools in another country to find how the people have developed and managed education to meet their needs. Keep notes.
12. Organize the findings from your study of Part I into notes as a recapitulation and review. You might classify under such heads as: (a) New Vocabulary, (b) Facts and Figures, (c) Ideas and Concepts, (d) Problems and Issues, and (e) Questions for Further Study.

SUGGESTIONS FOR GROUP WORK

Participate in some committee task or a group project as your share of the work to supplement the unit.

1. A good cooperative project for a committee would be to prepare a scrapbook on "American Education" or "Education in These United States" appropriate to be sent to a teacher or student group in some foreign country. It is a good idea to

show the significant features of American education by graphic means when possible.

2. Another worthwhile group project would be to compile a graphic booklet showing the historical development of the American common school. A booklet of this nature will prove useful to you later when and if you should teach history in a high school.

3. Devise exhibits of graphic data to show the impressive figures about education in the U.S.A.: expenditures, number of people affected and how, and similar relationships.

4. Make a collection of advertisements, clippings, pictures, posters, etc., about American education. Arrange an exhibit to show the vastness and variety of educational institutions and programs in the United States.

5. Participate in planning and carrying out a study of the history of the school system in your state and present a summary to the class.

6. Plan and take part in a symposium with class colleagues on "My Experiences in Educative Groups in ...." Describe and explain the significance of your experience in the various educative agencies of your home community to illustrate how children learn in our culture.

7. Prepare a group project to investigate the international organizations and relationships that affect American education.

8. Take part in a class project to study important leaders in developing and preserving America's common school systems and decide upon an "Educational Hall of Fame."

9. Help plan and participate in a project to write a series of brief articles on "How Our Common Schools Developed" for your community or college paper.

10. Take part in a panel discussion of a teaching film on the "History of American Education."

11. Set up a committee to study ways and means to illustrate the validity of the statement that *Public education is an investment.* Try to devise some proof.

12. Take part in a group discussion (or a panel) of "How American Education Is Distinctive and Why?" Keep notes.

II. PATTERN

Of Unity
and Diversity

Chapter 5

The Structure of
Public Education

The American people jealously guard their control over their schools. They want to keep their schools closely responsive to their needs. They will not permit too much control from the state capital, and they will permit no control from Washington. The local school board is one of the strong-holds of our American democracy. Despite the fact that education is a state function, the people have vested in their local boards of education far-reaching and final authority in practically all matters affecting their elementary and secondary schools. They have limited the state authorities largely to minimum standards. One of your most important functions is to continually inform the people of your district of the needs of their schools and what is being done for their children. A good public relations program will take many of the headaches out of your job. It is also one of the most effective ways to improve your schools—and the schools of the entire state.*

Introduction

Our study of the scope and character of American education has surely brought us to deeper appreciation of the varied beginnings of our schools and of the amazing diversity to be found among them. Each of these findings may be further confirmed when we study the structure and operation of our public school system. Historically, our schools have developed in response to needs and conditions in the experiences of widely separated states and communities. In spite of that, much similarity of purpose and organization has gradually evolved. Nevertheless, it is still true that the most pervasive characteristic of our schools is their diversity and variety. Even such prosaic features as school organization and control exhibit this fact. Decentralization and localization are generally recognized as

* L. E. Meece, "The New School Board Member," in *The Kentucky School Board Journal* (January 1953), p. 3. Reprinted with permission.

145

important features of educational organization. Evidence of growth toward a working partnership among local units and the state and federal governments in matters of control and support is becoming marked. We should watch for these as we study this aspect of American education.

Public Education and American Governments

The Federal Constitution (Tenth Amendment) reserves the control of education to the several states. Thus, no centralized national control of schools is possible under the American principles of constitutional government. This does not mean that the Federal government has had no interest in or influence upon American education. Remember that the term "state" in our educational literature does not mean the national government as is true in many nations.

It is commonly recognized that education in America is a state function. Several early state constitutions charged the legislature with responsibility for providing for schools—eight by the year 1800. As the states were developed in the old Northwest Territory, each received land grants for the support of public education. The long struggle within the states to provide free tax-supported schools was finally won by the turn of the century. State boards of education and executive officers (commonly called superintendents) were established, and varying patterns for state support were adopted. For more than a hundred and seventy years now, Americans have grown used to the idea of state responsibility for education and have made legal provision for state control of, and tax support for public schools.

Within the states, there is much of local control and initiative. Ordinarily, the state provides the constitutional and legal framework under which local units actually maintain and operate schools. Varying units have been designated within the states for the control and support of education. In the New England states, the town was the early unit of local control of schools. In some states, the township was an early unit. During the last century the idea of a school district was quite generally adopted. The old "Deestrict" school with its local trustee, or trustees, became a byword in American life. This was the little red schoolhouse of enduring fame.

In recent decades, the trend toward larger units of control has grown until changes have occurred in nearly all of the states. Now units of different size and legal status exist in the various states. One state, Hawaii, is a unit of organization; and two, Alaska and Delaware, have both state and local units. In the other states, the town, the township, the county, or some type of school district is the recognized unit for the administration of schools. In New England, the town is normally the unit for school administration and organization; in Florida and West Virginia, the county is the unit; in most of the southern states, New Mexico and Utah, the county is usually the administrative unit except for certain municipalities; Nevada uses groups of five counties as units; in some states, boroughs or townships are recognized; while in the remainder there are local school districts of varying sizes and purposes. Needless to say, the administrative organization is complicated and involved in such states. In a number of states, existing legislation permits districts to combine or unite, and the trend toward larger school units (particularly the county unit) seems clear. Effective organization and efficiency are so closely related as to make this trend of fundamental importance.

It is clear that students get a varied pattern when they seek to understand where and how the control of American education is placed. Although responsibility for providing and maintaining public schools is looked upon as a *state* function, there is much variation among the systems. Actually, there are 51 systems in the United States (including District of Columbia), or 56 if we include the territorial governments and other possessions. In all states, save one, there are local administrative units of varying sizes and types. In a good many states, the effort to improve the plan of organization of public education through more effective school districts must continue. Parents and teachers of the next generation should understand the nature and significance of an adequate pattern of organization for public school systems in the whole country.

THE LOCAL ORGANIZATION OF PUBLIC EDUCATION

A study of the organization of American public education should begin with the basic unit, the local school district. This is public education at the grass roots, the community level. Here the people live, send their children to school, pay taxes, and elect school boards to represent them in making policy for the operation of their schools. This unit must be close to the people, not too small to be economical in cost, nor too large to be responsive to the aspirations and needs of the patrons. As we have seen, there are about 32,000 school districts in the United States and the number decreases each year as small units consolidate or merge to form more equitable ones. Prior to World War II (1940) there were 117,000 school districts in the United States (counting those for one-teacher schools).

One clue to the understanding of local school organization is to see that our public schools are local institutions in the sense that they are organized, controlled, and partially supported by a unit somewhat related to local government. Be it a town, township, borough, a city, a district of some type or other, or a county, it is a unit calculated to be controlled and operated by persons closely in touch with and responsible to the people. For it is the people's children and the adults who are served by these schools. In colonial days these units were largely autonomous and started schools on their own initiative or under the mild stimulus of an early state law authorizing them to do so. Often early secondary schools were established by districts under charters from state legislatures. We now find that the local district or unit is definitely a part of a state school system and that its powers and responsibilities are provided by law. Its functions are definitely derived to those of the state government and provide for a division of power and of support between them. For example, you will likely find that the issuance of teachers certificates (or licenses) is done by the state, but that teachers are employed by the school authorities at the local level. You will find many other illustrations of the working relationship which exists between the state and local educational agencies.

In many states, the local unit of school control is the county. Some states have both county and city districts. In varius states school districts are composed of local units of government smaller than counties as in towns in New England, and townships in certain middle Atlantic and Midwestern states. Still other states use school districts of various size without references to units of local government. In a number of states, there are different districts for schools at each level, one board controls elementary schools; another board serving a larger district maintains high schools. In a few places, there are different districts to provide for the control and support of a public junior college. We will find a variety of organizational patterns if we but study the states represented in our class group. Members might share information about the kinds of school districts in which they live and the various taxes paid for education as one way to make this feature of American public education graphic.

It is important to understand education at the grass roots for many reasons. Here is where the American people have placed the responsibility. The Federal Constitution (Tenth Amendment) leaves education to the states. Most people have learned to say education is a state function. State constitutions generally charge the legislature with responsibility for maintaining a system of common schools. The legislatures have designated units of local control and support, the school districts, for this purpose. States *delegate* much of the responsibility and power for the public schools to local districts, actually to the people. There are both historical and psychological reasons for this policy.

Public schools originated in the old colony of Massachusetts Bay, when the early legislature (called the General Court) passed two laws requiring towns of a certain size to maintain schools. As towns grew, a number of children could not reach the central school, so portions of the town's area were set off as districts with their own little red schoolhouses. Thus, the typical small school unit began, a pattern that was widely copied in other states and used until in recent decades larger units of control became necessary. The local town meetings elected or appointed a school committee to manage their schools. This was the forerunner of local school-boards. These have been called variously, board of education, board of trustees, and board of supervisors, but their functions are similar.

Local school boards are usually elected by the voters of the school district for a term of years (four is common), to serve as the policy-making body for the public schools. The board usually appoints a professional administrator (usually called superintendent) to administer the policies for operation of the public school. Boards determine rate (levies) of school taxes, either directly or indirectly; they adopt a budget of planned expenditures for each school year, and account to the state for expenditures of school funds. The board acts on recommendations of superintendent and staff about matters affecting curriculum, school operations, building plans, purchase of equipment and supplies, and appointment of teachers and other school personnel. Members of school boards are *trustees,* that is, representatives of the whole public and should serve the interests of all the people of the district, regardless of race, religion, politics, social class, or any other factor. This is an ideal, to be sure, but all of us have known board members who served the public and the school unselfishly and fairly. There have been enough of such men and women to make American public school-board membership a symbol of prestige and respect in many communities.

Legislatures have usually spelled out certain requirements for board membership, such as residence in the district, nonpartisan elections, and minimum educational qualification. Other legislation affecting boards of education are common: nepotism and conflicts of interest are prohibited; meetings and records must be open to the public. School-boards serve the schools and the people that support them.

THE STATE RESPONSIBILITY FOR PUBLIC EDUCATION

Education is a state function. It is included in the powers reserved to the states by the Tenth Amendment to our Federal Constitution. This is an example of the "division of the powers" that characterize our constitutional systems of governments at different levels. There are also historical bases for this interpretation. In the earliest years of our independence the states adopted the Constitution and continued to legislate upon school matters as had the colonial legislatures. Thomas Jefferson proposed a complete state school system to the Virginia Assembly in 1779.

In general, it may be said that the state constitutions charge the legislature to make provision for state school systems. Laws enacted by the legislature comprise the general pattern or framework for the state school system. Under these provisions school units are empowered to establish, operate, and maintain schools with power to exercise the necessary authority for these functions. Usually the legislatures provide for the organizational machinery at the state level and for matters of broad general policy.[1]

Normally, state administrative agencies are constituted to exercise authority over education at the state level and to administer the policies and general practices which have been authorized by law. Many state constitutions include provisions for a state school board, a school fund and a chief state school officer (superintendent). The vast majority of states, now forty-six, have established state boards of education which have general control over the policies and management of the state school system. In some instances, the state board administers the state institutions of higher education, but usually a separate governing board (or number of boards) exercises this function. Members of the state boards of education are usually laymen appointed or elected for their ability and leadership. The number of members and the manner of their selection varies among the states. The number of members ranges from three to twenty-one, with a majority (29) having from 5 to 9. Some are appointed by the governor; others are elected by the people on a nonpartisan basis. Experience has demonstrated the necessity for protecting the state board from the rough and tumble fortunes of partisan policies. The trend seems to be toward smaller boards with

[1] See: Council of State Governments, *The Forty-Eight State School Systems* (Chicago: The Council, 1949).

fairly long overlapping terms for the members. It has been found that state boards make their best contribution by defining and developing general policy to implement the school law. The approval of budgets and matters of major importance, often the selection of the chief state school officer, are functions of the board.

TABLE 5–1. FACTS ABOUT STATE BOARDS OF EDUCATION*

Method of Selection	Number of States
Ex officio (other state officials serve)	2
Elected by the people	10
Elected by convention of school boards	1 (Wash.)
Elected by state legislature	1 (N.Y.)
Appointed by governor	30
Miscellaneous	2
State Board of Vocational Education only	4 (Ill., Mich., N. Dak., Wisc.)

*Source: Lee M. Thurston and William H. Roe, *State School Administration* (New York: Harper & Bros., 1951), p. 106.

Students should be prepared to find a good deal of variety in the plan of organization for public education among the states. The Council of Chief State School Officers recommends a single state board of education, elected by the people, with power to appoint the superintendent or commissioner of education.[2] There is evidence of a trend toward this policy.

The chief state school officer is the executive officer or administrator of the state schools under the state board of education. He heads the state department of education which administers the school laws and the policies developed by the state board. Usually he serves as the executive secretary to the state board, al-

[2] National Council of Chief State School Officers, *Our System of Education* (Washington: The Council), 1950.

though in a few states he may actually be a member of that body.

The title of this officer varies among the states, the following being most common: superintendent of public instruction, and commissioner of education. In most states, qualifications for this office are specified in such matters as education, professional experience, and character. Provisions concerning length of term and manner of selection likewise vary in the several states. Election by popular vote, appointment by the chief executive, or by the state board are the common methods. The term of office varies from very short term to an indefinite term in a half-dozen states, the most common being four years. In a few cases this officer may not succeed himself in office. Salaries of the chief state school officer have tended to be lower than the importance and nature of the position seems to justify. The median salary is lower than that of most superintendents of large city systems. This officer and his staff of assistants in the state department of education discharge important responsibilities; yet in many states appropriations and support have been meager in comparison with those for other functions and agencies of the state governments.

In every state, legislatures have established a state agency or office to exercise general oversight over public education. The responsibilities are threefold: (a) to *coordinate* the efforts of various agencies and the several districts, (b) to render needed *service* to the districts, and to (c) provide *leadership* of professional character. In some states the state department of education has direct control of certain institutions that serve special needs and groups—schools for the

TABLE 5–2. FACTS ABOUT CHIEF STATE SCHOOL OFFICERS

Title	No. of States	Method of Selection	No. of States
Superintendent of Public Instruction	28	Elected by the people	23
Commissioner of Education	16	Selected by the State Board of Education	22
Superintendent of Education	3	Appointed by the governor	5
Superintendent of Schools	3		
Total	50	Total	50

Source: *Patterson's American Education, 1962–63* (Mt. Prospect, Ill.: Educational Directories, Inc., 1962).

blind, the deaf, or the mentally retarded, and institutions for juvenile delinquents. In a few instances, public higher education is related to, or even controlled by, the state department of education.

The state department of education is one of the executive departments of the state government.[3] The discharge of its three functions involves *administrative*, distributing state funds, certificating teachers, approving building plans, reviewing budgets, and the like; *supervisory*, promoting curriculum development, evaluation, in-service teacher education, and other means of improving instruction; *research*, compiling statistics, making studies and surveys; *judicial*, advisory service to school administrators and boards, interpreting school laws and regulations of the state board, etc.; and *special* responsibilities. A more succinct way to state the functions of the state department of education is to lump them together into two categories: *leadership* and *service*.

In general, the state department of education is organized roughly to correspond to these functions. Bureaus or divisions of administration, finance, research,

[3] See: Beach, Fred F. and Will, Robert F., *The State and Education,* Bulletin, misc. No. 23 (Washington: U.S. Department of Health, Education, and Welfare, Office of Education, Government Printing Office, 1955).

and instruction are usually found, each with a staff of specialists or supervisors. The work and influence of the state department of education is an important factor in the growth and improvement of a state's schools. Its functions and responsibilities are becoming better understood and substantial support in the matter of appropriations will, in many instances, repay great dividends. In such cases, it may be a matter of spending a little to save or gain much.

As an informed citizen each of us will one day bear a part of the responsibility to help carry out the work of the schools of our state. We shall need to understand the constitutional, legal, and regulatory provisions for state schools. We should also assume some responsibility as a leader and active citizen in the community in matters affecting public education. Those who become teachers will find that their work with youth will be affected in after years by the help of a more interested and informed citizenry who will demand nothing less than the best the state can offer in the way of public education. Those who teach will have pupils who will one day serve on school boards and in the state legislature. In the last analysis, the schools belong to the people, but the people have the right to be well-informed if they are to make wise choices. The

KENTUCKY DEPARTMENT OF EDUCATION

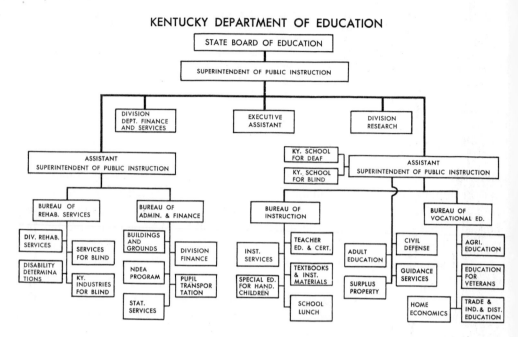

work of a teacher or community leader makes him partly responsible for this. Future leaders should begin now to get ready by becoming well-informed about education.

We should actively seek to understand the organizational pattern of our state school system, its constitutional and legal basis, the manner of its operation, and its relationships to the local schools in which you will be interested. One of the best ways to get an understanding of the state department of education would be to make a chart of its organization and functions. A good source of information would be the series of bulletins and other publications of the state department of education.

In summary, it may be said that each state legislature is responsible for establishing and maintaining an efficient system of public education. Most state constitutions use this language or words to the same effect. This has resulted in school codes, i.e., a body of laws setting up school districts, boards of education, detailing their powers and duties, regulations for the conduct of the boards' business, requirements affecting teachers, teacher education, certification, the courses of study, textbooks, school buildings and grounds, transportation, the levying of school taxes, budgets, and reports of annual expenditures. The state creates school districts, delegates authority and responsibility to the voters and to their school boards, and prescribes curriculum requirements for the operation of the public schools of the districts.

The state legislatures have provided a governmental organization to supervise and exercise necessary authority over public education at the state level. Many state constitutions include provisions for a state school board, a school fund, and a state superintendent.

All but four of the fifty states have a state board of education that serves as the policy-making body for public education at the state level. In some states the state board appoints the chief state school officer but in many, the superintendent is elected by popular vote. Some state boards are elected by the people, others are appointed by the governor.

The state departments of education vary in size, in organization, and in functions to a great extent. In general, their functions may be categorized as *coordination, leadership*, and *service*.

THE FEDERAL CONTRIBUTION TO PUBLIC EDUCATION

The principle of division of powers that obtains in our federal system of government makes education a state function. The Constitution, historical tradition, and many precedents all substantiate this generally-accepted principle. There is, however, a valid concern about education that should be expressed at the federal level. In the first place, the *federal government has a vital stake in popular education,* and this has been recognized from the start of the new republic. Education is so vitally connected with the proper functioning of our democratic institutions and way of life that all levels of responsibility —local, state, and federal—have an interest in effective educational programs.

The vital relationship between an informed citizenry and the success of representative government has been clearly recognized and voiced by statesmen since the days of Washington, Adams, Jefferson, and Madison. The profound changes and developments in our economic and social life have produced conditions that engender inequalities and deficiencies in educational opportunity among the states.

A modern interpretation of the perennial concern about an educated electorate would suggest that the federal government should have an interest in helping to solve the problems involved in keeping educational opportunity open to all, regardless of their creed, race, residence, place of birth, or economic status. This interest could be implemented as there is nothing in the Constitution that forbids the federal government to aid the states to provide for equal educational opportunity.

The current continuing debate over proposals for federal aid to education should not be permitted to obscure the true record. All the arguments *pro* and *con* upon this question must not suggest that the federal government has displayed no interest in education. The truth is that it has shown interest in education on many occasions in our national history. Before the Federal Constitution existed, the Confederation Congress in the Ordinances of 1785 and 1787 demonstrated strong interest in public education and set aside land grants for schools and higher education in the old Northwest Territory. To all save three of the states subsequently admitted to the Union, various grants of land were made for the support of schools. This practice was followed rather consistently for more than one hundred years, resulting in grants of approximately a quarter of a million square miles of land for schools. Subsequently, other grants of land were made to new states for the purpose of establishing universities. The Morrill Act of 1862 provided for grants of land to the states for the establishment of "colleges of agriculture and mechanic arts." These grants totaled over eleven and one third millions of acres to the states and territories. From this has resulted the great system of sixty-nine land-grant colleges, fifty-two for whites and seventeen for Negroes. Ever since the Hatch Act (1887) annual grants of money have been made to the land-grant colleges and the experiment stations attached to them. No piece of legislation in the history of American education has had more lasting influence or significance than this act of a wartime Congress.

During the 19th century there were two occasions when the Federal Congress distributed the treasury surplus to the several states, thus providing funds that could be used for the support of public schools. The proceeds of the Surplus Reserve Act (1837) provided money for the state school fund for some of the states. Later a small portion of the money realized from the sale of public lands in certain states was upon occasion granted to those states by the Federal Government. The first of these "five per cent funds" was granted in 1818; others followed from time to time. More than a third of the states used the money for education. The Federal Government indirectly aided in the establishment of several state public school systems by various grants of money.

Federal legislation in this century has provided further financial aid to the states in support of public school programs of vocational education. Among the landmarks in this series of legislation were:

1914—Smith-Lever Act—appropriated funds to assist the states in providing extension work in agriculture and homemaking. County agents, home demonstration agents, and 4-H Club leaders have been employed in this program of federal and state cooperation.

1917—Smith-Hughes Act—appropriated funds to assist the states for education in vocational agriculture, homemaking, trades and industries, and for teacher education in these fields.

1936—George-Deen Act—provided additional funds for vocational education, added distributive occupations to the program, and provided for its extension to the territories.

Other appropriations have been made to assist in the vocational rehabilitation of veterans of both world wars and of persons physically disabled. Obviously, one major financial provision involved in the GI Bill of Rights (P. L. 346, 78th Congress) related to education benefits for veterans. After the Korean War the Congress again made liberal provision for educational and other benefits for veterans. What this has meant to both the veterans and to the American institutions of higher education can hardly be overestimated. Suffice it to say that the federal government found itself providing scholarships for higher education for veterans for several years after end of hostilities at a total cost of over ten billions of dollars.

Another type of federal contribution to education materialized during the depression years. Problems of unemployment and relief were deemed at least partially amenable to treatment through programs of eductaion and several important programs included educational opportunities. The Civilian Conservation Corps (1933) attacked not only problems of unemployment, conservation and public works, but also provided functional education. The CCC trainees spent ten hours weekly at general education and vocational training programs. The National Youth Administration program

(1936) was multi-purpose in character, with programs which would provide relief work projects and employment, and vocational guidance and counseling. A great many of the experiences provided for youth through these programs were educative in nature. These programs were administered from the national level, and this fact raised much concern over the possibility of permanent educational agencies that would compete with the public school systems. These two programs were placed under the Federal Security Agency in 1939 but both were discontinued when the demands of the war rendered them unnecessary.

One important indication of the nature of the federal government's interest in public education was the establishment of the U.S. Office of Education. In 1867, the Department of Education was established by Congressional act. The new agency was to be a center for collecting information and statistics for reporting and distribution to the several states. Its title was changed to Office

(1869), to Bureau (1870), and to Office again in 1929. The U.S. Office of Education was in the Department of the Interior from 1869 to 1939 when it became a part of the Federal Security Agency. In 1953 it became one of the three components of a new cabinet department, the Department of Health, Education, and Welfare. The U.S. Office of Education has been headed by a Commissioner of Education, appointed by the President and confirmed by the Senate. A number of outstanding educators have held the office, beginning with Henry Barnard of Connecticut. Among them John Eaton, William T. Harris, Philander P. Claxton, and John W. Studebaker all served long terms and built up the functions and services of the office.

Through the years the original "clearing house function" of the Office of Education has grown through the addition of services and coordination activities. From time to time the Congress had provided for certain administrative responsibilities in connection with appropriations and

TABLE 5–3. U.S. COMMISSIONERS OF EDUCATION

Commissioner	Appointed by President	Term of Office
Henry Barnard	Andrew Johnson	1867–1870
John Eaton	U. S. Grant	1870–1886
N. H. R. Dawson	Grover Cleveland	1886–1889
William T. Harris	Bery Harrison	1889–1906
Elmer E. Brown	Theodore Roosevelt	1906–1911
Philander P. Claxton	William H. Taft	1911–1921
John J. Tigert	Warren G. Harding	1921–1928
William J. Cooper	Herbert Hoover	1929–1933
George F. Zook	F. D. Roosevelt	1933–1934
John W. Studebaker	F. D. Roosevelt	1934–1944
Earl J. McGrath	Harry S. Truman	1944–1953
Lee Thurston*	Harry S. Truman	1953 (2 months)
Samuel Brownell	Dwight D. Eisenhower	1953–1956
Lawrence G. Derthick	Dwight D. Eisenhower	1956–1961
Sterling McMurrin	John F. Kennedy	1961–1962
Francis Keppel	John F. Kennedy	1962–

* Died in office.

grants for research and various other programs. The vastly increased volume of Federal agencies and functions has created needs for coordination and assistance in matters related to education. Certain responsibilities for educational programs in the Territorial possessions, among tribes on Indian reservations, and relationships with school districts adjacent to federal defense projects and to military installations have brought work to the Office. Since World War II, there has been an increasing demand for cooperation with other agencies in programs of international education.

A quick look at the recent activities of the U.S. Office of Education will show what had been added to its traditional task of collecting data. In the 1961–62 fiscal year the Office was responsible for:

1. Administration of graduate fellowships and loans for college students under the National Defense Education Act;
2. Provision of foreign language institutes for elementary and secondary school language teachers;
3. Establishment of area study centers for work in rare modern languages;
4. Administration of grants to states and loans to private schools to purchase equipment for science, mathematics, and foreign language instruction, and for improved state supervision of these programs;
5. Making grants to states to strengthen guidance, counselling, and testing in secondary schools;
6. Provision for research and experimentation in more effective use of modern communication media in education;
7. Making grants to the states for vocational education related to national defense;
8. Aiding school construction and maintenance in areas affected by federal activities;

9. Assistance in programs for retraining of unemployed workers;
10. Beginning vocational training under the 1962 Manpower Development and Training Act (which will retrain up to 100,000 unemployed workers a year);
11. Administration of grants and fellowships to improve programs for the mentally retarded;
12. Extension of library service to rural areas;
13. Recruiting education technicians to work abroad;
14. Administration of international teacher exchange and technical assistance programs;
15. Making studies of foreign education; and
16. Cooperating with international agencies in projects and publications.[4]

The work of the U. S. Office of Education can be summarized by a glance at its present organization. There are three operating divisions headed by assistant commissioners: (1) Educational Research & Development (deals with all levels); (2) Financial Assistance Program Administration; and (3) International Education Program Administration.[5] School and college programs have benefited greatly from the leadership activities of the Office of Education. Its services include conferences, exhibits, radio broadcasts, loans of audio-visual aids, and consultative assistance. Among its recognized publications are the official journal, *School Life,* issued monthly, the magazine *Higher Education,* an annual series of bulletins, and reports of biennial surveys.

[4] Donald W. Robinson, "Commissioner of Education: Our Least-Most Important Government Post," *Phi Delta Kappan,* **KLIV,** No. 3 (December 1962), p. 107.
[5] Department of Health, Education, and Welfare, *Annual Report, 1962* (Washington: U.S. Government Printing Office, 1962), p. 236.

Despite steady growth of the Office of Education, it is obvious that its status in the federal organization is a handicap. Only one other major nation, Australia, has no national minister or cabinet secretary for education. Many educators favor a full federal Department of Education headed by a Secretary with cabinet rank.

The interest of the federal government extends further, into what might be considered another type of concern. This second concern might be termed *the national defense stake in education.* There are instances of this type to be found early in our national history—the Lewis and Clark expedition used federal funds as did the Mercury project of NASA. Through the years there have been evidences of this interest in research, in exploring, in gaining new knowledge in various fields. Maury did research to map the seas for the benefit of our Navy and our Ocean commerce. The Smithsonian Institution was established in 1847. The National Academy of Science originated during President Lincoln's administration, to name only a few landmark developments. In recent decades this interest has become recognized as one of the keys to the future of American institutions and our way of life. The national government simply has to invest heavily in scientific research and development. This illustration of the federal stake in education can be confirmed by study of recent activities of any of a number of government agencies and departments.

It is obvious to any student of the national scene that there are many particular needs and services on the part of various federal departments and agencies that must be served by educational programs. This is evident in the educational needs of the armed services, the demands for highly specialized personnel in the diplomatic service, and for technological and scientific experts in agriculture, forestry, wildlife, mining, aviation, commerce, engineering, and many other fields of responsibility. New agencies of the atomic and space age have accentuated the demands for top flight education in many specialized fields, many quite spectacular and dynamic. Families of service men and workers on government projects require education for their children. The long time responsibility of the federal government for the welfare of the Indian population on the reservations represents another concern for education. These are but a few examples of the manifold interests and responsibilities of federal agencies for education. It is said that every department of the cabinet has some kind of educational responsibility and program.

Since World War II, the dramatic developments in aeronautics, electronics, nuclear science, and space exploration, together with advances in public health and other areas, have stimulated broad programs of research in many scientific fields. The several federal agencies established to work in these areas have wisely chosen to utilize the research facilities and talents of recognized institutions of higher education.[6] Many major universities now have contracts for extensive research projects and derive a large share of their income from this source. This is an amazing recent development that involves the federal government and both public and

[6] The leading agencies with large contracts in higher education for basic research are Department of Health, Education and Welfare, the Atomic Energy Commission, Department of Defense, National Aeronautics and Space Administration, and National Science Foundation.

private higher education in a cooperative relationship of incalculable value to both.

The continuation of the Cold War with the prospect of continued emphasis upon defense measures has kept interest in scientific development and research at a high point both in the government and in educational circles. After the successful launching of Sputnik in October 1957, the ensuing discussion reached a new high in terms of demands and charges relating to education. One principal outcome was the enactment in 1958 of the National Defense Education Act. The Act marked a new milestone in the federal government policy of aid to education, specifically to assist the states to strengthen programs that had particular relation to national defense. Under the act grants were made for such specific purposes as: (1) educational materials, student loans, fellowships, and programs for the teaching of sciences, mathematics, and foreign languages; (2) for guidance and counselling; and (3) for research. The provisions of the Act strengthened the confidence of many that federal aid can be extended on bases that do not involve federal control of public education.

Organization of a School System

A school system includes all the schools and educational programs that operate under the control of a school board. In other words, the term refers to the schools maintained and supported by a given school district. In a sense, each school system (or the district) represents a unit in the organization of public schools in the state. The student of school organization must be prepared to find much diversity among the states in various matters or details related to this topic. The legal bases and composition of school districts vary. Their relationship with the state department may be somewhat different (direct or through an intermediate unit such as the county). There may be several kinds of districts for different purposes. A sound practice would be to make a special study of the organizational structure of public education in your state as a supplement to the general principles and practices that can be found in textbooks.

GENERAL FEATURES OF ORGANIZATION

The states differ in the degree of centralized authority and control exercised in the state boards and departments of education although one attempts to operate all schools from the state capital. The states have local school administrative units usually known as school districts. The schools operated in a district may be called a school system for purposes of this study.

Each district (or system) is responsible for the actual operation and control of its educational program under the legal and regulatory provisions set forth by the legislature and state board of education respectively. Local school systems are given latitude in most broad matters of policy and operation. Powers of the local school districts usually comprehend (1) determination of the educational program offered, (2) employment of educational and other personnel and the making of personnel policies upon retention, promotion, and compensation, (3) formulation of the school budget and of the tax levy needed to finance the program, (4) provision of the necessary school plant, equipment, and supplies, and (5) selection of competent educational leadership for administrative responsibility of the school system.

Local school districts are agents of the state, established under the statutes, to implement the state's educational responsibility. Local boards of education are elected by the voters within a given school district but their positions are determined by state law and their responsibilities are, in the last analysis, to the agencies and people of the entire state. This is the reason that state boards of education usually exercise some authority and general supervision and review over local boards.

In the event that this is mystifying, it may be helpful to recall that many of your fellow citizens do not understand the meaning of all these terms. This is simply an actual illustration of a major characteristic of American public education we shall mention more than once, namely that "American public education is *centralized in authority* and *decentralized in administration.*" The power, the responsibility, the authority belongs to the state; the state has assigned power to operate and control the schools to local units (districts) in order that they may better meet the needs of the people. Public schools are established both for the benefit of people and of the state. Local control is essential to the effective operation of schools which depend upon the inter-est, participation, and support of the people.

Criteria for local school districts

The number and variety of school districts pose a problem from the standpoint of effective administration. A marked trend in the revision of school districts is still in progress and the total number decreases each year. In a number of states the patterns of school districts and administrative units is complicated to the point that reorganization would be in order.

Various studies have been made of school districting problems and standards. A practicable set of criteria for local school districts has received wide acceptance in administrative circles.

School districts (or administrative units) should:

— not be smaller than the area of the natural sociological community;
— if possible, coincide with the local governmental unit;
— contain enough children to make possible a well-balanced but economical elementary and secondary school program;
— have a pupil population large enough to permit provision of many essential types of educational services on an economical basis (supervision of instruction, attendance, transportation, guidance, health services, lunch program, vocational education, and special teachers in fields of art, music, etc.);
— be large enough to locate high school attendance units within the natural community and permit elementary school attendance units at places which serve the children most effectively;
— be large enough to afford the necessary

administrative and supervisory staff at a cost deemed reasonable in terms of the total cost of the educational program;

— contain sufficient assessed valuation and taxing capacity to provide the revenue required, when supplemented by state and federal funds, to finance an adequate educational program;

— be large enough to attract and use to good advantage a high type of educational leadership (salary attractive to capable school leaders; program large enough to challenge best efforts of leadership).[7]

The local school district is a distinctive American institution. It is an agency, or "arm" of the state; at the same time it is a unit for the expression of the people's will at the community level. Everyone in the United States (outside of a federal reservation) lives in at least one school district and all property (save that of churches and governments) is taxed for support of school systems in the districts. The school district is both a type of local governmental authority and a corporation with limited powers.

Local District: Administrative Organization

The local district usually has an administrative organization that includes a board of education, a superintendent of schools (with assistant and staff depending upon size and needs), principals for the various schools (with assistants where needed), teachers, supervisors, and other professional personnel, and the nonprofessional employees needed to carry on its educational programs.

THE BOARD OF EDUCATION

The Board of Education is vested with authority from the state to control and maintain the schools of the local district. Usually, boards are elected by the voters of the district. This is part of the popular American tradition that the schools should be kept closely responsive to the will of the people and that the pro-

[7] See Leonard E. Meece, *A Manual for School Board Members* (Lexington: University of Kentucky, Bureau of School Service Bulletin, December 1961), pp. 11–12, for a digest of the NEA Department of Rural Education report *Your School District*, Washington, 1948. Used by permission.

gram of the schools should meet the needs of the communities they serve. No lesson in school organization is clearer than this, that the moment responsibility is removed from the people they begin to lose interest while interest is the motive power needed to effect needed changes and improvements. The term of office is set by law, commonly four years, and elections are usually on non-partisan basis. Boards of education range from five to fourteen members although there are districts with a single trustee. A number of titles are used in various states including: school "directors," "committeemen," and "district trustees."

Functions of boards

The major functions of a board of education are (1) planning, (2) legislation, (3) appraisal, and (4) interpretation.

Planning is the basis for and the process through which policy is formulated. It is a major responsibility of the board to promote sound studies on the part of the school staff which can be used as bases for planning. It is likewise good and sound policy for those engaged in planning important measures and policies to seek the cooperation and participation of the public through the help of community leaders and groups. The schools are *of* and *for* the whole community, not of or for a few individuals or groups. The community that participates in planning with its school leaders and its school board will be a community that understands, supports and works to improve its schools.

Legislation is the making of policy and making the decisions about how policies are to be carried out by the school administration. In effect, the school board is the community's school legislative body; it makes school regulations, major program decisions, and other policies all within the general framework of the state "school code" (school laws and state board regulations), and sets forth procedures for implementing policy. The board then leaves the actual administration of policy to the superintendent and his staff. The board should expect the superintendent to make recommendations about policy, program, and procedure for its consideration. A wise group always utilizes expert assistance. Sound teamwork is the clue to good leadership by a board, superintendent, and school staff.

Appraisal is a necessary sequel to policy-making. Policies made by the board and executed by the superintendent and staff must be evaluated to determine what results are forthcoming. The school board represents both the local community and the state and must be responsible for the economy, efficiency, health and safety factors, and general effectiveness of the instructional program, and the school

plant. All appropriate sources of information should be used and board members should seek to increase their information about educational programs for the sake of better appraisal. School board meetings can be planned to include some beneficial discussion and study of an educational topic. Board members should participate in regular activities of their state school board association.

Interpretation of the school program, its needs and problems, and plans for improvement to the public is the fourth major function of the board. In this task the board and superintendent cooperate, but it is important enough to enlist the best efforts of all. Board members should have adequate communication with their fellow citizens (who elected them), they should have the confidence of their peers because they represent the *whole* community (not the few, or a clique, or minority group, or political faction), and because they are known to be trustworthy and loyal to the idea and interests of the public schools. Board members of this character can interpret school needs and programs to the people who will listen.

Some specific duties of boards

There are many specific duties that boards will perform in carrying out their major functions. The most important single decision is that of electing an able superintendent who becomes the board's executive officer and school leader of the community. Acting upon his recommendation, the board appoints staff, principals, teachers, and employs other school workers. After study and with the superintendent's recommendation, the board adopts a budget for operation of the school system for the year and sets (or requests the setting of) the tax levy to provide the local funds for education.[8] It receives and accounts for the state and federal funds that supplement local taxes for the support of an adequate school program. This is often called the foundation program, a principle of school support utilized in many states. All business of the board must be transacted in full meeting, and in most states their meetings must be open to the public. The board must see to it that adequate minutes and records of the school operation are kept, and insure that all business matters, such as expenditures and accounting of funds, are handled accurately and promptly. Being a good board of education member is a real job!

Qualities of good board members

Most state school codes set forth qualifications for members of school boards. These usually require a minimum age, a minimum educational qualification, residence in the school district, state citizenship, and bar the holding of any other public office, or an interest in any business dealing with the school system. Beyond the legal qualifications there are some important characteristics and qualities that should pertain to good board of education members. They should be willing to devote time and energy to public business in a task which yields no pay but occasional headaches. They should be willing to represent the *whole* public, the entire school district and its best interests, rather than the particular desires of a neighborhood or section. The same prin-

[8] Boards of education in the several states are guided by state law in the matter of setting the school tax rate. In many states the board "requests" the city council or commission or the county commission or fiscal court to levy the necessary tax.

ciple goes for political affiliation, religious preference, economic interest, or social interests—the good school board member places his responsibility to the general public first. This is, in essence, *the concept of trusteeship* that should inspire good citizens to accept the responsibility of school-board membership.

Another important concept for the good board member is that of loyalty to the idea of the common school. It is manifest that only citizens who sincerely believe in public education—the common school in our democratic society, open and free to all, that accepts all and does its best for them regardless of race, creed, language, social class, or economic status, and teaching in the interest of the *whole* of our society—should accept posts of responsibility for educational leadership. This should be true for board members, superintendents, principals, and teachers if our schools are to make their full contribution to our pluralistic society and our democratic way of life.

Finally, the good board member should seek to grow in understanding of education as a process, and of the educational enterprise. He should be open-minded, willing to learn, even change his views for good reasons, and desirous of improving his competence as a civic leader and school policymaker.

THE SUPERINTENDENT OF SCHOOLS

The superintendent is elected by the board of education and serves as its executive officer. The position is now recognized as professional in nature, having developed from simpler beginnings. A good superintendent achieves recognition as the educational leader in his school district and community. The office requires men with broad backgrounds of education and experience and proven ability to lead the efforts of all forces of the community in the support of a good school system.

The American Association of School Administrators, the professional organization of America's superintendents has listed four basic assumptions concerning the role of the top school administrator:[9]

1. The superintendency is essentially the same work regardless of the size or nature of the community; it involves the same duties in metropolis, small town, or rural district;
2. The superintendency comprises a cluster of responsibilities and jobs to be discharged and done respectively; whenever the load is too much for one full-time person it is time to delegate the work and establish a central office for the system;
3. The superintendency best facilitates its work by utilizing sound principles of organization and management; it needlessly complicates its task by neglecting such principles.
4. The superintendency is devoted to the administrative and executive functions in behalf of the school system; the school board has responsibility for legislation and policy-making.

The relationship between the board of education and superintendent is extremely important, one that all concerned should try to understand and accept. It sounds simple: the board should make policy; the superintendent executes policy and administers the business of the school system in terms of that policy. Many good boards and competent superintendents

[9] American Association of School Administrators, *The American School Superintendency* (Washington: American Association of School Administrators, 1952), pp. 66–68.

have found it necessary to define their respective functions and roles in written statements of policy and procedure. Part of the problems arise from the continuing relationship of the superintendent as adviser to the board. He must recommend personnel to the board for appointment; he should provide information about problems and desirable policies; he should bring well-planned programs of studies and curriculum requirements before the board for study and approval; he must submit budget requests with supporting data for board action; and work closely with the members in all phases of planning and constructing school plant and other facilities. The fact that the superintendent makes recommendations to the board in important matters does not detract from the importance of its role. The competent superintendent realizes that the board has the final say. It must not become a "rubber-stamp" group if the school system is to make its best contribution to the people and the community.

Legal provisions affecting the superintendency

There is ample recognition of the role of the superintendent in school law but relatively little protection for the superintendent as an office-holder. Most states have tenure rights and minimum salary laws for teachers but few afford these protections to the superintendent. Normally, the superintendent is protected in his office for the duration of his contract with the board, typically a term of one to four years. State retirement systems often include superintendents, but retirement benefits rarely reflect the difference in salary compared to those paid to retired teachers.

State school laws specify qualifications for superintendents chiefly in the form of requirements for certificates (licenses) in school administration. In this regard, the office of superintendent has progressed rapidly since World War I. In general, it is recognized that the superintendent should have preparation for teaching and practical experience in the schools plus added professional study for the credential or certificate in school administration. Normally, this has meant at least one year of graduate study. The day approaches when membership in the AASA will require superintendents to have completed two full years of graduate study as minimum preparation for this professional responsibility. The salary of the superintendent is normally well above that for teachers and principals with comparable education. Most Americans would agree that the able superintendent abundantly earns and deserves his pay.

The chief appeal of the superintendency is the opportunity to exercise leadership in a demanding, difficult but exciting post of responsibility for the growth of all the children and the strengthening of the community. It is the kind of challenge that brings a wholesome response from many sincere and conscientious men. There is a growing recognition of this position in most communities and its prestige is rising. In most quarters, the superintendency is regarded as a profession.

ADMINISTRATIVE ORGANIZATION

Simplified concepts of administrative plans used in business, industry, and military establishments have contributed to the traditional schemes of organization of the administrative authority for school operation. The line and staff organization, as it was termed, was simple and direct. A diagram of this scheme had two dimensions: the vertical column listed roles and positions of authority from highest to lowest or *vice versa*; the horizontal items represent staff members who performed advisory, research, supervisory and specialized services. The vertical column represented the *line* of authority received from above and delegated to next below; the horizontal items represented *staff* positions and roles.

Under this plan the line and staff organization of a school system appeared to be clear and efficient. The citizens elected a board to represent them. The board made policy; the superintendent

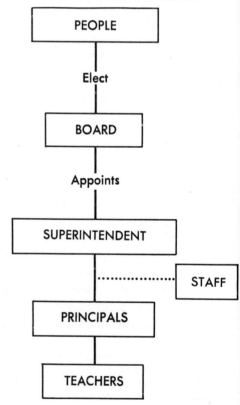

A SIMPLIFIED
ADMINISTRATIVE ORGANIZATION

executed policy, delegated power and authority for much policy to the principal of each school, who had authority over teachers and other school personnel, who, in turn, had authority over pupils. The staff personnel were located outside the line to the side just below the superintendent and assistant superintendent(s) (if any).

This simplified picture of administrative organization of local school systems resembles nothing so much as a diagram of a "peck order" of the animal life in a farmyard. Those who know how good school systems really operate in this country know how inadequate bare outlines and diagrams can be. The schools of this country have never been run quite as crudely as any such picture would indicate. The question about how much democratic citizenship can be taught in a school system run like a military establishment or a business for gain almost answers itself.

Many school systems have long employed modified plans of organization and approaches within the line and staff set-

ORGANIZATION OF A LARGE CITY SCHOOL SYSTEM

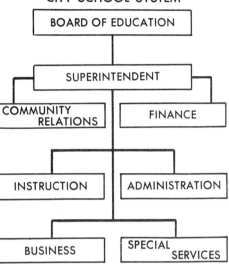

up to make for democratic planning and wide participation of teachers and other school personnel. It is not necessary to strip the authority from the line officials. It is appropriate for them to encourage means of enlisting all concerned with policy and programs at each level to plan and work cooperatively at the overall task. In this way, the skeleton line organization can acquire some live human content and thus be able to feel, act, grow, and improve.

Some principles of democratic approaches to administration of schools have been tested and proved in a variety of situations. These may be stated simply and concisely in eight phrases:

1. Authority inheres in the total situation, in what is required, and in what resources are available.
2. Authority, derived by persons from the situation, is shared by all who participate in the study, planning, and solution of problems of the situation.
3. Responsible educational leadership is superior to mere exercise of personal or legalistic authority. The superin-

A MODIFIED ADMINISTRATIVE ORGANIZATION

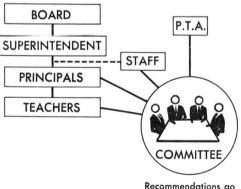

Recommendations go to administration and board for action.

tendent or any other designated leader should exemplify responsible leadership.

4. Educational leadership and responsibility are shared by all school personnel from board members to teachers. Any person may recognize a problem, exercise leadership in studying and taking action, and may be asked to assume formal leadership by the group.

5. Leadership is exercised by securing the full participation of all concerned—in formulating the policy of a program, in planning in its execution, and evaluation of the consequences.

6. New concepts of authority and responsibility are proved in practice through group determination of rules, organizational machinery, and procedures to be used.

7. Responsibilities and duties of administrative and supervisory officers are shared with all whose duties necessarily interrelate and overlap.

8. Democratic planning permits wide latitude in assumption of responsibility, for initiative, and for evaluation on the part of optimum number of persons.[10]

The cooperative approach to educational administration and supervision in public schools has been tested and proven in all sorts of conditions and types of situations. These principles have been found practicable in promoting democratic procedures of cooperation and participation in school systems where the line and staff organization exemplified responsible educational leadership.

School Organization

SCHOOL ORGANIZATION PROVIDES A LADDER OF OPPORTUNITY

In our country, public schools are organized as an "educational ladder." Children enter at a given early age, and move by fairly uniform steps through the elementary school and secondary education to graduation. This is possible in every community of the nation. There are some enterprising districts which have added pre-school programs at one end and junior college opportunities at the other end of the ladder. But their ladders are intact; they have merely added extra rungs.

Most education courses and textbooks refer to the three divisions of elementary, secondary, and higher education in presenting the organizational scheme. Elementary education typically includes grades 1 through 6; secondary education comprehends grades 7 to 12 inclusive;

and higher education includes curriculums of college grade pursued after graduation from high school. Here we encounter some immediate difficulties if we expect these levels to be inflexible uniform programs. What to call the rapidly growing fields of nursery and kindergarten education is one. It is pre-school education, but is it elementary? In many places and types of programs the elementary school still includes grades 7 and 8; in others, the junior college years (grades 13 and 14) are considered a part of secondary education. There are a good many programs of education beyond the high school years which are not thought of as higher education, usually termed as "programs for out-of-school youth." The infinite variety

[10] For full length statement see a modern "classic," p. 85 in A. S. Barr, W. H. Burton, and L. J. Brueckner, *Supervision* (New York: Appleton-Century-Crofts, 1947).

of adult education does not fit into any of our categories. These problems, briefly stated, reveal that it is no easy matter to classify and define divisions in our educational program completely and uniformly.

It is manifestly impossible to define education at any level except in most general terms. The usual designation of the various divisions in terms of grades or by chronological age of pupils is useful in some connections, but it is not always consistent. It is not always possible to say that the schooling given between the ages of 14 and 18 or 12 or 20 is secondary education. Another way to put it, is that secondary education is that provided for adolescents, whatever their varying chronological ages. This general statement is usually reasonably accurate but is subject to correction in certain instances.

The nature of the instructional content has also been used in the definition of the major divisions of American education. According to this view, elementary education provides instruction in the fundamentals, skills, or tool subjects required for meeting the daily life problems; secondary education offers opportunity to explore various fields of knowledge and develops further skills for solution of problems or advanced study; higher education comprises major areas of study in advanced, specialized, and professional fields. By now it will be seen that the various approaches to definition of the divisions of education encounter difficulty at the points of transition. Is a seventh grader in the elementary or secondary school? What about the 18-year-old youth who attends a community junior college, open to all and tax-supported, and housed in the same building with the senior high school? Whether you classify him as a student of secondary or higher education depends upon your definition. Certainly your point of view or conception of education makes all the difference in attempts to classify the junior high school or junior college years of education.

All this need not necessarily confuse us as we will likely work out our own conception of education along simpler and more consistent lines. One may say to oneself, "What's all the fuss about? Education is a long-time, continuous process achieved both without and within the school. Appropriate education for any person of any age or level is whatever is needed for and by that person at the time. Ideally, education should meet the needs and interests of the person of whatever age or grade or objective." From this viewpoint, the so-called divisions of education are mere conveniences or arrangements for administrative purposes. Education within each building or division should be as nearly commensurate with the needs, interests, and problems of the participants as possible. The abrupt dividing lines tend to disappear and we see instead a functional dynamic program growing and changing as necessary. As a starter it may be preferable to try to describe rather than to attempt to define major divisions in American education.

The diagram of the American ladder of opportunity will provide a convenient overview of the total school organizational picture.

Plans of organization

In former decades the traditional form of school organization in our country included an elementary school of

TABLE 5–4. LADDER OF AMERICAN EDUCATIONAL OPPORTUNITY

Traditional	Age	Grade	Typical
		20	
University	24	19	Graduate and Professional Schools
	23	18	
	22	17}	
	21	16	Senior College
College	20	15	
	19	14	Junior College
	18	13	
	17	12	Senior High School
High School	16	11	
	15	10	
	14	9	Junior High School
	13	8	
	12	7	
	11	6	
Elementary School	10	5	
	9	4	Elementary School
	8	3	
	7	2	
	6	1	
Kindergarten	5	k	Kindergarten
	4		Nursery School
	3		

eight grades serving children aged six to fourteen, and the high school of four grades for youth to about eighteen years of age. This was commonly called the 8-4 plan. Beyond this, the colleges offered additional educational opportunity for those who could afford it and who could meet entrance requirements. Finally, postgraduate education was provided in the graduate schools and professional schools offering three-or four-year programs. This program was not planned and developed deliberately and systematically. It grew up gradually over several decades. Our public high schools, for example, came into the picture relatively late in the nineteenth century after common schools and colleges were in existence.

The vast increase in the number of high schools and the growing enrollment of high school students in the late nineteenth and early twentieth centuries led to many studies and recommendations by NEA committees. The high school enrollment doubled each decade from 1870 to 1890 and continued to grow apace. In 1893 the famous "Committee of Ten" reported upon high school curricula and recommended that certain subjects be taught in 7th and 8th grades. Other reports on various aspects of secondary education by noted committees followed at intervals during this period. Research studies by leading educators and psychologists directed attention to the needs of adolescents, especially the early teen-agers, and to the nature of school programs for this age-group. By 1910 plans for reorganizing the upper elementary grades to provide richer educational programs for early adolescents were put into operation by enterprising schools in California and Ohio. These combined the curriculum of the 7th and 8th years with the 9th (from the old 4-year high school) into a new 3-year junior high school. It is difficult to decide among the claims of those who started junior high schools as Columbus, Ohio, Oakland and Los Angeles in California were innovators about the same time. At any rate, this development gave American public schools a new pattern of organization, the 6-3-3 plan. The idea gained acceptance in a number of places, chiefly city school systems, in the decade that followed. Meanwhile the junior high school plan received a significant boost from an outstanding group in secondary education. This support came in the final report of the NEA's renowned Commission on the Reorganization of the Secondary School in 1918. The Commission will be long-remembered for its list, the memorable "Seven Cardinal Principles of Secondary Education" and for its sponsorship of the junior high school as an idea whose time had arrived. This development gave strong impetus to the junior high school movement, and the plan gained wide acceptance during the 1920's.

The basic advantages of the junior high school were presented as follows: (1) Greater holding power for the schools by making transition from elementary to secondary school easier; (2) Gradual change from sheltered simpler environment of elementary to high school with many teachers, departmentalized curriculum, and complex schedule; (3) Opportunity for pupils to explore many occupational fields to discover their vocational interests and aptitudes; and (4) Provision for taking individual differences into account through guidance and counselling services, differentiated instruction, reorganized subject matter in new courses (general science, community civics, and the like) and attention to educational needs of exceptional children. These emphases caught attention in an era that had begun to find that high schools, like their predecessor institutions, the academy and the Latin grammar schools, stressed preparation for college and ignored interests and needs of many pupils. The high rate of "dropouts" alarmed many school leaders and parents. This was a time of concern about child labor legislation and compulsory school attendance laws, all of which contributed to the discussion of the new junior high school program.

The junior high school has become an accepted part of the total educational organization. Between 1948 and 1959 fifteen per cent of all school districts in the United States established for the first time a plan involving junior high schools. In the years 1952 to 1959 the total number of junior high schools in the United States increased over 50 per cent. The great majority of secondary school students (82.4% in 1960) lived in districts that have some kind of junior high school.[11]

The junior high school movement has declined, and people hear more about

[11] Harl R. Douglas, *Trends and Issues in Secondary Education* (Washington: The Center for Applied Research in Education, 1962), p. 67.

other emphases and programs of action but in some quarters, the idea is still debated and certain criticism is voiced. The idea has never been taken up by non-public schools to any great extent. Some superintendents and boards hold to a longer elementary school as more economical in cost and simpler to administer. In some places there are separate districts and school boards for the 8-year elementary and 4-year high school which perpetuates the traditional organization. Some say the social conditions that facilitate the movement have changed; that the economy of time is no longer a serious concern, and that the junior high has proved no panacea for the educational problems of the early adolescent.

The defenders of the junior high say that there is nothing wrong with the program that a good school cannot correct, that the shortcomings inhere in the carrying out of the philosophy, and not in the basic concept itself. Sometimes the point is made that the junior high schools that appear ineffective are found to have instructional programs that differ but little from the traditional ones it was to supplant—too much departmentalization, teachers not prepared for junior high teaching, formal bookish instruction, little use of the "exploration" function, and overstimulation of pupils by stress on sports, contests, and social affairs. It should be evident that the junior high concept should be judged by the performance of those schools that make the most consistent efforts to implement the basic philosophy. Furthermore, it is only fair to emphasize the preparation of teachers who are interested in early adolescents and the functions of the junior high school. It is of little consequence who wins the debate; it is far more urgent that the junior high school (or some other school) take serious and sincere interest in meeting the peculiar needs of early adolescents. In many communities, the junior high school is here to stay for a good while.

In a good many communities another scheme of school organization is found namely, the 6-6 plan. This means that grades 7 through 12 are grouped into a junior-senior high in the same building or school plant. This is particularly true of smaller cities and communities which can by this plan afford an economical high school. Other advantages are better use of faculty, broader curriculum and program of activities, and economical costs. The difficulties involve social adjustment problems of immature youth, wide variation among the choices of activities for pupils, need for standards of achievement fair to all age-groups, and the spread of teaching over a wide span of ages, interests, and needs. School officials in many communities defend the 6-6 plan in terms of the needs and realities of the school system—sparse population, transportation, space available, money for teacher's salaries, and other local conditions and factors. This is the second most influential plan.

It is possible to find a few school systems that utilize a 6-2-4 plan of organization, usually on a temporary or emergency basis. There appears no significant thesis for this particular scheme as it appears weak at the precise point it was designed to strengthen—the early adolescent years spent in school—and two years does not span that part of a teen-ager's experience. Another plan (5-3-4) has been tried in a few places but has not gained acceptance. The old 7-4 plan formerly used in a few states has disappeared.

There are two or three variations of a plan of organization that includes the 13th and 14th years of public education as a part of, or as supplementary to the secondary school program. These have been developed as the junior college movement, another American educational invention, gained headway over the nation. One phase of growth of the junior college has been fostered by certain public education systems that experimented with an extended curriculum for youth. The 13th and 14th years could be provided for all youth of the community at economical cost. In many places, this idea has been popular and the junior colleges have been in effect giving two additional and enriched years of general and technical education to late teenagers. This has given rise to what is called the 6-4-4 plan. An arrangement such as this frequently leads to problems and questions about the nature of the last two years— secondary or higher or something else? It would appear that the development of the two added years as part of secondary education has lost momentum, at least for the moment.

The extension of secondary education into the 13th and 14th years occurred in the same decade that saw the start of junior high schools. In 1902, the first public junior college was established in Joliet, Illinois, to bring post-high school educational opportunity closer home at economical cost. The new American institution provided lower division college work as terminal education for those youth who could or would not go to four-year colleges, and for adults who desired to further their general education. The junior college idea caught on as municipalities and larger school districts established their own programs. Often the plan was a 6-3-3-2 setup. California early proved the usefulness of the junior college and has established a pattern of cooperation with districts that sponsors over 70 institutions of this type. The movement has grown phenomenally since World War II.

In the junior college movement, what began as an upward extension of secondary education has, for the most part, been accepted as a new emphasis is the higher education scene. In recent years, the several states have turned to this plan as a means of meeting the unprecedented demand for higher education opportunity. There are several good arguments for the junior college in the Sixties that make sense. The first is realistic: How else can we provide college opportunity for the wave of students who deserve higher education? It is expected that the number of students entering some post-high school educational program will at least double by 1970. Furthermore, the parents of middle class American homes, and many others demand further educational opportunity for their children who will graduate from high school. Moreover, they appear to be willing to pay for it.

There is an increased respect for higher education among Americans generally. The term "junior college" gives the programs of the 13th and 14th years a far stronger appeal than they would have as part of a new-type secondary school at the crest of a 6-4-4 plan.

Those junior colleges that become truly community colleges make a contribution by providing diversified technical and technological programs of college grade. In certain respects, these are different from what have been called vocational education. The newer programs for technicians involve a high degree of skill and two years of training that depend upon mathematics and science subjects of college level. Programs for technicians in computer data processing, air conditioning technology, and electronics are examples of this type of offering. This type of institution—one that attempts to meet the needs of its community in this respect as well as by general education programs—has an appeal that gets the support of the public.

In recent decades the junior college has grown in amazing fashion. It has been accepted into many state higher education systems, and has been added to state universities as 2-year units on separate campuses. Entire systems of junior colleges have been established on a statewide basis. Florida, Illinois, and New York have set up statewide patterns of junior colleges. Indiana, Kentucky, Virginia, and Wisconsin have established many junior colleges as 2-year branches of their state universities. Georgia, Oklahoma, and Texas have junior colleges as units in the statewide system of higher education.

The junior college has become a prominent feature of postwar higher education in these United States. It bids fair to become a part of this generation's answer to the question of how to provide college opportunity for more and more of America's youth in the late teens.

INTERNAL SCHOOL ORGANIZATION

The great majority of Americans probably give little thought to the matter of school organization for instructional purposes. Most have graduated from or attended schools in a system that utilized grades and yearly promotions on one of the single ladder plans. Few know from our educational history that the graded school was itself an invention or discovery of the 19th Century. Early elementary classrooms were more informal in organization with pupils of various ages and the teacher arranged recitations and lessons by small groups according to the progress of the students. In the first half of the 19th Century as schools became larger it became easy to group younger children into a primary department, another middle group into an intermediate department, and a grammar department for the older pupils, all these followed by the high school. From this it was a logical step to a plan of one grade for each year's age group. Thus, the graded school developed, one which was hailed as a step forward, a step toward economy and efficiency. In its original setting and for the times these were the arguments that prevailed. Today, educators ask questions about other possible plans of organization that may better foster pupil growth and development.

Typical plans of school organization

The K-12 scheme of organization is common in the nation's school systems. This means that self-contained classrooms are found in the elementary schools; that is, a teacher and her pupils work together in their room for most of the time. The teacher is responsible for the instructional program, although in most school systems special teachers of art, music, and physical education are available to help enrich the learning experiences of the children.

The junior high school probably provides a homeroom for each group of

25 to 30 pupils with teacher who counsels and teaches part of their basic curriculum, while the other subjects are studied in separate periods and rooms with different teachers. Sometimes the subject matter studied with the homeroom teacher is known as the "core curriculum" and may be organized to cut across subject lines. Normally physical education, art, music, and certain other subjects are offered by special teachers. School authorities in general believe that the junior high school organization should permit pupils to have a home base, and, especially, a teacher who knows them well enough to lead, guide, and help them to be happy, relaxed, and achieving pupils. The proportion of the time spent with a homeroom or core teacher should be gradually reduced as pupils grow older until the great majority of time in senior high school is in specific subject areas with teachers specially prepared to teach their fields.

The senior high organization is usually departmental, i.e., by subject areas with teachers for each. A given pupil will take required and elective courses according to the curriculum he has chosen to follow. This may mean that he meets four or five or even more different classes in as many rooms with the same number of teachers in a school day. American high schools have followed inflexible schedules, i.e., with daily class meetings for the same length of time to meet the definition of a unit of credit. This practice became uniform after the Carnegie Foundation for the Advancement of Teaching sponsored studies that defined a "Carnegie unit" of instruction in 1909. Most states require that high school students complete a minimum number of required units (a year's course) in English, mathematics, science, social studies, and elective units for a total

of 16 or more. There is a recent trend to require 18 or even more credits for high school graduation.

American high schools differ from their counterparts in most European, Latin American and Oriental countries. A student in the German *Gymnasium*, the French *Lycée,* or the Japanese *Shensei Koto Gakko* will follow a weekly schedule of classes rather than a daily uniform round, and study more fields during his secondary school experience. Recent studies by leading American educators and groups have recommended more flexible scheduling for the high school programs to facilitate enrichment of curricular offerings, the strengthening of instruction by team teaching and other means, and the individualization of study programs to meet individual differences.

Newer plans of organization

As schools have endeavored to meet the needs and interests of pupils there has been experimentation with different plans of organization. One plan that has received favorable attention has been the "ungraded primary". There are several schemes of this type, but the general idea is to eliminate grade placement of materials and pupils and to defer promotions until the end of the primary years. Only at the end of three or four years of schooling is it necessary to decide upon "promotion" to what would be the fourth grade. During the K-3 years the child works with his age group or any other according to his maturity and ability. The pupils (and their parents) are spared the annual dread of "failure" or of "being held back," as children are not all expected to achieve a certain standard in each subject each year. This gives children with differing abilities and rates of maturation and growth a chance to develop more naturally and freely in a relaxed fashion. For many, school is a happier and satisfying experience. There are many reports of successful accomplishment through the primary years in schools that formerly expected a ten to twenty per cent rate of "failures" at the end of the first grade.

Here and there elementary schools are experimenting with various schemes of larger groupings of pupils in order to obviate the annual hurdles (promotion or retention) for pupils. Some have tried an intermediate block of 3 years similar to the ungraded primary plan. Others have tried various multi-grade plans of grouping children of different ages in one room for instruction. Some of the expected advantages are maturity, social learnings, and sensivity to others through the daily cooperation in living and working together. This was a feature of the old-time one teacher school although the age range of the pupils was much greater.

Still another type of newer organization for instruction purpose involves a varied curriculum with loose flexible arrangements so that children may undertake work at their own rate and make continuous progress. This has been called the "continuous progress" plan. Pupils may be placed in 3 blocks—kindergarten, primary, and intermediate—and work both in groups and individually upon subject matter suitable to his needs and level. The question of promotion comes up when pupils are ready to leave blocks. The development of auto-instruction devices will undoubtedly help teachers who use a continuous progress plan.

In recent years the success of experiments with team teaching in certain high schools has led to tryouts in certain elementary schools. A group of schools in downtown Pittsburgh has successfully used this general plan and the project is continuing.[13] This arrangement involves a common schedule for several class groups that permits (1) large group instruction by different teachers presenting their best and special field of competence, (2) smaller discussion (and participation) groups with teachers as helpers, and (3) generous but varied amount of individual study using latest devices and helps for study. The plan allows teachers time for helping pupils and the abler students can go further into topics and problems of interest to them.

Many schools have made use of plans to enrich the elementary curriculum by setting aside time for learning to use some foreign language or to share science experiences with another group. School buildings are being built to accommodate language laboratories, cubicles for individual study, space for programmed learnings and use of teaching machines, and team teaching plans. Some school systems have established camping facilities in which groups of pupils may spend a few weeks in outdoor learning experiences. Others have tried the 4-quarter school year, permitting most pupils to attend for 3-quarters for a normal academic year. Summer schools for those who need extra instruction and for those who wish an enrichment or accelerated program are available in certain school systems. In some communities where it fits the sociological needs of the area, the schools provide an extended day with voluntary activities that interest the children until

[13] *Pupils, Patterns and Possibilities, 1961:* Annual Report of Superintendent of Schools, Pittsburgh, Board of Public Education (1961).

it's time to find their parents at home.

Many of the newer plans of organization are found in some form in the high schools. Team teaching with its flexible tri-partite approach really originated in a group of high schools that worked with the original Trump Committee. At least one senior high school gained considerable notice with a continuous progress plan of studies in recent years. Older reorganized plans of curriculum such as the core program and unified studies are still subjects of tryout, adaptation, and use in various junior and senior high schools. The future look at the high school curriculum presented by experts in secondary education in *Education for All American Youth* has not been realized save in relatively few schools. The general pattern of the curriculum consisting of (1) Common Learnings, (2) Vocational Preparation, and (3) Individual Interest, could be best served by the comprehensive high school with its varied offerings and large faculty.[14] This ideal deserves serious study by more schools that now find many new devices and approaches that could be used to help carry it into successful use.

PATTERN OF ORGANIZATION

The principle of diversity in the pattern of control of education in the United States is clear. Education is basically a state function, organized into units of control at the local level with joint support. The relationship of the federal government to the state educational systems is another illustration of the diversity of American education. Often the "bogey"

[14] Educational Policies Commission, *Education for All American Youth—A Further Look* (Washington: NEA), 1952.

of federal control is raised, but there seems to be available evidence that a pattern of federal assistance to the states can be devised without impairment of that state function. It seems possible to view that relationship as a working partnership, one which can enable all the states to perform more *fully* their function of providing *adequate* free public education. Thus, the great strength of our public educational systems derives from the interest and control of the people expressed through the governmental machinery at various levels. Every teacher, every parent and every taxpayer should have a good working knowledge of the organization and control of our public schools and maintain that interest throughout life.

During the past forty years or so, a number of significant variations from the traditional 8-4 plan have developed in the organization of American education. Two plans have become fairly common; namely, the 6-3-3 plan and the 6-6 plan. The 6-3-3 plan provides for an elementary school of 6 years, a junior high school, and a senior high school of 3 years each. This form of organization has become popular in recent decades. Another common pattern in smaller communities has been the 6-6 plan; two schools, elementary and secondary, of 6 grades each. Another scheme of organization, the 6-4-4 plan appears to be coming into use in communities which provide public junior (or community) college programs. All of these patterns may be found with "K" prefix, meaning that the "Educational Ladder" begins with the public kindergarten as the first round of this way of educational opportunity.

Responsible young people of today can prepare to have public school districts of economical size and efficient organization, and school board members who exemplify the trusteeship concept; they can have loyalty to the common school idea and the willingness to study educational programs and principles. All of this can come tomorrow along with state legislatures and officials who appreciate and respect the vital role of public education in the extension and functioning of democratic institutions. It is clear that this can be realized if enough courageous, straight-thinking college youth begin now to get ready. If it can't be done any other way, they can do it for themselves in their generation for the benefit of their children in their time.

Selected Bibliography

American Association of School Administrators, *The High School in a Changing World*. Washington: The Association, 1958.

American Association of School Administrators, *Staff Relations in School Administration*. Washington: NEA, 1955.

American Association of School Administrators, *The American School Superintendency*. Washington: The Association, 1952.

American Association of School Administrators, *School Boards in Action*, 24th Yearbook. Washington: NEA, 1946.

Association for Supervision and Curriculum Development, *Action for Curriculum Improvement*. Washington: NEA, 1951.

Beach, Fred F., and Will, Robert F. *The State and Education*, Bulletin, Misc. 23, U. S. Department of Health, Education and Welfare, Office of Education. Washington: U. S. Government Printing Office, 1955.

Bell, John A., and Green, Arthur S. "What the Vital Services of Boards?", *American School Board Journal*, **CXL,** No. 3 (March 1960).

Bereday, George F., and Volpicelli, Luigi. *Public Education in America*. New York: Harper & Row, 1958, see Paul R. Mort "Federal Control for American Schools."

Brimm, R. P. *The Junior High School*. Washington, D.C.: The Center for Applied Research in Education, 1963. See Chapter 1.

Chamberlain, Leo M., and Kindred, Leslie W. *The Teacher and School Organization*, 3rd ed. Englewood Cliffs, N. J.: Prentice-Hall, Inc., 1958.

Chase, Francis S., and Morphet, Edgar L. *The 48 State School Systems*. Chicago: Council of State Government, 1949.

Commission on School District Reorganization, *School District Organization*. Washington: American Association of School Administrators, 1958.

Conant, James B. *The American High School Today*. New York: McGraw-Hill, 1959.

Conant, James B. *The Child, The Parent, and the State*. Cambridge: Harvard University Press, 1959.

Dean, Stuart E. "National Look at Elementary School Administration," *National Elementary Principal*, **XXXIX,** No. 5 (April 1960).

Educational Policies Commission, *Federal-State Relations in Education*. Washington: NEA, 1945.

———. *The Structure and Administration of Education in American Democracy*. Washington: NEA, 1938.

Fitzwater, C. O., and Roesch, Winston L. *Local Planning for Better School Districts*. Washington: U. S. Department of Health, Education, and Welfare, Office of Education, Government Printing Office, 1957.

Hanson, Earl H. "What is a School Superintendent?", *Saturday Evening Post* (April 8, 1961).

Meece, L. E. *A Manual for School Board Members* Bulletin, Bureau of School Service, **XXXV,** No. 3 (December 1961), Lexington, Kentucky: University of Kentucky, 1961.

Miller, Van, and Spalding, W. B. *The Public Administration of American Schools.* Tarrytown, N.Y.: Harcourt, Brace & World, Inc., 1958.

National Citizen's Commission for the Public Schools, *How Should Our Schools be Organized?* New York: The Commission, 1953.

National Council of Chief State School Officers, *Our System of Education.* Washington: The Council, 1950.

National School Boards Association, *New Approach.* Chicago: The Association, 1955.

Pierce, Truman M. *Federal, State, and Local Government in Education.* Washington: The Center for Applied Research in Education, 1963.

Progress of Public Education in the United States, 1961–67. Washington: U. S. Office of Education, U. S. Government Printing Office, 1962.

Reeder, Ward G. *The Fundamentals of Public School Administration,* 4th ed. New York: The Macmillan Co., 1958.

Shane, Harold (ed.) *The American Elementary School,* 13th Yearbook, John Dewey Society. New York: Harper & Row, Publishers, 1953.

The Federal Government and Education, Committee on Education and Labor, House of Representatives, 88th Congress, 1st Session. Washington, D.C.: U. S. Government Printing Office, June 1963.

Tuttle, Edward M. *School Board Leadership in America.* Danville, Ill.: Interstate Printers, 1958.

Chapter 6

The Support of Public Education

Public education in the United States is a community responsibility, a function of the individual states, and a concern of the Federal government. . . . The issue in education finance is to secure a well-balanced, stable, flexible, and adequate system of support, to which the local school, state, and Federal governments will contribute in accord with ability and need without destroying the traditional and highly valuable popular community control over public educational policy.*

We believe the American tradition of separation of church and state should be vigorously and zealously safeguarded. We respect the rights of groups, including religious denominations, to maintain their own schools so long as such schools meet the educational, health, and safety standards defined by the states in which they are located. We believe that these schools should be financed entirely by their supporters. We therefore oppose all efforts to devote public funds to support these schools either directly or indirectly.†

Introduction

Almost any discussion of public business or responsibility ultimately gets around to talking about money. Most of us have lived long enough to discover that little, if anything, is free. The great system of American free public education is no exception; it has to be supported and paid for by revenues raised by public taxation. It is true that public schools are free and open to the pupils who attend them. This privilege is provided by the general public—by the people who produce and pay taxes for the support of education. The responsibility of all the people to pay for the education of the children has been recognized and accepted during the past century or so. The struggle to accomplish this principle of public support for education was perhaps the fiercest of the seven great battles described in Cubberley's history of education in this country. Once established, this principle has been extended and made even more effective until a full system of fourteen or fifteen years of public education is poten-

* Arthur B. Moehlman, *School Administration* (New York: Houghton-Mifflin 1940), p. 738.
† Resolution adopted at the A.A.S.A. Convention, Atlantic City, 1952.

tially available to the children and youth of the nation.

The task of financing the schools has grown as the people have learned to demand more and better facilities, adequate teachers and improved learning programs for their children. School buildings now cost far more than the Little Red Schoolhouse or the old red brick graded school of grandfather's day. Both have given way to modern plants with facilities, equipment and programs that would surprise even Horace Mann. Instructional equipment and materials now cost more money than was formerly spent on the entire school system. Teachers' salaries and pay of other school personnel have risen steadily as better qualified persons have entered the profession. Many additional expenditures are now required in the operation of a modern school system. Vast numbers of children are transported to school in fleets of buses; lunchrooms are provided; and a host of other services are now common aspects of the school program. All of these cost money which must be raised by public taxation. It takes real money and a lot of it to maintain a modern public school system.

Each of us as a future citizen, parent or teacher needs to know something of school finance. For one thing, we will pay taxes like everyone else and should be interested in knowing how well and effectively our money is being used. Those who become parents will want the best educational opportunity that money can buy for their children. Those who decide to become teachers will derive their living from the money raised for the support of the schools, and it will be to their interest to know about school finance. It is possible that some may find the opportunity to become an administrator, a school board member, or a legislator whose job includes responsibility for the raising, spending, and accounting public funds for educational purposes. In any event the understanding and appreciation of our largest peacetime enterprise—public education—may be enhanced by a good working knowledge of school finance. The schools and the money belong to the people; we should be able to help interpret that intimate relationship to the public. We must first understand it all if we are to have a sound basis for our views.

The Cost of American Public Education

THE ANNUAL BILL FOR PUBLIC EDUCATION

Our first question will probably relate to the cost of public education. The answer in present day figures will open your eyes a bit, although it is not large compared to many items of Federal government expenditure.[1] Good education

[1] There are several informative and readable titles on this general topic. See National Citizen's Commission for the Public Schools

costs a lot of money and quality education will run even higher. Future citizens

publications (a) *Financing Public Education in the Decade Ahead* (New York: 1954); and (b) *How Do We Pay for Our Schools* (New York: 1954); (c) Educational Policies Commission, *National Policy and the Financing of Schools* (Washington: NEA, 1959); (d) Committee on Tax Education & School Finance, *Citizens Speak Out on School Costs* (Washington: NEA, 1959); and (e) John K. Norton, *What Everyone Should Know about Financing Our Schools* (Washington: NEA, 1960).

will be interested in noting how the total public bill has increased through years of this century. Data for selected years will make this clear.

TABLE 6–1. TOTAL EXPENDITURES FOR PUBLIC ELEMENTARY AND SECONDARY SCHOOLS FOR SELECTED YEARS 1900–1965*

School year ending	Amount
1900	$ 214,964,000
1910	426,250,000
1920	1,036,151,000
1930	2,316,790,000
1940	2,344,048,000
1945	2,638,665,000
1948	4,311,176,000
1950	5,837,643,000
1951	6,528,300,000
1952	7,344,237,000
1953	8,346,313,000
1954	9,092,449,000
1955	9,824,499,000
1956	10,955,047,000
1957	11,944,992,000
1958	13,569,163,000
1959	14,253,239,000
1960	15,643,519,000
1961	16,807,934,000
1962	18,222,842,000
1963	19,543,692,000
1964	

*Sources: (1) Research Division, NEA, *Research Reports,* R–22 (December 1961), see p. 15 for data 1951 to 1960 inclusive; (2) Research Division, NEA, *Research Reports,* 1962–R13 (December 1962), p. 5.

The annual bill for public higher education runs close to ten per cent of the total for public schools as shown by totals for the years:[2]

1959–60	1960–61
$1,342,698,000	$1,452,680,000
1961–62	1962–63
$1,645,438,000	$1,807,747,000

[2] M. M. Chambers, *The Grapevine* (October 1962), pp. 313–314.

These astronomical figures are to be expected in the "space-happy Sixties." The many billions of dollars for the annual bill for public education in the nation represents a great bargain for the people of these United States. A simple computation will give us the per capita expenditure for public education (schools and higher education) for a given year. We simply divide the census figure (or projection) for the year into the total expenditure for public education for that year. We should keep this figure in mind and use it in comparison with other expenditures of governments and by the people themselves.

Public school costs and the gross national product

Total expenditures for public education in 1958–59 comprised only a small percentage (3.1%) of the *Gross National Product* (GNP). The latter is a term used to express the total value of all goods and services produced in the United States in a given year. In the years preceding World War II the expenditures for public education approximated 2.4% of GNP and during the war it fell to 1.2% when total governmental spending was high.[3] In studying data on public school expenditures, you should be careful to note whether a given figure has to do with expenditures for *all* education, public and nonpublic, in the United States, and whether it refers to schools or higher education or both. You must check further

[3] Ralph Lazarus, *We Can Have Better Schools* (New York: Committee for Economic Development, 1960); see also *Financing Public Education in the Decade Ahead* (New York: National Citizens' Commission for the Public Schools, 1954), pp. 5–6.

CERTAIN PERSONAL CONSUMPTION EXPENDITURES COMPARED WITH EXPENDITURES FOR PUBLIC SCHOOLS, 1961

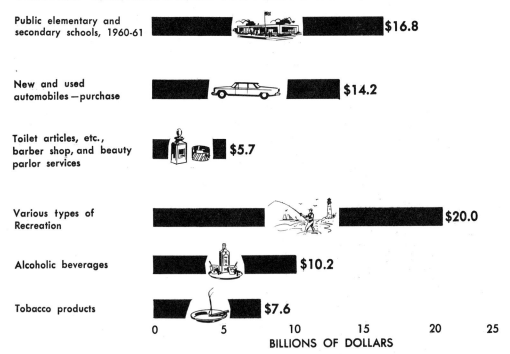

Public elementary and secondary schools, 1960-61 — $16.8

New and used automobiles—purchase — $14.2

Toilet articles, etc., barber shop, and beauty parlor services — $5.7

Various types of Recreation — $20.0

Alcoholic beverages — $10.2

Tobacco products — $7.6

0   5   10   15   20   25
BILLIONS OF DOLLARS

to find whether a given item refers to the total expenditure for public elementary and secondary schools or to the current expenditures plus capital outlay, interest on school debt and sometimes miscellaneous items.

An illustration may clarify this point. We have noted that total expenditures for public schools during the thirties comprised about 2.4% of the Gross National Product. During that same period the total spent annually on education—public and nonpublic—comprised about 3.9% of GNP. In 1955 the percentage rose to 3.6. The increased dollars expended for education have tended to keep the relationship of educational expenditures to GNP relatively constant. The swift rise in enrollments has outmatched the increase

in dollars, and the result is a proportionately smaller expenditure of GNP per enrolled pupil.[4]

The figures that you compile in comparing our national expenditures for education and especially public schools may not be as impressive as they appeared when you first noted all those billions of dollars. You have noted that a number of other governmental functions spend far more of public funds. After you compute the proportion of the GNP spent for public schools you may find that this figure compares unfavorably with the reported

[4] John W. Gardner, "The Pursuit of Excellence; Education and the Future of America," *Prospect for America*, The Rockefeller Panel Reports (Garden City, N.Y.: Doubleday & Co., Inc., 1961), pp. 574 ff.

HEALTH, EDUCATION, AND WELFARE EXPENDITURES
PUBLIC AND PRIVATE

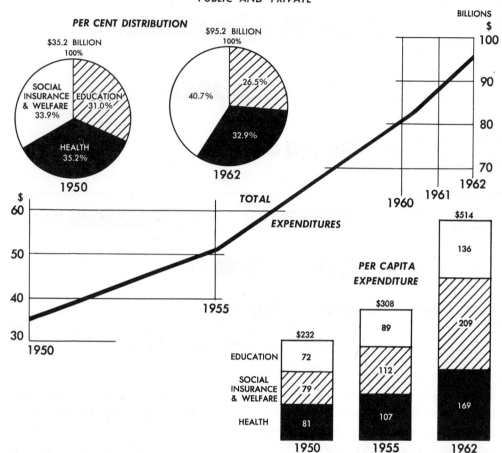

Source: *Road Maps of Industry*, No. 1379 (June 1, 1962), Reproduced by permission of The Conference Board, 460 Park Avenue, New York.

figure for certain other nations since World War II. After World War II it was found that Great Britain spent about 3% of her income for education and for Soviet Russia it was estimated at approximately 7%.[5] In recent years education is taking a rising share of the national income in most countries.[6]

We have had no consistent policy for the support of education. In 1929–30 we spent 2.1% of the gross national product for schools; in 1939–40 it was 2.4%; and in 1958–59 it amounted to 2.6%.[7] We need a sound and dependable policy for support of education.

Comparisons of school expenditures

Some other comparisons would be enlightening to the general public. We have already noted how the expenditure

[5] "Education," *Building America*, **XIII**, No. 3 (March 1948), p. 27.

[6] John K. Norton, "Education as Investment," *NEA Journal*, **LII**, No. 1 (January 1963), p. 55.

[7] Ralph Lazarus, *We Can Have Better Schools* (New York: Committee for Economic Development, 1960), p. 7.

for public education compares with the nation's yearly bill for amusement, cigarettes, alcoholic beverages, gasoline and oil, and for numerous luxuries. Something in the way of increased appreciation for the results obtained from public expenditures for education might take place in our thinking if we looked such facts straight in the eye. We could make a start upon this by studying some of the big items of expenditures of the American people and by the Federal government during a recent year: the military establishment, aftermath of war (interest on public debt, and veteran's benefits); personal consumption of luxury foods, beverages, and tobacco; housing, clothing, transportation, medical expenses, savings, accessories, entertainment, gambling, and others.[8] The results should provide some basis for visualizing and comparing expenditures for education, especially those for public schools. Facts and figures about expenditures tell the story concerning choices and decisions made by people and their representatives in our democracy. The chart on page 181 shows our real values.

Another interesting comparison can be made by inspection of the nation's total expenditures—public and private—for programs closely related to education. The years since World War II have seen greater increases for health and welfare than for education as shown by data for 1950–1962 in the chart on p. 182.

Ability to Support Education

A review of the annual expenditures for American education and the public schools reveals impressive figures. A further investigation into the current financial needs of education should suggest questions about the nation's ability to support public schools on a quality basis. This is a question well worth the time and effort required to find the facts.

Conscientious students will certainly want to know whether there are sufficient resources to provide for our school needs. Does the nation have the ability to pay for the education it should provide its children? Is the problem one of resources or chiefly a matter of policy? In short, can the American people expect to have what we would term quality education for their boys and girls? These questions lead right into a significant part of our study.

One way to approach this quest would involve checking how far short we now are in meeting the financial needs of public schools. Data for any recent year will illustrate this, but data for 1958–59 (related to the formula devised by EPC) will be used here. In that year the current expenditures for public schools amounted to 2.4% of the Gross National Product.[9] An increase of 1.7% would have made up the need according to the criteria for a quality program. Most authorities would agree that this represents a modest added price to pay for the quality schools we should have, especially in view of the importance of education in today's world and in the future of young Americans. It might be added that studies show that the

[8] See *World Almanac,* current edition, for data.

[9] This percentage was for current expenditures only; the total expenditures on public education (capital construction, etc., and higher education) amounted to 3.1% of the Gross National Product for the year 1958–59.

American people expend far more upon objects of lesser importance and worth.

The problem of financing education is not a question of wealth. As a whole, Americans have more money than ever before. It is also true that they are using it for more things and objects than ever before. A graphic picture could be drawn to show this general point. Over a twelve year period 1948–57 the American people spent:

For new and used automobiles	$110 billion
For alcoholic beverages, tobacco & cosmetics	$151 billion
For recreation	$127 billion
For public schools	$ 78 billion[10]

Taxes have increased during the post-war period but annual consumer expenditures increased 59% during the period 1947–58, an average of $11.8 billion each year. Similar figures can be used for other post-war years.

Indices of national ability

The basic problem is not that of resources to provide for education in the nation as a whole. Americans are energetic, their economy is productive, and the Gross National Product continues to rise each year. (See map on opposite page.)

An authoritative source sums up production and consumption by six observations: (1) total production of the U.S. economy is approximately 2½ times over that for the 1929 boom year and should continue at an increased rate in the years ahead; (2) production in terms of man-hour output has been increasing about 2.5% each year and should go higher as

[10] See insert "Can America Afford Better Schools?" in *NEA Journal*, **XLVIII**, No. 2 (February 1959).

new technological improvements continue; (3) more Americans share more of the benefits of large-scale production than ever before here or in any other nation; (4) consumption per capita has risen steadily since 1929 (about 60% allowing for inflation), far above that of any other nation; (5) ability to cope with economic instability has been greatly improved in recent decades; and (6) the U.S.A. with about one-sixteenth of the world's population produces one-third of the world's total industrial production.[11] Data that show that the per capita income in the United States is over twice that of most other industrialized countries, and that indices for both production and consumption are two to three times over many European nations, are good indications of

TABLE 6–2. PERSONAL INCOME PER CAPITA, PER CHILD OF SCHOOL AGE, AND PER CHILD ENROLLED IN PUBLIC ELEMENTARY AND SECONDARY SCHOOLS, 1900–1958*

Year ending	Personal income per capita	Personal income per child of school age (5–17)	Personal income per child enrolled in public elementary and secondary schools
1900	$ 199.23	$ 704.10	$ 915.63
1910	300.62	1,139.04	1,509.60
1920	712.26	2,708.96	3,309.18
1930	624.09	2,430.17	3,339.94
1940	595.51	2,641.24	2,865.61
1946	1,268.12	6,274.21	7,348.58
1950	1,506.22	7,434.69	8,295.60
1952	1,739.00	8,226.76	9,663.52
1954	1,784.45	8,056.74	9,696.50
1956	1,965.28	8,524.53	9,953.98
1958	2,030.29	8,458.39	10,387.78

*Source: NEA Research Division, *Status and Trends: Vital Statistics, Education and Public Finance*, 1959–R13 (Washington: NEA, August 1959), p. 18.

[11] See Gerhard Colm and Theodore Geiger, *The Economy of the American People*, Planning Pamphlet No. 15 (Washington, D.C.: National Planning Association, October 1961), p. 9.

GROSS NATIONAL PRODUCT, 1957 and 1970 (IN 1959 PRICES).

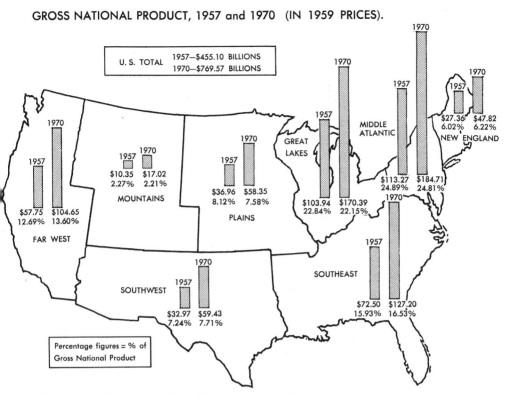

U. S. TOTAL 1957—$455.10 BILLIONS
1970—$769.57 BILLIONS

1970

FAR WEST
1957 1970
$57.75 $104.65
12.69% 13.60%

MOUNTAINS
1957 1970
$10.35 $17.02
2.27% 2.21%

PLAINS
1957 1970
$36.96 $58.35
8.12% 7.58%

GREAT
LAKES
1957 1970
$103.94 $170.39
22.84% 22.15%

MIDDLE
ATLANTIC
1957 1970
$113.27 $184.71
24.89% 24.81%

NEW ENGLAND
1957 1970
$27.36 $47.82
6.02% 6.22%

SOUTHWEST
1957 1970
$32.97 $59.43
7.24% 7.71%

SOUTHEAST
1957 1970
$72.50 $127.20
15.93% 16.53%

Percentage figures = % of Gross National Product

Source: *Financing the Public Schools, 1960–1970* (Washington: NEA, 1962).

the answer to our question. The source of the funds needed for quality education is evident in figures for personal income, and the amount of wealth per child of school age. (See Table 6-2.)

Studies of developments and trends in the American economy find potential for further growth. An illustration may be found in the upward trend in the national average of personal income payments.

TABLE 6–3. PERSONAL INCOME PAYMENTS PER CAPITA (1959 prices)*

Year	Dollars	Per cent of increase over 10 year period
1950	1801	
1960	2188	21.5%
1970	2840	29.8%

(1950 to 1970 increase estimated to be 57.7%)

*Source: *Financing the Public Schools, 1960–1970* (Washington: NEA, 1962), p. 13.

Evidence from studies of economic trends and the patterns of expenditures by the American people suggest that the nation as a whole has the ability to pay for the schools we need. The problem lies chiefly in the disparities and differences in ability to support education among the states which have the responsibility to maintain public schools.

Disparate ability among regions and states

The study of the nation's expenditures upon education has provided only one part of the overall picture. It is clear that the total expenditure for all education is increasing, as are the totals for public education at all levels and for public elementary and secondary schools. It is equally clear that the costs of education are climbing. Moreover the tide of increased enrollments continues to rise.

Can the nation and the taxpayers afford to support education at a level commensurate with our national and individual needs? A look at some of the economic indicators will help us frame an answer to this pertinent question.

The per capita personal income for 1960 ranged from $3,013 in Delaware to $1,173 in Mississippi with an average of $2,233 for the fifty states and the District of Columbia. Another indication of the ability to support education is the amount of personal income per child of school age (5-17). In 1960 the national average figure for this was $9,116. New York with $12,873 was high. Three other states—Delaware, Connecticut, and Nevada—were over $12,000 and near the top; at the other extreme were two states below $5,000; South Carolina ($790) and Mississippi ($4,083). The data for a third measure, personal income (1960) per pupil enrolled in public elementary and secondary schools in 1960, shows about the same disparity. Delaware with $16,459 was top, followed by New York, $16,126; lowest figures are for South Carolina and Mississippi with approximately one-third of the top figure. The national average was $10,670.[12]

Few people have probably appraised the national ability to support education well enough to answer the basic question positively. When we look into columns of data to pick out various states, you realize that the question cannot have the same

[12] Research Division, *Rankings of the States, 1962*, Research Report R-1 (Washington, D.C.: National Education Association, January 1962), pp. 33–36.

answer for every region and every state. A breakdown of data on Gross National Product by regions and states makes this clear.

Another good index of the ability to support education on the part of the several states can be seen in the relationship between their current expenditures for public schools and personal income payment.

TABLE 6–4. CURRENT EXPENDITURES FOR PUBLIC ELEMENTARY AND SECONDARY SCHOOLS AS PER CENTS OF STATE PERSONAL INCOME PAYMENTS, 1949–50, 1959–60, AND 1969–70 (projected)*

States	1949-50	1959-60	1969-70
	(%)	(%)	(%)
Recent high states			
La.	3.1	4.4	8.2
N. M.	3.4	4.2	7.8
N. D.	3.0	4.2	8.3
Wyo.	2.7	4.2	7.2
Ut.	2.9	4.1	8.7
Mont.	2.6	4.0	6.6
Recent middle states			
Alas.	1.1	3.3	5.7
N. C.	3.0	3.3	8.7
Vt.	2.4	3.3	5.4
Recent low states			
Conn.	1.6	2.5	4.7
Del.	1.5	2.5	4.7
Ill.	1.8	2.5	4.1
Mass.	1.7	2.5	3.6
Mo.	1.7	2.5	4.6
Ga.	2.2	2.3	8.2
D. C.	1.2	2.0	3.0
U.S. Total	2.1	3.1	5.5

*NEA Special Project on School Finance, *Financing the Public Schools, 1960–1970* (Washington: NEA, 1962), p. 145.

We shall make certain discoveries as we study the figures for the several states.[13] One is that huge disparities exist among the states in expenditures for schools. You might expect to find that these states which spend less for schools,

[13] See latest NEA Research Division reports for pertinent current data.

have fewer children to educate. *The reverse is usually the case.* You will find that these are the states which have less wealth to tax for the support of public education. Those states with more children and less wealth often spend a larger share of their income on education than do wealthier states. Many studies before and since World War II have reached conclusions to this effect.[14]

Data about expenditures for public education in a given state do not reveal the true situation until we have other information. We need to know the number of children of school age, the enrollments in public schools, and the amount of taxable wealth back of each school child. Only then can we tell how much effort a state makes to support good schools for its children. One of the best indices of a state's ability (or capacity) to support education is the income left to its taxpayers *after* they have paid personal taxes and purchased the basic necessities—food, clothing, and shelter. This *residual income* when divided by the number of children of school age shows the personal income available per child for all additional expenditures for whatever object, including education—public and private. Studies of this type show that states at the high end of the column (ranked by ability) may have several times as much ability as those at the low end to support schools, protect the health, provide for recreation or any other program for its youth.[15]

Data upon personal income and disposable personal income (income left

after taxes), more readily available, permit studies of the abilities of the several states to support public schools.

Columns of figures tell us part of the meanings. In other instances, a map shows related data more quickly, the national map of personal income per child of school age shows some regional patterns of highs and lows. This phenomenon has been one of the long argument for federal aid for public education. (See page 188.)

It is obvious that we cannot judge the educational efforts made by states unless we know a good deal more than the amounts of money that they expend upon public schools. States at the low end of the economic scale, find it difficult to maintain schools on revenues that would represent a relatively low effort for a state with high ability. It is unrealistic to suppose that each and every state can finance its own system of public education with its own resources. The wealth and the disposable income of the nation are not distributed uniformly among the states by population, or the number of children of school age, or any other scheme related to school support.

Disparities among local school districts

A study of public school finance within your own state may disclose disparities in the ability of the school districts or units to support education for their children. We may wonder whether anything can be done about equalizing the amount spent for the education of a child born on Swank Avenue in Cashtown and that expended upon the schooling of a youth brought up on Poverty Hill down in Hardtack County. It is possible that your state has provided some state support for all its schools and that part

---

[14] One of the explanations of this paradoxical situation may be found in the Education Policies Commission report, *National Policy and the Financing of the Public Schools* (Washington: NEA, 1959), pp. 15–21.

[15] See *National Policy and the Financing of the Public Schools, op. cit.,* pp. 15–18.

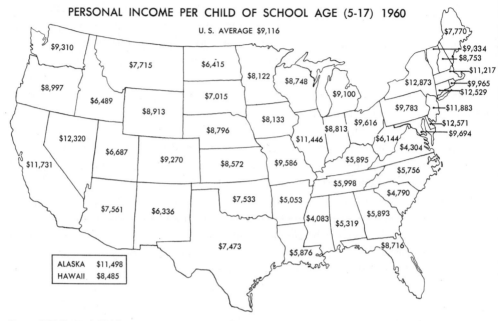

PERSONAL INCOME PER CHILD OF SCHOOL AGE (5-17) 1960

U. S. AVERAGE $9,116

Source: NEA Research Division.

of these funds are to be distributed to those districts less able to support an adequate school program for their children. This principle has been stated in simple terms: Tax the wealth wherever it is, spend it where the children live. It is a principle which has helped to improve the chances of a decent education for the children of poor parents in areas of little wealth.

Causes of differences in the ability of local school districts to support public education are many. One big problem is to be found in the tax policies and programs of state and local governments. Many tax programs are obsolete based on forms of taxation and bases no longer adequate for governmental needs. The property tax is typically the base of support of local units of government including school districts. It keeps up interest in local affairs and schools and makes people feel that they have responsibility for edu-

cation. In other words, local school taxes on property keeps many people interested in the schools, gets them to participate in school board elections, study groups, and school activities.

There are disadvantages to the property tax. It is no longer an equitable tax, i.e., the burden of tax support is not evenly distributed by the property tax today as it was in early agrarian communities. Persons with income from other sources and those who own little or no property may not carry their share of the burden of school support. Assessments of property, often made by local officials, are notoriously low in many districts and depress the revenue gathered from the property tax. Property assessments are exceedingly difficult to change once they are made. In many communities the base of school support would be greatly strengthened if assessments on local property were brought up to a reasonable percentage of its market value.[16] Often there are inequities among taxpayers of a single district that cause discontent. Provisions of some state constitutions make the matters of revision of the property tax extremely difficult, even impossible. Real estate is not the kind of property that increases along with the economic growth of the community.

The difficulties of finding adequate local tax revenue for schools has led some communities to turn to sales taxes, payroll taxes, and license taxes. Each of these presents problems because economic factors and operations are not governed by school district lines. Taxes on withdrawal of beverages from warehouses and other special levies are not a dependable source of revenue because their operation is unpredictable.

There is no escape from the finding that, do what they will, some school districts will not be able to raise enough money by local taxes to support an adequate public school system. This is the same old story of disparity in wealth— this time disparity in ability of the local districts to support public schools.

There are many reasons why the local school districts must turn to the state for help in meeting the need for adequate school support. The state can tax larger business enterprises that operate in several districts and sell products in all and make revenue available on an equitable basis to districts. Use of the state-wide

taxing power of the legislature combined with constitutional or statutory authority to distribute state school funds according to need of those districts, that have made a fair effort, is a fairer plan of support for public schools. The responsibility of the state is exercised here to insure that every local school unit gets the help it needs to maintain an adequate school system. The term foundation program is sometimes used for this general plan. The state guarantees enough funds, over and beyond the local taxes raised by the district that has made reasonable effort, to provide an adequate school program, to insure that no children shall be caught short on educational opportunity through no fault of their own. Many states now use some kind of foundation plans for distributing state school funds to the several districts according to a legal formula that defines units and amounts for each. The term equalization has been used to refer to plans whereby state school funds are distributed to school districts with low ability to support schools, and on a simpler basis principally according to index of need.

We have already noted that units of schools have but one place to turn when they have exhausted their own resources, namely the larger unit of which they are a part. The local districts have turned to the states in the great majority of cases. The states with least ability to support their schools have long attempted to gain assistance for their overall public education programs by appeals to the Federal government but to no avail.

Estimated U.S. average salary of classroom teachers for 1962–63 was $5,735. Examine the NEA research reports upon the rankings of the states to

[16] The revenue raised by taxes on true valuation of property in school districts varied widely. In 1961–62 the high-expenditure districts raised $1.24 per $600 of true valuation; low-expenditure districts raised $.49 on the same base. The national average was $.88 per $100 of true valuation. See *Phi Delta Kappan*, **XLIV**, No. 5 (February 1963), p. 236.

ESTIMATED AVERAGE SALARY OF CLASSROOM TEACHERS 1962-63

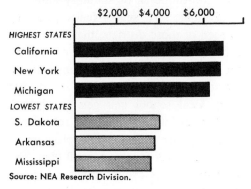

Source: NEA Research Division.

find what states tend to rank high consistently. Note that you find a number of states in relatively low position again and again.[17]

PER CENT OF SELECTIVE SERVICE REGISTRATION FAILING MENTAL TESTS, 1961

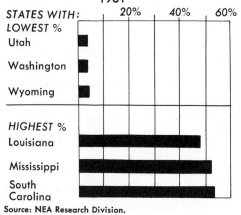

Source: NEA Research Division.

The total percentage of all men who failed the mental tests in the preinduction and induction examinations for military service in 1961 was 23%, in effect an average for the nation as a whole. Sixteen states had percentages under ten, in six the proportion of failures ran over 40%. Study of the rankings of the states on

the average educational attainment of adults of 25 years and older would show some of the same states in relatively high and low places.[18]

PERSONAL INCOME PER CHILD OF SCHOOL AGE, 1961

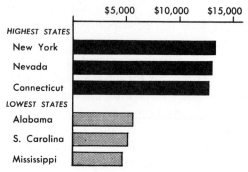

Source: NEA Research Division.

The nationwide per capita personal income was $2,263 in 1961. The national figure for personal income divided by the number of children of school age (5-17) was $9,174 in 1961. Comparable data for the number of pupils enrolled in public elementary and secondary schools in 1960 was $10,670. Various other indices of financial resources of the several states place many in the same relative position.[19]

The three graphs present a sample of the massive evidence that proves the wide disparities among the states with respect to ability to provide adequate educational opportunity for all.

The current dilemma in school support

Sometimes the study of facts and figures can be confusing, even disturbing. This may be the case as you review the data about expenditures for public edu-

---

[17] NEA Research Division, *Rankings of the States,* 1963, Research Report 1963 R-1 (January 1963), pp. 24–31. Chart was derived from Figure III, p. 25.

[18] *Ibid.* See Figure IV, p. 33, and tables pp. 34–38.

[19] *Ibid.,* see Figure V, p. 39, and various tables, pp. 40–43.

cation at local, state and national levels. It is obvious that the American taxpayers have paid billions of dollars in school taxes and that the annual cost of public education which had risen steadily by decades jumped after World War II. One can understand that the increased costs of education like everything else is partly due to inflation, the gradually rising price level in our economy. It is also recognized that there are many millions more children to be educated and that this calls for more school support by taxes. All available data indicates that the American economy is amazingly productive, that the Gross National Product increases steadily, and that the percentages of national and personal income devoted to education remain at a modest level. It becomes difficult to understand why there is so much talk and reference to crises in school support, classroom shortages, use of emergency teachers, and drives to get out the voters to increase school taxes or endorse bond issues for needed schools. We know the American people have money for installment buying, entertainment, recreation, new and used cars, alcoholic beverages, tobacco, and various luxury items. Why do we have this problem of inadequate support of public education?

The problem of school finance is really a complex of problems which, like the poor, are always with us. At the community or local district level the perennial problems of equitable tax rates and fair valuation or assessment of porperty for taxation purposes, still demand attention. At the state level the problems of initiating or of maintaining an equalization of support and the finding of additional revenue to meet the costs of improved and extended school programs are still imperative. The post-war years have brought or

heightened more financial needs including instructional space, increased teachers' salaries, more money to meet rising costs and the ever-increasing problems of inequality of educational opportunity among the several states. Rising birth rates have presented prospects of increased enrollments for several years; money will be needed to provide for teachers, equipment and buildings. Inadequate school buildings continue to present a grave problem. New capital construction has been unable to keep up with school population growth for the past few years and many plants are outgrown and obsolete. Many school districts have issued bonds for school buildings to the limit of their "ability" and may not incur further indebtedness. At the end of World War II, the NEA estimated that some seven billion dollars would be required to meet most acute needs—to replace worn out buildings, consolidate small schools, acquire suitable sites, and provide needed equipment.[20] That estimate is far too low in terms of recent studies and increasing costs make any estimate precarious. More than a billion and a half dollars a year for the next ten years would be a modest estimate of the outlay required to completely modernize the American school plant.

The problem of where to house the vastly increased number of young Americans when they go to school, must somehow be faced and solved by the American people. It begins to appear that some kind of working partnership of governmental action is necessary. In a given state some communities are rich enough to build the buildings and maintain good schools. Others simply cannot. The states can equalize educational opportunity among

[20] NEA, *The Public and Education*, **I,** No. 4 (February 7, 1946), p. 4.

school districts to the extent of their ability but inequalities will still remain. The traditional problem of regions with more children and less wealth will remain in spite of all the several states can do.

It appears that federal aid is the only major alternative. But there are some objections and problems and there are some groups that oppose federal aid on any basis. There are some objections by religious groups unless parochial schools can participate in any such program. Most people will want that federal aid to be merely *aid* without the threat of incurring federal control. The schools belong to all people; we must not remove from them the responsibility and the power to do all they can to provide good education.

Most public school leaders favor a program of federal assistance to the state, based on need, that will aid the states to more nearly equalize educational opportunity among the districts where the public live. A number of sound proposals to this have been introduced into the various congresses in recent decades but political considerations based on fear of alienating large blocs of voters have prevented action. Solution of the present dilemma probably awaits an effective program for giving the general public a realistic picture of the situation. When the people are close enough to the schools to see why good schools are important and that they are really an investment in the future they will expect their representatives at all levels of government to act accordingly. They will gladly foot the bill for a good program of education in our democracy.

Ways and Means of School Support

There is real need for an adequate way of developing popular understanding of school support. The traditional American way to support public education has been by popular vote in the local districts. This was accomplished in the open town-meeting or by an annual election of school trustees, but the taxpayers (who were also the school patrons and voters) understood what was needed. They acted accordingly and they could determine what their local officials were doing to carry out the policies and programs they had approved. The people felt their responsibility and took steps to meet it.

No one needs to be told that the days of grass roots control of public schools (or of any other public function for that matter) have gone the way of mud roads, horse and buggy travel, and a dollar a day wage scale. An understanding of the ways and means of school support today involves consideration of local, state, and federal sources.

SOURCES OF SCHOOL SUPPORT

The public schools are controlled by the states, which means that the policy of school support is determined by the state legislature. All states raise money for public schools by taxation. Certain other sources are available in some states such as interest upon state school funds and income from public lands granted for the support of schools. The states provide about 39.2% of the total support for public schools in the entire nation. In 1960 the several state governments spent more than six billion dollars for public schools and over eighteen billion for all other purposes.[21] There is a wide range in the proportion of support for public schools among the states. Nebraska and New Hampshire rank lowest with about 6%, and Delaware the highest with as high as 81%.[22]

The states also delegate authority to the local school districts to raise funds for education by taxation and the major share of school support is raised at this level. Local school districts now provide over 57% of the total cost of public schools for the nation as a whole. In Nebraska the percentage of support by the local districts would run very high, in Delaware very low.

There are also certain funds available to the states from Federal appropriations for specific purposes, notably vocational education, the school lunch program, and the National Defense Education Act objectives. The total amounts to about 3.7% of the total cost of public schools over the nation. During the depression years some Federal funds were made available to assist school districts to build school plants under various public works programs. In the war years other appropriations were made to aid schools in defense areas to meet the unusual demands they incurred by the influx of war workers and this program has been ex-

tended to more centers. It is clear that emergency measures such as these cannot be counted upon in the planning of policies of school support.

School leaders have long sought the enactment of legislation by the Congress to provide federal aid for public schools as a means of assisting the states to provide reasonably adequate programs of education for all children. This proposal has been strongly pressed for many years by the National Education Association and other professional groups. Discussion of this movement, possibly comparable to some of the seven great battles of our educational history is one which we will hear many times. At this stage the subject is highly controversial since various economic and religious groups are strongly opposed to federal aid for public education.

In summing up we should note that the support of public education is essentially a partnership of local and state units with some help from federal sources for specific purposes. It is clear that this pattern has changed a great deal since the beginnings of American public schools when schools were financed entirely from local revenues. For the past few years the proportion of support from the three levels of government has remained approximately the same. The percentages are approximately 57%, 39% and 4% for shares of public school support by local, state, and federal funds respectively.

[21] See *Financing the Public Schools, 1960–1970, op. cit.,* pp. 76–82 for tables and data. Counting public higher education costs borne by the states the total for all public education would exceed $9 billion of state money.

[22] *NEA Research Bulletin,* **XL,** No. 1 (February 1962), p. 6; see also *NEA Research Bulletin,* **XLI,** No. 1 (February 1963), pp. 8–9 for recent data.

SCHOOL SUPPORT AND TAXPAYERS

All American taxpayers live in some kind of a school district, some in two or more. These are actually units of government for a specific purpose and functions, i.e., the maintenance of public education. In many instances, the local unit of government—town, township, county or municipality—is the school district, and the schools are operated as a department of the unit. In any case it is at the local level that the problem of financial support for public education comes close to the taxpayers and citizens.

School districts and school taxes

Local school districts are governmental units in a limited sense (their functions and powers are limited), and have their own governing bodies similar to village boards of trustees, town councils, city and county commissions, or the state legislatures. Its legal title may be the Board of Education, the School Committee, or the Board of School Directors. It is often popularly known simply as the school board. It is elected by the voters of the school district or governmental unit in most states of the union. In some, the board may be appointed by the governing body of the local unit of government. It differs from most governmental bodies in that its members usually serve without pay. The school board members are elected by their fellow-citizens to have general charge of the limited functions of the school district. It plans with the help of its chosen executive, the superintendent, decides upon policy and maintains general oversight of the school system of the district. One of the major specific duties is to adopt the budget for operation of the school, set the tax rate (or levy), and authorize the expenditure of school funds for budgeted purposes.

The school board is composed of persons willing to give time and energy to public service. Sometimes they may even incur criticism from their fellow-citizens if they disapprove of school policies or practices. School tax levies and proposed expenditures are not always popular with some citizens of some communities. Board members need to have the strong conviction that our free system of public education is a basic ingredient in American culture and an essential agent in maintaining our democratic way of life.

The schools cost money and school boards have no source of support, other than public funds raised by taxation. This means that boards must levy taxes upon the taxable property and assets of their fellow-citizens and neighbors. Local tax funds for public schools have paid for more than half their total cost (57%) for the entire nation in recent years. Local school taxes have gone up during the postwar years but only enough to maintain approximately the same proportion of public school support. Education's share of all taxes—local, state, and Federal—has been significantly lower in recent decades than it was before World War II.

PERCENTAGE OF ALL TAXES DEVOTED TO EDUCATION

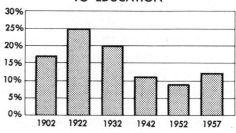

Source: "Can America Afford Better Schools?" NEA Journal (February 1959).

School boards have to depend upon the revenue from local school taxes to a much greater degree in certain states than in those which distribute state tax money to the districts. These foundation programs or equalization funds do not replace local taxes, but do supplement them to the extent needed to support an adequate school program.

State foundation programs are even more needed where the local tax base is principally the real and personal property of the citizens. Probably 90% of local school support is derived from local taxes on property.[23] Moreover the schools must compete for the same tax dollar that supports other local governmental units, the county, and their activities. This is strong competition and this situation, coupled with the chronic low ratio of assessed valuation of real property, represents an acute problem in school finance.

Legal powers and organizational features of school districts enable us to separate them into two categories dependent upon their taxing power. Many school districts have fiscal independence, i.e., they have autonomy in the matter of levying and collecting school taxes subject to state legislation relating to school districts, boards, and taxation. This was an ideal that was advocated as a way to remove school policies and programs from the rough and tumble scene of local politics. Frequently this feature was one of several state legal or constitutional provisions for education that stipulated separate elections of school board members, and non-partisan ballots. Fiscal independence simply means that the school board of a given district has authority to fix local school taxes as it sees fit, subject to pertinent state legal and constitutional provisions. Educators have generally favored fiscal independence for school boards.

[23] "Can America Afford Better Schools?" *NEA Journal* (February 1959), p. 33.

Another type of school district is found in some states that use the municipal or local unit of government for the provision of schools. In this case, the school system represents a department of the local government. This makes the school board fiscally dependent upon the city council, or commission, which sets the local tax rates for all purposes. The superintendent of schools in this type of district is comparable to the head of any other department of the local unit, such as public works, law, finance, safety and welfare, usually headed by a commissioner. This type of school system is not directly responsible to the people because taxes are levied by the elected council or commission. Frequently this local governing body selects the school board or confirms the appointments made by the mayor. This plan makes no special provision for keeping public education apart from other governmental machinery and functions. It does not recognize any unique function of public education as often argued by those who favor fiscal independence for public school districts and boards of education.

The matter of levying local school taxes is relatively simple. This is how it generally works in districts with fiscal independence. After due study the Board of Education knows how much it needs to operate the school system for the next year. It develops its budget and formulates the budget as the basis for its tax levy, or for the levy it requests the governing body to make. The school board also knows how much property it has that is taxable—this is called the assessed valuation. By a simple computation the tax rate is found—by dividing the total budget figure into the assessed valuation. The quotient is the tax rate. This figure may be expressed in terms of mills, per hundred dollars, or per thousand dollars. For example, if our district had a tax rate of $20.00 per thousand dollars, and if real property (house) was assessed at $10,000, our school tax bill would be $200.00. Our share of the school tax plus those of our neighbors and fellow-citizens would be the local school revenue. When the local districts' school revenue falls short of paying the bill, state aid must make up the difference.

The state and school taxes

The people pay for public education in the last analysis, a fact that should emphasize the importance of having citizens participate in the decisions of who should control their schools. In other words, it has been proven, many times over, that popular support and backing for education depend upon the feeling of responsibility. That sense of responsibility is lost when the control of the schools are removed from the citizens, when voters and taxpayers do not actively participate in school elections and the big decisions that count, such as special elections on additional school tax levies, or bond issues. This sense of participating-that-makes-a-difference is lost when the responsibility is vested in officials that are not chosen as the people. It is easy to lose this simple feeling of responsibility and concern; its revival depends upon more than a smooth public relations program.

Tax funds raised for education at the state level are levied by action of the legislature and collected by the department of revenue. State school funds may come from the general fund revenues by appropriation acts of the legislature. In some instances the state legislatures may levy a tax for a specific educational purpose or program, or it may earmark a portion of revenue from a specific tax for education. States employ a number of tax programs to get revenue for many functions including public schools and higher education. Most states use a combination of two or more major tax programs.

We can see that the support of public schools involves citizens and public officials and representatives from the local level all the way to the State Capitol. All citizens should be interested in having the best schools that their tax money will pay for, and in strengthening the support of public education. Parents and interested citizens can find ways to make their wishes for better schools and adequate school support known to their representatives on the school board, the tax-levying authority of the city or county, and in the state legislature. The voice of the people is always heard.

Problems of School Support

THE INCREASING COSTS OF EDUCATION

Enrollments continue to mount

Education of children and youth costs more in the sixties because there are so many more of them. Enrollments rose sharply in all levels of education during the 1950's but especially in the high schools. This great upsurge continued into the college level. The education of more children always costs more money. The larger increase of secondary school pupils

PERCENTAGE INCREASE IN PUBLIC SCHOOL
ENROLLMENTS, 1952-53, 1962-63

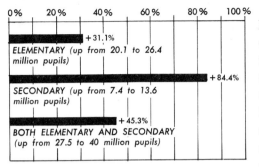

More teachers and better salaries

Teachers' salaries which were never high, remained at a relatively low level during the war years, lost ground until they were below the average earnings of all employed persons. Much of the increase in teachers' salaries after the war has been absorbed by inflated price levels and their relative position has improved only slowly. This has contributed to a chronic shortage of teachers that has marked the post-war period. Many school boards have undertaken to attract teachers with good preparation and to provide them with adequate classrooms, instruction supplies, technical equipment, and other assistance in order to achieve a quality school program. This costs more money but those who have tried it find that it pays dividends.

Competent studies have been made to find what it would cost to provide the minimum essentials for a quality school program. A formula for calculating the cost of this kind of program in a given school district and the criteria upon which it is based are available for study by professional and lay groups.[24]

costs still more because of higher per pupil costs (estimated at 50% above elementary level) are higher.

Growth of enrollments during most of the 1950's provides a graphic illustration of these factors. Various population projections into the next decade and the increasing percentage of children of school age in the total population indicate that the problem of mounting enrollments will be with us for some time to come.

Inflation and rising prices

School costs, like everything else, are affected by the inflationary spiral in our economy. The decreased buying power of the dollar necessitates provision of more dollars to supply school facilities and equipment, pay teacher's salaries, provide school transportation and other services, and build the new classrooms needed for rising enrollments. The 1959 school tax dollar bought only 52¢ worth of goods and services that the 1949 school tax dollar provided. The annual school bill for 1958–59 included nearly $3 billion to cover the inflated costs over the 1944–49 level. Inflated costs have continued into the Sixties.

Additional buildings and equipment

An acute need of education at all levels in the post-war period has been the shortage of classroom space. New buildings and equipment required by the mounting enrollments have come at the time when other costs were rising sharply. Costs of capital construction rose rapidly as expenditures increased five fold during the 1950's. Other contributing factors

[24] Educational Policies Commission, *An Essay on Quality in Public Education* (Washington: NEA, 1959), pp. 27–29.

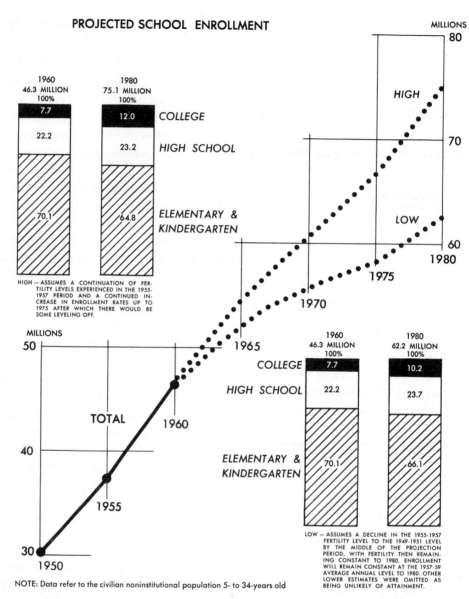

PROJECTED SCHOOL ENROLLMENT

MILLIONS 80

1960
46.3 MILLION
100%

1980
75.1 MILLION
100%

7.7

12.0

COLLEGE

22.2

23.2

HIGH SCHOOL

HIGH

70

70.1

64.8

ELEMENTARY &
KINDERGARTEN

LOW

60

1980

HIGH — ASSUMES A CONTINUATION OF FER-
TILITY LEVELS EXPERIENCED IN THE 1955-
1957 PERIOD AND A CONTINUED IN-
CREASE IN ENROLLMENT RATES UP TO
1975 AFTER WHICH THERE WOULD BE
SOME LEVELING OFF.

1975

MILLIONS
50

1970

1965

1960
46.3 MILLION
100%

1980
62.2 MILLION
100%

COLLEGE

7.7

10.2

HIGH SCHOOL

22.2

23.7

TOTAL

1960

40

ELEMENTARY &
KINDERGARTEN

70.1

66.1

1955

30

1950

LOW — ASSUMES A DECLINE IN THE 1955-1957
FERTILITY LEVEL TO THE 1949-1951 LEVEL
BY THE MIDDLE OF THE PROJECTION
PERIOD, WITH FERTILITY THEN REMAIN-
ING CONSTANT TO 1980. ENROLLMENT
WILL REMAIN CONSTANT AT THE 1957-59
AVERAGE ANNUAL LEVEL TO 1980. OTHER
LOWER ESTIMATES WERE OMITTED AS
BEING UNLIKELY OF ATTAINMENT.

NOTE: Data refer to the civilian noninstitutional population 5- to 34-years old

beside that of increased enrollments, were a backlog of building needs that had accumulated during the war and depression years, the shifting of population during and after the war, the deterioration of old buildings and equipment, and the rising costs of sites, construction, equipment, interest rates and everything related to building. There has not been a time since the war when many public schools have not been handicapped for lack of classrooms and other facilities. Despite policies of double shifts, lengthened school days, and longer school terms the classroom shortage continues.

ACUTE NEEDS OF PUBLIC EDUCATION

There is some danger that Americans will live with some of their problems so long that some bad situations may be

STATE-LOCAL TAX DOLLARS REQUIRED TO PURCHASE THE EQUIVALENT OF $100 IN 1948 PRICES

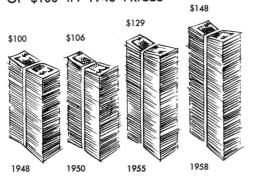

Source: NEA Committee on Educational Finance, *What Everyone Should Know About Financing Our Schools,* 1960.

ANNUAL EXPENDITURES FOR SCHOOL CAPITAL OUTLAY AND INTEREST PAYMENTS

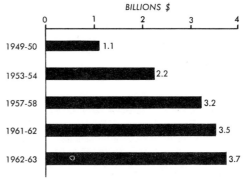

Sources: U.S. Office of Education, *Digest of Educational Statistics,* 1962; NEA Research Division, Research Report, 1962 R–13, December 1962.

accepted as inevitable. It must sometimes look that way to perplexed school boards and superintendents when they study the unmet needs of the post-war period. Communities have been on double shift plans for use of school facilities for years, the chronic shortage of teachers continues (with a sizeable number of emergency teachers each year in the schools), and teachers' salaries, although much improved, do not enable us to hold many good teachers whose training is valuable in other fields. These are some of the chronic problems and needs that people should not view with complacency if our schools are to meet the challenges of the years ahead.

Continuing shortage of teachers

There has been no permanent solution of the emergency teacher problem. The number continues to represent about 7% of all teachers.

Teachers' salaries are not competitive

Beginning salaries in teaching are not competitive with other fields open to college graduates, a factor that contributes to the continuing teacher shortage. The

ANNUAL AVERAGE SALARY OF INSTRUCTIONAL STAFF AS A PER CENT OF AVERAGE EARNINGS OF ALL EMPLOYED PERSONS, 1939-1962

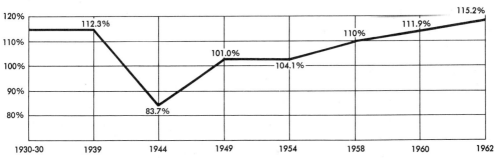

TABLE 6–5. BEGINNING SALARIES PAID MEN COLLEGE GRADUATES IN 1962, IN INDUSTRY AND IN TEACHING*

Men Graduates, in Industry		
Engineering	$5,616	
Accounting	4,992	
Sales	4,944	
General Business	4,846	
Other Fields	5,148	
Average—all fields		$5,160
Men and Women in Classroom Teaching (Est.)		$4,208

*No data for women later than 1958. Estimated average beginning salary in teaching for both men and women.
Sources: (1) Frank S. Endicott, *Trends in Employment of College and University Graduates in Business and Industry*, Seventeenth Annual Report, Evanston, Illinois, December 1962. (2) NEA Research Division.

picture has improved in some communities but there is room for improvement.

Teachers' salaries have increased during the Fifties and Sixties but there is still a great differential with other professions. Typical teacher income ranks low in any study of median income of professional persons. Experienced proven teachers are often in demand for other fields for which their education has equipped them. Many of these are teachers the school boards and superintendents would choose to hold. In short, boards of education and school administrators are not in position to compete for personnel with education and experience necessary to achieve a quality program of education.

Unmet and emerging needs are at hand

Many communities have delayed action upon needs that have been recognized earlier. Some have temporarily abandoned kindergartens because of costs and space needs, hoping to restore them at a later date. Here and there pressures for retrenchment and elimination of frills have led to deletion or the limiting of such subjects as art, music, physical education and general shop. A clear need is the restoration and strengthening of kindergartens and enrichment of elementary and junior high school curriculums.

A great many school systems have found it impossible to implement the findings and recommendations that have been recognized as essential to a good program of instruction. The need for guidance counsellors in both elementary and secondary schools is an example. Facilities and equipment for the exploratory functions of the junior high school and for the new emphases upon mathematics, science, and foreign languages in senior high schools are needed in many school systems.

Community colleges are overdue in a number of centers in various states. The need for a variety of new technical and semi-professional programs in community colleges and technical institutes is apparent. Increased opportunity for up-to-date vocational preparation for out-of-school youth remains a need in many areas and communities. The whole field of adult education must be developed in terms of the growing needs and interests of persons, who wish to continue education. Public education cannot evade responsibility for action upon these emerging needs. They make sense in our changing society and it is reasonable to expect the people's school to accept this responsibility. Added programs will require added support.

The cost of quality education

Studies of minimum standards to insure quality in public education and of the anticipated costs have been made in recent years. The NEA Special Project on School Finance estimated that the achievement of minimum standards for quality in public education will cost $720 per pupil for current expense in 1970.[25] The national average in 1962 was under $400 per pupil. The projected estimates for 1965–70 were based on the $720 per pupil current costs for public elementary and secondary schools and a total enrollment projected at 46,700,000 pupils. The estimated total of the figure for current expenditures for 1969–70 reached $33.6 billion. This figure represented an estimated price for a minimum standard of quality education. The minimum standard included:

1. Adequate instructional staff and services;
2. Adequate staff salaries (beginning and continuing); and
3. Proportional increases in other current costs.

This proposed program set a goal for the educational and lay leadership of public education to work toward in the Sixties.

FINANCIAL NEEDS OF PUBLIC SCHOOLS

Questions about the expenditures for education preface still others about the adequacy of the support provided for our schools and colleges. There are many reasons for this concern of professional and lay persons interested in public education. Appropriations for education are often outrun by needs and pressures upon the schools before the funds are expended. Analyses of the situation by many responsible study groups have unanimously con-

cluded that America must devise policy for more adequate and consistent support of public education.

The citizens and taxpayers who foot the bills should understand the factors that contribute to the financial needs of public education. Those who are concerned about this problem should be prepared to explain the most important facts and factors that relate to the needs of the school to the general public in intelligible terms.

The financial needs of public education have been studied extensively by responsible agencies and groups since 1950. Reports of a half-dozen of these agree that the needs of the schools require the doubling of expenditures for education. These included the National Citizens Commission for the Public Schools (1954), the White House Conference on Education (1955), the Problems and Policies Committee of the American Council on Education (1958), the Panel on Education of the Rockefeller Brothers Fund Special Studies Project (1958), the Educational Policies Commission (1958), and the President's Science Advisory Committee (1959).[26]

Useful yardsticks by which a community might estimate the current needs of its school have been proposed by the Educational Policies Commission.[27] The formula proposed assumed that the quality of the school teaching staff and the total cost of operating a school system

[25] "A Minimum Standard of Quality Education" in *NEA Research Bulletin,* **XL,** No. 4 (December 1962).

[26] See quotations from the reports of six groups from 1954 through 1959 in an appendix to Educational Policies Commission, *National Policy and the Financing of the Public Schools* (Washington, D.C.: National Education Association, 1959), pp. 27–29.

[27] See *An Essay on Quality in Public Education* (1959), pp. 25–29.

can be proportional to the salaries of that professional staff. Size and salaries of the faculty can be estimated by the following criteria: (1) at least fifty professionals per 1000 pupils; and (2) a beginning salary for new college graduates that competes with other agencies that employ persons of similar preparation and experience and salary advancement at least comparable to those of competing agencies in the community. In 1958 data for average salaries of college graduates and for civil service positions led to a suggested beginning salary of $4500. That yardstick, if applied throughout the nation would have raised the per pupil expenditure to $540 in 1958–59; the actual average figure for the year was $310. Other expenditures for public education, such as professional services and current operations, could be calculated in terms of percentages of the professional salaries item ratios, derived from analyses of costs in previous years. The financing of public schools in 1958–59 according to the formula of the Educational Policies Commission would have required nearly eight billion dollars more than the ten and seven-tenths billion dollars that were spent. Communities that have shortages of classrooms and facilities would have to add costs of capital construction to this total under the formula. Increased school population would require yearly revision of the program according to the criteria of the formula.

A Policy for School Support

THE PARTNERSHIP
SHOULD BE EXTENDED

It is important that all of us think this whole problem through while we are still concerned about the need for equalization of educational opportunity for the children. We must ponder the problem of securing increased support for schools in the effort to determine how we could have an adequate financing of education. We have noted that the responsibility now rests upon the states. Local districts, units, or communities raise varying proportions of school revenues. Some trifling aid is received from federal appropriations. This at least suggests the idea of a working partnership for the financing of education. Would it be possible to develop cooperatively a more consistent policy for the support of our schools, which will guarantee every child everywhere, at least a minimally decent educational opportunity, with each level of government bearing its fair share of the cost?

It is possible that some group will come forth with the proposal that the whole program of education should be controlled and paid for with federal funds. Only the Congress can tax the wealth of the nation as a whole, they will say. Let the states and the numerous school districts turn the problem over to the federal government. The needed money could be raised and spent upon the schools where the children are, thus providing each with an equal opportunity for education.

That sounds logical and simple to people with minds that crave uniformity and sameness at any cost. But there are few educational leaders or social scientists who would favor a shift to the federal government of the responsibility of the state for maintaining education. It would mean a national system of education with the inherent dangers of centralization, standardization, strict uniformity, and dead level mediocrity. The prospect of federal control which would follow, would deter most educators from advocacy of any such scheme. The same kind of argument could be used to advocate centralized federal control of any other human activity or enterprise. All the children *could* be reared more economically in government orphanages, to use an extreme example.

Our political system of government grew from local and state beginnings into a Federal Union which provided for division of powers between state and national levels of government. It is now conceded that education is one function for which the state is responsible. The needs and problems of education vary widely over the country; one system or way of doing things will not suffice. It has been demonstrated that people do not maintain an interest in activities which are handled too far away from them. Take education out of the hands of the states and the local communities and efforts to help improve the schools would gradually cease. People place value upon these programs and activities which they have participated in and contributed to and thus accept as their own. Washington is too far from grassroots to provide an educational program which will meet local needs and elicit the efforts of people in the communities. The public schools owe much of their origin as such to devoted concerned parents and neighbors who built schools with their own hands. That delicate thread of interest and active concern between people and their own institutions is needed if we are to have schools good enough for today's children.

Community support for education

There are sound reasons for the position that the local community should carry major financial responsibility commensurate with its ability to support public schools. The schools are for the people; their interest and cooperation are essential to the functioning of a good instructional program. They will feel a sense of pride and participation in a school which is theirs in a tangible way. Our schools are needed as community centers and efforts are being made in many communities to get people to use the buildings, facilities, and equipment their money paid for. This is all the more reason why the local community should carry as much of the financial load as possible and fair. Historically, the local community has been the chief source of school revenue; it is a sound policy and needs modification only because of the inequalities which exist in their ability to support an adequate program of education.

Figures for the entire nation show that in recent years, more than half of all school revenues are raised at the local or county level. State sources account for nearly forty per cent and the remainder comes from federal appropriations for specific purposes. In some states the percentage of school support from local sources is very high.

You should go into a thorough study of the part of the local community or school district in public school support for your state. We shall need to find out

TABLE 6–6. HOW THE SCHOOL TAX DOLLAR IS SPENT IN A LARGE CITY SYSTEM*

* Current Operating Expenses	
Instruction	66.6%
Operation	11.1%
Fixed Charges	8.1%
All Others	7.5%
Administration	2.4%
Auxiliary Services	2.4%
Capital Outlay	1.9%

Source: *Investment in Youth*, Report of the Superintendent, Cincinnati Public Schools, 1960.

what legislation governs the levying of school taxes, how it is collected and handled, and how the school boards and administrators budget and account for school expenditures. One way to get started would be to bring in a local superintendent who could explain how this is handled at the district level in your state. An illustration of an interpretation to the general public is provided by figures from a large city system.

State responsibility for education

The next phase of our study should consider the role of the state in school finance. The keynote is the term responsibility. The state is responsible for the maintenance of adequate schools and many state constitutions charge the legislature with the responsibility of maintaining an efficient system of public schools. Financial support is the opportunity for the state to exercise its responsibility for maintaining adequate schools. The state must use its taxing power over the entire wealth of its people and be able to supplement the money which is raised by the local school districts. Sometimes the state school funds have been distributed chiefly on a per capita basis, so much per child to be educated, but sounder plans of state aid according to effort have been developed in many states. State aid has been a great help to the local districts, and it has enabled the states to require higher standards and thus improve the schools.

This policy can not be expected to fully eradicate all the inequalities of educational opportunity within the states. State school funds distributed on a per capita basis can do nothing to remove the differences in ability to support schools. These funds only raise the high and low districts an equal amount per child, but do not bring them nearer together in ability to provide schools. The best plan which has been devised by the states to meet this need is some form of the equalization principle. This means that part of the state school funds are distributed to the local school districts *according to need*, rather than the per capita basis. We can readily see how this practice does get right at the problem of inequalities among the school districts. Wealthy Gold Coast School District with a reasonable tax rate gets only the per capita distribution of state funds, but the Hardscrabble School District with little wealth and a higher tax rate gets the per capita state fund and an exra fund for equalization purposes. This last part makes a lot of difference in the ability of the poorer districts to support a decent program of education for their children.

The equalization principle has not been used sufficiently to solve all the problems of unequal ability and support. The share of the state funds distributed on an equalization basis are often too small to do the job. Often the state legislature finds that constitutional provisions prevent or limit the use of this principle. It has proved its worth by showing an effective way for the state to discharge its responsibility to ensure good schools for all the people. States that learned this lesson have proceeded to devise a foundation program of support for school districts that provides the funds needed for an adequate school program *after* the local system has made an *effort* to support its schools.

We should try to get an accurate picture of the pattern of financial support for schools in our state. There should be helpful materials in bulletins of the state department of education and in collections of the college library. It may be practicable to invite in as consultant a well-informed state or local school official who will answer some questions as we try to develop this idea of the working partnership between local districts and state governments in matters of school support.

Federal aid for public education

Most public school leaders want just what the above title says; no more, no less. Federal aid is needed, because grave disparities exist among the states in their ability to support adequate programs of education. School people do not want federal control for American education for obvious reasons. Citizens may wonder whether we can have federal aid without federal control. Most educators believe this is possible, but there are some who doubt that this desired end can be guaranteed.

The advocates of federal aid point out that Congress has provided land or money grants to the states upon a number of occasions in our history and that education has remained in the hands of the states. The famous Ordinances of 1785 and 1787 authorized land grants for education in the old Northwest Territory. Other grants of lands followed until 30 states in all received such help for their schools. Eleven million acres of land were granted to the states for higher education purposes under the Morrill Act of 1862. Grants or advances of money were made to the states on three principal occasions more than a century ago. In this century some of the revenues from forest reserves and oil-mineral leases have been granted to states.

Direct appropriations for specific purposes have been made by Congress on several occasions. Most familiar to students are those which provide aid to land grant colleges and agricultural extension services and for vocational education in the schools such as the Hatch Act (1887), Smith-Lever Act (1914), Smith-Hughes Act (1917), and the George Deen Act (1936). These appropriations have been continued by the Congress and account for a small part of the school revenue of each state.

Advocates of federal aid point out that federal control has not followed in the cases cited. They believe that federal aid to the states can be provided on a basis calculated to help equalize educational opportunity in the same manner that state funds are used to assist poorer districts. In view of the American constitutional principle of separation of church and state, federal funds could only be used to improve public education.

On the other hand, there are some educational interests that strongly oppose further trends of federal participation in education. In support of their view, they cite evidences that federal government agencies exercise strong controls over money appropriated for various other programs carried on in cooperation with the states. Some put it this way, "Send a tax dollar to Washington to get back 80 cents for a program."

For several decades the National Education Association has strongly urged and worked for the enactment of the federal aid principle. This would grant money to the states upon basis of need to improve public education. Several times since the 80th and the 81st Congresses, there have been serious considerations of bills which would provide money to be distributed to the states according to need. This legislation has been strongly urged by organizations of school people. Each time various questions of possible use of federal funds for nonpublic education in some states have tended to prevent concentration upon the real need. The most frequent questions have arisen from interests related to segregation problems and to proposals for aid to parochial schools and colleges. Recent sessions of Congress have given more attention to bills that would provide federal funds for capital construction for public school and higher education. Progress has been slow due to strongly expressed interests of certain groups interested in parochial schools, nonpublic higher education, conservative politicians, business groups, and critics of public schools. No experienced politician or lobbyist would rate the chances very high under the present circumstances for early favorable action upon a comprehensive bill for federal aid.

The enactment of federal aid along the lines which have been suggested would complete the pattern of a working partnership among all levels of government—local, state and national—to provide adequate educational opportunity for all American children.

ANALYSIS OF THE COST

Through this entire treatment of support for education one logical question has been hovering around like an uninvited guest: Is Education Worth Its Cost? Since public education is supported by taxes paid by the people, they have the right to know what they are getting for their money. Citizens should be well-informed about education in order to help interpret true facts about the work of the schools. One answer to the above question would show that a democracy such as ours cannot afford to neglect education for all the people. All citizens have the right to vote and to participate in public affairs; they must have education in order to read and learn about their rights and responsibilities and the issues of our times. The Founding Fathers saw this clearly as expressed in quotations from Washington, Jefferson, Madison, and others. It is equally true and essential for our day as for theirs. Even in the Twentieth Century we cannot have a democracy without public educational opportunity for all. This costs money.

Public education can never be fully evaluated in terms of dollar returns although a good case can be made for the expenditure of school funds as an investment. A provocative illustration of the tangible worth of public education may help to answer the typical question about the worth of education in dollars and sense terms. The 19,000 public high schools graduated approximately 1,700,-000 seniors in 1961. It has been estimated that the total cost of their 12 years of public school experience was $7,855,054,-000. A brief calculation indicates that the average per graduate cost was $4,626.[28] It is not difficult to discover that the average earnings of these 1,7000,000 young citizens will be larger and their increased tax returns to their communities and states will soon pay for the public investment in their future.

The cost of public education is not the only consideration for the taxpayers and their legislators to recognize. Another is the high cost of ignorance and neglected talent in the lives of people. Ignorance and poverty are universally related. Low educational levels are associated with unemployability. Poor educational standards and high rates of selective service rejec-

tions are linked as data for certain states clearly show. It costs more in the long run to neglect education and human well-being than it does to maintain excellent schools and colleges.

A concise summary of the current situation with respect to support of public education may be found in a recent provocative study by the Educational Policies Commission:

It has long been an article of faith in America that public education, if universal and excellent, would help immeasurably to eradicate social ills, elevate the tenor of human life, and strengthen democracy. But America has yet to test, through full support of its schools, the validity of that faith.[29]

[28] *NEA Research Bulletin,* **XL,** No. 2 (May 1962), pp. 42–43 for data.

[29] Educational Policies Commissions, *An Essay on Quality in American Education* (Washington, D.C.: National Education Association, 1959), p. 26.

Selected Bibliography

Abrams, Frank W. *The Stake of Business in Public School Education.* New York: National Citizens Commission for the Public Schools, 1951.

"Are School Costs Getting Out of Hand?" *Suburbia Today* (November 1960).

"Can America Afford Better Schools?" *NEA Journal,* **XLVIII,** No. 2 (February 1959).

Carson, Ruth, "More Time for Your Money," *Parents' Magazine,* **XXXVII** (February 1962).

Educational Policies Commission, *An Essay on Quality in Public Education.* Washington: National Education Association, 1959.

Educational Policies Commission, *The Contemporary Challenge to American Education.* Washington: National Education Association, 1958.

Heller, Walter W. "Education and Economic Growth," *NEA Journal,* **L,** No. 7 (October 1961).

Lazarus, Ralph, *We Can Have Better Schools.* New York: Committee for Economic Development, 1960.

National Association of Manufacturers, *Our Public Schools and Their Financial Support.* New York: The Association, 1954.

National Citizens Commission for the Public Schools, *Financing Public Education in the Decade Ahead.* New York: The Commission, 1954.

National Citizens Commission for the Public Schools, see titles:
How Can We Help Our School Boards?
What Are Our School Building Needs?
How Do We Pay For Our Schools?

National Citizens Commission for the Public Schools, *How Do We Pay for Our Schools?* New York: The Commission, 1954.

National Industrial Conference Board, *The Economic Almanac, 1962.* New York: The Conference Board, 1962. See current edition.

Norton, John K. *Citizens Speak Out on School Costs.* Washington: National Education Association, 1959.

————. *What Everyone Should Know About Financing Our Schools.* Washington: National Education Association, 1960.

————. "Education as Investment," *NEA Journal,* **LI,** No. 1 (January 1963).

Peterson, Le Roy J., Flanigan, Jean M., *et al., Financing the Public Schools.* Washington: NEA, 1962.

Research Division, *Estimates of School Statistics, 1962–63,* Research Report 1962–R13. Washington: NEA, December 1962.

Research Division, *Rankings of the States, 1963,* Research Report 1963–R1. Washington: National Education Association, January 1963.

Research Division, *Status and Trends, Vital Statistics, Education, and Public Finance,* Research Report 1959–R13. Washington: National Education Association, August 1959.

"Will Your Child Get a Quality Education?" *NEA Journal,* **XLIX,** No. 1 (January 1960).

"Your Money's Worth in Schools," *Changing Times,* **XV** (September 1961).

Aids for Part II

AUDIO-VISUAL MATERIALS

FILMS

Board of Education, United World Films (28 min. b & w). Title is descriptive. [5]

Design of American Public Education, McGraw-Hill Text Films (16 min., b & w). Title is descriptive. [5]

Design for Learning (Sound, 20 min., color). School buildings project. [6]

Fight for Better Schools, March of Time (20 min., b & w). Story of citizens' group fight to recover control of schools from political machine and for improvements. [5]

Pop Rings the Bell, National School Service Institute (23 min., b & w). Directed to the American taxpayer. [6]

School Board in Action, National School Boards Association (27 min., color). [5, 6]

Schoolhouse in the Red, Encyclopaedia Britannica Films (42 min., color). A rural community faces problem of school district consolidation. [5]

Schools March On, McGraw-Hill (18 min., b & w). How a midwest community improved its school system. [5, 6]

Way of Life, Harvester (21 min., color). A community deals with problems of finance. [6]

FILMSTRIPS

Design of American Public Education, McGraw-Hill (35 frames). [5]

QUESTIONS FOR DISCUSSION

1. What are the duties of school boards in your state?
2. How are local school board members selected in your state?
3. Are the qualifications adequate? Why?
4. What do you believe about the local control of public schools? What are the advantages? The disadvantages?
5. What types of school districts are provided by your state School Code? Describe.
6. Are school taxes adequate in your community? Why?
7. Are school taxes equitable in your state as a whole? Why?
8. What are the major problems, if any, of local school organization in your state? Explain each suggestion.
9. What does your state Constitution say about public education?
10. What are the principal functions of your state department of education? Where do you find this stated in official conclusive form? Explain.
11. How does the organization of the department of education in your state differ from the example provided in the text?
12. What are the differences in the work of the state and local boards of education?
13. How is public higher education organized in your state?
14. What control does the state have over nonpublic schools and other educational institutions?
15. What are the principal provisions governing the chief state school officer in your state? What are the strengths and weaknesses of this position?
16. Can you explain how and why education is a state function? Just what does this mean? What difference does it make?
17. What word would you use for the part the Federal government has (or should have) in public education? Why?
18. Why are there so many educational activities and programs in so many federal agencies?
19. What historical and development factors have brought the great change in the role of the Federal government in education? Explain your ideas.
20. What do you see as the arguments about Federal aid to education, *pro* and *con*? Explain.
21. What issues are involved in the controversy over Federal aid to education?
22. How are the public schools supported in your state? Are there any inequities and disparities?
23. How could support of public education be improved in_____?
24. What is the typical plan of school organization in_____? What are the advantages? Disadvantages?
25. What new plans of school organization appeal to you? Why?
26. What is the status of the junior high school in_____?
27. What does the term "equalization of educational opportunity" mean? Does it mean identical opportunity for everyone? Explain.
28. Should everyone pay taxes for public education? Why?
29. What do you mean by the term "quality education"? Explain.
30. Can the American people afford to support good public schools? Support your views.

IDEAS FOR INDIVIDUAL STUDY

1. Follow the newspapers for one month for clippings relating to educational organization and support.
2. Prepare an organizational chart of local school organizations in your state.
3. Prepare an educational ladder for your state.
4. Prepare a diagram of the state department of education.
5. Study the educational system of another large nation. Prepare a graphic exhibit to explain its organization and important features.
6. Prepare a research paper on "The History of Federal Aid to Education Bills in the U. S. Congress."
7. Study the proposals for and pending bills upon education in the Congress and report upon same.
8. Investigate the most important Supreme Court decisions that have affected public education and prepare report for the class group.
9. Do research upon the development of the state board of education and report.
10. Do a research paper upon the historical development of the state school system.
11. Prepare a chart to show "How School Taxes are Levied, Collected, and Used."
12. Prepare a research paper on the historical growth of the U. S. Office of Education.
13. Chart the course of a congressional bill relating to education through its entire history from drafting to final signature.
14. Devise a graphic representation to show the number and variety of groups, organizations and other influences that affect educational legislation and policymaking in the national capital. Or, do such a study for your state capital.
15. Make a study of the office of chief state school officer in the 50 states, noting the manner of their selection, duties, powers, and other basic information.
16. Make a list of the changes and improvements that you would recommend in state and local school organization in your state. Support each.

SUGGESTIONS FOR GROUP WORK

1. Arrange for committees to visit boards of education in regular meetings to be followed by a report (by the chairmen of the groups) to the entire class.
2. Invite a superintendent of schools to describe the organization of local school districts and school organizations in your state.
3. Participate in a group discussion on "The Distinctive Characteristics of American School Organization."
4. Take part in a committee project to collect documents and publications about your state school system and exhibit these for the class.
5. View an appropriate film on American school systems such as "Design of Public Education" and keep notes.
6. Invite an official to discuss the process of getting school legislation drafted and passed in your legislature.
7. Take part in a group study of the various Federal educational activities and programs. Develop a chart or use an overhead projector to show your findings to the class.
8. Take part in a research project to trace out and report upon the long series of Federal government appropriations to the states for educational objectives.
9. Participate in a debate upon a pending bill in the Congress for Federal aid to education.

10. Take part in a committee project to discover differences in the ability of school districts to support schools in your state and prepare a map to show any disparities.
11. Take part in a group study of "The Sources of School Support in_____."
12. Make a group study of reasons for the increasing costs of education and report your findings to the class.
13. Take part in a research project to discover the nature and extent of lobbying on educational legislation in your state legislature and report to the class.
14. Participate in a committee interview with two superintendents (city and county systems) to gather information about their responsibilities.
15. Do the same for principals of elementary, junior, and senior high schools.
16. Debate the question: Resolved, that there should be a Department of Education with full cabinet rank.

THE IMPERATIVE NEEDS OF YOUTH

1
All youth need to develop salable skills and those understandings and attitudes that make the worker an intelligent and productive participant in economic life. To this end, most youth need supervised work experience as well as education in the skills and knowledge of their occupations.

2
All youth need to develop and maintain good health and physical fitness.

3
All youth need to understand the rights and duties of the citizen of a democratic society, and to be diligent and competent in the performance of their obligations as members of the community and citizens of the state and nation.

4
All youth need to understand the significance of the family for the individual and society and the conditions conducive to successful family life.

5
All youth need to know how to purchase and use goods and services intelligently, understanding both the values received by the consumer and the economic consequences of their acts.

6
All youth need to understand the methods of science, the influence of science on human life, and the main scientific facts concerning the nature of the world and of man.

7
All youth need opportunities to develop their capacities to appreciate beauty in literature, art, music, and nature.

8
All youth need to be able to use their leisuretime well and to budget it wisely, balancing activities that yield satisfactions to the individual with those that are socially useful.

9
All youth need to develop respect for other persons, to grow in their insight into ethical values and principles, and to be able to live and work cooperatively with others.

10
All youth need to grow in their ability to think rationally, to express their thoughts clearly, and to read and listen with understanding.

Adapted from Educational Policies Commission, *Education for All-American Youth—A Further Look* (Washington: NEA, 1952), p. 216.

III. PROGRAM

A Ladder
of Opportunity

Courtesy Cincinnati Public Schools

Chapter 7

The Purposes of

Democratic Education

We need not retreat one step from our goal of providing education for all (and I mean all) American youth. Equality of opportunity for all children and equality of respect among all educational groups are two doctrines that are as significant for our future as for our past. These are the fundamental premises of American education. Every citizen needs to realize how they differ from the premises in other lands. He will then see how our American educational philosophy differs from the European and reflects the special nature of our own free society. He will then be more ready to support in every possible way the further development and improvement of our American schools. If one understands why and how their schools differ from those of other free societies, one will be more ready to support them and make the sacrifices that are required to improve them, even at a time when they face the staggering problem presented by the drastic up-rising in the size of our population.*

Introduction

More and more as we continue our education and thinking about our life's work we shall become concerned with purposes. *Purposes come first* in adequate programs of education. This is true from both the standpoint of the society that sponsors the educational enterprise and that of the individuals who benefit from the educational opportunity provided. We can expect to find, when parents and

* James Bryant Conant, Address before final dinner, National Citizens Commission for the Public Schools, January 9, 1956. Used by permission.

teachers stimulate pupils to desire an adequate education, that the question of "Adequate for what?" must inevitably arise. Adequate educational opportunity and programs can hardly become reality until and unless we determine clear and appropriate purposes.

Schools do have purposes even though these may be outmoded or may be taken for granted by the general public. These purposes are rather clear at the outset of an educational program; they may become inadequate or obsolete as time goes on and conditions change. We

215

shall find that the purposes of our schools have changed a great deal in the three hundred years of American public education, growing ever more varied and complex. Even greater changes are in prospect as our society moves faster and faster, and people face new problems and adjustments. Educational programs and schools adequate for an age or one set of conditions are often found to be grossly inept and ineffective in results and returns needed in our time and society. Good teachers for one day may even be found lacking when the schools are faced with new and greater demands. More and more these social changes and the problems of the people must come to find a place on the agenda of education.

There are significant developments in the American scene that reflect a growing popular interest in what our schools should do and try to accomplish. Informed persons will be familiar with the recent great debate over American public education, its problems, its strengths and weaknesses, and various questions by critics and spokesmen, friendly and otherwise. They will recall the work of the National Citizens Commission for the Public Schools and of thousands of local groups at work on school improvements. Such profoundly different groups as the National Association of Manufacturers and the American Federation of Labor-Congress of Industrial Organizations have both given attention to the purposes of American Education. The noteworthy studies by Conant, the Gardner Committee for the Rockefeller Brothers Fund Panel reports, the President's Commission on National Goals, the current work of the Trump Committee, and various curriculum studies have all given emphasis to

purposes. In recent years many church groups have re-expressed their concern about and support for strong public schools and for effective programs of instruction. On the other hand, there have been attempts by certain groups to dictate to our common schools in matters of curriculum, method, and with respect to their goals. These suggest the primary importance of the purposes of public education; few persons would bother to discuss the purposes and program of something insignificant.

The tremendous rate of social change and novel developments in our way of life present continuous need for recent review of purposes, curricula, methods, and programs in our schools. Here busy educators find more headaches than in nearly any aspect of education one can name. The reason is that common schools are *in* and *of* this modern society, itself casually patterned and full of contradictions. Public schools derive their support from that dynamic society and, at the same time, contribute toward a new and improved social order. If the school or the teacher can not do this with masterly skill they may precede their society too far and defeat their purpose. Advanced too far, they lose communication with the general public and the support needed to maintain their positions. On the other hand, timid and uncritical leadership in the schools is even more dangerous in that it offers no stimulus to improvement and allows old evils to become aggravated. Ultimately obsolete, such schools have to be replaced by new-type institutions which will grapple with societal problems and the needs of the time.

Hence, the need for wise, farseeing teachers. Teachers must teach and lead in desirable directions without losing the support and approval of the people they serve; without getting either too far out in front of a mere procession, nor yet back in the crowd with the unseeing, complacent followers. Surely of all people, teachers need to have *purposes* and functions of their work clearly in mind. Teachers for our time need, more than anything, a fine sense of direction and purpose as they teach adequately for today and lead toward tomorrow. The parents and school supporters for the next generation need to understand educational objectives if they are to give the meaningful cooperation and backing that their democratic society and the common schools will need.

General Role of Schools

ROLE OF THE SCHOOL IN SOCIETY

Schools exist in, and because of, a society. There is no society or culture anywhere which has not provided some institution or program for education. Even primitive societies have developed definite, often elaborate, educational programs for their youth in order to make them adequate members of the group. Often these programs are largely carried out by direct experience with an experienced, mature adult serving as the guide or teacher. The content of education consists of the skills, knowledges, and beliefs needed for participation in the group life. Schools in the sense we know them are not common among primitive peoples, but education is always present in any society. Advanced societies have always found it necessary to develop and maintain schools.[1] If the need for education in the society was (or is) confined to a few objectives, schools were developed along such lines. Perhaps this was true of most ancient and medieval cultures. Indeed, this is true even today of education among some peoples and nations.

History indicates that education has presented tough problems in many cultures and times. *Change* is one unchanging fact of human life. The content of education has needed to be revised and kept up to date lest its supporting culture suffer. In long periods of static conditions educational programs did not tend to become inadequate or obsolete, and the content of education tended to be looked upon as fixed and final. The subject matter came to have great validity and even to be regarded as an end in itself. This uncritical view of the traditional curriculum has persisted even among people of today in mid-twentieth century American democracy.

For this mid-twentieth century American democracy of ours is the last society which should try to use a cut-and-dried curriculum! We can readily see the sense of that when we consider the nature of our society and tempo of the times in which we live. We shall certainly find that this society of ours is the most complex and varied culture the history books mention. So many skills, so great a variety

[1] Documentation of this section is hardly necessary in view of the references listed in Chapter 2. A good general reference for this section may be found in Ralph L. Pounds and Robert L. Garretson, *Principles of Modern Education* (New York: The Macmillan Company, 1962), pp. 135–146.

of knowledges, so wide a range of human abilities to be developed pose seemingly impossible tasks for American education. Here are more than one hundred and eighty-five millions of people, each with different abilities and capabilities to be developed. Furthermore, in this democratic culture, each has the right to expect educational opportunity to develop his abilities. Never have the schools of any people and culture been handed such a mandate. Little wonder that education ranks as an important public enterprise!

We next discover that the tempo of social change has been stepped up, especially in the past century and a half. Someone has said that the everyday life of Julius Caesar and Benjamin Franklin were much more alike than is ours compared with theirs. Far more material change has taken place in the past 150 years than occurred during thousands of years preceding. All this means that education has had unprecedented demands placed upon it in matters which previously could be dealt with when teachers got around to it. Changes do affect present-day education by requiring additional content and even thoroughgoing revisions of curricula. In this case it is not necessarily true that "Time makes ancient good uncouth," but that the times require the addition of other "goods" and truth. In a fast-changing society education must change to keep in step; to influence and affect social changes, it must move even faster.

Finally, we must observe that American democracy is inextricably enmeshed in the affairs and problems of this global world. Never again will it be possible for our leadership to concern itself with policy and practices confined to the national or even continental scene. "All the world's a stage" and there's not even an audience; all are participating in the world drama. There's no escaping this fact, time and distance have been so nearly eliminated by our modern means of communication and transportation, that all men are physically close to each other. Since we can not escape it, we shall have to live up to its demands. The first of its demands seems to be that all men must become close to each other in ways other than physical. Of such magnitude is this modern task of education!

Primary role of our schools

American schools have the mandate to educate the younger members of our society to fit them for active, intelligent participation in a democratic social order. It is also true that persons participate best in a free society by developing and making the most of their potential. Hence, the premium on optimum personality development, self-realization, you may call it in democratic society.

The culture of that democratic society is changing, and changing at a rate hitherto unknown. Moreover, our democracy is immediately and vitally affected by what happens elsewhere on this planet. We see, then, why it is imperative for education to keep pace with change, rapid change, and with global conditions. Clearly, public education must meet far greater challenges and demands today than has ever been the case in our history. It must accept people of all groups, all races, all creeds, all parties, and teach them to live and work together in a pluralistic society. It must help them to appreciate common values and agree upon common loyalties. It must help to open up opportunity for each child of democracy to make the most of his potentiality. It must be the school of all the people and of the community. Small wonder that we place emphasis upon quality in our search for capable youth for teaching in such a day and age!

Upon the general statement of the primary role of the school in our society there is practically uniform agreement. But agreement upon any one detail is a different matter. Since our society changes shall the schools try to determine the future of our society by educating for this or that? That's good for an argument any time, anywhere. Shall the schools indoctrinate for democracy? Reactions to this run the whole gamut from fierce approval to savage denunciation. Shall the schools teach values? Again, there are strong but irrevocably opposed views as to what values, how much, and how. And so it goes.

People are rather inconsistent about their views on education as we will find if we ask several persons a few questions. There is a vague, general feeling that nearly every problem which arises is a matter for the schools to do something about. But, the fellow who says this is likely to be just as insistent that the schools teach what he thinks or advocates about the matter. So we see where this gets us—to the point where teachers must be the wisest and sanest persons among us. We cannot determine what the curriculum should be by taking a straw vote; the majority will probably favor the introduction of any important problem to the curriculum, but it will hardly agree upon what should be done about it. So we are back where we started—on our own. What does the teacher do in such a case? Well, what can she do; what choices does she have? She can: (1) Ignore the problem; teach them the three R's; (2) Teach the view favored by the most people; (3) She can teach her own view of what is right and take her chances; (4) Teach the problem, giving all available information and showing the various proposed solutions and let pupils reach their own conclusions. Now what should she do?

There is another controversy about schools in our society. Many people see that the schools are gradually forced to take over more functions because of changes in other institutions and because of things which have not been done by other agencies. The hot lunch program is an example of the former; summer playgrounds of the latter. A recent one is: Shall new schools be built underground to serve as fallout shelters? These demands upon the school are not lessening; in fact, they tend to be enlarged and increased as our society turns up new problems and changes. There seems to be no lessening of this trend. We must go on working to justify the people's belief in the school and its role. We must justify their faith in the school as the short cut to active participation in society, as an effective and economical means of acculturation of the new members of our democracy. In short, the schools can never escape from their task of helping to remake society each generation or so. Youth will have part of the responsibility to keep from making another generation with many of the faults and problems we now have to plague us.

Education is a co-responsibility

In our society, indeed in any modern society, education is a function of a number of institutions. Both public and private agencies have educational responsibilities and functions in a democracy.

Their education programs may be formal, informal, or both. In any community some of these characteristics may be observed. All of us recognize the primary and most essential role of the home in the education of a child. The family background and early experiences of a child provide the most effective aspects of his education. By the time a child is ready to enter the kindergarten or the first grade, much of the basic patterns of attitudes toward other people and institutions of society and habits are relatively established. Hence, the importance of pre-school educational opportunity for children. Although educators since the days of Aristotle have often referred to the effectiveness and desirability of good early education of children, we have not yet made any consistent nationwide effort to provide for publicly-supported programs at this level.

Other early educative institutions are to be found in the play groups where the child learns some socialization and adjustment to others. Church school programs often have some part in the early growth and development of the child. Contacts with persons and businesses who serve the needs of the neighborhood are educative influences. A trip to the grocery or the drug store, seeing the postman or milkman make deliveries, or a bus ride downtown are illustrative of informal educative experiences.

The child in school continues to be educated by a number of agencies. Often learnings from informal, uncontrolled sources may seem more effective than those which occur in school, much to the teacher's chagrin. What teacher has not wished for the power to teach constructive values as effectively as slang terms and sayings are acquired by children. After school and on Saturdays the school child picks up much education from play groups, from the movies, the comic strips, television and the radio, visitors, and numerous contacts. Learning, whether accurate and desirable or not, is going on all the time—in school and out. In the heyday of radio, children learned theme music and signatures as tunes connected with favorite programs and not for what they really were.[2] Far more children learn singing commercials than ever learned an old English ballad. The child who has trouble with spelling sees many words spelled out in commercial advertising that do not follow the book. No wonder that teachers often wonder how they can do teaching of equal effectiveness to the influence of informal casual educative agencies and experiences.

The multitude of educative agencies and institutions is vastly increased for the later adolescent and adult members of our society. Added to the formal programs of the school and church are the services of numerous governmental agencies, even more private groups and institutions and a welter of commercial influence in the forms of advertising, radio programs, television, movies, circular letters, and propaganda in many forms. Industry and labor unions alike sponsor extensive training programs often with aid from public funds. Numerous correspondence and evening schools offer the adult courses in everything from how to read blue-prints to ballroom dancing in ten easy lessons. Small wonder that there is much confusion and controversy concerning the

[2] Students should investigate such former radio programs, such as *The Lone Ranger,* for examples of this kind of learning.

function of the school in our society and time!

Public schools have significant functions

Education is a social force, especially in a free society; everyone should be concerned about education. Parents and teachers must be particularly aware of the educational needs of individuals; citizens and teachers must be concerned that the schools serve the needs of society at the same time. In our pluralistic society public education must accept all learners, help them develop, and teach them what is necessary for the *whole* of society; especially, appreciation of and loyalty to the great guarantees and rights that make diversity possible, and the responsibilities that follow.[3] This marks the significance of the school as compared to other educative agencies in our time and society.

We cannot expect to find that public education always performs so capably and effectively in the fulfillment of the responsibilities which society delegates to it. Sometimes society has not definitely settled upon what its policy is or should be and this often leads to confusion in educational policy. It is not difficult to see how this happens in a democracy since all groups and interests may vigorously present their own preferences in matters of policy. Indeed, pressures are often placed directly upon the schools by groups, interests, and individuals. But this does suggest that schools must be free to explore and present all points-of-view, all the information, and all sides of important issues if the necessary, sound poli-

cies are to be developed *in* and *for* our democratic society. The responsibility of public education to contribute to social policy through *constructive criticism* is an important function in democracy.

Education has been said to have a unique function in American democracy.[4] We see that it *makes effective the work of other institutions* and agencies; the school teaches people what is necessary to make the other societal institutions and programs work. Public health, welfare, public works, conservation, and many other types of agencies find their programs of action depend upon education and especially public education. Anyone can study this question for himself by trying to find whether other local, state, and national agencies, both public and nonpublic, depend upon the work of the schools for their effectiveness.

The public school must accept and seek to accomplish its responsibility in the light of a clear understanding of the nature of its task. Teachers and members of boards of education are literally *trustees* since they represent society—the general public—all of us. This responsibility they must understand, accept, and discharge competently if public schools are to make their essential contribution to democratic society.

Our stake in public education

When we review our own understanding of this question we can hardly fail to have a positive attitude toward the school as a significant institution. It is clear that education is important in every culture; the school may or may not be

[3] Ellis Ford Hartford, *Moral Values in Public Education* (New York: Harper & Row, 1958), pp. 42–46.

[4] Educational Policies Commission, *The Unique Function of Education in American Democracy* (Washington: NEA), 1937.

important, depending upon the nature of its program and its effectiveness. The character and the quality of what the school does determine the significance of the school in our culture. Education was provided for in societies before schools came into being; it goes on in and through other agencies even after certain types of schools disappear. (Remember the Latin grammar school and the academy?) Whether the traditional high school can "hang on" is becoming a debatable issue, and we remember that the form of institutions changes more than do the functions. Teachers must learn to see the relation of the school to culture: culture changes, so the school must; culture accumulates, so the school has more to do; transmission of the culture is necessary for social control. The school must play its part in that along with other "agencies." If we accept, further, that new culture patterns are to be developed, the school should make its contribution to that end. Let's see how far we can go toward accepting this view: the school reflects the culture of the community or the nation; it should be a major force in changing the culture. This is its role in the culture.

How does this sound? The school reflects the culture of the community or the nation; it *should* be a major force in improving and guiding the changes within the culture. In American democracy, our diversity and dynamism have resulted in the marvelous public school which serves the educational functions of the whole society—John Q. Public and *all* his folks. John Q. Public's schools deserve teachers who appreciate this role; also, citizens and parents who understand and support good schools for everybody's children.

Future parents and teachers will be encouraged to know many of our ablest community and educational leaders have devoted attention to this basic concern. A good illustration may be found in a large city school system that summed up its position upon the basic philosophy of public schools by stating six basic principles as follows:

1. The schools serve all the people
2. The schools are concerned with the whole person
3. The schools are concerned with improving the quality of all aspects of living
4. The schools furnish continuing educational services
5. The schools make provision for thoughtful adjustment to social change
6. The schools cooperate with all educational agencies[5]

THE SCHOOL ACHIEVES AIMS AND OBJECTIVES

The nature of aims, objectives, and purposes

Educational *aims* or goals represent the desired direction of the programs and efforts of schools and teachers. *Objectives* are frequently specified as particular points or stages of accomplishments to be attained through a program or effort. *Purposes* is a general term used for all of these types of end-results the schools are trying to accomplish.[6]

The importance of aims and objectives can hardly be overestimated. They indicate the direction of educational effort

[5] *School and the Means of Education in Cincinnati* (Cincinnati: Board of Education, 1954), pp. 4–5. Used by permission.

[6] See Pounds and Garretson, *op. cit.*, pp. 175–178 for a discussion of these and related terms.

and specify particular desired results for a given program. Teachers plan and select materials and learning experiences in terms of these goals. Evaluation of progress and results would be meaningless without aims, either expressed or implied. Through all educational activity, the influence of accepted aims and objectives is felt in terms of interest, incentives, and efficiency of effort.

Aims and objectives are developed from the experiences and needs of people and society. The goals of a society relate to the interests and influence of the controlling groups of that society. Likewise, the educational goals of the schools reflect the nature and purposes of the sponsoring society. The nature and quality of the culture itself make the difference in the educational purposes of its schools and institutions of higher education.

Aims or purposes of education change because of social change, although frequently at a slower rate. Revolutionary movements in certain societies have effected drastic changes in educational agencies and systems. Examples of the French Revolution, the Revolutionary government of Mexico after 1917, and the reorganization of Japanese education after World War II illustrate the point. Conversely, the educational agencies have sometimes influenced the direction and change of societies, either by deliberate or inadvertent means.

The traditional aims of western education

Schools and colleges of the 20th century derive much of their purpose and programs from the long tradition that originated in the Mediterranean area of the globe upwards of six thousand years ago. Understandings of this character are some of the soundest reasons for study of cultural and intellectual history, and future leaders of our communities and nation should be sophisticated and perceptive in this respect. Those who would cherish our way of life and strengthen its environing social order need to appreciate the hazards that other Western and Oriental civilizations have experienced and their eventual decline or downfall. Analyses of civilizations and their records have often cited errors and weaknesses in their education as contributors to their unhappy ends.

Schools of modern-day America owe a great debt to the schools of ancient Greece and Rome and to the provisions for education among the Hebrews. The educational history of the Greeks reveals a remarkable diversity of educational goals and provisions ranging from the ideal of a responsible citizen in Athens to the single-minded fighting man of Sparta. The incredible artistic, intellectual, philosophical, and political accomplishments of ancient Greece have provided Western civilizations with imperishable subject matter, inspiration, and aims for school and higher education programs. The ideal of a liberal education for the well-rounded free man who could and would participate in managing the affairs of his city-state has contributed to the aim of education for citizenship in Western nations ever since Greek learning was revived in Renaissance times. The Western heritage from the Judeo-Christian tradition from the ancient Hebrews through the early Christian era and the Middle Ages that presents many emphases and forms of education in and for *religious aims* is another major contribution to the educational purposes of today. Our own early educational history in America reflected these two broad general aims or purposes, as is evident from the time and languages of the first school laws of Massachusetts Bay Colony.

Education in modern Europe was strongly shaped and influenced by the religious, economic, and political developments of the 16th and 17th centuries. The Reformation gave great impetus to the aim of popular literacy in order that people might read the Scriptures and find salvation. This inspired real progress in the establishment of schools for the common people with instruction in the vernacular. Religion was taught but there was also a strong emphasis upon nationalistic purposes. Loyalty to country and monarch, obedience to laws of the nation, service in the armed forces, were typical goals of schools for the children of commoners. The demands and needs of the mercantile economy and rising trade brought new emphases upon commercial and practical skills such as bookkeeping, mapmaking, navigation, penmanship, and surveying.

The new folk schools grew up as a parallel system to the Latin grammar schools that prospered after the models set by Vittorino de Feltre's famous "court school" in Mantua, Italy, in the fifteenth century. This dual system—separate schools for the common folk and for the privileged classes—became commonplace in most European nations in the post-Reformation period.

The earliest schools of New England and the New Netherlands reflected the educational ideas and institutions of the settlers' original homelands. Central in their provisions for education in their new homes were the goals of popular literacy for religious purposes and as the basis for knowledge of the laws of the province. Religion and citizenship were closely related in the early theocratic society of New England; they were likewise intermingled as the goals of education in the schools established by the town meetings in the colonies.

The schools of the colonies changed gradually as colonial communities grew more diverse and cosmopolitan. This process of ethnic, social, and religious growth toward heterogeneity made it necessary for the schools to change religious indoctrination to moral instruction and to open their doors to all the children. The end-result of several decades of social and educational change was that each state established a system of common schools, open to all children, tax-supported, and committed to provide educational opportunity for rich and poor alike.

The American common school inherited the Western tradition in education, but its sponsors—the people and representatives—refused to discriminate in favor of a class or a few or any particular group. All of its purposes and programs were freely shared by all its pupils, the children of all the people.

The lengthy chronicles of modern educational developments in Europe and America include many influences, innovators, and institutions that stand out prominently for important or significant reasons. Some of the "Great Educators" of all times would be included in a review of educational history. John Amos Comenius, Richard Mulcaster, John Locke, Jean Jacques Rousseau, Johann Heinrich Pestalozzi, Friedrich Froebel, and Johann Friedrich Herbart belong in any catalog of thinkers whose ideas later influenced educational purposes and programs of the young Republic. The great upsurge of new scientific discoveries and theories of the 19th century brought new concerns and content to education. Herbert Spencer's famous essay, "What knowledge is of most worth?" in 1860 raised questions about the priority schools should give knowledge, which could be placed in five categories of activities related to: (1) self-preservation, (2) securing the necessities of life, (3) rearing and discipline of the young, (4) proper social and political relations, and (5) miscellaneous leisure activities. The work of education was to prepare the individual to perform these activities as effectively as circumstances permit. The overall purpose of education was to prepare people for "complete living."[7] These ideas may be found in some form in various statements of educational purposes.

The discriminating student of history can see the long attenuated strands of traditional purposes and programs of education derived from classical civilization that survived and were revived to compose the starting point for modern secondary education in Renaissance times. Elementary education derived, in large part, from consequences of the Reformation period and the complex of social-economic and intellectual developments that followed. The rise of science and the intellectual revolution, that gradually transformed old subjects and brought new knowledge into existence, came to affect education profoundly. That potent leaven of democratic ideas and concepts implemented in the 18th century by the American and French revolutions and in the common school systems of the 19th, represents another great source of purposes for education in these United States.

Our national life has witnessed dramatic and profound transformations through the Industrial and Technological Revolutions of the past one and one-half centuries; the effects and consequences have brought new challenges and demands to American education that must be recognized as potential purposes and goals. Those who have not found the exciting new insights into the relationship of our educational systems and our historical tradition have missed one of the best chapters in the records of mankind.

Other sources of educational purposes

A brief review of the educational traditions we have inherited through Western civilization reveals sources of certain educational purposes. Other sources may be disclosed by study of the significant economic, intellectual, political, and social developments in American life. The great documents of American liberties and our constitutional form of government afford implications for democratic education that cannot be ignored. An educational system committed to the kind of social order envisioned and characterized by the Constitution will find basic purposes to pursue.[8] Appreciation of the "premises" of democracy should be the heritage of every American.

An important source of goals and

---

[7] Consult any recognized history of education for information on these and other great educators.

[8] See the broad purposes of the preamble and the guarantees of the Bill of Rights for example. See also, George C. Kyte, *The Elementary School Teacher at Work* (New York: Dryden Press, 1957), pp. 10–16.

purposes for education, particularly public education, is available in the studies and analyses of our democratic society. The findings show needs, problems, and changes in the educational goals of the schools and higher education. Many official study groups, named at the national level, bring in reports that merit consideration in this connection. The President's Committee on Recent Social Trends in 1932 was followed by findings of many other groups, under both official and private sponsorship, during the depression, war, and postwar decades. Reference has been made to the President's Commission on National Goals, the Panel Reports for the Rockefeller Brothers Fund Study, and comparable studies that have made fine contributions in recent years.

One of the most provocative studies of this type by an educational organization was that of the NEA Committee on Social-Economic Goals of America.[9] The study committee functioned in the early stages of the Great Depression and problems of economic distribution, disparities, and emergency conditions were current. The objectives framed by the Committee were designed to strengthen the American way of life and to underwrite the kind of educational outcomes that would enhance its survival and progress. The report found that every individual was entitled to the following: (1) hereditary strength, (2) physical security, (3) participation in an evolving culture, (4) an active flexible personality, (5) suitable occupation, (6) economic security, (7) mental secu-

rity, (8) equality of opportunity, (9) freedom, and (10) fair play. These goals were expected to direct the energies and efforts of leaders and educational institutions into the task of improving our society by education of people for these objectives.

Certain educational leaders and school groups have derived educational purposes from noteworthy studies and analyses of democratic society. The needs and values of democracy, once identified, can be recognized as goals for the educational programs. These may reflect both individual growth and development and a quality of social living. One experimental school faculty undertook to identify the characteristics of a democratic society and of a democratic personality in parallel columns and proceeded from this to formulate seven purposes directly related to democratic values. These were the development of: (1) social sensitivity, (2) cooperativeness, (3) ability and zeal to utilize the method of intelligence in solving all problems, (4) creativeness, (5) skills in democratic living, (6) interpretation of democracy, and (7) self-direction.[10]

One of the noteworthy studies of this kind was the Citizenship Education Project of Teachers College, Columbia University, in cooperation with over 500 school systems over the nation (1949–1955). Among the pertinent findings was an emphasis upon the "premises" of American democracy, explicit or implicit in the documents and structure of our democratic society. Premises were expressed in terms of beliefs, rights, guar-

[9] Fred J. Kelley, "Social-Economic Goals of America," *NEA Journal*, **XXIII**, No. 1 (January 1934), pp. 6–12; see also Fred J. Kelley, *et al.*, *Implications of Social-Economic Goals for Education* (Washington: NEA, 1937).

[10] Florence Greenhoe Robbins, *Educational Sociology* (New York: Henry Holt and Company, 1953), pp. 470–475.

antees, and responsibilities of "The Free Individual, The Free Government, The Free Economy, and The Free World."[11]

The needs of children and/or youth have been subjects of many authoritative studies in recent decades and the findings represent another significant source of educational goals and purposes. Among these may be mentioned the Children's Charter of the 1930 White House Conference on Children and Youth and subsequent pledges and statements formed by that decennial gathering. The 1937 report of the American Youth Commission announced a comprehensive statement of the needs of the youth of the nation.[12] Youth's needs were expressed in seven areas: (1) congenial companionship, respect, and admiration of their fellows; (2) opportunity to experience satisfying achievement; (3) an opportunity for economic independence; (4) instruction in family living and responsibilities; (5) to understand political and economic conditions; (6) instruction in maintaining and improving their physical and mental health; (7) many worth-while ideals and inspiration.

Another approach stressed the preparation of children for life in democracy by a program of democratic living in the schools. Group participation, shared choices and decisions, and the mutual acceptance that derives from these processes represented the essential needs of children who will become citizens of a democratic society. The overall aim was to enhance growth in accepting responsi-bility. The four main areas of growth toward this general end were: (1) ability and desire to control conduct toward worthy ends; (2) understanding of important relationships existing in the life of the community and society; (3) broadening their interests to include high types of esthetic experiences; and (4) ability to use the tools of learning and to find joy in their use.[13]

The schools of thought represented in American philosophy, particularly the philosophers of education, and the formulations of notable scholarly groups provide another major source of purposes of education. Many schemes and pages of classifying and characterizing these are available for study and reflection. A convenient brief classification that will illustrate this general source utilizes six alternatives:

1. *Perennialism* (or neo-humanism): Education teaches the eternal verities, trains the intellect;
2. *Essentialism* (or social evolutionism): Education is made up of the timeless essentials of the social heritage;
3. *Social realism.* Education is preparation for living in present-day society.
4. *Experimentalism*: Education of critically-minded individuals for critical thinking and use of problem-solving methods;
5. *Reconstructionism*: Education for the new society based on the findings of the scientific methods and findings to the end, and
6. Educational *"laissez-faire"*: Education of the individual for his own maximum development.[14]

[11] See *Citizenship Education Project, When Men Are Free: Premises of American Liberty* (Boston: Houghton Mifflin Co., 1955).

[12] H. R. Douglass, *Secondary Education for Youth in Modern America* (Washington: American Council on Education, 1937).

[13] John A. Hockett and W. E. Jacobsen, *Modern Practices in the Elementary School* (Boston: Ginn & Co., 1943), p. 4.

[14] See Pounds and Garretson, *op. cit.,* pp. 202–208, for a helpful discussion of this source of educational objectives.

The small but influential organization, chiefly known as the Progressive Education Association (1918–1954) early formulated seven "principles" that represented the new or changed emphases that American education should make. The original list appeared in 1924 and reveals little that appears controversial to those who read it today. It stated that children should have *freedom to develop naturally,* learn to govern themselves rather than be under arbitrary law, have free use of an environment rich in materials, and full opportunity for initiative and self-expression; *interest* should be the motive of all work. The teacher should *guide* rather than serve as taskmaster. Teachers should *encourage use of all the senses and the study of real life activities* rather than exclusive use of books. They should stress the *use of information to draw sound conclusions and to express them clearly and effectively.* The scientific study of child development, including growth and health, improved reporting upon all aspects of school work, and closer cooperation between home and school in the interest of all children were favored. The school should become a *laboratory* where worthy ideas are to be encouraged and tried out. Such were the original principles of the most provocative and controversial groups ever to exert influence on the American educational scene during the period between the two World Wars.[15] It is probably true that no other group in American education has ever been criticized and judged by so many who had never read the basic principles for which the organization stood.

During the Thirties decade of the Great Depression, a number of important groups made reports and pronouncements that expressed or implied purposes and goals for American education. One of these, the Essentialist Committee for the Advancement of American Education, presented its platforms in 1938.[16] Study of this position in comparison with the publications of various other contemporary groups reflects the diversity of opinions and views of modern American education.

Still other sources and examples of purposes of education could be examined if necessary. At this point, it may be well to reiterate some observations about purposes and practices: (1) schools do have (or had) purposes but these grow outmoded and may be neglected in practice; (2) the purposes should be re-examined and revised by those concerned about schools in the light of changes in societal and individual needs; (3) the purposes and programs of American schools have changed materially in more than three centuries of public concern about education; (4) although purposes and programs of American education grow ever more complex and varied, these are frequently left to be accomplished in casual or haphazard fashion; (5) as our society changes even more drastically and ever more rapidly, the necessity for consistent attention to logical and systematic study and revision of educational purposes and programs becomes imperative; (6) the responsible leadership of our schools and

---

[15] The original statement is in the first issue of *Progressive Education,* (April 1924). A brief account may be found in H. G. Good, *A History of American Education,* (second edition), (New York: The Macmillan Company, 1962), pp. 391–396.

[16] William C. Begley, "An Essentialist's Platform for the Advancement of American Education," *Educational Administration and Supervision* (April 1938), pp. 241–256.

colleges must enlist the support and participation of thoughtful citizens in studies of their purposes, lest our nation suffer for lack of programs and teachers adequate for the times and the functions that education should serve—both individual and societal.

Public education serves individual and social purposes

The common school carries out its role in our democratic society through its efforts to achieve aims and objectives. These may change or be modified from time to time in particular details but they include both *individual* and *social* purposes. Parents and teachers desire to help each child develop as fully as possible physically, mentally, emotionally, socially, morally, and spiritually into well-rounded, adequate personalities. In this process it is expected they will become competent persons for themselves, and for their home, economic, ethical, and civic responsibilities. The other aspect of the general aim of education is the improvement of society through the growth of a more competent and effective generation able to deal with local, national, and world responsibilities. As this oncoming generation lives, makes choices, and works toward desirable individual and social goals, the demand for and know-how of a better society are being developed. This double-edged goal of education was expressed rather effectively by the Commission on the Social Studies over three decades ago:

Education . . . is concerned with the development of rich and many-sided personalities capable of cooperating in a social order designed to facilitate the creation of the largest number of rich and many-sided personalities.[17]

A dozen years later something similar was expressed in the famous Harvard Report entitled *General Education in a Free Society* as follows:

The quality of alert and aggressive individualism is essential to good citizenship; and the good society consists of individuals who are independent in outlook and think for themselves while also willing to subordinate their individual good to the common good.[18]

Statements of general aims leave much latitude to schools and teachers in working toward specific objectives. It is here that changes and revisions become necessary as faculties, study groups, and individual teachers formulate their immediate goals and provide for their implementation through learning experiences. This must continue until those who teach have expressed their purposes and goals clearly and accepted them as important to work toward. Unless teachers develop and accept goals that motivate their work the study of purposes is little different from an oldtime copy book exercise!

The two general statements serve to emphasize the dual nature of purposes and objectives of education in American society. Our schools must be concerned with both kinds of objectives, *individual* and *societal*. Democracy means *people,* concern about people, their optimum development, and self-realization. Therefore,

[17] American Historical Association, Commission on the Social Studies, *Conclusions and Recommendations* (New York: Scribner, 1932), p. 31. Used by permission.

[18] Report of the Harvard Committee, *General Education in a Free Society* (Cambridge: Harvard University Press, 1945), p. 77. Used by permission.

an emphasis upon individual development should characterize the purposes of American education.

The other side of the list, societal goals and purposes, may be thought of as complementary rather than antipathetical or unrelated to the individual goals. This might well be true of social goals in another type of society. Democracy places a premium upon individuality, richness not sameness, diversity not uniformity, and versatility. The individual goals need only be complemented by the necessary purposes designed to strengthen and extend the pluralistic and permissive social order that prizes personal fulfillment. An examination of the purposes of American public education then may well be undertaken from both standpoints, *individual* and the *social*. Many of the formal statement of aims, objectives, and purposes of education tend to stress the former; the principal element of the latter should be the essence of democracy, the minimum essentials that comprise democracy. The beliefs and values are to be understood and lived by those who would cherish and retain the democratic way of life.

Statements of Purposes of Education

SOME SIGNIFICANT GENERAL LISTS

The past half-century has produced many statements of this kind. A review of education textbooks will provide evidence of many statements and revisions of educational objectives during the past fifty years. Many of these reflected the views of Herbert Spencer which were far in advance of his time and received little attention before the turn of the century. The work of this frontier thinker and the famous Seven Cardinal Principles that appeared in 1918 have had tremendous influence upon educational aims and curriculums. Since then we have had many noteworthy statements of aims and objectives for education. Among them was the list of six great concerns of education by Chapman and Counts in 1924: (1) health, (2) family life, (3) economic life, (4) civic life, (5) recreation, and (6) religion.[19] This, together with the "Seven

[19] James C. Chapman and George S. Counts, *Principles of Education* (Boston: Houghton Mifflin, 1924), pp. 195–364.

Cardinal Principles" (1918) and Parker's list of aims for the elementary school (1919) represented influential statements as American education entered a period of vast growth after the First World War.

The number and variety of statements of aims and purposes have become profuse in recent decades. A number have been selected to show something of the scope and nature of the many expressions and statements relating to public education.

The most notable statements of educational aims and objectives have not appeared in any logical order or sequence. Purposes of education in general, no matter how clear in the early stages, tend to become confused and to be taken for granted at later periods. We have noted that certain themes or motives have dominated American education at various times in our history. As the areas or levels of American education became better developed, more consistent objectives were found necessary, although they were sometimes belated in appearance. It happened that we had for twenty years a fairly well-accepted statement of objectives for the high school before we had a comparable general list of aims. This finally appeared in the fourfold list of "Purposes of Education in American Democracy" issued by the Educational Policies Commission in 1938. The statement received wide attention and was relatively favorably received by our educational leadership.

Purposes of education in American democracy

At this point, it seems desirable to have a good look at the general objectives of education expressed by the Educational Policies Commission of the NEA in 1938, which will serve to illustrate specific objectives which influence the work of the schools. These are expressed in four groups of purposes as follows: (1) self-realization, (2) human relationships, (3) economic efficiency, (4) civic responsibility.[20] You may wish to study carefully the complete list, noting the skillful blending of individual and social aims of education in each group.

Here is the list adapted for brevity:

I

The educated person—
—has an appetite for learning
—can speak the mother tongue clearly
—reads the mother tongue efficiently
—writes the mother tongue effectively
—solves his problems of counting and calculating
—is skilled in listening and observing
—understands the basic facts concerning health and disease
—protects his own health and that of his dependents

[20] Educational Policies Commission, *The Purposes of Education in American Democracy* (Washington: The Commission), 1938.

—works to improve the health of the community
—is participant and spectator in many sports and other pastimes
—has mental resources for the use of leisure
—appreciates beauty
—gives responsible direction to his own life

II

The educated person—
—puts human relationships first
—enjoys a rich, sincere, and varied social life
—can work and play with others
—observes the amenities of social behavior
—appreciates the family as a social institution
—conserves family ideals
—is skilled in homemaking
—maintains democratic family relationships

III

The educated person—
—knows the satisfaction of good workmanship
—understands the requirements and opportunities for various jobs
—has *selected* his occupation
—succeeds in his chosen vocation
—maintains and improves his efficiency
—appreciates the social value of his work
—plans the economics of his own life
—develops standards for guiding his expenditures
is an informed and skillful buyer
—takes appropriate measures to safeguard his interests

IV

The educated person—
—is sensitive to the disparities of human circumstance
—acts to correct unsatisfactory conditions
—seeks to understand social structures and social processes

—has defenses against propaganda
—respects honest differences of opinion
—has a regard for the nation's resources
—measures scientific advance by its contribution to the general welfare
—is a cooperating member of the world community
—respects the law
—is economically literate
—accepts his civic duties
—acts upon an unswerving loyalty to democratic ideals

Other noteworthy general lists have appeared in our educational literature but most which have appeared since 1938 show the influence of this statement by the Educational Policies Commission. We may note, for example, the aims expressed in the Report of the Inquiry into the Cost and Character of Education in New York State or the reports of surveys of schools in St. Louis or Pittsburgh as illustrations. In the Fifties the work of the National Citizen's Commission for the Public Schools, in cooperation with numerous local citizen's groups, resulted in searching inquiries and studies of the aims and purposes of our common schools.

A culminating effort to focus the attention of citizen's groups upon public education needs at local community levels, followed by conferences in each state, reached its climax in the White House Conference on Education in 1955. Hundreds of small study-groups reported findings upon several major questions about American public education in the future.[21] A consensus of the reports that defined the task of the elementary and secondary schools in the face of expanding enroll-

[21] *The Reports of the White House Conference on Education,* Washington, D.C., November 28–December 1, 1955 (Washington: U.S. Government Printing Office, 1955), pp. 1–2.

ments and new responsibilities yielded a total of 14 aims.

The schools should continue to develop: (1) the fundamental skills of communication; (2) appreciation of our democratic heritage; (3) knowledge of American institutions, civil rights, and responsibilities; (4) respect and appreciation for human values and for the beliefs of others; (5) ability to think and evaluate constructively and creatively; (6) effective work habits and self-discipline; (7) social competence as a contributing member of family and community; (8) ethical behavior based on sense of moral and spiritual values; (9) intellectual curiosity and eagerness for lifelong learning; (10) aesthetic appreciation and self-expression in the arts; (11) physical and mental health; (12) wise use of time including constructive leisure activities; (13) understanding of the physical world and man's relation to it as represented through basic knowledge of the sciences; and (14) an awareness of our relationships with the world community. The concern of the Conference embraced both individual and societal goals for American public education. The Conference view as expressed in the preface to the Reports noted that education is necessary for the optimum development and enrichment of persons, and that it is a sound and required investment in the future well-being of the nation and its citizens.

SOME REPRESENTATIVE SPECIFIC LISTS

Objectives for the elementary school

Aims and objectives for elementary education have not received as much attention in our educational literature as one might expect. This has probably been due to a tendency to take this part of the educational program for granted. Many people think the job of the elementary school is the teaching of the "3 R's" and let it go at that. There has never been an effort to study the elementary school on a scale to compare with several studies which have been made in the fields of secondary and higher education, a situation that will undoubtedly be corrected in the years ahead. Already two interesting developments may be noted. Early in 1948 the Educational Policies Commission published its *Education for All-American Children,* destined to become a classic in our educational literature. In twelve states of the South, a Cooperative Study of Elementary Education was carried on from 1947 to 1953 by the Southern Association of Colleges and Secondary Schools and eight other regional groups.

One searches the literature for any statement of objectives of elementary education which has received general acceptance or attention comparable to those we have noted in other fields of education. Perhaps this is partly due to the prevalent notion that most people have a pretty good idea of the purposes and functions of the elementary school. One writer defined elementary education simply by saying it referred to attitudes, skills, ideas and insights that everyone needed to live in the American social environment.[22] In effect, it has been the common denominator in preparation for life for the American people in past generations.

Early views of the great educators had much influence upon the thinking on purposes and goals of elementary education as did the Seven Cardinal Principles

list for the secondary schools. One of the early influential statements on the aims of elementary education appeared shortly after the First World War. Dr. Samuel C. Parker proposed that the overall aim should be the achievement of *happiness.* His analysis of the factors in the achievement of happiness led to four broad social aims of teaching: (1) good health, (2) harmless enjoyment of leisure, (3) good will, and (4) social service.[23]

The lack of a commonly-accepted set of aims for the elementary schools does not mean there was no concern or discussion of purposes. Study of the various statements and pronouncements of groups and thinkers reveals a variety of implied aims and purposes. In view of current discussion of public education there is ground for differing interpretations of the aims of the elementary school. A list prepared during a study by New York City school administrators will serve as a point of departure.[24]

According to this group study every child should:

1. understand and practice desirable social relationships;
2. discover and develop his own desirable individual aptitudes;
3. develop the habit of critical thinking;
4. appreciate and desire worthwhile activities;
5. gain command of the common integrating knowledge and skills;
6. develop a sound body and desirable mental attitudes.

This list of aims or goals for elementary education may appear formidable at first but some discussion and thought should

[22] John T. Wahlquist, *Introduction to American Education* (New York: Ronald Press, 1958), p. 341.

[23] Samuel C. Parker, *General Methods of Teaching in Elementary Schools* (Chicago: Ginn, 1919), pp. 34–50.

[24] Curriculum Bulletin No. 1, *Changing Concepts and Practices in Elementary Education,* New York, Board of Education, 1945.

prepare you to visualize what the terms mean. Some of the best aids to this insight are in the form of illustrative programs

The great upsurge of interest in the public schools stimulated by the National Citizens Commission for the Public Schools led to many studies of what our schools should do. A great number of these local study groups brought their work to a formulation-of-findings stage in time for participation in the conferences held in preparation for the 1955 White House Conference on Public Education. Many useful illustrative statements from communities of all types over the nation were available to show the kinds of goals and purposes local citizens groups formulated for the elementary school. A report from *Better Schools* summarized the strongest beliefs and views as they appeared in this type of studies.[25] The ten most important objectives for the elementary school were reported as follows: (1) mastery of essential skills; (2) mastery of essential knowledge; (3) good health; (4) good citizenship; (5) good character; (6) good home life (develop the skills and personal traits that strengthen the American home); (7) ability to think; (8) ability to get along with others; (9) personal adjustment; and (10) development of individual abilities and talents. Other lay groups have given increasing attention to the basic purposes and goals of our schools, many of which have been reported in popular magazines as well as educational journals. The public schools are the people's school and many people have ideas about what they should try to accomplish.

[25] See *Better Schools*, **I**, National Citizens Commission for the Public Schools, for this and other reports.

All citizens should know about the work of professional groups and leaders in the development of goals and purposes of the common schools. Some of the best work has been by the Educational Policies Commission whose epochal volume *Education for All-American Children* listed some enduring values, with implications for goals of elementary education.[26] The following statements contain general objectives:

1. A good elementary school, therefore, will help to develop those basic skills and that sturdy independence and initiative which will enable our citizens to attack the problems that face them and to press forward toward ever-improving solutions.
2. A good elementary school, therefore, strives for the discovery and full development of all the human and constructive talents of each individual.
3. A good elementary school, therefore, emphasizes social responsibility and the cooperative skills necessary to the progressive improvement of social institutions.

Implicit in these values are important goals for the elementary school which good teachers recognize and accept. Other postwar studies of elementary education that provide challenging and helpful objectives for the common school are available in the literature of the field.[27]

[26] Educational Policies Commission, *Education for All-American Children* (Washington: NEA, 1948), pp. 2–4.

[27] See *A Good School for Children* (Nashville: George Peabody College for Teachers, 1951), for a helpful statement; see also Nolan C. Kearney, *Elementary School Objectives* (New York: Russell Sage Foundation, 1953), and George C. Kyte, *The Elementary School Teacher at Work* (New York: Dryden Press, 1957), pp. 26–29 for a brief summation.

Aims for the secondary school

America's early secondary schools had a single aim, the preparation of young men (and later, women) for college. Later secondary schools established for broader purposes have tended to emphasize the preparatory function although the multi-purpose high school is clearly the choice of most American communities. The story of the growth of the comprehensive high school is related to the long catalog of school purposes.

Many noteworthy and influential statements of objectives have been made at the level of secondary education. Among those commonly mentioned are the Seven Cardinal Principles set forth by the NEA Commission on Reorganization of Secondary Education in 1918.[28] Note the familiar sound of these: (1) health, (2) command of fundamental processes, (3) worthy home membership, (4) vocation, (5) citizenship, (6) worthy use of leisure, (7) ethical character. This statement of some thirty-five years ago grew out of a period of readjustment and revision in education during and after World War I.

No statement has had greater influence upon the aims and content of American education than these Seven Cardinal Principles of Secondary Education. The list still meets the views of many teachers; the only note of recent criticism has been constructive, viz., that an eighth item—*"world citizenship"*—should be added.

One of America's greatest leaders in secondary education, Alexander Inglis of Harvard, formulated a comprehensive set of aims and functions of the secondary school that appeared almost simultaneously with the Cardinal Principles. His general aims were three in number:

1. *The civic-social aim* (knowledges, habits, and ideals that make the good citizen);
2. *The economic-vocational aim* (knowledges in economics, human relationships, aptitudes, etc. and competence in vocational skills); and
3. *The individualistic-avocational aim* (development of higher cultural interests, personal habits, and traits, and leisure activities with social benefits).

The school should implement the accomplishment of these aims by and through six kinds of procedures which Inglis termed "functions": (1) The *adaptive* or adjustive function (aid pupil to adjust to physical, human, and social environment); (2) the *integrative* function (help students to have shared interests and accept normative practices and behavior to make for societal cohesion); (3) the *differentiative* function (help pupils to develop differing capacities to meet society's need for variety of talent); (4) the *propaedeutic* function (prepare pupil for next step whether it's a job, the army, or college); (5) the *selective* function (opportunity to gain work experience and select among interests); and (6) the *diagnostic* or directive function (pupil evaluation of own strengths and weaknesses).[29] The work of Inglis left its imprint upon secondary education in these United States.

A continuation of our study of the aims and objectives of secondary schools

[28] Commission on the Reorganization of Secondary Education, *Cardinal Principles of Secondary Education* (Washington: U.S. Government Printing Office, 1918).

[29] Alexander Inglis, *Principles of Secondary Education* (Boston: Houghton Mifflin, 1918), pp. 367–375.

should disclose challenging statements by great leaders in the field, pronouncements by educational groups such as the North Central Association of Colleges and Secondary Schools, the Educational Policies Commission, the American Youth Commission, the Commission on Life Adjustment Education for Youth, and many others. One of the most recent of these is the Educational Policies Commission publication *Education for All-American Youth,* a report which will repay time spent in careful study.[30] It would be a good experience to study this statement to discover what purposes of education the Educational Policies Commission expressed or implied. Here we shall find "The Imperative Needs of Youth," (see page 212) one truly distinctive way to express secondary school goals and purposes.

Other provocative statements about the purposes of secondary schools are available; others will surely be formulated if the teachers and parents of American youth keep alert to their responsibility. We can make our contribution to the improvement of secondary (and other) schools in our own community by helping all concerned to set sound and adequate purposes first.

Objectives for higher education

Concern about aims and objectives of the colleges is very old in this country but there have been long periods when comparatively little re-examination and revision have taken place. In recent years,

this has become a matter of serious study by certain leaders and groups in higher education. It is certain that some form of study concerning the purposes of higher education programs is currently underway in a large number of institutions of various types. During the past 25 years a number of colleges and universities have experimented with programs of general education and this has involved the re-examination of aims and objectives. The ever-increasing junior college movement has stimulated review and further study of higher education programs at many institutions. Recent statements such as those by the Harvard Committee and the reports on the American Council on Education have occasioned a great deal of discussion and controversy.

A concise list of broad objectives for general education has received much attention. There were four in number as stated by the Harvard Report: (1) to think effectively; (2) to communicate thought; (3) to make relevant judgments; and (4) to discriminate among values.[31]

For purposes of comparison one list of objectives for general education has been adapted from a statement by a representative group:

General education should guide the student to:
1. *Health*—improve and maintain health; help protect the health of others;
2. *Communication*—communicate in his own language (oral and written) at a level adequate for an educated person;
3. *Adjustment*—make sound emotional and social adjustments;
4. *Family and Marriage*—understand problems and gain basic orientation

---

[30] Educational Policies Commission, *Education for All-American Youth* (Washington: NEA, 1944), p. 421, or see the pamphlet *Planning for American Youth* (Washington: NEA, 1944), p. 64. See also the enlarged recent revision entitled *Education for All-American Youth—A Further Look,* 1953.

[31] *General Education in a Free Society* (Cambridge, Mass.: Harvard University Press, 1944).

for satisfactory adjustment to family and marriage;

5. *Citizenship*—do his part as an active and intelligent citizen;
6. *Scientific Attitude*—understand and use his natural environment for human welfare; use a scientific approach to problem solving;
7. *Literature*—find self-expression in and derive ideas and ideals from literature;
8. *Fine Arts*—find self-expression and appreciations in and from fine arts;
9. *Clear Thinking*—practice clear and integrated thinking about life's meanings and values;
10. *Vocation*—choose the vocation best suited to his talents and offering his best contribution to society.

Effective lists and statements of higher education abound in our educational literature. The catalogs of many good colleges may offer evidence of this. The *Education Index* will give many leads on recent articles on this subject.

Views concerning the purposes of higher education would vary widely even among the students and professors on a given campus. At present, there is no authoritative statement of purposes which has received acceptance comparable to some of the statements for secondary education.

Work really begins here

Many other useful and thoughtful lists of objectives could be brought in for attention if time and space permitted and if it were necessary. In any case, we shall, as education students, have opportunities to learn more about these statements. It is vastly more important here and now for everyone to begin his own thinking and study of aims and objectives of education. We should always have an interest in education. We may work in schools with boys and girls when our views and theirs will become the real aims and objectives we will strive to accomplish. Our own best ideas about the purposes of education should emerge and develop as we teach, or when we work with parents and teachers in the schools and the community. One significant kind of opportunity is that of working with groups of parents and teachers in considering the goals and purposes of our schools. Those citizens who take an alert and interested part in such movements in the school community will share many common understandings gained from cooperation with other interested persons.[32] Participation helps people to realize their potentialities as community leaders; this will happen to us if we continue to think and work for our ideas about quality education for today's democracy.

One of the most significant kinds of understanding is that of appreciation of the true nature of democracy and of its values. This and the potential for human development and happiness are taken for granted by many persons who enjoy these boons without knowing their full significance. Those who have the opportunity for a good education, especially a college education, should endeavor to appreciate the society that has so generously afforded so many privileges to its youth.

We must understand the real nature of democracy, its essential beliefs and assumptions. We can then make better sense in our efforts to explain that indispensable role education must play in our society and discern more clearly how this is to be accomplished.

[32] A useful guide for local study groups is available in *What Should Our School Accomplish?*, National Citizens Commission for the Public Schools (1953).

Education *in* and *for* Democracy

Education in a democracy is unique and different because only democracy permits expression of and tolerance for other points of view. In a totalitarian society education is forced to indoctrinate for one point of view. This is an easier role for schools because it can utilize all the sanctions, taboos, and compulsions necessary to accomplish the desired purpose. In a democracy, it is sometimes difficult to see how far the schools can go either toward indoctrination for one viewpoint or toward permitting full freedom to those interested in undermining democratic society. If we indoctrinate solely and completely for democracy, do we still have a democracy? On the other hand, if we permit the enemies of democracy to exercise civil rights will they not destroy the very values which we prize most highly? Is this the either-or question that it may have appeared to be?

One possible answer we can see is this: we should have academic freedom, to be sure (democracy can stand a healthy diversity of opinion and values), but let's put equal emphasis upon teaching and experiencing democracy so as to give the latter an even break with its competitors. Emphasis should also be given to the real evaluation of rights; each one is counter-weighted by a responsibility that goes with its exercise. Along with academic freedom the teacher also accepts academic responsibility. Both of these also relate to the student's right to have access to all sources of possible truth. Some of our schools could do a great deal more along this line. Such an education would enable more people to do more of their own thinking about democracy and other systems and their deliberate choice should govern. If we insist upon having full knowledge about all systems, if we rule out the specious comparisons of the advantages of some other system to the disadvantages of democracy we can give an adequate and satisfactory answer to the critics of democracy.

CENTRAL BELIEFS AND VALUES OF DEMOCRACY

What are those essential beliefs and values which characterize democracy? These have not always been stated as clearly nor understood as extensively as they should be. The following list of important understandings that citizens should have will serve as a starting point for further study and consideration. It is a product of the renowned Teacher Education Study sponsored by The American Council on Education:

1. *Faith in freedom.*
2. *Faith in popular government.*
3. *Respect for human personality*—as unique and different, yet similar—thus offering strength to society. Each has worth of its own.
4. *Recognition of the social nature of people.* Men live by interdependence. There is no person who lives completely apart or alone. The individual is really an individual-in-society.
5. *Faith in reason as a means of solving problems and making decisions.* Thus, the common purposes of men are the methods of intelligent democracy.
6. *Possibility of self-improvement.* Men's potentialities are almost endless; by faith, by reasoning, by experiment, we can improve and grow.

7. *Possibility of improving our democratic society.* Admittedly, our democracy is not perfect, not even complete; there is much to do to make it work better. But, a democratic people can do this, working under the above faiths as rapidly as they choose. "The sky's the limit" for a dynamic democracy.[33]

Another list of essential beliefs about democracy was formulated and used in the Teacher Education Study by Dr. Karl Bigelow of Columbia University, who served as the Director. These essential characteristics of democracy are as follows:

1. A belief in the unique worth of each individual. Each person may be thought of as possessing potentialities to which no limit may in advance be set. These dynamic and creative qualities of persons may be seen as a fundamental asset to society. Democracy then must provide freedom of opportunity for all in order that these diversities and strengths may be developed and used.

2. Balancing the first is the *recognition of the interrelatedness of human living.* No man can live to himself· alone. People cannot realize their potentialities except in relation to others. The inescapable fact that human existence is of a social character is the centripetal force balancing the centrifugal force of No. 1.

3. The third characteristic of democracy is a *profound faith in reasonableness as the sovereign means for the solution of conflicts.* Of course, there are and will be differences of opinion and clashes of interests in democracies. But democratic men believe that differences can be dealt with through reflective thinking, in a spirit of good will, and without resort to violence.

This implies reliance upon facts, upon inferences drawn from facts, upon discussion of those inferences, and friendly persuasion.[34]

The nature of these essential characteristics of democracy requires a delicate balance between individual development and social responsibility. Making democracy work and grow is infinitely more difficult than maintaining a regimented totalitarian social order. Democracy makes diversity inevitable but draws added strengths and richness from that same diversity.

Democracy is the only social system which can endure a plurality of values and healthy diversity of beliefs and practices. In social evolution it is a relatively high type of an organization characterized by diversity and versatility but in what we may call balance. In this democratic system of plural values and diverse strengths self-discipline becomes the ideal.

Professor John Brubacher of Yale and Michigan, an outstanding educational philosopher and writer, has noted that democracy underlies all aspects of our society, that it means infinitely more than a form of government that makes decisions by "nose-counting." Four of the meanings democracy has for the earnest student.[35]

1. A form of government of, by, and *for the many,* based on moral and ethical concepts of human worth. Sources of this view go back to classical Greece, to the early Christian belief in the brotherhood

[33] The seven points listed above have been adapted from *Teachers for Our Times,* a report by the Commission on Teacher Education (Washington: American Council on Education, 1944). Used by permission.

[34] *Cultural and Social Elements in the Education of Teachers,* a report by the Commission on Teacher Education (Washington: American Council on Education, 1940).

[35] John S. Brubacher, *Modern Philosophies of Education* (New York: McGraw-Hill, 1939), pp. 147–164.

of men as God's children and in their worth. American sources in the Declaration of Independence and the Bill of Rights serve to emphasize that democracy is more than a form of government resting upon popular suffrage, depending on discussion, debate, and voting for its decisions. It is also the view that every human being must count and that the unique, distinctive, potential value of each must be realized. (Does this imply anything concerning the teacher's attitude toward the child?)

2. Democracy is truly a way of life— a kind of human association in which purposes are shared. No one should be barred from full participation in the community enterprise; all classes, races, sexes, or ethnic groups should take part in democratic society to which each one contributes his abilities and experience. In a real sense, the worth of a society can be judged by the number and variety of interests consciously shared within the groups and with other people. (Does this imply anything for the organization of schools, and grouping?) This is a respect in which our society is not perfect; it is an ideal of what society should become. Thus, we have a dynamic future for democracy—we have much to work for. Democracy is not decadent as the Nazis claimed, it is not even full-grown.

3. Democracy is a distinctive method of thought by voluntary choice. Experiment, tested thought, and reason—these are methods of democratic-minded persons. Democracy, then, is as versatile, facile, and effective as the number and variety of the thoughts of its people. No wonder Hitler lost; he lost by throwing out much of the capacity for thinking and problem solving. Democracy has something there!

4. Democracy has a new metaphysics of its own. It affirms that the whole is more than the sum of its parts, that our democracy is better and stronger than the sum of 185 millions of people. Moreover, the strengths and diversity of all these people can do things. We can almost literally create our own destiny. In effect, "the sky is the limit."

Recently, a great foundation started to make an educational film about the meaning of democracy. Some of the best scholars of the nation were asked to suggest the "very essence" of what democracy is. That decision took nearly a year, but it was significant. Democracy, they finally said, depended upon *shared purposes* and *shared decisions.* Of course, there are many implications in these two essentials. Two conditions serve to facilitate democracy: namely, *economic balance* and *popular enlightenment.*[36]

One of America's revered and respected philosophers, Professor William H. Kilpatrick sums up his views of democracy in simple terms, in language which could be discussed with high school students:

1. Respect for people.
2. An attempt to run society upon a moral or ethical basis.
3. Reliance upon tested thought as the means of decisions and action.
4. Belief in the improvability of people and of society.[37]

These seemed to this great educator to comprise the essence of a democracy. We can readily see the implications for education which may be drawn from such a philosophy.

Another noted educator, L. Thomas Hopkins, summarizes the democratic way of life in terms of six major groups of beliefs. The following is an adaptation of his list:

[36] See this in two short films: *Democracy* and *Despotism* (Encyclopaedia Britannica Films).

[37] See William B. Kilpatrick, *Education for a Changing Civilization* (New York: The Macmillan Company, 1926), To read this in his own words, see also his *Philosophy of Education.*

1. Belief in the worth of the individual as a human being; belief that every person can achieve creative individuality; respect for the personality of each individual;

2. Belief that everyone has the capacity to learn how to act on thinking (reason);

3. Belief that all who must abide by decisions have the right to participate in making them;

4. Belief that the control and direction of democratic action lies in the situation, not outside of it;

5. Belief that the process of living is the interactive process (each individual and/or group works with other individuals and groups);

6. Belief that changes in our culture should be accomplished through deliberate social action rather than by uncontrolled violent methods (reasonableness).[38]

Enough has been suggested to provide us with a basis for much discussion and thinking about the nature of democracy as the setting for our lives. We may then go on to consider what this means for the schools in a democracy and the functions which they should perform in that society. What do the characteristics of democracy impose upon education in the way of responsibilities and functions?

The foregoing ideas should come to have meaning for us as we study and develop our own philosophy of education By meaning, we refer to the implications for actual practices, what teachers and pupils do, the ways people act toward each other, the nature of the learning experiences which take place in the school-community. We will know when we really

begin to see what these statements mean in actual practice. Take the first one, for example. What does it mean in a concrete instance? Does it mean that the most attractive young daughter of the chairman of the local school board deserves more attention and consideration than the underprivileged little boy from a shantytown family who comes to school in need of some grooming? The stirring film *A Desk for Billie* is an answer to that kind of question. Some of the episodes from the book, *Elmtown's Youth,* illustrate the need for actual use of democratic ideas and principles in the schools.[39] We should think about these until each means something in terms of what the teacher understands, feels, attempts, and does in his work with people.

Our schools are democracy's schools. Democracy means the people—all of the people. All of the children of all of the people are served by the schools. The common school must accept all children and teach them terms of equal respect, teach them the understanding, loyalties, and values that are in the interest of the *whole* of democracy. There should be no favorites among the pupils; no preference for any vested interest in society. Such is the view of the democratic-minded teacher. We should get ready to support public education—perhaps to teach in the light of that belief and conviction.

What goes on in the schools?

We have considered some ideals for a genuinely democratic system of education. We do not always find that the schools we know show up very well in terms of these standards and practices.

[38] L. Thomas Hopkins, *Interaction: The Democratic Process* (Boston: D. C. Heath, 1941), pp. 102–103.

[39] See August B. Hollingshead, *Elmtown's Youth* (New York: Wiley, 1949).

And we ask, "Why?" All the people have the right to ask that question.

The answer varies from one situation and time to another. Many teachers have not been really concerned about it. Practices sometimes ran counter to these ideas. Some talk about educating for democracy but run some of the classrooms and schools as little dictatorships. Some of our early schools were largely copied from older European models and change has been slow. Another point is that young children have to learn self-controls by graduated experiences. Teachers seem to continue dictation because they started in schools which taught that way. We need a generation of young teachers with the vision, the desire-to-do, and the intestinal fortitude to carry through this great task. We can do much to make the schools in which we teach little democracies of free minds cooperating in daily living. When we do, we shall be worthy of the title, "Teacher for democracy." This applies to teachers and for that matter to future parents as well.

The Central Purpose of American Education

A recent statement by The Educational Policies Commission submits the thesis that education should be interfused with attitudes of thoughtfulness and the thinking process as freely as possible.[40] Educational programs should promote creativity, inventiveness, and innovation. Any suggestion of narrow and exclusive intellectualism was clearly repudiated. The central purpose of education should be realized by all, not by the few who have academic aptitude. All persons have unrealized aptitude, and latent talent for creative activities. Education of all persons able to participate in formal school programs should stress the achievement of as much *rationality* as possible for each in the conviction that it is the thinking person who brings the several worthwhile purposes into an integrated whole of measurement.

Freedom in our democracy exalts the

[40] Educational Policies Commission, *The Central Purpose of American Education* (Washington: NEA, 1961). Used by permission.

individual and enhances the values of the society that maintains it. It has many dimensions and phases. It must be understood, believed, accepted and acted on to be best supported by people. Citizens who examine the values of freedom in the free society, understand them, in their own lives and in democracy, and who accept them to be supported and lived by, are those who exemplify the central purpose of American education. They have become truly free.

Freedom depends upon the protection and promotion of the institutions of democratic society and upon the personal commitment of people which gives it force in action. These two conditions depend upon one characteristic condition within the people of democracy, namely *freedom of the mind*. This condition— freedom of the mind—must be developed by each individual for himself. The provision of circumstances favorable for this development and the fostering of it through appropriate experiences is the responsibility of democracy's schools. This is the central purpose of public education.

Let us hear the Commission upon this point:

The purpose which runs through and strengthens all other educational purposes —the common thread of education—is the development of the ability to think. This is the central purpose to which the school must be oriented if it is to accomplish either its traditional tasks or those newly accentuated by recent changes in the world. To say that it is central is not to say that it is the sole purpose or in all circumstances the most important purpose, but that it must be a pervasive concern in the work of the school. Many agencies contribute to achieving educational objectives, but this particular objective will not be attained unless the school focuses on it. In this context, therefore, the development of every student's rational powers must be recognized as centrally important.[41]

This challenging document concludes with an expression that summarizes a point of view consistent with the purposes of this whole chapter. Every word carries its part of this message for the comprehending student of American education who started with the challenges of today:

Man has before him the possibility of a new level of greatness, a new realization of human dignity and effectiveness. The instrument which will realize this possibility is that kind of education which forces the mind and enables it to contribute to a full and worthy life. To achieve this goal is the high hope of the nation and the central challenge to its schools.[42]

[41] *Ibid.,* p. 12.
[42] *Ibid.,* p. 21.

Selected Bibliography

Advertising Council, *On the Basic Elements of a Free Dynamic Society.* New York: The Macmillan Co., 1952.

American Association of School Administrators, *This We Believe.* Washington: NEA, 1958.

Bayles, Ernest E. *Democratic Educational Theory.* New York: Harper & Row, 1960.

Colorado State Department of Education, *Goals for Education in Colorado.* Denver: The Department, 1962. An excellent statement of eleven goals for public schools of a state.

Conant, James Bryant. "False Education for Many Slum Children?" *Ladies' Home Journal,* **LXXIX,** (January, 1962), pp. 6, 62.

Educational Policies Commission, *The Central Purpose of American Education.* Washington: NEA, 1961.

———. *Moral and Spiritual Values in the Public Schools.* Washington: NEA, 1951.

———. *The Purposes of Education in American Democracy.* Washington: NEA, 1938.

———. *The Unique Function of Education in American Democracy.* Washington: NEA, 1937.

Ehlers, Henry and Lee, Gordon C. *Crucial Issues in Education.* Rev. ed. New York: Holt, Rinehart & Winston, 1959.

Gardner, John W. "National Goals in Education," in the Report of the President's Commission on National Goals, Goals for Americans. New York: The American Assembly, Columbia University, 1960, see chapter 3.

General Education in a Free Society. Cambridge: Harvard University Press, 1944, chapters 1–4, 6.

Graham, Grace. *The Public School in the American Community*. New York: Harper & Row, 1963. See chapters 2, 7, and 15.

Hook, Sidney. *Education for Modern Man*. New York: The Dial Press, 1946.

Hopkins, L. Thomas. *Interaction: The Democratic Process*. Boston: D. C. Heath, 1941. See chapters 3 and 5.

Jones, Howard Mumford. "Goal for Americans," *Saturday Evening Post,* **CCXXXIV,** (July 1, 1961), pp. 32–33, 62, 64.

Kilpatrick, William H. *Philosophy of Education*. New York: Macmillan, 1951.

King, Edmund J. *Other Schools and Ours*. New York: Holt, Rinehart & Winston, 1958. Readable treatment of education in a half-dozen nations including the U. S. A.

Knight, Edgar W. *Fifty Years of American Education*. New York: The Ronald Press, 1952.

McMurrin, Sterling M. "A Crisis of Conscience," *Saturday Review,* **XLIV,** No. 37 (September 16, 1962), pp. 58–59, 77–78.

National Association of Manufacturers, *This We Believe About Education*. New York: The Association, 1954.

Peters, Herman J., *et al. Introduction to Teaching*. New York: Macmillan, 1963. See chapter 11.

"The Pursuit of Excellence," *Prospect for America*, The Rockefeller Panel Reports. Garden City, L. I.: Doubleday & Co., Inc., 1961, pp. 337–392.

Rockefeller Panel Reports, *Prospect for America*. Garden City, N. Y.: Doubleday & Co., Inc., 1961, see report V.

Ross, Alf. *Why Democracy?* Cambridge: Harvard University Press, 1952.

Sayers, Ephraim Vern. *A First Course in the Philosophy of Education*. New York: Holt, 1952.

Sayers, Ephraim Vern and Madden, Ward. *Education and the Democratic Faith*. New York: Appleton-Century-Crofts, 1959.

This We Believe About Education. New York: National Association of Manufacturers, 1954.

What Should Our Schools Accomplish? New York: National Citizens Commission for the Public Schools, 1955.

Williams, Charl Ormond. *Schools for Democracy*. Chicago: National Congress of Parents and Teachers, 1939, chapters 1–4.

Chapter 8

Some Basic Principles
of Education

Educational psychologists now feel that learning—because it is a developmental process—must be so directed and evaluated that the needs of the individual are met. This principle is in accord with the even greater one that the learner is the focal point in the learning process. Thus the present trend is toward utilizing knowledge of the past only insofar as it assists in meeting the problems of the present and the future. Most students of the learning process now recognize the fact that the learner also is a human being enmeshed in a society which influences his every action.*

A good learning situation consists of a rich and varied series of learning experiences, unified around a vigorous purpose, aimed at a number of different learning products, and carried on in interaction with a rich, varied, and provocative environment.†

Introduction

There are numerous principles in educational literature. The term is current in almost any field and whole books have been written on the subject.[1] Principles refer to basic laws governing an operation or process, to fundamental statements about what appears to be true, or to be most consistent in terms of a given set of conditions and purposes, to settled rules of action that experience has found dependable or proven; in short, to the best generalizations we can make about an object, or process, and the relationships between and among them. Most of us have to develop our principles through the school kept by Dame Experience. We finally learn to generalize a principle from many specific instances or items. This is the inductive part of logical thinking, i.e.

* Louis P. Thorpe and Allen M. Schmuller, *Contemporary Theories of Learning*, p. 41. Copyright 1954 The Ronald Press Company, New York.

† William H. Burton, *The Guidance of Learning Activities*, 3rd ed. Copyright 1962 Appleton-Century-Crofts, New York.

[1] One great classic was J. Crosby Chapman and George S. Counts, *Principles of Education* (Boston: Houghton Mifflin Company), 1924.

245

that we proceed from the particular items to the formulation of a general law. The other part of the process is to utilize a generalization (law) or *principle* that fits a situation or group of data by reasoning from the general to the particular. In other words, deductive reasoning involves thinking about specific actions, behavior, data, and situations in terms of whether a given law fits the case.

The principles that have most significance at this point—midway between the purposes and programs of American schools—are those that refer to the learner and learning in the surrounding democratic society. All that we know about modern education tends to emphasize the importance of learning in human growth and development, in personal adjustment and adequacy, in rich purposeful living. Learning begins at the very threshold of human experience and continues throughout an active participating life. As a famous psychologist put it, "The individual learns his way through life."[2] Principles that relate to learning and living in democratic society would appear to be the most important ones for parents and teachers to understand.

As a starting point, consider what we mean by learning. Do we mean *facts*? *Information*? A conclusion reached by seeing relationships among several facts (a *generalization*)? A *skill* such as drawing geometric figures or typing? A belief in something as worthwhile or important? Should we include *attitudes*? *Appreciations*? Should we consider the desire to get out and do something about a social

[2] Robert J. Havighurst, *Developmental Tasks and Education* (Chicago: University of Chicago Press, 1948), p. 6. Copyright 1948 by The University of Chicago.

problem as learning? Are any or all of these comprehended in what is meant by learning? Our conception of the scope and breadth of learning outcomes is important as we begin to study how it takes place.

Consider a few more questions: Is the learner aware of what goes on as he learns something? Should one be aware of the process by which he learns? We can put these questions to ourselves and use our ability to analyze our own experiences. Consider what was going on while we each scratched on a piece of paper until the result could be called writing? When we repeated

Tiger! Tiger! burning bright
In the forests of the night . . .

until we knew William Blake's classic by heart? When boys stood at the free throw line for hours perfecting that push shot form which finally spelled extra points for their team? How one felt during one's first experimental steps when someone taught one a new dance? Were these learning experiences?

All this brings us to the following situation: *how people learn* is one of the most important understandings educators should have—yet quite often teachers have an inadequate or obsolete understanding of the whole process. Many students seem to accept the whole process as something to be endured, although they could improve their own learning if they really were aware of its nature. It is reasonable to suggest that a careful study of this problem will really pay big dividends when we teach. Let's study the learning process:

We might start by noting what it is

that people learn, and thus become better able to define and understand learning. We should then investigate what is known about how people learn. Next, we might consider some of the significant principles involved in learning to live in a democratic society. Finally, we may profit from consideration of the teacher's part in the total learning situation and process. All of this will be helpful when we begin to think of ourselves as teachers. Indeed, most adults are, in some respect or other.

What People Really Learn

SOME REPRESENTATIVE VIEWS

A half-dozen statements from educators widely separated by time, geography, and point-of-view serve to indicate the wide variety of the concepts of learning that have been held. This is another of the profoundly important and significant phases of education which almost everyone believes that he understands. This is a fallacy, of course, as in the case of health, politics, foreign policy, military strategy, and other topics upon which many people consider themselves to be experts. The lack of popular understanding and the wide variety of concepts of learning which have been presented suggest its importance for the student of education. Future parents and career teachers should endeavor to become skilled observers and students of the learning process.

The concepts of learning may be indicated by study of the outcomes that follow in the process as some selected examples will show.

Isocrates, the great Sophist teacher of ancient Athens, answered his own question about what constituted an educated man by five major characteristics that indicate various types of learning outcomes. The educated person controls circumstances, meets all occasions manfully, acts in accord with intelligent thinking, is honorable in all dealing, treats disagreeable persons and things with good nature, keeps his pleasures under control, and is modest about success. What kinds of learnings would the educated person have according to the views of this great Greek educator?

The late Nicholas Murray Butler, widely known as a president of Columbia University (whose field was philosophy), once suggested five tests of education in a person. These were: correct and precise use of the language; refined gentle manners as the result of habitual thought and action; appreciation of beauty and of worth as bases for sound character; the power and practice of reflective thinking; and the power to do, which he called efficiency. How do his ideas compare with those of Isocrates even after twenty-four centuries of Western history?

A group of outstanding leaders in another democracy which emphasized public schools delineated several desirable products of school experiences on the part of pupils. Among them were a zeal for further knowledge, for the quest of the truth with skills in pursuing it; attitudes of cooperation toward one's fellows; willingness to express oneself and to assume responsibility; appreciation of beauty in life; ability to lead a healthy life; and capacity to handle practical affairs. In this fashion, the Australian Council for Educational Research dealt with different outcomes of the educational process.[3]

Quotations from three modern works by leading educators in as many fields will indicate the variety of learning outcomes that may be recognized by the student.

1. The real contribution of the new psychology . . . lies in its indication of the great diversity of the types of learning. While all learning may be said to have certain common principles, it is equally important to emphasize the different procedures required in different fields and for various purposes in the same field. Obviously, learning to play the violin is not the same as learning to understand the social problems of our day. Even within one field, that of music, there may be a great difference: learning to play an instrument is not the same as learning to appreciate music. The fault of the traditional system lay in that it attempted to apply methods of memorization and habituation to fields of learning when inquiry and judgment were essential.[4]

2. The concept of an educated man as one who has a "trained mind" has little educational significance today. Philosophically, we are coming to realize that the educated person is much more than one who knows. We now specify that the educated person possess useful skills and abilities, be interested in a variety of activities, manifest proper attitudes, hold value systems that are consistent with the Judaic-Christian ethic and the democratic way of life, and at all times translate these attitudes, interests, and value systems into right conduct.[5]

3. Many definitions of learning have been given from time to time. As viewed by some teachers learning applies primarily to academic growth or growth in the ability to perform the various school tasks including growth in the acquisition of knowledge. Such a description of learning is too narrow. Growth in reading ability and in arithmetical skills are examples of learning. The early emotional and social conditioning of the child . . . are examples of learning which appear during the first year of life. Then, there are examples of learning to be found in the applications of knowledge to the building of roads and bridges, to the teaching of growing boys and girls. The child learns to roller skate, the musician learns to play a musical instrument, the man learns to lay bricks, and the housewife learns to cook and sew.

There are types of learning which are more subtle in nature . . . such as those involved in creative writing, specialized interests, attitudes toward other people, and appreciation for some of the things about us.[6]

There appears to be a common awareness of a number of learnings in the writings of the philosopher of education, the administrator, and the educational psychologist. Most students will need to read and think further about this topic. A great many have simply taken it for granted that learning occurs in school when they have completed an assignment,

[3] Australian Council for Educational Research, *A Plan for Australia* (Melbourne: Melbourne University Press, 1943).

[4] I. B. Berkson, *Education Faces the Future* (New York: Harper & Row, 1943), p. 210. Used by permission.

[5] G. Lester Anderson, *Learning and Instruction,* 45th Yearbook, National Society for the Study of Education, Part 1 (Chicago: University of Chicago Press, 1950), p. 9. Copyright 1950 by The University of Chicago. Used by permission.

[6] Karl G. Garrison and J. Stanley Gray, *Educational Psychology,* p. 228. Copyright 1955 Appleton-Century-Crofts, New York.

memorized some facts or a poem, learned to solve an equation, to recall an irregular French verb, or to perform some other directed task. Some may have had the impression that learning is chiefly a matter of mastering certain facts which the teacher thought was important; that learning is a much simpler response than it is. In the case of many persons learning has been accepted in the light of their own school experiences and there has been no occasion to study it. It appears simple: the teacher assigns, the pupils study the material and recite it back upon demand. It is simply a matter of being able to read and to memorize. Now it is evident that there can be no simple or single answer to the question: what do people learn? It is time for us to look further into this basic question.

We should read, discuss, and think about some of the actual learnings that do take place in schools, especially in classrooms. This can be an interesting and even amusing topic. Find several different examples to discuss, as for example: What did the Indian boy who learned to repeat sounds that resembled words in the "Pledge to the Flag" actually learn? What does the junior learn who reads one of Emerson's essays because he must do so to pass? What does the pupil learn who earns a good mark in geometry by copying the exam? Or, when the parent pays money for A's on report forms? What actually is learned in a study hall under strict supervision? Do all pupils learn the same, are the outcomes the same, from the same episode in school? Let us consider these and other questions of comparable significance and see what we can make of these puzzling problems. Should

one recognize some different "kinds" of learnings?

Getting a concept of learning

The limited concept which holds that learning is a matter of memorizing and retaining factual information or the attainment of specific skills and of being able to recall or to use them upon demand has been challenged and modified. A recent writer quotes several penetrating criticisms of this limited view.[7] It has been termed the "cold storage" concept of learning and referred to as the process whereby pupils learn their lessons but do not learn. Burton concedes that the teacher can prove she gets results by such methods but notes that the results are not worth anything.

A better view of learning can be developed from analysis of what people do in order to learn. A detailed list of learning experiences is to be found in educational literature on the "activity" concept.[8] Mossman's list of 83 learning experiences arranged in ten categories represented wide diversity. The first terms in each of the ten groups were as follows: (1) adventuring, (2) creating, (3) cooperating, (4) judging, (5) consuming, (6) recreating, (7) recording, (8) repeating, (9) obeying, (10) dictating. Note that the last three terms are the experiences which pupils of the traditional school are most likely to remember. Another list

[7] See William H. Burton, *The Guidance of Learning Activities*, 3rd ed., pp. 90–100. Copyright 1962 Appleton-Century-Crofts, New York.

[8] See Lois C. Mossman, *The Activity Concept* (New York: The Macmillan Co., 1938), pp. 54–55. Quoted in Burton, *The Guidance of Learning Activities*, p. 49.

used four groups: (a) knowledge and understanding; (b) skill and competence; (c) attitude and interest; and (d) action pattern.[9] Some idea of the wide variety of learning experiences may be gained from study of such lists.

Learning experiences are many and varied. Something happens or comes out of each of these types of experiences. These may be thought of as learnings. Note, too, the relationship between the words *learning* and *experiences*. The two are in many instances synonymous since we learn something from experiences always. The learning which results may or may not be significant or even desirable but it happens.

Concepts of learning, like the outcomes and evidences of learning, are varied and different in the views of various students of the subject. Serious students must continue to give attention to this major concept.[10]

TYPES OF LEARNING OUTCOMES

It is time to consider some of the outcomes of learning which can be started by a look at the different kinds of learnings we have experienced and observed. These should serve to illustrate rough types of learning which may go on in the educative process. An example can be made of almost any list of facts and figures about an education topic which we

[9] See Nolan C. Kearney, *Elementary School Objectives* (New York: Russell Sage Foundation, 1953).

[10] See for example, an interesting chapter, "A Theory of Learning for Teachers," in H. Gordon Hullfish and Philip G. Smith, *Reflective Thinking: The Method of Education* (New York: Dodd, Mead & Co., 1961), pp. 169–191.

have assembled for our notes.[11] Looking back we can see that what was gained from that experience was *information— a number of facts*.

Consider, for example, the data about the number of emergency teachers for the postwar years, 1946–1961. As a result of acquiring these facts—fifteen pieces of information—we were able to see a certain relationship among them. We noted, for example, that the figure for each successive year was smaller than the preceding one until 1955 when it reversed. In other words, it was quickly discovered that the number of emergency teachers had decreased each year for a decade, then began to rise again. So the problem of emergency teachers is still unsolved and is actually growing slightly. We drew a conclusion from the relationship which existed among these fifteen facts. We made a generalization which appeared to hold good—that stated the general meaning of those facts for us. We had developed an *understanding* of the significance and meaning of several facts.

All can understand that this step is very important—the drawing of valid conclusions from facts which are related in some way or ways. Otherwise, the many individual facts and figures may be simply isolated items meaning little to anyone unless they happen to fit questions on the "giveaway" radio and TV programs. And, that doesn't happen often enough to justify memorizing an encyclopedia! We must have *understandings* as well as *facts*.

But facts and generalizations are not the only kinds of learnings we acquire.

[11] See tables in Chapters 1, 4, 6, 12, and 13 for good examples. Table 12–1 provides a good illustration of this point.

What about the dexterity and coordination involved in typing? in playing the piano? in using a compass to describe geometric figures? or the ability to use a complex tool of some sort? Can you think of any such ability that we have acquired recently? What about learning to start, stop, and use the movie projector? Any of these would represent a new *skill* someone has learned. This is another type of learning—skills. Sometimes certain clusters of varied skills may be thought of as comprising broader competences, a term often used in designating desired outcomes for planned educational programs and experiences.

One's own experiences will probably afford an example of another type. Let us try to recall some of the strikingly beautiful or impressive scenes in a movie we have seen in recent weeks. For example, many may remember the NEA film, *A Desk for Billie*. They will recall the artistry involved in some of the photography in the film, the closeups, and the sequences late in the picture, in particular. The group probably discussed the effect which the film had upon individual members of the class. Some of its features had given pleasure, or enjoyment, while others had appealed to one's liking for the beautiful and the artistic. This may be seen as an example of an *appreciation* lesson. We learned not mere facts, nor a generalization, nor a skill. We simply gained total impressions, some of which were charged with traces of emotion. That is, we liked or disliked it, and may have been "for" or "against" somebody or something in the story. This will do to illustrate appreciation as a type of learning outcome. We may recall some other looking and listening experiences we have had and some appreciation outcomes from these experiences.

Many have probably anticipated the next type of outcome, namely, *attitudes*. How many ever sat before a tape recorder or mike ready to record their voices? Or, waited to take part in a TV show? What were their reactions? Wonder? A mild curiosity? Certainly, but there were some others. Some were a bit anxious and concerned about how they were going to sound. They may have thought, "Goodness, this will sound like Gravel Gertie for sure!" Maybe some voices shook a bit as emotion (just a little nervousness) got in the way. In any case, the new experience left persons with a feeling toward what had happened. They may have enjoyed it, suffered through it, or merely endured it, but something happened. Most came out of that experience with an attitude—a pattern of their reactions toward it. This is an important kind of learning outcome, but all too few students recognize this. It's an important fact to know about teaching. The teacher can make children do this or that, but she can't keep them from feeling as they please about it afterward. If the professor bores the class day after day, they may keep on coming, but they won't like it. Some of these may be thought of as *concomitant* learnings, i.e., they appear to accompany other learning outcomes. Put simply, this means that we may learn some outcome that was planned or desired by the teacher, but we learn at the same time some other outcome(s) that may or may not have been anticipated or expected.

Perhaps all have seen on the playground specific instances of the teacher at work in the building of an attitude. Remember why the gym teacher said she chose Sammy to lead the games—how she explained to the class that he had shown an attitude of good sportsmanship on the playing field the day before. So she rewarded him by her approval. She was making him feel that this attitude "paid off" in teacher approval and praise. She was re-enforcing desirable learning! This is an all-important principle of teaching. In fact, it is just about the most important one we know about. The teacher knows that people often try *this, that,* and *the other* response to a learning situation until they get the right one. She "rewards" that correct response to re-enforce it—so that it will come more quickly next time. When it comes at once, we say that the person has *learned.* Let's get this fact and its teaching implications clearly in mind for it will make us better teachers.

These are all important kinds of learnings or outcomes of the learning process. These come out of an educative experience. Are there any others? Perhaps three more may be mentioned. There is the kind we call "values," which the learner builds and integrates into his system of beliefs about things and ideas. These come more rapidly with the intelligent person; some people never seem to pull them together in their thinking. These are not simple outcomes—they are complex and appear to result from several or all of the foregoing outcomes. Suppose that as a result of the learning experiences he has had someone arrive at a point where he says, "You know, I believe that love for little children is the *most* important quality of the good teacher." That is a value which has been

arrived at as he grew in personality adjustment to the whole pattern of teaching as a career. It is a conclusion which tests out best or highest after all of his quantitative and qualitative standards of judgment have been applied to it.[12] It has, then, in his total personality makeup a certain weight; it means a lot; it is important. It is a value. Ideals, ethical principles, truths—these are values in and for people. People have to have something in the way of a set of values in order to be emotionally and psychically healthy and happy.

There is another term for a kind of learning outcome that is highly important, one related to the example used for values. We may try to get at it by trying to remember occasions when we sized up some person or interpreted a new situation in unique fashion, in our own very special way. We may have been able to think about it and to recall how it linked up with or related to some image we already had like an earlier impression of and about people who look a certain way, for instance. This is difficult to explain unless we can find illustrations that are meaningful. And this will be true only if our perceptions are much alike. This is the concept we have been leading up to— that people learn what they perceive, i.e. they learn what they see in a situation. Remember the great Prussian general von Moltke who could not see the beauty on the autumn hillside pointed out by his wife; he saw only a set of tactical problems involving artillery, strong points for

[12] See various definitions for the term *value* in John Dewey Society, *Seventh Yearbook,* p. 29. Here you find that a value is ". . . a good which has passed through a process of examination and evaluation . . ."

defense, cover, and the like! We learn what we are able to perceive and what we perceive depends largely upon our "self-concept." Children become who they are and what they are by the way they are treated according to perceptual psychology.[13] In many learning situations, pupils gain perceptions. They see a situation not as it really is, but as they perceive it; they see others and themselves in terms of their own perceptions. Teaching helps children to get better perceptions (meanings) from experiences.

Teachers must know children well enough to sense problems of learning that arise from limited perceptions. They must be able to see situations as they appear to the pupils and be able to help accordingly. Teachers who empathize can really feel and understand as the child does in a given situation, can do the really constructive building of the better person he is capable of becoming. Parents need to understand that children become what their experiences make of them and that this depends on their perceptions including preceptions of themselves (the self-image). Learn about this in psychology courses.

We need to consider another kind of learning outcome by reviewing what happens after a person has learned something or many "somethings" through an educative experience. Does the whole business stop right there? Suppose we see a film about starving children in a distant land or hear a radio program about "saving a loaf" for the hungry little ones whose

plight is no fault of their own. We check up on the things we saw and heard, and get convincing proof that these allegations are true: therefore, they are facts. One accepts the fact that these people are in a bad way; he concludes that they need help. He finds that his emotions are involved; that he feels deeply about it. He has an attitude (pity) toward the victims. His sense of values—justice, fairness, kindness is at stake. There are two forces in conflict: he feels uncomfortable, and he cannot keep from thinking about it. He has the *urge to do something about it.* He feels a *drive to action.* What can he do? Cry? His intelligence tells him that this will not solve the problem. Should he write a letter to his Congressman? Suppose good judgment indicates that this official cannot or will not do what is needed. So it goes until he figures out the action to take which is right for him and *does it.* Only then does he feel at peace again. Note that one's emotionalized *attitude,* one's system of *values* and one's *judgment* all united in the decision and the action. For intelligent people then, learning means action—knowledge is for use. A *drive to action* may be an important outcome of a learning experience.

It will help if we can relate these outcomes to incidents or episodes in our own experience. We may observe evidence of one or more of these in the classrooms or other school situations that we visit.

Learn to recognize outcomes

Emphases upon simple and single outcomes are giving way to better understandings of what comes out of learning experiences. No longer are teachers satisfied to have pupils learn some isolated facts, develop certain commonly

[13] This topic will be discussed further elsewhere in this chapter. For brief discussions see Burton, *op. cit.,* pp. 8–9; and "Perceptual Psychology" in *Education Digest* (December 1962), p. 22.

useful skills, and memorize a few formulas. The modern school is concerned with a wide range and variety of learning experiences and outcomes.

Facts and information have not lost their place in modern schools but that place is no longer the chief outcome of learning. Neither are the skills neglected. *Facts* are learned and used in connection with each other and to other information; it is the emphasis upon the learning of isolated, unrelated facts which is on the wane. Facts mean something when we can use them to tell us more or to provide better information which really counts. A number of facts may add up to a rather significant understanding.

Understandings appear as generalizations, principles, theories, or concepts which are organized or interpreted from the various aspects of a given situation, or interpreted from a number of specific instances.[14] Generalizations may vary from statements of broad principles or concepts to simple declarative sentences which interpret personal experience or local data. Understandings are important; they represent some of the meanings we get from our experiences.

Appreciations involve a *liking for* and tendency *to choose* something. It is thought of as a satisfying emotional response. It is often difficult, even impossible, to draw clear distinctions between appreciations and attitudes.

Attitudes are relatively constant tendencies to act in certain directions and in conformity with certain behavior patterns. Attitudes are usually thought of as primarily emotional in nature, but they can be intellectual to the extent of their bases

[14] This definition has been adapted from Burton, *op. cit.*, p. 99.

in knowledge and understanding. Attitudes toward the subject matter being studied are developed by pupils. This is an example of what has been called "concomitant" learning, i.e. something learned concurrently or which accompanies some other learning outcome. This means that a positive attitude of interest in what is being learned is desirable if we are to have best learning outcomes.

Perceptions are individualized interpretations of situations, of elements in the situation, others, and the actions of others. These depend upon the person, his self-image, images of others, and previous learnings. Actually, this may be influential in most of the other outcomes we have noted.

Skills and *abilities* may be regarded together. Ability is the generalized power to carry on an integrated complex of related activities. This may be made clearer by some illustrations such as: The ability to read, the ability to write, to sight-sing, to play the piano, or to lead a group discussion.

Values are outcomes of our experiences and learning. These may relate to the worth, goodness, beauty, desirability of the company of a person, object, process, or belief. Values are determined by the way in which they satisfy our purposes, desires, aspirations, or ideals. Thus, they are built up gradually as we generalize from our experiences (the way things work out in meanings for us) and are constantly re-tested and strengthened or modified as we learn from living and doing.

Implications for teaching

From all this, we may begin to draw some implications for teaching. For one thing, we shall see that learning is not the simple, single-outcome, compartmentalized process many people have thought. (Actually, the person learns many different kinds of outcomes by and through experiences.) These are complex, varied and interrelated. Logically, then, the school program should recognize these facts about learning outcomes. It means, too, that the learning is what happens as pupils (or anyone, for that matter) derive something from novel experiences. These may be desirable or undesirable, but they are learnings. The teacher naturally wishes to get as many of the former and as few of the latter as possible. Pupils get more of the former when they do carry out activities (have experiences) which mean something to them. The outcomes are what happen or result in improved or changed behavior and ability to improve behavior or acts. Pupils can be made to go through the motions of doing something they do not like, and have no interest in *but* the outcomes are quite likely to be undesirable learning. For example, the pupils can be required to study *Idylls of the King* or *Julius Caesar* even though they want to do something else. The trouble is they may come out with a dislike for study of the "classics." We may sometimes teach in such a way as to get outcomes radically different from those desired. What do you think?

An excellent treatment of popular misconceptions of the concepts of learning has been offered by Burton.[15] These include: (1) learning has too long been regarded as confined to the experience of memorizing; or to the outcomes regarded as facts or skills which the pupil is expected to reproduce from memory; (2) type of learning stressed produces other than the desirable outcomes, e.g. facts and verbalisms are often accepted as satisfactory outcomes when certain abilities, habits, skills are the necessary outcomes; (3) outcomes are thought to be simple and single rather than complex and varied; (4) the symbols of learning (marks, credits, "parroting information") are often mistaken for the outcomes of learning. It would do many persons good to give careful consideration to these points since the misconceptions these represent are widely held. These misconceptions of learning should be traded in for clearer and more useful concepts, more nearly the converse of each of these statements. It is important that a more intelligent concept of learning experiences and outcomes be developed by teachers, professors and parents.

What has been presented here has been streamlined and simplified for purposes of clarity. Some of these outcomes are taking place concurrently, and they interact upon each other and in the learner during the learning experience. What we need to do as adults is to get a picture of what goes on during educative experiences and to know how and what outcomes may emerge from this process. We need to appreciate that learning is a personal response or adjustment or adaptation or achievement. It represents a wide variety because of individual differences and variation in all the many factors of situations. Knowing these things, we may better plan our part as teachers in fostering and providing educative experiences. We may also acquire masterly skill in making the learner *aware* of all this so

[15] Burton, *op. cit.,* pp. 85–122. This Chapter is a classic treatment of an important subject.

that he or she may more quickly *learn* and learn with less effort, and learn (grow) in desirable directions and dimensions. With this understanding, we shall never be the same parents and teachers; we shall be immeasurably better ones. As better teachers and parents, we shall have power, but knowing this we shall ever take care to use that power wisely and conscientiously.

Some Definitions of Learning

There are few phenomena more common than learning in the lives of people but a great many receive more attention. Adults take the learning experiences of children for granted, forgetting or ignoring the difficulty and even anxiety that may be experienced. Adults frequently experience frustration in learning some new skill like a foreign language, or almost anything, when under pressure. We go on learning as we live, if we live meaningfully and richly.

Concern about learning should be universal among teachers. It is likewise a potentially important concern of parents and pupils for various reasons. The term has wide use both in popular discussion and in our educational literature. This general concern about learning is not matched by common agreement about its nature and how it takes place. The history of education shows that several different concepts and definitions have held sway at various times. Today there are various concepts and theories which are held by individuals and groups in educational circles.

There are a number of ways to characterize the different concepts and theories of learning.[16] One way is to place them into two big categories, namely, the "association" and the "field" theories. Another similar brief classification places all views under either "behaviorist" or field theories.

Another identifies two streams of research that yield "*behavior* theory" and "cognitive theory."[17]

Some maintain that learning is the formation of fixed habits and patterns of behavior. To others certain principles of learning appear important and significant. In one view, conditioning appears as an important process in and for learning; consequently, the teacher's task is that of guide for the learner in the acquisition of habits, and information. Others believe that learning means a more and greater variety of desirable changes in the individual. Emphasis upon the total of the child's development—attitudes, interests, understandings, and all aspects of behavior is implied in this conception. The goal is a resourceful and adequate person after his school life is over, and his teacher is no longer available to guide one's growth and behavior. Ability to react to problems and situations is stressed. Creative thinking is thus the most significant outcome of learning thus viewed.

Education is responsible for promot-

[16] Most educational psychologies offer some help, upon this subject. See, for example, Karl C. Garrison and J. Stanley Gray, *Educational Psychology* (New York: Appleton-Century-Crofts, Inc., 1955), pp. 227–248.

[17] Ralph Garry, *The Psychology of Learning* (Washington: The Center for Applied Research in Education, 1963), pp. 1–12.

ing the sort of learning which results in desirable behavior and participation of the members in our democratic society. The cooperating, participating, and social being learns desirable behavior through experiences which provide understandings, appreciations, attitudes, and values of and for democratic living. There is no guarantee that democratic citizenship can be learned in terms of fixed habits and a prescribed body of factual information. It is possible to find well-informed persons who are not cooperative, participating citizens, and even a few who are criminals. You could also find persons who would make a low score on an achievement examination whose behavior *in* and contribution *to* society is cooperative and useful. What one *does* rather than what one is able to repeat from memory (verbalism) is a most significant clue as to what one has learned. Teachers are concerned with learning as it is shown by or reflected in desirable useful behavior in society.

Our present task is to explore more fully what learning is, to try to arrive at a good working definition for it, and to gain an adequate picture of how people learn. This is one of the most important sets of understandings we need as adults. By the same token it is one of the most difficult problems we shall encounter as we study to become good teachers and parents.

Defining what learning is

Educational literature abounds in explanations about learning and how it takes place. Each of these is based on a psychological interpretation of what is known of how people learn and what happens as a result of learning experiences. We shall find several points-of-view, prin-

ciples, and even "laws" of learning set forth in numerous books upon the subject. A few selected statements will serve to illustrate this point:

1. From the *Dictionary of Education*:

learning: change in response or behavior (such as innovation, elimination, or modification of responses involving some degree of permanence) caused partly or wholly by experience, such experience being in the main conscious, but sometimes including significant unconscious components as is common in *motion learning* or in reaction to unrecognized or subliminal stimuli. . . .[18]

2. From a book on learning:

Learning is the development and modification of the tendencies that govern the psychological functions.[19]

3. From a writer who has analyzed the various positions:

Learning is a change in the individual, due to interaction of that individual and his environment, which fills a need and makes him more capable of dealing adequately with his environment.[20]

4. Here is another view held by some but not by the author cited:

Learning is acquiring by conditioned and associative responses, mastery of facts, skills, and other logically organized subject matters set out by adults for children to learn on the assumption that the children may have occasion to use them at some future time.[21]

[18] Carter V. Good (ed.), (New York: McGraw-Hill Book Company, 1948).

[19] Howard L. Kingsley, *The Nature and Conditions of Learning* (New York: Prentice-Hall, 1946), p. 31.

[20] William H. Burton, *The Guidance of Learning Activities* (3rd ed., New York: Appleton-Century-Crofts, Inc., 1962), p. 13.

[21] L. Thomas Hopkins, *Interaction: The Democratic Process* (Boston: D. C. Heath and Company, 1941), p. 139.

5. A philosophy of education professor gives this definition:

To learn should mean to build up the whole self, achieving self-control and self-direction in the conduct of life, becoming capable of utilizing opportunities for creative work and the enrichment of life.[22]

6. From a leading writer and theorist:

In the most general sense, learning is any change in the behavior of an organism.

Learning is sometimes defined as any *desirable change* in the behavior of an organism.

Learning is . . . the progressive changes which an individual makes in the logic of his experience due to his increasingly purposeful efforts to resolve his own personal problems of living more intelligently.[23]

The foregoing samples of definitions of learning from recent well-known books on education may serve to illustrate something of the diversity of opinion which exists at this time. Although students may be confused by the language used and by the differences in viewpoints they should persist, for this is one of the most essential understandings.

It may help to make an analysis of the different concepts of what learning is and to note several points which are common to each of these definitions. Each mentions *behavior* (or response) on the part of the organism (or individual). *Change* (or modification) is either expressed or implied in the various statements. Thus far, there is fairly good agreement.

The concept of *desirable* change is found in some definitions but not in the others. The definitions can now be separated into two groups on this basis. Note, however, that the point of *desirable or useful* change may not necessarily be in conflict with other statements. All would admit that changes in behavior are *learned* for the most part[24] and that some may be undesirable rather than desirable or useful. Could it be that some of these statements refer only to the kind of learning we wish to foster or promote? If so, we find these positions more tenable than first appeared.

Further study and critical thought will be your best means of working out better understandings of these concepts and principles. Various courses in educational psychology and/or human growth and development should provide excellent opportunities for furthering this understanding.

Stating a conception of learning

Since the position taken in this discussion is that of substantial agreement with the last definition quoted, it may be well to show why this particular one has been accepted. One of the reasons is found in the inadequateness of the stimulus-response concept as an explanation of human behavior. Note the implication of the theory that the organism makes a definite response to an external stimulus. This would seem to mean that behavior should be definite and uniform given identical stimuli and a number of organisms to respond to them. This turns out to be inadequate; such a concept makes of people quite monotonous machine-like

---

[22] I. B. Berkson, *Education Faces The Future* (New York: Harper & Row, 1943), pp. 153–4.

[23] L. Thomas Hopkins, *op. cit.*, pp. 136–7, 140.

[24] This is not meant to exclude changes in behavior that emanate from maturation, changed motivation, or even fatigue factors which lead to easier ways of acting or doing something. Even here there is no way to exclude effects of learning.

individuals played upon by chance stimuli. There are too many evidences that persons in the same environmental setting respond in different ways to the same stimuli. There must be other factors in the situation which affect the responses of the different individuals. It has been pointed out that the previous experiences of the individuals may serve to provide such factors. In this connection the concept of individual perceptions must be considered. The goals or purposes of the organism play a role in the behavior (or responses) which is observed. We should recall what we have heard about individual differences, and the way people differ so much that each is unique. These factors indicate a much greater role by and for the individual in responding to stimuli than was originally suggested by the stimulus-response concept. Interaction of the individual and the environment seems more nearly to be the key word in an explanation.

It appears that we can expect to have a conception of learning which comprehends the *environment* (stimuli) which may include other individuals and groups, the *individual* (with all his individual differences including capacity to perceive and to interpret a wide variety of background and *previous experience*) and goals or purposes which are served by behavior. Certainly some persons appear to gain understanding of the relationships in a "field" to form cognitive structures; insight plays an important part in this theory.[25]

How Learning Takes Place

SOME EXPLANATIONS AND THEORIES

Many explanations and theories of how learning takes place in terms of types of learning have been offered. Still the final word has not been written inasmuch as investigation and research continue at full speed.

It is obvious that there can hardly be a simple standardized explanation of learning in view of the fact that individuals differ profoundly, that perceptions are peculiar to persons, the environmental conditions vary widely, previous experiences are never identical, and there is great diversity among the purposes (or goal set) of the learners. An explanation of learning is further complicated by the fact that so many different kinds of learning outcomes are to be found. Here it is possible to provide only a generalized, somewhat streamlined description of learning processes which may give a better understanding of how people learn.

The following situations may represent only part of all that is known about how people learn, but they do illustrate common types and principles of learning. When we become students of educational psychology we should be better prepared and motivated to learn more about this important problem.

We learn much by trial and error

Much animal and human learning takes place as the result of varied activity in problem situations. This is often termed trial-and-error learning. Perhaps it should be called "trial-error-and success" learn-

25 See Ralph Garry, *The Psychology of Learning* (Washington: The Center for Applied Research in Education, 1963), p. 9.

ing. Psychologists show that behavior involves varied activity by the organism at first, and that from this, specific forms of response are selected (learned). It is noted that infants exhibit mass movement at first, and that coordinated, specialized responses are gradually developed. Look at the movies made in Dr. Gesell's clinic to find illustrations of this in young children. An infant of a few weeks moves "all over" as he tries to reach for a small toy; by the end of his first year he is able to exhibit more specialized reaching and grasping movements with the hand and finger. The useless and unnecessary movements have largely disappeared.

It has been pointed out that this principle of varied activity followed by specific response applies when children or adults are faced with a new situation or problem.[26] Faced with a problem to be solved or a situation to be mastered, there is varied behavior (many useless and wasted responses). From repeated trials there emerges a response which does the trick. You might observe that the learner performs in ways pertinent to the problem as he sees it; he does what he perceives as leading to the goal and this is learned. We can give a child or an adult a puzzle to work and note what happens; or watch a young child learning to draw, or to write; or ask an adult to trace a figure by observing its image reflected from a mirror. Such observations will serve to show this principle in operation.

Most descriptions of this principle

[26] See the following references for descriptions of the process: Kingsley, *The Nature and Conditions of Learning* (New Jersey: Prentice-Hall, 1946), Chapter 4; Miller and Dollard, *Social Learning and Imitation* (New Haven: Yale University Press, 1941), Chapter 2.

are of experiments in animal learning, but you can find illustrations of its use in human learning. Four characteristics or components are found: (a) some form of motive (or drive), (b) thwarting occurs, some sort of block is encountered, (c) varied (sometimes called random) behavior occurs until, (d) the successful response occurs. This successful response does the trick, tension is reduced, and the organism goes on about its business. When this happens often enough for the organism to make the correct response immediately upon encountering the problem-situation (thwarting) we say it has learned that specific behavior.

A rough diagram (opposite) may serve to illustrate this principle in operation.

After successful experiences we find that tension (anxiety) is reduced because the correct response is made immediately.

This over-simplified picture of the principle of learning through varied activity (trial and error) may serve to start you toward an understanding of much human learning.[27] It is employed when we do not know what to do when faced with a problem-situation, or when we are unable to make the correct response even if we know what it is. Even in thinking out the solutions of problems, we may consider and reject many trial solutions until we find the one which does the trick.

We may conclude that often we learn by trying, by doing something (this, that, and the other) until we get the answer or find the correct solution. As we learn to eliminate unsuccessful and useless responses we learn to come at once to the

[27] For an excellent description of an experiment in animal learning see Kingsley, *op. cit.*, pp. 63–66.

B. Encounters problem situation

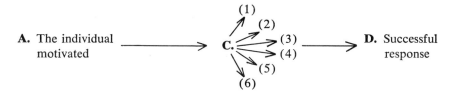

A. The individual motivated ⟶ **C.** (1) (2) (3) (4) (5) (6) ⟶ **D.** Successful response

C. Makes varied responses

Again, when successful response occurs at once, we say learning has taken place. Note what happens while this goes on:

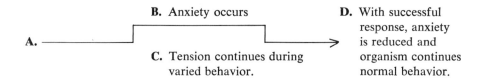

A. ⟶

B. Anxiety occurs

C. Tension continues during varied behavior.

D. With successful response, anxiety is reduced and organism continues normal behavior.

successful one. When this occurs, we say that we have learned to solve the problem.

This is an important principle. We learn by vigorous attempts to accomplish our purposes (reach the goal). There is no learning unless we make responses to the problem situation. Students who do nothing ("I don't know how to do it.") when faced with a problem situation cannot learn how to handle it. We must do something, even if it is wrong and keep on until we hit upon the solution!

It is obvious that human beings learn much from the trial-and-error process which has been described in simplified terms. Yet we shall be able to see that this process will rarely operate as crudely as this in human learning for rather obvious reasons. Human learning will tend to be far superior to animal learning because an individual will have a repertoire of more responses. In other words, the more intelligent organism will be able to try more responses in the problem-situa-

tion. Furthermore, the individual may be able to utilize previous experiences in solving problems. Skills once learned and learning acquired previously provide a fund of experience which can be brought to bear upon a problem. Thus, the human learner can become more skillful and adept at problem-solving because of this. Old methods and experiences may be brought to bear upon a new situation and a quick effective adaptation made which solves the problem. Many interesting reports of problem-solving of this sort by animals are available. Some of this has been termed learning by insight. Obviously, the human learner utilizes this higher form of learning even more effectively.

We learn many conditioned responses

The foregoing simplified account omits much which has been written about learning. For example, much emphasis has been placed on *conditioning* as an important kind or means of learning.[28] Through experimentation and study different forms have been identified and described. There is no doubt that much is and can be learned through conditioning experiences. Many habits, fears and other responses have been learned by conditioning experiences. These may be especially important in early years of life. Conditioning has many uses in the classroom. The successful athletic coach uses this principle widely. Students should try to recall learning experiences which were examples of conditioning.

A trite definition is that conditioning is the process which results in the learning of a conditioned response. A conditioned response is elicited by a stimulus that originally would not cause this response. This stimulus having become substituted for the original stimulus through association comes to have the same effect in that it elicits the conditioned response.

Two rough diagrams, below and on page 263, illustrate this principle:[29]

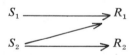

When S_1 and S_2 occur simultaneously or in some consistent relationship, R_1 is learned so that S_2 will elicit R_1 even without S_1.

A crude illustration of this principle may be found in the learning of terms for pets or animals, something which occurs in the early experience of nearly everyone.

[28] E. R. Hilgard and D. G. Marquis, *Conditioning and Learning,* second edition, revised by G. A. Kimble (New York: Appleton-Century-Crofts, Inc., 1961).

[29] Stimuli are designated S_1 and S_2; responses in like fashion.

A child sees his parent point to the dog and say "dog." The child says "dog" and may be praised, "That's right," or "Mama's smart boy." After some trials, the random response the child would make is replaced by the response "dog" when the child sees the animal, even though the parent is not present.

You can probably think of many examples of this from your early school experiences, especially when you were drilled by the teacher to learn certain responses. Remember occasions in arithmetic, spelling, new words in reading, and how you learned correct responses. These were probably conditioning experiences. You can see now why this principle can be called a common type of learning experience.

One experience from real life may serve to illustrate the strength of conditioning experiences early in life. Years ago, as a child one parent learned fear of lightning and thunder from his grandmother who exhibited emotional behavior when these phenomena occurred. This irrational behavior continued until later in life when it was extinguished by the learning of other responses, in other words, "reconditioning" took place. Afterwards, when he became a parent, it became his purpose to prevent learning of unnecessary fears through conditioning experiences by his own children. When each of the children were young, he took care to display no outward signs of fear of lightning and thunder. Instead, he tried to show interest and to use exclamations which indicated pleasure. For example, he would say, "Bingo! That was a good one, wasn't it? We certainly had a pretty flash of lightning that time. Now listen

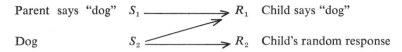

Parent says "dog" S_1 ⟶ R_1 Child says "dog"

Dog S_2 ⟶ R_2 Child's random response

to the thunder roll." Each of the children learned to take lightning and thunder as a normal happening. The daughter learned to call it "bingo-bango" and this same expression was later used by a younger son. The important point is that each sleeps by a window with no fear whatsoever of lightning flashes or the heaviest of thunder rolls. Many fears are simply a matter of being conditioned early in life to make responses which remain indefinitely. Parents can do much to prevent learning of fears, undesirable attitudes, and poor speech habits, if they understand that many of these are results of early conditioning experiences.

Teachers should study these and other recognizable episodes or instances that represent illustrative learning situations and endeavor to develop a comprehensive and overall view of learning theory. Actually, there is no immediate prospect of an agreement upon or formulation of a single theory or explanation of learning. Certainly these "kinds" or types of learnings will continue to be recognized and used by teachers without the necessity of accepting or rejecting either or both as the final or single view.

Learning by insight

Another broad or general category of learning theories should be presented in this brief survey. For convenience only, this group of three or four major explanations has often been termed the "field theories" in educational literature. Recently, the term "cognitive" theory has

come into use. Here it is our purpose to set forth a simple brief description under the heading of *learning by insight*.

Every student can recall instances when the problem before him suddenly became clear and the meaning or solution was apparent. Teachers have had many experiences with pupils who have spontaneously exclaimed, "Oh! I see!" when the flash of insight made sense and meaning out of the baffling or complicated problem situation before them. These are crude illustrations of the broad view or approach to learning theory popularly known as "field" or learning by insight. Actually, the learner acquires understanding (often very quickly and dramatically) into the patterns of structure and relationships in the "field" and forms cognitive structures of them. In brief, a flash of insight enables one to see the innate "meanings" in a total pattern.

There are actually three or four related theories in this broad category which we will study in some psychology courses. Our present purpose is merely to build interest and to develop purposeful motivation in preparation for that study. We shall deal quite briefly and generally with "learning by insight" as a kind or type of "learning theory."

According to this general concept, experience is possible because there are patterns (figures, configurations) that the learner can recognize through a power or a potentiality called insight. Insight has been defined as ". . . a special kind of neural or cortical organization that is established as soon as the organism achieves its purposes."[30]

Among the views comprehended in this broad group of learning theories are those which stem from Gestalt psychology. This is closely related to others of this category but deserves identification here because of its currency and frequency of mention in educational circles. The Gestalt position on learning can be briefly described. The learner perceives the situation. He acts on that perception and thereby comes to redefine the situation in a new perception. Again, action is followed by redefinition and new perceptions. This goes on until suddenly there is—insight![31]

These brief examples and descriptions may serve to present the kind of concept which is called learning by insight. Learning, then, is a psychic process, to put it in grossly simplified terms. It may help to note the contrast to other theories which stress association of parts or elements in the learning process.

Learning by insight has some distinctive characteristics which have been recognized by students of learning theory.[32] In the first place, insightful learning depends upon the capacity of the learner; the mature organism achieves insight more readily. Second, previous experience is prerequisite to insight, although it does not guarantee it. Third, the situation may be so designed or arranged that the learner can structure it, else there can be no insight. Fourth, insight follows earlier trial-and-error efforts and attempts to solve or understand the problem-situation. Fifth, problems solved by insight can be solved again if the conditions are the same. And, sixth, insight achieved can be used in other and new situations. This is a crude description of a whole group of learning theories. In field theories are concepts which view insight as perception of what is present in. the universe as configurations (*Gestalten*), which see learning as dependent upon the individual's ability to perceive and to structure situations, and to utilize innate ability in this respect.

Teachers will recognize much that is familiar and accepted in this general view of learning. The significance of perception, the "wholeness" of learning and the "quality" of objects are aspects of learning that tie in with the experience and observations of teachers the world over.

As a future parent or teacher one can begin now to be conscious of concepts and theories of learning as one observes and engages in teaching and other laboratory experiences. Awareness and interest will enable one to gain background for meaningful and perceptive inquiry into this later in the educational program.

Principles affecting learning have received attention

The foregoing simplified discussion of some general types of learning leaves much to be desired but it will have served

[30] G. W. Hartmann, *The Psychology of Learning,* 41st Yearbook, Part II, National Society for the Study of Education (Chicago: University of Chicago Press, 1942), p. 192. Copyright 1942 by The University of Chicago. Used by permission.

[31] See Cole and Bruce, *Educational Psychology* (New York: Harcourt, Brace & World, 1950), p. 477, or any comparable book for teachers for a concise explanation of this.

[32] See Ernest R. Hilgard, *Theories of Learning* (New York: Appleton-Century-Crofts, Inc., 1948), pp. 189–195; or Thorpe and Schmuller, *op. cit.,* pp. 219–221 in this connection. See also Ralph Garry, *op. cit.,* pp. 10–11 for "principles" of cognitive theory.

its purpose if students go from this course into their studies of educational psychology and related fields with more interest and a better background. As we continue our study, abundant references will be found to "types" of learning in books and articles on education and psychology. We shall discover that "laws" or principles of learning formerly received much attention in the literature of this field. But all of this hardly needs to be explored here; it more properly belongs in such courses as educational psychology which we may take as we continue our studies.

In this connection the principle of "reward" (law of effect) is universally regarded as of highest significance. It simply states that the response (behavior) which has the most satisfactory effect will be learned most rapidly. Why? Because it is rewarding; it brings relief from anxiety (tension is reduced); the effect is satisfying. Each time this happens, the learning of that response is re-enforced. This principle is an important guide for the teacher and the parent.

Learners Become Personalities

Any investigation of learning should not proceed too long without consideration of the nature and purposes of the learner. After all the learner has the most significant vested interest in the nature and processes of learning. Thus it is necessary to review briefly the concepts of personality and to note that these relate to certain principles that are emphasized in or related to the theories and principles of learning.

Many concepts of personality are current

The diversity of concepts and definitions of personality ranges from excessively-worded phrases to involved descriptions of social behavior. Many approaches to the measurement or assessment of personality have been used—adjustment and interests inventories, graphs, rating scales, pencil and paper tests, multi-phasic tests, projective techniques, ink blots, sociograms, and various others. The truth is that personality is a broad concept that comprehends so much that it is difficult to entertain all of it or to deal with it in its entirety at a given time. When we talk of personality we include ability, intelligence, looks, physigue, learning, memory, emotions, attitudes, habits, motivation, and many other attributes and traits that, taken totally, comprise the person. This is the term we apply to the totality of the individual person. It represents the synthesis of all the physical, emotional, mental, social, and other factors that make up a given person.

Much of the confusion about the nature of personality arises from its different aspects, one of which may be stressed or referred to in a given instance. What is true of one aspect of personality may not be accurate or sound with respect to another. Failure to communicate clearly and precisely what concept of personality or what aspect of a given personality one is talking about is the cause of difficulty. Sometimes we hear that someone has "a good personality" when the reference is really to the *social aspect of personality*. This is what has been called the "stimulus effect" one has on other people, meaning that one makes a favorable impression and gets a positive response from others.[33] This is important, but it is only one aspect of personality.

Another phase of personality, often used as if it were the totality, is the general reaction or response that one makes. We may hear someone termed as an "emotional" or an "intellectual" personality, some as calm and collected, even poised, others as spasmodic and impulsive. Terms like this are frequently used: "a likeable personality," one that is "dignified," "aggressive," "coldly calculating," "temperamental," "pushy," "methodical," and many others depending upon the way persons react to situations. This aspect of personality—a behavioral aspect —is important but it is only a phase or part of the whole concept of personality.

A third aspect of personality may be referred to as the *inside* component. This may be viewed as the psychological base or nature of an individual that impels him to be sociable or unfriendly, outgoing, or retiring, and the like. Note that the behavior may be seen as the response aspect of personality but it stems from the "cause" aspect, which is the basic psychological nature of the person. This is little more than a popular, simplified explanation, but it is intended to throw some light upon the various aspects of personality, none of which are more than part of the whole concept. Unfortunately, much that is heard and read about the person as his friends see him, or as they view his overt behavior, or as his attitudes and "inner state" cause and affect his

actions, tend to confuse parts of the personality for the totality of his personality.

Representative definitions of personality

We can find some helpful definitions and theories of personality in the work of some of our outstanding psychologists.[34] Among the popular views of personality are some social or "outer" ones that define it in some such fashion as: (1) the sum-total effect an individual makes upon others; (2) patterns of habits and action that impress and influence others; (3) the ways that other people respond to a person as a stimulus; (4) defined as what other people think of a person. In other words, this view is of personality in terms of the impression one makes on other people and of their response. As we shall see, this is an aspect, but only an aspect, of personality.

Other definitions of personality from psychologists tend to define personality more objectively, that is, to refer to something that really exists, not to mere appearance. Personality is affected by others, by the objective world around us, and it has an effect upon environment and people, but these are not all. Some definitions refer to a kind of dynamic unity that characterizes or exists among the components of personality as the essence. It is also an entity or state of unity to be prized, held as valuable, and distinctive. Its integrity must be respected. Philosophers and great leaders of religious thought have placed premium upon this

---

[33] See Paul C. Garrison and J. Stanley Gray, *Educational Psychology* (New York: Appleton-Century-Crofts, Inc., 1955), pp. 177–178, for a good introduction to this subject.

[34] The serious student should read about the origin, development, and implications of the concept. See, for example, Gordon W. Allport, *Pattern and Growth in Personality* (New York: Holt, Rinehart & Winston, 1961), pp. 3–82. A treatment of concepts and definitions may be found on pp. 22–30.

kind of concept of the person. It has become central to the basic beliefs and essential concepts of democracy. This may sound convincing but it still does not say clearly what personality is or how it is defined.

Another group of definitions refers to personality as the sum-total of biological appetites, impulses, instincts, mechanisms, innate tendencies, and mental abilities, plus all the characteristics and dispositions that have been acquired by learning and life experiences. This is an omnibus definition, sometimes called the ditty-bag type. Other ways of stating the concept give more weight to structure by citing the "entire mental organization" of an individual at a given period in his growth or by calling it "the organized aggregate" of mental states and processes of the person. These three types of definitions that originated with various psychologists and anthropologists and other specialists have been adapted to show the diverse views held but even these are not all.

Still another type of concept is held by psychologists and behavioral scientists who will attempt merely to describe "operations" of the person. These operational definitions question the validity of the structural and other essentialist definitions. Personality in this view is not what one is (or has) but is the perception of someone else. Personality might well be phrased as the most adequate and detailed "conceptualization" of the behavior of another person that the scientist can give at a given time. One brief description termed personality as an individual's unique pattern of traits.[35]

One of the best-known psychologists, Dr. Gordon W. Allport, who has long studied in this field, defined personality as possessing an internal organization or structure, recognizably its own. The dynamic organization of the psycho-physical systems that determine the individual's characteristic behavior and thought—this is personality.[36] Note key terms in the definition that refer to important concepts: *Dynamic organization, psycho-physical systems, determine, characteristic, behavior* and *thought.*

The concepts and ideas of a large number of specialists — psychologists, physiologists, psychiatrists, philosophers, and sociologists—who attended the Mid-Century White House Conference on Children and Youth contributed to a new definition of personality. In this view, personality meant the human being who feels, acts, and thinks, who understands himself as an individual distinct from other persons; this individual human *is the* personality instead of merely having one.[37] The development of healthy personality was seen to be the major purpose of child-rearing in the home and of education in the school.

The nature of personality and its development

Those who have responsibility for home and school experience of children should appreciate the nature of personality and know something about the process of personality development. This understanding should begin with some basic facts about personality. First, each is

---

[35] See, for example, J. P. Guilford, "Creativity," in Jerome M. Seidman, *Readings in Educational Psychology* (Boston: Houghton Mifflin Co., 1955), p. 223.

[36] Gordon W. Allport, *Pattern and Growth of Personality* (New York: Holt, Rinehart & Winston, 1961), pp. 28–29.

[37] See William A. Fullagar, Hal G. Lewis, and Carroll F. Cumbee, *op. cit.,* pp. 353–356.

unique, different from any and every person. Even identical twins exhibit many differences apparent to the skilled observer. This does not deny the fact that people are similar, alike in many respects, and that some resemble others in a given respect so much that they may be grouped together for certain purposes. But individuals are literally *that*; they cannot be catalogued on any defensible and stable basis. Even "types" like extreme extroverts differ in many respects; they grow and change at different rates, and it is not possible to generalize about them. Everyone has this quality and characteristic of uniqueness. This means what it says and provides the basis for belief in the worth of people. Remember what the little girl wrote about her insight into different people after reading about life in several countries, "Remember that everyone *is as special as you*." That is profoundly true.

A second important fact is that personalities are patterned, in that each is comprised of aspects, appearance, temperament, attitudes, habits, emotions, learned responses, and other factors in a structured whole. These are not conglomerate, or chance arrangements. There is significance and pattern to the totality that composes the person.

Another primary fact is that each personality is a product of its own functioning and growth. Personality is continually becoming; what it is like in the future depends upon what it is and how it is functioning now. In other words, personalities do not suddenly become what they are; they are determined by what has been happening, by their manner of functioning in the long view. It is also true that personality is not tied to its status as of today; its functioning and growth can determine its future.

Most theories of personality development reflect the influence of Freudian theory which can be traced in many fields and applications of psychology and education.[38] Many persons have some awareness of unconscious aspects of personality and recognize that there are depths and factors not under conscious control. The need for satisfaction of basic urges and personal wants, possibility of conflicts with societal standards and customs, and the process of becoming socialized in the course of satisfying wants are generally accepted. Children must reach adjustment to conflicts between their personal wants (from biological needs to spiritual cravings) and the customs of groups to which they belong. All must somehow effect adjustment of their ways of satisfying personal wants with those of the other individuals in their families and groups. The satisfactory arrangement may be looked upon as a kind of adjustment.

The normal personality has achieved some degree of adjustment to the societal customs, and within or to itself. There is no prolonged tension, due to continued failures, unresolved problems and conflicts such as marks the disturbed person. Well-adjusted persons grow from well-adjusted children who grow normally in a suitable cultural environment. Normal personalities develop best in wholesome and challenging environments. This suggests the significance of the quality of the home and the school environments where

[38] Reference is made to the contribution of Sigmund Freud whose theories have profoundly changed and influenced most fields of modern scholarship and thought.

children experience most of their growth and development.

Some characteristics of well-adjusted persons

Wholesome personalities exhibit relatively effective adjustment with habits and skills that stand them in good stead in social and personal relationships. Many studies have recognized several traits and qualities that characterize the normal well-adjusted person. These include: (1) *Happiness* is one of the best indicators of mental health; (2) *Emotional control* does not mean absence of emotions or even of emotional behavior, but what it says, *control,* rather than lack of control; (3) *Physical health* which is closely related to the other characteristics; (4) *Freedom from serious self-conflicts* due to reasonably good agreement between one's own ideas and habits and practices; (5) *Social status* to the extent of deserving and enjoying the approval of one's peers; (6) *Challenging work* is a necessity; the nature of one's occupation does not matter so long as it is enjoyable; (7) *Intellectual honesty* on whatever level one can achieve it, is a significant trait of mature personalities. The ability to face reality honestly, to avoid wishful-thinking, and to leave off pretending even to oneself are all marks of the honest-with-himself person. It is a good sign of mental health and of a high level of adjustment.

Various other significant characteristics could be added to complete an adequate list. Certainly a "zest for living," many active interests, and sense of purpose would be appropriate additions to our list of characteristics of well-adjusted persons.

Personality development as an educational goal

Most Americans have little difficulty in accepting ideas about the significance and worth of individual persons until it comes time to implement them with appropriate action. Concern about people —their dignity and worth—is central to democratic institutions and values; this concern is inherent in the acknowledged responsible role of the school in promoting personality development. This has been expressed in a variety of ways, but it is important to consider it from the standpoint of developing healthy personality. This connotes balanced, all-round, wholesome development that means fully effective, vigorous, purposeful, achieving persons as the end-product of the educational system. Obviously, the school is but one of a number of educative agencies that contribute to personality development. It enters the interaction process several years after the home, the play group, neighborhood, kinfolks, and church or synagogue have exerted greater or lesser influences upon the child's growth and development. But the school does have a discriminating role to play; it has more resources and leadership for undertaking its share of the total process and it must frequently correct, modify, and supplement some of the educative experiences and outcomes that the child has had elsewhere. The school must accept the responsibility to study the learner— his background, interests, needs, and potential—and make possible a program that will foster optimum development of the person he can become, i.e. self-realization.

Teachers and parents who see the

significance of this major task of the school will be concerned about the components of a healthy personality as a part of the philosophy that motivates good teachers in this endeavor.[39] These included three that should become prominent in the pre-school child, another that should develop from the time of entering school, two that are especially significant for adolescents, and two that should be achieved in adulthood. These follow in that order: (1) *The sense of trust*—should be learned in infancy from parents and other adults who accept the child and give affection; (2) *The sense of autonomy*—children begin the effort to establish independence as a human being—with mind and will of their own—early in the second and third years, and this process continues. Parents and teachers who want them to develop mature personalities must respect their desire and need to assert themselves and help them to keep the desire for independence in reasonable bounds; (3) *A sense of initiative*—shows in about the fourth and fifth years in efforts to recreate some adult activities and to share in same. Eagerness to learn and readiness show up and this should be fostered. Restriction of initiative yields bitterness, resentment, and vengeful attitudes that may become part of the developing personality; (4) *A sense of accomplishment*—children who have developed the three "senses" in pre-school years may be expected to show development of a sense of accomplishment. At six they are ready for real tasks that they can successfully complete. Exuberant imagination comes under controls and the primary grades are a period of calm steady growth, a time when respon-

[39] William A. Fullagar, Hal G. Lewis, and Carroll F. Cumbee, *op. cit.*, pp. 354–356.

sible citizenship is developed in the children of the group. Home and school should be on guard to prevent experiences that lead to feelings of inadequacy and inferiority. The sense of successful accomplishment is the bright side of the situation and one to be valued and worked at; (5) *A sense of identity*—with adolescence the individual seeks clarification of his own selfhood and of his future role; the peer-group opinions are important to him; previous accomplishment and the other "senses" developed can afford basis for a feeling of self-esteem and healthy emotional growth; (6) *A sense of intimacy*—the sense of identity is almost a prerequisite for this desirable development, successful entrance into human relationships of friendship, love, and inspiration; (7) *The parental sense*—achieved in adulthood substantially as other senses have been developed, features qualities of creativity and productivity; and (8) *The sense of integrity*—gradual and continuing acceptance of the dominant ideals of the culture—courage, courtesy, fairness, honor, self-discipline, reliability, and the like—tend to approximate integrity, a key to the integration of a healthy personality. This kind of bird's-eye view of the progress toward the goal of wholesome personality development is important for parents and teachers to know, understand, and use as a guide to their own roles in facilitating this process of growth.

SOME CONDITIONS OF DESIRABLE LEARNING

The preceding discussions have prepared the way for an understanding of what may be expected of principles or guides to action concerning learning. But "principles," however sound, will not do our work for us; principles are merely guides or helps for our own action and use. In the work of teaching, an understanding of sound principles of desirable learning can be a great help if they are regarded as such, not as "laws" or infallible rules to follow without decision and action on your part. Perhaps these may be best described as "conditions" which promote desirable learning.[40]

Responsible adults need to understand conditions which promote effective learning:

First, *the learner must have purposeful goals to guide his learning activities.* Behavior is always purposive in nature, i.e. it is exhibited for the purpose of reaching a goal, doing something, or getting results. Purposeful behavior (when the goal is clearly in mind) is more effective than impulsive behavior. The purpose must be the pupil's purpose rather than the teacher's purpose. Purpose implies interest and interest is the motive power which gets things done. Ideally, the two should accept or desire the same purpose or goal. This may explain why the athletic coach and his teams get results while the teacher of academic subjects has much difficulty with the same pupils.

Second, *the learner must be free to create or select his own responses to the problem-situation which he is in.* A learner facing a problem-situation is the essential unit of learning. This is the life

situation. People grow (learn) and change, conditions and situations constantly change. Thus, old responses and learnings tend to be inadequate or inappropriate in more and more situations. Hence, the learner needs to have freedom to act creatively (intelligently) to make the best response in the problem-situations he will face in living.

Third, *the learner must have the freedom to make his own organization of the materials needed to reach his purposeful goals.* Desirable learning means that the child creates for himself the subject matter and the methods he uses to reach goals of his own activity. Ready-made curriculums, subject matter packages, pre-arranged techniques are not adequate for him; they are not his own work and can have little meaning for him. He may be able to discover some of these for himself. If so, well and good, but we cannot expect individuals to be able to take and use effectively something created by another.

Fourth, *the learner needs cooperative sharing of experiences with other learners under adult guidance rather than control.* Children can share in the management of their affairs including learning experiences. To be sure, this degree or extent of this varies with their ages but it is essential to social growth and development. Incidentally, much of our learning is in a social situation, which includes other individuals and groups. There are relatively few learning experiences which approximate a laboratory experiment where a solitary learner works a problem-solving situation. Cooperative interaction with other learners is an essential condition of desirable learning in and for the social world which the learner experiences.

---

[40] See Hopkins, *op. cit.,* pp. 160–171 for a good discussion of this. Another good discussion of this general topic may be found in Earl A. Johnson and R. Eldon Michael, *Principles of Teaching* (Boston: Allyn & Bacon, Inc., 1958), pp. 109–165. A useful summary of eleven principles may be found on pp. 162–164.

Fifth, *the learner must have sympathetic understanding as a growing personality.* Children can quickly sense sympathy and sincerity in adults with whom they come in contact. All persons behave more normally and feel freer in the company of others who accept them for what they are. Teachers and parents who expect to help children learn must make them "feel at home." Doctors, nurses, school psychologists and other adults who work with children know the importance of establishing rapport with them. You may observe the importance of this by watching a good nursery school or kindergarten teacher work with her pupils. Such teachers understand the growing personalities of the learner and accept the fact that learning (growing) is a genetic process. Learning for the moment is not finished behavior; it is behavior on the way to becoming better behavior. Sympathetic adults who understand this represent a condition for desirable learning.

Sixth, *the learner accepts and uses the learnings which he finds personally valuable or useful.* All learnings are not related to and used by the learner. Those which fill a need, which can be used, which prove valuable are selected because they tend to be used in meeting new experiences. This is the creative principle which was referred to in our conception of learning. This has been best expressed by Kilpatrick: "We learn what we live, what we in our hearts accept as our way of living; and we learn it as and in the degree that we accept it."[41]

We must study learning

Our best cue is to resolve to become a student of learning. We shall have further opportunity as we read and discuss materials in this course, and as we observe schools. Later, many will have courses in educational psychology and methods of teaching where they will make a more systematic study of learning and applications to typical classroom situations. The practice teaching experience will provide students with some laboratory experience in helping pupils learn. Meanwhile, if all can become more aware of their own learning problems and experiences they may profit from them. All of these experiences can further your understanding if you have this as your own purposeful goal. As a good teacher you must know how to aid learning.

The parent or the teacher who learns to appreciate and act upon five basic needs of children will do much to promote wholesome, balanced, and relaxed growth of children.[42] All of these relate to the whole child, and they contribute to a warm, friendly, interesting, social environment that will encourage the participation, the best efforts, and the cooperation of boys and girls. This "Big Five" of basic needs are: (1) *Acceptance*—of each child as he or she is, fully, freely without patronizing or conditions, permitting the feeling of security of children to release their energies to try, to participate, to achieve, and to grow; (2) *Achievement* —should be in terms of what is best and

---

[41] Frequently quoted by Dr. William H. Kilpatrick in addresses and writings. See for example, his book, *Philosophy of Education* (New York: The Macmillan Company, 1951), pp. 221, 242–245, 296–298, 424–427.

[42] See Gladys Gardner Jenkins, *Helping Children Reach Their Potential* (Chicago: Scott, Foresman and Company, 1961), pp. 11–153, for an interesting and helpful treatment of this view.

fair in terms of each child's potential, recognizing that achievement depends largely upon the child's image of himself and that his perceptions must be taken into account, helping him to build from this point; (3) *Participation*—is important for several reasons—to provide group acceptance and cooperative experiences, for emotional and social growth, and to develop skills and attitudes for living in an interdependent society; (4) *Expression of Feelings*—for the sake of emotional growth and mental health, recognizing that emotionalized behavior represents symptoms that should be studied and followed up intelligently, to foster develop-ment of emotional maturity, all the while accepting and promoting the all-round growth of the child; and (5) *Self-Discipline*—as an ideal to be achieved by and through the growth in the understanding of this goal and of their own development by the children. Teachers should be willing to accept each day's incidents as opportunities for some good learnings and progress in the realization that children can learn from their mistakes. Problems that arise are means through which the important self-controls can be developed and accepted by each child as he grows and learns by choice rather than being forced into conformity.

Democratic Living in the Schools

It has seemed wise to devote attention to some basic principles that relate to education that are important in the learning experiences of children as they grow up to participate in our democratic society. This has necessitated choice among the numerous principles that relate to all aspects of education—both as an institution and as a process. In view of the primary concern of democratic institutions for people and of the central role of learning in their development, the choice of learning principles seemed most appropriate.

Another major concern about principles related to American education stems from the need for experiences in social living that will promote democratic citizenship. There are many approaches and facets to the total problem but the immediate question has to do with the nature and quality of the experiences of democratic living in the schools of these United States.

Education in and for democracy

There are and should be many different viewpoints on a basic question like this, especially as to ways and means. A starting point for further explanation of this subject can be presented in the form of a few simple propositions to consider:

1. Education in our democratic society should be *education in and for democracy.* In other words, schools of the United States will necessarily be different, in many respects, because of that fact.

2. Education in a democracy should be based upon a philosophy of democracy, i.e. the central beliefs and values of a democracy.

3. Education in a democracy should mean having experiences in democratic living, thinking, and values for teachers and learners.

4. Democratic education presents challenging beliefs in the improvability of people and of society. In other words, democratic education has a job—a mission to perform. In this respect, it is dynamic, alive, and growing.

5. Schools in a democracy should be organized, financed, and administered in a manner consistent with democratic principles and values.

All of these propositions have merit but the priority should be given to those with implications for the living experiences within the school. The school is a "little community" where many people follow many roles; a great many persons have to accept and relate to each other, and most aspects of personality development can be served in some degree. Moreover, it is a social environment in which there can be some controls and modifications to foster desirable learnings. The common school should be deeply committed to the task of providing experiences in democratic living for all the children of the people. Whether this is the generally accepted view and how well this function is being carried out are natural questions to raise and to follow up.

Hallmarks of democratic education

One of the best explorations of this subject came during the years immediately preceding World War II. The Educational Policies Commission conducted a study of "education for democracy in American high schools," seeking to find how well our schools were accomplishing this important objective. The report entitled *Learning the Ways of Democracy* was published in 1940.[43] All will be in-

[43] Educational Policies Commission, *Learning the Ways of Democracy* (Washington: NEA, 1940), pp. 35–39. Used by permission.

terested in what this report presents as the "Hallmarks of Democratic Education" as follows:

1. Democratic education has as its central purpose the welfare of all the people. This means nothing, a little, or *everything,* depending upon one's philosophy.

2. Democratic education serves each individual with justice, seeking to provide equal educational opportunity for all, regardless of the intelligence, race, religion, social status, economic condition, or vocational plans.

3. Democratic education respects the basic civil liberties in practice and clarifies their meaning through study. Here, what is lived in the daily life of the school is tied in with the subject matter of the social studies.

4. Democratic education is concerned for the maintenance of those economic, political, and social conditions which are necessary for the enjoyment of liberty. People want to be free—able to hold up their heads unafraid—not "beholden" to anyone—in the economic and social sense as well as free and able to vote.

5. Democratic education guarantees to all the members of its community the right to share in determining the purposes and policies of education. The schools belong to the people—all the people.

6. Democratic education uses democratic methods, in classroom, administration, and student activities.

7. Democratic education makes efficient use of personnel, teaching respect for competence in positions of responsibility.

8. Democratic education teaches through experience that every privilege entails a corresponding duty, every authority a responsibility, every responsibility an accounting to the group which granted the privilege or authority. Learning this is a long and difficult task for the people or any group; it cannot be begun too early. Failure to accomplish this invites a dictator to take over in an emergency.

9. Democratic education demonstrates that far-reaching changes, of both policies and procedures, can be carried on in orderly fashion, when the decisions to make the changes have been reached by democratic means.

10. Democratic education liberates and uses the intelligence of all. This reminds us of Dewey's definition of freedom—essentially the opportunity to use our intelligence freely and liberally.

11. Democratic education equips citizens with the materials of knowledge needed for democratic efficiency. Note that efficiency in democracy is defined more generously than in a dictatorship—it means more than Mussolini's making the trains run on time or Hitler's building of wide auto roads which planes could use as runways.

12. Democratic education promotes loyalty to democracy by stressing positive understanding and appreciation and by summoning youth to service in a great cause. Our schools do too little of this. We need an enthusiasm for and in behalf of democracy. Hitler gave purpose to his youth, so did the Nips. How much more important it is for American youth to have a faith in the liberal principles of system that tries to make *free men*.

Keep these distinctive marks of democratic education in mind as you visit and observe in schools later in your experience.

A social philosophy for our schools

Should the schools live and practice democracy in their programs? Professor Kilpatrick is quite eloquent on this subject. Following is a brief summary of his suggestions which will serve as a starting point for your thinking and discussion.

The schools must believe and practice according to this view:

1. Respect for human personality as such;
2. The moral obligation to take account of all the consequences of one's acts;

3. Each human is inherently social in origin and character;
4. Rapid change in our time and society makes strategic demands upon thought and education (social change);
5. Personal integration depends in good measure on the character of the surrounding life (culture);
6. The individual can in creative intelligence rise above his culture (social mobility);
7. We must always have regard for the *whole* child (the organism acts as a whole, not by parts);
8. The school cannot stand apart from life (community school).[44]

PRINCIPLES AND PEOPLE

Actual performance of its role by the school rather than the lip service which is freely given in many instances is necessary. Some of our great educators have long urged the importance of living what we learn. For this view children (and adults) learn anything as they accept it to act upon or use it; they learn it better and more readily if it is deemed important. This major principle, long current in certain philosophy of education circles, suggests that we must allow children to have experiences in the development of democratic methods and values if they are to grow up to accept it as a way of life. Telling them about Thomas Jefferson and exhorting them to be good citizens of democracy will not suffice for most of the pupils. They must have actual experiences *and be conscious* of the real significance and meanings they derive from living in democratic fashion with others in the school. When teachers can help children

[44] W. H. Kilpatrick, "A Social Philosophy for Progressive Education," in *Progressive Education*, reprinted by PEA, 1935.

to have experiences that have meanings for democratic living and get them to intellectualize about what they mean they can be sure that they are promoting the democratic way of life.

What we know about the importance of living and learning democracy is further supported by many psychologists who have consistently shown that children become what they experience. The feelings of being unwanted, rejected, unworthy, unacceptable, and of failure are learned through experiences that led to these perceptions by children. These negative concepts and the unwholesome self-image they accompany are results of ways these children have been treated and they have learned what they lived. Practices by parents, teachers, and adults (even peer group leaders), that make pupils feel inferior, degraded, and rejected are unsound and dangerous in their effects upon personality development. Good teaching requires learning experiences broad and varied enough to permit something of interest and challenge to all pupils, the change to have some success, and satisfaction. This should go forward and deeper until pupils are challenged to think to the level of their potential. When pupils discover that they can solve their problems by critical thinking, we may expect changed perceptions of self, of others, and of the social environment in which they participate. This is the way teachers help build better people and democracy.

Selected Bibliography

Allport, Gordon W. *Pattern and Growth of Personality*. New York: Holt, Rinehart, & Winston, 1961.

Association for Supervision and Curriculum Development, *Learning and the Teacher*, 1959 Yearbook. Washington: NEA, 1959.

Brubacher, John S. (Ed.) *The Public Schools and Spiritual Values*, Seventh Yearbook, John Dewey Society. New York: Harper & Row, 1944.

Brumbeck, Cole S. *The Discovery of Teaching*, Englewood Cliffs, N.J.: Prentice-Hall, Inc., 1962.

Burton, William H. *The Guidance of Learning Activities*, 3rd ed. New York: Appleton-Century-Crofts, Inc., 1962, pp. 4–167. See pp. 18–23 for a good discussion of general principles of learning.

Bruner, Jerome S. *On Knowing, Essays for the Left Hand*. Cambridge: Belknap Press of Harvard University Press, 1962.

Clement, Stanley L. "Seven Principles of Learning," *The Clearing House*, **XXXVI**, (September 1961), pp. 23–26.

Cole, Lawrence and Bruce, William F. *Educational Psychology*. New York: Harcourt, Brace & World, 1950.

Cronbach, Lee J. *Educational Psychology*, 2nd ed. New York: Harcourt, Brace & World, 1963.

Chapman, J. Crosby and Counts, George S. *Principles of Education*. Boston: Houghton Mifflin & Co., 1924.

Fullager, William A., Lewis, Hal G. and Cumbee, Carroll F. (Eds.) *Readings for Educational Psychology*. New York: Thomas Y. Crowell Co., 1956.

De Huszar, George B. *Practical Applications of Democracy*. New York: Harper & Row, 1950.

Educational Policies Commission, *Education of the Gifted*. Washington: NEA, 1950.

————. *Learning the Ways of Democracy*. Washington: NEA, 1940.

————. *Our Democracy*. Washington: NEA, 1941.

Garrison, Karl G. and Gray, Stanley J. *Educational Psychology*. New York: Appleton-Century-Crofts, Inc., 1955.

Garry, Ralph. *The Psychology of Learning*. Washington: The Center for Applied Research in Education, 1963.

Havighurst, Robert J. *Developmental Tasks and Education*. Sec. ed. New York: Longmans, Green & Co., 1952.

Hilgard, Ernest R. *Theories of Learning*, Rev. ed., New York: Appleton-Century-Crofts, Inc., 1956.

Hopkins, L. Thomas. *Interaction: The Democratic Process*. Boston: D. C. Heath & Co., 1941.

Hullfish, H. Gordon and Smith, Philip G. *Reflective Thinking: The Method of Education*. New York: Dodd, Mead & Co., 1961, see especially chapter 11.

Jenkins, Gladys Gardner. *Helping Children Reach Their Potential*, a Teacher's Resource Book. Chicago: Scott, Foresman & Co., 1961. An excellent readable book for future parents and teachers.

Johnson, Earl A. and Michael, R. Eldon. *Principles of Teaching*. Boston: Allyn & Bacon, 1958, see chapters 5–6.

Kingsley, Howard L. *The Nature and Conditions of Learning*. New York: Prentice-Hall, 1946.

McGeoch, J. A. and Irion, Arthur L. *The Psychology of Human Learning*. 2nd ed. New York: Longmans, Green & Co., 1952.

Melby, Ernest O. *The Teacher and Learning*. Washington: The Center for Applied Research in Education, 1963.

Miller, Neal and Dollard, John. *Social Learning and Imitation*. New Haven: Yale University Press, 1941.

National Society for the Study of Education, *Learning and Instruction*, 49th Yearbook, Part I. Chicago: University of Chicago Press, 1950.

————. *The Psychology of Learning*, 41st Yearbook, Part II. Chicago: University of Chicago Press, 1942.

Pratt, Caroline. *I Learn from Children*. New York: Simon & Schuster, 1948.

Peters, Burnett, and Farwell. *Introduction to Teaching*, New York: The Macmillan Co., 1963. See chapter 6.

Rasey, Marie I. and Menge, J. W. *What Do We Learn from Children*. New York: Harper & Row, 1956.

Raths, L. E. *An Application to Education of the Needs Theory*. New York: Modern Education Service, 1949.

Redl, Fritz and Sheviakov, George V. *Discipline for Today's Children and Youth*. Washington: NEA, 1944.

Seidman, Jerome M. (ed.) *Readings in Educational Psychology*. Boston: Houghton Mifflin, 1955.

Thorpe, Louis P. and Schmuller, Allen M. *Contemporary Theories of Learning*. New York: The Ronald Press, 1954.

Townsend, Edward Arthur, and Burke, Paul J. *Learning for Teachers*. New York: The Macmillan Co., 1962.

Travers, Robert M. W. *Essentials of Learning*. New York: The Macmillan Co., 1963.

Trow, William Clark. *The Learning Process*, What Research Says Series. Washington: NEA, 1954.

Watson, Goodwin. *What Do We Know About Learning? NEA Journal*, **LII**, No. 3 (March 1963), see pages 20–32 for articles on learning.

Weber, Julia. *My Country School Diary*. New York: Harper & Row, 1946.

Chapter 9

The Practices of Good Schools

The classroom is a small community where children should learn satisfactory relationships with others. In such a classroom, the teacher is a friend and guide of each child, and each child learns to assume his share of the responsibility for the success of the group undertakings. Valuable opportunities for learning are found in daily conferences when children and teachers plan the work of the day together, discuss problems which arise, listen to reports of group progress, and evaluate their work as it proceeds. Children who work under wise teacher guidance on significant, worthwhile undertakings in a school environment which is pleasant, stimulating and not unduly restrictive have the best opportunity for acquiring those traits of cooperation, initiative, originality, leadership, and respect for the opinions of others which are so greatly needed in the world today.*

Introduction

Our need to have first-hand experience in good schools provides the cue for that important next step namely, observation and visitation in both elementary and secondary programs. Experiences that we may acquire in this unit should help us to approach the matter of deciding about our own interest in teaching with confidence and adequate knowledge of the opportunities ahead.

Observations and other experiences in schools may well be one of the most helpful and effective ways for each to learn something about teaching opportunities. Certainly we cannot now think of the questions we shall want to have answered when we begin to teach two or three years hence. Neither can we get the understandings, skills, attitudes, and all else we shall need for teaching from education textbooks unless we have had enough background to make the texts meaningful.

We need to learn something about schools and the whole process of education by seeing it in action. We should see many children, every one different with his or her own problems, good and poor teachers, various kinds of organization,

* *School Days,* Maine Department of Education, Curriculum Bulletin No. 6, 1948, p. 16. Used by permission.

diverse methods, all sorts of activities—in short, the works. From this we should begin to really see the problems we will meet one day as teachers, and at least learn some of the important questions to ask; possibly find some of the answers! Then we shall be more nearly ready to make a sound decision concerning our own place and our role in the schools and in the community.

Descriptive presentations of elementary and secondary school programs have been prepared for our consideration, pen pictures of schools and practical suggestions about ways to carry our study into actual practice. After a good experience in studying how many teachers work with boys and girls in various schools we shall have a better basis for making our respective decision about teaching.

Learning to make the most of an observation in an elementary school is something worth trying to develop. Many people see very little of the school, even though they go out and in year after year. Too many people just accept schools as a matter of course. They have always been used to them, and they have never really considered fundamental reasons for or questions about the educational programs they have known.

Since we must make the most of our limited time for observing and studying schools, we should prepare ourselves to that end. It would be a good idea to set down the most important things we should like to know as one means of getting the most out of this experience.

A few questions might help at the start. What is the school for? What are its purposes? Why is it located as it is? How and by whom is it supported? How is it organized? Who is responsible for its ad-ministration? For its policies? Does it have a basic philosophy? Is it developing a program to accomplish its stated purposes? How can its work be evaluated?

What will we do while at the school? Should we go at once to a classroom and visit first one and then another all day? Would it be well to see someone who can explain the school organization and program first? Should we make a brief tour to learn our way about, before beginning our classroom observations? Why? Shall we talk to teachers and students? Why? Should one make notes during any of these conferences? Should one do so during a classroom visit? We must raise, discuss, and decide about such questions as these beforehand.

Consider further, what values should we expect to get from our school observations? We should have a real purpose if this kind of experience is to be of most help. Perhaps the greatest help we should derive from school observations is a visual picture of what teaching is like, or what it should be like. We shall be able to visualize the problems of teaching and to raise *real* questions which otherwise might not occur to us until some years in the future. We must try to get this kind of help from our observations. Each should bring up in class the practical questions he thinks of and discovers, so that our education courses will give us the greatest possible help in preparing to teach or to become informed citizens and parents.

All prospective teachers need real experiences of a wide variety in actual schools as a part of teacher education. The medical student gets much of his training in the clinic and in the hospital. The dental student gets a great deal of actual practice, and so does the student nurse. The young engineer works in laboratories and shops. Teaching should profit from real practical experiences by student teachers. These real experiences should increase gradually in frequency and purpose until the student teacher is actually participating in the school program—doing directed teaching (often called practice or student teaching).

But the day for your directed teaching is still in the future. We have not yet determined whether to teach or the kind of teaching we should do. In preparation for that, we should see different schools and learn about the work of many teachers. We should start by visiting an elementary school, preferably one with a good kindergarten.

Know Good Schools for Children

We might remind ourselves about some important things to do before we go to visit a modern elementary school. There are at least three.

Pointers for advance planning

We should get a good picture of the community setting of the school. Locate the community on a map, and get general information about it—area, relief, population, housing, neighborhoods, economic data, highways, industries, recreation, and community life. One can tell a good deal about some of the socio-economic conditions which affect the work of the school by referring to the census data for the county. Some of the most important data is that about the people—what they are like, what they do for a living, how they live, their general educational status, and comparable facts. What the school is doing or should be doing will make sense only when viewed in terms of its community orientation.

The second important step is to find some general information about the school. This is as good a place as any for us to begin using the directory, courses of study, and other publications from the state department of education. Here we will find much helpful data. We may also be able to find annual reports of the school system particularly if it is a good-sized one. Some schools have a handbook for new teachers which would be helpful for the group to read beforehand.

Finally, all should collaborate both with classmates and instructors in planning the visits. If possible the principal or a supervisor of the school system should have a conference with the group. All will be interested in what the school staff believes it should do (philosophy); what the program is like; how it is evaluated; and the problems it now faces. We shall need to prepare questions and suggestions to be followed up at the school. It would be smart for the group to be on its toes in this preliminary planning. This is the sort of thing we will be trying to do with boys and girls when we teach. Why not make our own participation as full and as complete a learning experience as possible. Does this make sense?

Making our visits count

As we approach the school we observe the location well off any main traffic route. The building is a low sprawling structure, attractively landscaped, and a credit to the community. It takes up little or none of the good playing space on the school grounds which cover an area of some 12 acres.

We begin to wonder at the cost, but recall that we were told how much the community got for its money. Beauty, simplicity, safety, utility, and adaptability are terms which seem to apply as we study the building and site. We see that the lawn is well kept, the shrubbery neat, and the whole location gives a pleasing effect. The parking space provides room for many cars away from the space where children play. Here is the shelter where the buses are loaded. Out on the play areas are several groups of children at games and using the outdoor play apparatus. A teacher is moving around and helping when needed.

Inside the school we are directed to the school office by one of the children. The principal immediately arranges for us to be shown around the school by a committee of pupils. Off we go to see the school and to hear about it from an eleven-year-old girl. There are four large rooms with partitions that can be separated into smaller rooms, which are used for some team teaching. There are several rooms for group work (we called them classrooms), a sunny, cheerful room they call the library, a shiny cafeteria, a small auditorium with a stage, and a large playroom. We also find two suites of rooms used for administrative purposes and health activities respectively. We notice there are stockrooms for supplies and books, a small room for meetings, and a room for health exams adjoining a room with cots. We find that the stage can be utilized for music groups and activities; that films can be shown either in the auditorium or in the larger rooms for groups; that each of the latter has space for easels and a work bench. We wonder how much it all cost and how it is kept so much better than the dimly lighted old grade school we remember so well.

By the time our groups have gained a general knowledge of the building, we learn that we are lucky—we are to begin observing the nursery school group and see other groups during the day. As we observe the three-year-olds, and later the kindergarten group, we begin to see what we missed as a preschool child. Somehow the time passes rapidly as we observe the group and the individual activities of the children. By midmorning when the children prepare to have a glass of milk or fruit juice, to be followed by a rest, we go on to an older age group.

Here we see a large room which can be used for different purposes. Several small groups are working, with the teacher staying with each as needed. We wonder about all the materials we see and about the paintings on the display space. Bookcases, pictures, a large frieze, growing plants, many things seem to have a place here. The week-schedule informs us that three large group meetings will be held with smaller groups at work on alternate days, and some ETV lessons.

After we go to the library with the group, it is time to meet our friends and the principal in the cafeteria for lunch. The time passes quickly with a good hot lunch and a chat about our morning. Then some questions, and a brief discussion of the school's statement of philosophy and purposes, a copy of which the principal has distributed. We note that lunch has been scheduled for various groups on some staggered plan and that there is no confusion or waiting. The recollections we have of noisy lunch periods and hasty eating in order to get out to play seem very far back in the past. It appears that lunch is as much a part of the daily living together as any other part of the school program, and we see that it has its merits.

In the afternoon we find the auditorium in use by a group which has arranged a short play from a story they liked. Another group has been invited to enjoy it with them and we see how hard the children have worked to carry out their plans. Several older people, probably parents, are present. We have noticed adults around the school all day. Some had lunch in the cafeteria. We saw a committee meeting in a room near the principal's office. Two were working with the school nurse in the health suite, and one was simply reading in the library. We wondered if there was any special reason for so many people around. We recall how rarely we ever saw a parent in the elementary school we attended.

After the play we circulate around a bit more. The library has users in the eleven-year-old group. The twelve-year-olds are going out to work in the school garden. We want to see this, so off we go. We find that they have a visitor, the county agent who has been asked to help plan a winter garden. We think it's smart to call in someone-who-knows, to serve as a consultant when you need expert help. When we talk with one of the older boys later, he tells us that the school often brings in someone to help; that they go out in the community quite often to learn more about some part of its life and even to work on some project. Thus we learn how the little park area further down the street happened to have some lovely flower plots. The kids did it with some advice and tools procured from the president of the local Garden Club.

Back in the building we have just time to meet at the principal's office for a brief conference with the secretary and nursery teacher who explain how children enter school, and show us some of the records in their folders. We begin to see how seriously this school takes its own philosophy—"to do all within its power to help each child, each day and each year, to grow and to develop toward the purposes of education as much as his talents and capacities permit."

After the buses have started to leave and most of the children have gone, we talk to some teachers who are coming together in the committee room. One remarks that she has just finished viewing a film she will use next week and another has talked to a parent about a child who has just returned to school after an illness and needs care. Shortly, several parents come in and a brief meeting begins. We learn that this is a committee of the PTA to plan further details of entertainment for a large district meeting to be held at the school the next month. When it ends we look at our watch and note it is 4 p.m. It is time for all teachers to go home, including would-be teachers like ourselves.

As we leave the building we see a ball game in progress with an older boy serving as umpire. It was explained that the play space is used most of the time and that older boys from the nearby high school are dependable volunteer help for such activities. The principal is still around the building when the group leaves the premises. Many reflect and think "what a day!" Some wonder whether their feet will hurt. When suddenly they realize that all is well everyone is encouraged. Teaching in a good school would be like teaching in Farmville—that ideal school that has been described in recent years. When we realize that good teachers and cooperative parents are trying to provide better schools for children as fast as they can it causes one to wonder if he is big enough to help do that job.

Observe in different schools

A visit to one elementary school, even to an excellent one, is not conclusive for the purposes and needs of college students. The great Aristotle once said that it takes more than a swallow or one fine day to make a spring. So it is with observations to learn about teaching in elementary schools and the characteristics of a good school program. It is necessary and desirable to visit enough schools in different communities, serving a diversity of people, under varying conditions, to get a good sample of experience. The interesting point is that we can learn a great deal in any and all of these different kinds of schools.

Those who aspire to teaching and the role of parents of the next generation should know that schools and devoted teachers serve all manner of Americans. Thus it is possible to visit schools that serve the culturally deprived children of an underprivileged neighborhood in a metropolitan center and to find some of the same instructional content that you would find in swank suburban classrooms. Discriminating instructors and alert students can find live vigorous teachers and good instruction in old school buildings that present a dreary external appearance. One of the promising experimental programs

with team teaching in elementary and junior high schools is being carried out by a number of older institutions in downtown Pittsburgh.[1] The "Big Cities" movement to revitalize many school programs in depreciated areas has made an impressive start.[2]

Prospective parents and teachers will know more about schools in middle-class neighborhoods and the suburbs from first-hand experience, but they will learn more from visits after planning in terms of purpose(s). Excellent schools must be recognized and evaluated in terms of what the school attempts to do, its performance in terms of its personnel and resources, and the quality of the experiences it provides for the learners. We must learn to find these no matter where they may be.

Hallmarks of a good school

Some of the authorities and reports of studies have listed the characteristics of a good elementary school.[3] We may set

[1] See *Pupils, Patterns, and Possibilities, 1961 Annual Report,* Superintendent of Schools, Board of Education, Pittsburgh, Pa., 1961.

[2] See for example Ralph E. Loewe, "Who Makes a Menace Out of Johnny?" *Saturday Review,* **XLVI,** No. 24 (June 15, 1963), pp. 64–65, 80.

[3] See for example, Hollis P. Caswell, *Education in the Elementary School* (New York: American Book Co., 1942), pp. 67–71; Educational Policies Commission, *Education for All American Children* (Washington: NEA, 1948), pp. 1–8; Maine Department of Education, *The Good School,* Curriculum Bulletin No. 8, August 1948; Southern Association Cooperative Study of Elementary Education, *Good Schools for Children* (Atlanta: Southern Association of Colleges and Secondary Schools), 1951; Arthur D. Morse, *Schools of Tomorrow—Today* (Garden City, N.Y.: Doubleday & Co., Inc., Dec. 1960); Virginia Department of Education, *The Characteristics of a Good Elementary School* (Richmond: March 1949).

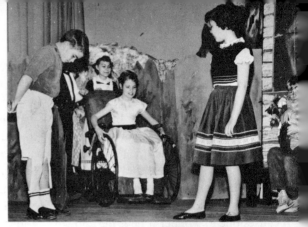
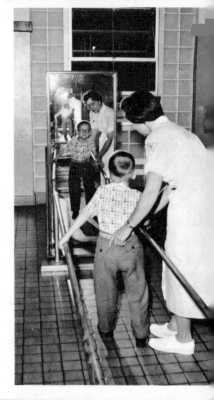

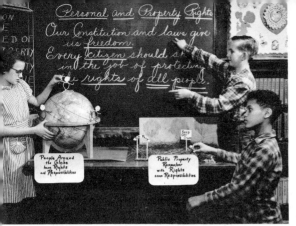

THE
ELEMENTARY
SCHOOL
CURRICULUM
IS ENRICHED
BY MANY KINDS
OF
EXPERIENCES

forth three kinds of illustrative features which should serve our present purposes.

A good school fits into its own place in the complete school system and in the whole pattern of educative agencies of society (community). The program of the good school is viewed as part of the life-long process of living and learning which normal personalities experience, and it is developed in full knowledge of this relationship. In plain language, the good school is part of the community, and its work takes into account the wider community process of education which continues throughout a person's lifetime. The *good school has a community orientation.*

The school must be concerned with all that happens before schooling begins, inside and outside the school during the years of attendance, and with adult education. This means concern about the level of living and the quality of living in the community. Such a school works with other agencies; it supplements and strengthens other instructive educative activities all to the end of improved living by people.

The good school bases its program upon adequate understanding of the learner, of growth, development, and maturation, and of learning. This means that the needs, the interests, the abilities and capacities, and the maturity level of the child provide the criteria for the school program. The knowledge of how people learn is of fundamental significance in the instructional work of the school. The *good school is child-centered* as it is willing to take the child as he is and provide for his education in terms of how learning takes place.

This means that physical facilities, arrangement of equipment, instructional materials, and everything related to instruction, are utilized to the end of effective learning. It means that learning experiences are provided in terms of the maturity level of the learner. It means that the teachers are content to foster optimum growth and development of a child in terms of what he or she is like instead of being concerned with mastery of pre-arranged subject matter content. This makes the school a place *of* and *for* living, where the child can have experiences at his own level of understanding, and where his needs and interests are used in planning learning experiences. The learning proceeds at varying rates and degrees according to the different capacities of the participants.

The good school develops its program in the light of the best and highest values of the culture. School purposes and programs reflect judgments and decisions regarding worth, quality, goodness, soundness, desirability, among many alternatives and choices. Ethical values have an important place among these criteria and represent much of what has been deemed important in the history and experience of the people.

In other words, the good school utilizes and fosters the most important values of the race experience and culture from which it derives. For Americans, a good illustration might be noted in the responsibility of the school to reflect and to exemplify democratic values. The way of living (and learning) in the school should be democratic in nature which proves to be an effective way to teach these values. The *good school is value-conscious,* committed to the ideals of the good life for everyone.

An inspiring but concise statement that characterized a good elementary school will serve for a summary:

A good school—

. . . this miniature of democracy, wherein pupils, teachers, and parents work together to solve their common problems; where learning activities literally teem with opportunities for critical thinking; where children are required to face facts and do what they do in the face of facts; where decisions are made and responsibilities assumed; where fundamentals and honesty and social concern are the guiding principles of daily living; where the whole community provides a laboratory for learning; where children and teachers are led out into the stresses of life and find the security which comes with the awareness and understanding of the things around them.[4]

That goal will be reached when we have the clear understanding which makes sense out of the educational literature about good schools. We may readily visualize what is meant by twenty characteristics of good schools for children.[5]

Good elementary schools

— develop needed skills
— teach moral and spiritual values
— meet needs and broaden interests
— foster personal and community health and safety
— teach wise use of resources
— develop democratic citizens
— continue to improve
— provide adequate instructional materials
— provide adequate and safe transportation
— have good buildings, equipment, and grounds
— provide for the guidance of children
— have small classes
— provide learning experiences for children under six
— provide special programs for exceptional children
— never close
— have good teachers
— have good principals, supervisors, and superintendents
— have a good school board
— have interested cooperative parents
— have adequate financial support.

We will know when these begin to make sense; we shall have at hand good illustrations and examples from our own experiences to help our understanding. In other words, we should be ready to have an informed opinion about what constitutes a good school for children.

Mark Good Schools for Youth

All teachers in our schools should come to an appreciation of the American high school and what it is all about. That is true for teachers irrespective of the area or field, grade, or age-group which they expect to teach. We will be able to check such a sweeping statement as we get into the study of this question.

High schools, an American institution, have come a long way since the first one opened nearly one-and-a-half centuries ago. This new type secondary school rapidly outstripped the older academy in popularity and won the battle for public support. During the first half of the twentieth century it gained popular

[4] J. E. Windrow, in *Professional Laboratory Experiences,* 27th Yearbook (Association for Student Teaching, State College of Iowa, Cedar Falls, 1948), p. 89. Used by permission.

[5] *Good Schools for Children* (Atlanta: Southern Association of Colleges and Secondary Schools, 1951).

acceptance as the agency for meeting the educational needs of youth. Each decade since 1870 the high school population has doubled, a rate of growth far ahead of that for the general population. Indeed it now enrolls more than 80% of youth of high school age.

The high school may be seen as an important agency of education in a democracy. Enrolling millions of youths who will receive no further education, it must provide for their overall growth and development, and for the major roles they will perform in our society. In this compound sentence we will find both tasks of the people's high school: individual growth and social needs. In democracy all youth are deemed important and deserving of the chance to make the most of themselves, and to realize their potentialities. At the same time, the democratic society needs to have its youth grow up to be good citizens, able workers, wise consumers, cooperative members of groups, tolerant, healthy and happy persons and responsible members of families. The high school tries to do these two major jobs in our culture. We will need to see some good high schools and to study their philosophies and programs in order to get an adequate picture of secondary education. Our next step should be that of visiting and getting acquainted with the work of some good high schools in various communities.

Can one tell much about a high school by a brief visit? How long would it take for us by observing its work to decide whether a high school was a good one or not? What do we want to know about a school anyway? Should we prepare for a visit to a school beforehand? Are most schools pretty much the same,

or does each have an individuality which one can recognize? Do high school faculties have a clear purpose in mind? What could one determine about a school from seeing the building after the children and teachers had left for the day? What can one learn by observing some high schools at work? Should one like to visit a school? How do high schools show the public the results of their work? We should not worry if we do not have answers to the above questions right on the tips of our tongues for that's what we are doing here —learning about these and other questions about teaching.

Getting ready for our visit

Before we begin to observe in any kind of high school, there should be careful preparation. We must first find out all we can about the community served by the school. Is it a "Farmville" or more like "American City"? Some general information about the school may be available in the public school directory and other publications of the state department of education. A copy of the handbook provided for the high school students would be a good source of information particularly about the school activities. If the instructor can arrange to have the principal come in to confer with the class, it would be a great help. We can get some idea of the school's point of view (philosophy and objectives), its guidance program, its curricular offerings, and its student activities. Plans for most effective use of our visitation time can be made beforehand with the school authorities.

We should make and arrange our notes from this advance information for later use. Then we shall be ready to prepare questions for which we will try to find answers as we visit and observe in the high school. Work out with the rest of the class some of the more important points you need to understand in order that your observations may be as helpful as possible.

Making our trip pay learning dividends

We can learn something by close observation in the community as we travel. Here is the chance to see something of the community: its size, its general character, its appearance, and its economic bases. This is an opportunity to see whether we can tell something of its economic status, the ways the people earn their living, the kinds of homes they have, and the roads and streets. There may be some evidences of civic pride or unconcern, and some clue as to the sort of amusement facilities available to the people. If we learn how to make the most of every opportunity, we can get some ideas about the needs and opportunities which the school serves. Do these give any indication as to what the school program should be like?

Suppose there are no recreational facilities in the community at all, save a cheap-looking movie theatre with bills of second-run films. Our inquiries elicit the information that our suspicion is correct. There are no facilities. Would this give us any ideas as to one function the high school should perform in that community? It should.

Let's take another possibility. Suppose there are several unsavory looking jive joints along the highway just outside of town. Would this suggest a possible problem for the parents and teachers of the high school pupils? Other possibilities

should occur to us if we are on the alert.

We should watch for further information and suggestions as we approach the school itself. Note its general setting in terms of the community it serves, and any evidence as to the size, adequacy, and accessibility of the site. Are there any serious traffic hazards? Are there adequate play spaces, parking areas, and room to expand for a school of this size? Note any evidence as to the probable cost of the plant, the care it receives and what use the general public makes of it. It is not ostentation or obvious costliness, or even beauty which makes a school building valuable to a community. It is rather what it means to the people in terms of community improvement and the needs of growing youth. Our alertness will enable us to get much evidence of the high school's community setting and of its place in the local scheme of things. We shall see even more evidence as we enter the school and observe its activities.

Make the whole day count

In high schools we should try to get an idea about every aspect of the school and its work. Perhaps it would be a good idea to have a general tour of the building to get a general orientation. There are some advantages in having this tour conducted by students as it will give some insights into the school program we may not get by more formal means.

One can tell much about the school program by the facilities and equipment, partly by what is available, but far more by the way it is used. We can tell whether the gym is used for anything except basketball teams and whether the commercial subjects room is open to the people of the community. Up-to-date equipment in the homemaking department is costly indeed if it serves only small classes of girls taking the usual courses; it could be the place where the high school boys and the adults of the community learn a great deal. Does anyone save the boys taking vocational agriculture ever use the elaborate farm shop? What value does the library have for people who have already graduated or quit school and those who never attended the high school? Is the cafeteria the scene of community affairs replete with good food, fellowship and friendliness? Look for such evidence as this. Its presence or absence will tell us far more about the worth of this school to the community than any amount of unctuous talk by administrators or teachers.

Sometime early in our observation we want to get a fairly good picture of the daily program or schedule. Visualize what the typical student does during the day. Perhaps it would be a good idea to make a chart of the daily programs for several students to be used in subsequent study.

We should be shown illustrative folders and records kept for each student. These will give much evidence as to the real concern of the school for its pupils. We will feel better if our study reveals health records, reports and test scores, etc., from the elementary school. Later aptitude, personality, mental ability, and achievement testing results, work records, student activities records and other pertinent material should be in the cumulative folders. If the school has counselors, we should get an adequate understanding of how they work to help teachers to improve guidance and counseling services to pupils, and how they give supplementary assistance when and where needed. We will also want to learn how homeroom teachers come to know the members of their group and how they work together. They will probably give us a helpful explanation of how pupil records are used and also a description of the procedure of the school for receiving and orienting new students. Some will remember their own first days in high school and the adjustment they had to make after leaving elementary school and hope that this problem is being met in good high schools.

Observe classes and home room groups as much as possible, making an effort to see the scope and nature of the teacher's work. We will note that records are one little task of the teacher; that personal attention to the pupil must often be given. Clubs and other student groups have teachers as sponsors or advisers, and some duties in the actual running of the school are assumed by the faculty. It appears that this business of teaching is far more than preparing a few lessons to present to pupils. When we try to list the various things that we saw these busy teachers doing, the diversity will be impressive.

Our observations of the pupils at work in classrooms, laboratories, library, and elsewhere should also provide some opportunity for learning more about adolescents. Of course we will be careful to be as casual and matter-of-fact about our classroom observations as possible because we want the students to be natural and to go about their work in a normal manner. This will give our class many interesting and practical points to discuss when we get back to our own classroom.

We must not fail to see what goes on in the student activities program. Attend assembly if there should be one. See a club meeting; observe a working group in committee, or some other activity. We should be able to give our views as to the learnings which take place through these varied experiences. Try to see how all this is an important part of the pupil's real curriculum. We remember that he learns from all his experiences whether they are what pupils should learn or not and that these are concerns of the school which takes its job seriously. These activities formerly were called extra-curricular, then they were termed co-curricular; now the better schools tend to regard them as quite as much a part of the school's program as is an algebra course. Is it clear as to why this is a part of the school philosophy?

Our observation should not be concluded without some attention to the general morale and climate of opinion of the school. It is actually a little community made up of many people who must relate to each other in many ways. A pupil who never passes a course learns something there, good, bad, or mixed perhaps, but he does learn. The quality of the daily living in school corridors, rooms, and playgrounds is a part of the pupil's real learning.

The visitors should raise some questions which they have brought along. It would be a good plan to have a final conference with the principal or some other staff member to discuss these points before leaving. This would be a good way to round out the days' observations. The group may wish to discuss the school's promotion policy, the means of evaluating its program, and the work of pupils and many such questions.

We should not fail to look for evidence as to the effectiveness of the school program toward meeting the objectives it has stated. We found that *health* and *citizenship* and *wise use of leisure time* were among these objectives. What was actually going on by way of accomplishing these objectives in the growth and development of pupils? This question demands an answer.

Perhaps the chance can be found to ask some questions about these points. How do the teachers and the principal know when these objectives are being realized or when the school is failing to accomplish them? That is certainly a fair question. Would the answer: "By the marks pupils make on tests," satisfy? Doesn't it go further than that? The real test is the improved behavior of pupils along these lines. Put down in some notes all of the things you saw or heard which indicated these were being accomplished.

HOLD FOLLOW-UP
DISCUSSION SESSIONS

After school visits, it will pay to discuss all observations and impressions with the instructor and classmates. We will agree upon many points and probably differ upon various others. In any event we will be starting to get the realistic picture of what teaching is like, and of life in a high school. Two other suggestions may be in order for this part of your study. In the first place, we are now ready to do some careful reading about high schools and the work of the high school teacher. We have framed some intelligent questions which may be partially answered by good books on secondary education. We should try to come out with an understanding of the kind of high school we would like to see for all the youth of our nation.

The second is to make a list of all the duties which high school teachers perform. This should be discussed with instructors and classmates until we can arrange a fairly complete picture. Further reading about high schools and the study of this list will give a much better idea of what it is like to teach youth in a secondary school.

It is wise to organize all information and questions for use as guides in later visits to other schools and for future reading. As our background of information and understanding becomes more complete, we shall be able to derive much more from books and printed accounts of school programs.

GOOD SCHOOLS FOR
AMERICAN YOUTH

A school for all youth

An excellent description of an ideal school for youth of high school age has been prepared for us by the Educational Policies Commission. We should discover it in the course of our reading about high schools. It has been clearly outlined in *Education for All-American Youth* and in a briefer account in a digest entitled *Planning for American Youth*.[6]

This excellent school for all youth is described as it would operate in two American communities "Farmville" and "American City." It is to be a school for youth, boys and girls of high school age everywhere in the nation. Remember that we found that about 89% of our youth enroll in high school. The chief reason for our failure to get all of them is that the

high school has not offered programs to interest them and to meet their needs. We must have a school which does this. We may recall that two fine old institutions have largely disappeared from the American education scene—the Latin grammar school and the academy. They were once deemed adequate, but they failed to help all youth needing education. So the high school took their place. Will the high school, too, pass out of the picture and a new "youth school" take over? Possibly, unless the present day high school succeeds in meeting its responsibilities to all youth. This is the case for comprehensive high schools.

The Farmville youth school is pictured as a comprehensive high school. It accepts its responsibility to all youth of high school age regardless of background, family, money, social class, or any other basis. It is a school which tries to meet its responsibility to the community which supports it. This means facilities and activities for adults. All who can be served by the school are welcome at the Farmville school.

The school would be in many respects the community center. Certainly for education, recreation, health services, library service, and public meetings, it would be open to all during the day and evenings. On the grounds would be shops and cooperatives for the adults of the community. We shall read much of the "community school" idea; if Farmville becomes a reality, we may look forward to teaching in such a school.

The school program for youth may cover a period of eight years—grades seven through fourteen. In other words, secondary education is tending to include the junior college years. In the larger communities, free public education for all

[6] Educational Policies Commission 1944, 1946; National Association of Secondary School Principals, *Planning for American Youth* (Washington: The Association, 1944).

MAJOR CURRICULUM AREAS

Periods Per Day	GRADES							
	Early Secondary School			Middle Secondary School		Advanced Secondary School or Community Institute		
	7	8	9	10	11	12	13	14

1 — PERSONAL INTERESTS — Exploration of personal abilities and individual interests, discovery of interests in art, music, science, languages, sports, crafts, home and family problems, and leisure activities.

INDIVIDUAL INTERESTS* — Election by the pupil under guidance of teacher in fields of avocational, cultural, or intellectual interests.

2 / 3 — VOCATIONAL PREPARATION — Includes the study of science, mathematics, social studies, literature, and foreign languages, in preparation for advanced study in community institutes, colleges, and universities, as well as education for industrial, commercial, home-making, service, and other occupations, leading to employment, apprenticeship, or home-making after grade 12, 13, or 14.

4 / 5 — COMMON LEARNINGS — A continuous course in social living to foster growth in personal living and in civic competence. Guidance of individual students is a chief responsibility of social living teachers.

6 — HEALTH AND PHYSICAL FITNESS — Includes games, sports, and other activities to promote physical fitness, together with the study of individual and community health.

* Broken line indicates flexibility for youth who need to spend more time in either of those areas, depending upon their occupational or future educational plans.

Source: *Education for All American Youth—A Further Look* (Washington: Educational Policies Commission, NEA, 1952).

youth is to be extended by what is often called the community college. During the first three years the curriculum would stress these major areas:

1. Developing as a citizen.
2. Building health and physical fitness.
3. Exploring personal interests and abilities.

For the last five years its emphasis would be:

1. Preparing for an occupation.
2. Developing civic competence.

3. Developing personal interests and aptitudes.[7]

The above diagram shows a general scheme for the school curriculum over the eight year period.

Comparisons of various program proposals and recommendations of groups for high school curriculum may be helpful. Studies of the Educational Policies Commission and the Harvard Committee

[7] *Planning for American Youth*, op. cit., pp. 47–56.

EDUCATIONAL POLICIES COMMISSION

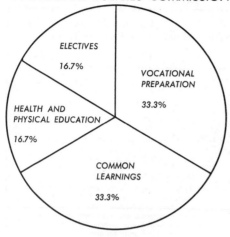

ELECTIVES 16.7%

VOCATIONAL PREPARATION 33.3%

HEALTH AND PHYSICAL EDUCATION 16.7%

COMMON LEARNINGS 33.3%

HARVARD COMMITTEE

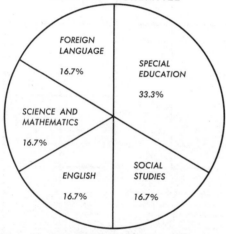

FOREIGN LANGUAGE 16.7%

SPECIAL EDUCATION 33.3%

SCIENCE AND MATHEMATICS 16.7%

ENGLISH 16.7%

SOCIAL STUDIES 16.7%

Source: *The Rand McNally Handbook of Education.*

recommended general and vocational (or special) education in the ratio of 2 to 1. The chief difference is found in the subject area emphasis of the latter in the provision of general education.[8] Other interesting comparisons can be made with the recommendations of the nationwide study by Dr. James B. Conant and of the Association for Supervision and Curricu-

[8] See the Harvard Committee, *General Education in a Free Society* (Cambridge: Harvard University Press, 1946).

lum Development of the National Education Association.[9]

The school studies the needs of the youth of "Farmville" and surrounding areas. It finds that its youth have immediate goals in about the following proportions:

10% go to work in the community at the end of 12th grade.

18% will remain in the 13th grade in Farmville.

17% go away to junior colleges, vocational schools, or trade schools, then go to work in cities.

10% go away to colleges and universities.

9% go away directly to the cities to work after the 12th grade.[10]

The school then tries to provide for each of these groups the educational opportunity they need. Guidance and counseling services are an important aspect of the school program. Work experience and direct participation in community life are deemed important parts of the youth's experiences in the school. Participation in student activities and in school government are regular parts of the school program.

In many ways the community participates in making the school program effective. It supports the school supplemented by state and federal funds. It sees

[9] See *The American High School Today* (New York: McGraw-Hill Book Co., Inc., 1959), and *The High School We Need* (Washington: NEA, 1959), respectively.

[10] These figures represented approximations of estimates made more than a decade past, but are still worthy of consideration. Some allowance might be made for service in the armed forces but even these years may include some education.

to it that all facilities, equipment and materials, even textbooks, are furnished free to pupils. It transports the rural pupils to school in safe buses. Work experience programs are geared to the school program so that youth may earn money for personal expenses. There is no artificial line between the school and the community activities. Farmville is truly a community school.

The Farmville Youth School is envisioned as the kind of school we should have to serve parts of our population living in small towns and rural areas.

An equally significant picture of the type of school we should have for youth who live in our cities is presented. This is termed the school for American City. Its program has purposes similar to those of Farmville but the activities are geared to fit the conditions and opportunities of a large urban community. As potential teachers of youth we should know these schools well enough to bring equally good schools into being when and where we teach.

Discover the teacher's role

One of the big factors in one's decision about his teaching field or area will be that of the duties and responsibilities of the teacher in that type of position. It is well to begin early to set down one's findings and reactions to the work of the teachers. We should get the good picture —the positive and constructive teacher in the happy relaxed environment for youth—in our thinking as clearly and definitely as the other kind, lest we get a distorted view. Too many teachers forget the many significantly sound and valuable experiences because of annoyances and petty items. Remember that teaching is a way of life for many, many thousands of fine folk who have lived and learned with the best young people. We may recall that the best brief philosophy of teaching known is—"living with children." That goes, too, for living and working with youth.

It is sound to arrange one's observations of what good teachers in high schools do into the broad categories that we find. Perhaps it will be discovered that there are up to a half-dozen big kinds of responsibilities. We have an adviser-counselor-guide, big brother or sister category. The guide of systematic learning activities is another. Still another is the minor role of administrator helper to which classroom teachers give time. Further the teacher serves as stimulator and leader of evaluation by pupils and parents. Moreover the teacher is a school citizen and participant in the living-together that comprises the school environment and an example for youth. The teacher is a sharer of hobbies and recreational interests of young people. Ideally the high school teacher will be a friend to many people, youth and adults. Finally the teacher should be an active participating citizen of the community.

We must study our own findings with members of other class groups and compare them with ideas from our reading. From all this we should have a good mental picture of what it means to be a teacher of youth. Whether we teach or not, we should go from college with an appreciation of the nature and significance of public education. In this the American public high school has a distinctive place. A good reminder of this has been chosen in these words:

America's policy of providing high-school opportunities for all children and youth and adapting the schooling to each pupil's needs, within the scope of the general demands of life today, is unique among the nations of the world. Although in several foreign countries elementary education has been universal for years and secondary education recently has moved definitely in that direction, none has gone as far as America in making secondary education effectively free and available to all, and in the effort to adapt education to the needs of the individual. While this country still has much progress to make in that respect, it has led the way by at least decades if not a half century. In brief, the United States has the only truly public secondary schools, devoted to the aims of a democratic people.[11]

A LOOK AT THE JUNIOR HIGH SCHOOL

Good junior high schools for today

Visits to schools for pupils in early adolescence should provide acquaintance with some good junior high schools. Junior high schools and curricula need to change a great deal to meet their challenging tasks in the next few decades. So do all other types of schools and educative agencies, but we shall have greater appreciation of that after we have come to understand the strengths and contributions of the best junior high schools of today.[12]

The junior high school of the Sixties at its best is a lively place to work and live with youth. Junior high schools have

[11] Leslie L. Chisholm, *The Work of the Modern High School* (New York: The Macmillan Co., 1953), p. 15.

[12] See Jean D. Grambs, *et al., The Junior High School We Need,* Association for Supervision and Curriculum Development (Washington: NEA, 1961).

grown rapidly in number and size in recent decades. Some controversy and a great deal of discussion have been continuing concerning the functions and program of the middle section of the American school program. Many lay leaders and parents who study American society recognize the gravity of the task of the schools that serve adolescents and pre-adolescents in an age when there is no real place for youth, save in school. For a great many educational and lay leaders it makes good sense to have schools genuinely devoted to the needs and potentials of teenagers. Junior high schools here and there have shown something of the possibilities now before us.

The junior high schools that offer leadership are characterized by extraordinary activity and experimentation. A number of curriculum projects have been undertaken in reorganization of curriculum content in mathematics, science, and foreign languages, in development of flexible curriculums for many different groups of students, adaptation of counselling to the realities and potential of today's social scene and the participants.

Visits to some of the best junior high schools would reveal certain desirable characteristics and features that might challenge other schools.

1. Size—moderate to the extent that program is sound and students feel security and participating membership.

2. Faculty—competent, prepared specifically for junior high school careers, concerned about purpose and role of the school, committed to concern about the wellbeing of students and prepared to understand, assist, and guide the young adolescent.

3. Library and Materials Center—central in the planning and practices of competent teachers.

4. Substantial Block-of-Time Instruction—adequate for meeting needs of adolescents during each of the three years should be provided. This provision should vary by years and for different groups to permit optimum use of both subjects and fused curriculum offerings.

5. Flexible Scheduling—to permit best possible use of all resources and offerings for meeting individual needs in terms of abilities and interests of pupils. The traditional departmentalized daily program of uniform rigid class periods and separate subjects is not well adapted to programs that are designed to provide as much individualized instruction as possible.

6. Adequate Guidance Services—serve a critical need during the early adolescent years. This becomes a major function of the junior high school, to be served by both teacher-counsellors and by guidance specialists in appropriate ways.

7. Adequate Laboratories and Workshops—to house suitable programs of exploratory experiences for boys and girls in various vocational and avocational fields.

8. A Modern Instructional Program—to meet the demands and challenges of the space age. This requires ample provisions for sciences, mathematics, and other curriculum areas to make best use of reorganized and modernized content now becoming available. There are many areas of instruction that must be served by different programs to meet the needs of groups of students.

9. Strong Physical Education Progress—represent a must for junior high boys and girls. This does not mean competitive athletics but a comprehensive program of a variety of sports and games for optimum physical fitness of youth.

10. Adequate administrative, clerical and instructional personnel—must be provided if the junior high school is to do the strategic job it is responsible for any youth of the Space-Age Sixties.

Students who learn to find evidences about characteristics and features of the junior high school through the media of study, observation, and conferences, will have the best background for understanding the educational challenges that come to future parents and teachers. Further reading and study will pay good returns in form of understanding the middle segment of America's ladder of educational opportunity.[13]

Our future junior high schools

It is clear that the junior high schools have won acceptance in the organizational structure of American public education. An overwhelming majority of children (82%) attend school in systems that provide junior high schools. Whether the junior high school is to be the dominant program for early adolescent pupils of America's school depends upon the vision and quality of its leadership and the support it receives from parents. None who read and think can doubt that the nature and imperativeness of its task suggests *urgency* in every respect. One of the greatest sources of help in the endeavor to have the best possible junior high schools for tomorrow's children would be an informed concerned group of parents and teachers.

[13] Good general references on the junior high school include: James B. Conant, *Education in the Junior High School Years* (Princeton, N.J.: Educational Testing Service, 1960); Educational Policies Commission, *Education for All American Youth—A Further Look* (Washington: NEA, 1952), pp. 214–244, 321–344; *The Junior High School Program* (Atlanta, Georgia: The Southern Association of Colleges and Secondary Schools, 1958); and Mauritz Johnson, Jr., "School in the Middle—Junior High: Education's Problem Child," *Saturday Review*, **XLV**, No. 28 (July 21, 1962), pp. 40–42, 56–57.

THE
JUNIOR
HIGH SCHOOL
PROVIDES
EXPLORATORY
EXPERIENCES

ALL PHOTOS COURTESY DALLAS INDEPENDENT SCHOOL DISTRICT

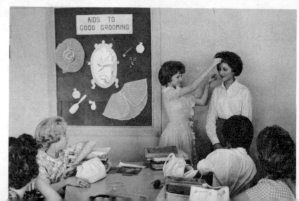

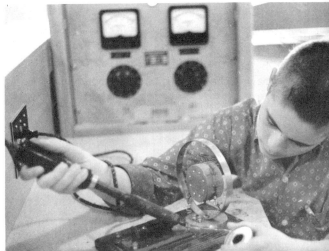

The Commission on Secondary Curriculum of the Association for Supervision and Curriculum Development has made suggestions concerning desirable features and characteristics of the junior high school of the future.[14] Today's good practice must be made better for tomorrow and other good practices must be developed. The group presented a statement of some fifteen beliefs about what the junior high school of the future should be and do: (1) Its central commitment must be to the development of democratic values; (2) Its instructional program should be developed experimentally; (3) Its arrangements of time and scheduling should be in the interests of effective learning and teaching; (4) Its instruction should be developed expressly for youth at the junior high school level; (5) It should be an ungraded school; (6) It should utilize patterns and routines that foster refined and responsible living; (7) Its instructional procedures should be diverse and flexible enough to fit the varied purposes; (8) It should afford various means to enable pupils to see themselves as significant individuals in an ever-expanding societal setting; (9) Its school term should be extended to permit enrichment and strengthening of the learning experiences of pupils; (10) It should provide an abundant variety of aesthetic and cultural experiences; (11) It must provide comprehensive guidance for all pupils; (12) Its faculty should be organized and assigned to make optimum use of their talents and interests; (13) Its instructional program should make full utilization of new technological and instructional development and equipment; (14) Its administrative responsibilities and organization will reflect the major function(s) of the school; and (15) Its basic goals will emphasize knowledges, skills and understanding on the part of all pupils. Communities will make better progress in efforts to have quality programs in their junior high (and other) schools by fostering citizen participation in educational studies and planning, by encouraging effective cooperation between educators and lay leaders and groups, and by supporting courageous school leadership that has constructive viewpoint toward change—that inevitable concomitant of our economic growth and cultural life.[15]

A LOOK AT SENIOR HIGH SCHOOLS

Good senior high schools for today and tomorrow

The American high school has been deliberately developed and supported by the people to meet the educational needs of all youth. Many states have extended compulsory attendance laws while school boards have established comprehensive high schools with curriculum offerings for pupils of diverse interests and needs. Provision of the needed experiences for all youth is the best possible means of insuring the necessary competencies and problem-solving potential—personal, social and vocational—for our future society. This is the one-sentence way of stating the continuing role of secondary education in our diversified pluralistic democracy.

Since democratic society requires all youth to attend high school it is mor-

[14] *The Junior High School We Need, op. cit.*, pp. 19–29.

[15] *Ibid.*, pp. 31–35.

ally responsible for the fullest provision of opportunity for each to find and choose his own vocational and educational goals and to make progress toward self-realization. The American high school serves both social and individual purposes through its comprehensive program of offerings.[16]

Good high schools should be alike but different. There should be distinctive features and provisions in terms of community resources and needs, the student population, and the school leadership. On the other hand, many of the distinctive features will represent a variety of characteristics and qualities that will be found in some form in all good schools. It is important that we learn to recognize a variety of high quality provisions with expecting uniformity of provisions.

The good high school should exhibit several characteristics, features, and qualities that make a difference.[17] (1) It should offer a *comprehensive program* to meet the needs of all persons and groups. It does this and provides all these different individuals with experiences in living and working together in preparation for maintaining a free pluralistic society in the future. (2) It should help all youth to realize *some common outcomes*, viz., better understandings of self and one's social responsibilities; of democratic values; of economic institutions and principles; of civic and political rights and duties, or esthetic appreciations; and the ability to think effectively and rationally. Stu-

dents will neither begin nor complete their growth toward these common objectives at the same point, but the school must make this contribution if our future democratic society is to cohere and function. (3) It should provide class and extra class activities and experiences to meet the broad range of human capacities found in the students. (4) Student programs should be developed on the basis of individual needs. This means more than the mere selection of one of several pre-planned tracks (or streams or paths) in the curricular offerings to be followed to graduation. Individual differences can not be met fully unless there is much flexibility and adaptability in the curricular and co-curricular provisions of the school. It is important that growing adolescents be able to change goals (for good reasons) without undue loss of time and effort, and the good school does not penalize pupils for learning more about themselves and making better choices of goals. (5) All individual programs must provide for both general and specialized education. General education is essential in the preparation of citizens in a democracy and for the assumption of responsibilities common to all persons. All must be made ready for the duties and privileges of citizenship, employment, marriage and family, consumership, esthetic, moral and spiritual experiences, and opportunities to participate in and contribute to the cultural and social life to which they belong. Simultaneously, specialized education, essential to the development and realization of individual abilities, interests, and needs, must be provided. This will include, to varying degrees, vocational, technical, or professional education for many different

[16] See *The High School We Need, op. cit.,* pp. 2–5 for a good discussion of beliefs about the American high school.

[17] *Ibid.,* pp. 5–20, for discussion of these and related ideas.

persons. (6) General education should receive adequate attention in school offerings and in the planning of individual programs. Recommendations of all important groups and studies emphasize this provision and suggest that one-third to one-half of each student's program be devoted to required courses in general education. (7) Individual student programs should provide for elective courses and experiences to develop their talents and to further personal goals. Studies recommend that one-half to two-thirds of programs be devoted to this purpose. (8) Elective courses should be available to qualified students whenever their individual programs can be best served thereby. So-called grade placement of many courses is meaningless. More attention should be given to assessment of students' aptitude and qualifications for courses (e.g. reading rates and levels, depth of interests, particular aptitudes, etc.) than to traditional time for choosing an elective. Contemporary high schools that use much individualized study under team teaching and ungraded programs have opportunity to use their elective offerings widely and wisely for the benefit of individual students. (9) The school should provide testing and guidance services that provide each pupil and his parents an adequate appraisal of his general ability and achievement level. This is essential from the standpoint of both home and school. Parental aspirations and pupil purposes must be based upon reasonably accurate estimates of ability and potential which a good testing and guidance program should provide. Many high schools have much work to do upon this phase of their programs. (10) Curriculum pro-

grams for individuals should be jointly determined by pupil, parents, and school staff persons in terms of the aptitudes, achievement levels, and purposes of the student. These should be reviewed annually and revised whenever necessary to fit changes in purpose or better evidences of student's abilities.

(11) Every pupil should belong to some kind of homeroom (or other home base) group on a continuing, participating basis. This group affords experiences in cooperating, relating-to-others, the give-and-take, and responsibility for participating in common activities for a purpose that all citizens of a free society should have. It should be the school unit for intramural activities, and student government. (12) Good high schools must utilize new instructional media and techniques that have resulted from the technological developments of our society. Future high schools should adapt, devise, invent, and utilize even more aids and techniques for instructional purposes, and teachers should have freedom to undertake experimentation of this kind. (13) High school schedules should be made to fit the learning experiences needed in the instructional program. All too often daily schedules are rigid frames into which the instructional program must be made to fit regardless of the nature and purpose(s) of a given learning experience. (14) School faculties should maintain an organization for continuous evaluation and revision of the school's instructional program. (15) The school plant should be planned, constructed, and used to further the achievement of the instructional goals and purposes of the school. This means instructional units of such size and ar-

rangements as to facilitate close relationships among students and with teachers and staff. Certain comprehensive high schools such as Evanston Township High School have developed schools-within-the-school to this end. (16) Teachers of adolescents must develop special teaching skills and understandings related to their responsibilities. The education of high school teachers should be of professional nature, based on cooperative efforts of the teaching profession, representatives of the general public, and of faculties of institutions of higher education that accept responsibility for teacher education.

These points have been presented as some of the characteristics and features that responsible educational leaders recognize in good high schools, both present and potential.[18] High schools with all of these qualities well developed are yet largely in the future, but all of them can be cited somewhere in schools that are leading the way toward quality education for adolescents. The challenge lies in helping to create many good high schools.

Learn about Higher Education

Students are already on the site to observe higher education, since college study is their chief occupation. This should afford an excellent opportunity to become aware of higher education and its place in the whole picture of American education. The practice of getting into the meanings and significance of things will stand us in good stead now. We are on the inside of a college or university; we should not leave the institution without a real appreciation of its purposes and programs, and the general principles and procedures employed in its operations. One can look around to learn much, and it is possible to learn how to look to find out even more.

Higher education is an old and respected part of American education. Most Americans believe in it strongly (but vaguely), and want their children to have the advantages that derive from college experience. A brief resume of the rise and expansion of higher education in this country may give us a background for discussing the findings we obtain in our college observations.[19]

Developments in American higher education

American higher education had its beginnings early in the colonial period.

[18] Some good general references would include the publications of the Association for Supervision and Curriculum Development and of the National Association of Secondary School Principals already cited and such works as: James B. Conant, *The American High School Today* (New York: Mc-Graw-Hill, 1959); Harold B. and Elsie J. Alberty, *Reorganizing the High School Curriculum* (New York: Macmillan, 1962); J. Lloyd Trump and Dorsey Baynham, *Focus on Change: A Guide to Better Schools* (Chicago: Rand McNally & Co., 1961); and J. Lloyd Trump, *Images of the Future*, National Association of Secondary School Principals (Washington: 1959).

[19] Most standard works on America's educational history deal with the origin and growth of higher education. A useful book is Richard Hotstadter and C. Dewitt Hardy, *The Development and Scope of Higher Education in the United States* (New York: Columbia University, 1952).

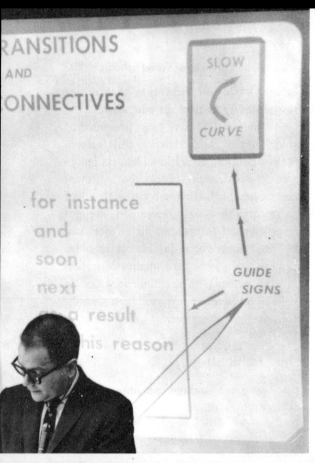

RANSITIONS
AND
ONNECTIVES

for instance
and
soon
next
a result
his reason

SLOW
CURVE

GUIDE
SIGNS

FRESH
FISH

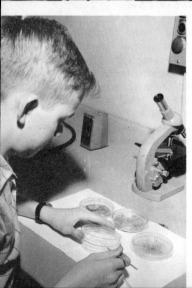

STOP

YIELD
RIGHT
OF
WAY

TRAFFIC
SIGNAL
AHEAD

THE COMPREHENSIVE
HIGH SCHOOL
PROGRAM
MEETS INTERESTS
AND NEEDS
OF ALL
YOUTH

Shortly after the first Latin grammar schools opened in Massachusetts and well in advance of the famous early school laws, the Massachusetts Bay Colony took the steps that led to the founding of Harvard College in 1636. Virginia established William and Mary College just before the 17th century closed, and in Connecticut Yale opened in 1702. A total of eight colleges represented higher education in the colonies at the start of the Revolution.

The curriculums of the colonial colleges consisted of the traditional liberal arts plus the philosophies (natural, moral, and metaphysical), and one or more of the classical languages. The influence of the old English universities—Oxford and Cambridge—was pronounced as most of the early faculty were graduates of one or the other.

Students lived in austere fashion in the early colleges with few activities save impromptu sports, some debating, and pranks typical of college youth. In the early years students were listed in order of the social rank of their families. Discipline was strict; orthodoxy of belief was prized; and there were no facilities for research and scholarly study comparable to modern universities. Higher education was dominated by the religious motive and controlled by denominational governing boards.

By the end of the eighteenth century, new institutions had appeared and there were additions to the curriculums of the older colleges. Medicine, some biological and physical sciences, navigation and surveying, geography and history, additional subjects in the classics, came to be offered in various institutions. Before the century ended, two states had opened state universities—Georgia and North Carolina—and colleges had been established in the new states west of the Alleghenies—Transylvania in Kentucky (1798).

Perhaps the greatest innovation in higher education of the 19th century was the rise of the state university. After the famous Dartmouth College case (1819) which prevented the New Hampshire legislature from gaining control and the successful start of public institutions, a number of states established public universities. The crowning achievement of Jefferson's leadership was the University of Virginia in 1821. Ohio used some of its public land grants to establish state institutions as did other midwestern states. The University of Michigan opened in 1837. The early state universities stressed secular studies—the classics or humanities studies—but added offerings in the sciences. The colonial emphasis upon the training of ministers was balanced by preparation of leaders for the law, medicine, teachers, military service, and business. Before the end of the first half of the nineteenth century, the woman's college had come into existence with Mt. Holyoke, Wesleyan (Mason, Ga.), as the pioneers. Numerous small denominational colleges were founded by the circuit riders and settlers in the midwestern and southwestern states during this period.

The public stake in higher education received its greatest recognition and stimulus in the passage of the renowned Morrill Act in 1862. This wartime act signed by President Lincoln granted public lands to the states to be used in support of college for the encouragement of agriculture and the mechanic arts. Few investments have ever paid off so handsomely. The land-grant institutions brought into existence centers for research in agriculture, engineering and technology that were to facilitate the industrial and technical advance of the economy. Early sneers and jibes at the "cow colleges," "book farming," and "boiler makers" have long since passed into limbo as great state universities developed the trilogy of functions—teaching, research, and service to the state. Every state has used the assistance provided by the Congress to found or adapt a total of 69 institutions and their influence has long been comparable to that of the older Ivy League institutions. Some of the largest of American universities and most noted universities started as land-grant colleges—California, Wisconsin, Minnesota, Illinois, and Ohio State to name only a few.

There were other noteworthy events in higher education in the nineteenth century. One of these was the founding of co-educational institutions beginning with Oberlin. The establishment of institutions for education of Negroes—Hampton Institute, Howard University, Tuskegee Institute, Fisk University—was a marked step in the spread of educational opportunity. The rise of the normal school for the education of teachers paralleled the establishment of state school systems. The first at Lexington, Massachusetts, was followed by myriad institutions that grew in the twentieth century into teachers' colleges. More recently most of these have outgrown their limited curriculum and become state colleges offering a variety of degree programs.

Other types of higher educational institutions developed in this country include the technical or engineering school (M.I.T., Cal Tech, Rensselaer), and many types of professional schools at the collegiate or graduate level. Early in the twentieth century, the distinctly new public junior college developed. The first junior college was in Joliet, Illinois (1902). The growth of this type of general education opportunity close to the homes of students has been phenomenal, particularly in recent decades. California, Florida, and New York have developed extensive statewide programs of junior colleges.

Expanded programs reflect purposes

The long story of American higher education reflects many changes and developments that relate to the growing needs and demands of the American people and culture.[20] Other professional goals were added to the original one of preparing ministers in colonial colleges: physicians, lawyers, engineers, scientists and many others. The most convenient place to check this is by study of your state university general catalog. Listing of the various professional, semi-professional, and preprofessional curriculums will give an impressive list which you will find relates to the past growth of American culture—industrially, technologically, scientifically, and professionally. We may also note the comparative recency of some programs reflecting the dynamic developments still under way in American society. This is one side of the vast social change that has affected the college curriculum principally by expansion and growth.

The other major type of change in higher education programs has stemmed

[20] See Paul L. Dressel, *The Undergraduate Curriculum in Higher Education* (Washington: The Center for Applied Research in Education, Inc., 1963).

partly from the increasing specialization and narrowing-of-the-scope of college curriculums. It has been effected by efforts to change, reorganize, and develop new curriculum patterns that will in some degree complement the narrow but deepened programs of studies prescribed for professional students. In essence, many of the colleges and universities have endeavored to provide a broadened curriculum with specially designed courses in most major areas of learning for all students. In this manner, all graduates might be expected to gain a balanced well-rounded education plus a modern specialized field. This has often been designated as the program for *general education*. There are a number of well-known approaches especially since World War II.

Three types of programs are found in the junior colleges (often called community colleges). One type is the two-year program of general education and liberal arts offerings that can be transferred to a four-year institution or represent a terminal program for others. A second type of program featuring various new semi-professional and technical fields that require some mathematics and science beyond high school level are often called technical institutes. These are popular in communities where the offerings can be related to industrial and other local needs. The third type of junior college program offers some or all of the programs noted but also provides opportunity for individuals and groups in the community to study what is needed. This type of institution makes studies of community needs for education beyond the high school, and develops educational offerings accordingly. There have been several outstanding successful programs of this type

in recent years which brought wide use of the term community colleges. Unfortunately the name has been applied, sometimes by legislative action, to two-year institutions that have no particular reference to the community in which they are located. This is another good illustration of a common error, the mistaking of the symbol for the reality.

College teaching stresses method

Teaching in colleges and universities has a tradition of emphasis upon method. Faculties of many institutions rely chiefly upon methods of teaching that have been used more or less continuously for generations. Two of these have very old traditions of use namely, *explication of the text* and *lecturing*. The lecture has been the most universally used method in European and American universities. It is also used in Asiatic and Latin American institutions. British universities have long used the tutorial conference as an effective method. American colleges and universities have used discussion sessions, laboratory experimentation, and field projects as means of enlisting the intellectual participation of students. The seminar has been a standard practice for instruction at upper class and graduate levels. These approaches in adapted and modified form will be found in certain classrooms and institutions, but these represent the major types of instructional techniques employed in higher education. The statement that college professors are more consistently devoted to a single method of teaching than any other group of instructors is probably true.[21] This is an in-

[21] Algo D. Henderson, *Policies and Practices in Higher Education* (New York: Harper & Row, Publishers, 1960), pp. 176–178.

teresting observation because of the common criticism by academicians of the professional educators' reputed concern with methods and techniques of instruction.

Observations of college teaching on a planned basis are probably not feasible in most institutions. Nevertheless, students are participants in many different classes and have ample opportunity to observe various methods of instruction. There are some newer approaches to teaching that have received attention in recent years. Experiments with large group instruction using closed circuit television presentations plus small group discussions with leaders and individual study projects have proved encouraging in a number of institutions. This employs techniques like those in the *team teaching* projects we have noted. Many varieties and plans for group participation have been employed ranging all the way from unplanned bull sessions to elaborate arrangements for a series of small discussion groups with summary sessions. The wide variety of plans include the *reading period* followed by a formal report or paper, the *case method* of instruction in professional fields, the actual practice of skills as in *moot courts, speech events, student teaching,* and *internships,* and many others.

Recent developments in the areas of mathematics and sciences have stimulated experimentation with method of instruction as well as curriculum development. Emphasis upon foreign language instruction has brought wide use of language laboratories in which students can speak and hear the language they seek to master. New type teaching materials and instructional films have been emphasized since World War II. The recent development of auto-instruction devices (teaching machines) and of programmed learnings plans should have a great impact upon college teaching.

This whole area of instruction can provide us with an interesting opportunity to observe and to learn during our college years. We shall find some instructors who will discuss methodology and explain their approach in terms of objectives and course content. There will be others who will not be approachable on the subject. One's good judgment will have to be the guide. But we can learn something from almost any teaching situation.

Practices Are Principles in Action

Extended observations of teachers and pupils at their work in elementary, junior, and senior high schools should help us to visualize what teaching is like in each school and to develop concepts of what constitutes a good school program. After observations and study, we might try to bring our findings together by attempting some kinds of lists or written descriptions. It would be manifestly easy to jot down all the kinds of specific actions we saw teachers take during our school visits. This could be discussed with other experienced teachers, then classified into several broad categories as a basis for an estimate of how much time teachers spend marking tests, reading themes, making out objective tests, checking homework, and keeping records. This might be done meticulously—only to represent a relatively minor accomplishment. If these were to be our major findings about the nature of the teacher's work, the result would be a tragedy. Teaching is too strategically important, too significant in the lives of free men of the potentially free society to be reduced to a series of chores that can be set forth like those regulated by time and motion studies. True enough that some people have this notion about the nature of the teacher's work, but they are utterly mistaken and wrong.

The idea of the importance of education to both individuals and to our democratic society has been presented more than once in this book. It is true that education does improve the earning power, the employability, the job opportunity, and the status of individuals in a general sense. It is also true that nations that invest in education have higher standards of living and stability. It has been shown that American education has made indispensable contributions to the unity and unprecedented progress of this country. But this does not mean that just any kind of education would make that kind of contribution. This is a terribly important matter, so let it be said as simply and clearly as possible. It is not only the amount of education but *also the kind of education that makes free men and fosters a free society.* A great deal of education, full of indoctrination and propaganda, might well undermine our democratic institutions. It is important to remember that the great contribution of American teachers and schools in general has been to respect their academic freedom and the right of students to all possible sources of information and truth. Teachers should do this and should try to develop a loyalty to those overarching freedoms guaranteed to all Americans in the Bill of Rights, the Constitution, and other documents of our liberties. Those who do these things are the special guardians of the future of our free people and of this nation. This is an image of teaching that should appeal to youth with intelligence and ideals.

Teaching is people and principles in action

It would be ideal if we could visualize a good school program and the teacher's role in such fashion as to see how principles are exemplified and used. Our quick test of our own findings may be made by reviewing them in the light of sound principles. A list of seven challenging statements provides a useful yard stick.

According to this authority, learning should have seven characteristics, evidences of which we should be able to discern in the schools. Learning should be:

1. An active process
2. Meaningful
3. Useful
4. Interesting
5. Individualized
6. Satisfying
7. Unified[22]

Our observations in the schools will provide a number of illustrations of the ways that teachers planned, arranged, and guided experiences in terms of principles. This kind of review can go on in our own thinking and study until we see the significance of this section on *teaching is people and principles in action.* When we do see this clearly it will make all the

[22] Stanley L. Clement, "Seven Principles of Learning" in *The Clearing House,* **XXXVI** (September 1961), pp. 23–26.

difference in our concepts of what teaching is and of its significance as a calling. Should we feel more inclined to make teaching our goal, we will have an informed basis for a choice of the kind of school where our contribution will be greatest, and in which can be found the satisfaction the teaching life should hold.

Selected Bibliography

Association for Supervision and Curriculum Development, *Organizing the Elementary School for Living and Learning*. Washington: NEA, 1947.

Brim, R. P. *The Junior High School*. Washington: The Center for Applied Research in Education, 1963.

Chisholm, Leslie J. *The Work of the Modern High School*. New York: The Macmillan Co., 1953.

Conant, James B. *Education in the Junior High School Years*. Princeton, N. J.: Educational Testing Service, 1960.

———. *The American High School Today*. New York: The McGraw-Hill Book Company, 1959.

Dehaan, Robert F., *Accelerated Learning Programs*. Washington: The Center for Applied Research in Education, 1963.

Department of Elementary School Principals, *Elementary School Organization—Purposes, Patterns, Perspective*, 1961 Yearbook. Washington: NEA, 1961.

———. *The Flexible School*. Washington: NEA, 1957.

Douglass, Harl R. *Trends and Issues in Secondary Education*. Washington: The Center for Applied Research in Education, Inc., 1962.

Educational Policies Commission, *Education for All-American Children*. Washington: NEA, 1948.

———. *Education for All-American Youth—A Further Look*. Washington: NEA, 1952.

———. *Higher Education in a Decade of Decision*. Washington: NEA, 1957.

———. *Social Responsibility in a Free Society*. Washington: NEA and A.A.S.A., 1963.

———. *The Central Purpose of American Education*. Washington: NEA, 1961.

———. *The Contemporary Challenge to American Education*. Washington: NEA, 1958.

Goodlad, John T. and Anderson, Robert. *The Nongraded Elementary School*, Rev. ed. New York: Harcourt, Brace & World, 1962.

Goodlad, John T. *Some Propositions in Search of Schools*. Washington: Department of Elementary School Principals, NEA, 1962.

Grambs, Jean D. *et al.*, *The Junior High School We Need*. Washington: Association for Supervision and Curriculum Development, NEA, 1961.

Handlin, Oscar. "Live Students and Dead Education," *Atlantic*, **XXVIII** (September 1961), pp. 29–34.

Henderson, Algo D. *Policies and Practices in Higher Education*. New York: Harper & Row, 1960.

Hill, Gladwin. "A Father Looks at Progressive Education," *Atlantic Monthly* (December 1954), reprinted by National School Public Relations Council, NEA.

Hollingshead, August B. *Elmtown's Youth*. New York: John Wiley & Sons, 1949.

Johnson, Mauritz, Jr., "School in the Middle," *Saturday Review*, **XLV** (July 21, 1962), pp. 40–42, 56–57. Reprinted in *Education Digest* (November 1962).

Joint Study Committee, *The Junior High School Program*. Atlanta: Southern Association of Colleges and Secondary Schools, 1958.

Lambert, Hazel M. *Elementary Education* (Washington: The Center of Applied Research in Education, 1963).

Mayer, Martin, "Last Chance for Our Schools," *Saturday Evening Post*, **CCXXXVI**, No. 31 (September 14, 1963), pp. 24–36.

Morse, Arthur D. *Schools of Tomorrow—Today*. Garden City, N. Y.: Doubleday & Co., Inc., 1960.

National Association of Secondary School Principals, *Planning for American Youth*. Washington: NEA, 1944, 1951. An abridgment of *Education for All-American Youth*.

————. *Junior High School Today and Tomorrow*, Bulletin No. 259. Washington: NEA, 1960.

————. *Overall View of Secondary School Practices*, Bulletin No. 251. Washington: NEA, 1959.

National Citizens Council for Better Schools, *Yardsticks for Public Schools*. New York: Better Schools, 1956.

Pinous, Hannah M. "Changes in Teaching the 3 R's in the Early Grades," *Parents' Magazine*, **XXXVII** (September 1961), pp. 45, 77–78, 80.

President's Committee on Education Beyond the High School, *Second Report to the President*. Washington: U. S. Government Printing Office, 1957.

Robbins, Jhan and June. "Do Our Schools Demand Enough of Our Children?" *Redbook*, **CXVII** (October 1961), pp. 50–51, 94–96, 98–101.

Rummel, Frances V. "These Children Love to Read," *Saturday Evening Post*, **CCXXXIV** (September 9, 1961), pp. 24, 53–54.

Thurston, Mildred. *Helping Children Live and Learn*. Washington: Association for Childhood International, 1952.

"The Junior High School Years," *Saturday Review* (October 15, 1960).

Trump, J. Lloyd and Baynham, Dorsey. *Guide to Better Schools*. Chicago: Rand McNally, 1961.

Trump, J. Lloyd. *Images of the Future: A New Approach to the Secondary School*. Urbana, Ill.: Commission on the Experimental Study of the Utilization of the Staff in the Secondary School, 1959.

————. *New Horizons for Secondary School Teachers*. Urbana, Ill.: Commission in the Experimental Study of the Utilization of the Staff in the Secondary School, 1957.

————. *New Directions to Quality Education, the Secondary School Tomorrow*. Washington: National Association of Secondary School Principals, n.d.

Virginia Department of Education, *The Characteristics of a Good Elementary School*. Richmond: The Department, 1949.

Weber, Julia. *My Country School Diary*. New York: Harper & Row, 1946.

Wiles, Kimball and Patterson, Franklin. *The High School We Need*. Washington, Association for Supervision and Curriculum Development, Washington: NEA, 1959.

Wright, Grace S. *Core Curriculum in Public High Schools*. Federal Security Agency, Office of Education, Bulletin 1950, No. 5. Washington: U. S. Government Printing Office, 1950.

————, *et al.*, *Education Unlimited: A Community High School in Action*, Federal Security Agency, Office of Education, Bulletin 1951, No. 5. Washington: Government Printing Office, 1951.

———. *Block-of-Time Classes and the Core Program in the Junior High School*, U. S. Office of Education Bulletin No. 6. Washington: U. S. Government Printing Office, 1950.

Wrightstone, J. Wayne. *Class Organization for Instruction*, No. 13 in series "What Research Says to the Teacher," by Department of Classroom Teachers and American Educational Research Association, Washington: NEA, an informative series of pamphlets for teachers.

Aids for Part III

AUDIO-VISUAL MATERIALS

FILMS

Broader Concept of Method, Parts I, II (15–20 min. each; sound). Developing pupil interest and cooperative planning. [8, 9]

Defining Democracy, Encyclopaedia Britannica Films (1½ reels, sound). Title is descriptive, combines parts of next two films. [7]

Democracy, Encyclopaedia Britannica Films (11 min., sound). Essentials and conditions of democracy. [7]

Despotism, Encyclopaedia Britannica Films (11 min., sound). Characteristics and features of despotic governments. [7]

Dynamic Learning (2 reels, silent). Dr. William H. Kilpatrick explains modern education. [7, 8, 9]

Education of Exceptional Children, University of Illinois (22 min., b & w). Title is descriptive. [8, 9]

Experimental Studies in the Social Climates of Groups, Iowa State University (32 min.). Compares various methods and settings in terms of learning outcomes. [7, 8]

Freedom to Learn, NEA (25 min.). Academic freedom is for both students and teachers. [7]

Guiding the Growth of Children, McGraw-Hill (17 min., b & w). Importance of knowing children in the teacher's work. [8]

High School: Your Challenge, Coronet (12 min., sound). The high school as viewed by the teenage pupil. [8, 9]

James B. Conant, Encyclopaedia Britannica Films (30 min.), Reviews problems of today's high schools.

Junior High School Story, Junior High School Council, Inc. (28 min., color). An overview of a good junior high school program. [9]

Learning Through Cooperative Planning (2 reels, sound). Group planning and projects in an urban elementary school. [9]

Lessons in Living, National Film Board of Canada (2 reels, sound). Shows a Canadian elementary school program. [9]

Living and Learning in a Rural School, Teachers College. (2 reels, b & w), Title is descriptive. [9]

Motivation Through Unit Teaching, Iowa State Teachers College (25 min., b & w). Title is descriptive. [9]

Near Home, British Information Service (2¼ reels, sound). A British elementary school studies its own community. [9]

Practicing Democracy in the Classroom, Encyclopaedia Britannica Films (22 min., sound). An excellent illustration of principles in use in high school class. [7, 8, 9]

School—The Child's Community, Wayne University (17 min., b & w). Title is descriptive. [9]

Secure the Blessings, NEA (25 min., sound). Role of schools in a democracy. [7]

Skippy and the 3 R's, NEA (3 reels, sound). Excellent presentation of elementary school teacher's work in light of a sound philosophy. [8, 9]

The Elementary School, Part I, Virginia Department of Education (25 min., sound, color). [9]

The School, United World Films (21 min., sound). A full day in an elementary school. [9]

The Teacher as Observer and Guide, Metropolitan School Study Council (2 reels, silent). Shows part played by wise teacher in helping children to develop and grow. [8, 9]

The Time of Their Lives, NEA (30 min., b & w). Documentary on modern kindergartens. [9]

The Wilson Dam School, TVA (22 min., sound). Excellent story of an outstanding elementary school program; also useful for study of roles of teachers and parents, and examples of good teaching. Request from: TVA, Education Relations and Training Division, Knoxville, Tennessee. [8, 9].

Three R's Plus, McGraw-Hill (27 min., b & w). Describes elementary school program. [9]

Time to Spare (2 reels, sound). A rural school teacher improves the daily program. [9]

FILMSTRIPS

Democracy at Work, Curriculum Films, Inc. (38 frames, silent, color). [7, 8]

Education for All-American Children, National Education Association (52 frames, silent). Excellent resume. [9]

Trip Through Our Schools (54 frames). John's first day at school. [9]

We Go to School, Young American Films (25 frames, silent). A full school day. [9]

RECORDINGS

Face to Face, Institute for Democratic Education (15 min., 33⅓ rpm). [8]

The Goal Beyond, NEA (6½ min., 33⅓ rpm). The schools teach moral values. [7]

The Kindled Spark, NEA (6½ min., 33⅓ rpm). Function of schools in teachng democracy. [7]

Threshold, NEA (6½ min., 33⅓ rpm). Reading readiness in the first grade group. [8, 9]

Yes, Your Honesty, Institute for Democratic Education (14 min., 33⅓ rpm). [9]

QUESTIONS FOR DISCUSSION

1. Does every teacher have a philosophy of education? Why do you believe your answer?
2. Should everyone be concerned with philosophy? With philosophy of education? Why?
3. What are the best indications of the teacher's beliefs and philosophy? What can you tell about a person's philosophy? How?
4. How much time and energy should teachers give to discussion of aims and purposes of education? Explain.
5. Should the aims of education in a democratic society be significantly different from those of schools in a totalitarian state? Basically different? Why?

6. Why should there be more statements of purpose for secondary education than for elementary schools? Discuss.

7. How would you express the distinctive role of the *common school system* in our democracy? Does the common school have any distinctive responsibilities?

8. What do you believe about democracy? What constitutes democracy? Explain your concept of democracy.

9. What does a democratic philosophy of education imply for the work of the teacher? Administrator? Parent?

10. What stand should teachers take upon controversial issues?

11. What is your concept or definition of learning? (If not original, indicate the source.)

12. What is meant by "learning what we live"? "learning by doing"?

13. Is learning the same as problem-solving?

14. What learning outcomes do you view as important? Is the work of the teacher made more difficult if he accepts responsibility for all the outcomes of learning?

15. How can we tell when learning has taken place?

16. What effect does each of the following have upon learning: environment? other pupils? interest? purpose? previous experiences?

17. Some educators would say that teaching is largely a matter of learning along with the pupils. What is your reaction to this view?

18. What is your concept of teaching? Explain your views.

19. Do good teachers need to continue to study learning? Why?

20. Should the organization and curriculums of American schools be different from those in other countries? Why?

21. How would you rank the school among the influential educative agencies in our democracy? Support your answer.

22. How and by whom should school policy be determined? What does democratic planning mean?

23. What are the best statements of the purposes of public schools in our democracy that you know? Why?

24. What groups and organizations have been consistent supporters of public schools? Which have been in opposition?

25. What have you learned from visits to good elementary schools?

26. What have you learned from visits to good junior high schools?

27. What have you learned from visits to good senior high schools?

28. What were the best examples of learning that you observed in schools? Explain.

29. Were there examples of democratic living? Explain.

30. Can you describe a good school in terms of concepts and principles you have been studying? Explain your ideas.

IDEAS FOR INDIVIDUAL STUDY

1. Do some research to find definitions of education which have been widely accepted in American education. Why have these tended to change emphasis at major intervals? Explain.

2. Show by some kind of a chart or outline the important aims and objectives which have been stated for American public education at various times in our history.

3. Choose some important foreign or historical source of educational ideas and show how the thinker (or movement) influenced America's educational history. Report to your group.

4. Examine textbooks to find available explanations of the meanings and essential components of democracy. Develop your own summary statement on "What Democracy Is." Invite criticisms and suggestions.

5. View the films *Democracy* and *Despotism*. Write up notes for discussion in class.

6. Examine statements of beliefs and principles of education by various organizations and groups in our society. How do these compare in positions taken toward important issues and values? How well do they reflect the interests of the *whole* of our democracy? What can you learn of the special interests of the respective sponsoring organizations? Keep notes here.

7. List below the most significant statements upon democracy, democratic education, and education for a democratic society that you can find. Arrange chronologically, identify the source and the content by appropriate phraseology.

8. Prepare a series of statements which present your own beliefs about education. Ask for criticism from your classmates and instructors.

9. When you have done some reading and discussion about this subject, try to recall something of your own learning experiences. Take an experience which resulted in learning one of the outcomes which has been explained and write a brief account. Continue to do that until you have written enough to show the different outcomes of learning.

10. Observe a play period for children and write an account of the learning which took place.

11. Observe a group in the library noting exactly what happened. Try to identify the actual learnings that resulted.

12. Do the same for a gym class group during a period of activity or games, and a group on the playground. Study these experiences in terms of the learning(s) that occurred.

13. Do the same for a music group, an appreciation period, a dramatic production, or some other comparable activity.

14. Attend a club meeting or organization at work for the purpose of observing behavior and learning. Try to analyze the observations you make.

15. Visit also an informal group that has come together for no specific purpose and observe proceedings with an eye for what is learned. Keep notes for your reports and discussions below.

16. During a school visitation observe the operation of different class groups to discern what learnings result. Describe what the teacher did during one of the observation periods. How would you characterize the role? Does the part or role a person plays have any effect upon the learnings?

17. Formulate a list of the best practices used by the good teachers you have known.

18. Read up on some of the experiments about the effects of the social environment upon the learning that took place and report your findings.

19. Summarize your present concept of what learning is, and use in a panel discussion before your class.

20. Develop a list of questions to pursue further in this field, presumably in later courses in educational psychology, learning, personality, and related topics. Discuss with the instructor.

SUGGESTIONS FOR GROUP WORK

1. Participate in a group discussion about the meaning of philosophy of education and its significance.

2. Participate in a group study of the most important American philosopher of education and make a report upon the ideas of one that appeals to you.
3. Take part in a group discussion of the question, "How can you identify democratic practices in a school or classroom?"
4. Participate in a group study of the groups and organizations that influence American education today. Make a report upon one of these groups.
5. Participate in a group project to study what is meant by creativity and creative student. In what ways can the school foster the development of creativity in pupils with this potential?
6. Participate in a study of the statements of philosophy preferred by faculties of schools in your vicinity. Submit an evaluation of one from your point-of-view to the group.
7. Summarize one part of your reading about learning and use in a report to your group.
8. Arrange to see selected films about learning. Write a brief report of each.
9. Recount episodes from your own experiences that illustrate some of the learning outcomes and principles. Use in class discussion and keep notes.
10. Try some simple learning experiences such as working a puzzle, finding something, or making a generalization from several related facts. Can you duplicate some of the learning experiences which you read about in references? Team up with another student to try some of these and compare notes on the result.
11. Compile a list of questions about learning to be discussed with your instructor and group.
12. Arrange to see the film *The Wilson Dam School*. Take part in a panel discussion of the ideas gained from the picture.
13. Participate in a committee assignment to preview and choose an appropriate film about a junior high school program to be shown to the entire class.
14. Participate in a committee assignment to preview and choose an appropriate film about a senior high school program to be shown to the entire class.
15. Make a collection of articles and booklets that describe "The Good School." Study these and prepare a comprehensive list of the important characteristics and/or features of good schools.
16. Prepare a graphic exhibit to show the historical growth of the American school curriculum.
17. Collect and arrange an exhibit of instructional materials (other than books), to illustrate the development of the modern school curriculum.
18. Participate in a committee project to make a brief outline of the most important concepts and understandings about American public education that you believe should be presented in a unit of study for high school seniors.
19. Make a survey of the criticisms of public education during the past 10–12 years. Classify the major changes and criticisms into appropriate categories. Prepare a chart to present these showing groups and individuals responsible for each, changes, and your comments. Discuss noting particularly how many are related to differing aims and philosophies of education.
20. Participate in a series of 3 panel discussions "What we learned from visiting schools" (elementary, junior high school, and senior high school). Prepare summaries for your notes.

IV. PEOPLE

All the
Children of
All the People

Chapter 10

The Pupils Served by
the Schools

As every teacher has reason to know, each child is unique. In spite of the fact that there are basic human needs common to everyone which are essential for growth, each person is a distinct and separate personality. One of the most important human needs is the need to be an individual, to be oneself. Belief in the worth and dignity of every individual is the cornerstone of both democracy and emotional health. For both to be realized, it is essential that every child feel he is important, and has something to contribute to his classmates, his school, his parents, and his community.*

Actually, all children and youth have problems, each in his own way; for the stumbling blocks in the road to the pursuit of happiness have no respect for social, economic, or biological boundary lines. Youth with problems, therefore, are found among all levels of economic and social backgrounds, all nationalities, all races, all creeds, the complete range of abilities or almost the complete range of interests, ambitions, and home environment, a wide range in health and physical fitness, and a very great range in the scholastic accomplishments in the previous grades of our schools. In fact, to live is to have problems.†

Introduction

The child is central in home, community, and national interests. Perceptive parents and teachers see this and more; they regard children highly, and see in them the potential persons they may be in a better society realized largely by their efforts.

The job of responsible adults is to guide the growth and development of the young and to facilitate desirable learnings. Success in this endeavor surely requires that their efforts be based upon clear and accurate understanding of the learner. Many teachers fail for lack of such insight; others manage to keep their jobs

* National Institute of Mental Health, *The Teacher and Mental Health,* U.S. Department of Health, Education, and Welfare, P. H. S. Publication No. 385 (Washington: Government Printing Office, 1954).

† Leslie L. Chisholm, *The Work of the Modern High School* (New York: Macmillan, 1953), pp. 100–101.

321

but fall short of accomplishing the purposes, which should be attained in their work with children. Parents are not fired for failure in this role, but the best parents take this matter seriously. The best parents and teachers are characterized by intelligent insight into the nature of the learner and by ability to assist the all round growth and development of the pupil.

Such knowledge on the part of the adult comes from diligent study, keen observation of children, and experience. It can hardly be expected that we will get more than a good start in that direction through this course. We shall need to make the most of biology, psychology, and sociology courses, as these present an opportunity to learn what the major studies of human growth and development have found. Education students should grasp every opportunity to work with children and to learn from and about them. Those who find themselves in a school position should continue to study as they teach children and youth.

All teachers, all adults in fact, have an important stake in the education of our youth, one of the most significant and indispensable functions of our society. Teachers in elementary schools taught the youth of secondary school age only a short time ago. Parents look to adolescents with pride and even anxiety in the hope that they will grow up and achieve far more than today's adults have been able to do in their times. All of the American nation looks to its high school youth as an incalculable resource, as the coming front line of new citizens. The education of youth then must rightly be an acknowledged high priority task and responsibility of all American communities. Youth are tomorrow.

Pupils Are People

Children and youth are important people. This statement is to be taken seriously, no matter how trite or even amusing it might appear. Children are people, persons with all human attributes save what has to be added and developed through growth and experience. Youth are human beings further advanced in their growth, to the point of transition into adulthood. Children and youth afford parents their greatest satisfaction (and disappointments), and teachers, their very *raison d'être*.

CHILDREN ARE IMPORTANT

Children are important for numerous reasons; each of them is important as an end in itself. In general, they are strategically important to society. In the first place, they are young, their future is ahead, they can learn and be taught. This constitutes a concern so important that society provides formally for meeting the educational needs of children.

Second, children, like everyone else, have individuality. Each is a unique person.[1] By that we first mean that the

[1] There are many useful references on this general topic. See, for example, Marian E. Breckenridge and Elizabeth L. Vincent, *Child Development*, 2nd edition (Philadelphia: W. B. Saunders Co., 1949), pp. 54–62; see also Willard C. Olson, *Child Development*, 2nd edition (Boston: D. C. Heath & Co., 1959), chapter 1. For a concise statement see Gladys Gardner Jenkins, *Helping Children Reach Their Potential* (Chicago: Scott, Foresman & Co., 1961), pp. 158–162.

biological inheritance of each one is different. Our biology studies should have given us elementary facts about the conception and growth of the young. We recall that this process results in unique patterns of physical inheritance—no two people come from the same "shuffling of the chromosomes." Persons then are born with varying patterns of potentialities for physical and mental development. Another important concept points up the profound variations and differences in the nurture of children.[2] Since they are born into different families of widely varying circumstances, socio-economic conditions, and opportunity their experiences will differ a great deal. Thus, they will acquire differing patterns of learned behavior, attitudes, and the like. The end result of the difference in physical inheritance and in the social environment of children is uniqueness and individuality for each. We might go on to philosophize a bit about this, noting that uniqueness should make each person valuable to society. Who is to say that this or that person is worth more than another? Who knows which *person* has an ability or a potentiality which our society may need? As teachers, a great responsibility rests upon us because of this fact.

The keynote is growth

The personalities of children, like adults, are complex; they are many-sided entities. Many qualities and characteristics are found, all integrated in some fashion. The growing personality does not develop consistently and consecutively. Among the various aspects or components of one's personality there may be observed differing rates and degrees of growth or development. These differing patterns of growth have been observed and studied by students in many fields of research that deal with human growth and development.[3] Several aspects and stages of development have been identified and designated in terms of indices or "ages." Thus, we will note frequent references to *chronological age, mental age, educational age,* and the like. We should have little difficulty with the meanings of these terms. When we read articles by authorities on child development we will run into many other terms for stages of development. We may encounter terms like anatomical age or even carpal age, dental age, and grip age. One may find a term *physiological age* which relates to the growth of bodily organs, particularly to the maturing of sex organs and functions. There are still other specific terms relating to educational aspects of child growth such as *achievement age, reading age,* and the like. Usually the meaning will be clear from the context and the discussion, if one reads and checks carefully.[4] The important point to appreciate and to remember is that people vary a great deal in all these respects. And, especially that children grow in each of these respects but at uneven and varying rates among them. A modest bit of observation plus careful reading

---

[2] For a brief helpful introduction see Gladys Gardner Jenkins, *op. cit.,* pp. 172–187.

[3] A good reference for the physical growth and development of children and youth may be found in Jerome M. Seidman, *Readings in Educational Psychology* (Boston: Houghton Mifflin, 1955), pp. 7–15.

[4] These may be found in many references. A good one is Breckenridge and Vincent, *op. cit.,* pp. 16–40; see also William A. Fullagar, Hal G. Lewis, and Carroll F. Cumbee, *Readings for Educational Psychology* (New York: Thomas Y. Crowell Co., 1956), pp. 99–110, or Willard C. Olson and John Lewellyn, *How Children Grow and Develop* (Chicago: Science Research Associates, Inc., 1953), p. 10.

should better enable us to understand this. A talk with the best informed elementary school teacher that you can find may help to comprehend the meaning and significance of this data and information about child growth.

Growth is natural and normal for all living organisms. Natural growth or maturation is thus an especial consideration in an understanding of children. Growth is normally continuous and gradual. However, it is uneven among the various traits which compose the total personality. At times there appear to be sudden "spurts" of growth (at puberty, for example) but these are the results of rather consistent growth which has been going on. Hence, we can conceive of growth as being a continuous, gradual process taking place in all aspects of the personality. At any given stage, we have the right to think of growth in terms of what is normal for persons of that age.

Growth or development then is the result of two important influences which interact and affect each other as the organism lives and grows.[5] These are *maturation* (or natural growth) and *influence of environmental factors*. In other words, both nature and nurture are involved in the process of growth of the organism. One's inherited qualities and potentialities determine limits of growth which may be reached; the strength and quality of the environment in which he lives and grows affects the rate and degree to which these potentialities are reached.

By way of summary, we may say that

[5] See for example, Breckenridge and Vincent, *op. cit.*, pp. 16–26; Fullagar, Lewis and Cumbee, *op. cit.*, pp. 99–101; Karl C. Garrison and J. Stanley Gray, *Educational Psychology* (New York: Appleton-Century-Crofts, 1955), pp. 22–32.

growth is a complex, many-sided process. The "Y" suggests 3-way development of boys and girls. The 4-H Club offers four clues. Are these all? It really does not matter so long as we understand that growth is an all-round process and that the result should be a well-rounded personality.

Intelligent parents and teachers have come to view child growth as largely a phase or stage of development—one's place at a given moment being somewhere along in a continuum that began at conception and stretches on through life. The stage of development for a child of given age may well represent lags from earlier stages and uneven progress or growth in various aspects of personality achievement. A given stage of development for a child may frequently approximate further maturity that commonly is achieved at older chronological age. There are hardly any fixed or definite "norms" that may be expected in children of a given age as the calendar has it. This is but a way of saying that children grow at different rates. They grow in different ways; some aspects of personality change more or faster than others. Individual differences are not erased by even the normal processes of human growth and development.

Children do pass through substantially similar stages of growth and development but at their own individual rate and way of "growing up." Teachers have observed this and assisted it as a great privilege; parents who have lived with their children closely have an interesting appreciation of this.

This appreciation has helped teachers to arrange schools to foster and to promote positive and all-round "growing" by boys and girls. All else the school is expected or requested to do must take second place to this compelling task and privilege of the teachers.

The dynamics of growing up

Competent studies of infant and child behavior and growth are becoming available to the interested teacher and parent of today.[6] These prove invaluable aids to the teacher who tries to learn about children. We cannot see many children grow up and follow them over a long period of time, but we can take advantage of what careful researchers in child growth and development have provided us.

Even with these aids our task will not be an easy one. Many teachers testify to the experience of successful completion of courses in child psychology only to find later when they had children of their own that they knew relatively little about rearing and caring for children. Can we explain how this could happen? And, more important, can we discover ways to keep it from happening to us?

If we could actually watch some children grow up we would undoubtedly make several interesting observations. We would certainly note this key concept of *growth,* which human beings have in common with all living things. We would see that their rates of growth varied, that the little girls seem to acquire maturation in some respects a bit earlier than do the boys. Also, that there is much variety in growth among children of the same age reckoned by the calendar. Those who have wondered at the sight of alert little children and tall gangling adolescents in

the same junior high school class, should now see how it happens.

One should soon begin to note the many ways the children differ. Gradually we would find that some of our psychology reading seemed to make sense.[7] For example, we should be able to note differences in *physique,* the actual physical inheritance of the child. To be sure, it is modified somewhat by environmental factors of health care, nutrition, and the like, but it is recognizable. We would also be likely to observe differences in what is sometimes called *temperament.* Of course, we recognize the futility of trying to classify everyone as "introverts" or "extroverts"; it is not as easy as that! But we should come to see that children vary widely in the general pattern of temperament. Here is an excitable youth; there one quite easy-going, whom nothing seems to knock off his feet, emotionally speaking. We would wonder how much environment and education affects this business of basic temperament of people. And we would quickly discover the wide variations among children in the matter of native ability to learn and to solve problems—*intelligence.*

All of this would give us the basis for understanding the concept of *individual differences.*[8] This simply means

[6] The bibliography is extensive. The student may examine many listed in the selected titles at end of this chapter. One of the best known studies has been continued for many years at the Yale Clinic by Dr. Arnold Gesell, Dr. Frances Ilg and others. See Breckenridge and Vincent, *op. cit.,* pp. 40–51.

[7] See Gordon W. Allport, *Pattern and Growth in Personality* (New York: Holt, Rinehart & Winston, 1961), pp. 33–35, 57–82.

[8] A concise treatment can be found in many books on educational psychology and human growth and development. See, for example, Morris L. Bigge and Maurice P. Hunt, *Psychological Foundations of Education* (New York: Harper & Row, 1962), pp. 110–139; Breckenridge and Vincent, *op. cit.,* see index; Allport, *op. cit.,* pp. 15–21; Fullagar, Lewis and Cumbee, *op. cit.,* pp. 124–125, 235–236. See also John P. Lubek and P. A. Solberg, *Human Development* (New York: McGraw-Hill, 1954), pp. 108–110, 146–148, 207–214, 306–307.

that children—all people—are different in nearly any respect we can name. They vary in height, weight, motor coordination, ability to run the 50-yard dash, age at which they are ready to begin reading, and dozens of other ways. Their ability to learn new meanings and understandings varies widely, as one can see from the scores upon many tests. Their interests are different, too, because of a wide variation in the home environment, and of their previous experiences. The teacher of a typical group of boys and girls has at hand a widely varying pattern of human abilities, aptitudes, interests, and problems. Her work is greatly conditioned by the *individual differences* among her pupils. Good parents and teachers understand and accept this and approach their tasks in the light of that fact. Each child and each pupil is seen as a person— unique and different, with abilities and needs to be used and met, respectively. It is the responsibility of the school and of teachers to do their best to meet this great challenge. All are important, each is important and valuable. It is no less important for each home to practice this same philosophy. Who is to say that this *one* ability is more valuable and important than another? We cannot give the answer, unless we wish to be arbitrary about it. All children have the right to be accepted, to have a reasonable degree of success in the school program. If all teachers really understood and accepted this viewpoint, our schools would become the happy, blooming, buzzing places that Pestalozzi dreamed of nearly a century and a half ago. We can get a forceful impression of this concept from seeing the film *Twins Are Individuals*. All future parents and teachers should see it, read some refer-

ences, and discuss this concept until it is clear.

What has been noted concerning *individual differences* should not obscure the corollary of that concept. Some may be thinking about the difficulty of teaching twenty-five or thirty youths—all different—if each is to have a different program. It is not as bad as all that. Of course, the abilities of children differ, so do their needs.[9] But note that these differences may often be differences of degree. Take health, for example. In any group of children, one will find many kinds and degrees of health needs, ranging from minor dental care to severe malnutrition. At least these differing needs do serve to show up a common problem, namely, health. The teacher is on safe ground if she tries to meet these varying needs by making health an important part of the school program. How do the different abilities of children fit into all this? Again, it is a matter of using these different abilities in an overall approach to the general problem. Suppose Johnny reads poorly for his age level; then we depend more upon audio-visual aids than a textbook in health in his case. Susie likes to use paints and color so she is encouraged to develop a poster which expresses the health problem as she learns it. Billy makes a contribution by getting an interview with a local health expert and makes a report to the group. Sally reads a fine story in an advanced book and adapts it for telling to the other children. Henry goes to the science teacher in the high

[9] Fullagar, Lewis and Cumbee *op. cit.,* pp. 121–137; Breckenridge and Vincent, *op. cit.,* pp. 105–113; Allport, *op. cit.,* pp. 203–206, 313–370; Garrison and Gray, *op. cit.,* pp. 200–204; Bigge and Hunt, *op. cit.,* pp. 204–221.

school and arranges for a conference with the group. And so it goes! The capable teacher uses these different abilities and needs in a concerted attack upon problems of general concern.

If we go on to analyze this we will begin to see that children are *alike but different.* Their abilities differ but they do have abilities. That's common among the group. Their needs vary but they tend to have needs in several large areas. Again these needs are seen to be common for the group, as in health, as we have seen. We look at some others to find that learning to get along with each other, a matter of elementary citizenship, is certainly a common need for the group. Learning wholesome beneficial ways of playing and using spare time is almost certain to be another.

Keep this up and we shall soon have a list comparable to the seven cardinal principles of education or some other commonly accepted list of purposes of education. The important thing is that we should now see that these are really based upon the varied abilities, interests and needs of children. In this sense purposes really illuminate the task and responsibility of teaching.

YOUTH ARE TOMORROW

Those who are interested in youth have questions to ask: Who are youth? How many youths are there? What is the significance of this period of growth? What are the needs, interests, responsibilities, and aspirations of this vast crowd of young Americans? And how do public schools translate these into effective school programs? These questions will naturally come to the fore as we get into the matter of learning about pupils in general and adolescents in particular.

How well parents and teachers understand about youth depends upon a good foundation of interest in and appreciation of both children and adults. Youth are people—important, interesting people in the process of growing from childhood into adulthood. Teachers and parents appreciate this fact as they learn to accept and to work sympathetically with growing young people in the exciting and serious experiences and concerns that make up life. This kind of appreciation of youth is a cornerstone, a distinguished feature of the good teacher's equipment. It should be the goal of your study of the adolescent learners, the youth of America.

This is a period of significant and varied growth—physically, mentally, emotionally, socially, and in all other aspects of personality. Unprecedented problems may appear, but these should be seen as incidental to the processes of growing up.[10] By and large, youth are interesting and exciting persons to know and to work with. As they grow normally and naturally they settle down and achieve wonderful things. One of the nicest things that can happen to a discerning and sympathetic adult is to be accepted and rewarded by the affection of youth. For there is nothing more important than the need of adolescents to be understood, accepted for what they are, respected for their varied abilities and aptitudes, considered in terms of their interests and needs, and helped

[10] H. H. Remmers and C. G. Hackett, *Let's Listen to Youth* (Chicago: Science Research Associates, 1950); also John W. M. Rothney, *The High School Student* (New York: Dryden Press, 1955), pp. 249–268; see also Bigge and Hunt, *op. cit.,* pp. 182–201; and Allport, *op. cit.,* pp. 124–127.

in these respects by discriminating, friendly, and relaxed teachers.

Teachers of younger children and of youth alike have important interests in children of all age groups. For what now concerns the teacher of the elementary school group is prerequisite to what the high school faculty member needs to understand. All teachers need to know children and youth and to see them as interesting, different, and worthy persons growing up, becoming unique and valuable personalities.

How many youth of high school age are there? There can be an answer to this question but the minute it is given it grows obsolete. We can only point to the latest available census figures and estimates, and to the current rates of population growth. In 1950 the number of youth ages 15-19 inclusive was 10,671,327 (7.1%); in 1960 the same age group numbered 13,219,243 (7.4%) Percentages of 1960 enrollments in secondary schools for the 14-17 year age groups were as follows: 14- and 15-year-olds 94.1%, 16- and 17-year-olds 80.9%.[11]

Diversity is the word for youth

What differences must the teacher appreciate in youth? In what respects may youth differ significantly enough to require special attention by the school? The most obvious differences, of course, are those of *sex* and *race*. America is the most cosmopolitan of nations. People of all racial stocks live together here and meet freely in our common schools. Boys

and girls attend the same schools in the United States in contrast to some school systems abroad where the sexes are separated in most of their educational institutions. Thus, the American teacher expects to accept, understand, and respect pupils of all races and both sexes with all the other differences they will have as they come together in the school.

Pupils differ in native ability—in *intelligence* and *aptitudes*. These differences may be profound and varied. Teachers are prepared to accept pupils of widely varying native ability, seeing that this is but one of the ways people are "fearfully but wonderfully made."[12] Formerly, secondary schools were chiefly designed to accept pupils of superior mental aptitude for academic subjects; today the high schools of America try to offer some challenging and meaningful subjects for all adolescents. This does not mean that the needs and interests of superior students are neglected, but rather that more is offered to appeal to the interests, needs, and abilities of more young people. Teachers now see that people are vastly different and that they differ widely in their aptitude to do and to learn different things.

The modern high school is likely to provide a wide variety of curriculums for the great numbers of teenagers that make up its student body. The philosophy of the comprehensive high school expresses concern for the growth of pupils with artistic as well as academic ability, for those with mechanical aptitude as well as for those

---

[11] Source: United States Bureau of the Census. *U.S. Census of Population, 1960.* General Social and Economic Characteristics, U.S. Summary, Final Report PCCDC (Washington: U.S. Government Printing Office, 1962). See Table 114, p. 1–259.

[12] Fullagar, Lewis and Cumbee, *op. cit.,* pp. 159–186; Seidman, *op. cit.,* pp. 86, 134–135; Garrison and Gray, *op. cit.,* pp. 75–88; Zubek and Solberg, *op. cit.,* pp. 272–291; see also Lawrence E. Cole and William F. Bruce, *Educational Psychology* (Yonkers-on-Hudson: Harcourt, Brace & World, 1950), pp. 125–158.

of scientific turn of mind. It cares for those with creative potential as well as those who excel in following directions, and for those who are studious and reserved, as well as for those who exhibit talents for leadership. This point of view considers all wholesome and worthwhile aptitudes of youth as legitimate subjects of instruction. Teachers recognize that people are different—superior in some respects, average in others, inferior in still other ways—but that all are worthy of respect as unique and important persons. Most persons have some aptitude or other that is outstanding or above average.[13] Contrast this with the older view that prevailed in secondary education, one that placed premium only upon superior aptitude for academic subjects of classical studies, the scientific fields, but little else. This narrow concern of past school programs was one reason for the rapid growth of student activities. In the extracurricular activities of the school there was tacit acknowledgment of the wider variety of pupil abilities and aptitudes that were not served by the traditional curriculum.[14] The modern high school takes in that wide range of interests because it accepts the fact that youth vary widely in native ability (intelligence), and that intelligence includes many kinds of aptitudes.

Closely related to intelligence are factors of physical, emotional, and mental health and wellbeing which are present in varied combinations and degrees in different personalities. Teachers expect to find physiques that range from frail to robust (and some with physical disabilities) in every classroom. Likewise, there will be a wide variety of personality adjustment in the form of emotional poise and balance. The adequate personality, the pupil with problems, and the unstable ones are all present in any age group. The teacher learns to recognize symptoms of problems of mental health such as aggressive pupils, those given to undue fantasy, others that seek to retreat from activity, those who have learned various mechanisms and complexes. These problems are present in any roomful of young people. Mental health is seen as one of the important phases of human growth and development, one closely related to other factors.

Any group of youth represents a variety of home backgrounds and early family experiences.[15] The local community may be a farming area, a mining town, a suburban development, a crowded midtown section, a small village with quiet streets and trees, a slum area near the waterfront or an orphan's home. Some have learned to carry responsibility for chores on the farm and with their pets; another carried papers early in the morning hours, one worked for a truck farmer during vacations, others caddied for a

[13] An outstanding high school principal wrote that one major discovery from his long experience was that over 90 percent of all the pupils he had known had some aptitudes, quality, or potential that was above the average, i.e., nearly all could excel in something.

[14] See for example, Earl A. Johnson and R. Eldon Michael, *Principles of Teaching* (Boston: Allyn & Bacon, 1958), pp. 255–265, 286–306; and Educational Policies Commission, *Education for All American Youth—A Further Look* (Washington: NEA, 1952), pp. 1–11.

[15] See National Asociation of Secondary School Principals, *Planning for American Youth* (Washington: NEA, 1944); or Educational Policies Commission, *Education for All American Youth—A Further Look* (Washington: NEA, 1952), pp. 106–146.

brief time. A few have never done anything much but looked at television. Some have learned to improvise play and later to loaf in crowded streets and cluttered alleys of blighted areas. These are the culturally deprived. At the other end of the scale, students have money to spend, clothes, poise, and cultural advantages. These are indices of the wide variety of home conditions and experiences that boys and girls of a high-school group have.

Consider Development

We can see stages of development

Children differ even at birth and show their individual differences as they grow. Their growth is continuous but gradual. Therefore, we need to be cautious in making too many generalizations about them at any given age. But there are some very helpful studies available which have been reported after capable students studied thousands of children. Thus, their findings may be regarded as dependably typical for children of a given age. The extensive work of Gesell and associates provides parents and teachers with useful information about child growth and development from birth.. The published studies include useful summaries of behavior of infants and children at monthly (or longer) intervals.[16] These include motor development, language, adaptive behavior, and personal-social behavior. We should find an opportunity to read and study this material as background for better understanding of the school child. Perhaps your best introduction to these studies should be through use of the films made for this purpose.[17] Of course, the child will be older when he is ready for school, but the wise teacher can understand present behavior much better if she knows how the child grew and learned as an infant. Certainly this is of utmost importance for parents. Since the informed teacher finds it necessary to work closely with them she needs to be able to ask intelligent questions about the early growth and learnings of the child.

Everyone may have heard that the first five years of a child's life are the most important in the formation of his personality and character, or that the child's habits and attitudes are so well fixed by the time he comes to school that little can be done about them. There is some truth in these statements but we should not be certain that the child cannot learn better habits and attitudes, especially if parents and teachers work intelligently and cooperatively. The trouble has been that few teachers have really understood total child behavior and what it means. Since the traditional school merely tried to provide formal learning anyway, it made little difference what the child's previous experiences had been. We may see much improvement in the work

[16] A. L. Gesell and others, *The First Five Years of Life* (New York: Harpers, 1940); A. L. Gesell and Frances Ilg, *The Infant and Child in the Culture of Today* (New York: Harpers, 1943); A. L. Gesell and Frances Ilg, *The Child from Five to Ten* (New York: Harper & Row, 1946).

[17] See for example, *Life with Baby,* a March of Time film that summarizes a number of others on child growth and development.

of schools, particularly if we have more nursery and kindergarten programs for three-, four- and five-year-olds.

THE PRESCHOOL CHILD

Usually we speak of the child from three through five as the preschool child, whom we find to be an interesting little person, already well developed.[18] Their oral language skills have developed a great deal and they have learned to care for simple bodily needs and habits. They can understand simple language and can learn regular habits of caring for belongings, clothes, and toys.

This is the golden age for socialization as the child likes to be with others. Here is the time for play and other social activities with other children from which much is learned. The child is dependent upon his parents; yet he responds to other adults whose interest in him can be recognized. Although still dependent, the preschooler is fast developing some independence and may even be labelled as "contrary" by parents. Affection and care tempered with understanding are his especial needs.

The preschooler enjoys play with other children, much of it imitative of the adult activities he knows and accepts. It is often true that a parent can see his or her

[18] See many good references on preschool age children: Eva Knox Evans, *Children and You, A Primer of Child Care* (Chicago: Julius Rosenwald Fund, 1945); Edith G. Neisser *et al.*, *How to Live with Children* (Chicago: Science Research Associates, Inc., 1950); and Gladys Jenkins, Helen Schater, and W. W. Bauer, *These Are Your Children* (Chicago: Scott, Foresman & Co., 1949); and James L. Hymes, *Enjoy Your Child—Ages 1, 2, and 3* (New York: Public Affairs Committee, Inc., 1948).

own behavior and voice reflected in the talk of the child to her dolls. The child likes to help the parent do this or that simple task, but it is play for him.

Among the strongest characteristics of this age are the imaginative and dramatic activities. There is much "pretending" or "play-like" and later, perhaps some pretty wild stories. Another strong characteristic of this age is curiosity. The preschool child who has a chance to live normally is a veritable chatterbox. Innumerable questions, some far beyond the parent's ability to answer may be asked. These questions are sincere and represent the rich native curiosity of the child—he simply has to learn so many things. It is important for adults to remember this—the child has to get answers because he has a great deal to learn. Children have interest until ignorant adults stifle it by discouraging their questions and natural curiosity. Teachers and parents should answer their questions sincerely and honestly, using terms and illustrations on their level of experience. Sometimes they may have to say, "I'm sorry, but I don't know." This will not hurt if it doesn't happen too often, and if it is *true*. Now that we have mentioned it, it is well for the young teacher to learn that it may be necessary to say "I don't know" now and then. We should learn to do it honestly and in matter-of-fact fashion. We don't lose face if we do it naturally. It is important to add, "Let's find out together."

Preschool children need much free activity and a variety of experiences. A school program for them should provide a good rhythm of work, play, and rest periods. Emphasis should be placed on satisfactory group living, principles of cooperation and respect for rights of others, such as "taking turns." The child should never be talked down to; good teachers simply use the vocabulary and example which they understand. Most of us have noticed that the good teacher in the nursery or kindergarten sits on the little chair with her group and that she gets down so she is near the child's face when she talks to one.

THE ELEMENTARY SCHOOL CHILD

The subject of this section is the term used to refer to the six-year period usually spent in grades 1 through 6, or roughly from ages six to twelve inclusive. The youngster who comes to school at six for the first time normally is anything but naive and underdeveloped.[19] First graders come to school with many learnings and traits already strongly developed. It is true that school is new and different; it may even be a bit frightening for a time. That may be because the school is formal and restricts the normal range and character of the child's activities.

The elementary school child is normally quite active and gets restless if kept confined by sitting for long periods. The wise teacher provides plenty of variety and a rhythm of activities for children. On the playground organized play becomes more and more skilled and advanced. Competition in games is quite pronounced, but cooperation is not difficult to get if the teacher knows how to meet children at this level.

Motor control and physical development are achieved during these years. Many skills can be easily developed, especially if they are seen as needed or desirable. Reading is increased both in rate and comprehension, and written language, first as manuscript writing and later in cursive style, becomes a usable tool. Children have a great many interests and the "collecting urge" is often quite pronounced. You have often heard fabulous tales of the contents of a small boy's pockets. The wise teacher uses the interests all this represents to advantage in her teaching.

During this period the children come to have greater interest in others of their own age group. This is the stage for gangs of fellows and all sorts of escapades and adventures. Little girl cliques and crushes are another illustration of this lessening dependence upon adults. Again, the wise teacher guides these group interests into wise channels and desirable activities.

Children of this age do accept adults, but chiefly those who are sincerely interested in them and the things they like. Authority must appear to be just and must be understood to be accepted very well. Parents sometimes fail to understand why boys of this age are embarrassed by shows of affection which they welcomed as a preschool child. Both boys and girls at this period may not welcome solicitude and demonstrations of affection, especially before others. The wise parent and teacher

[19] There are many useful references for this group. See Nina Ridenour, *The Children We Teach* (New York: Mental Health Materials Center, 1956); Clara Lambert, *Understand Your Child—From 6 to 12* (New York: Public Affairs Committee, Inc., 1948); Gertrude M. Lewis, *Educating the More Able Children in Grades Four, Five, and Six,* Bulletin 1961, No. 1, U.S. Department of Health, Education, and Welfare, Office of Education (Washington: Government Printing Office, 1961); and Arnold Gesell and Frances L. Ilg, *The Child from Five to Ten* (New York: Harper & Row, 1946).

understand that this is perfectly normal.

During the pre-adolescent years children begin to show some sex consciousness. Boys and girls tend to play together less and exhibit some shyness toward each other. There may be a good deal of "putting on a show" for the benefit of the other sex, such as pretending to ignore, boisterousness, loud criticism or "razzing." Competition between the sexes can be aroused, and teachers who know no better have even used it for motivating study and achievement in the classrooms.

These later years are characterized by much changeableness, fleeting interests, "crushes," and other previews of adolescence. Bubble gum, comic books, movie magazines, favorite TV shows, distaste for piano practice, skipping one's turn at doing the dishes or washing the family car—all these and more may be expected. The teacher and parent who understand the elementary school child are not often bored. Adults should learn to understand them and to enjoy them at this period. Normally these should be happy and secure years. All teachers should understand and try to help, for all children have the right to these happy undisturbed years of growth.

The discerning parent and the wise teacher find children of early school years to be exciting and appealing little persons. Different in various ways from their infant and preschool years, they bear close acquaintance and friendship equally well, and their needs and interests can well bring out some of the best that adults have to offer. By this time most of the hazards of common childhood diseases have been met or passed; physical growth has slowed down appreciably, but skills

have begun to increase; all sorts of interests, kinds of expression, and the urge to "try things out" are on the upswing. Early school years find children still close to parents, needing them in many respects, but beginning to strike out along new lines and to grow in their own abilities. Interests, at home and outside, are wider and there are marked signs of competence in handling pets, in learning to master wheeled vehicles, in trying out skilled games with whole body movements, and in meeting the school routine. In brief, the primary school child's whole personality has become more complex than previously.

THE SECONDARY SCHOOL PUPIL

Usually the high school pupil is referred to as an adolescent, or youth. In any event, we are referring to those between the ages of thirteen and eighteen inclusive or those in the period usually spent in junior and senior high school. Some youth spend an additional two years in junior college as further education beyond the high school, but, in any case, this is a later adolescent period.

The adolescent pupil formerly received far more attention in educational literature than any other age group.[20] Adolescence has been termed the age of

[20] The bibliography on youth runs to great lengths. Useful general references are plentiful, such as Evelyn Millis Duvall, *Keeping Up with Teenagers* (New York: Public Affairs Committee, Inc., 1948); H. H. Remmers and C. G. Hackett, *Let's Listen to Youth* (Chicago: Science Research Associates, Inc., 1950); *Understanding Your Teen-Ager* (New York: The Metropolitan Life Insurance Co., 1953); Editors of Coronet, "How to Raise a Young Teenager," *Coronet*, **XLIX**, No. 3 (March 1961), pp. 149–170.

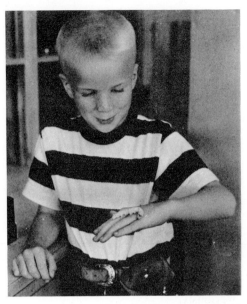

What is a boy?

What are little girls?

conflict and turbulence. The teenage youth is moving out of childhood into a stage is involved in a complex, often incon- of independence and participation in adult responsibilities. Attitudes and habits of the child have to break up into new patterns of independence, self-reliance, dependability, and initiative. The youth sistent total situation when home mem- bership is changing, and the peer group relationship is growing, yet he finds both difficult to cope with. No more strategic and interesting period can be selected by

They grow—

—and change

teachers who are willing to really try to understand the pupils they teach.

Secondary school pupils have been a favorite topic of study by psychologists, sociologists, educators, and other specialists. This is one index, perhaps, to the significance and importance of youth and a clue to one of the big "understandings"

a teacher should achieve while in preparation for her profession.

The attention devoted to adolescents since the work of Dr. G. Stanley Hall has disclosed much that is helpful about youth, but the books should never be closed on this kind of research. This is important for many reasons. We know all

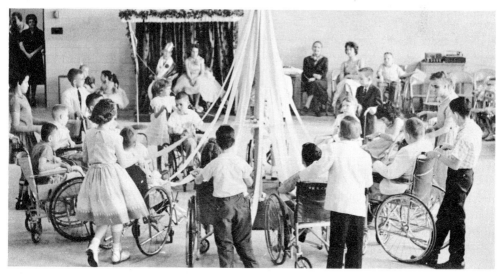

Accept all children

too little about how people grow and develop into unique and important personalities; study of that amazing process, partly sociological and partly psychological, must go on, and all teachers should be in on it. Moreover, we have made mistakes, settled for partial answers and hasty conclusions in the past, and need to improve our findings and the implications for our work as teachers. Too, we need to learn how to help parents (and other adults) to understand youth better and to accept them as good teachers do. Finally, we should become far more skillful in assisting youth to take increasing responsibility for directing and controlling more of their own growth and development in various ways.

The very physical makeup of the youth is changing rapidly. Often youth do not fully understand the physiological changes and the great demands which rapid growth makes upon their bodies. At this stage, health needs of youth are of great importance. Intelligent guidance as to habits and practices in diet, sleep, exercise, and dress is indispensable. Teachers, especially physical education teachers and coaches, have a great responsibility toward youth of this age.

Mental and emotional maturity are gradually achieved during this stage. These are not accomplished easily and automatically. Self-assertion, it is said, often precedes self-confidence; braggadocio covers up insecurity; enthusiasm and noise make up for lack of ability to master and to follow up numerous interests to complete satisfaction. Youthful enthusiasm needs wise guidance and help from understanding adults. Parents should carefully examine their admonitions and judgments of teenagers to be more consistent.[21] The youth may blame others or conditions for his own failure and shortcomings. He blows hot and cold alternately. He does not understand his own abilities, nor his limitations. But he does have energy and puts it out unsparingly. Helped and guided wisely, the adolescent pupil can accomplish an amazing amount of school work.

This is the age for strong vocational interests and for the development of hobbies and leisure time interests. These can be a source of great motivation for successful school experience and adjustment. Conversely, they can be sources of grave conflicts within the family circle, especially if parents oppose or try to dominate their decisions.

Romance enters the picture at this age level. Hero worship, strong admiration for teachers and other youth leaders often develop; likewise, there are strong aversions to some persons. Interest in the opposite sex is intense and the well-known "puppy love" stage may be expected.

The teenage pupil is often quite unpredictable and full of contrasts and contradictions. They are idealistic but may profess the utmost sophistication. Language may be extreme, showing strongest approval or utter distaste for something. Security is strongly needed and desired, but adolescents also wish to stand on their own feet. Recognition as *somebody* seems to be of supreme importance.

Adolescents who grow normally and naturally tend to settle down. That is, they

[21] For example, think about this question: How many parents have told teenagers that they should do something because "You're grown up now," but in the same day have forbidden another undertaking because "You're too young for that. Wait until you're grown up." This is confusing to youth.

do if their adjustment proceeds satisfactorily. It is the great opportunity of teachers and parents to help them accomplish just that. They are great folks, these adolescents. They are easily motivated; tend to accept others at their valuation, but demand sincerity and fairness. They detect pretense and condescension instantly and will have no part of them. You will like them when you really get to know them.

What your observations do tell

Teachers, whether beginning or experienced, must keep in mind some very important considerations and principles in their study and observations of children. In the first place, it is easy to view growth and development as a series of "stages" and to expect children to be understood in terms of a simple still picture. Teachers must remember that the characteristics and features set forth for various age groups are merely *normative,* that they are found for the greatest number at these age intervals. A child may be at the norm or somewhere in a wide range of variations, with respect to a given place of growth and development and *still be absolutely normal* and educable in every way. Actually, an average or mean is only a way of examining and getting new insights into the meaning of a set of data; it tells us nothing about a given individual.

Adults who are concerned about the wholesome growing up of children should resist the temptation to use a simplified and extreme kind of generalized picture of that process. It is too easy and too misleading to say, "All twelve-year-old girls are like that" or that "Three-year-olds always say 'no.' " Remember that wide differences exist among individuals within the same chronological age groups. Every teacher learns to recognize a range of two or three years in various phases of growth and abilities within her group of children. It is unsound to regard sex differences among children as uniform and profound as norms might indicate. It is true that girls in childhood grow earlier toward most phases of maturity than boys, but this tells us nothing definite about a particular Johnny or a specific Susie. The essential point for adults to remember is that what is known about child growth is general, normative, and important. However, it is only a guide to the understanding and guidance of an individual pupil. The real skill and insight of the teacher must be given to the use and application of these general guides to the study of a pupil. Real appreciation of human growth and development discloses where the teacher can begin to look for help in getting a good understanding of a child; it does not automatically tell one what to think without applying the pertinent information.

Sometimes, teachers and parents attribute to the three or more aspects of growth more validity than is justifiable. There is no final and proven validity to the common practice of listing characteristics of growth under the headings of physical, intellectual, and social. Some lists add another aspect (emotional), and still other headings are used for various purposes. This does not mean that aspects of growth are clearly distinguishable and separate. Actually, they are often closely related; some phases cannot be entirely separated, except for purposes of organization of a list for study. Adults who work with children should not expect to separate growth into three or more consistently separate categories. Neither should they gain the impression that physical growth is *more* or *less* important than, or preliminary to, the others. At a given moment there may be reasons for giving more prominence to a particular aspect of growth. Physical growth might be more discernible at one time, or social development might be relatively prominent at another. It is merely for the sake of consistency and convenience that a given aspect of growth is listed first or last in summaries of human growth and development.

EXCEPTIONAL CHILDREN AND YOUTH

Exceptional children are those with mental, emotional, social, or physical characteristics sufficiently different to require special educational programs for their optimum educational development. Children and youth of all ages may be found in these groups. Groups usually included in provisions for special education are the mentally retarded, the blind and the partially seeing, the deaf and the hard-of-hearing, the crippled, the delicate, the cardiopathic, the epileptic, the speech defective, the cleft-palate, the emotionally or socially maladjusted children and youth.[22] In some instances "culturally-deprived" children may be temporarily included when their experience has contributed to maladjustment in typical school situations. The mentally gifted have frequently been grouped with exceptional children although the provisions for special education would differ in degree and kind.

[22] N. S. S. E., *The Education of Exceptional Children*, 49th Yearbook of the National Society for the Study of Education (Chicago: University of Chicago Press, 1950).

The mentally retarded groups

Estimates of the number of mentally retarded children and youth in the total school population usually run above 2 percent, i.e. those that require special education programs. There are slow learners in all school situations and the differences among them are so great as to require a variety of modified instructional practices in regular elementary school classes or in special classroom programs for mentally retarded children of comparable mental ages. Mental retardation is measured and studied by specialists in the education of exceptional children for the purpose of arranging placement in an appropriate group. Mentally retarded pupils with I.Q.'s from 50 to 75 may be classed as "educable" and special education programs are provided by school districts or by the state. Mentally retarded pupils with I.Q.'s from approximately 25 to 50 are usually classed as "trainable" and programs for this purpose are provided in institutions for their care and instruction. The educational objectives are limited but much can be done to help the trainable child to help himself. The mentally retarded child who is educable can be identified early: he will not be ready to read in the first grade and tends to fall further behind his age group in mental age. Parents need to learn to seek competent help in studying children who are mentally retarded, to accept them wholeheartedly, and to plan for their optimal development through an appropriate program of special education.

The physically handicapped child

Physical conditions that constitute a handicap contribute to many cases of maladjustments among the school population. Most parents and teachers believe that children with physical handicaps should be educated with their own age groups in regular school classes whenever possible. In many modern schools we can find many thoughtful provisions that make it possible for crippled children and others to attend classes and other school functions with their own groups.

Parents and teachers need to understand pupils with physical handicaps and need to be able to help them choose personal goals that can be realized. Crippled children, pupils with cardiopathic conditions, the cerebral palsy victim, the child with severely limited vision, and others must learn to accept themselves as they are and to choose worthy goals accordingly. This becomes easier and works better when adults and other pupils accept them as they are without being either over-solicitous or indifferent.

Children with defective hearing or vision comprise a good-sized fraction of the school population. Estimates of the number of school age children with hearing defects have run to over three million. Unfortunately, some are not discovered promptly, and maladjustments may occur because the child does not hear what is going on. Sometimes children considered "dull" have been revealed as bright pupils when defective hearing has been corrected.

Defective vision occurs frequently in school-age groups. Parents and teachers must watch for problems that require attention. School health examinations have served a useful purpose in this respect.

Children that may be classed as physically crippled include those suffering from cerebral palsy, congenital malforma- tions, crippling accidents, and the after effects of poliomyelitis, encephalitis, or brain injury. The National Society for Crippled Children and Adults estimated that over 400,000 children and youth had orthopedic handicaps requiring plastic surgery and that 150,000 had cerebral palsy.

Many children have speech defects

Speech defects are commonly found among young children and some continue throughout childhood and adolesence. There are several causes of speech defects: faulty habits (lisping, baby talk, etc.), emotional instability or maladjustments (stuttering is the major defect), a definite physical basis (cleft palate, etc.), and defective hearing. Lispers and those who learned baby talk usually make better speech adjustments in early school years. Stuttering is probably the most serious speech problem for most teachers. The peak periods of stuttering come when the child begins to talk freely and when he enters school. Greater need for language in social situations and the tensions that are felt in new demands lead to confusion and stuttering. Parents and teachers need to understand and to be able to help keep the new social situations from becoming too tense and threatening for children that develop maladjustments and the stuttering pattern. It is difficult to see how adults can expect children to be relaxed and to meet new demands in their stride unless they can exemplify this attitude in their relationships with children.

Many specialists are needed to develop the necessary insight, skills, and competences that are needed for the special educational programs that we must provide for all our exceptional children.

Implications for Adults

There are many insights and understandings about children and youth that have important implications for parents and teachers.[23] Adults who can and will help young people to grow and to develop their potentialities need to become wise in the ways of children and youth. They should be able to understand, to accept, and to guide by constructive help and by example.

GUIDES MUST UNDERSTAND CHILDREN

Adults who contribute the most to the growth and development in the broadest sense are effective as counsellors and guides. Obviously, the minimum prerequisite for this role is a clear understanding of children. But this elicits the question: What does it mean to understand children? The answer will involve more than one big concept and understanding.

In the first place, we need to know how children grow and develop, "grow up" in effect, at rates that can be seen as similar, yet at the same time, as different for different individuals. Then, we must be able to see that growth involves a number of aspects or facets—physical, mental, social, and emotional—which do not de-

[23] There are many good references for parents and teachers. See, for example, Gladys Gardner Jenkins, *Helping Children to Reach Their Potential* (Chicago: Scott, Foresman & Co., 1961); Lawrence and Mary Frank, *Your Adolescent at Home and in School* (New York: Viking Press, 1956); and Sidonie M. Gruenberg, *et al.*, *Our Children Today: A Guide to Their Needs from Infancy through Adolescence* (New York: Viking Press, 1952).

velop symmetrically but vary among different personalities. These two concepts enable us to better appreciate how personalities are truly and actually unique; each is not like any other; people are not copies of a master model. Thus, the philosophy that stresses the worth and dignity of each child of each person which is the philosophy of democracy, really stems from a solid foundation of fact.

Another point to be appreciated is the widely varying factors that have a part in the growth, development, and learning of children: home and parents; social environment and playmates; possible church and Sunday school experience; urban, rural and social class values; economic advantages or limitations; emotional and social factors in early experiences; work; travel; friends and peer groups. All these and more enter into the achievement of personality.

Finally, we need to understand that all behavior is *caused*. There is a reason or a number of reasons for what we see and call behavior. Sometimes the pupil is unaware of the real reason or motive for his behavior, but it is there in his "living space," and must be considered if constructive changes are to be made through learning. Behavior is, in one sense, a reflection of the characteristics of the child. In another sense, it is an index of the needs of the young person. Often, it is helpful for the teacher (and parent) to remember that the behavior problems and incidents that occur are helpful indicators of what children are at a given point in their growth and development; that here is a signpost that indicates some need, motivation, or drive that should be understood and served in an improved and better way. In other words, here is a chance to make good with a better learning outcome(s) than is now being achieved by this growing, sometimes baffled, or confused child.

Approach learning through needs

This presents the teacher with a practicable and valuable opportunity to use knowledge of pupils in studying and developing ways to improve learning in the school. An effective way to start this is to list on separate sheets of paper brief statements of an individual pupil problem or kind of behavior that is of concern to the teacher. Divide the top half of each page into two columns; at top left write one problem, in the space at top right briefly characterize the best information about children of that age group. Usually this space should have far more information than is supplied about the problem. The bottom half of the page should be used to summarize the implications for the program of instruction that follows from analysis of the foregoing material. Finally, a number of possible approaches, things to do, in appropriate order may be set down by the teacher. It would be helpful to keep a file of analysis and study pages of this kind as a teacher grows in experience and in competence.

The needs of children and their problems are individual. Obviously, this awareness on the part of the teacher means a mandate to study and learn about a child fully and carefully enough to enable sound analysis and planning for his improved behavior through better learning experi-

ences. Study of the learner is a truly functional part of equipment for teaching.

What has been suggested implies that teachers should be concerned about far more than the child's success with the academic subjects taught in school. These are only a part of the wide range of educative experiences which the child and youth must have in order to become the persons they can be in our culture. This responsibility for helping the child to grow in all aspects of personality is challenging, and too many teachers fail to meet it. But you must try to understand this challenge and be ready to meet it because more parents and educators are learning to expect this from good teachers.

What is involved when we speak of the whole child, well-rounded personality, and well-adjusted people? How many sides or facets are there to this thing called personality, anyway? Well, it's not a geometric figure, a polygon of some sort. We're talking about live people with abilities, interests, and potentialities for growth and needs. Here we seem to get a clue that will help us as teachers. What are these needs? If we can get a working knowledge of what the child really needs to be adequate, to be well-adjusted, and to get along in life, we'll be able to take our share of responsibility for his well-rounded personality development.

We have been told that child needs are individual, as indeed they are. They apply to an individual and mean so much that we must be concerned about his needs because that specific child is important, valuable, and unique. However, many children have problems that can be recognized as similar or comparable for many practical purposes. It is possible to consider certain characteristic needs of individuals at different levels. One useful compilation provides a helpful illustration.[24]

A Child of 5, 6, 7, 8 Needs:

> Assurance that he is loved and valued at home and at school.
>
> The right combination of independence and adequate support.
>
> Space and opportunity for plenty of activity; equipment for large muscle exercise.
>
> Alternate periods of rest and activity.
>
> Guidance in group living, sharing, give-and-take, and good work habits.
>
> Chances for participation in concrete learning situations.
>
> Wise channeling of interests; opportunity to develop personal powers.
>
> Help in adjusting to more vigorous ways on the playground.
>
> Opportunities for discharging simple responsibilities.

A Child of 9, 10, 11 Needs:

> Praise and encouragement of parents and teachers; assurance that he is needed and wanted.
>
> Friends and membership in a group.
>
> Active rough-and-tumble play.
>
> Training in skills but without undue pressure.
>
> Reasonable explanations; answers to questions about coming physiological changes.
>
> Definite and increasingly important responsibilities.
>
> A sensible rhythm of rest and activity.
>
> Longer periods of time for sustained efforts in pursuing interests and hobbies.

[24] *Schools and the Means of Education in Cincinnati*, 1954, p. 17; see also Gladys Gardner Jenkins, *op. cit.*, pp. 13–31.

It is necessary to be discriminating in use and application of this list. Obviously some needs could be stated in different terms. Some you find relate to the others, and it is difficult to set them down as separate items. But we do have to have a starting point and this approach gives the young teacher plenty to think about. We should examine the list carefully to see if we can suggest one or more implications for the teacher's work for each of these needs. What about this "assurance of being valued"? This might be termed a "sense of personal worth." Does it imply that each child must have adequate recognition by the teacher and be accepted in the group? Can we think of school practices which run counter to this basic need? Can we suggest constructive practices which would more nearly meet this need? As we move on to the last items of the second list, it appears that we might phrase this as a need for "varied experiences," or an "interesting life." What do these suggest about the daily program of the classroom group? It should be helpful to complete this kind of analysis in terms of what the teacher and the school can do to help meet the needs of children. Similar attention might be given to ways that parents can serve these needs in home and family life.

Some other explanations of basic needs, wants, urges, drives of people are available. As we continue our study we may be able to identify specifics which fit into these broad categories or areas of need. For example, we may begin with physical-biological needs which require various foods, water, certain mineral salts, vitamins, protection from extremes of temperature, and rest and sleep. Note that these are primarily met by the most important educative agency, the home. They become a school responsibility later. So the hot lunch programs, the rest periods, the work-play-rest rhythm of early school years, health examinations, and appropriate playground equipment are all needed.

Consider the emotional-social aspects of living, an area of needs of normal people. They can be identified as needs for affection, for security, for status in the group, for recognition, and for interesting experiences (variety). These are understood by our best teachers. How the teacher recognizes the child with unmet need in this area is not easy to explain. Those problems are the teacher's cues to find out causes and to help find solutions. Behavior of children and youths are useful indices to needs for emotional wellbeing which the wise teacher learns to recognize. Aggressive behavior is not the important problem for a teacher; rather, she tries to find what causes the confused little boy to act like that. The shy, retiring little pupil who tries to get in a corner with a book is a child who needs an understanding teacher. Mannerisms which indicate insecurity, "attention getting" devices, a tendency to run to parent or teacher for support, sulking, tattling, whining, and other behavior are all cues for study of causes and positive measures which may help. Home and school have a tremendous coresponsibility; we begin to see why teacher and parent should be friendly co-workers if children are to be understood and helped to all-round growth and stability.

We must never forget the mental-intellectual aspects of child growth and development. Many of the needs of pupils are related to the abilities and skills necessary for adequate living in modern society. An emphasis upon "fundamentals" has been a part of the school's answer but it is clear that today's needs go much beyond that. Perhaps the ability to do sound thinking is the most basic need for people who try to solve their problems. Adults can help children to learn to think and to reason by providing them chances to use their ingenuity and initiative on problems appropriate to their level of maturity: i.e., not just on arithmetic problems, but rather on all kinds of problems. These may be experienced in daily living together in school and on the playground, through the human relations in the family, and with playmates. Most schools could provide a rich and stimulating learning environment which invites children to explore and to develop intelligent interests. The curiosity of children is one of their significant characteristics; it is a "natural" for the imaginative teacher. There should be in every school enough variety of things to do that all children can discover and follow up some of their interests. What's more, each of these must be deemed worthwhile by the teacher; there must be enough "recognition" of accomplishments to go round the whole group.

Parents and teachers should take time to share creative activities and experiences with children. Time thus spent is a sound investment in the mental growth of children. The wise teacher finds motivation here for even better accomplishment in the hallowed "tool" subjects.

Good teachers learn to depend upon sounder means of motivation than competition and rivalry. If sincere approval and recognition are given for honest effort by the child, there will be sufficient incentives. The child knows when he is doing his best; that is enough for anyone. Thus there are no good reasons for putting children under pressure in competitive situations. Finally, nothing goes over better with children nor helps them more than to give them complete acceptance and sincere respect as persons. Those who have the chance should try it when they teach young boys and girls or adolescents in the secondary school.

How can we begin to see that the needs of people, especially of children, provide teachers with an intelligent approach to curriculum development? It is only when we see problems and needs as the bases of selecting and focussing the content of the curriculum, the program of living in the schools, that we can begin to make our maximum contribution as teachers.

Who Helps Youth Must Understand

UNDERSTAND YOUTH TO HELP

Adults who have been most helpful to youth recognize that there are some simple but subtle understandings that are essential. For example, usually we do not guide or direct youth by an obvious means very long or harmoniously. We can learn how to be of some help, a great deal of help, in fact, but we have to earn the right to render it. Acceptance goes both ways in the contemporary peer culture; it is given and taken. Too few adults seem to realize this is so; fewer still see that it is reasonable. The important point is, that those who can and who wish to help youth must really take every opportunity to learn about adolescents, their places in their cultures, their roles, their systems of loyalties and values. Study and concern for these marvelous young folk will repay the richest dividends to more parents and teachers and other community leaders who will take the time and trouble to make that investment in tomorrow.

One highly significant kind of evidence is to be found in the questions that keep recurring in communication with those who are trusted and respected by youth. These reflect the important concerns and problems that challenge and perplex adolescents in a world that is not fully intelligible to adults.

Perennial questions and concerns of youth

The high school teacher and the parent of the adolescent can develop mutual understandings with present-day youth and gradually acquire greater skills in working with them. For instance, notice the questions that youth are perennially concerned about:

How does one get out of here and get into the money?

What courses shall I take?

Will football hurt my chances with the baseball scouts for good teams?

How can I be popular, make friends, have good pals, and be liked and accepted by them?

Shall I quit school and go to the city to work?

Shall I join the Army?

How does one get a job and money after one gets married while still in school?

Where and how can we have any fun?

What is there to do here, anyway?

What can I do for my life's work?

How can I solve my problems?

These are the kinds of problems the teacher who knows youth can begin to spot among the group. Later, these will come out in conferences after the teacher has proved to be approachable and discreet. When this begins to happen, teachers know that their study of youth was worthwhile and that the experience has begun to pay off.

Teachers must remember that youth's problems have an immediate use in their work. These problems serve to outline one dimension or boundary of the curriculum to be lived in the school—by teachers and their youthful friends. Another dimension or boundary line of the curriculum is the catalogue or total compilation of abilities, aptitudes, and experience backgrounds of the adolescents. Within these confines or bounds the living and learning experiences of the school take place.

Basic needs of people provide an approach

How can we get at these needs of people? Some recognized writers in these fields have prepared helpful lists of fundamental needs of people. In his popular book on psychology Dr. Wendell White suggests the following list of basic needs:[25]

a. *A sense of personal worth.* This is described as the deep-rooted desire to amount to something among our associates

[25] Wendell White, *Psychology in Living* Third ed. (New York: Macmillan, 1955), p. viii. See also, Herbert Sorenson and Marguerite Malm, *Psychology for Living* (New York: McGraw-Hill, 1948), Chapter 5, for a helpful discussion of these types of needs.

and in society. We all want to feel that we are "somebody."

b. *An interesting life.* This is relief from monotony, sameness, drudgery; we must have a variety of experiences, many of which must be pleasant and worthwhile if we are to be happy and well-adjusted.

c. *Love.* This is a composite of sexual and other needs which compose this important aspect of living.

d. *Activity.* This means the need to be doing something, sensory and motor experiences, especially important to children; the need to be engaged in something deemed worthwhile.

e. *Physical well-being.* This is a composite; you can think of several factors and conditions which contribute to this side of growth and life.

f. *A livelihood.* In other words, making a living, security in economic and material sense.

g. *A sense of security.* This is another composite and comprehends several factors.

You will recall previous discussion of the teacher's necessity for seeing the needs of pupils as individual on the one hand, yet to recognize their general character at the same time. For instance, a given fifteen year old high school boy with the problem of shyness has an *individual* problem, one very real and perplexing to him. This problem provides the homeroom teacher with a beginning point for working with the individual pupil to the end of better adjustment and improved achievement in other areas. So it is an individual problem; it affects a live human being, an individual; it is an opportunity to help that person really learn something better, something he needs.

Yet, that same individual problem may be simply one datum, that added to many other specific ones, similar in nature, constitutes a general type of problem which can be said to be characteristic of youth or groups of adolescents. Perhaps, then, we are prepared to consider some of the characteristic needs of youth as a further example of the approach to effective educational programs. It may be briefly catalogued as follows:

Characteristic Needs of Youth[26]

For ages 12, 13, 14

> Continued training in skills.
>
> Knowledge and understanding of the physical and emotional changes that are about to come or are taking place.
>
> An individualized program to meet the needs of those who are approaching puberty as well as those who are not.
>
> Warm affection and a sense of humor in adults.
>
> The assurance of security and provision for both dependence and independence.
>
> Increasing opportunities for independence from adults in performing responsibilities.
>
> Sense of belonging and acceptance by groups.

For ages 15, 16, 17, 18:

> Continued training in skills.
>
> Conformity with and acceptance by the group.
>
> Adult guidance that is kindly, unobtrusive and does not threaten the young person's feeling of freedom.
>
> Adequate understanding of social relations and attitudes.
>
> Opportunities to make decisions, to be on one's own and responsible for one's acts, and to earn and save money.
>
> Provisions for recreation in mixed groups.
>
> Provision for constructive activities related to a worthy cause.

[26] *Schools and the Means of Education in Cincinnati, op. cit.*, pp. 17–18.

For purposes of further study along this line the list has been extended to include the characteristic needs of adults as identified by the same source.[27]

Characteristic Needs List

> Provisions for continuing the formal education program.
>
> Opportunities to acquire technical skills needed to earn a better living.
>
> Chances to gain awareness of problems and the social skills needed for effective community participation.
>
> Opportunities to engage in group recreational activities.
>
> Opportunity to study and discuss wholesome family living.
>
> Help in overcoming or adjusting to physical handicaps.
>
> Instruction in learning the English language and facts needed to become an American citizen for those who have adopted this country as their own.

The goal is well-rounded personality

One result of your study of the growth and development of children and youth should be the appreciation of the goal for all young people, the achievement of personality. We might well reflect upon the meaning and significance of that goal.

One teacher borrowed words from a song made famous during World War II to put it this way, "Bless 'em all. Yes, bless 'em all, the long and the short, and the tall"—meaning both children and youth. Elementary school children and high school pupils are interesting persons to know and to understand. They are interesting to study, too, but it is not wise to let them know that they are under observation. Sometimes when groups get the

[27] *Ibid.*, p. 11.

idea they are being studied, they put on a show that gives an unnatural picture, to say the least. But if we can take them in our stride we will find them interesting, important, and valuable.

Before we agree or disagree, we should reconsider what we know about youth. When we look them over we recall that they are alike in some respects, but so very different in others. Take any one characteristic; for example, height and measurement. We will have some boys way over 6 feet, many around 5′ 6″ to 5′ 11″ and a few way down at 5 feet plus. Can we say that any one of these is better than the others?

The reason for raising this question is that some adults think all youth should be alike—carbon copies of the best bookworm. Think about this question for a minute. Our answer as to which height was best had to depend upon "best for what?" The tallest were obviously best for rebounding a basketball or picking apples; the shortest were better for close body work in airplane factories or for a jockey's life. It all depends upon what the purposes are and how many purposes there are. If there are enough and they are all considered worthwhile then there are enough significant places to go around for the whole group. It is possible to see what this means for the conscientious teacher. She can't say that this or that pupil is best, most valuable, or indispensable. She can only give recognition in terms of something specific. Suppose Jimmy is best in algebra—what of it? Is Bert any less valuable because his strong points lie in getting along with people; he may be a potential chain store manager or topnotch insurance salesman. Doris is crazy about young children and earns

good wages as a baby sitter, but she does have trouble with the dates of the Punic Wars! Is she any less valuable as a prospective housewife and mother of part of the next generation? Betty is slow to get her homework done and her collateral reading reports come in late, but she is the best person in the class to get things done when there is a party to be given, or a picnic, or money to be raised for the annual or any other practical problem. Is this less valuable than an "A" in a space on a narrow card at the end of each six-week grading period? It all depends upon how broad is the teacher's understanding of young people and how sympathetic he is toward their total growth and development. It is a great privilege and an opportunity to work with them.

The teacher who accepts youth and who tries to provide learning experiences that help pupils to achieve their potentialities becomes keenly critical of ways and approaches to this responsibility. One of the most promising approaches that can be found is that of utilizing what is known about the basic needs of people as the starting point. But, first, one must know what is available upon this broad general topic of study and investigation by many capable researchers and thinkers.

Emotional health and maturity are central

Sometimes parents and teachers are preoccupied with their own problems and cannot really help the teenagers. Problems are normal in the lives of people, and all adults may expect to have their share. Parents and teachers should be able to face their problems realistically and courageously and work constructively to solve them. They cannot hope to be perfectly adjusted and without a care in the world before they are ready to help youth to cope with problems. Actually a frank acknowledgment of one's problems with an honest expression of how one is trying to solve them makes a good impression. Young people can get their own concerns and problems into better perspective when they realize that they are not coping with these calamitous matters without the counsel of consultants who have learned about problems, too.

Parents and teachers who live fully and qualitatively with youth should be able to be mature and relaxed in their attitudes toward the "growing up" phases of adolescence. Youth needs to grow up and into emotional maturity and perception; relaxed parents are able to put in an "assist" when it is needed. Emotional maturity and emotional health are hard to define but some characteristics show that one is on the way. The person who is emotionally healthy is:

1. able to and does love someone besides himself;
2. able to and does accept disappointment;
3. able to and does cooperate with others;
4. able to judge a situation as it really is; and not as he wants it to be;
5. self-reliant; and
6. able to make effective use of his abilities.[28]

These criteria are applicable to adults as well as to teenagers. Future parents and teachers can make use of this kind of personal "yardstick" as they continue to grow into other phases of life.

[28] *Understanding Your Teen-Ager* (New York: The Metropolitan Life Insurance Co.), p. 20.

Learn to look for help

One can hardly be expected to become an authority in child study even after one successful introductory course in education. Competence in this respect will be developed gradually if we begin now and if we utilize every opportunity to learn. Our future courses in psychology and in education should be helpful in this respect. We may also get much good from a course in sociology which explains the process of social interaction, namely, how the individual becomes a person and the work of the various educative agencies of the culture. We should remember that the school is only one of these and that the teacher must see her work in relation to the wider educative processes in society.

This suggests further that the teacher in service should utilize as much information as possible from the other educative agencies which are important contributions to the personalities of pupils. The home is universally considered to be the first and strongest influence in a person's growth and education. When this fact is understood, can one doubt the wisdom of close cooperation between the teacher and parents? We see, then, why the best teachers visit the homes of their pupils and become well acquainted with the community. They are following up their efforts to know the children; they seek help wherever it may be found.

We should see clearly that there is much for the adult to learn about children of all ages; this is the continuing responsibility of all those who help children grow and learn. We must keep it up as we continue in our general and teacher education courses. It is possible to find ways to continue: One might get out during vacation and find a job working with children, see films on children, read what the best students of human growth and development have to say, and observe at every opportunity. Later, we shall be able to help parents to learn more about their own children if we have acquired the understandings we need as a teacher. It will not be difficult if we really love children and see that the chance to work with them is what we really want to do. In re- turn for the hard work and study, it is possible to become a great teacher. Understanding teachers find indescribable rewards in the trust, the love, and gratitude of all the children they will teach. Remember! Every child needs to be understood. When we begin to try to understand children we shall have made the first long step toward becoming good teachers. If we do not decide to teach, we will have what it takes to be a constructive parent and community leader who supports what is needed for children and youth.

Selected Bibliography

Baruch, Dorothy M. *How to Live with Your Teenager,* New York, McGraw-Hill Book Co., 1953.

Beyer, Evelyn. "What Every Pre-schooler Wants," *Parents' Magazine,* **XXXVII** (February 1962), pp. 62–65, 82–84.

British Ministry of Education, *Seven to Eleven.* London: H. M. Stat. Office, 1949.

Bossard, James H. S. *The Sociology of Childhood,* rev. ed. New York: Harper & Row. 1953.

Breckenridge, Miriam E., and Vincent, Eliz. L., *Child Development,* 3rd edition, Philadelphia: W. B. Saunders & Co., 1955.

Children's Bureau, *Infant Care,* U. S. Department of Labor, Pub. No. 4, 1942.

Children's Bureau, *From One to Six,* U. S. Department of Labor, Pub. No. 30, 1945.

Children's Bureau, *Guiding the Adolescent,* U. S. Department of Labor, Pub. No. 225, 1933.

Children's Bureau, *Your Child from Six to Twelve.* U. S. Department of Labor, Pub. No. 324, Washington: Government Printing Office, 1949.

Chittenden, Gertrude. *Living with Children.* New York: The Macmillan Co., 1945.

Commission on Teacher Education, *Helping Teachers to Understand Children.* Washington: American Council on Education, 1945.

Cosgrove, Marjorie C. & Josey, Mary I. *About You.* Chicago: Science Research Associates, 1952.

Cruze, Wendell W. *Adolescent Psychology and Development,* New York: The Ronald Press, 1953.

Davis, Mary Dabnery, *Know Your School Child,* Leaflet No. 51. Washington: U. S. Office of Education, 1939.

Duvall, Evelyn M. *Keeping Up with Teenagers.* New York: Public Affairs Pamphlet, 1948.

Editors of Coronet, "How to Raise a Young Teen-Ager," *Coronet,* **XLIX,** No. 5 (March 1961), pp. 149–170.

English, O. S. and Finch, S. M. *Emotional Problems of Growing Up*. Chicago: Science Research Associates, Inc., 1951.

English, O. S. and Foster, Constance J. *Your Behavior Problems*. Chicago: Science Research Associates, 1952.

Frank, Mary and Frank, Lawrence K. *How to Help Your Child in School*. New York: New American Library, 1954.

Frank, Lawrence and Frank, Mary. *Your Adolescent at Home and in School*. New York: The Viking Press, Inc., 1956.

Gallup, George and Hill, Evan. "Youth: The Cool Generation," *Saturday Evening Post*, **CCXXXIV**, No. 51 (December 23–30, 1961), pp. 63–80.

Gardner, John W. "All Children Are Born Talented," *Parents' Magazine*, **XXXVI** (September 1961), pp. 43, 116.

Gesell, Arnold and Ilg, Frances. *Infant and Child in the Culture of Today*. New York: Harper & Row, Publishers, 1943.

————. *The First Five Years of Life*. New York: Harper & Row, Publishers, 1940.

————. *The Child from Five to Ten*. New York: Harper & Row, Publishers, 1946.

Giese, Donald John. "I Was A High School Drop-Out," *Coronet*, **L** (September 1961), pp. 174–175, 178, 180–181.

Grafton, Samuel. "The Tense Generation," *Look*, **XVII**, No. 17 (August 27, 1963), pp. 17–23.

Havighurst, Robert J. *Human Development and Education*. New York: Longmans, Green & Co., Inc., 1953.

Hurlock, Elizabeth B. *Modern Ways with Children*. 2nd ed., New York: The McGraw-Hill Book Co., 1955.

Jersild, Arthur T. *The Psychology of Adolescence*. New York: The Macmillan Co., 1963.

Kallenbach, W. Warren, and Hodges, Harold M., Jr. *Education and Society*. Columbus: Charles E. Merrill Books, 1963, pp. 123–142, 178–195.

Keliher, Alice. *Life and Growth*. New York: Appleton-Century-Crofts, Inc., 1938.

Lambert, Clara. *Understand Your Child—From 6 to 12*, Public Affairs Pamphlet No. 144. New York: Public Affairs Committee, 1948.

Laughton, Grace and Stout, Irving W. *Those Well-Adjusted Children*. Chicago: Science Research Associates, Inc., 1951.

Leonard, Edith M., Emiler, Lillian and Vandirkar, Catherine S. *The Child at Home and School*. New York: American Book Company, 1942.

Lewis, Gertrude M. *Educating the More Able Children in Grades 4, 5, & 6*, U. S. Department of Health, Education and Welfare, Office of Education Bulletin 1961, No. 1. Washington: Government Printing Office, 1961.

MacKenzie, Catherine. *Parent and Child*. New York: William Sloane Associates, 1949.

Martin, Frances. *Know Your Child*. New York: Hinds, Hayden and Eldridge, 1945.

Millard, Cecil V. *Child Growth and Development in the Elementary School*. New York: D. C. Heath & Company, 1951.

Mitchell, Lucy Sprague (Ed.). *Know Your Children in School*. New York: The Macmillan Co., 1954.

Neisser, Edith C. *How to Live with Children*. Chicago: Science Research Associates, Inc., 1950.

Olson, Willard C. *Child Development*. Boston: D. C. Heath & Company, 1949. Excellent book, modern viewpoint.

Pierce, Wellington G. *Youth Comes of Age*. New York: The McGraw-Hill Book Co., Inc., 1948.

Pratt, Caroline. *I Learn from Children*. New York: Simon and Schuster, Inc., 1948.

Remmers, H. H. and Hackett, C. G. *Let's Listen to Youth*. Chicago: Science Research Associates, Inc., 1950.

Reynolds, Martha May. *Children from Seed to Saplings*. New York: The McGraw-Hill Book Co., Inc., 1939.

Rothney, John W. M. *The High School Student, A Book of Cases*. New York: Dryden Press, 1953.

Rusk, Howard A. "Square Pegs in Round Holes," *NEA Journal*, **XLVII** (December 1958), p. 608.

Schacter, Helen. *How Personalities Grow*. Bloomington: McKnight and McKnight, 1949.

Strain, Frances B. *Your Child, His Family, and Friends*. New York: Appleton-Century-Crofts, 1943.

Taylor, Harold. "The Whole Child: A Fresh Look," *Saturday Review*, **XLIV**, No. 50 (December 16, 1961), pp. 42, 43, 57–58.

"The Good American Teen Agers: Their Problems, Their Achievements, Their Life," *Newsweek*, **L** (November 15, 1959).

Weitzman, Ellis. *Guiding Children's Social Growth*. Chicago: Science Research Associates, Inc., 1951.

Zubek, John P. and Solberg P. A. *Human Development*. New York: The McGraw-Hill Book Co., Inc., 1954. Up-to-date summaries, good bibliography.

Chapter 11

The Parents Look to the Schools

True progress in the neighborhood or large community is dependent upon intelligent cooperation between educational forces and citizens in general. Neither group may forge far ahead and leave the other far behind if the local community is to be made a better place in which to live and rear children.*

Introduction

Teachers and most other adults have a common interest in the well-being and growth of the children and youth of this country. Parents are vitally concerned about the growth and education of their young folk and this means a working relationship with school people. The teachers of a given school should be alert to help parents know their children better, to understand their problems, and to help youth meet the acute needs that accompany growing up. Sometimes study and discussion groups help. Again the right kind of recreation and entertainment opportunities must be arranged, and the work of all community agencies must contribute to the end of constructive growth for all youth. Teachers will be active and helpful in all of these. The school program should be based upon the best knowledge of youth and of their needs that teachers can attain in their preparation for their work. Students will prepare for their part in that endeavor by studying to learn how to guide children and to help youth.

What Parents and Teachers Share

Teachers and parents have mutual interests and responsibilities of the utmost

* C. O. Williams (Ed.), *Schools for Democracy* (Chicago: National Congress of Parents and Teachers, 1939), p. 191.

gravity and significance. These are represented in the children and youth that seek an education and a future in our schools and colleges. Parents and teachers are linked by the strongest bonds—human ties of affection, concern, respect and understanding—in their common responsibility to today's youth and the future of America. Every consideration then would call for a large measure of common understandings, clear communication, and effective cooperation between teachers and parents.[1] Since this is not always the case, it becomes more important to try harder to attain this ideal.

This mutual interest is the child, son or daughter to one and accepted pupil of the other. Their mutual concern for the future achievement and well-being of the child motivates their respective best efforts. An account of a great lesson taught by the Master Teacher presents a graphic picture of a little child set down in the midst of adults.[2]

The child is in the middle when parents and teachers fail to understand or to communicate, or when there are conflicts of values between the home and school environments. In another sense, the child is a bridge between the school and home, a line of communication between teacher and parent.

Children are expected to bring their homes to school with them, not literally, of course, but as part of themselves as young personalities already well along the way of growing up. The children come from early years in home, play group and neighborhood into nursery school or kindergarten with social and emotional development according to the experiences they have had. Skilled teachers know and expect differences in social skills and emotional adjustment because of the differing family and neighborhood environments of the children. The values, esthetic standards, habits and attitudes of children reflect the educative experiences children have had prior to entering school. Competent teachers know and expect this from the very start of the child's school experience.

From the time the child enters school —sometimes even earlier—the teacher becomes an important figure in the child's world of living and growing. In a great many instances, the teacher comes next to parents, even closer than other relatives. The teacher's influence and ideas enter the home whether she has ever visited it or not. "Teacher says" is a preface to many sentences uttered by the new pupil. Reactions of parents and siblings to the frequent reference to "my teacher" differ according to the pattern of home life. In some there will be derision and even hostility to teachers and school in general. In others the teachers will be held in high regard. Other reactions will run somewhere between the two extremes.

It is easy to see how there can be misunderstanding at either end of the road which children have to travel—living and learning. Often it is mere lack of understanding but this too needs to be corrected. There must be a common understanding of this whole growing up process and of the roles of parents and teachers in it for the sake of the child. Children need *both parents and teachers*. All should strive for a common goal.

[1] Concise general discussions of this topic may be found in (1) Martha Piers, *How to Work with Parents* (Chicago: Science Research Associates, Inc., 1955), and (2) Irving W. Stout and Grace Langson, *Parent Teacher Relationships*, No. 16, What Research Says to the Teacher Series (Washington: NEA, 1958).

[2] See *Matthew*, 18: 2–6.

Common Understanding Is the Ideal

The ideal school would have several distinctive characteristics but one would be common understanding of the children and their growing-up experiences plus shared views of how parents and teachers could best facilitate and assist that educational objective. Many schools exhibit good examples of this kind of harmonious working relationship among the adults who are dedicated to the well-being of their children. It is hardly necessary to add that there are schools that exhibit little evidence of the desirable relationship between parents and teachers.

This ideal is more than a pretty phrase; it has a sound basis in what is known about sound educational practice and about the emotional and mental health of pupils. The bases are simple and clear. Teachers need to know their pupils as thoroughly as possible and parents should be their best source of much of the needed information. This would include the obvious items about health—childhood diseases, immunizations, and allergies; the family background—siblings, adults and kinfolks; early childhood experiences; the cultural level of home life; the neighborhood influences; and related information. Informal talk with parents can elicit more subtle information about the experiences and influences that have contributed to the personality development of children. Teachers learn to recognize such clues as these: an only child with doting parents; children kept by over-indulgent grandparents when both parents are at work; those with no siblings and a sheltered home life; the harsh realities of a broken home with privations and precarious existence as the rule; evidence of an insecure home, continually threatened by factors beyond children's comprehension; problems resulting from many changes, moving, and lack of security anywhere; early childhood as a struggle for survival in and outside the home in a disadvantaged area; pupils who have always been sickly, never able to play like other children; and other leads of like significance. Results of efforts to get information will not all be sweetness and light to be sure, but how else could the conscientious, courageous teacher acquire a sound basis for understanding the child?

A second imperative follows clearly from the first: Teachers need this information about children in order to plan for learning experiences, activities, and materials to meet the needs and interests of the group.

There is every reason to believe that the vast majority of parents will react favorably to the teacher who desires to know about their children in order to help provide a better school program for them. In many instances this happy state of affairs will not materialize in a first meeting or a few hours *but come it will,* if the teacher is sincere and genuinely interested. This brings the third major consideration into the total picture. When children recognize that parents and teachers are communicating and that both are interested, most problems of adjustment between home and school and others, too, tend to dissipate. This is a homely truth but vitally important: children need both parents and teachers that they can be sure of, and count on and trust. What *more* does any normal child need?

There is a fourth consideration, very

much like the converse of the second. The home environment and living pattern can be intelligently modified and improved in terms of the child's progress and problems therein. Does the child need to concentrate on some particular skill, a series of drills? Or have someone help with a homework task? A simple explanation and request from a teacher who can be trusted and believed, will often result in modifications of evening home life to make these adjustments possible. Many TV sets have been darkened, and lights turned up at study stations in family situations as result of clear mutual understandings of what is needed by both sets of adults that the child can trust.

These are considerations that clarify and illustrate the significance and need for broad common understandings by parents and teachers, and sound working relationships between home and school. To put it as simply as possible, this means that the home and parents come to appreciate the "school side" of problems and issues; the school people, especially the teachers, understand the "home side" of the same matters. This is as our psychology students will say a good illustration of the differences that perception can make. Better perceptions by all concerned in a situation help enlarge the area of common understanding and the basis for agreement.

THE PARENTS' SIDE

Teachers as parents see them

It does make a difference how parents view teachers because children usually reflect and perpetuate the image and impressions of parents. How many children have started to school with the reiterated phrase ringing in their heads: "Just wait until you get to school! Miss Jones will make you walk a straight line (or 'toe the mark')!" Some other uncritical and subjective phrases may have been used, but the picture Johnny or Susie got was one that lived in parental heads long after the days of harsh discipline and poorly-trained teachers had passed. Many school people have not recognized this elementary fact—that some of the misunderstanding of teachers and modern school programs is a carry-over from the school days of two or three decades ago. Isn't it quite plausible to expect that some of the negative attitudes toward contemporary public education as shown by recalcitrant groups of taxpayers and anti-school bonds campaigns, come from unfortunate school experiences of certain adults in schools a good many years ago? Some folks have voted against increased school taxes in referendums on building needs and increased school costs to get even with some minor tyrant of a classroom who long since yielded up his hickory stick "scepter" and faded away. In brief, some parents may harbor an old unfavorable or hostile attitude toward teachers that no longer has any rational basis.

Parents may even be afraid of the teacher for other reasons. Teachers who are unapproachable and who brush parents off without courteous consideration, although few in number, have complicated that relationship with parents for a great many other teachers. Teachers who are naive with respect to the subtle but real differences in family living patterns and values in different neighborhoods and social class often arouse apprehension on part of both parents and children by insistence upon the typical middle class behavior and values often deemed normative. The unsophisticated, even crude teacher who resorts to sarcasm, ridicule, and rash threats of failure wreaks immeasurable harm to the good relationships of home and school. To be sure, the group of teachers whose performance falls so low is small (thank goodness!), but the result is all out of proportion to the number. The intelligent, emotionally-mature teacher will understand the bases of such problems as these—irrational as some may be, and take pains to clear the way for better understanding, positive attitudes, and genuine cooperation.

There are parents who are unable to be objective about their child. Many factors and experiences could contribute to this phenomenon which is relatively common. These parents often feel that the teacher doesn't know how to deal with or treat their child. Children are often quick to sense lack of parental confidence in or regard for teachers and to act accordingly. Accounts of happenings in school and the child's own part in incidents may be reported in distorted or biased fashion. In this way, the misunderstanding grows and extends. Parents who lack confidence in teachers or who are unable to see any "side" except that of their own child, may complain of unreasonably hard discipline, especially when they have been indulgent themselves. Sometimes parents go to the other extreme and expect the teacher to impose the rigid discipline that they have not maintained during the early years of their children's experience. Some parents who have been too busy and preoccupied to give full attention to their children, may feel that the teacher has *come between* them and their son or daughter. It is a lot easier to face up to some such explana-

tion than to undertake the long process of developing a real basis of sharing life with one's children. There are parents who seem to resent the teacher's efforts to explain some of the problems of the children. They even become threatening and hostile. The teacher who avoids all such difficulties would probably be a master diplomat or capable psychologist.

The teacher who is well-informed, confident, and honestly interested in the child, can usually find ways to work out misunderstandings with parents. How to do it in any specific situation cannot be set forth in a handbook for teachers as the factors and circumstances of similar problem situations will differ as will the capabilities of different persons involved. The clues to success include inventiveness and sound information before any decisions. Raise questions until the picture becomes clearer to all concerned, and avoid ultimatums and threats. Keep in mind the proverbial wisdom about the virtue of a "soft" answer and a long supply of patience. Remember that the time spent in developing better understanding at one time will save time and facilitate progress the next time. Good teachers teach children indirectly through parent conferences and *vice versa*.

Teachers sometimes fail to see the parents' side of certain problems. A common complaint of parents is that the teachers do not realize the heavy load parents already carry, else they would not expect help to be given to Tony on his homework, or that Sally's costume for "the program" be readied in a hurry. Teachers who think about this will see the point and be able to handle it. A simple straightforward statement of commendation for the hard work the parents do to raise their children, sincere thanks for what parents have done to help with homework, the preparation of properties and costumes, and any other contribution go a long way toward realization of a good relationship with the home. It is an amazingly effective, although simple, approach to request the help of parents if it can be done with sincerity. An ancient truth can be put bluntly, "A little sincerity goes a long way toward solving problems of human relationships." Genuineness is the best preparation for dealing with people of high, low, or middle degree. Teachers can use a lot of it and those who try genuineness, find that it frequently is returned by the parent.

Home life affects school progress

Sophisticated teachers understand the effects of home conditions and the family experiences of the school child upon his adjustment to, and performance in the school.[3] Poised teachers can understand why the attitudes of children toward them and toward the school may be due to parental views and family experiences, but does not hold resentment toward them. The teacher with deep understanding of these factors and influences will not take refuge behind an oversimplification about the schools' function to teach. She will not try to solve the social problems of the community. Instead, she will be more likely to study and seek ways to help the child with problems to make a better adjustment and to successful experiences in school.

[3] A useful book is James L. Hymes, *Effective Home-School Relations* (Englewood Cliffs, N.J.: Prentice-Hall, 1953). See also John A. Bartky, *Social Issues in Public Education* (Boston: Houghton Mifflin Co., 1963), pp. 127–162.

Teachers who have learned to study children recognize symptoms and evidences of need that mislead or escape most persons. The aggressive child, the child who craves attention constantly, the apathetic child who just endures the school day, the shy, timid, introverted child who withdraws, the child literally sick with anxiety, the child whose parent is gravely ill—compels attention and understanding. How can one shine in the reading group when the family integrity is so threatened that Tommy doesn't know what he will find when he returns home after school? Little wonder that Jane failed to bring a homework assignment back today since her mother is gravely ill in a charity ward at general hospital. Susan sits ever so quietly and day-dreams of going away to fame and fortune. Milly's speech patterns were learned in an early rural home environment in a distant state before her parents moved to the Milltown section, and the ridicule of classmates hurts her deeply. Allen tries very hard to do what is expected of him. He constantly wants to know how he stands and his prospects for marks. He recalls that his older brother and a sister are both straight "A" students in high school. All of these symptoms and evidences tell the perceptive teacher a great deal. She recognizes possible problems that preclude the free exercise of his aptitudes and interests—pressures, threats, friction, continued tensions, and harsh conditions—in the child's home environment.

Teachers who study children and who seek the help of modern knowledge know that the child's perceptions of himself, of his schoolmates, the teacher, and of other adults have much to do with his adjustment. The attitudes and values of the parents and other adults in the home have a bearing upon those of the child. Not until the teacher has a reasonably accurate knowledge of such factors as these can she expect to work effectively to bring about constructive change in the situation.

Ideally, the answer to problems of the home and family life that affect the child's adjustment *to* and progress *in* school, should be solved by cooperation of parents and teachers. In cases where the goal of wholesome understanding and mutual consideration has been achieved, this cooperation can start and continue as needed. Those problems that must be tackled without benefit of any previous understanding may possibly become the means of achieving a cooperating relationship as efforts to improve the situation are made. In those disappointing instances when neither problems are solved nor any cooperation achieved, the teacher will have a better self-image if she can honestly say that she has given it her best efforts.

What parents expect of teachers

Every teacher has probably considered questions of this type. Parents do expect a number of contributions to the education of their children on the part of the teachers.[4] Some expectations may be considered general, although they may be expressed in various ways.

In the first place, parents expect teachers *to be competent and capable* guides for their children. In other words, teachers are expected to know their jobs and do them well. Parents who know

[4] See Cole S. Brembeck, *The Discovery of Teaching* (Englewood Cliffs, N.J.: Prentice-Hall, Inc., 1962), pp. 225–230 for a discussion of this general question.

nothing of the fine art of teaching or teacher education courses, get a quick impression of whether teachers know their business or not. This is normative human behavior; it is easy for laymen, including teachers, to make up their minds about the performance of professional and public officials from meager information.

Parents expect teachers *to be interested* in their children. Probably "concerned about" may be a better expression for this statement, which is obviously a significant key to the relationship between parents and teachers.

A great many parents would place strong emphasis upon and expect teachers *to teach fundamentals*—knowledges and skills—that all people need to live in today's world and to continue their educational progress. Opinions would differ sharply about the nature of the content, but all would expect teachers to teach what the *children should know*.

Many parents expect teachers *to challenge their children* into accomplishing what they are capable of doing. This is a frequent source of misunderstanding as parents may fail to see that teachers must challenge, motivate, and help twenty-five to thirty other children as well. Common reactions are that the school program is paced too closely to the ability and rate of the slow students or to the average pupil.

Parents expect school teachers *to be dedicated* to their work. This is not easy for some parents to express, but there is general interest in this point. It shows when parents sense that a teacher is not committed to his work in statements about "teaching only for the money" or "not really interested in teaching." Teachers who are committed, who derive real satisfactions from teaching, and whose enthusiasm begins to be shared by pupils need not fear that this will be noticed. Parents can tell even when they do not make it explicit.

The great majority of parents expect teachers *to emphasize character* development of their children. American parents generally recognize that the public school cannot indoctrinate pupils in any particular religious faith or even give instruction in religion. They expect to provide for religious instruction through educational programs sponsored by church, synagogue, or temple. But they also expect that teachers will emphasize those moral and spiritual values that undergird human society and enrich personal living, and which are acceptable to major faith groups in American society.

Parents who care about the education of their children—and the vast majority of them do—expect teachers *to report* upon their progress. In other words, parents wish to be informed about the school experiences of their children and to have a meaningful evaluation of the child's performance. This has been the source of a great deal of discussion between parents' and teachers' groups. Discussions of the reporting system or plan frequently disclose the great gap that must be closed by more effective communication between lay and professional groups that work on school problems. Parents cannot be expected to know what educators mean by the numerous terms and phrases that comprise the professional terminology sometimes known as "pedaguese." Neither can they be expected to appreciate the philosophy or theory that supports a comprehensive pattern of reporting pupil growth and progress. Some of the "report forms" may tell parents more than they want to know, as many

have the impression that a numerical grade or letter mark is all that matters. This is an important problem area for the schools and homes of a given school system to be concerned about. More cooperative studies should be in order.

Certain other expectations of parents might be included if our list could be extended indefinitely. For example, a number of parents would expect teachers to discipline their child. This brings up problems, some would object to punishment, others object to corporal punishment, and a few would view this as part of the teaching. This is a good example of the complications that arise—the varied concepts of and meanings of discipline, among parents and teachers alike, make communications and policy-making difficult. In early American schools, everyone knew what discipline meant—ability to keep order by physical force if necessary (as it usually was). This is a reasonably good illustration of the change that has come in American life and in the schools. People know too much and expect too much to be satisfied with uncritical and oversimplified answers and solutions of a different era.

There are some conflicting expectations of teachers on the part of parents upon such matters as homework, relative importance of subjects, grouping of pupils, and extra class activities. These may frequently be logical choices of parent-teacher study groups for study in a given community.

Parents' views are important

The significance of the parent-and-teacher relationship can hardly be stressed too much. A few quotes from parents will serve as a reminder of this phase of the teacher's work:

"Teachers treat me like a child and I don't like it."

"Teachers act like they know everything about my child, but I know they don't."

"Teachers do not seem to feel that parents have any intelligence."

"They (teachers) seem to think they know all the answers."

Some parents often feel that the schools do not hesitate to ask them for more money but seldom for advice. They say: "Why should teachers be unwilling to talk about how the school could be changed to help the children? They always want to tell us parents how to change the home."

It is easy to see that these are extreme statements albeit each is authentic. Many school people take offense at any word of criticism and statements like these would frequently scuttle chances for cooperative home-school relations for good. It is fortunate that few opinions of this character come to the ears of teachers. This does not mean that teachers and principals should want to live in a fool's paradise, unable to discern valid criticisms and even to evaluate statements about the school whether favorable or not. The truly intelligent person does not cut off the sources of information and takes the bad with the good. Educators who are reasonably mature in emotional growth will wish to know how people really feel and what they believe about education, schools, and the progress of their children. In other words, intelligent school people should try to understand what the parents' perceptions of the school situation are and to act accordingly in matters of communication.

Reflection upon this point will bring the problem into better perspective. It will be clear that anger, hurt feelings, and harsh rejoinders are equally unwise when we learn that parents have been critical. The soundest reaction is to endeavor to find whether there is basis for criticism and what brings it about. This should be followed by constructive action. There is no easy way out, but a way can be found, namely to develop a school program of such character that parents will be able to recognize its quality. Parents can be requested to help initiate or improve features of the school. Co-workers have a far better chance to understand *each other* and *what* the others are doing, and *why*, and *how*. In such cases, the perceptions of all participants will have more in common and misinformation and misinterpretation will be reduced. In this way the schools receive some good help on projects, a sounder basis of community support, and a favorable press when parents and teachers find ways to cooperate.

Teachers must learn to be more objective in their judgment of parents. There have been instances of hasty judgment, quick criticism, and unwarranted generalizations about parents by school people. In this event there is less likelihood that parents will develop long-range plans to effect an improved situation. Teachers must learn to accept parents as they are, even with shortcomings and problems they are the only parents the children have. They are the best parents in the eyes of the children in most instances and this should be enough for school people. Their opinions are important, as they represent the real basis of public support of education. Their views on education are largely determined by what and how school people do in the schools. This is a simple truth but it is sometimes taken for granted.

Parents are real people

Parents are real people, live human beings, with all the normal attributes and characteristics of people, plus a potential interest in education for their children. Everyone knows this, in a sense, but not everyone knows it with conviction. Parents are alike in many general respects; they have numerous individual differences as do their children. They should be understood and accepted—all of them—as human beings with capacities, needs, interests and motivations that range the whole scale of human characteristics and qualities.

Parents and teachers who have developed an adequate background of knowledge and understanding of human growth and development will find use for it in their relations with other adults as well as children. There will be instances when it will be evident that certain adults are immature in some respects and their behavior interpreted accordingly. They have the basic need(s) which they endeavor to satisfy with varying degrees of success and failure.[5] They adjust to the demands and challenges of life as best they can with the physical, mental, and emotional strengths at their command. Parents each have their own self-concept. They try to maintain it by a variety of means. Each as an individual lives in an "experiential field" which exists around about him as the center. This private world of experience can be known fully only to oneself. Other persons perceive an individual or a situation in their own ways from the center of their own respective private worlds of experience. Obviously, the "perceptions" of different persons vary in many details and degrees but they also have something in common. When we have a fuller appreciation of this, we begin to understand the nature and significance of communication with others.

Each person perceives the external world, persons, behavior, and everything individually, and this perception (or the interpretation of it) is *reality* for him. It is not absolute reality but his perception of reality. We see how different persons can perceive the same phenomenon and interpret it differently. Herein lies the problem of relating to and communicating with other people. This is a part of the self-knowledge that parents and children need to better understand each other, likewise for teachers and pupils and for parents and teachers.

This sample of illustrations of the understandings that parents and teachers need, serves some useful purposes at this point in our study. In the first place, these are examples of basic understandings each person should have of himself and of others; understandings that we should seek in future courses in psychology, human growth and development and human relations fields of study. Future parents and teachers should elect courses of this nature with the express purpose of gaining insight into the meaning of self, personality, human growth and development, and behavior. Teachers and parents who have these understandings should be able to relate to other adults and to their children. Ideally, there should be cooperative study groups of parents and teachers working in

[5] Some authorities stress the one basic need of the organism is to actualize, maintain, and enhance itself—all else is an aspect of this. See Carl R. Rogers, *Client-Centered Therapy* (Boston: Houghton Mifflin, 1951), pp. 476–491.

these fields in most school districts over the nation.

Parents are real people, so are teachers. When individuals of both groups have real understandings of themselves as persons and apply this knowledge, there can be cooperation among adults who accept each other in mutual respect and empathy.

THE TEACHERS' SIDE

Parents as teachers see them

Much of the material relating to parental attitudes and views about teachers could be related with the direction reversed. Some teachers may hold resentments toward parents that stem from their own childhood. The image of parents that some adults carry may be a domineering, harsh, and demanding person. An old pattern from one-teacher schools days is still recalled when parents punished children a second time after any corporal punishment at school. Old half-forgotten experiences of being deprived of participation in social functions and athletics, of being reprimanded publicly, of nagging—may still be harbored by some. Happily few teachers carry such images of parents, but those that do can be badly in the wrong without realizing it. Mature teachers would not generalize about *all parents* because of their own experiences.

A more frequent problem is caused by teachers who "cannot be bothered" with parents. This is a superior attitude in title, although it may indicate anything but an actually superior person. Sometimes this kind of attitude shows itself in the refusal to talk in terms that unsophisticated parents can understand, in brusque statements and attitudes that are intended

to terminate the conversation, and in crude efforts to establish a dominant relationship. There have been cases where teachers have underestimated the education and sophistication of parents who were not given to affectation and have made themselves slightly ridiculous as a result. A sound rule for teachers—and everybody else—would be to concentrate on becoming superior and let other people discover (perceive) it for themselves.

Another misunderstanding on the part of some teachers is the over-simple explanation of children's behavior as due to parental influence. This is too pat and too exaggerated to be accepted by a mature teacher but it does happen. According to this notion, all the child's difficulties are due to the parents—their heritage, their influence, their bad attitudes, their shiftlessness—it's all their fault somehow. Teachers who seek easy and inflexible answers to important questions cannot be expected to further the education of many boys and girls, to say nothing of the kind of understanding and relationship the school should have with parents.

Mature intelligent teachers avoid such obvious and simplified notions of parents. They would be more likely to feel that most parents wish to do well by their children, and that they want them to succeed in school as a step toward adulthood and success in the workaday world. Intelligent teachers recognize that parents may act differently for different reasons and motives. They would be willing to meet all parents without pretense or posing, to talk with them honestly and as clearly as possible, and seek to understand and to be understood. They would acknowledge that parental influence is a factor in all children's growth and development but would be careful to study each problem of each child fully before reaching any conclusion. They would deny themselves the luxury of an oversimplified and meaningless explanation that fools no one who has really learned anything from psychology, social sciences, or just plain straight thinking. There are more teachers who approach these brief specifications than were included with those who hold misconceptions of the parents of school children.

School programs affect home life

Teachers should be realistic in considering how many features and requirements of the school program have some effect upon the home life of the pupils and their families.[6] Also, how much and in what ways. We could begin by noting that the very start of the family's waking hours may be due to the daily time schedule of the school. Children have to be in school on time. This means the family must make its rising, bathing, eating, transportation and other schedules to fit. Teachers can find explanations for sleepy-eyed pupils, for others who are half-starved by midmorning, and some who have been up for hours. Within the home many afternoon and evening activities have to be modified to fit Harry's school program. His home work requires use of the dining table, the TV set must be dark lest he neglect to study. Others resent the disruptions caused by those unreasonable teachers who probably never check all that stuff he is writing anyway. We can expect this process to become a two-way one in many instances.

Children take new learnings, likes and dislikes, and needs into the home

[6] Irving W. Stout and Grace Langson, *op. cit.*, pp. 6–7.

from school. A simple matter like a meal with the family may provide an illustration. Need for another book to be read and reported on in English class calls for plaints how teachers must think that parents are made of money. Class rings, school parties, money for the bus ride and field trip with the class, and a host of other special needs come up during the year. There are trips to follow the team. There is depression because teenager romances break up or never get started. Teacher says bring so many samples of this or that for the class tomorrow. Schools even introduce ideas and questions that are downright upsetting at times, and parents wonder about this.

Teachers should make every effort to see this kind of situation as the parents and pupils see it. When they can and do get closer to the perceptions of others, there is a better basis for understanding. Much can probably be done by most schools to prevent some school practices from disrupting home and family living at all. In any event, some carefully planned programs during which the school principal or teachers explained the reasons for these practices to parents, would pay dividends in better understanding and cooperation. Teachers should discuss and make clear to the children whatever it is that the school wants done at home, making sure the pupils understand and can explain to parents. It is desirable to make plans involving the home that will minimize the inconvenience to the family insofar as possible.

What teachers expect of parents

One could probably develop a good list of the teachers' expectations of parents by stating the converse of those expected of teachers. There are some that have particular significance or relevancy to the educational task.

Teachers universally desire and expect *the strong support* of the parents in providing for and guiding the education experiences of their children. This needs little explanation beyond the suggestion that we consider the difference to the teacher's work and the school program in general, when parents exhibit and/or express indifference to education, or even deprecate the school or teacher's work. Teachers quickly see the effects of this attitude in the home and recognize many problems that arise or are complicated thereby.

Teachers expect parents *to supply information* that is necessary or useful in planning and implementing good programs for the growth and education of the children. Reporting should be more of a two-way process than is often the case.

Practically all teachers expect parents *to accept their responsibility* for the total growth of their children.[7] This is a many-sided kind of responsibility, and various facets of it may be involved in the concerns that teachers express. Frequently, problems arise because parents tend to shift part of their own responsibility to the school and the teacher(s). Discussion with experienced teachers will afford a variety of examples of this type of problem.

A great number of teachers would add a number of other expectations of parents to this list. One expectation might be that parents should respect the professional *role* of the teacher, at least to some degree, as they do that of the pediatrician or the public health nurse. This would imply that the professional findings of teachers should be respected. Teachers are expected to be *professionally* competent by most parents as we have noted.

Ideally, teachers should be able to expect that parents would study their children and learn to be consistent in guiding their overall growth and development. Most teachers can relate numerous instances and type of school problems that originate in the home and family experience of children. For example, parents should be consistent in the disciplining of children, regardless of the manner and method used; they should not compare performance of older and younger children as if they were identical in abilities, interests, and motivation. Teachers and parents would have much to teach and to learn from each other if the opportunity, and an adequate medium of communication, were forthcoming.

Teachers are only human

What has been said about parents as human beings and the need for all adults to have real understandings of themselves as persons goes double strength for teachers. It has been clearly shown that teachers with deep insight into themselves and the ability to interpret themselves as persons, their need(s), motivation, and behavior are better able to understand pupils and other adults.[8] Modern programs of teacher education place stress upon foundational fields of study designed to yield understanding and competence in this field but only a start has been made.

[7] See Cole S. Brembeck, *op. cit.,* pp. 230–238.

[8] A discussion of this may be found in Arthur T. Jersild, *When Teachers Face Themselves* (New York: Bureau of Publications, Teachers College, Columbia University, 1955), pp. 82–85.

The need for teacher competence in this area has long been evident. Students of research will recall the celebrated study by Wickman (1928) which showed that teachers viewed as most serious those patterns of children's behavior that mental hygienists considered to have least significance. Moreover, those rated least serious by the teacher (behavior indicating social and emotional maladjustment) were deemed most serious by the panel of mental hygienists.[9] Teachers expressed most concern over behavior that violated their own moral standards, their authority in the classroom, their standards for study, or behavior that disturbed other students. Problems of greater significance identified by mental hygienists as serious were indicated by behavior such as shyness, unsociability, sensitivity and other recessive traits. This study provided a needed reminder for teacher education institutions. Some evidence of progress on the part of teachers was shown by a second study by Stouffer (1952) that repeated that of Wickman.[10] Again there were great discrepancies in rating the seriousness of 50 childrens' behavior problems by a sample of teachers and a panel of mental hygienists. In this study some items moved upward from the bottom and down from the top (most serious). In the teacher's list (four of the first five rated highest by teachers in Wickman's study moved down in the comparable list by Stouffer's sample, and one moved from second to top place; the five lowest items moved up while the 47th moved to last place respec-

tively in the second study).[11] This is but one example of some of the basic understanding that future parents and teachers should gain as part of their general education. Those who have this background are prepared both for parental and teaching roles and for cooperation with adults in the other field. Adults who lack this kind of preparation for understanding and guiding children should make this field a subject of study.

Teachers are only human, not supermen, they cannot be paragons of everything desirable. They should be able to accept themselves with their limitations and go on from there to richly qualitative lives. This means constructive efforts to realize themselves, to maintain the "self" image, and practices of good mental and emotional health. They can acknowledge their own backgrounds, try to identify and allow for bias, and endeavor to understand the other fellow's perceptions. Teachers can cope with most problems. Some even manage under conditions like "Blackboard Jungle." Teachers and parents can learn to recognize the humanness of each other and work constructively for the benefit of all children of the community.

THERE IS A PUPIL'S SIDE

All of the concern about getting parents and teachers to see the others' point of view should not preclude consideration of children and their interest in cooperation between home and school.[12] Children

---

[9] E. K. Wickman, *Children's Behavior and Teachers' Attitudes* (New York: The Commonwealth Fund, 1928).

[10] George A. W. Stouffer, Jr., "Behavior Problems of Children as Viewed by Teachers and Mental Hygienists," *Mental Hygiene,* **XXXVI** (April 1952), pp. 271–285.

[11] See a brief account in Earl A. Johnson and R. Eldon Michael, *Principles of Teaching* (Boston: Allyn & Bacon, 1958), pp. 311–326.

[12] There are many useful references. See Nina Ridenour, *The Children We Teach* (New York: Mental Health Materials Center, 1956); Edith G. Neisser, *et al., How to Live with Chil-*

must be dependent upon both, chiefly on parents but some on teachers, must accept both, and must suffer if there is conflict between the adults. The nature of growing children and the changes that occur among them at various stages adds new complications to the problems of parents and teachers. Some children go overboard for teachers at certain stages of their normal development, and the home life may reflect this transitory attachment. Teachers and parents need to know this stage and expect it. See it for what it is—it's nothing to get excited about.

Teachers who know child growth and development are prepared for the stage when boys boast "my daddy can whip your dad," and when little girls exaggerate their mother's attentions toward them to get attention. The skillful serene teacher learns to hold many childish confidences about what goes on in the home. A calm listening ear attached to a good teacher is a real necessity for children at times.

The home gets the benefit of childish enthusiasms and extremes. Many times parents have grown tired of "Miss Jones says this," and "my teacher thinks that" so many times a week. They should learn to view this in a broad and long time perspective and to relax and enjoy good normative behavior of children. As a matter of fact, it is not likely that children with problems will find these convenient normal means of expressing themselves.

It is the child who has no way to release tension that should give concern to knowing adults.

The problems that reveal children's perceptions of parents, teachers, and other adults, will probably increase in intensity during the teenager stages. Then, the gang's values and practices lead to misunderstandings with parents *and* teachers. The teenagers are beginning to assert their independence and grow into adulthood. But adolescent behavior continues to the extent that we find some amazing contradictions and incongruities in lives of teenage students. Through all of this hectic era of growth, both parents and teachers are judged and often found wanting by a panel of their child's peers. Somehow, if parents and teachers can keep their balance and be patient, there comes a day when most adolescents have a better perception of self and of others. Then, parents and instructors get a better break.[13] "They are not so bad, after all," is a discovery that many a late teenager has made on his own. Who once remarked that youth was such a wonderful thing that it seemed a pity to waste it on the young?

Parents and teachers can help each other to really understand that the children and youth are vitally interested in having them work together. They can also learn more about children and youth by sharing and strengthening their respective efforts.

---

dren (Chicago: Science Research Associates, 1950); Robert S. Havighurst and Bernice L. Neugarten, *Society and Education,* sec. ed. (Boston: Allyn & Bacon, 1962), pp. 113–123; ASCD, *Fostering Mental Health in Our Schools,* 1950 Yearbook (Washington: NEA, 1950), chapter 2.

[13] This has been expressed by an unknown sage in this fashion "Teenagers first judge parents, later they are able to *accept* them, finally they *forgive* them." Most experienced guidance counsellors and school psychologists have witnessed this kind of understanding on part of teenagers in course of contacts over a period of time.

Develop Good Relationships with Parents

Teachers who find little enthusiasm for the opportunity to get to know the parents of the children they teach, should be reminded that teachers in earlier American schools had no such need. The reason was that they knew (or quickly learned) all the families served by their one-teacher school. Enough parents had to accept a teacher before he could expect to get the job. The teacher had to try to please everybody lest the school committee or trustees award the school to another instructor next year. Teachers lived in the homes of their patrons in turn, a week or two in each home represented by children. This was known as "boarding round" and constituted part of the pay. It involved sleeping in all kinds of rooms with a variety of bedfellows from hired hands to young children of the family. Many diaries of teachers report the rough "bills of fare" they found at the tables of their patrons. Often, they split wood, milked cows, and did other chores as their share of the life of the family. Colonial and early American teachers needed to develop no "working relationships" with parents of the children they taught, they already had it.

The incredible "cultural distance" our nation has moved from the agrarian way of life to the 1960's has made these old ways appear foreign and strange to teachers whose pupils come from homes she has never seen. Reflection will help any teacher to understand how provision must now be made to supply means of understanding the home experiences of children and of working with parents for the sake of a good education for all the children.

PROVEN PRINCIPLES ELICIT COOPERATION

There are no unique feats or tricks of magic involved in the approach to improved relationships between teachers and parents.[14] Principles of sound human relationships are as good here as in any other situation. Actually, there is reason to believe that there are some advantages because both parents and teachers have common interests and commitments. Education of all the children of all the people is a distinctively human enterprise. There are none of the "commercial enterprise for gain" elements involved. The motivation and a high degree of good will would appear to favor efforts to develop sound working relationships with parents.

Teachers should probably expect to take the initiative more often than not in effect to effect good relationships with parents. Teachers are paid from public funds. Their educational preparation is consistently above average for a typical community, and they are concerned about all the children of a classroom group rather than only one pupil.

Teachers should utilize approaches and ideas that have been proved sound and valuable by many leaders and groups in other human relations projects. No technique or device works magically;

[14] Some helpful references are: Mauree Applegate, *Everybody's Business* (Evanston, Illinois: Harper & Row, 1952); Eva H. Grant, *Parents and Teachers As Partners* (Chicago: Science Research Associates, 1952); Marcia Piers, *How to Work with Parents* (Chicago: Science Research Associates, 1955); and James L. Hymes, *Effective Home-School Relations* (Englewood Cliffs, N.J.: Prentice-Hall, 1953).

many worked exceptionally well because the user knew what he was trying to do, believed in it and in his own motives, and conveyed some of his sincerity to his co-workers. This is the real point. No ideas will solve our problems or carry out a program for us unimplemented. We must take action and do what is judged most needed or urgent to make ideas operate. This will be true for teachers who work to improve understandings and working relationships with parents.

Start with sound assumptions

Ideas that have paid off in many attempts to effect good working relationships should prove equally useful to teachers and parents. Teachers and parents should think of each other as people, each distinctive and different, but sharing many interests and exhibiting common characteristics. There is enough of common interest for a start in working together. This would appear to be a good starting point.

Another worthwhile suggestion is that teachers (and parents) should assume the interest of all who are concerned with the child, and keep this clearly in mind at every step. When there are problems, it will be helpful to get back to the basic question of—just what is this whole enterprise (public education) about, anyway —and the answer gives all a better perspective. Along with the factor of parental interest, teachers may also assume the willingness to cooperate. Normal people desire friendly relationships and most enjoy working together on something worthwhile. It is reasonable for teachers to assume that the parents will be interested and cooperative.

It helps greatly when both or all participants in a human relationship can feel that they are making a distinctive contribution to the outcomes. This should be kept in mind by teachers who work with parents. Parents are also vitally engaged in the education of their children, and the teachers who appreciate and respect that fact, develop better communication and rapport. When teachers fully appreciate the nature of this relationship they will be considerate of statements and requests that may inadvertently give offense to parents. For example, should teachers ever issue a request that parents not teach arithmetic or spelling at home because so much of it is done poorly? Would it be better to have a general question raised about what areas or bodies of subject matter should parents be asked to teach at home? This is a good illustration of the important concept of joint or cooperative responsibility to promote the child's learning experiences.

Efforts in communication pay dividends

Teachers need to spend time on real communication with parents. One form letter or one brief talk to PTA group per year is not enough.[15] Much can be done through the reports that children give orally to the family at dinner. Time spent in making clear to children what and why they are doing or attempting, is well spent in most instances because most parents listen to these youthful interpreters of the school program. Teachers should utilize every opportunity to explain the instructional program in plain simple language.

[15] A useful reference is Grace Langdon and Irving W. Stout, *Helping Parents Understand Their Child's School* (Englewood Cliffs, N.J.: Prentice-Hall, 1957).

Her attitude should be sincere, straight-forward, and cooperative. Questions should be welcomed and answered candidly and fairly. There should be enough enthusiasm about the questions raised to encourage others by parents who hesitate to speak up. Many fine teachers deliberately arrange for group meetings for purpose of communicating with parents. There are communities and schools that may require very informal and opportunistic talks with parents, but usually some way can be found.

Sophisticated teachers are not distracted and disturbed by seeming indifference or kinds of mechanisms parents sometimes use to cover up real reasons for their actions. There may show up as indifference, raising of a false issue, delaying tactics, and an appeal to tradition of the community. The real reason may be lack of complete acceptance of the teacher, a carryover from earlier experience with a teacher (or other public servant) who did not treat them right, or a threat to a vested interest or special privilege. Efforts to help them to learn more about the school program and the teacher's methods often help. A simple personal request for help in something the teacher knows a parent can do is a good starting point for getting truly acquainted. The point is—learn to look beyond the surface appearance of a situation that seems unpromising to find real reasons that have not come out. This also includes being able to see one's own behavior and motives more accurately for possible clues to understanding a part of the problem.

Remind ourselves to remember

There are a few tried and tested pointers from the work of successful teachers with parents that we should be able to use. It is reassuring to know that most parents really want teachers they can respect and look up to. Sometimes the early contacts with parents are feelers for the purpose of reassuring themselves that Mary and Tom have a good teacher, one their parents can trust to handle their educational advancement. It makes a difference in the interpretation of some of the first impressions teachers may get when this possibility is recalled.

Some other obvious reminders hardly need mentioning. Parents like teachers to be honest and straight-forward in talk and dealings, doubletalk and evasiveness do not wear well in human relations anywhere. Parents also like to be reassured, and the teacher who can identify their anxieties and offer some encouragement is a great help. Teachers who live up to parental expectations know the importance of accepting and treating all children as real individuals. They know the importance of recognizing individual differences, needs and interests. Parents like to feel that the school is doing its job competently, that their children are in safe hands. This is a part of the teacher image many parents have and they want to keep it.

Being one's self is best practice

The matter of requesting help of individuals when progress seems blocked deserves further mention. This is really a general approach or principle capable of being used in many situations. Stated simply, it means call on and use the talents and capabilities of parents and other adults in the community when they can make a real contribution to the instructional program for the pupils. The very ringleader of a group that deplored the passing of traditional teaching of the "Three R's" can become an innovator when used to illustrate ways of living in an earlier historical period in which he is interested. Teachers and pupils can have the benefit of collections, exhibits, special skills, consulting service, and other help from those in the community with hobbies and interests that lend themselves to this purpose. Every community has far more resources for curriculum enrichment than most schools have used. This is an illustration of a way that teachers can work soundly with parents. Imaginative teachers can find others equally appropriate for their communities and school situations.

RESPECT THE RESPECTIVE ROLES

Many problems in parent-teacher relationships arise from the failure of one or both to understand their respective roles. There is no question that both have roles, necessary ones, but they are different and for various reasons. It is essential that this be recognized to avoid unnecessary conflict and problems.[16]

Responsibilities of parents

Parents are responsible for bringing children into the world and the provision for most of their needs of infancy and early childhood. As children grow older parents enlist the help of religious, recreational, and educational agencies in providing for the growth and development of children.

Parents continue to provide physical

[16] A useful reference is Irving W. Stout and Grace Langdon, *Parent-Teacher Relationships,* No. 16, What Research Says to the Teacher Series (Washington: NEA, 1958).

needs: food, shelter, clothing, medicine; health care, exercise, play, and recreation; affection, emotional security, attention and recognition, acceptance as a person; early experience in getting along with others; discipline; moral, ethical, and religious instruction (often with assistance of religious agency); family ways of living, traditions, and values; experiences in sharing responsibilities of family life, chores, duties, etc.; opportunity for cultural growth, books, music, pictures, etc.; preparations for formal education. These are the big areas, the breakdown could run on to great length. *Clearly the role of the parent is primary, permanent and paramount.* Everyone ought to understand this. Teachers cannot and should not take over the parent's role even though it is obvious that part of their responsibilities have been neglected or evaded. Efforts to help bring about improvement of the home situation would be better than to substitute for the parental role.

Responsibilities of teachers

Teachers are principally responsible for providing for the child's formal learning (academic); discipline in the school; provision for school experiences commensurate with the child's needs—physical, mental, emotional, and social; and study of the child to find bases for planning school program. Sometimes there is an added function of formal or informal adviser or counselor. The teacher may also become the trusted co-worker and adviser to parents, but this role has to be earned. After having been accepted by the community's parents they have greater opportunity to advise and help parents to improve the total situation that affects their children's education and growth.

Some overlapping responsibilities

Parents and teachers share responsibility for some aspects of the growth and development of children in school. Both should emphasize character development —ethical sensitivity and choice and responsibility; each contributes guidance by helping children to discover their abilities, interests and special talents, also problems and needs; sound habits and practices in matters of health, safety, personal hygiene; growth in responsible citizenship; desirable human relations; exploratory experiences in economic and vocational interests; provision for sound study habits; instruction in personal development including sex; preparation for marriage and family living. These areas represent the opportunities for parent and teacher cooperation following the initiative of either. Detail steps and procedures for this are not available in handbooks, only tested principles and encouragement. Yet, good teachers have been doing a lot of this right along.

When we observe an extraordinary and able teacher who works capably and effectively with parents, we will probably find that the techniques hardly show at all; it seems to come naturally. Closer study may disclose that this teacher has hit upon some basic general ideas and depends upon them over and over, like being free and relaxed and sincere with people, actually liking them and finding this returned, so that the relationship is one of mutual respect and trust.

A distinctive task for the school

It is time that teachers and interested parents who will take time to study curriculum problems got to work upon realistic and sound programs of instruction for family living in our high schools. The faculties and the community agencies see evidence of the need for helpful teaching of boy-girl relationships, planning for major life responsibilities, preparation for marriage and problems related to these universal needs of youth. This is not being done consistently and effectively in most communities. A few clergymen, priests and rabbis do a conscientious job with a fraction of young couples prior to marriage. Some parents pay some attention to aspects of this but little is accomplished as a rule. Those youth who lack the opportunity to learn what is involved in marriage are least likely to find any help in this matter. And every year counsellors learn of many youngsters who get caught. Hasty ill-advised marriages and a long train of tragic consequences follow in many instances. This unfortunate trend can be reversed, at least improved, if the schools could develop a full-scale program of preparation for marriage and family responsibilities for all youth.[17] Teachers who deplore the tragic lot of many children, products of unwise marriages, can do no more important job than to help provide a realistic program that will prevent so many ill-advised, ill-prepared and insecure families in the future. Somebody must make it clear to young marriage partners that it is easy to become a biological parent, but no one has a moral right to invoke that privilege without assuming the emotional, moral,

[17] An old but valuable treatment of the role of schools in family life education is Joseph K. Folsom, *Youth, Family, and Education* (Washington: American Council on Education, 1941). A popular text for college courses is Henry Bowman, *Marriage for Moderns*, 3rd ed. (New York: McGraw-Hill, 1954).

and practical responsibilities that go with parenthood. This will not be a popular topic of conversation in every quarter but it is illustrative of some of the critical problems our culture must begin to solve.

Teachers cannot jump on a soapbox and urge crusading programs at the very start of their careers in a new community. Textbook writers who have had long experience have a great advantage in this respect. But young teachers can acquire status and acceptance and become co-partners in planning and working to improve the instructional program of the school. One of the orthodox ways to begin to be on the team of the school-community is through the parent-teacher organization.

Teachers and Parents Cooperate

The Parent-Teacher Association

School people recognize the strong and indispensable source of help available to education in the National Congress of Parents and Teachers. The nationwide body is now over 65 years old and enrolls over twelve million members yearly. Organized in 1897 as the National Congress of Mothers, reorganized ten years later as the National Congress of Mothers and Parent-Teacher Associations, it took its present title in 1924. Each of the states has an active organization and local chapters are found in larger communities all over the country. In 1945, there were over 27,000 local chapters over the nation; in 1954, no fewer than 39,000; in 1960, approximately 47,000. This total suggests that the parents of a large fraction of America's school children are represented in this great organization. About one-third of the members are males, nearly 86% of teachers in schools with PTA belong to the group.

Purposes of the PTA are: (1) to know the child through child study and parent education; (2) to cooperate with the school and other educational agencies in his training through shared participation with teachers and educators; and (3) to control and balance his environment through the development of public opinion and civic activity.

The PTA brings together those adults who have interest in and responsibility for the child's growth and education. United in their belief upon the importance of the child and his education in our society, these groups have rendered invaluable aid and support to educational forces and movements. No aspect or level of education is foreign to the scope of work of the National Congress of Parents and Teachers. Its national officers testify before Congressional committees on proposed legislation; officers of the state chapters are likewise active before legislative and other official bodies. And at the local level, its activities may include almost any task which is calculated to improve the schools.

In its organization the PTA permits the necessary latitude and freedom for the local association to direct its efforts upon problems which need attention in the community. Each local association subscribes to the general objectives of the National Congress of Parents and Teachers, but it works out its own program of action according to the needs of its school com-

Nichols Junior High School, Evanston Community Consolidated Schools

Parent-teacher committee plans joint study groups.

munity. Local chapters are chartered by the state chapters and send representatives to district meetings and state conventions. All adults who are interested in the schools are eligible for membership. The official journal of the Congress is *The PTA Magazine*. In addition, there may be state journals or space in the state education journal allocated for the organization's use.

Earlier incidents of friction between school authorities and PTA groups have practically disappeared. Instances of cooperative study upon educational problems have increased enormously and most school authorities have found the help of PTA groups to be well-nigh indispensable in efforts to improve and strengthen edu-

cational programs. The National Congress of Parents and Teachers has taken a strong stand upon matters which formerly were causes of friction. Today it favors absolute non-interference with school administration; intelligent support of the school program, emphasis upon parental attitudes and home conditions which will increase the effectiveness of the school, cordial and cooperative relationships between parents and teachers in all matters of mutual concern for children, and joint action for improving community conditions. The days when the PTA had to make valiant efforts to raise funds to help equip schools are happily past. Those efforts have helped to show boards of education that such items were legitimate, necessary expenditures for public tax funds. Thus, the PTA has entered upon a period of larger usefulness and responsibility.

At the local level, PTA's have often led in public campaigns for the issuance of bonds for school buildings, and programs to induce state legislatures to increase appropriations for public schools. At the national level, the PTA has fought valiantly side by side with NEA for Federal Aid legislation by the Congress. Recently, the PTA has given strong support and leadership to efforts for the solution of the teacher crisis. In many states PTA's have led in teacher recruitment programs and given publicity to needs of the schools. Clearly, American public education owes much to the work and accomplishments of the National Congress of Parents and Teachers.[18]

We should have a good idea of the work and program of the local PTA chapter in our school community. Undoubtedly, we shall wish to affiliate and to find a place to work alongside the interested, active parents of the children we teach. Remember that people who work together learn to understand and to respect each other. The PTA can be our best open door to real acceptance by the people of the community where we will teach.

---

[18] Some idea of the scope of interests of the National Congress of Parents and Teachers may be gained from: Charl O. Williams (Ed.), *Schools for Democracy* (Chicago: National Congress of Parents and Teachers, 1939), pp. 188–199.

Teachers of education courses may request an excellent unit of instructional material about the PTA from its national headquarters for use with students. The title, "The Parent-Teacher Organization, A Unit for Education Classes," may be had from the Chicago headquarters at 700 North Rush Street, Chicago 11, Illinois.

Common concerns and study groups

Opportunities for parents and teachers to work upon common problems are present in almost every community. Ways and means of approaching the solution of problems can be devised if there is freedom for groups to exercise their intelligence as widely as possible. This is the clue to the real meaning of freedom which means that people can be creative in working on solutions to real problems they have the opportunity to use their intelligence without restriction. Leadership develops in a truly free situation, and the leaders tend to come from more individuals as different purposes and needs are followed up.

One of the soundest approaches to the solution of a community or school problem is to undertake a thorough fact-finding and analytical study to clarify the situation and disclose the possible alternatives for its solution or improvement. A modern sage has said that once we see our problems clearly we know what to do about it. This is the sound sense behind the policy of sponsorship of joint study groups by educational and lay leaders interested in the community.

Parents and teachers need not dread the effort needed to deal with problems nor feel that they should already be stocked with answers for every major question that is encountered. Every generation of this century has faced new problems and changing conditions and the prospects are clear that this will continue. Answers for these concerns and problems are not stored up in people through their educational experiences. The capacity to deal with problems by critical thinking should be developed through education. This and freedom to think are all that most groups need, to do a good job of improving and strengthening their schools and the community.

This potential approach lends itself excellently to the needs of parents and teachers who discover common concerns or interests. The PTA organization can sponsor any number of voluntary study groups to deal with all manner of problems about family living, child growth and development, discipline, curriculum and co-curriculum, peer groups, character education, and reporting to parents. This kind of project would help participants to find better ways to handle their problems, gradually develop an informed opinion about joint concerns of home and school, and revitalize the functions of the local PTA chapter.[19]

Teachers often wish there were more parents who could apply sound knowledge in fields of the behavioral sciences in guiding the growth and development of their children. The problem of communication about some of the difficult questions would then become simpler, and both parents and teachers could cooperate more intelligently in helping pupils. Of course, a great many teachers lack adequate background in this big field or their subject matter is no longer up-to-date. It would make sense to arrange study groups to meet probably one evening each week for careful study of some basic understandings that both parents and teachers need.

Appropriate topics for study groups of this kind might well include: (1) understanding ourselves, (2) understanding our children, (3) understanding our school. Planning, careful selection of interesting sound reading materials, choice of some teaching films, and full participation of group members could make these invaluable and mutually helpful programs of study. There is every indication that the problems of parents will continue to be many and serious in future decades. Until such time as adequate programs in family living are provided in our high schools, there is little indication that most parents will be any better prepared for their responsibilities than are those of today. This is the strongest plea for the encouragement of PTA's, school boards, and citizens' committees to sponsor study groups of parents and teachers to study their common concerns and needs.

The day should come when the typical PTA (or some other community agency) should sponsor and support several continuing study groups and seminars each year. The pattern should cover a wide range of problems and needs and be repeated as often as necessary. In most communities there should be simultaneous groups for pre-natal parents, parents with infants, parents of pre-schoolers, and for parents of all age groups in the school. It would make real sense to have a special group for out-of-school youth who would give some serious study to preparation for engagement and marriage. A program of opportunity for both parents and teachers would do more for the future children than anything we could name.

Adult education makes sound progress

Adult education has become part of the total public educational enterprise in several states and many communities and the movement to tax-supported programs

---

[19] It would appear to be preferable to call this kind of projects "joint study groups" or some other title that does not place parents in an unfavorable light as does the old "Parent Education" label.

is growing.[20] Where the organizational framework already exists for it, parent and teacher study groups can be arranged as part of the overall program of offerings. In other instances, there will have to be beginnings made by those with wisdom and courage to be both enterprising and effective.

Adult education is of especial significance in a free society, particularly one that expects all citizens to participate actively and fully in the duties and rights that constitute citizenship. Our democracy was founded on the conviction that free men could and would make sound decisions when informed. In a free society it should be everyone's right to be educated and to have access to information. Various forms of adult education, formal and informal, have existed in the United States. In colonial days Benjamin Franklin organized popular libraries, a discussion club (The "Junto"), and used his newspaper and *Poor Richard's Almanac* for educational ends. Town meetings, colonial committees of correspondence, pamphlets on political and religious questions, the battle to have a free press in New York, all were instruments of adult education. Certain adult education institutions grew up alongside the establishment of the state school systems in the 19th century. The most extensive was the American Lyceum (1831) that sponsored

[20] Some general references are (1) John W. Powell, *Learning Comes of Age* (New York: Association Press, 1956); (2) National Association of Public School Adult Educators, *How Adults Can Learn More-Faster* (Washington: NEA, 1962); (3) Malcolm S. Knowles, "Adult Education in the United States," *Adult Education,* V (Winter 1955), pp. 67–75; and (4) Charles H. Radcliffe and John B. Holden, "Adults in the Public Schools," *School Life,* XL (April 1958), pp. 7–10.

series of lectures (followed by discussion) in numerous cities and towns. One of its principal objectives was the promotion of public school systems. The Smithsonian Institution in the national capital (1846) and the Cooper Union (1859) in New York City were principally concerned with adult education. Two popular movements of the late 19th century with most influence were the Chautauqua Institution (1874) and the national farmer's organization known as the "Grange" (Patrons of Husbandry). After the land-grant institutions grew into strong institutions, their early work with farmers led to the Smith-Lever Act (1914) that provided for agricultural extension work on a permanent basis. Privately sponsored programs of industrial corporations and labor unions have emerged in recent decades. The public library movement and the pattern of adult education opportunities therein have likewise grown rapidly.

Public schools here and there had offered educational opportunity for adults in the 19th century. Their greatest contribution in this field came in seaboard cities in form of "Americanization" classes for immigrants who came in increasing streams to the "land of opportunity." Various correspondence and other commercial-venture schools offered education for adults, especially in vocational and trade fields. The period of the First World War brought to light the educational needs of adults for literacy, job training, physical fitness, and Americanization. Programs for eradication of illiteracy were stressed in many states such as the famed "moonlight schools" started by Cora Wilson Stewart in Kentucky (1916).

The decade immediately following World War I marked the modern beginnings of the public adult education movement in the United States. Similar developments had begun in Great Britain a few years earlier. The American Association for Adult Education was organized in 1926. Slowly states enacted legislation to permit support of adult education with public funds. The depression period of the 1930's brought a number of developments in adult education in form of Federal programs of relief, public works, and conservation. The adult education programs sponsored by the TVA, through its employee and job training programs, and in the construction camps and villages, provided an impetus to the movement.

The community school movement of the 1940's and 1950's included adult education using the school as the community center. Public higher education from junior colleges to universities have established evening colleges and programs for part-time study by adults. Most public colleges have policies to admit mature students to special basis and permit them to continue if they can successfully do college work. It has been reported that public adult education courses enrolled five million Americans in 1962.

Parents and teachers should encourage sound programs of adult education and participate in activities and courses that meet their needs. Many study groups and seminars for parents and teachers can be assisted as part of the community's public adult education program.

The teacher works with parents

No teacher can do effective work without adequate contacts with parents and the home environment of the children. The best effort of the teacher can be nullified by the attitudes and actions of parents who do not understand or who are uncooperative. Conversely, those efforts are vastly enhanced and strengthened by the best relationships with and the cooperation of the parents. Relationships of teachers and parents in the best schools are vastly different from the good old days when the teacher lived in fear of irate parents after corporal punishment had been meted out to miscreant pupils. That relationship can best be expressed as one of mutual respect and helpfulness.

Teachers simply must know the home background and the opportunities of the children they teach. Wise teachers have always made it their business to learn this. Young teachers will do well to seek the earliest possible opportunity to visit the homes of their pupils. Teachers who can meet and associate freely and naturally with the parents are certain to be accepted and held in high regard in the community. More important than this, is the fact that the teacher can do a superior job of helping her pupils only when she knows the educative influences of the home and the community.

Teachers will also wish to welcome the parents at the school. Better schools now make great effort to get the parents to visit and to know the school and its program. But this endeavor should not be confined to American Education Week or to brief PTA meetings; it should take place whenever it is needed. A friendly interest in talking over the problems of the children is the best way to get parents to feel welcome in the school.

It may well be that an approach to high quality teaching will include parent conferences as needed for teachers to know their pupils and as means of developing cooperative evaluation of child growth. Teachers can learn to do a lot of good by work with parents.

Parents have the right to be consulted in the planning and developing of school policies and programs. More and more it is expected that parents of the community will serve on committees to study curricula, building needs and all the other matters which a school system must think through. It is the people's money which pays for all this; it is the people's children and the people whom teachers serve; the people are the most important ends. The parents of the children are precisely those people that teachers can meet on common grounds naturally and normally because of their joint task in helping their children to grow. Courtesy, respect and thoughtfulness are important and effective if they spring from an inner quality—sincerity.

Reports to parents and vice versa

The problem of reporting pupil progress to parents has probably been the most frequently-studied of the common concerns of home and school. This problem is difficult at best and the solution is further complicated by several popular misconceptions about the purpose and nature of marking and reporting practices. No single plan or scheme for reporting to parents now known would be appropriate for all school systems even of one state. It is clear that the educational and lay groups that support public schools should have the right to make decisions that represent the best judgment of those who must utilize the plan.

Groups that enter into any extended study of the complex of problems related to marking and reporting inevitably find that they become concerned with bases for promotion, the curriculum experiences, and even the objectives of the whole program.[21] This involves a lot of time and effort. Meanwhile the criticisms and controversy over the marking and reporting system continue. Many citizens who can not or will not participate in the study have no informed basis for judging the recommendations that come from the group, and the problem is rarely settled to everybody's satisfaction. After a few years when today's parents are no longer active in PTA and school affairs, this matter will again need to be studied and clarified. This is as it should be. The American tradition guarantees each generation the right to make its own decisions. Each generation should accept the responsibility that goes with their right, namely to study the matter thoroughly; consider alternatives; try and test practices as basis for reaching decisions.

Sometimes school people wonder why school marks and report forms are so important to parents. The answer is complex and involves many factors and influences. Much of it is tradition—the old numerical grades people remember from school days, and the practice of awarding honors and prizes on basis of marks, the publication of honor rolls, dean's lists, and the honorary societies for students who make top grades—all these are examples. Another cluster of reasons relates to current practices and values that tend to reward students that earn good marks. Marks enter into decisions

[21] See Jerome M. Seidman, *Readings in Educational Psychology* (Boston: Houghton Mifflin Co., 1955), pp. 311–335; see also Ruth Strang, *How to Report Pupil Progress* (Chicago: Science Research Associates, 1955), for example of modern report forms.

about admissions to further study, employment, and the type of recommendation the school makes for its graduates. There are strong attitudes, often unconscious, shown on part of parents and even teachers that place a premium upon good marks. Parental projection of their own aspirations and feelings into their children's school careers is common and a high mark is gratifying to proud adults. High marks gain approbation at home and in school, earn prizes and indulgences, increase one's prestige with adults (if not one's peers), and bring satisfactions that our cultural experiences have taught us. Most teachers believe in marks although many would find it difficult to explain why. Clearly the practice of assessing or evaluating pupil performance in school by means of marks is entrenched by tradition and uncritical attitudes of the general public.

When people ask what marks mean, those who advocate numerical or letter marks are neither clear nor convincing as to the answers. The truth is that marks are based chiefly on subjective judgments and decisions of teachers. Studies have shown that different teachers who graded identical mathematics papers gave widely varying marks.[22] Numerous investigations have proved this point repeatedly. Even pupils know this. They also know that many factors unrelated to scholarship may enter into grading and marking. Anyone who hears teenagers discuss teachers and marks can get information on this point. Some teachers grade "easy"; others mark

[22] A nationwide study showed that 111 different teachers graded identical arithmetic papers and gave marks ranging from 21 to 88. Similar results were found for a plane geometry examination paper.

"hard." Students who have moved to different schools know that marks vary widely. College admissions officers have good evidence of the differences in marking standards. Pupil performance upon standardized tests provides a means of checking the validity of school marks. The truth is that school marks are not reliable or consistent and often command more respect than is warranted.

Faculties and study groups have considered means of separating achievement in subject matter from other factors that complicate the marking system. Personal, social, and emotional factors and citizenship deemed important to school performance and pupil growth have been reported by other means. It appears that teachers encounter the same problems of what the marks for conduct and emotional stability mean and how to make them consistent. Other faculty groups have tried joint marking of exam papers, themes, and other written work in the effort to improve consistency. Progress has been reported by some studies, but the time and administrative details involved tend to restrict this approach.

Parents are willing to have teachers decide upon appropriate bases of marking but many do wish for an appropriate and consistent plan that they can understand. School faculties, with help of parents' committees if desired, should study the methods of marking and come to agreement upon what seems desirable and possible at the moment for a given school or school system. Three methods in common use are (1) marks given on a comparative basis; (2) marking only on an ability basis; and (3) marking on a dual basis. No method pleases everyone and the debate continues as to their merits. Often the superior students favor comparative marking asserting that the colleges expect traditional marks, that parents want comparative marks, and that all pupils need reports with marks, for incentives to work harder and to compete. A whole cluster of questions about related matters is frequently brought into this debate. This includes proposals for grouping pupils according to ability, or separate curricula for pupils with academic, general, vocational, and other objectives, and the demand for a "prestige" high school.

Pupils with less aptitude for academic subjects and their parents see justification for marking in terms of the students' ability and effort. Many schools do not provide curriculum offerings to fit the needs and interests of all pupils and many cannot compete in academic courses with the college-bound students. Despite the fact that the potential voice of students in this category would usually be in the majority, it is typically far less articulate than the smaller number favoring comparative marks. This is a phenomenon that school faculties might well study for their own school communities.

Dual marking plans sometimes encounter difficulties due to traditional attitudes and expectations of adults. Failure to appreciate the reasons for and the methods used in dual marking has led to some disapointing results and abandonment of the plan in some places. On the face of it the idea appeals to many, but the factor of popular acceptance must be reckoned with.

Grading in terms of ability depends upon consideration of more factors by the teachers. Such factors as the achievement in subject matter as shown by tests, the effort made by student in preparation of course work, his attitude toward class work, and evidence of his progress may be considered by the teacher in the light of information about the I.Q., reading grade level, and other data related to his ability. Teachers keep the information about students' ability in the class roll book and use it as guides when determining marks for each grading period. A number of school systems have used some form of this general approach with success and apparently without alienating parents, college admissions officers, or employers.

A plan for appraising pupils' achievement in terms of their ability and their own purposes, allows them to compete against their own record. It is clear that some pupils have derived real satisfactions from the sense of work done to the best of their ability and that the extrinsic rewards have not been necessary to motivate them. Such plans sound almost ideal but they do not always work out well in practice. It is not an easy plan to administer; teachers, administrators, and counselors alike must make consistent and effective effort if it is to be successful. As with other programs, some do; some don't.

Faculty and parent groups that study this whole question would come finally to consider what form of reporting should be used. All are familiar with various types of report cards. Some have used a letter-form report written by the teacher to parents. Sometimes a combination of the two is used plus a parent and teacher conference. Advocates of the letter-form report frequently find it difficult to explain the terms used. It is doubtful that teachers generally appreciate the effects of an unfavorable report card on a child. Other criticisms of reports to parents are frequently made; tactless expressions and snap judgments about pupils antagonize parents and destroy pupil morale; poorly-written reports incur unfavorable criticism in the community; teacher opinions are not based on adequate observation of pupils; overuse of meaningless clichés and stereotyped expressions; reports reflect the "power structure" and prestige of the community; the report is a one-way report only. It is obvious that the mere form of report is not the sole determining factor.[23]

The practice of conferences between each parent and the teacher has been used with varying degrees of success in differ-ent schools and communities. In communities where this plan fits the family living patterns, it may be successfully used provided the teacher and parents understand each other. On the other hand, there are schools in communities that find it impossible to get parents to come in for conferences on any basis. Again, it seems necessary to repeat that the plan for reporting to parents must be determined after thorough study in which all those affected participate. This is imperative if reports are to be meaningful, intelligible, and helpful to parents who wish to assist the school to provide the best possible program for their children.

Schools Are a Community Enterprise

NEW PATTERNS AND
POINTS OF VIEW

The school is a community enterprise. It is a cooperative undertaking involving the authority of the state, the funds of both state and local governments, the voters and taxpayers of the district, the school board, the administrative officials, the faculty, and the parents. Everyone should appreciate this cooperative undertaking, and most of all, the school people. Parents provide the reasons for the school. Intelligent teachers can learn to work with parents and like it.

Early American schools needed no explanation to both parents and teachers. Everyone knew they represented a cooperative undertaking; the people gathered and built the school house. They met in town meeting (or went to polls) and elected school committees or boards. Parents took turns boarding the teacher to provide part of his pay. They visited the school for spelling or "ciphering" matches, debates, and "speakin's" for entertainment. It was their school in every sense of the word. Communication among parents and teachers was the least of their problems. Sometimes the pupils thought there was too much of it.

The school of today, so radically changed in many external features and internal arrangements, is in need of a comparable degree and consistency of support. Modern America is specialized to a degree that even Horace Mann could not anticipate with the result that the school leadership must devise ways to keep in touch with the community. Teachers must perfect means of working together with parents often and long enough to gain common understandings and interest, sufficient to make and keep communication

[23] See, for example, Earl A. Johnson and R. Eldon Michael, *Principles of Teaching* (Boston: Allyn & Bacon, 1963), pp. 370–389.

going. This at once suggests the obvious focal point—the child.

One of the dangers to the community and its common school system is that the specialized responsibilities public officials and private citizens bear tends to deprive all the people from active participation in the work of the schools. The tendency of a very few school people to feel that they run the schools is an example of what the community should not want. The common school is the property of all, should be the concern of all. No one nor any single group has any vested interest, not even the "middle-class" values and patterns of the typical teacher's own background have any special validity in the curriculum. The public school is the common school for all the "uncommon" children of the district—all colors, creeds, ethnic groups, economic circumstances, language backgrounds, political persuasions, social classes and talents are equally entitled to its facilities and offerings. Indeed, they are not only entitled but are required to avail themselves of the education provided in the common school or its equivalent elsewhere. This common, free, secular school makes sense in that pluralistic American democracy with its diverse communities and patterns of living. But everywhere, it brings parents and teachers together in common concerns and responsibilities.

COMMUNITY PROBLEMS INVOLVE SCHOOLS

Teachers like other adults, often lose their perspective on problems and wish for release from the many concerns and pressures that they experience on this account. Reflection upon the status of the persons and those societies that are no longer concerned with problems usually disabuses most minds about this way to relief. Parents and teachers can only expect to recognize the problems of their communities and to merge their best efforts toward improving the conditions and situations that affect their homes and lives. Both will have a special concern about those problems and conditions that affect or implicate the schools.

All communities have problems of change, growth, and decline that may be expected in the normal course of events. There are some types of American communities that have encountered problems that are novel or unusual in certain respects. Those who will be heads of families or teachers should be concerned about community problems, both ordinary and extraordinary.

The past decade has brought the American people to face up to the problem of racial desegregation of school facilities and programs.[24] No less than seventeen states were affected by the Supreme Court decision of May, 1954, that struck down the older "separate, but equal" doctrine of *Plessy vs. Ferguson* (1897). In the border states desegregation took place on schedule and without untoward incident in most places. After various moves and approaches school

[24] Bernard N. Meltzer, Harry R. Doby, and Philip M. Smith, *Education in Society: Readings* (New York: Thomas Y. Crowell Co., 1958), pp. 428–453. See also Robert J. Havighurst and Bernice C. Neugarten, *Society and Education,* sec. ed. (Boston: Allyn & Bacon, 1962), pp. 393–407, and John A. Bartky, *Social Issues in Public Education* (Boston: Houghton Mifflin Co., 1963), pp. 130–142).

districts in most Southern states have achieved some desegregation. Only in two states have no attempts at desegregation been permitted to this time—1963—one hundred years after the Emancipation Proclamation. Accounts of the progress and problems of desegregation can be studied in various social science courses and individually in preparation for appreciation of the peculiar problems parents and teachers face in communities affected by this phenomenon of social change.[25]

The school systems of a great many communities—urban and rural—are affected by the comings and goings of migrant workers. A complex of educational and other problems is presented by this form of social change that brings hundreds of farm, orchard, or other seasonal workers into an agricultural community. Many families make seasonal harvesting jobs and brief living in temporary housing their way of life. In different regions of the country, many families of Mexican, Puerto Rican, or other West Indian origin may be found at given seasons of the year. The problems range from administrative concerns about facilities, shifting school populations, increased costs without added school revenue for the school board and administration, to those of communication with parents for the teachers. This socio-economic complex of problems should be studied in an appropriate course in the teacher education program. Various experimental projects and studies have been undertaken by the United States Office of Education and various state departments of education to find ways to deal with this type of problem.[26]

Metropolitan centers have unprecedented problems

It has been suggested that those who teach young folks to become teachers should take them to visit schools in metropolitan centers where slum conditions and problems have become acute. Here they would find minority groups living under crowded conditions in unwholesome, even hazardous quarters, with serious problems of communication and adjustment on part of adults and children alike, as they seek to find a place in a setting that is bewildering, frustrating, and threatening. The elementary school serves large groups of children from homes with a cultural level not far removed from the old-time tenement conditions. The average I.Q. may appear to be around 85 insofar as popular tests show, and there are grave problems of human relations, and personal adjustment. Dr. Conant's study of schools in urban slums concluded that the conditions represented "social dynamite."[27] Teachers in difficult neighborhoods of cities often feel that their work is too much, and prefer easier assignments in economically-favored parts of the city. One reason for "the flight of teachers to the suburbs," as some city authorities have put it, is the opportunity to work with parents who are more cooperative and students with better, cultural back-

[25] See for example, B. J. Chandler, Lindley J. Stiles, and John I. Kitsuse (editors), *Education in Urban Society* (New York: Dodd, Mead & Co., 1962), pp. 83–104.

[26] Paul E. Blackwood, "Migrants in Our Schools," *Educational Leadership,* **XIV,** No. 1 (January, 1957), pp. 207–212. See also Meltzer, Doby and Smith, *op. cit.,* pp. 491–495.

[27] James Bryant Conant, *Slums and Suburbs* (New York: McGraw-Hill, 1961).

grounds. The challenge to the professor and prospective teachers is obvious; what to do about it takes a great deal of consideration, self-searching and preparation.

Some observations may come as a shock to youth who have typical middle-class suburban and small-town backgrounds. One who has always held a mental picture of a parent meeting the teacher who comes visiting at the door with out-stretched hand and pleasant chatting over coffee or an iced drink finds it difficult to understand a home situation where teachers may be received with suspicion or apprehension. It is not easy to accept the picture of teachers who have appeared at homes in crowded neighborhoods and introduced themselves to be greeted with "Well, what's he done now?" or some other less-than-cordial response. Seeing and reading about "Blackboard Jungle" may upset more than a few preconceptions of the educational task in this fair country. Rough as this awakening may seem, there appears to be no reason to avoid it. The kind of teachers America's children and their parents need is capable of facing facts, of trying to gain understanding about *real* conditions, and to gain understanding of people in all situations without loss of faith or perspective. Teacher education that is oriented to only a part—and the favored part—of American life and to the needs of children and adults in middle-class and privileged homes is a luxury contemporary society cannot afford.

What future parents and teachers can do

What can and should be said and done in the educational guidance and curriculum of youth who can visualize the compelling problems and needs of people in America's blighted and disadvantaged areas and communities? Fortunately, there are many constructive ideas and potentialities that should be included in the larger perspective all students should try to achieve upon social problems, "problem areas," and education. In the first place, desperate as these situations appear, the outlook is not hopeless. College youth should study their social history, sociology, political science, and psychology with the purpose of getting understanding of the realities of community development, especially the urban centers. They will find that these have been more than one form or manifestation of slums, that much has been done to change the urban environmental conditions and areas where great numbers of recent immigrants from southern and eastern Europe congregated a few decades ago. Many of these people and their children made excellent adjustments to American life and *moved* into better economic opportunities, different neighborhoods, and fuller participation in the larger community. The recent migrants to the metropolitan centers are chiefly Latin American (Puerto Ricans, Mexicans, lately Cuban exiles) native white "hillbillies" and Negroes from Southern states. Is there reason to believe that America's capacity to provide opportunity is any less than in the days of Edward Bok, Andrew Carnegie, Jacob Riis and Charles P. Steinmetz. Solutions of complex problems are never easy to come by but the American genius for cooperative effort should not be underestimated.

An important second point is that college youth who will become the parents, taxpayers, and teachers of the next generation ought to become capable students of people, human behavior, and human relations. Good grounding in the behavioral sciences for students with real sense of purpose may provide essential equipment for those who have the courage to become community leaders for the whole community, not merely the more exclusive suburbs or the stable middle-class neighborhoods. Persons who gain real insight into the ways other people behave and live—their perceptions, motivations, and values—can learn how to work effectively and constructively with them, requiring neither condescension nor censure in their approach. This is more than mere wishful thinking, community leaders including some teachers have demonstrated that it can be done.

Another potential step that future community leaders should take is to gain as much experience as possible while in college in learning how to cooperate in and work through organizations for useful objectives and purposes. It is obvious that the removal of the blighted areas and the slums of our cities, suburban, and rural communities, will require cooperative efforts of many persons of a wide variety of competences and responsibility in diverse committees and projects. Future teachers can find opportunities to gain experiences in work with community groups, and on worthwhile projects by volunteering during vacation periods, on part-time basis on weekends during the college year, and by helping on programs sponsored by the college for this purpose. There is reason to believe that intelligent college youth with purpose can learn to be effective and imaginative in coping with problems of our time no less well than they comprehend those of other peoples in other times and circumstances.

In the last analysis, the development of the needed knowledges, skills, and attitudes for venturing to work with the parents of "disadvantaged" pupils is a matter of learning to accept other people, people different from us in some respects —language, home background, religion, economic opportunity, and education. Those teachers who can learn to do this by coming to *know and to accept* these parents with compelling problems will make a constructive contribution to our democratic institutions by extension of educational opportunity. They may find a sense of satisfaction that few persons ever comprehend.

Parents study their schools

A continuing major concern of parents is for the quality of the educational experiences provided by the schools for their children. Parents usually do not regret paying school taxes for good schools for Johnny and Susie. But when they think it through all of them desire a good school for their own and for their neighbor's children.

How can parents determine whether their community has good schools or not? There is no definite single standard or yardstick by which the layman may judge a school. State departments of education have standards for approving and accrediting elementary and high schools, but these are not suitable for use by parents. The same difficulty applies to the accreditation standards of the regional association to which many high schools belong. School faculties spend many months in committee work, making studies, preparing reports, and other preparations in advance of evaluation committees from the regional accrediting organization. The guide used for this kind of study is a huge volume that outlines the work of several committees called *The Evaluative Criteria*. This is not practicable for use of an individual or even a lay group unless there is unlimited time and adequate personnel to make the study. Parents should know that these evaluation programs exist and that their schools do participate in them. But they do not afford the busy citizen and parent the informed basis he needs to answer the basic question about whether his child's school is a good school.

This same question has occupied the attention of both educational and lay groups during the past 12 to 15 years and some progress has been made by a number of citizen's groups in various states. The National Citizen's Commission for the Public Schools and many state and local community committees worked on this problem, published some handbooks, and passed on the task to its successor, the National Citizen's Council for Better Schools. This group developed, in cooperation with the National School Boards Association, a guide for parents' and citizens' groups, who wished to evaluate their schools.[28]

Seven yardsticks for the use of citizen's groups are provided: (1) The goals of your school; (2) The school program (elementary, secondary, exceptional children, guidance, classroom tools, and library); (3) Teachers and teaching; (4) School buildings and equipment; (5) Finances; (6) Organization and administra-

tion; and (7) Citizen action. After study and survey of the schools members of the committee may check their findings by means of a self-quiz—a check list of 80 items grouped to fit the standards set forth by the yardsticks. A study group should conclude a study of their school(s) by use of this plan with an informed basis for an opinion about the quality of the school. Another desirable outcome might well be the discovery that evaluating a school or school system is not done quickly using quantitative measures that yield a definite mark or grade such as are used in marking goods for consumers benefit in the markets. This growth in sophistication is often found on the part of parents who really make a serious study of their schools.

Another practicable approach to the study of schools by citizens' groups was developed by an NEA seminar on evaluation in 1958. It was suggested that a local PTA or citizens' committee should use the instrument for interviews and studies to collect the facts and information needed for further study by all groups interested in a project of learning about their schools. The elements of a good school system provide a preface to the detailed questionnaire. Since education is a complex process there is no single definition of a good school that can be applied in all districts and communities.[29] The major elements in a good school system

[28] *Yardsticks for Public Schools* (Evanston, Illinois: National School Boards Association, 1959), 26 pages. Copies may be procured from the Association, 1940 Sheridan Road, Evanston, Illinois.

[29] See for example: (1) *Schools Are What We Make Them: A Handbook for Citizens* (Chicago: Bell & Howell Co., 1949); (2) Jacquelyn Gross, "Finding the Best School for Your Child," *Pageant*, **XVII**, No. 3 (September 1961), pp. 98–105; and (3) Alice V. Keliher, "Environment for Learning," *The Education Digest*, **XXVIII**, No. 6 (February 1963), pp. 12–15.

include: (1) a clear and sound set of educational goals; (2) a balanced program planned to serve all the learners; (3) a faculty of competent, qualified professionals; (4) a competent staff for administrative, supervisory and special services; (5) a variety of modern instructional materials; (6) a school climate that promotes high morale on part of the pupils; (7) an adequate plan of financial support; (8) a truly representative, forward-looking school board; and (9) an active and continuing citizen interest. Desirable standards and questions about the schools(s) are grouped in sections with these headings for use of fact-finding and study groups.

Another useful instrument for parents' study groups has been developed by the National Congress of Parents and Teachers.[30] There are several booklets and materials that may be found helpful by citizens' and parents' committees that undertake to study how to understand and to improve their schools.

A COMMON CAUSE FOR COMMON SCHOOLS

Parents and teachers have much in common, a common cause for common schools for uncommon children, all the children of all the people. This can be spelled out in many details. All have the present best interests and the future well-being of the children at heart. Parents are

[30] *Looking in on Your School,* Questions to guide PTA fact finders (Chicago: National Congress of Parents and Teachers, 1958).

the child's first teachers, no matter whether they recognize it or not. Home is the primary setting for learning. Throughout America's history parents have expressed their belief in educational opportunity for their children and for the neighborhood children, as well as in a wider community, and in the state. Early schools were built by the work-hardened hands of pioneer fathers as beginners were taught to read by tired mothers about the fireplace at day's end. The theme of America's educational history has been the wish-thought of parents: "I want my child to have a better chance than I've had." Teachers had their part in helping and guiding children from colonial school days to the edge of space.

America's amazing growth and the opportunities for her people have been such that "Space Age" parents may realistically desire and expect more in their hopes and aspirations for the children. Teachers and parents find new and better ways to complement their contributions to the education of democracy's children just as they have stood together in battles to save the school tax funds from reactionary forces or to lay up one side of the log schoolhouse at the crossing of the trails. Each has a distinctive part to play in democracy's educational enterprise; both should endeavor to give young Americans an appreciation of the nature and significance of the opportunity which is their heritage in the hope that they, too, will become informed active parents and teachers.

Selected Bibliography

Allen, Charles M. *Combatting the Dropout Problem.* Chicago: Science Research Associates, Inc., 1956.

Applegate, Mauree. *Everybody's Business—Our Children.* Evanston: Harper & Row, Publishers, 1952.

Asbell, Barnard. "Not Like Other Children," *Redbook,* CXXI, No. 8 (October 1962), pp. 64, 114–120.

Barclay, Dorothy. "Meeting the Test of Testing," *New York Times Magazine* (January 7, 1962), p. 56.

Baruch, Dorothy W. *How to Discipline Your Children.* New York: Public Affairs Pamphlet, 1957.

Brembeck, Cole S. *The Discovery of Teaching.* Englewood Cliffs, N.J.: Prentice-Hall, Inc., 1962, pp. 208–240.

Conant, James B. *The Child, the Parent, and the State.* Cambridge: Harvard University Press, 1959.

Cunningham, Earl C. "My Child's Teacher and I," *Phi Delta Kappan,* **XXXVII** (March 1956), pp. 254–258.

Derthick, Lawrence G. "Four Ways to Better Schools," *PTA Magazine,* **LVI** (September 1961), p. 19.

Foster, Constance J. *Developing Responsibility in Children.* Chicago: Science Research Associates, Inc., 1953.

Gallagher, James J. *The Gifted Child in the Elementary School.* Department of Classroom Teachers, American Educational Research Association. Washington: NEA, 1959.

Glessner, Chloe Holt. "Teachers Can Do a Better Job When Parents Cooperate," *Saturday Evening Post,* **CCXXXVI** (September 9, 1960), p. 8.

Grant, Eva H. *Parents and Teachers as Partners.* Chicago: Science Research Associates, Inc., 1952.

Gross, Jacquelyn. "Finding the Best School for Your Child," *Pageant,* **XVII** (September 1961), pp. 98–105.

Gross, Neal C. *Who Runs Our Schools?* New York: John Wiley & Sons, Inc., 1958.

Harris, Raymond P. *American Education—Facts, Fancy, and Folklore.* New York: Random House, Inc., 1961.

Harvey, Evelyn. "The Best Jobs for Your Child in 1975," *Pageant,* **XVII** (January 1962), pp. 90–99.

Hechinger, Grace and Fred, "Why Do They Have to Take All Those Tests?" *Parents' Magazine,* **XXXVII** (February 1962), pp. 46–47, 139–140.

Jersild, Arthur T. *When Teachers Face Themselves.* New York: Bureau of Publications, Teachers College, California University, 1955.

Johnson, Earl A. and Michael, R. Eldon. *Principles of Teaching.* Boston: Allyn & Bacon, Inc., 1958, pp. 370–390.

Kaplan, Bernard A. "Issues in Educating the Culturally Disadvantaged," *Phi Delta Kappan,* XLV, No. 2 (November 1963), pp. 70–76. See other related articles in same issue.

Kawin, Ethel. *A Guide for Child-Study Groups.* Chicago: Science Research Associates, Inc., 1952.

Kvaraceus, William C. *Juvenile Delinquency.* Department of Classroom Teachers, American Educational Research Association. Washington: NEA, 1958.

Ladd, Edward T. and Sayers, William C. (eds.). *Social Aspects of Education.* Englewood Cliffs, N.J.: Prentice-Hall, Inc., 1962.

Lambert, Clara. *Understand Your Child—From 6 to 12.* New York: Public Affairs Pamphlet, 1948.

Levine, Milton I., M.D. and Seligmann, Jean H. *Helping Boys and Girls Understand Their Sex Roles.* Chicago: Science Research Associates, Inc., 1953.

"Making the Grade with Parents," *NEA Journal* (April 1953).

Mayer, Frederick. "Parents as Teachers," *Phi Delta Kappan,* **XLI** (February 1960), pp. 216–219.

Meltzer, Bernard N., Doby, Harry R. and Smith, Philip M. *Education in Society: Readings.* New York: Thomas Y. Crowell Company, 1958.

Mohr, George J., M.D. *When Children Face Crises.* Chicago: Science Research Associates, Inc., 1952.

National Association of Public School Adult Educators, *How Adults Can Learn More —Faster.* Washington: NEA, 1962.

National Citizens Commission for the Public Schools. *How Can Citizens Help Their Schools?* New York: The Commission, 1954.

National Citizens Commission for the Public Schools, *What Do We Know About Our Schools?* New York: The Commission, n.d.

Neisser, Edith G. *How to Live With Children.* Chicago: Science Research Associates, Inc., 1950.

Ojemann, Ralph M. *Personality Adjustment of Individual Children,* Department of Classroom Teachers, American Educational Research Association. Washington: NEA, 1954.

Piers, Martha. *How to Work With Parents.* Chicago: Science Research Associates, Inc., 1955.

Remmers, H. H. and Hackett, C. G. *Let's Listen to Youth.* Chicago: Science Research Associates, Inc., 1952.

Ribicoff, Abraham, "The Battle for Better Schools," *Parents' Magazine,* **XXXVII** (February 1962), pp. 45, 130.

Riednour, Nina. *Building Self-Confidence in Children.* Chicago: Science Research Associates, Inc., 1954.

———. *Some Special Problems of Children Aged 2 to 5 years.* New York: The National Association for Mental Health, Inc., 1947.

Rosten, Leo. "Don't Just Sit There—Do Something," *TV Guide,* **IX** (September 2, 1961), pp. 14–16.

Rothney, John W. M. *What Research Says to the Teacher.* Department of Classroom Teachers, American Educational Research Association. Washington: NEA, 1955.

Schools Are What We Make Them. Chicago: Bell & Howell Company, 1949.

Seidman, Jerome S. *Readings in Educational Psychology.* Boston: Houghton Mifflin Co., 1955, pp. 85–98, 129–132, 286–293, 311–335.

Sloan, Fred A., Jr. "Helping Parents to Help Their Children," *NEA Journal,* **XLIX** (March 1960), pp. 49–51.

Smiley, Majorie B. and Diekhoff, John S. *Prologue to Teaching.* New York: Oxford University Press, Inc., 1959. See pp. 492–506, 556–590.

Stout, Irving W. and Langdon, Grace. *Parent-Teacher Relationships,* Department of

Classroom Teachers and American Educational Research Association. Washington: NEA, 1958.

Strang, Ruth. *How to Report Pupil Progress*. Chicago: Science Research Associates, Inc., 1955.

Trachtman, Gilbert M. "Should Parents Know the Results of Intelligence Tests?" *PTA Magazine*, **LVI** (January 1962), pp. 4–6.

Yauch, Wilbur A. *How Good Is Your School?* New York: Harper & Row, 1951.

Chapter 12

The Professionals Who

Serve Schools

. . . the whole child (emotional, social, moral, intellectual, etc.) reacts to an entire situation, which in a given case may include arithmetic problems, the teacher's attitude and actions, the temperature of the room, the attitudes of other pupils, and the like, confronting the pupil as a total stimulus pattern. In this sense, learning concerns the whole person and results in an entire reorganization of the individual's patterns of behavior. The guidance of learning thus is more effective when the pupil's interests and attitudes, as well as his fundamental organic, personal and social needs are considered in determining the pattern of his learning experiences.*

Introduction

Teaching is a complex and challenging role in any good school today. The statement about the nature of the learner and what is involved in learning is a good starting point for an appreciation of the significance of teaching. Teachers must accept all learners, keep them, and give equal consideration to the gifted, average, and slow; they accept students and their varied interests; their individual needs plus differences of home, social class, and community backgrounds; their diverse faiths and ethnic groups; they accept exceptional children of many types. It is obvious why teaching is a job for professionals.

* Louis P. Thorpe and Allen M. Schmuller, *Contemporary Theories of Learning* (New York: Ronald Press, 1954), p. 461.

Some people think that teaching is a routine task: assign, hear recitations, give tests, and marks, keep order—the impression is as outmoded as the picture of Ichabod Crane. This inadequate picture of teaching persists because of older misconceptions of learning and of the nature of the learner. Today we should know better, should be able to prepare teachers for a more significant and skillful role as guides and helpers in this lifelong business of everyone's learning. When you consider what is known about learning, the learner, and how people learn, you begin to see how teaching can be regarded as a creative, highly skilled role in our society.

Professional teaching must come from several basic understandings plus the willingness to use imagination and

391

initiative. The teacher must understand human growth and development and how all of its aspects are interrelated. She must know how the social process of inter-action results in the individual becoming a personality. She will know what learning is and see its results in improved behavior. She must understand how learning takes place and develop skill in planning for and guiding those experiences which result in desirable learning by the child. This implies close cooperation with parents and appreciation of the work of other educative agencies. The creative skilled teacher is an artist in human relations and social interaction, an "understander" and a cooperator with few equals. This kind of background of understandings and skills will mean that the teacher sees her role as that of guide, helper, and friendly counsellor. One of the best teachers who ever taught in an elementary school ex-pressed her whole philosophy in one crisp sentence: "Teaching means to live richly with children." It would be difficult to improve upon that statement.

Teaching Is Living with Learners

Key concept of teaching

Our conception of the work of the teacher must have a sound basis in what is known about the learner, learning, and how people learn. From these conceptions we may be able to visualize what the teacher does to help or guide the learner and learning. We may get our clue, in the key words *helping* and *guiding* and con-sider some representative statements con-cerning teaching for evidence of these concepts. Burton gives the following gen-eral definition of teaching:

Teaching is the guidance of the natural activities of the learner, and the stimulation of desired activities, directing them through educative experiences to the acquisition of socially desirable controls of conduct.[1]

Hopkins puts it this way:

. . . teaching is guiding children through their experiences so as to increase their ability to use better the process of achieving intelligent behavior.[2]

Note the terms of "guiding" and "stimulating" in these statements. The latter authority goes on to point out that every person is both a teacher and a learner in a desirable learning situation. All members of the group, including the teacher, learn from each other. Parents, too, enter into the learning situation as they help teachers to understand their children better; they are learners as they get from the teacher a better picture of the child's problems at school. By the same token the supervisor and superintendent are both teachers and learners as they fit into, or contribute to the learning situ-ation. Hopkins sums up this view of the teaching process in terms of six statements:

(a) The teacher is a guide in the learning situation rather than a controller and director of it;

[1] W. H. Burton, *The Guidance of Learn-ing Activities* (New York: Appleton-Century-Crofts, 1944), p. 213.

[2] L. Thomas Hopkins, *Interaction: The Democratic Process* (Boston: D. C. Heath Co., 1941), p. 40.

(b) His administrative authority is moved to the background and he becomes a cooperating member of the group;

(c) His mature experience is placed at the disposal of the group as an aid toward more adequate study of their problems;

(d) He emphasizes improvement in the process of inquiry, attaining greater validity of judgments and making reasonable choices of action;

(e) He helps the learners develop their command of subject matter in the process of inquiry into their problems; and

(f) He aids learners to evaluate by increasingly better means the results of their work.[3]

This seems to sum up quite well the conception of teaching which follows the definition of learning which has been presented. The teacher is a guide, a helper, and a co-learner and sharer with the learners. He reads, studies, thinks, plans, advises, leads and evaluates, but he helps and expects the pupils to grow in and through each of these same activities. He realizes that the different pupils and adults perceive the learning situation differently and that this complicates the task of learning.

Implications for teaching

The foregoing concepts of learning and teaching suggest some important implications for teaching. Educational literature abounds in lists of suggestions or pointers for teachers, but the following digest will suffice for our present purposes. Remember the key concepts of learning as experiencing-doing-acting, as well as teaching as guiding and helping

[3] Hopkins, *op. cit.,* pp. 142–43.

that process toward ever more desirable experiences (and learning). The initial step may be that of helping the learner to see the various factors in the learning situation and what is involved, i.e., the problem. In the light of these considerations you might examine the following implications for the teacher:

1. *The learner must have freedom of opportunity to choose appropriate responses in the problem-situation*

Obviously, the learner who is free to engage in more varied behavior can find solutions to more problems. His "repertoire" of responses is utilized more fully. He can become a more versatile person. Learners will make mistakes (wrong choices, poor selection of responses), but each instance is a teaching opportunity. Our goal is not the prevention of mistakes by the learner but rather the utilization of such situations for better learnings. Notice that the teacher's role is not to control rigidly, but rather that of guide, helper, and mild challenger-to-the-learner-to-make-good-choices.

2. *The interest of the learner should be utilized for more effective and better learnings*

Along with this must come an attempt by teachers to understand *interest* better. Some people have believed that all of this must come from children spontaneously, and that it must be direct and immediate. On the other hand, many have thought that the teacher could and should induce interest by motivating, or selling children on what was to be taught. We need not go to either extreme. Interest may well come originally from either the learner or the teacher. The important

Nichols JHS, Evanston Community Consolidated Schools

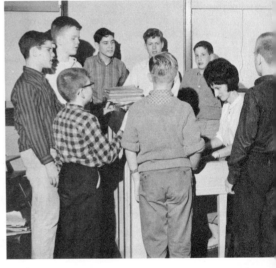

RESPONSIBILITIES
OF
TEACHERS
TODAY

Photos courtesy Cincinnati Public Schools or as noted.

Nichols JHS, Evanston Community Consolidated Schools

point is that interest must be present for effective learning. The teacher must know children well enough to identify their purposes.

3. Teaching should imply concern for the unity of the learning experience

Learning involves thinking, feeling, and willing—all aspects of human personality. These can be in conflicts or they can be integrative in terms of all around growth and development. Desirable experience then is integrating experience in that it contributes to fuller growth and better adaptation. The whole organism learns and all the learning outcomes are involved. Thus learning experiences must be utilized to result in as great and as varied learning as possible. Learning is naturally unified. That is, the learner responds and acts as a whole in problem situations. Unless we artificially delimit the learning situation the learner gets the fullest benefit from the experience. The teacher must be able to provide and guide learning experiences which observe the principle of unity. All of the learner is affected; all aspects of the learning experience should be involved.

4. The attitude of the learner is a great factor in the results of learning experience

The total effect of the teaching-learning process means that the whole child is affected. Attitudes, for example, are modified and all aspects of personality may be involved. Whatever the result in terms of subject matter gains attitudes are affected in or by the learning experiences of the child. Attitude of the learner is a most important concern of the teacher.

5. Learning experiences should be such that all pupils have some degree of success

The above principle is so important and so universally true that further discussion seems superfluous. Yet, there are many traditional schools which fail to practice this. You can readily see the injustice or inconsistency of requiring all learners to do exactly the same things and to meet the same standards. This is a basic implication from our concept of individual differences. It is just as logical and intelligent to require all pupils to run the fifty yard dash in the same time as to expect all to achieve at the same rate in school. The narrow academic school program is just as intelligent and sound as would be a dinner composed entirely of one type of food.

Working with pupils

The conceptions of learning and of teaching which have been presented include some points which will bear repetition. Teachers need to remember that their job means working with people, especially parents and pupils. It also will help to recall that people should always be regarded as ends in themselves, never as means.[4] Pupils are people, the ends which

[4] This basic principle from Immanuel Kant's work on ethics states that man exists as an end in himself, not merely as a means to be used by this or that will. This practical imperative is frequently quoted as follows: "So as to treat humanity, whether in thine own person or in that of any other, in every case as an end withal, never as means only."—Immanuel Kant, *Fundamental Principles of the Metaphysic of Ethics*, trans. Abbot (London: Longmans, 1895), pp. 55–56.

Many philosophers of different schools of thought have expressed a paramount regard for people and the concomitant view that institu-

the schools and curriculums are provided to serve. Clearly, the buildings, equipment, supplies, money, materials, and all the other thousand and one *things* are merely means to be used *by* and *for* the real ends of education. Even our principles, theories, and techniques exist for the same purpose, to be used. It is sometimes difficult for some adults to remember this.

Learning is an individual matter since it is *by* and *for* individuals. Sometimes teachers become extremists, expecting one theory or technique to accomplish the work of teaching. There are several important ideas and theories advanced about the teaching of reading. Sometimes there is controversy among teachers as to which of these is the answer. Our answer would be that learning to read is an individual problem; since there are so many individuals, all different, we may need different approaches and techniques.

Learning should be viewed as a rich creative experience. Narrowly-conceived curriculums, limited freedom to respond, meager materials, restricted environment, all detract from the quality and degree of learning which can take place. Thus, the most interesting stimulating environment for the learning experiences of children is best.

Attitudes of the learner are important. The free, relaxed, and secure person behaves better and learns more desirable outcomes. This implies freedom from anxiety or tension. Teachers who use fear or threat of punishment are adversely affecting the learning experiences of the

learner. Anxiety or a feeling of tension are damaging to all of us.

Learners will learn something from their experiences if those experiences involve activity. Any group of normal children will respond to problem-situations as freely and intelligently as the conditions permit. Therefore, we teach well when we permit pupils to have experiences, to observe the results, and to learn. Especially do we need to reward desirable learnings in order to re-enforce that sort of behavior. Reward does not mean prizes or favoritism; it simply refers to approbation, recognition, and encouragement by the teacher. It is the strongest and most versatile tool of the understanding teacher.

Illustrative situations show principles

You will find many discussions of principles and techniques of teaching although these terms are not as prevalent as they once were. For our present purposes it may be desirable to vary our presentation a bit. Suppose we set up some questions which are based on principles the teacher should utilize in her efforts to guide and assist her pupils to learn. Consider as many of these as you can and try to state a principle which is involved.

(a) Do we teach well when we get Johnny to memorize as many facts and bits of useful information as possible because we know he will need them; or when we help him to get the facts, skills, etc., needed to meet problems he feels now, even if he doesn't get as many as the boy across the table? Put another way, does learning take place as we put something into the child or as we help to bring out potential ability and growth from within him?

---

tions exist to serve individuals. See, for example, Bertrand Russell, *Political Ideals* (New York: Century, 1917), p. 14; also, John Dewey, *Reconstruction in Philosophy* (New York: Holt, 1920), pp. 196–198.

(b) Which is better as a learning experience for second-grader Susie—to have her adored teacher start the day with a talk about how much we can see on our way to school, or to have Susie tell what she saw on the way to school? In other words, does learning come from an active or a passive role?

(c) Should we use uniform methods with Sally (IQ 110) and Dick (IQ 109)? Shall we teach all members of the class in the same way, or must we remember that their backgrounds of experiences, environments, and native abilities all differ widely? In more formal terms, can we consider the learner except in terms of what he is and what has made him like that?

(d) Which brings better learning—to assign a task to be completed, or to help Ann find what must be done to solve her problem? Does the pupil work for himself or for the teacher?

(e) Shall we begin ninth grade English readings with Margie who likes *Silas Marner,* Jim who reads only comic books, Ann who has read voluntarily *Seventeen,* or Dick who has finished Churchill's memoirs? Shall we follow the prescribed course of study, ignoring the plus and minus signs which indicate student levels of interest above and below the recommended readings? Do we begin where the pupil *is* or where the teacher is if we are to teach effectively?

(f) When the teacher notes that several remarks indicate a good deal of interest in wildlife should the children enter into planning and evaluating the work as well as doing it or should these steps be done by the teacher? In practical terms, do children learn more by participating in each phase of a learning experience or by doing the part which is assigned to them?

(g) How shall we keep the children from forgetting facts and skills which they will need, by drill and repetition over and over, or by providing fresh activities and experiences in which these need to be used? Or put in another way, should we drill to remember, or should we learn through actual use?

(h) As we try to help Jane, Jeanie, Betty, Skippy and Mike to learn, which should we use—praise and recognition for progress, or blame and criticism for failures? Which incentives work best in our work with pupils—encouragement or censure?

You can think of other illustrations and examples which will show how the teacher can aid the learning process. You will progress as you come to understand more clearly that learning results from an active, participating, sharing process in a situation which is real and meaningful for the learner. Incidentally, the teacher has a lot of fun as she participates in this dynamic process of learning.

Understand what really happens

Your appreciation of teaching will be evident when you can visualize what really goes on in that exciting social environment we call a good school. Take any aspect or phase of growth and learning, and try to imagine how it goes on in the live school. This quotation offers such a clue to what you may be able to perceive:

Character education takes place every hour of the school day. It takes place when the five-year-olds learn to take turns with the new toy rather than to fight for it; in the opening exercises of the country school as the children are asked by the teacher to explain the meaning of '. . . with liberty and justice for all'; on the playground when the 'gang' tells the trouble-maker to play by the rules or get out;

. . . in the eighth-grade history class which makes posters to illustrate the immortal ideals of the American Declaration of Independence—'all men are created equal . . . endowed by their Creator with certain inalienable rights . . . life, liberty, and the pursuit of happiness';

. . . in the high school homeroom as the students decide what message to send to the girl who has been stricken with polio;

. . . in the English class that studies *Macbeth* or *The Vision of Sir Launfal*;

. . . on the class picnic, on the football field, in the rehearsal for the senior play, in the social-service project of the sociology class, in the community beautification project of the civics class;

. . . in the developing insights into the nature of truth in the geometry class and the physics laboratory;

. . . when a disturbed adolescent shares his troubles with a trusted counselor . . . when youth observe exemplary character in their teachers.[5]

The important point is that you cannot lose if you have such a view and concept of the school and of its work. The door to any schoolroom can be the entrance into such an exciting and significant way of life.

Analyze and think it over

Any good student who is genuinely interested in people and in teaching should not be pessimistic about the role he will be expected to perform. Teachers do not have to be the mechanical know-it-all automatons that some people have thought they should be. It does not matter if the teacher has to say, "I don't know," but it does if she does not follow by saying, "Let's find out together." Genuineness, sincerity, helpfulness—these are virtues in the work of teaching.

The teacher sees education as the process whereby human behavior is changed *for the better*. Learners come to school with their learning already well advanced—many habits, attitudes and patterns of behavior are formed. The school attempts to re-enforce and to extend desirable learning already acquired; it seeks to promote the development of other desirable learnings. The wise teacher seeks to understand the child and his behavior as he enters school and to begin at that point to promote further desirable behavior. Teachers are guides and helpers to the pupils; they grow and learn together. This is the work of an artist, a creative person. This is the work of the teacher.

Schools Need Many Professionals

You have been impressed with the fact that teaching offers today greater opportunity to capable young people than ever before in our history. Not only is this

[5] Willard E. Givens, *The Public School,* Annual Report of the Profession to the Public, (Washington: NEA, 1952). Used by permission.

true in the sense that the need for teachers is unprecedented with resultant chance of promotion, but also because of the wide range of abilities and interests which are required. The present situation spells opportunity for many young people of widely varied capabilities, interests, and preferences. Your experiences have shown that good teachers are no more the stereotyped sort of person that has been presented in comics and in glib statements any more than are doctors or other professional persons. Teachers are often found to be inspired persons, capable specialists, and effective leaders. The best ones are trying to find even more effective ways to pool their skills to provide the best possible educational opportunity for our children and youth. Your observations in schools and your study of educational programs have served to remind you of this point.

It should now become more and more your purpose to determine *whether* and *where* and *how* you may fit best into the educational profession in the years ahead. It is wise to make that decision as early as possible in your college career. For those who will teach, the decision between the elementary and secondary levels should be made as early as is practicable after this course. It would be wise to begin careful consideration of that problem now. You should read, observe some more, talk to successful teachers, evaluate your own interests and abilities as means to that end. The next step would appear to be a recapitulation of the kinds of opportunities teachers may find in our best schools.

It is also important to have a more accurate conception of the work of the teacher than most people have. Too many people tend to think of teaching as a routine process of assigning work, holding classes, checking papers, examining and grading pupils during a six-hour school day. Many believe that the teacher's work is completed with the close of her day's teaching. Such narrow and inadequate views of what teaching is have misled

many people as to its importance and significance and have deterred able youth from entering the profession. You should know better and for good and sufficient reasons. Consider now what teaching really is and means in each of the large areas of service in our schools.

Elementary teaching is strategic

It is for real and convincing reasons that educational leaders speak of the grave shortage of capable classroom teachers. As you have seen, it is the classroom teachers who carry the major burden of American education. For the children and the work which the excellent teacher does with the child all the other factors and elements in the educational program exist.

It is hardly necessary to remind you of the grave shortage of competent classroom teachers today. That same fact turned around spells "opportunity" for capable youth who are getting ready to teach. Never has there been a greater opportunity for capable youth to get a good education for teaching our children and start as an elementary teacher. Young men in great numbers are needed for a great many years to come. It matters not where you look at the elementary school program, teachers are needed, women for the pre-school, primary, and intermediate years, men for the latter.

You will recall the phrase used by the Educational Policies Commission in referring to the teacher, "The Teachers: A Strategic Factor." In the elementary school she is all that and more. Teachers are found to contribute most to the elementary school program if they really understand how children grow and develop, if they have a clear knowledge of how learning takes place, if they themselves are rich personalities of broad cultural background, and if they keep up and utilize teaching opportunities. Such a teacher is the best possible guarantee of an effective vital school program. This is the sort of person able to carry her part in planning groups, and guiding and leading children. She plans her own work, to be sure, but so soundly and fully as to be prepared for any worthwhile interest of the children. For she really knows the children—their backgrounds, interests and needs—and can utilize these in her teaching. She knows, too, the society which the children will enter and make contributions to one day. Skillfully she weaves the individual and the social dimensions of the curriculum into unique patterns of personality growth. Such a teacher is an artist. Any attempt to present a full and adequate description of the work an excellent elementary teacher does would fall short of realization. Your best understanding will come from close acquaintance with some master teachers and full knowledge of their contributions. Another way is to go to the best literature written by the ablest classroom teachers themselves. Some outstanding teacher educators have given us excellent pen pictures of the good teacher.[6] These should serve to give you a better idea of what great teaching can be in the elementary school.

[6] See, for example: Julia Weber, *My Country School Diary* (New York: Harper, 1946). Also, the following: (1) *Education for All-American Children*, pp. 121–156. (2) Dorothy McCuskey, "How Do You Know A Good Teacher?" in Arthur Foff and Jean D. Gramps (eds.), *Readings in Education* (New York: Harper & Row, 1956). (3) Barbara Biber and Agnes Snyder, "How Do We Know A Good Teacher?" in *Childhood Education*, February 1948, pp. 281–85; and (4) Francis V. Rummell, "What Are Good Teachers Like?" *School Life*, June 1948, and July 1948, pp. 4 and 7, respectively.

Capable students who have the first prerequisite of a genuine love for children need no longer hold back to enter the elementary teaching field. All we learn about the good teacher serves only to re-enforce that regard for others as the one great characteristic of the best teachers. Findings of studies such as those done at the University of Minnesota are convincing in this respect. Children have always known this.

Potentially good teachers may enter the elementary education field with confidence. Standards for qualifications are being raised more rapidly than the supply of teachers increases. Salary schedules are being placed on equality with teachers of other levels in most states and cities. Finally, it is being recognized that the broad general education needed by the elementary teacher and supplementary work in psychology, sociology and other foundational fields should insure a capable well-rounded professional teacher. Teaching in the elementary school requires maturity of thinking, emotional poise, and a high quality education. It is a challenge to the best.

Secondary teaching offers variety

On the surface it may appear that teaching in the high school is radically different from the work of the elementary teachers. Perhaps it is true that the subject matter teacher who thinks of her job as presenting content does do an entirely different kind of work. Your study and observations have given you an opportunity to see better teaching than this and to note that the two levels have much in common when the teachers accept their responsibility for guiding and helping optimum pupil growth. That is precisely and concisely just what we mean by teaching.

Teaching in the high school is not merely a matter of presenting subject matter in English, social studies, science, mathematics, or any other field. It is helping boys and girls to grow and develop to their fullest capacities, and this process does involve using the subject matters of the curriculum purposefully. Simultaneously, adjustment or adaptation to the social-cultural environment must be accomplished.

It is true that one teacher will have unusual competence in the field of English, another in the area of social studies, still others in mathematics and science, but the group taken together compose a working staff. Teachers are then used or called upon to make the particularly strong contributions they can make in these different areas. The science teacher is called in to help another teacher with a group which needs that particular competence at a given time. All teachers then must take primary responsibility for helping to meet the needs of the pupils they teach. Each takes the initiative on all this for the group with which they work most closely. Often these are termed "homeroom groups," or "core groups." Such a teacher sees her job as that of helping meet the health needs of pupils, or helping to solve the problems of "growing up," or finding out more about a pupil's aptitudes for different kinds of work. This teacher is thus concerned with guidance and counseling, with the day-to-day chores of running the school, with helping to evaluate the work of the group and of pupils, with student personnel problems and records, and perhaps with a club or other activity. She also teaches classes but this is not considered all of the teaching job; it is only one aspect of teaching. All these tasks and activities of the teacher comprise the modern high school teacher's job.

Many teachers, of course, do not accept any responsibility beyond the presentation of subject matter in the field they have chosen to teach. It will probably be some little time before the modern conception of the teacher's job is universally accepted. Meanwhile American democracy is stuck with some teachers who do not meet the needs and opportunities which are right under their noses. But in our best situations real creative teaching is to be found.

Actual instruction in the best classrooms has changed much from the older formalized methods of a few decades ago. The old routine of "assign-study-recite," graphically described by Burton,[7] has given way to many newer methods and, in some cases, to more flexible procedure which is not characterized by any particular methods. For many years the Morrisonian "unit mastery technique" was a commonly accepted teaching procedure, but it is not generally pervasive in our schools today. In the modern approach the teacher and pupils plan together, do whatever is necessary to accomplish their agreed-upon-purposes, and jointly evaluate the outcomes. Thus, teachers and pupils share experiences and learnings that are not possible under more inflexible methods and procedures.

Methods, both general and special, are not so much stressed as formerly in teacher education. You will find that more general discussions of the teacher's procedures in recent textbooks deal with the

[7] W. H. Burton, *The Guidance of Learning Activities,* Third Edition (New York: Appleton-Century-Crofts, Inc., 1962), pp. 289–325.

flexible approach we have mentioned. If you can begin to visualize the educative process in which teacher and pupils engage, as a live, learning-together situation in which each participates to the extent of his ability and learns accordingly, you will have a pretty good picture of modern teaching. This does not mean that our best teachers do not know and use good methods and techniques, unit plans of organizing content, and the like. It does mean that such a teacher can and does use any which fit her need and the needs of the group at the time without being bound slavishly to a particular procedure to be followed at all times.

The role of the high school teacher thus runs the whole gamut of the problems of youth. At various times the teacher handles the homeroom, helps in guidance, does counseling, testing, keeps records, sponsors and advises student activities, visits homes of pupils, serves on committees, helps in PTA work, and attends to numerous other details. One cannot say that all this is done besides teaching, all this *is* teaching!

Administrative and supervisory talent hunt

Positions of educational leadership offer the better recognized professional opportunities in education. The positions of superintendent and principal are natural goals for many teachers who acquire sufficient experience and the necessary training. The attractions are the more favorable income and relatively greater prestige among educators and in the community. On the other hand, there are considerably greater handicaps in the form of less security, and the carrying of final responsibility for smooth operation of a

system or school. It is noted that the average term of a superintendent has been relatively brief.

The superintendent is the legal and official head of the educational system. He is elected, normally, by the board of education and serves as its executive officer, sometimes as its secretary. He advises the board on matters of broad school policies and administers the policies and regulations of that body. In most states, his duties are outlined by law. He recommends teachers for appointment, is responsible for preparing budget proposals and financial records, and for the general oversight of the school system. A good superintendent occupies a significant position for community leadership.

School administration was formerly a far more arbitrary and centralized responsibility than now. Our best school systems are no longer run by edict from the superintendent's office. Not so often does one find that the schools are operated as a big business corporation with a superintendent, instead of the general manager. A healthy trend is seen in the increasing number of systems which provide for staff participation in the making of school policies. The function of administration is seen as that of aiding and abetting the best possible program of instruction in the schools. All else is secondary and incidental to that.

Principals are designated for schools of sufficient size to require full time services of an administrator. Usually, this position is full-time responsibility for the management of the school unit. In some schools the principal teaches part of the time but this is becoming increasingly rare. The principal is responsible to the superintendent and enjoys something like professional status. The pay and the relative prestige in the community are rather better than for most teachers. The functions of the principal are professional in nature—day-to-day administration of school policies, supervision of instruction, and contacts with parents. Ideally the principal delegates most matters of business and details to his clerical and administrative assistants. Principalships are open to successful teachers who have done successful teaching for a prescribed number of years and who have studied administration and supervision on the graduate level.

Supervisors are employed by many school systems to help inprove the instructional program. Even the very title has been changed in many places to that of "consulting teacher," or "teacher consultant." The newer terms suggest a far far more accurate impression of the functions of this type of leader. At one time supervision was more closely connected with the administration of schools. It was found that teachers tended to regard the supervisor as an administrator—one who has power to hire and fire, in plain language. Obviously a free and natural relationship between supervisor and teacher was difficult under those conditions. Many school systems now attempt to free supervisors of any administrative chores, giving them a better and freer opportunity to work with classroom teachers on problems of instruction. Now it is far less likely that a supervisor can be found who believes her job is to observe the teacher and pass judgment upon her work. The more modern view is that the learning situation is one which concerns children, parents, teachers, supervisor, even administrators. Teacher and supervisor both try to have better understanding of it and to find ways of improving it. Under this arrangement the teacher feels a partner in the whole program of improving instruction. Supervisors are employed at all levels of public education, but the greatest number are found in the elementary schools.

The capable supervisor should have a considerable background of successful experience as a classroom teacher. Unusual ability to work with other people, genuineness and sympathetic understanding are other qualities of the good supervisor. To sum it up, the good supervisor measures up to the title many of them have been given of "teacher consultant." The new title is symbolic of the changed concept of the supervisor's role and function in many places.

Supervisory staffs of larger school systems provide a number of specially trained staff services. In these systems the teachers are given help in the use of audiovisual aids, education by radio and other mass media, health and safety, art and music fields, and in vocational education programs. Opportunity for such work may be sought by successful teachers who acquire the necessary graduate preparation for leadership in their specialties.

Many specialists are needed

Our study of children and youth will give a background for an understanding of the need for specialized services in modern schools. Exceptional children have needs and problems which must often be met by services and procedures not possible in an ordinary age-group program. It is often noted that our schools fail to do all that should be done for exceptional children. Professional teachers for today's best schools who accept responsibility for helping children grow and develop in all phases need help and assistance from a number of trained experts. We find represented on the staff of the modern school system a number of specialists once unknown in education.

Teachers of special pupils are found in larger school systems. Handicapped children are usually placed in schools provided by the states, often in conjunction with hospitals or institutions providing the care they need. Such teachers must have adequate training for the skilled teaching they must provide for these children. Among the personal qualities needed are unusual patience, sympathetic understanding of children and their problems, a strong belief in the value of their work, and marked ability to help youth find opportunities to fit into society. Larger school systems often employ teachers to instruct children who cannot attend school because of physical disability. Such teachers should have a broad general education, exceptional teaching skill, and a strong sense of service. These "bedside" teachers are in position to see results of their work in the opportunities enjoyed by the children who otherwise would have little chance in life.

Larger school systems provide skilled service for schools in the form of school psychologists who help develop testing programs, guidance and counseling specialists, speech correctionists and visiting teachers. The nature of the work of these specialists is fairly well indicated by their titles. Often these staff members are persons who have developed strong interests in one of these fields while teaching and sought specific training for their additional tasks.

Critical needs in college teaching

In spite of all the discussion we hear about the needs in higher education, we shall likely find that effective instruction is a need not fully met. Our colleges and universities are badly under-staffed at present. Lack of money is a great drawback certainly, but it is also true that capable instructors are hard to find. After all that has been said about the pupil coming first, and subject matter second, you may have thought that the only place left for subject matter experts was in higher education. It is true that teaching in colleges and universities requires scholarly persons. But it is also true that college teaching could greatly benefit from the use of instructors who understand how people learn and know how to guide learning. Mere scholarship is in itself no guarantee that one will be an effective college teacher despite the first-rank importance of broad knowledge. In other words, make the old saying read, "Good teachers are made, not born."

The usual road to college teaching involves successful high school and/or junior college teaching, plus the necessary progress in graduate study. The doctor's degree has become practically a prerequisite for entrance into the college teaching field in major institutions. Experience in actual teaching appears to be indicated before a young person should attempt to decide upon this type of teaching.

New opportunities are emerging

In addition to the great demands for teachers in the elementary school now and the expected increased need for secondary school teachers, there should be other new opportunities which have received little notice. We remember that the community college idea is taking hold very rapidly in several states. That means teaching opportunity for well educated teachers. In recent years, a few outstanding universities have established programs to train instructors for the junior college level.

At the preschool level, the need for public-provided education is evident in most communities. Here and there educational leadership is placing emphasis upon the need for legislation and public support for preschool programs. Before World War II, about 10% of the two- to five-years-olds were enrolled in nursery schools and kindergartens. About nine-tenths of these were in cities and most progress has been made in Pacific Coast states. In 1952 about one and a half million children were enrolled in our kindergartens, 85% of these were in public schools. By 1960 nearly one-half of elementary schools had kindergartens and somewhat less than half of the five-year-olds attended. In 1960 nearly 64% of all five- and six-year-olds were in school.[8] Eight states have improved their laws on preschool education in recent years. A trend seems to be in the making. We can readily see the great opportunity for teachers of young children when the American people decide that they want preschool education enough to begin paying for it. When that day dawns in the near future attractive positions for trained leadership will be available.

We should seek other clues to worthwhile opportunities by keeping informed about developments in American education. Reading, attendance at professional meetings, and discussion with educators are obvious ways to keep informed. It is not necessary to make opportunity knock on the door; let's keep it wide open.

Open any door

The next generation of teachers should be emotionally stable and happy to a degree not usually found because they can choose the teaching opportunity they like best. The teaching field offers opportunity to persons of widely varying abilities and interests. The profession has been called on to provide so many services and types of programs that all sorts of persons are needed. All of which means that teaching is more challenging and significant than ever before. There are many doors for you to open, but there is some kind of opportunity on the other side of each of them.

Most likely, that opportunity means the chance to live with children, see them, and help them to grow and develop. If not with children, at least it means working with people. For if teaching means anything, this is it. Let all who consider teaching be prepared to accept that fact about it, otherwise they will miss most of what it has to offer. When we think about it, that's about the best that life itself has to offer.

Professional Human Relations

Teaching means working with people. This has been suggested in a number

[8] U.S. Bureau of the Census, *U.S. Census of Population, 1960,* General Social & Economic Characteristics, U.S. Summary, Final Report (Washington: U.S. Government Printing Office, 1962), pp. 1–259.

of places; it is worth repeating as we turn to the consideration of the teacher's relationships with other teachers, administrators, and parents. Although it is often said that teachers are interested in books and ideas, it is even more important that they be concerned with people and how to work with others.

Persons interested in teaching can do a great deal to learn and develop skills in human relationships. But there is no simple, surefire way, even though advertisements of Dale Carnegie's books may suggest the contrary. Most important are an interest in people, the willingness to see the other fellow's viewpoint, and the desire to learn how to work with other people as equals and in groups. The role of the teacher in the school-community can be expressed in one good and much-used word: cooperation.

The teacher and his colleagues

Teachers are human beings much like other people you meet on the street. Their personalities and backgrounds vary and they have their little individual ways just as other people do. There is no reason to feel that relationships among teachers are fundamentally different from adequate adjustments elsewhere in society. Teachers probably get along as well with each other as any other groups of persons and much better than some. This may be due to their relatively comparable educational and professional backgrounds and experiences which provide many common interests and standards.

But this does not keep the young teacher from wondering just how he or she will fare in associations with colleagues, many of them older and more experienced. I remember quite vividly a conversation with a superintendent of schools who told me that his assignment was to a school which had many older teachers, concluding, "Now be careful that those old crustaceans don't ruin your philosophy of education." Yet there proved to be no real difference in making

friends in that school from any other place. As a matter of fact there is no good basis for feeling that basic habits of courtesy, regard for others, and cooperation are less important and effective in school work than in any other association or place.

There are few formulas for making friends and getting people to accept one's work unless the user actually likes people and conducts himself naturally and sincerely. Even children can spot a "phony" —one who pretends to be something other than what he is. It is best to avoid kidding ourselves that we can get by with a pretense of interest in others; we simply must feel that way. Then we do not have to put on an act; it goes over naturally. The best formula for getting along well with people is to *actually like people and act that way!*

The beginning teacher faces many problems, among them the desire to be accepted and respected by his colleagues. Self-respect and poise are obviously essential to the making of a good impression at the very outset. The new teacher would do well to be prepared with plans and carefully developed programs which will enable him to feel adequate and confident. It is pretty nearly axiomatic that other people take a person at his own valuation. Adequacy and the quiet confidence it gives somehow are subtly broadcast to other people when we ourselves feel that way. If young teachers could understand this, there might be less apprehension and concern about the matter of relationships with colleagues. Respect and courtesy are always necessary attributes of decent human beings. Among your associates who are educated, intelligent people these are cardinal points of personal conduct. Interchange of questions and ideas are common items of teachers' conversations; questions about school activities are usually good "openers." It is also remarkable what a single but simple and honest request for information or help will do to assist one to get acquainted with colleagues. Young teachers would do well to know and to follow the implications of the professional code of ethics in relationships with other teachers. One does not criticize other teachers before colleagues, parents, or pupils. Criticism should first be taken directly to the person involved and then only when it is important. In instances of serious offenses, the teacher should first be approached and the matter taken to administrators only if necessary to get things straightened out. One common offense of teachers is to criticize or make derogatory remarks about the work of a predecessor. Often the new teacher hears many stories and reports about preceding teachers which he would do well to ignore. Remember it is possible that some reports about you and your work will be made which are not accurate. The keynote of the successful teacher's relationships with colleagues is cooperation. We will hardly go wrong if we play this note over and over. Should we wish to add some variations on this theme, we can try honest regard for others, real acceptance of those we work with, and practice the Golden Rule. We will do well to put it mildly.

The teacher and administrators

What has been said of the teacher's relationships goes for the contacts one has with administrators. Modern administrators are not looking for subservient docile teachers who merely take orders. They prefer intelligent, alert teachers with initiative and ability who can use all the freedom and opportunity they get. There seems to be little need to approach one's principal as if he were a military leader or a dictator. It is well to understand clearly the responsibility of the principal to the superintendent, board of education and the general public and to see that loyalty and support are essential. On the other hand, it is one's right to expect the loyalty and backing of the principal. The best principals recognize their role as that of facilitating, promoting, and aiding the instructional program of the school. Teachers and the principal should be able to find a common ground of interest in that process.

Relationships with supervisors are becoming far more natural and wholesome in our best schools. For one reason supervisors are seeing their own position more nearly as that of a "helping teacher" or a consultant to teachers. Outmoded techniques of the nature of an inspection have given way to constructive helpful suggestions and cooperative planning by both teacher and supervisor to improve the learning environment and process for the pupils. In this revised and improved relationship the teacher need feel no trepidation at visits by the supervisor. Teachers have the right to feel that it is the teaching situation which is under study; that they are among those cooperating to improve it; that supervisor, principal, and interested parents wish to help. Even the children help in their planning and evaluating with the teacher. The teacher finds it as easy and rewarding to work with the best supervisors as with a trusted friend and adviser. The relationship should be one of mutual respect and helpfulness, a great advance over the days when teachers felt it necessary to put on a good show because the supervisor was due for a look in to see how she was doing.

Teachers need to belong in community

Young teachers often make their worst mistakes in their failure to appreciate or to adapt to the community in which they teach. Communities are different and there are good reasons why they should vary in many respects. No matter how poor or backward a community may appear, there will be found many loyal persons who will resent any disparagement or criticism by an outsider. And the new teacher may be an outsider *until* he fits into the community and is accepted by the people. The best way to do this is to find a way to make a contribution by helping out in the community. It may be a PTA committee or a program of some civic group in one of the churches but ways are usually open. Parents who want to help can anticipate this need of new teachers.

Teachers often find that changes and improvements are needed in the community. Usually it is wise to go slowly and carefully in inaugurating abrupt changes. People will go much further toward accepting one's ideas and suggestions after they have accepted the person. In teaching, teachers will know they have put something over when their pupils see the idea for themselves. It is just as true in working with adults. Of course, this does not mean that young teachers should never do or risk anything; it merely counsels sagacity, forethought, and good sense. It also counsels parents to be sympathetic and helpful to teachers who have good ideas that need a "tryout."

Community standards and patterns of personal conduct expected of outsiders have sometimes been quite unreasonable and even unfair to teachers. This was once more common and even today one might find that simple harmless amusements may occasion unfavorable comment in some places. It may be irritating to find that card parties or cocktails are taboo in certain communities, but these are hardly major issues worth making a fight about. Few school administrators and boards of education now try to lay down meticulous regulations concerning the private social lives of teachers. This is a sensible trend and it may be that one of the few constructive gains from the teacher crisis is a more tolerant attitude toward the teacher's right to live as a person in the community. This has not yet occurred in some communities, and young teachers who would find such conditions uncongenial should seek a different locale. Regardless of our opinions about the mores of a community, there is no denying the fact that teachers are public servants, and that they have much influence. It would seem far wiser to try to do something positive about the conditions which prevail than to spend one's energy fretting and fuming about them. For example, if the teacher learns that it is unwise to visit local juke joints or bars it is equally true that parents would prefer a better environment for their children. What's to prevent that teacher from helping to start a wholesome youth canteen, a fit place for teachers and parents to sponsor parties and get-together affairs for the young people of the community? Such constructive effort would represent a real contribution to the community and partially satisfy the teachers' need for social contacts and fun.

Teachers often find a great demand for their services by groups and organizations in the community. Often it is the matter of teaching in Sunday School or working with some outside youth group. The teacher cannot afford to evade any responsibility at all, but he must also remember that his first obligation is to the school program. Perhaps the school administration and board of education should help formulate policies to guide teachers upon such matters when and if these demands become excessive. The teacher should expect to be a fully participating citizen in civic and public affairs. At least the active participating teacher finds himself making friends and wielding influence in the community—he counts. This is one of the rewards of teaching, and, in the long run, it pays even in terms of salary checks. For the active teacher is acquiring leadership abilities which in turn qualify one for positions of greater responsibility and pay.

Other things being equal, the teacher would do well to live in the community where he teaches. Current housing conditions may make this impossible but it is preferable to live among the people with whom you work. Teachers who "live out of a suitcase," arriving Monday morning and leaving after school on Fridays have fewer opportunities to fit into and contribute to the community. Small wonder that they count for little with the people. Another possible constructive gain from the current teacher shortage may be the provision of adequate living quarters for teachers by many communities.

The last word on this subject cannot be set down here. The adjustment of the teacher to and within the community is important, and it is proper that he is expected to provide leadership. Many communities can afford few publicly-supported agencies and leaders. The people look to the schools and to teachers for more than nominal leadership. If we think this is unreasonable and feel that we cannot be happy under these conditions, we may need to reconsider the choice of teaching. Remember, we have said from the very start that *teaching means working with people.*

Teachers should be effective group members

Everyone has heard of group dynamics and much about human relations in his own educational experiences. Chances are that many already have some of the insights and skills that belong in these categories. In any event, we should begin to develop awareness of each and to become skillful as a member of the various groups we need to work with and serve. Actually, our profession is making great strides in this respect.

Teachers learn more about group behavior by working on programs and problem-solving as persons really concerned with results. We can learn much about effective and valuable ways to get things done or improved by trying to facilitate and improve the interaction and performance of the group of people who are responsible or concerned with an objective or a problem. We come to learn many things as we try to work as a fully participating member of a professional or community group. We learn to accept and to respect other people, that is we can learn this, and it is a great discovery to find that it is fun and richly rewarding. We can learn to be conscious of our own behavior as a group member and to improve as a participant and contributor. We can see that any group, by taking conscious stock of itself and of its functioning, can improve its performance. It is comforting to discover that democracy can sharpen up its processes and procedures by this means. A sloppy or careless group can become a more responsible, consistent, or effective one by voluntary effort. Democracy does not have to be "mobocracy."

The teacher's responsibility to cooperate and to work with colleagues, administrators, parents, the PTA, and the community may seem to present a heavy burden. But this is only one side of the picture. The other side is that each of these bears the same responsibility to cooperate and to work with us. Besides, working together comes to have a great fascination for people who have tried it. We remember that the ability to get into things, to participate, is a pretty sound index of good personal adjustment. Successful teachers come to find that some of their greatest satisfactions come from the human relationships and friendships of life. Things and money are important only as means to serve people, the real ends in this business of living. When we learn to like other people, and to enjoy working with them, we find much that is real and satisfying in the process. The best plan is to try it and see. Each person will be a far greater teacher when his own "cooperating" is high and the friendship he gives is surely returned.

Giving Teaching Serious Consideration

The challenge for many youth may be found in the ideal of having professionals in our schools. A variety of persons capable of leading the various aspects of the educational growth and development of America's children are imperatively needed. A report to the parents of America puts it concisely:

There is the attractive, quickly sympathetic, alert young teacher who is always surrounded by a group of pupils who are coming back for the special response and help that the teacher is sure to give. There is the older teacher, rich in understanding and skill, to whom pupils and parents alike constantly go for counsel and information. There is the scholar-citizen who combines the best of general education and pedagogical skill with the whole-hearted devotion to the building of a better society—in local community, state, nation, and the world. There will be more and more teachers . . . of these truly professional types as the pub-

lic provides conditions under which greatness of spirit and service can develop.[9]

When the typical school is in the capable hands of professionals backed and supported by alert, interested parents, public education in these United States will be making its full contribution to the well-being of all the people and to the future of this fabulous nation.

TEACHER CRISIS AND OPPORTUNITY

The American people have become used to the term "crisis" in education since 1940. During the Second World War and since, there have been shortages in buildings, classrooms, many equipment

[9] Willard E. Givens, *Our Children*, Annual Report of the Profession to the Public (Washington: NEA, 1946), p. 14. Used with permission.

items, tax money for public schools, and, especially, *teachers*. The last is the most important shortage and it has continued so long that people probably consider it chronic, a condition to be endured.

The loss of teachers during the war, the increasing enrollments due to higher birth rates, the lag in improvement of teachers' salaries, continued demand for professional personnel in industry, on top of the normal annual loss of teachers, all have contributed to the prolonged teacher shortage.

The practice of using teachers without full qualifications on an emergency basis gained headway during the war. After the war the practice continued, but the number dropped off for a time. By the mid-Fifties, the number had climbed again and reached above the 90,000 mark, where it has remained well into the Sixties. It is clear that the problems of finding and preparing enough capable teachers for the vastly increased school populations of this nation have not yet been solved. What had been considered to be a wartime emergency condition has continued along with the national debt, the cold war, and inflation.

Many studies of the supply and demand of teachers have been made since World War II. The National Commission on Teacher Education and Professional Standards reports annual studies of this subject. The findings of the 1962 report included three significant facts: (a) there is no sign of relief in sight in the teacher shortage; (b) there continues to be an imbalance in the division of the new supply between elementary and high school; and (c) there is some prospect of an improved supply of teachers in the fields of gravest high school shortage.[10] There are in service over 876,000 elementary and 578,000 high school teachers, a ratio of 8 to 5. The prospective new supply of teachers from the graduating classes shows a ratio of 5 for elementary to 8 for high school teaching.

Estimates of the number of new teachers needed during the Sixties run well above the expected number of graduates who will enter teaching. In 1959 total estimates for school years from 1960–61 through 1964–65 were above the 190,000 mark: 192,117 for 1963–64 and 192,541 for 1964–65.[11] It is generally recognized that five kinds of needs for new teachers comprise the "demand": (a) to replace teachers who retire or leave classroom service; (b) to take care of increased enrollment; (c) to relieve overcrowding and part-time sessions; (d) to replace the "emergency" teachers now being used; and (e) to provide instruction and other services that should be added to the school program. Recent studies show that some 40,000 teachers retire each year and

TABLE 12–1. NUMBER OF EMERGENCY TEACHERS EMPLOYED IN PUBLIC SCHOOLS BY SELECTED YEARS 1946–1962*

School Year	Number	School Year	Number
1946–47	108,000	1957–58	94,732
1947–48	101,612	1958–59	94,010
1949–50	93,146	1959–60	93,543
1952–53	69,600	1960–61	96,799
1953–54	78,850	1961–62	91,522
1954–55	80,674	1962–63	91,556
1956–57	86,616		

*Sources: *Teachers for Tomorrow* and NEA Research Reports.

[10] NEA Research Division, *Teacher Supply and Demand in Public Schools, 1962*, Fifteenth Annual Survey, Research Report 1962, R8, April 1962, NEA, p. 5.

[11] See NEA Research Report, *Estimates of School Statistics, 1959* (Washington: NEA, December 1960), p. 5.

that the total annual loss is about 110,000. The studies show that the first two needs are most likely to be met by the "supply" of new college graduates prepared for teaching. In 1962 approximately 73% of the new crop of graduates educated for elementary teaching and 68% of those prepared for high schools actually entered the field.[12] The outlook is for a continued teacher shortage with insufficient new teachers to meet the last three kinds of needs. There continues to be disparity between the numbers of teachers needed in and the supply for the elementary schools. The annual supply of new teachers for the high schools comes closer to meeting the demand. In certain fields of high school teaching the acute shortages have been eased somewhat, in foreign languages and the sciences in particular. It would appear that the publicity the teacher shortages in certain fields has received has had some affect.

This is the teacher shortage, a major aspect of the school "crisis" that has gripped American communities in the postwar period. In many respects, it means crisis for children, headaches for superintendents and school boards who must staff our schools, and danger for the future growth and wellbeing of our democracy. It does spell opportunity for thousands of capable American youth with aptitude to enter the important profession of teaching at a time when needs are so great.

Teaching is always important; in these days of world insecurity and grave problems it is even more significant and necessary. But the facts are clear that our

[12] NEA Research Division, *Teacher Supply and Demand, 1962.* Fifteenth Annual Survey, Research Report, 1962, R8, April 1962, p. 5.

current shortage of teachers amounts to a crisis situation. That crisis offers capable serious-minded youth a great challenge and opportunity. You may do well to consider teaching now; *the time is right.*

GOOD TEACHING IS AN IMPERATIVE

One of the most important considerations about a profession has to do with its significance, whether it makes a difference to people, our national wellbeing, or the future. In this respect the profession of teaching would rate positive answers from most persons you might ask about its importance. We might well reach the logical conclusion that teaching is significant for the reason that education is vitally important. In a modern democracy education makes all the difference; teaching bears the same brand of responsibility and significance. This suggests some essential requirements for the teaching if it is to contribute toward democracy—people—and better living.

This is what is back of our democratic philosophy of education. There is no single, final formulation of this philosophy; thousands of teachers and parents and community leaders ought to be working to develop and express their best ideas about it and its use. A democratic philosophy is a set of working concepts—about people, about how people grow and learn, about the importance of freedom in learning situations, about *responsibilities* and rights, about groups and group processes of thinking and working together, about experimentation and critical thinking, about improvement of experiences and the meanings we derive from these, and about the values (our best meanings) of the human spirit. This is a statement or summary of the elements in a modern point-of-view toward education in a free society. Education in terms of such a philosophy, and teaching from such a viewpoint are imperative needs for the extension and preservation of what we call democracy in today's world, on the edge of space.

The American public in general does not exhibit the same degree of belief in the importance of modern education as our best-informed teachers view it. Shall they then stop and wait? Earlier generations of Americans viewed new developments in medicine no more favorably until professional standards and the performance of better trained doctors convinced them. Capable doctors have, after decades of leadership and action, won true professional status and the responsibilities that go with this position.

Teachers must see clearly for themselves the worth and importance of their work, and they must, by excellent performance and professional action, clearly demonstrate to the public their role in and importance to democratic society. This is not to say that there has been no recognition of the true significance and importance of teaching. Great discerning leaders and some great teachers have seen this clearly and expressed it in convincing fashion. We can find excellent illustrative statements by great thinkers, influential professional groups, presidents, popular stars, some top-notch teachers, and from a variety of tributes to teachers and good teaching. We can find many challenging expressions of faith in and concern about our democratic way of life that show the imperative role of great teaching. Consider this view by a great public educator and leader:

The American people, led by our profession of teaching, seriously need to rebuild a faith in and better understanding of democracy itself. Belief in ourselves and respect for others must be preserved. The primary values on which our nation was founded, along with the process by which these values may be achieved, must again occupy the thoughts and minds of citizens everywhere and dominate their acts. Among the most basic of all is the concept that ours is an evolving, dynamic society which permits the discovery of new values and an understanding of and devotion to these concepts.[13]

Select representative views from a variety of sources and "sum up" the evidence to answer the question implied at the start of this study.

It is interesting to check upon the findings of public opinion polls for the views of the general public upon teaching and its importance. The celebrated Roper Poll for *Life* magazine revealed greater respect for teaching than many expected to find. The sample population questioned ranked occupations in order of importance to the community as follows: teachers, 31.3%; clergymen, 27.1%; public officials, 19.1%; merchants, 12.8%, and lawyers, 9.7%. Today's teachers were rated superior in training and capabilities to those of twenty years ago by two-thirds of the poll.[14]

Another way to approach this question might be to consider the kind of society that we want and what can be

[13] Finis E. Engleman, "Teaching: A First Line of Defense," in *Report of Palo Alto Conference* (Washington, D.C.: NEA, National Commission on Teacher Education and Professional Standards, 1951), p. 7. Used with permission.
[14] NEA Research Division, *Public Opinion Polls on American Education* (Washington: NEA, May 1958).

provided for the young in that desired society. The overwhelming evidence that most of us desire to maintain our democratic way of life seems unmistakable. Most of us probably believe the best way to maintain it is to work continuously for its extension and improvement. Since democratic society gets things done by the people through proposal—discussion—decision—action, it follows that a high level of education is necessary. Most of our great leaders have seen this clearly and have pointed out the need for popular enlightenment through education and unfettered channels of communication. If a high level of education is necessary for the maintenance of rational society at any time, it becomes even more basic in times of crisis and unprecedented problems. Thus, both the nature of our society and the temper of our times appear to indicate a basic role for popular education.

Most Americans would agree upon some basics which are the right of every child. Some of the White House Conferences have framed highly valuable statements. Think about some of the most basic rights which should be served in our society. These would probably include: (1) *a good home*—with affection, care and guidance, security, and early learnings; (2) *a wholesome community*—safe, healthful, stimulating, cultural opportunities, and further learning; (3) *an excellent school*—which offers optimum growth in terms of his capacities and opportunity to adjust to life responsibilities; (4) *adequate economic opportunities*—the chance to earn a decent living and to make his contribution to the economic strength of our society; and (5) *responsible citizenship*—which develops through chances to practice democratic ways as he learns both duties and privileges of adult citizenship. When you think of all that these mean in terms of informed, responsible parents, community leaders, business men, workers, public officials, leaders and *teachers*, you begin to realize the strategic importance of teaching.

Let's each draw his own conclusions

The important judge of the question discussed in this chapter is the reader. Each has had to investigate for himself, to gather the evidence, think it through and make his own judgment. Each and everyone can check for himself all that has been suggested by doing some further reading, by conferences with experienced teachers, by and contacts with public-spirited citizens.

It is too much to hope that we will find a unanimity of opinion. We will find much indifference and ignorance on the part of many persons and traces of cynicism and bitterness among disillusioned teachers. We would find the same attitude toward and within any other profession. Perhaps that is really a good thing; it takes all kinds of work and workers to make a world. On the other hand, we believe that we will find a high regard for teaching on the part of the top-notch leaders in most fields of work. Finally, we may discover that the best teachers generally have a sincere confident faith in the importance and worth of the social role they are performing. Our conclusions should be our own, but you will find abundant support for the position that teaching is as important a job as any intelligent, idealistic youth could hope to find. *The task is imperative.*

TEACHING RETURNS
ARE GRATIFYING

We have considered whether this is a good time to be interested in teaching and have thought of some basic questions to answer as we follow up that incipient interest. Among the most important matters to be considered about teaching (or any other field of work and service for that matter) is that of the rewards and satisfactions that may be expected. We are on the right track when we start after this big question; it is one that deserves a high priority in our thinking and study.

Let us begin by looking at all angles. Capable people derive various satisfactions and rewards from their work. Pay is important, up to a certain point, but there are other fundamental questions to be considered about a profession. Is it an interesting kind of work? What satisfactions does it bring? Can one keep alert and active in it? Are there "intangible" rewards that gratify and please one who makes a career of the profession? To these and similar questions teaching offers answers which will impress some youth very much and others not at all. The same is true for each of the other important professions. There is simply not one uniform answer to such questions which would be acceptable to everyone. The answer lies in the person. All have read many statements by people who believe that teaching is a great profession. Many of them stated that teaching offered many satisfactions aside from material things. If one is the kind of person to whom these statements about teaching seem important, well and good. If not, that probably means that one should look elsewhere for one's future. In other words, some persons are able to see the rewards and satisfactions of teaching as an enduring basis for a worthwhile life. Others are not impressed because the material advantages offered by teaching are not impressive. For that reason we may wish to look carefully at both the advantages and disadvantages of teaching before we try to decide how the profession stacks up in our own estimation.

We should also try to understand what some of the best teachers and greatest persons derive from teaching. This can help us to discern and get a better evaluation of some of the factors. All of this can help us to a better idea about our own purposes, interests, and values. Maybe there are some big intangibles we need to give more consideration. Anyway, we must give this a good try. It will help us to get our purposes and directions straight.

Solid satisfaction and rewards

Teaching as a way to live is exceptional in many respects. Like other professional fields of service it offers both tangible and intangible satisfactions and rewards. In tangible rewards, those from the work of teaching are not impressive when compared with the peak returns from many business enterprises, industrial concerns, certain skilled occupations and high prestige professions such as medicine. Even here may be found wide variations and discrepancies among the earnings of persons in professional and business fields that do not get the headlines. It should be noted that the tangible rewards of teaching, although lesser than for certain fields, are relatively uniform, stable, and dependable. The real case for the satisfactions and significant outcomes of teaching is not to be made in terms of job security, kinds of leave, retirement, tenure, vacations, and the like although these are relatively good. Teaching has its good points in those respects if we are not completely taken in by quantitative measures. There are more significant and lasting values in the form of intangibles that have much to do with the life of excellence.

What we and our values are will have much to do with our evalution of teaching as a way to make a life. If one is strongly concerned about the externals—the status symbols in the community—one should look rather skeptically at the teacher's way of life. It can hardly mean big cars, winters in Florida or California, mink coats, country club atmosphere, house servants, and man-about-town contacts. In good time it can come to mean modest, increasingly comfortable but plain living, interesting challenges, civic and other activities, and fine friendships. One should see that it is a matter of getting all the big, little, and in-between factors and considerations identified and then evaluated in terms of one's approach to life—one's goals, one's motives, one's needs and interests, and one's values. Only then can the judgment be valid *by* and *for* that person.

Beyond these considerations are the biggest and most important concerns and values that life can bring. We cannot often weigh and measure them fully but they do count in the lives of fine, highly intelligent and perceptive people. We should let these reminders and suggestions have a place in our own thinking as we consider the best returns from teaching.

One of the simplest ways to get some of these before us is to call upon some of the "master spirits" of the human race for samples of their views and values. Two

or three selected expressions may illustrate what we can find in this vein.

A fitting tribute to teachers by a great public figure and friend of public schools who acknowledged her gratitude in eloquent fashion is:

> On graduation night as I looked at the row of solemn teachers and wondered if they realized the potential power of their influence to shape a life, to change a destiny, to free a world, I wished I could help them to recognize their power and to encourage them to use it.[15]

A great teacher and former dean of a college of education, speaking from a long career that began in a one-room school in 1903 said:

> Teachers find satisfaction in their work for the simple reason that the pupils, the parents, and the general public appreciate good teachers and good teaching. Yes, teaching is fun! The satisfaction that comes from work well done, from being able to use one's leisure time pleasantly and helpfully, from the delightful associations with stimulating people and from being able to help mold young people into desirable citizens in a democracy—all these make teaching fun. Few professions offer more challenging opportunities for pleasant work and happy rewards than teaching.[16]

What top-notch teachers think

Teachers have provided many voluntary statements about their chosen field of work and their reactions to its challenge. One class in education made a survey of the columns of two professional journals for a few months to collect material of

[15] Billie Davis, "I Was A Hobo Kid," in *The Saturday Evening Post*, **CCXXV**, No. 24 (December 13, 1952), p. 108. Used with permission.

[16] Statement by the late Dean William S. Taylor, University of Kentucky, to the author, March 13, 1946.

this kind. An average of nine articles per issue testified to the strong sense of satisfaction derived from their chosen profession by many thoughtful teachers. We can find many other reminders of the big things that make a rich life as other teachers have interpreted their experiences. Numerous articles and books have appeared on this subject.[17]

It is not expected that any intelligent young person should settle all the motivations and purposes of living in his early years, leaving only the implementation and follow up to occupy the remainder of his experiences. Ideally, life should continue to include and involve all the purposing, evaluating experiences, and the revising of purposes and means that is possible for a sensitive, responsible, and growing person. This should go on as we live and teach, but it might well begin now.

Effects of teaching upon teachers

Another approach to the desirability or attractiveness of teaching as a career is the effect it has upon teachers after several years of experience. Some people get the impression that teaching tends to ruin one's disposition; that it makes cranky old maids out of comely young ladies who enter hopefully upon the task. Doubtless there are some cranky, frustrated, disillusioned persons in the field of teaching, but no more than in other fields. The notion that teachers are odd, cranky, ill-tempered old maids is nothing more than a stereotype. Neither were Ichabod Crane and Mr. Chips any more typical of teaching than was Scrooge of the business man or Shylock of his ethnic group. The best way to check up on this is to investigate for oneself.

Some reputable studies have been made of this problem. One of the most useful studies was reported in 1947 by Hartman. The vast majority of 110 experienced teachers who cooperated in this study were convinced that whatever personality changes had occurred in themselves as a result of their work were preponderantly beneficial. In brief, they believed that teaching has made them better human beings. Here are sample results:

> 5 out of 8 believed they had grown more cheerful;
>
> 5 out of 6 believed they had become kinder, more tolerant, and democratic;
>
> 6 out of 10 believed they had become more diligent, original, and had gained more insight in public affairs;
>
> 1 out of 2 believed they had become more convinced of the worth of education and their jobs in teaching.[18]

So far as people in teaching are able to detect and to report changes in their own personal qualities, there is evidence that teaching may strengthen agreeable characteristics and weaken unpleasing ones. That is true for the great majority of teachers. In only four out of twenty-six traits were there any considerable percentage of teachers who stated that they were uncertain as to whether changes had occurred or not.

---

[17] See for example, Calvin O. Davis, "The Rewards of Teaching," *School and Society*, **L**, No. 25 (1939), pp. 691–694 for a good discussion. See also an anthology of selected articles and statements on teaching, D. Louise Sharp, *Why Teach?* (New York: Holt, Rinehart & Winston, 1957).

[18] George W. Hartman, "Effects of Teaching Upon Teachers," in *Phi Delta Kappan*, **XXIX** (December 1947), pp. 178–182.

Another bit of evidence may be found in the report of a study of the Educational Dynamics Committee of the Metropolitan School Study Council. This research found that fifty-nine per cent of the teachers questioned stated that they would again choose teaching if they had the opportunity to select their life's work now. Over thirty per cent of the teachers felt that the satisfaction of working with children was the strongest reason for entering the profession. The largest number of complaints referred to inadequate salaries.[19]

Other corroborating evidence comes from studies of the polls that sample opinion of the general public which indicates that many well-educated parents would encourage their own child to teach.

Why students choose teaching

Leaders in education and the thinking public hope for a great increase in the number of young people who choose to prepare for teaching. Some people can't understand why anyone would select teaching as a career. They say it isn't *glamorous* like the movies, not *romantic* like the work of an airline stewardess, not *exciting* like aviation, not *creative* like the work of a composer or a painter, and certainly not as *well paid* as the medical profession. Others have been so unkind as to say that teaching is for those who cannot do or achieve. In view of these popular reactions to teaching there must be some compelling reasons why intelligent, able young men and women are interested in becoming teachers. There have been a number of studies that disclose something of the motivation of youth who choose

teaching. An illustration from teaching experience of a university professor will indicate students' views and understandings of the choice they had made. The following list is derived from the written responses of 207 students in the introductory course in education of a state university over a two-year period.[20] Teaching looked satisfying and attractive to these students for a variety of reasons. The total number of reasons listed was forty-nine but this included some possible duplications. The most frequently listed reasons were as follows:

		No. Students Mentioning
a.	Teaching is important work	106
b.	Interest in and liking for children	92
c.	Teaching is interesting work	80
d.	Teaching offers great personal satisfaction	80
e.	Teaching offers opportunity for advancement	75
f.	Teaching keeps you learning and growing	71
g.	Teachers pay is adequate or improving	70
h.	Teaching offers relative security	64
i.	Teaching is an opportunity to help others	50
j.	Teaching affords much leisure time	49
k.	Teaching offers favored status and respect	48
l.	Teaching offers opportunity to serve democracy	45
m.	I enjoy working with people	43
n.	Conditions affecting teaching are favorable	36
o.	I like the subject I will teach	31

No conclusion can be drawn from so small a sample but the findings do suggest

[19] For this data see *Bulletin of the National Association of Secondary School Principals,* **XXXIII** (March 1948), pp. 169–175, 260–261.

[20] E. F. Hartford, "Why Two Hundred Chose Teaching," *Phi Delta Kappan,* **XXX** (December 1948), pp. 126–127.

that a function of the introductory course in education should be to bring out clearly good and sufficient reasons for choice of teaching as a career.

Many college youth will share something of the view of a young teacher, one who had gained teaching experience, to determine how his reasons for choice of teaching seemed to stand up after a year's work. Consider this frank and sincere statement:

I Chose Teaching

I chose teaching as a profession, a lifetime career, because I want to make a contribution to the development of society and the perpetuation of freedom and democracy. I believe that as the world is taught so life will become. I believe that education can be the greatest force for good known to civilized man. I want to lend my influence and my talents to making just a little less ignorance and a little more understanding. I want to do all I can to help develop happy, competent, well-adjusted young men and women who love a little more and hate a little less.[21]

EXPERIENCE IS THE BEST TEACHER

The foregoing lists offer some help but they provide no substitute for the one best teacher each will have—his own experience. Since that will not be available until you have taught for a time you may be able to draw upon the real experiences and reflections of successful teachers. Lists put down on paper are impersonal and academic so we should supplement what we have selected here by arranging some interviews with the ablest and best teachers we know. We may find from

[21] By a young teacher from South Dakota, quoted in *NEA Journal*, **XXXV**, No. 7 (October 1946), p. 4. Used with permission.

their testimony evidence of the satisfactions that good successful teachers derive from their work. We should observe all we can of their work from time to time, and be on the lookout for the gratifying returns and rewards which they receive from teaching.

We should find that there are many teachers who would not trade jobs with anyone although they probably make less fuss about it than do a few disappointed and cynical persons who have not achieved success in the profession. Some of them will show that there are more or less intangible feelings and satisfactions that come from working with other people and learners in particular. The importance and significance of the teacher's work in our world today and the need for better education as a means of solving some of our problems will doubtless be named. One view which will be suggested is that a teacher (or anyone else for that matter) gets from his work about what he puts into it. That's a point worth keeping in mind as we go along in life.

After we have both sides of the ledger filled out, you will be in a much better position to evaluate and make up your mind about our basic question. Certainly we shall wish to avoid the all too common practice of comparing the *disadvantages* of teaching with the *advantages* of some other profession. All will readily recognize that the only fair way is to compare advantages with advantages and disadvantages with disadvantages. After we have carefully analyzed the evidence and evaluated the situation, we can find our own answer about the attractiveness of teaching in terms of personal satisfactions and rewards. This will shortly become your major concern.

Selected Bibliography

Alexander, William M. *Are You a Good Teacher?* New York: Holt, Rinehart & Winston, Inc., 1960.

Association for Supervision and Curriculum Development, National Education Association, "The Teacher's Role in Educational Leadership," *Educational Leadership,* **XIV** (December 1956).

————. *Toward Better Teaching,* 1949 Yearbook. Washington, D.C.: The Association, 1949.

Barnes, Melvin. "More Time to Teach," *Atlantic Monthly,* **CCVI,** No. 5 (November 1960), pp. 128–131.

Beecher, Dwight E. *The Teaching Evaluation Record.* Buffalo: Educators Publishing Company, 1956.

Brembeck, Cole S. *The Discovery of Teaching.* Englewood Cliffs, N.J.: Prentice-Hall, 1962, pp. 3–37, 57–105.

Caldwell, Sarah, "Teaching is Hard Work," *Atlantic Monthly,* **CXCV,** No. 5 (November 1954).

Chase, Francis S. "Teaching in the Sixties," *Tomorrow's Teaching.* Report of a symposium sponsored by the Frontiers of Science Foundation of Oklahoma, Ind., 1962, pp. 10–15. Reprinted in *Education Digest,* **XXVIII,** No. 3 (November 1962), pp. 5–7.

Education Department, *Our Teachers, Their Importance to Our Children and Our Community.* New York: National Association of Manufacturers, 1958.

Elsbree, W. S. and Reutter, E. Edmund, Jr. *Staff Personnel in the Public Schools.* Englewood Cliffs, N. J.: Prentice-Hall, Inc., 1954.

Filbin, Robert L. and Vogel, Stefan. *So You're Going to be a Teacher.* Great Neck: Barron's Educational Series, Inc., 1962.

Franseth, Jane. *Supervision in Rural School,* Bulletin 1955, No. 11, U. S. Department of Health, Education, and Welfare, Office of Education. Washington: United States Government Printing Office, 1955.

Graham, Grace. *The Public School in the American Community.* New York: Harper & Row, 1963. See Chapter 14.

Handlin, Oscar. "The Crisis in Teaching," *Atlantic Monthly,* 198:33–37 (September 1956).

Hanson, Earl H. "What Is a School Superintendent?" *Saturday Evening Post* (April 8, 1961).

Hill, Henry H. "Wanted: Professional Teachers," *Atlantic Monthly,* **CCV,** No. 5 (May 1960).

Jenkins, Gladys Gardner. *Helping Children Reach Their Potential.* Chicago: Scott, Foresman & Company, 1961.

Kearney, Nolan. *A Teacher's Professional Guide.* Englewood Cliffs, N. J.: Prentice-Hall, Inc., 1958.

Kinney, Lucien B. *Measure of a Good Teacher.* San Francisco: California Teachers Association, 1953.

Muuss, Rolf E. *First-Aid for Classroom Discipline Problems.* New York: Holt, Rinehart & Winston, Inc., 1962.

Peters, Herman J., *et al. Introduction to Teaching.* New York: The Macmillan Co., 1963.

Reed, Donna. "What Greater Service?" *NEA Journal,* **LII,** No. 1 (January 1963), p. 29.

Riccio, Anthony C. and Cyphert, Frederick R. *Teaching in America*. Columbus: Charles E. Merrill Books, pp. 171–230.

Sharp, D. Louise. *Why Teach?* New York: Holt, Rinehart & Winston, 1957.

Sheviakov, G. V. and Redl, F. *Discipline for Today's Children and Youth*. Washington: Association for Supervision and Curriculum Development, NEA, 1956.

Smiley, Marjorie B. and Diekhoff, John S. *Prologue to Teaching*. New York: Oxford University Press, 1959, pp. 3–83.

Spaulding, William E. *How Shall We Judge Them?* Boston: Houghton Mifflin Co., 1961.

The Ford Foundation, *Time, Talent, and Teachers*. New York: The Foundation, 1960.

The Fund for the Advancement of Education, *Teachers for Tomorrow*. New York: The Ford Foundation, 1955.

Wynn, Richard. *Careers in Education*. New York: The McGraw-Hill Book Co., Inc., 1960, pp. 106–186.

Vander Werf, Lester S. *How to Evaluate Teachers and Teaching*. New York: Holt, Rinehart & Winston, Inc., 1958.

Aids for Part IV

AUDIO-VISUAL MATERIALS

FILMS

A Day in the Life of a Five-Year-Old, Metropolitan School Study Council (20 min., sound). Title is descriptive. [10]

Before They Are Six (22 min., sound). [10]

By Experience I Learn (25 min., sound). [10]

Children's Emotions, McGraw-Hill (22 min.). [10, 11]

Children Learning by Experience, British Information Service. [10, 12]

Fight for Better Schools, March of Time (20 min., b & w). Story of citizens' fight to regain control from political machine and for improvements. [11]

Human Growth, Brown (15 min., color). [10]

Individual Differences, McGraw-Hill (22 min.). [10]

Learning to Understand Children, Part I (21 min., sound). [11, 12]. Part II (23 min., sound). (From the McGraw-Hill series of text films.) [11, 12]

Life with Baby, March of Time (18 min., sound). [10, 11]

Parents Are People, Too, McGraw-Hill (15 min., b & w). Relationships with parents essential to mental health of pupils and to solve problems. [11]

Preface to Life, United World Films (28 min., sound). [11]

Principles of Development, McGraw-Hill (17 min., b & w). Outlines the fundamentals of growth. [11, 12]

School and the Teenager, University of Michigan (30 min., b & w). Relationship of the teenager to the school. [10]

Social Development, McGraw-Hill (16 min., sound). [10, 11, 12]

Teachers at Work (22 min., sound). Presents several classrooms and show work of elementary and secondary school teachers. [12]

Teenagers As They Are, University of Michigan (30 min., b & w). Three-way discussion of teenagers and their problems in home, school, and community life. [11, 12]

The Elementary Teacher as a Guide (20 min., sound). Two noted authorities, Professors Bode and Zirbes, use classroom situations to show role of the elementary teachers problems in home, school, and community. [11, 12]

This Is Robert, New York University (75 min., sound). A study of growth in a preschool child. [11]

Understanding Children's Play, Caroline Zachary Institute (11 min.). [12]

You and Your Child (20 min., sound). [11]

You and Your Family, Association Films (1 reel, sound). Useful for students of adolescent behavior. [10, 11]

You and Your Friends, Association Films (1 reel, sound). Useful for students of adolescent behavior. [10, 11, 12]

Your Children and You, British Information Service (30 min., sound). Excellent for young parents. [10, 11, 12]

Two groups of films:

A. *Adolescent Development,* McGraw-Hill (15–20 min. each, sound). Five titles: *The Meaning of Adolescence, Physical Aspects of Puberty, Age of Turmoil, Social-Sex Attitudes in Adolescence, Meeting the Needs of Adolescents.* These are useful films frequently used in later courses in psychology and human growth and development. [10]

B. *Child Development,* Encyclopaedia Britannica Films (12–11 min. each). Ten titles available; see especially: *Behavior Patterns at One Year, Growth of Infant Behavior, Life Begins, Learning and Growth.* [10]

These are useful films which are frequently used in later courses in psychology and human growth and development.

FILMSTRIPS

Your Child and College, NEA (20 min.). Answers many questions of pupils about college. [11]

Your Child's Intelligence, NEA (20 min.). [10, 11]

RECORDINGS

A Forward Look for the Teaching Profession, Educational Recording Services (30 min., 33⅓ rpm. microgroove). Comparison of teaching with other professions, explains professional standards and goals. [12]

QUESTIONS FOR DISCUSSION

1. Why should teachers study and understand children in order to facilitate their learning? Be explicit.
2. Why is it that some teachers who pass difficult courses in human growth and development and educational psychology are not able to promote the wholesome growth of pupils?
3. What is meant by the phrase: "The Whole Child"? Explain.
4. How well do parents and teachers "communicate" when they talk? Explain.
5. What do teachers need to know about the children they work with?
6. What happens to your conception of discipline as you learn more about children?

7. Have your ideas about examinations, report cards, and promotions been changed by your study of children and parents?
8. What illustrations of teaching procedures that definitely showed the teacher's knowledge of children can you describe?
9. Whose responsibility is it to evaluate pupil growth and progress? Explain.
10. What is your understanding of "guidance"? What is its purpose?
11. Should teachers undertake those responsibilities which parents have not met in helping their children? Why?
12. How much effort of the PTA should go to raise money for school equipment and instructional materials?
13. How much PTA work should teachers be expected to do?
14. How can the new teacher determine the social activities in which she should engage in the community?
15. Can one be a good teacher without deep and sincere regard for people? Can this be learned?
16. Is there actually an "average" pupil? Explain your view.
17. What is your evaluation of the "study guides" available from certain magazines for parent groups?
18. What kinds of records should you have as aids to understanding and helping children to grow and learn best?
19. What can one learn about other persons by trying to better understand himself?
20. What is meant by "individual differences"?
21. What do you believe about the uniqueness of individuals?
22. Who should have access to pupils' cumulative file of records and information?
23. What should be the basis of the marking system?
24. What should teachers report to parents? Why?
25. What are the methods used to report to parents? What are the strengths and weaknesses of each?
26. Should public funds be used for adult education? Why?
27. Should men and women teachers teach the same grades and receive equal pay? Explain.
28. What are the most important returns that persons derive from their work? How do these apply to teachers?
29. How are the different fields of work in education regarded today? Explain.
30. What fields of educational service hold some interest for you now? Can you tell why?

IDEAS FOR INDIVIDUAL STUDY

1. Plan and participate in a series of trips to local schools, day nurseries, playgrounds, and other suitable places to observe children at play and at work. Develop systematic ways to organize notes and other information for study and discussion.
2. Plan and complete some kind of an individual project which will provide you close contact with children. You might volunteer to tell stories one afternoon per week at a branch library, help on a playground, work at a settlement house, assist a den mother with Cub Scouts, become an aide in a day nursery or a nursery school or do some baby-sitting. Keep a "log."
3. Make a report upon one of the special references on child growth and development for this step. Keep notes and questions.
4. Visit any convenient place to study the products of manufacturers that supply "educational playthings" for children.

5. Make a brief study of the magazines available for parents and the features or services they provide. See, for example, *Parents' Magazine* for October 1950.
6. Do a survey of helpful magazines for children.
7. Keep a list of important new terms that you learn in connection with human growth and development. Keep these on cards and file alphabetically until your study is finished. Enter in your notes.
8. Do a brief survey among "baby-sitters" in your neighborhood to find what appears to help them to be successful. Ask what they have learned about children. How do they find out what they need to know about their charges?
9. Review a recent volume of an education journal to find what is presented on human growth and development, parent-teacher relations, or human relations in general. Keep notes for report of "highlights" to class.
10. Read and report upon one reference to some aspect of human growth and development or some age group of children that interests you.
11. Make a special study of "sociometries" as used by teachers to study class groups. Prepare a sample "sociogram" and explain it to the class.
12. Choose, read, and report upon a reference to school problems in a metropolitan center.
13. Participate in a group discussion of "The Role(s) of the Teacher." In other words, discuss the full scope of the teachers' responsibilities.
14. Investigate the history of the PTA movement and make a brief report using graphic materials.
15. Study the origin and programs of the public adult education movement in your state and make a report.
16. How has the teacher's place in the community changed in recent years?
17. How should one prepare to decide upon his field of service in education? Explain.
18. What are the best fields of opportunity in American education? What is the basis for your opinions?
19. Study the criteria for determining professional fields of work. What are the characteristics of a profession? Do you consider teaching a profession? Why?
20. Make a list of further questions to be followed up in the course on "Human Growth and Development" to be taken next year. Discuss with the instructor.

SUGGESTIONS FOR GROUP WORK

1. Help your group to arrange for talks or interviews with specialists in your college community upon various aspects of human growth and development. For example, a pediatrician, a public health nurse, a clinical psychologist or psychiatrist, a guidance counsellor, a psychometrician, a top-notch nursery school teacher, and a competent parent could be included. Keep notes upon the questions and discussions.
2. Help your group to select and use a number of the available films upon child growth and development listed for this unit. Help plan the showing; keep notes of the discussion.
3. Collect useful catalogs (such as one on "creative playthings") and magazines with ideas for parents for the use of education classes and parent groups in your college and in the neighboring community.
4. Attend any available exhibits of furniture and equipment designed for children's play and schoolroom use.

5. Help in a committee assignment to select helpful recent magazine articles on content related to this unit and order reprints for the class.

6. Arrange with your instructor to exhibit testing materials on "Human Growth and Development" at the conclusion of your study.

7. Prepare a group discussion to bring out examples of how "perceptions" of reality by different people differ. Discuss what this means for parents and teachers.

8. Make a survey of several books about human growth and development find what "needs" common to people they present and report to class.

9. Participate in "role-playing" to show what the various "professionals" of a given school system do. Arrange a "committee" meeting to discuss "school dropouts," include administrators, teachers of different fields, supervisors, guidance counsellors, visiting teachers, director of pupil personnel, psychologist, and research director, etc.

10. Work as a committee member to develop some graphic materials to illustrate child growth and development at various stages for an exhibit to the class.

11. Collect and exhibit materials showing the public adult education program and offerings in your state.

12. Participate in a panel discussion of the "responsibilities" of parents and of teachers for the educational program and wellbeing of the child. Keep notes.

13. Collect report cards and other forms of reporting to parents from various school systems and prepare a discussion and exhibit for the class.

14. Participate in a group discussion of "What I have recently learned about my parents (i.e., since leaving home for college?)."

15. Attend a PTA meeting with a group to observe the roles of participants. Discuss the teacher's part in PTA work in a class session.

16. Take part in an experiment in role playing to show how teachers might handle problems raised by parents of children in the school. Plan this with the instructor for presentation before the class. Episodes might include: a displeased parent calls upon the teacher to protest about Johnny's report for last month; the teacher calls upon a child's parents that are not interested in school; the teacher is stopped on the street and asked how to discipline a child, etc.

17. Participate in a panel discussion of the topic "What We Have Learned About Human Growth and Development."

18. Invite a PTA official to address the class upon the purposes and program of the PTA movement. Keep notes.

19. Participate in a committee study of the needs for teachers and other school personnel in various fields and levels in your state and report to class.

20. Participate in arranging interviews with some outstanding teachers to get their ideas about the most valued satisfactions of their work.

"If ever there was a cause,
if there ever can be a cause,
worthy to be upheld by all of
toil or sacrifice that the
human heart can endure, it
is the cause of education."
— HORACE MANN

V. PROFESSION

The Cause

of Education

Chapter 13

The Planning

of Teaching

The Teacher Holds the Destiny

I thought if every teacher in every school in America could inspire his pupils with all the power he had, if he could teach them as they had never been taught before to live, to work, to play and to share, if he could put ambition into their brains and hearts, that would be a great way to make a generation of the greatest citizenry America has ever had. All of this had to begin with the little unit. Each teacher had to do his share. Each teacher was responsible for the destiny of America, because the pupils came under his influence. The teacher held the destiny of a great country in his hand as no member of any other organization could hold it. All other professions stemmed from the product of *his* profession.*

Introduction

America needs many capable, devoted teachers. Desperate as that need appears to be, it is imperative that only those who really believe in teaching be educated for the profession. Those who do not see their future vocational choice as teaching should be encouraged to select other fields. No one should enter teaching who does not see it as important work, as interesting work, as satisfying work, and as a chance to get ahead in life. But there are many capable college youth who should think very seriously about choosing teaching as a career. We are not talking about

* Jesse Stuart, in *The Thread That Runs So True* (New York: Scribners, 1949), p. 82.

mediocre students or persons who have no better choice available; America needs youth of better-than-average ability to come into the teaching profession. It is gratifying to be able to say to them that this is a good time to be preparing to teach and that teaching is becoming more attractive as a vocation for capable youth.

Students who are considering teaching for the first time will certainly want to know what teaching is. There is a quick, short answer but it is not easy to understand fully without experience. Teaching means *working with people,* not just *telling* them as teachers once did (and still do in some schools and colleges), but

431

working together. Teachers, real teachers, do more than teach algebra, or English, or history, or physics, *they teach boys and girls!* And they must *really like boys and girls, really accept people,* if they are to be helpful and effective teachers.

Teaching involves working with people. Teachers must know better than anyone else how to discover and help meet the big and little needs of people. Real teachers see each child as unique, different, and important; they consider people as the most important resource we have. All the books, tools, gadgets, materials, buildings, schedules, courses of study, and subject matter specialties that we have in education exist for the purpose of helping children and adults to grow, develop, and learn. That may sound elementary, but it is not always really understood and remembered.

There are some other ways of looking at teaching that should offer encouragement. Teaching can be *fun.* Many teachers see in it the opportunity to render invaluable *service.* In some communities it is, and in many others teaching may become, a really *desirable way to live,* with adequate pay, the respect of the public, and recognition as tangible rewards. But these depend largely upon the teacher. As Professor George D. Strayer used to say: in the long run teachers are usually paid just about what they make themselves worth to the community. Teaching is *important;* it makes a difference to people and the lives they lead. Effective teaching is *power,* power to change people and society. Conversely, it is power to destroy or inhibit progress and growth if used badly. Teaching is really decisive; it cannot be neglected if our democracy is to be strong and to grow better. The American public is slowly beginning to grasp this understanding. Let's be sure that we, as future teachers and parents, understand and act in the light of that fact.

These are concepts and convictions that one must reach for as one continues to study beyond this first course in education. Now is the appropriate time to go into a careful study of the work of the teacher and of the teaching profession from which one can draw one's own conclusions. Too many people judge teaching by *one* unfavorable point or instance, neglecting the other facts which should be considered. It would be a good idea to make a thorough study of the advantages and disadvantages of teaching before we decide finally for or against it as a career. That's what this unit is all about—the future and teaching.

The material included in this unit has been assembled to provide information concerning some important questions which we may wish to ask as we study teaching as a profession. We considered some basic questions about the profession: the importance or significance of teaching, its satisfactions and rewards in our study of the professionals who serve in the schools. It is time for some further questions on the pay and security factors, the future prospects for teachers, the qualities that make a good teacher, and how one may assess his own aptitudes for teaching.

It is hoped that everyone will find this a helpful and stimulating experience. If one finds that his decision to teach is strengthened, he can go right on to the next step. Assuming that he finds himself well-fitted for the profession the student can give all he has to the task of preparing for the work of a teacher. This orientation experience should be helpful to other students who do not choose teaching. For them and for the work of the teaching profession it is far better that they face the issue squarely now and choose a life career in a field related to their interests and aptitudes. This study can be the means of considering the alternatives open to persons who should find their future in some other calling.

Those who should elect a field of professional service other than teaching should know more about American education, especially the great public school enterprise. Some will serve as school-board members, as P.T.A. officials, even as legislators; all will be taxpayers and voters concerned with public policy. All will need to appreciate what education means to our communities and to our democratic way of life. This course can be helpful in that respect for those who go into other fields of study besides education. Teacher candidates and those who prepare to enter other fields will be better

"appreciators" and cooperators in their future roles as community leaders and participants in public affairs for the experience of studying together.

Those who find their initial interest in teaching confirmed and are ready to go into further study of teaching in a serious way will then be ready to start the second important step. That will be one which will help them to assess their aptitudes and capabilities for the professional life and work of the teacher. *Interest* is one absolutely important prerequisite; *having what it takes is* the second. As we go on we can determine whether these two big questions can be answered affirmatively *by* us, for we are making sure that we have both the interest and the ability. It's too important to be taken lightly or settled quickly. Teaching is for those who believe in it and see in it their future work. Those who should not choose teaching will want their own progeny taught by teachers with both interest and ability.

Consider Some Practical Factors

Some of the most practical questions to raise about teaching have to do with its appeal as a way to make a living. These include salaries, security factors, advantages and disadvantages, and the future prospects.

TEACHER PAY IS IMPROVING

The logical question about the pay for teaching always involves discussions of the profession and life of the teacher. It is time to consider the money angle, which is important to most people. Teach-

ers who have long been underpaid cannot live in genteel poverty or be expected to teach for pure love of their work as Socrates once did in ancient Athens. The pay for teachers has been traditionally inadequate, but many people formerly found that it offered a steppingstone to other fields. Teachers' salaries have risen gradually during recent decades, principally in those states and districts with favored economic status and for those teachers with educational background. Pay for teaching has been notoriously inadequate in those areas least able to support good schools and in communities where schools are dependent upon the vagaries of political changes and fortunes. Modern emphases upon foundation programs for state support have been instrumental in raising teachers' pay in many states.

Since World War II the teacher shortages and crises in school problems have brought the matter of adequate pay for teachers to the attention of parents and the general public. Teachers' salaries have been increased in all states and certain other benefits have likewise been improved. The continuing inflation of prices and increased living costs have prevented expected improvement in the purchasing power of teachers and their families. We shall need to acquire a good background of information about the whole matter of teacher pay and an understanding of present trends if we are to find the answer to the big question.

Teachers' salaries in perspective

A general perspective on teachers' salaries may be gained from the figures for annual average salaries for all instructional personnel in public schools in the continental United States.

Teachers' salaries rose appreciably following the First World War, only to regress during the depths of the depression of the Thirties. The average salary for teachers increased each year after 1912 except during 1931–34. The average did not reach the pre-depression level until 1939–40.

During the Fifties average annual salaries of teachers increased at a rate of approximately 6% per year. This meant an increase of about 76% in current dollars, but only 47% in purchasing power.[1]

[1] NEA Research Division, *Research Bulletin* (April 1958), p. 30.

TABLE 13–1. AVERAGE ANNUAL SALARY OF PUBLIC SCHOOL INSTRUCTIONAL STAFF BY SELECTED YEARS, 1900–1962*

Year Ending	Average Salary
1900	$ 325
1910	485
1918	635
1920	871
1930	1,420
1932	1,417
1934	1,227
1936	1,283
1940	1,441
1944	1,728
1945	1,846
1946	1,995
1948	2,639
1950	3,010
1951	3,126
1952	3,450
1953	3,554
1954	3,825
1955	3,950
1956	4,156
1957	4,350
1958	4,720
1959	4,935
1960	5,174
1961	5,449
1962	5,710
1963	5,940

*Source: NEA Research Division, *Research Report 1959*, R.13.

Like Alice's friend, The Red Queen, teachers' salaries would have had to move twice as fast as possible in order to effect a gain in purchasing power during this period of inflation and increasing costs. In 1939 the average purchasing power of teachers was 11% above that for the average of all employed persons in the United States. In 1952 despite increased teachers' salaries, the averages for teachers and for all employed persons were the same in purchasing power according to 1939 levels. In recent years teachers' salaries have risen to a level 14% above the level of all wage-and-salary workers and have caught up with the average employee in manufacturing for the first time since 1940.[2]

Unusually vigorous efforts have gone into the struggle to obtain better pay for teachers. In many places teachers are doing more to improve conditions and to secure adequate salaries than ever before. But there are some points which we need to remember as we study these figures. An average salary includes all salaries—low, middle, and high—many lower than the figure quoted; many inadequate salaries are masked in an average. The range among the states in salaries for principals and other instructional personnel, who are included, also tends to make the average figure look better. The disparity among average salaries in the states is great; the highest being about double that in the lowest state for the year 1961–62.[3] We must remember that costs have increased so rapidly as to wipe out much of the gain as far as purchasing power is concerned. The teacher's average salary since 1921 has increased about five times in current dollars but only three times in purchasing power.[4] Since 1939, teachers' salaries have been subject to Federal income tax which has absorbed a part of the increases they have received. These considerations make the improvement in teacher pay all the more significant. As a whole, teachers' average salaries are now increasing faster than the cost of living.[5]

Some comparisons among salaries

Recent increases in teacher pay have been encouraging and represent the first appreciable gain in the race against inflation and living costs for some twenty years. Teachers' salaries have moved on a parity with employees in manufacturing but still compare unfavorably with those in technical and professional fields. Civilian federal employees have an approximate 14% salary advantage over teachers. The average salary paid to members of professional occupations in 188 standard metropolitan areas in 1961 was $9,474, which may be compared to $5,926 average salary for teachers in urban districts over 30,000 population.[6] Although comparisons of salaries among personnel in professional and technical fields is difficult it appears that teaching is probably somewhere about the 63% level for the seventeen professions that have been used in previous studies.[7]

The annual Endicott survey of the starting salaries of selected college graduates for 1961–62 indicated that male graduates entering teaching had beginning salaries about $1,000 under those for men recruited by business and industrial companies through college recruitment programs. Further studies indicate appreciable disparity between beginning teachers' salaries and those for certain technical, scientific and engineering fields. Other studies show that the gap tends to widen over periods of five and ten years of employment. It is clear that the classroom teacher starts at a lower salary and that the rate of increase does not equal

[2] NEA Research Division, *Economic Status of Teachers in 1961–62*, Research Report 1962, R–7 (May 1962), p. 5.

[3] *Ibid.*, p. 5.

[4] T. M. Stinnett, *The Profession of Teaching* (Washington: The Center for Applied Research in Education, Inc., 1962), p. 55.

[5] NEA Research Division, *Economic Status of Teachers*, Research Report 1962, R–7 (May 1962), p. 5.

[6] *Ibid.*, p. 5.

[7] *Ibid.*, pp. 14–15. See also Stinnett, *op. cit.*, pp. 56–57.

that for other technical and professional fields as a whole.[8]

Salaries of women teachers show about the same level as for men because of the nearly universal policy in public education of equal pay regardless of sex. This long time policy of the NEA has gained ground in other fields of public employment and to a lesser degree in nonpublic enterprises. The single salary schedule has not gone far enough to equalize earnings between the sexes. Where comparisons are available among women in professional fields, the median salary of elementary teachers was slightly below that of women therapists, dietitians, and librarians, and approximately $1,200 below those of women mathematicians and chemists.[9]

Prospect for teachers' salaries

Studies generally show that teachers' salaries have increased substantially in the past decade, including the first real gain in purchasing power. Teacher pay has moved ahead of certain other occupational groups but is not comparable to that for most professional and technical fields. The progress of recent years and the quickened interest of the general public lends encouragement to the professional organizations and leaders who plead the case for adequate teachers' salaries.

The overall situation with respect to salaries is improving with the universal adoption of a single salary schedule, and with the requirement of the bachelor's degree for teaching at any level now true of nearly all the states. Many states with poorer districts have established "foundation" programs of school support that

provide state tax funds to supplement tax revenues of local school systems that have made a reasonable "effort" but are still unable to maintain an adequate school program. In this way states have sought to equalize the grave disparities among rural and urban schools, and between poorer and richer communities by granting financial aid on a basis designed to promote equalization of educational opportunity for children. We can see how this helps to erase disparities in teacher pay by enabling less favored districts to afford better educated teachers. A major argument for Federal Aid to education is that funds appropriated by Congress to states could be used to further equalize the support of education. This would help to further reduce the glaring disparities in teachers' salaries over the nation.

There are some further aspects of the problem of teacher pay that should be considered. We should analyze what columns and tables of figures mean, especially the significance of *average* (or *mean*), and *median* when referring to salary. There are low, medium, and high salaries included in every average; there are as many above the median as there are below it. This means that there are many thousands of teachers whose salaries are on a respectable level; some communities have teacher salary schedules that run up to $8,000 and $10,000 a year for experienced people. The teacher shortage and the migration of teachers will keep the matter of teachers' salaries on the agenda of school boards and before the parents who want their children to have good teachers with adequate pay.

There are some additional points to consider before one comes to a conclusion concerning the outlook for teachers'

[8] Stinnett, *op. cit.*, p. 56.
[9] *Ibid.*, p. 17.

salaries. Although it is true that teaching does not rank high in comparison with average earnings in other professions, it does not show too unfavorably in the matter of beginning salaries. There is no initial "starving period," such as often faces the beginner in some of the leading professions. Neither does the young teacher face an initial outlay of money for office facilities, equipment, and helpers such as are required for beginners in some professions. The teacher's pay is normally quite stable; one can count upon receiving the monthly pay check regularly. Usually teachers are paid on a monthly basis for 9-10 months, although some school systems follow the practice of paying twice each month. In a large number of cities, teachers receive their salaries over a period of twelve months. Finally, you must remember that the higher average annual earnings of doctors and lawyers represent many lower incomes. One factor in the high income of the top physicians is that they have spent many years in graduate study. Their earnings should be compared with the top pay of university professors.

What all this really means is that we should do a complete study of this matter, get the full picture, compare advantages with advantages, and disadvantages of various fields with those of teaching, in preparation for reaching our own conclusions.

We may observe that the recent experiences of the profession in working for more adequate teaching salaries and to arouse public interest in adequate support for education has had, and is having, beneficial effects upon our educational systems. The general public has shown signs of greater awareness of the primary importance of education and of its role in the growth and strengthening of the national life. It seems to be shaking off its reputed indifference toward the schools. No longer is the teacher taken for granted. Among teachers there are evidences of heightened self-respect and pride in their profession. The NEA has provided strong, vigorous leadership throughout the postwar crisis, and its membership has reached an all-time high during this period. It is fair to say that teachers have achieved significant gains in the face of great odds —gains that will prove hopeful for the future years of American schools.

Teacher Security Provisions Are Favorable

Teachers and those who consider teaching should be concerned about other practical matters of an economic nature besides pay. Conferences with teachers often reveal concern about many practical questions that relate to job security, welfare provisions, fringe benefits, income protection and the like. This turns out to be one of the strong points of teaching as a calling. Get your questions ready and look to the answers.

Teachers raise basic questions

The realistic questions of teachers relate to a half-dozen basic problems of people in all walks of life: Can I count on keeping my job? What will happen if I become ill? What can I look forward to when I am too old to teach? How does one avoid getting into a rut of monotonous routine? All of these matters have been grave problems in the past. The gratifying progress that has been made toward their solution is a tribute to the leadership and efforts of members of the teaching profession aided by some far-seeing conscientious legislators and public officials.

Job security through tenure

The old days of job insecurity for teachers are receding into our history, but the problem was a very real one for teachers. Little wonder that teachers were represented as migrants, moving from year to year, trying to please local trustees and everyone in the district. Summary dismissal by the school board or superintendent was a possibility until recent decades in many states. This is no longer true because of *tenure* policies.

Tenure provisions are now quite generally accepted as a part of educational policy. This has long been advocated by the National Education Association, the various state education associations and the American Federation of Teachers. Various proposals for tenure have been advocated, viz., life tenure, permanent tenure and indefinite tenure. Objections raised to the first two have been noted especially in the matter of professional inertia and lack of incentive on the part of some teachers under these plans. Some form of indefinite tenure now seems to be the most widely accepted. Such a plan provides for a trial period, followed by appointment (continuing contract) for an indefinite period unless removed for cause. Most commonly specified grounds for dismissal are immorality, insubordination, in-competence, and neglect of duty. The intent of tenure laws is to prevent summary dismissal of teachers, to set fair rules to govern necessary dismissals, with notice, statement of charges, and the right to a hearing in such cases. Thus acceptable moral standards and continuing professional growth have become the keys to satisfactory tenure on the part of teachers.

As a general rule, tenure legislation has proved quite effective at times, actually making it extremely difficult to dismiss even partially inefficient teachers. It should be noted that the privilege of tenure imposes an ethical responsibility upon teachers to continue to grow in professional competence and effectiveness.

More than a half century has passed since enactment of the first state tenure law (New Jersey, 1909) and at least forty-four states have attempted some form of legislation upon the subject. Thirty-two states and many large city systems have adopted laws which provide for permanent tenure after a probationary period, usually three years. Four states do not specify a probationary period.[10] In many states tenure provisions vary among the various school districts and systems. Another common plan is to give teachers continuing contracts which mean retention from year to year unless dismissed by board action for cause.

One indication of tenure for teachers may be noted in the gradual increase in average age of teachers in service. The median number of years of service has likewise shown an increase. Teachers have the protection of contracts for a definite period of time without loss of time from layoffs or dismissal.

[10] T. M. Stinnett, *op. cit.,* pp. 49–50.

All states have teacher retirement systems

Retirement is a serious matter for workers in all occupations. It has been a perennial concern of teachers at all levels. The relatively low pay and the lack of opportunity to "save for a rainy day" have required special attention to the problem of pensions or other retirement benefits for elderly teachers. It is good to find that provisions for retirement benefits have been improved greatly in recent decades. Before 1900 several large city systems and a few states had established retirement plans on a voluntary, mutual aid basis. New Jersey set up the first state plan in 1896; others followed until there were twenty-two in 1930. Since then the movement has grown and been improved until all states have adopted some plan for this benefit.[11] In most of the states funds are provided by joint contribution of the teachers and by the state legislature. In thirty-eight states teacher retirement programs have been converted to or related with the Social Security program.

Age of retirement usually varies from 50 to 65, at option of the teacher and with mandatory retirement at 70. Sometimes it is provided that optional retirement may be elected after a specified number of years of service. Provisions for retirement because of disability after a specified length of service are found in most of the plans. Amount of pay under retirement plans varies but it is usually computed from such factors as number of years taught, average salary for the period prior to retirement, and the percentage of salary contributed by the teacher. Most colleges and universities have adopted sys-

[11] T. M. Stinnett, *op. cit.,* pp. 58–59.

tems of retirement for faculty members in connection with the state system or by arrangement with private annuity plans.

Teachers who leave the profession recover their total contribution plus accrued interest. If a teacher dies in service the amount paid in plus interest is payable to the designated beneficiary. Many of the state systems now provide certain other benefits for survivors and other features. It is impossible to describe one typical plan. It is possible to note that the progress made in this phase of teacher security in a period of three decades is remarkable.

Some problems remain, notably that of providing adequate pensions for teachers whose service has been in more than one state. The great need is for a workable universal plan for reciprocity among state retirement systems. Other tough problems have been solved by interstate agreement; the teacher certification agreement for reciprocity is an example.

The overall benefits to teachers from adequate provisions for retirement can hardly be overestimated. Progress in this respect has been heartening and teacher morale has received a substantial boost as a result of these achievements.

Insurance programs are emerging

Added security for teachers has become available in recent years in the form of various types of group insurance. Most large urban school districts make provision for group coverage for hospitalization and other benefits, usually on a shared cost basis. About one-fourth of large urban school districts pay the full cost of insurance for personal liability against damage suits that might arise from pupil injuries. A growing number of districts are establishing programs for insurance protection against hazards of accident, health, hospitalization and surgical benefits, and others.

Professional organizations have sponsored various group insurance programs for teachers in many states as has the National Education Association. In 1961 state education associations provided insurance groups as follows: Income Protection (32); Hospital and Surgical (29); Life (24); Automobile (23); and Liability (16). The National Education Association successfully initiated a voluntary group term-life insurance program in 1961.[12]

The National Association of Retired Teachers has worked upon a program of low-cost health insurance for its members with some success.

Leave policies are increasing

Leaves of Absence are a factor worth considering in thinking about a vocational choice. Teaching shows up favorably in this respect. Provisions for leaves of absence for temporary emergencies, for illness (sick leave) or for rest, and study and travel (sabbatical) are to be found in various forms in many school systems. Legislation providing for certain of these privileges is appearing more frequently in the states. Most school systems readily grant a leave of absence for brief periods to enable teachers to meet emergencies such as personal illness or death in the family and maternity leave. Most school systems grant brief periods of absence for purposes of attendance at major educational conferences and conventions, which are permitted by most state school laws and regulations of boards of education.

Sick leave and disability benefits are two of the most important items affecting

teacher welfare. Few provisions could offer more reassurance and a feeling of security than the knowledge that most illness can be faced without a loss of income. The various states and school systems have different policies on this. Nearly half the states (23) have general or permissive laws or regulations upon this subject. Some provide for accrued leave; if the teacher does not require sick leave in a given year that much time is added to the allowance for the next and so on. Approximately eighty-four per cent of urban systems provide cumulative sick leave; over ninety-five per cent have full pay during sick leave. Others permit from two to four weeks but do not extend it beyond the end of the year. Unfortunately, the privilege under the latter plan sometimes is subject to abuse by teachers. Closely related to the subject of sick leave is the matter of disability benefits for teachers. Nearly all states have some form of legislation on this problem. About two-thirds of urban systems cooperated in some group hospitalization plan.

Sabbatical leave provisions are common in colleges and universities but are now coming into greater use in public school systems. Eighteen states and the District of Columbia have laws authorizing sabbatical leaves.[13] Teachers may be absent with pay each seventh year of service for purposes of exchange, study, rest, research or travel. Sometimes a shorter period of absence is permitted at more frequent intervals or on half-time pay.

All in all the teaching profession has more adequate provisions for necessary leaves of absence than most other professional workers enjoy. More adequate

[12] T. M. Stinnett, *op. cit.,* p. 61.

[13] NEA Research Division, *NEA Research Bulletin,* **XL,** No. 4 (December 1962), p. 118.

policies are being developed in leading school systems and the state legislatures are becoming more favorably disposed toward legislation for this purpose.

Other fringe benefits are found

Other economic benefits for teachers have been provided by certain school districts and professional organizations. Nearly 1200 districts and 200 colleges have credit unions with an aggregate membership of 750,000 teachers. Credit unions are designed (1) to encourage saving and investment by teachers and (2) to provide convenient economical loan service to members when needed.

Homes for retired teachers have been provided by some state education associations (California and Indiana are examples) and by several large city school systems. The National Association of Retired Teachers has developed a colony and recreation center for members in California and Florida respectively. There is growing interest in developments of this kind.

CONSIDER ADVANTAGES OF TEACHING

When old Sir Roger de Coverly was confronted by a debatable issue he used to say, "There's much to be said on both sides." So it is with teaching. Reactions to teaching vary greatly among individuals. Viewing the same set of facts or conditions, some people see teaching as desirable; others will have none of it. It appears to be impossible to prepare an answer to our question which will be acceptable to everyone. You will have to decide for yourself after reviewing all of the pertinent facts and considerations.

Phases of teaching most generally listed as attractive to teachers are job security, chance to work with young people and to help them grow, the respect shown teachers, and the warm appreciation often shown by some pupils or their parents for the helpfulness shown. Some of the more tangible features frequently approved are short hours, long summer vacations, stimulating work with ideas and books, chances of self improvement, comfortable and attractive working environment, and friendly associates. The freedom teachers have to study and experiment, and the pleasures of working with people, especially children, are often deemed important.

The NEA Commission on Teacher Education and Professional Standards presented the following strong points in favor of teaching in one of its early reports:

a. Teaching is full of personal satisfactions and joys;
b. Teaching is a lot of fun. Consider the happy relationships of pupils and teachers in the classroom and laboratories, on the playgrounds, trips, etc.;
c. The teacher's time is relatively flexible—weekends, summer vacation time, etc.;
d. Community respect for the teacher in terms of his contribution;
e. Teaching offers wide opportunities, all types of work and chances for advancement;
f. Teaching is a challenge, a service in a world needing dynamic leadership;
g. The teacher is the real builder of America.[14]

Certain other practical factors are often mentioned in connection with the

[14] *America's Children Deserve Capable Teachers* (Washington: NEA, 1947), p. 7. Used with permission.

advantages of teaching as a profession. It is often stated that the hours of work in teaching are favorable, being likened as "bankers' hours" by wags. This may or may not be true depending upon the teacher. Often the public fails to realize how much time good teachers spend in planning and at homework, how much they contribute to community life, and how much time is spent in cooperation with parents. Some teachers may punch the time clock or belong to the T.G.F.F. Club (Thank God For Friday) but most work overtime. The average number of hours of work by teachers was given as 48 in an NEA study. Average number of hours "on duty" was 32, but the sample of teachers surveyed reported 16 hours of outside work on preparation for teaching.

The matter of long vacations is often mentioned as a favorable aspect of teaching. Vacations are desirable, even necessary, but the long summer months have usually been enjoyed by teachers without pay. The evaluation depends upon one's point of view. There is a growing movement in some systems to undertake twelve months' employment of teachers with provision for about one month's vacation. During the other two months teachers would hold summer classes for children, handle health problems, do research, plan school work, direct playgrounds, or other community activities. This is an emerging practice of great promise and teachers can give it greater impetus by working to justify their worth to the community throughout the entire year.

One interesting means of highlighting the basic characteristics of the teacher and of her work has been suggested by The New York Times. All too often teaching is described in terms that stress the negative, when the need and the opportunity alike suggest that the positive approach should be accentuated. As an illustration, The Times article suggested how the metropolis might set forth the careers open to teachers in its schools through a "want ad" like this:

WANTED

Young men and women to enter attractive profession. . . . Steady, automatic increases. Pleasant associations. Make new friends. Be paid while learning. Three month vacation each year. Retirement pension. Leave of absence every seventh year. Advancement to high executive positions possible.[15]

Professional organizations and school boards might well consider ways to present or express the positive features of teaching to the general public.

Check out the disadvantages

All important decisions have two sides, and the same situation can be viewed from different vantage points. When we study teaching fully and look at the other side, some may want to take some of the above statements and cite instances which indicate that there are disadvantages. Sometimes the same picture has two possible interpretations.[16]

There are some teachers who find teaching monotonous and non-creative; who are interested in paychecks, not service; who do not make enough to live on; who have been fired summarily; who haven't learned a thing for forty years.

[15] Quoted in NEA News, 6, No. 12 (October 17, 1952), p. 4. Used with permission.

[16] See Margaret Wasson, Teaching Is Exciting (Washington: Association for Childhood Education, 1951), pp. 26–28, for a brief illustration of this.

Many of these teachers have naturally turned "sour" on the whole business. What others see as advantages are to them quite the reverse. It is definitely true that lack of tenure, low pay, public criticism and meddling, lack of free time, poor working conditions, and "little Hitler" administrators have often been cited as disadvantages of teaching. No one will deny that these exist. It is believed that they are not nearly as common as formerly. Conditions are better in many school districts which were once exceedingly poor. One benefit from the teacher shortage has been the lessening of community interference in personal lives of teachers. It is not too much to hope that even further improvement will come as teachers improve themselves and as they learn to work together and with their communities for better schools. Teachers, like all other active citizens, must work to improve our society if they are to enjoy better living and improved conditions of work. Few good things come to him who sits and waits and howls about his bad luck! The teacher who takes an active participating role in school, in the community, and in professional activities will find ways to help bring about those improvements that are desired. Yet many young teachers come up with questions about how can one live a normal life as a human being in a goldfish bowl environment of the teachers. That is a problem in some places, but it is not nearly as bad nor as common in recent decades.

In past decades public school teachers were expected to set the example in matters of conformity to the community morals and standards of personal behavior. Anything regarded as sinful or questionable from the standpoint of the influential groups and leaders was not permitted for the teachers. Dancing, playing cards, games, smoking, even "dates" were often taboo in certain communities. Many young teachers were unjustly condemned for nothing worse than being human and desirous of living reasonably normal lives. All told, the lack of freedom was one important cause of teacher turnover. Elsewhere we may read an early example of a rigid harsh contract which was actually used in a school district. But even these ways have changed.

According to all evidence, including some recent careful studies, this aspect of the teacher's life has changed markedly in recent years and for the better. In 1954–55 an extensive study of first year teachers reported that two-thirds felt no restriction upon their personal lives, nearly one-third felt slightly restricted, and only two percent felt seriously restricted in their personal lives.[17] By and large, teachers in small towns, or away from home, and those who were single tended to feel restrictions more than those from larger towns or those in their home communities, or those who were married.

About half of the first-year teachers liked their work about as they expected; over forty percent liked teaching more, and only nine percent liked their work less than they had thought they would.[18] Nine out of ten young beginners found older teachers were friendly to them. Only one in eight were ready to quit or seek other work after that first year of teaching. After that the chances of wishing to quit or change are much less.

[17] NEA Research Bulletin, *First Year Teachers in 1954–55* (Washington: NEA, February 1956).
[18] *Ibid.,* pp. 37–39.

So the matter of disadvantages of teaching also depend upon us, our values, our interpretations and our evaluation. Two members of a group may differ upon a given feature of teaching to a marked degree. And, each could be right, for him or her. It depends upon the person.

Add up the final score

For many persons the answer to teaching is a flat and final negative response because the salaries of teachers appear to be inexcusably low. Sometimes this is the case, but there are other and valid conclusions which can be drawn. Teachers' salaries have shown a definite trend for the better; this will continue *if teachers make their organized efforts count* and if teaching can be made so vital to our society that people recognize that fact. These are two big "ifs," but each of them can be licked. Let no one suppose that doctors, dentists, lawyers, and other professional people have achieved greater than average earnings by sitting and howling about their bad fortune. Not only the Lord, but legislatures and the public help those who try to help themselves.

It is reasonable to assume that pay for teaching will appear more adequate (in purchasing power) if and when the postwar inflationary period ends. What if there is a depression? It may be helpful if we recall the figures for the last experience. Teachers' salaries were retrenched, but not to the point they were after World War I. And, usually, teachers' salaries are steady and certain.

But this is primarily a matter to study, investigate, consider, and decide for oneself. Each person should now have a fairly good general background of facts on this question. Each person should make his own study of the situation in his state and community to supplement the overall picture. One should obtain copies of the salary schedules, leave policies, and retirement plans for the state and its representative school systems to study. School authorities, experienced teachers, and instructors will gladly answer sound questions. We can begin to frame our own answers to the questions about teacher pay and security.

THE FUTURE SPELLS OPPORTUNITY

Prospective teachers are naturally concerned about the future outlook for the teaching profession. This is one question that can be answered definitely and positively. Opportunity for teachers exists in every field and the overall demand promises to remain heavy for the foreseeable future.

The concern about a future in teaching should not obscure another important one, namely the responsibility to make the greatest possible contribution to others and to America's future. Everyone has something important in the way of ability and in aptitude for some big and constructive role in our society. It may be teaching. It is important for a person to recognize that future, for his own happiness and for the welfare of others.

A nation takes out the best insurance it can have by establishing and maintaining a first-rate educational system. It underwrites and provides for its future. This means that education in America must have a great future. It will require fine people, and they must discharge an indispensable vital function. They can have a great future in a great profession in a great society.

The natural concern of would-be teachers about the prospect for teachers

TABLE 13–2. NUMBER AND RATE OF BIRTHS
BY YEARS IN U.S. 1940–1961*

Year	Total	Rate (per 1000) population
1940	2,360,399	17.9
1945	2,375,456	14.5
1950	3,544,149	23.6
1955	4,047,295	24.6
1957	4,254,784	25.0
1958	4,203,812	24.3
1959	4,244,796	24.1
1960	4,257,850	23.7
1961	4,282,000	23.4

*Source: World Almanac, 1963.

is a fair question. One clue to the answer may be to study the birth rate and expected school enrollments for the future.

All studies indicate increasing need for over and above the number needed for normal replacements to the profession. The annual turnover of teachers continues at a rate somewhat above 10%. The phenomenon of "emergency" teachers continues, and additional teachers are needed to relieve overcrowding in certain school systems. Back of all the factors is the project of rising school enrollments based on the rates of births in our expanding population. All projections of school enrollments show this.

One can draw his own conclusion by counting a few years ahead from a given year and estimating what the number of

TABLE 13–3. ESTIMATED ENROLLMENT IN
PUBLIC SCHOOLS 1965-71.

School year ending	Total number
1965	41,484,000
1966	41,888,000
1967	42,514,000
1968	43,148,000
1969	43,840,000
1970	44,497,000
1971	45,223,000

*Source: NEA Research Report, Status and Trend, Vital Statistics, Education, and Public Finance (August 1959), p. 9.

births will mean in terms of beginning enrollments.

Both time and opportunity

The next big question related to this one is also very practical and important to us and our college friends interested in teaching. That next question is: What are the chances of advancement in teaching? Or, is this a good time to get into teaching? There are some rather convincing evidences about these which should be investigated and considered.

At the end of the first postwar decade the picture of *demand* for teachers and of *opportunity* for prospective teachers were even greater in numbers, so great had been the growth of the nation. A comprehensive study concluded that the patterns of recruitment and utilization used in 1955 could not possibly "secure anywhere near enough good teachers for our schools and colleges over the next 15 years."[19] This study matched the best estimates of teachers needed against the prospective supply of qualified teachers in the years ahead. The demand exceeds probable supply so widely that at least one-half of all college graduates of every variety would be needed to meet the need. Such a prospect is fantastic since business, commerce, engineering, government, industry, professions, science and technological fields are likewise in need of qualified manpower.

Demands for teachers in future years promise to be so acute that various groups have begun to study ways to better utilize the qualified teachers we now have. Some

[19] The best single reference on this is the report by the Fund for the Advancement of Education entitled *Teachers for Tomorrow*, which gives estimates and projected figures through 1965. See pp. 20–24 for this discussion.

have advocated the use of "teacher aides" to relieve classroom teachers of many routine duties, the increased use of television for instruction purposes, longer school terms, and various other proposals.[20] Anyway we look at it, the demand for qualified teachers spells opportunity for jobs.

The men-wanted sign

An important and allied question relates to the need for a greater total of men teachers, particularly at the elementary and secondary education levels. The composition of the teaching profession became predominantly female during the latter part of the 19th and early 20th centuries. In early America the typical teacher was a "school master" and males dominated in the profession. The growing emancipation of women and the economic conditions which obtained in the 19th century were factors in the gradual change in the ratio between male and female teachers. War periods show losses of men teachers, particularly during the War Between the States. Published figures show that, since 1880, the number of men teachers has never challenged the predominant number of women in the profession. Note that only minor changes are observable since that date.

Educational leaders have commented upon some obvious effects of the changed composition of the profession. For a long time it operated to keep salaries at a relatively low level. Many have deplored the lack of men teachers in the elementary school, noting that children have had few contacts with adult men during their formative years.

The picture remained very much the same during the first postwar decade as women teachers predominated at all levels of education save the collegiate. In 1948 the percentage of men teachers in public schools—elementary and secondary—dropped to 18.8. The decade of the Fifties brought a marked change. By 1960 the total percentage of men teachers had reached its highest point since the Gay Nineties. In the 1960–61 school year the number of men teachers in public high schools exceeded women for the first time in many years. In the public elementary schools, the numbers of women teachers and men teachers in public schools in 1960–61 was 476,000 and 1,013,000 respectively.[21]

There appears to be little room for doubt as to the need for additional men in the teaching profession. The matter of recruiting a greater proportion of men into the profession presents both problems and opportunities. The unprecedented demand of today indicates that greater emphasis should be placed upon the attraction of men into the profession.

All fields and levels are open

Another way of looking at the opportunities in education is in terms of the types of positions that may be chosen which are as broad as the entire educational program of the nation. Consider the various types of schools and institutions (formal or organized education), the kinds of training programs, the public and private agencies which conduct informal educational activities, and you will see the possibilities.

The other dimension may be recognized from a survey of the continuous character of education and of the provi-

[20] See *How Shall We Get Enough Good Teachers?* (New York: National Citizen's Commission for the Public School, 1953), pp. 16–25, for descriptions of various proposals.

[21] T. M. Stinnett, *op. cit.,* p. 17.

TABLE 13–4. PERCENTAGE OF MALE AND FEMALE TEACHERS
IN PUBLIC SCHOOLS OF U.S.*

	1880	1890	1900	1910	1920	1930	1940	1950	1960
Males	42.8	34.5	29.9	21.1	14.1	16.5	22.2	21.3	32
Females	57.2	65.5	70.1	78.9	85.9	83.5	77.8	78.6	68

*Sources used: L. M. Chamberlain and L. E. Meece, Women and Men in the Teaching Profession (Lexington: University of Kentucky, 1937); NEA Research Bulletin, Teachers in the Public Schools, XXVII (December 1949), p. 135; T. M. Stinnett, The Profession of Teaching (Washington: The Center for Applied Research in Education, Inc.), pp. 17–18.

sions we have made for lengthening and extending it. Educational programs are expanding rapidly at either end—in preschool years and at the adult education level. Draw a diagram (by years) of the opportunity for education which is open to the average person. Remember that opportunity for students means opportunity for teachers. All the way along from nursery schools for the two-year toddlers to adult education classes and Ph.D.'s, teachers are needed. Few states have really begun to provide for the education of preschool children. Likewise, the movements for public junior colleges and opportunities for adult education are only getting under way in this country. These are broad fields of educational need and opportunity which must be extended and developed in the years ahead. Here will be found the fields of opportunity for young people interested in educational service.

In the school systems of the present, opportunity beckons to qualified teachers in all fields or levels. A great number of additional instructors will be needed in our colleges in the years ahead. The need for high school teachers has far exceeded the supply during recent years. In such fields as science and mathematics the supply is still short although there has been some increase in the number of teacher candidates in recent years.

In the elementary schools, there continues to be a critical shortage of qualified teachers. It has been noted that all of the teacher candidates now in our teacher education institutions would not meet the demand for trained elementary teachers even if they were to choose that field of service.[22] Demand has far outrun supply for the past few years, and present trends of enrollment in teacher education institutions indicate that no relief is in sight. Remember that the present supply of graduates represents only a fraction of the annual demand for fully qualified elementary teachers. Never has there been opportunity so great for teachers who are capable of guiding the education of young children. So great is the need that vast numbers of "emergency" teachers are being used to keep our elementary schools going. This emergency policy is recognized as dangerous to our society, because no aspect of our educational program is more important than the early years of a child's education.

Our educational leadership accepts the view that requirements for certification of elementary school teachers should be as high as for teachers at other levels. The minimum should be a four-year college education including adequate professional work and experience. Legislation in many states providing for certificates based on two years of college work is now regarded as inadequate and temporary. Yet there are those who feel that even if

[22] M. Margaret Stroh, Find Your Own Frontier, p. 43.

requirements cannot be raised while the critical shortage exists, there should be no cheapening of desirable professional standards for certification of teachers for our children.

In most states students in teacher education institutions may elect a curriculum leading to the *provisional* and *standard* certificates (or licenses) to teach in elementary schools. The former is valid for a term of years; the latter is good permanently or subject to renewal after a period of successful teaching and graduate study. In addition, opportunity is open to students who wish to specialize in art, public school music, and physical education work in the elementary schools.

Candidates for high school teaching may choose majors and minors from a wide variety of offerings roughly equivalent to the comprehensive programs offered in the secondary schools. Teacher education institutions offer various opportunities for the choice of teaching fields or combinations of fields. These may be called majors and/or minors, areas of concentration, or teaching fields. The college catalog is our best source of information about specific details of this sort. It is a good idea to discuss this with an advisor or instructor in education who will know about the laws and regulations governing the issuance of certificates (or licenses) by the state department of education.

Thus opportunities in teaching may be seen as unlimited. Capable youth interested in teaching may look forward with confidence to finding themselves a place at almost any level or in any field of teaching which appeals to them. The need for teachers is great at all stages: for the tots, the teens, and the grownups. It is especially critical at the elementary school level, where the shortage will remain acute for years. Such demand can mean only opportunity for some years to come.

A Magna Carta for teachers

One of the most perceptive and appreciative studies of the work of good teachers appeared in *Look* early in 1956.[23] It concluded with what may become a "classic" in recent educational literature. The opening paragraph of this "Magna Carta" envisions a great future for teachers in a great society:

To govern himself, man must decide; to decide, he must understand; to understand modern civilization, he must learn. We therefore entrust to our teachers the minds and hearts of our children; and, through them, our nation's survival. But survival alone is not enough. We hold the pursuit of happiness to be a natural right. In today's world, the fruits of happiness are not within reach of the ignorant. We therefore believe that no profession is more essential to our life or more deserving of respect than that of teaching.

Appraise Your Teaching Potential

Everyone interested in America's future is concerned with having good teachers for our children. Every college student that recognizes the importance of this will see the necessity for getting youth with aptitude to consider teaching as their occupational choice. This choice may well be a pertinent matter for thousands of

[23] See *Look*, **XX**, No. 4 (February 21, 1956), p. 45. Used with permission.

youth in colleges and universities today. That number may include us. As a start we shall need to consider what makes a good teacher.

Most people would agree right off that "Good teachers make good schools." As the great Massachusetts educator, Charles S. Brooks, used to put it, "As is the teacher, so is the school." But there would be far less agreement upon any single list of qualities that every good teacher must have. And there is room for several lists because there are many kinds of teaching situations and because there is enough variety in teaching to accommodate different personalities. As schools try to meet the needs and problems of living in our time, it is possible that our standards of good teaching change to some extent. Teachers are not alike any more than are members of other professions. In other words, teachers are no more "carbon copy" personalities than are artists, clergymen, lawyers, physicians, social workers, or public officials. We may think of the really good teachers we have had. Were they exactly alike? Of course not, not in every respect; yet each was effective in her own way. So there is room for many interesting, alert, attractive, but varying personalities in this great work of teaching.

One may wonder why all this preliminary build up is necessary. Why be concerned if many different kinds of persons can become good teachers? When we recall our good teachers and reflect about them a bit, an answer may be forthcoming. It is true that good teachers were not exactly alike. Their voices were not the same; one can almost hear them now. We'd never mistake Miss Jones' for that of Mrs. Smith, would we? But what was there about those different voices? They

were not the same, but each was pleasant, nice to listen to, and effective. That will do for an illustration of what we mean. Certainly good teachers vary in personality, but the total effect of each is attractive, pleasing, stimulating, and helpful.

We may find another example in those good teachers we had who liked boys and girls. Did they show this in exactly the same way? Certainly not, but one could tell; we knew that they did, after we learned to know them well. Perhaps one had a way of smiling that told volumes, showing she was glad to have us around; another went to bat for us when we needed a real friend; and still another used to talk to us in preference to doing something else interesting. But each way was enough; it was genuine and convincing. So again this quality of friendliness, or liking for children, was there, although the personalities which expressed it were different.

The next logical step involves making an effort to study those personal qualities which good teachers have. After that will come some consideration of the kind of young person who should choose to teach and be selected for the profession. Then we should be ready to take a good look at ourselves to analyze our aptitudes and capabilities for teaching, to see if we are on the way.

QUALITIES OF GOOD TEACHING

All history records the lasting influence of great teachers upon their pupils and their distinctive and profound contributions to human society. Teachers have influenced the course of history as an apt student discovers for himself. There has been no decline or eclipse of the great teachers' role and influence in our society and time; if anything, their contributions have more significance than before World War II and the new postwar age which our culture has entered. Teaching has an important and strategic role in America today; it demands the best abilities and talents of our best potential young leaders. Even though the recent and current crisis in education has resulted in the use of persons not particularly fitted for teaching, there should be no compromise upon qualities desired in teachers. Let us look at this question with the idea that nothing is too good for education; no type of personality or character too dear when we choose teachers for our children. A good start might be to review some of the characteristics of the best teachers we have had.

Approaches to the study of teachers

A variety of ways have been used to study the characteristics and qualities of good teachers. A. S. Barr has classified them under four types of evaluative studies as follows: (a) *performance,* (b) *personal qualities,* (c) *mental prerequisites to teaching efficiency,* and (d) *pupil growth and achievement.*[24] Studies of teaching efficiency and of the personal

[24] A. S. Barr, "The Measurement of Teaching Efficiency," in *Growing Points in Educational Research* (Washington: American Educational Research Association, 1949), p. 251. See also, A. S. Barr, *et al.,* "The Measurement and Prediction of Teaching Efficiency: A Summary of Investigations," *The Journal of Experimental Education* (June 1948), pp. 207–214. Some of the best known early studies were: Charters, W. W., and Waples, Douglas, *The Commonwealth Teacher-Training Study* (Chicago: University of Chicago Press, 1929); W. G. Bagley, *School Discipline* (New York: Macmillan, 1914); Ray Franklin, "What Superintendents Ask Applying Teachers," *American School Board Journal* (April 1930), p. 51.

and social traits of teachers alone number in the hundreds. Samples of the various studies have been briefly described or summarized here for your information.

Many studies have involved pupil evaluation and views. An extensive study of the qualities of good and poor teachers made nearly thirty years ago (based on responses of 10,000 seniors in sixty-six high schools over the nation) showed interesting results. Here are some of the qualities the seniors listed:

Disliked Teachers Were

1. Too cross, crabby, grouchy, sarcastic, never smiles, nags, loses temper and flies off the handle.

2. Not helpful with homework.

3. Does not explain lessons and assignment clearly.

4. Does not plan his work.

5. Partial, has pets, and picks on certain pupils.

6. Superior, aloof, haughty, snooty, overbearing; does not know you out of class.

7. Mean, unreasonable, hard-boiled, intolerant, ill mannered, too strict. Makes life miserable.

8. Unfair in marking tests and exams and in grading.

9. Inconsiderate of pupils' feelings and bawls them out in class; pupils are afraid and ill at ease.

10. No interest in pupils, and does not understand them.

11. Makes unreasonable assignments.

12. Too loose in discipline, has no control of class; does not command respect.[25]

[25] The original study was published in 1934 in: Frank W. Hart, *Teachers and Teaching* (New York: Macmillan, 1934); see Ward G. Reeder, *A First Course in Education,* Fourth Edition (New York: Macmillan, 1958), pp. 501–505, for a summary of this study.

Best Liked Teachers Were

1. Helpful with homework.
2. Explained lessons and assignment clearly and thoroughly.
3. Used examples in teaching.
4. Cheerful, happy, good-natured.
5. Had a sense of humor and could take a joke.
6. Human, friendly, companionable; "he is one of us."
7. Interested in and understood pupils.
8. Makes work interesting and creates a desire to work.
9. Strict, commands respect, has control of the class.
10. Impartial, shows no favoritism, and has no pets.
11. Not cross, crabby, grouchy, nagging or sarcastic.
12. We learned the subject.

A nationwide contest by the "Quiz Kids" radio program revealed traits of teachers who had helped them most:

1. Cooperativeness—democratic attitude
2. Kindliness and consideration for the individual
3. Patience
4. A multitude of interests
5. Pleasing personality, appearance, and manner
6. Fairness
7. Sense of humor
8. Good disposition and consistent behavior
9. Interest in pupil's problems
10. Flexibility
11. Use of recognition and praise
12. Unusual proficiency in teaching subject[26]

[26] See "The Good Teacher," *Time,* August 21, 1950; also similar article in *Phi Delta Kappan* (December 1950), p. 160; and Paul A. Witty, "The Teacher Who Has Helped Me Most," *Proceedings* of the 15th Annual Guidance Con-

Another study of characteristics of teachers conducted by Professor Arthur T. Jersild found that teachers "liked best" were most frequently described by (1) kindness, (2) teaching skill, (3) sympathy. Teachers "disliked most" were most frequently criticized for:

1. Sarcasm.
2. Scolding.
3. Poor discipline.
4. Uninspired teaching.[27]

The prominence of traits which relate to personal relationships and attitudes seemed to suggest that the children liked the teacher as a person first. Subsequent studies over a period of five years served only to strengthen this finding. In 1950 *Time* magazine summarized the results of study of 90,000 replies from children by noting that pupils admired most those teachers with "a cooperative, democratic attitude," one who is well adjusted and genuinely responsive to people. We can find helpful discussions of this continuing study in periodicals and in libraries.

Children had another way of characterizing the good teacher; they list what the good teacher does not do in crisp unmistakeable language. The good teacher does not get mad or fly off the handle; she never pounds the table or gets into a rage or tries to bite one's head off; she finds it unnecessary to scream or shout or fuss to get things done. Children like good teachers

ferences Studies in Higher Education, No. 76 (Lafayette, Ind.: Purdue University, April 1951), pp. 13–20.

[27] Arthur T. Jersild, "Characteristics of Teachers Who Are 'Liked Best' and 'Disliked Most'," in *Journal of Experimental Education,* **XII** (December 1940), pp. 139–151.

because they do not play favorites or make fun of students. Good teachers do not dress the same every day, they don't talk too much; nor do they use words that children cannot readily understand.

Studies of successful teaching

A great many studies of successful teachers by analysis of their teaching have yielded many attributes that enter into effective teaching personality. The noteworthy Commonwealth Study resulted in a list of 25 "traits." Another study used the questions that twenty-five successful superintendents asked of applicants for teaching positions. A study by a leading American educator enlisted the judgments of one hundred school officials and employees on the most important elements composing teaching personality. The first ten were as follows:

1. Sympathy
2. Personal appearance
3. Address
4. Sincerity
5. Optimism
6. Enthusiasm
7. Scholarship
8. Physical vitality
9. Fairness
10. Reserve and dignity[28]

A noteworthy study in recent years identified important generalizations about the successful teachers who were interviewed. There were several specific and different views but many general convictions and attitudes were clearly pervasive among the group. All of them saw "teaching as the way to make a rich life

if barely a living."[29] Next, these good teachers had "plenty of convictions about their profession." Another surprising finding was that the teachers voiced no complaints about infringements or "taboos on personal liberties." Apparently, restrictions upon the teacher's life were no greater than for persons in other professions; adequate persons make a go of it anywhere. The teachers tended to be strongly enthusiastic about their communities and their own places therein. The good teachers possessed a final distinctive cluster of characteristics best termed as *artistry in human relations*. The study observed that the classroom was a veritable gold mine for observing and practicing human relations. Included in this general "artistry" was an unusual "sensitivity to children's emotional problems," and a realistic view of the high calling of the teaching profession.

Findings by experts and groups

Educational literature affords many lists and suggestions on this general topic which may be sampled.

1. The Commission on Teacher Education of the American Council on Education proposed the following list of qualities of a good teacher:

(a) Respect for personality
(b) Community-mindedness
(c) Rational behavior
(d) Skill in promoting learning in others
(e) Increasing knowledge
(f) Friendliness with children
(g) Understanding children
(h) Social understanding and behavior

---

[28] W. C. Bagley, *School Discipline* (New York: Macmillan, 1914); summarized in Ward G. Reeder, *op. cit.,* p. 510.

[29] Frances V. Rummel, "What Are Good Teachers Like?" *School Life,* **XXX** (June 1948), pp. 4–9; (July 1948), pp. 7–11.

(i) Faith in the worth of teaching[30]

2. The 1948 National Conference on the Education of Teachers formulated a list of qualities for an ideal teacher. The list follows:

(a) Appreciation of humanity and essential values of individuals
(b) Emotional stability and adjustment
(c) Native ability plus adequate professional training
(d) Intelligent alertness and curiosity
(e) Pleasing appearance and personality
(f) Love for democratic processes
(g) Critical thinking and objectivity
(h) Healthy physical and mental views
(i) Knowledge of educational trends and philosophies, and
(j) Knowledge of the importance of human relationships[31]

3. A leading American educator sets forth his ideas of the personal "equipment" the beginning teacher should have as follows:

(a) High intelligence
(b) Good health
(c) Ethical character
(d) Pleasing and well-rounded personality
(e) Broad education (general)
(f) Knowledge of subject matter
(g) Desire to teach
(h) Professional competence[32]

A modern teacher should be a person who lives a rich, full life. His experience and education should include travel and adequate information in the sciences,

the social sciences, the humanities, and on the current problems of society. The psychology of learning, ability to guide learners in the educative process, and a viewpoint of education's role in our society are minimum aspects of his professional preparation. He enjoys creative work and gets much out of life. In the community he is an active participant and leader in organizations and groups. He develops worthwhile relationships to local business and cultural institutions in the community. His character is dependable and worthy of emulation. His personality is well-balanced, mature, and adequate. In brief, the modern teacher which we desire is an all-round person, a real fellow.

But some say there are not enough teachers such as these in our schools. If teachers meet the demands we have noted for personal qualities and characteristics, they will be ready to teach, as interesting and effective personalities. To summarize, good teachers should have: (a) well rounded, pleasing personalities; (b) high intelligence; (c) physical fitness; (d) a social philosophy; (e) professional competence; (f) a good general education; (g) emotional maturity; (h) ethical character; (i) a faith in teaching, and (j) a scientific attitude. At the conclusion of our study we may come out with a better list. The most important point is that all this is helping us to understand better the essential characteristics of the excellent teacher.

[30] American Council on Education, *Teachers for Our Times* (Washington: The Council, 1944), pp. 158–173.

[31] *The Education of Teachers as Viewed by the Profession* (Washington: NEA, 1948).

[32] Ward G. Reeder, *A First Course in Education,* Fourth edition (New York: Macmillan, 1958), pp. 491–509.

RATE YOURSELF FOR TEACHING

The many attributes, characteristics and qualities of good teachers afford many specific opportunities to check upon our

PREPARATION OF TEACHERS

0% 20% 40% 60% 80% 100%

No Degree
- 2.5%
- 9.9%
- 7.6%

A diploma or degree, but less than 4 years
- 1.7%
- 9.4%
- 7.0%

Bachelor's Degree
- 55.1%
- 65.1%
- 61.9%

Master's Degree
- 39.8%
- 15.5%
- 23.1%

Doctor's Degree
- 0.9%
- 0.1%
- 0.4%

MEN
WOMEN
ALL

AGES OF PUBLIC SCHOOL TEACHERS

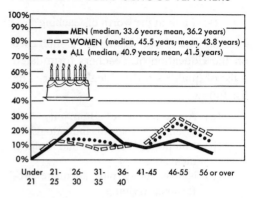

MEN (median, 33.6 years; mean, 36.2 years)
WOMEN (median, 45.5 years; mean, 43.8 years)
ALL (median, 40.9 years; mean, 41.5 years)

Under 21 | 21-25 | 26-30 | 31-35 | 36-40 | 41-45 | 46-55 | 56 or over

PER CENT IN VARIOUS AGE GROUPS

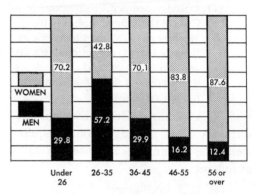

WOMEN
- 70.2
- 42.8
- 70.1
- 83.8
- 87.6

MEN
- 29.8
- 57.2
- 29.9
- 16.2
- 12.4

Under 26 | 26-35 | 36-45 | 46-55 | 56 or over

SEX OF ALL PUBLIC SCHOOL TEACHERS

0% 20% 40% 60% 80% 100%

SEX OF ALL PUBLIC SCHOOL TEACHERS
MEN — 31.3%
WOMEN — 68.7%

SEX OF ELEMENTARY TEACHERS
MEN — 12.1%
WOMEN — 87.9%

SEX OF SECONDARY TEACHERS
MEN — 56.8%
WOMEN — 43.2%

American Public School Teachers—A Profile.

Source: *The American Public School Teacher, 1960–61* (Washington: NEA Research Division).

MARITAL STATUS

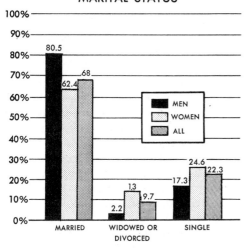

PER CENT OF ALL TEACHERS WITH AND WITHOUT CHILDREN

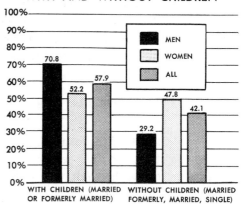

PER CENT OF TEACHERS ACTIVE IN VARIOUS COMMUNITY GROUPS

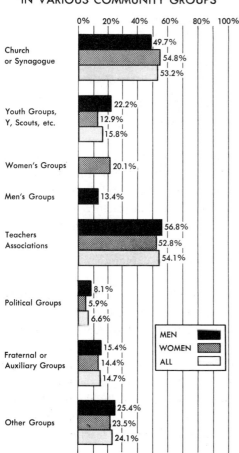

WOULD YOU CHOOSE TEACHING AGAIN?

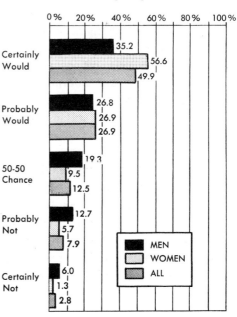

own aptitude for teaching. When we study the many specific items to find they comprise several large categories of personal qualities, we will be close to the point of doing some self-appraisal to find what is our own potential for teaching.

Important abilities from little items grow

We should study the many ideas and suggestions about good teachers and successful teachers to find out who should choose teaching. Many would find that prospective teachers should rate high in terms of *personality,* ethical character, scholarship, initiative, and leadership potential.

As we study and think about these suggestions, we shall probably agree that they are important, but that their application should be investigated. Some of these abilities and qualities can readily be recognized in a person; in other instances we need more definite evidence. Take *leadership* or initiative as an illustrative example. We shall need to know a great deal about the background and experience of a person before we can judge him. Since, in this instance, the matter relates *to us,* we should have first hand information. We should each be able to evaluate our own experience and personality in terms of such specifics as these.

Use the available evidence first

The first step should be to make explicit the abilities we mean by use of "initiative" and "leadership." How does one recognize these qualities in or by the student who should be encouraged to become a teacher? Some clues for consideration are:

1. Watch for leadership and ability to work in clubs, various co-curricular activities, scouting, and other youth organizations. Who is it that gets things done?

2. Look for experience and work in Sunday School groups, especially with younger children. See which adolescents are most successful with these activities.

3. Notice to whom pupils go for help at review and examination times and when other hard jobs are to be done. Usually the high school groups themselves have already discovered the best student sources of extra help.

4. Study the attitudes and work of those who care for younger children at home. Find out who the babysitters are and how they feel about this work. These experiences may be useful indicators of young people who have developed qualities valuable for teaching.

5. Try to determine their degree of understanding of the children with whom they have informal contacts on playgrounds, at camp, and similar opportunities.

No great number of final answers may be expected from these clues, but their use should give some fairly good indications of potentialities for teaching. Students should carry this further by thinking it through and discussing it with classmates and instructor.

One can feel fairly certain that a student is a good bet for teaching if he has had some exploratory experiences in his school life which gave him an insight into a teacher's work and if he found them interesting and enjoyable. Has he worked with children a great deal? Can he help other students with their school work? Does he get satisfaction from seeing his work with other people show up in what they do? Does he really like people, especially children? These answers will show evidence of fitness for teaching.

Use pertinent suggested questions

We may read the foregoing lists with interest, but still may want something more specific. There is no single authoritative check-list. There are many lists of clues and questions that may be helpful, but these must not be considered other than tentative suggestions and reminders.

One approach to the appraisal of potential for teaching started with the assumption that it should be possible to recognize a high school graduate who has the qualities and characteristics that seem to be required for success in teaching. An interesting set of questions for youth interested in teaching was prepared for a national honorary organization of teachers for this purpose:

1. Are you interested in children?
2. Do you care what happens in your community?
3. Do you enjoy study?
4. Have you originality?
5. Are you objective in your attitude? (Do you analyze situations without emotion?)
6. Can you laugh at yourself?
7. Have you vigorous habits?
8. Do you make the most of your appearance?
9. Have you a pleasant voice?
10. Have you a code of ethics?[33]

A student may find that he has been nodding his head rather vigorously as he reads the questions which good teacher material should be able to answer in the affirmative.

Another list of considerations prepared by a state group of educators interested in the selection of capable youth

for teaching may stimulate your own questions.

Important Considerations for Teacher Candidates:[34]

1. *Better than average intelligence.* Teaching for today requires the best brains and abilities we can muster; we must deliberately seek out and select the best.

2. *Ability to help other children with their problems and to explain difficulties to children.* Such experiences indicate maturity, poise, adequacy on the part of the student. It may be a good clue to potential ability as a teacher.

3. *Initiative* or willingness and ability to undertake a job without waiting to be told what and how. This quality is essential for teaching of a high order.

4. *Persistence* or ability to see a job through even when the going is hard—tenacity of purpose. This is the "companion" requirement to initiative.

5. *Good sense of justice and fairness in dealing with others.* The best teachers have exemplified these qualities. All evidence points to the need for these in satisfactory human relations. Teaching is nothing if human relations are left out.

6. *Patience with persons and things.* The former is of primary importance in teaching. Patience with learners implies a faith in their ability to grow and develop.

7. *Good physical health* is of manifest importance. Teachers work directly with youth and must exemplify healthful living.

8. *Average attractiveness.* Teachers do not have to be candidates for the "Miss America' title but they should not be "repulsive," as young people use the term.

9. *Emotional stability.* A fundamentally important quality. Well-adjusted, balanced persons with stability and tolerance are needed.

[33] M. Margaret Stroh, *Find Your Own Frontier* (Austin: Delta Kappa Gamma, 1948), pp. 10–13.

[34] Kentucky Committee on Teacher Recruitment, mimeographed, no date. Used with permission.

10. *Willingness to work.* This certainly applies to teaching; teaching means work.

11. *Use of good English.* Ability to communicate effectively is essential in teaching. It also indicates ability to think accurately and effectively.

12. *Leadership.* We need a generation of leaders in teaching. This can be observed in the experience and work of youth.

13. *Liking for people and the desire to work with them.* This is always recognized as an essential requirement for teaching.

What should one think?

What were the reactions to these questions? Perhaps the lists can help us to form our own views about important items and questions to consider. What changes do we suggest? After we have formulated and revised our own list as far as necessary, we may think carefully about the evidence. Can we be sure of all the answers as applied to ourselves? If we are not sure we may need to find more facts. In other words, we should find ways to study ourselves.

As we start this last procedure it is well to remember a few important items. This can be an interesting and helpful experience. It is a good time to do this because we are still in school and have the chance to work on any point which we may decide needs attention. Our college has advisors and counsellors who should be able to help. We should remember that all this is for our benefit and that we are doing it. There are some testing instruments that the advisor may wish to use in the class.[35]

It is not necessary to debate what should come first. What is most important: physical fitness? intelligence? general knowledge? your special field (major)? emotional maturity? All of these are but different aspects of one's *personality,* and we can hardly say that one is more important than another. We may start with any point and keep working until we have considered all "sides." That should be our next task—finding whether we have what it takes to teach.

We should use our own questions and ideas in our self-appraisal and discuss them with an advisor. As we make progress we may compare notes with other interested students. The group may wish to study a number of other instruments as a further guide to understanding of fitness for teaching. Many such scales are available from various publications and professional sources, but it may be well to do some work in selecting and adapting certain scales to the group's present purposes, but that should not prove difficult.[36]

Some relatively comprehensive programs of assessment of teaching aptitude have been developed in certain colleges of

[35] Research work at the University of Minnesota resulted in development of the *Minnesota Teacher Attitude Inventory,* a promising instrument used in many pre-professional courses in college of teacher education.

[36] See for example: (a) Mildred Sandson Fenner, *The Growing Teacher* (Washington: NEA Personal Growth Leaflet No. 20); (b) Robert L. Filbin and Stefan Vogel, *So You're Going to Be a Teacher* (Great Neck, N.Y.: Barron's Educational Series, Inc., 1962), pp. 9–13; (c) E. F. Hartford, *A Plan Book for Future Teachers* (Evanston, Ill.: Row, Peterson & Co., 1961), see pp. 48–68 for "self-appraisal" scale; (d) Margaret Lindsay, "Ask Yourself Some Questions," *NEA Journal* (March 1951), pp. 173–175; (e) Michigan Education Association, *Teacher Rating Scale* (Lansing, Michigan); (f) Ruth Wolozin, *Careers in Teaching* (Washington: B'nai B'rith Vocational Service, 1955); and (g) *You'd Like Teaching,* Ellensburg (Washington: Central Washington College of Education, 1946), pp. 35–39.

teacher education.[37] The class might well take this opportunity to learn about some of the instruments used for this purpose.

Consider findings and follow through

When everyone has completed a careful self-appraisal, he should have some good ideas for the next steps which should be taken. The exact rating of each person can not be strictly accurate; the chief value is the thought and study which entered into it. In this exercise, we should have received rather definite and useful impressions of what enters into the teaching personality. We are not concerned with a mere rating of a given numerical value but rather with the *promise* which begins to show up through such a study of ourselves. Each person is his own answer, and the answer shows promise. One may say to oneself: "Look at *this* and *that* and still another aspect of personality! Here is good background experience as a leader." Another may definitely begin to realize that he values people highly, and sees that working with them will be easy and gratifying. This sort of analysis will give us real insight into capabilities and resources for the master profession—teaching.

Now for another step to follow the self-rating experience we have completed. We should review our responses to the various items, noting those which we

[37] A program might well include the *Minnesota Teaching Aptitude Inventory,* along with other instruments, such as a Group Participation Scale, the *Mooney Problem Checklist,* a vocational interests inventory (like Kuder, Cleaton or Strong), personality inventory (California, Heston, etc.), academic interest inventory, certain sociometric tests. Tests of general ability and comprehensive achievement will usually be available from the college testing service for all students.

could not clearly and promptly evaluate and reconsider these items carefully. It is perfectly acceptable for us to decide that we "don't know" *now.* But it does mean that we need to find out. Some ways to do that will occur to us as we go over these points with the instructor and get suggestions. We may decide to use some simple testing materials which will give each of us additional information about ourselves.

Take some constructive action

The culminating point of all this is that we should each begin to work for improvement on those items about which *we can do something.* Take appearance, for instance. As they say, "Everyone looks at your hat but you." Now that we have looked at ourselves, as it were, are there some details which we can definitely improve? The thing to do then is to begin on intelligent programs of self-improvement. Each person can find other little points which have not concerned him before that he can profitably try to change and improve.

What about that participation record? If one has tended to go it alone, now is the time to get into things to gain social experience and more skill in working with people. We know it is almost impossible to dislike or to fail to appreciate people with whom we have worked on a common task. Many can recall how a person's face would light up when asked whether he knew someone as he replied, "Oh sure, I've worked with him." Teachers do a lot of working together with people. We should get some valuable experience in this group of skills now.

To take another illustration, suppose one begins to realize that he needs to learn to take criticism. That's not easy for anyone to learn but it must be developed if one is to become an adult in emotional stability. There are many great big babies running around in grownup dress. These folks are not good candidates for teaching. We do not need to accept every criticism that we may hear, but we must learn to react to it objectively. Let's say to ourselves, "Just how accurate is that criticism? How much truth is in it? Am I really like that?" When we can do that, get and review the facts, accept the truth and act upon it without feeling hurt or angry, then we are adults. There's no easy way to learn to do this but an earnest attempt to practice it will pay real dividends.

Other possible items may be selected for your efforts at self-improvement. It may be relatively simple matter of weight control or a better time schedule, a rhythm of work-play-study-rest. It may be the need to keep in better touch with current affairs and what's going on in the world about us. These are fairly obvious or common problems and the solutions are not difficult to find. But everyone should follow up self-study with the necessary program of self-improvement in order to make the most of potential capabilities and personal resources. Whether he teaches or not, everyone wants to be the person he is capable of becoming, and not one who merely "gets by."

A final word

One should not stop with a brief inventory of himself. Each should discuss his personal biographical sketch with an advisor or instructor. It is well to recall the various tests, physical examinations, questionnaires, and other forms of getting basic information about ourselves which we have had. Each should record and study what is known about the results with all comments upon each. In other words, each person should try to discover what he really knows about himself. It will prove a fascinating subject.

Then one should plan carefully and begin to do something positive about any items which he needs to learn more about, or which he may wish to improve. For example, there may be some tests which will help to teach one more about interests and capabilities; there may be some physical education or health needs which he can meet; or he may desire to plan additional studies in professional or academic fields. Each person should work out his own program and do something about it. Such an investment in oneself and in one's own future effectiveness will pay important dividends. One result will be a more convincing answer to that all-important question of whether one has what it takes.

By way of summary we may wish to remember five basic qualities that distinguish any good teacher: (1) A strong desire to learn; (2) A strong desire to teach; (3) An interest in people, especially children; (4) The ability to get along well with people, especially young folks; and (5) Good character. We can check ourselves on these major basic qualities by various means. The most important points are to be thoroughly honest in appraising ourselves and to do something constructive and definite to grow, develop, and improve as persons. Many students probably have already much of what it takes to be a good teacher. One's contribution will be constructive and one's life will be happy if one really has what it takes to be a good teacher. American democracy doesn't need any other kind.

Selected Bibliography

Adams, Beatrice. "The Magic Ingredient," *NEA Journal,* **XLVII** (November 1958), p. 571.

Cushman, Jack. *Young Man's View of the Teaching Profession.* Reprint from American National Red Cross Journal, Washington: Future Teachers of America, National Commission on Teacher Education and Professional Standards, 1961.

Davis, Billie, "I Was a Hobo Kid," *Saturday Evening Post,* **CCXXV,** No. 24 (December 13, 1952), p. 108 ff.

Davis, Hazel. "Facts and Issues in Merit Salary Schedule," *Journal of Teacher Education,* **VIII** (June 1957), pp. 127–135.

Deuel, Leo (Ed.). *The Teacher's Treasure Chest.* Englewood Cliffs, N. J.: Prentice-Hall, Inc., 1956.

Eckel, Howard. "How Can We Get Quality Teaching?" *The School Executive,* **LXXVII** (June 1958), pp. 19–21.

Evans, Eva Knox. *So You're Going to Teach.* New York: Hinds, Hayden & Eldridge, 1948.

Fuess, Claude N. and Bashford, Emory S. *Unseen Harvests.* New York: The Macmillan Co., 1947.

Highet, Gilbert. *The Art of Teaching.* New York: Alfred P. Knopf, Inc., 1950.

Holman, Mary V. *How It Feels to be a Teacher.* New York: Columbia University Press, Teachers College, 1950.

Huggett, A. J. and Stinnett, T. M., *Professional Problems of Teachers.* 2nd ed., New York: The Macmillan Co., 1963.

Jersild, Arthur T. *When Teachers Face Themselves,* 2nd Ed. New York: Bureau of Publications, Teachers College, Columbia University, 1957.

Lambert, Sam M., "Angry Young Men in Teaching," *NEA Journal,* **LII,** No. 2 (February 1963), pp. 17–20.

Leonard, George B., Jr. "What Is A Teacher?" *Look* (February 21, 1956), pp. 29–39.

Lynham, Adria B. "Teachers Are People," *NEA Journal,* **XLVII** (October 1958), pp. 503–504.

Mathews, Marcia M. "A Wonderful Profession," *Saturday Evening Post,* **CCXXXV** (January 27, 1961), pp. 34–36.

Mayer, Frederick. "A Letter to a Teacher," *Phi Delta Kappan,* **XL** (February 1959), pp. 216–218.

National Commission on Teacher Education and Professional Standards, *Invitation to Teaching.* Washington: NEA, 1960.

Newlon, Richard and Lee, Betty Jean, "Denver Achieves Professional Negotiations," *NEA Journal,* **LII,** No. 2 (February 1963), pp. 14–16.

Peters, Herman J., *et al. Introduction to Teaching.* New York: The Macmillan Co., 1963.

Redefer, Frederick L. "Factors That Affect Teacher Morale," *The Nation's Schools,* **LXIII** (February 1959), pp. 59–62.

Research Division, *Estimates of School Statistics, 1962–63,* Research Report, 1962, R-13. Washington: NEA, December 1962.

————. *The American Public-School Teacher, 1960–61,* Research Monograph, 1963, M-2. Washington: NEA, April 1963.

Riccio, Anthony C. and Cyphert, Frederick R. *Teaching in America.* Columbus: Charles E. Merrill Books, Inc., 1962. See Chapters 3–5.

Rummel, Frances V. "What Are Good Teachers Like?" *School Life* (July 1940).

Russell, William F. "Should You Be a Teacher?" *Career Opportunities*. New York: New York Life Insurance Co., 1958.

Sharp, Louise D. (Ed.) *Why Teach?* New York: Holt, Rinehart & Winston, Inc., 1957.

Stiles, J. Lindley, *et al. The Teacher's Role in American Society*, Fourteenth Yearbook, John Dewey Society. New York: Harper & Row, Publishers, 1957.

Stinnett, T. M. *The Profession of Teaching*. Washington: The Center for Applied Research in Education, Inc., 1962. See chapters 1–4.

Stroh, M. Margaret. *Find Your Own Frontier*. Austin: Delta Kappa Gamma, 1948.

Stuart, Jesse. *The Thread That Runs So True*. New York: Charles Scribner's Sons, 1949.

Teunien, Frederick W. "Who Thinks What about Educators," *American Journal of Sociology*, **LIX,** No. 1 (September 1953), pp. 150–158.

The Shape of Education for 1963–64. Washington: National School Public Relations Association, NEA, 1963, pp. 35–47. See especially the digest entitled "Good Teachers Are Very Unusual People."

Wasson, Margaret. *Teaching Is Exciting,* Bulletin No. 88. Washington: Association for Childhood Education International, 1951.

Weber, Julia. *My Country School Diary,* New York: Harper & Row, Publishers, 1946.

Whitelaw, John B. *et al. Teaching as a Career,* U. S. Department of Health, Education, and Welfare, Office of Education, Pamphlet No. 122. Washington: U. S. Government Printing Office, 1959. See also rev. ed. of this pamphlet dated May 1963.

Wilson, Charles H. *A Teacher is a Person*. New York: Holt, Rinehart & Winston, Inc., 1956.

Wynn, Richard. *Careers in Education,* New York: McGraw-Hill Book Co., 1960, pp. 192–238.

Chapter 14

The Preparation

of Teachers

A good teacher is one who has an active interest in children and youth; has a broad educational background; is professionally qualified and competent; possesses good physical and mental health; has a good moral character; manifests a desire for self-improvement; can work constructively with other professional workers, parents, and the community; and is proud of teaching as a profession.*

Introduction

The education of teachers is of the profoundest significance to our democratic society and to the future of its institutions. Likewise, it has the deepest or closest connection with the purposes, aspirations, and destinies of people, the most important entities we know anything about. This concerns the growth and development of future teachers. Therefore, careful and capable attention should be given to growth of students into competent, skilled, and professional persons. Good teachers for democracy's schools will need to have clear concepts about education and certain big understandings about the nature of their work and the issues before American education. This may be clearer if we consider the other extreme. A pas-

sive student lets things happen to him with the result that learnings are incidental, may be hit-or-miss or unreliable. Students can do more than anyone to see to it that the important objectives for this introductory course are realized. They do this to the extent that they take an active interest in what goes on, and keep themselves aware of what happens, and consider what it all means. It is possible, by conscious attention and thought, to facilitate what we learn. By this means, one moves into the driver's seat, so to speak, and takes over more control of what happens to him and of the learnings that result from his experiences.

Check this point thoroughly and extensively; it will stand up as a dependably good principle. It may be agreed that one good purpose of education is for the stu-

* *Report,* White House Conference on Education, p. 11.

dent to grow and develop control of his own purposes and learning experiences. This is part of what we mean when we talk about "developing self-control," and about "discipline coming from within."

This unit represents an approach to better understanding of the processes and activities that provide learning opportunities for each of us. All of these are expected to help us gain many learning outcomes of many different kinds—information, skills, attitudes, appreciations, and values. Beyond these, there is one more understanding we can and should gain from our activities. That particular one is the subject matter of this chapter.

The important point is: Can we gain here from our own experience a working idea of how people learn concepts? How does one learn to understand a principle, a generalization, or an outcome from a number of experiences and meanings? An approach to the answer can be had if we are aware of our own learnings and growth in the understanding of a concept.

Perhaps an illustration will make this point more convincing. We have had some experiences—observations in schools, visits to study the work of teachers, use of films showing a classroom situation—planned to give us understandings such as "how children grow and develop," and "how people learn." The point is that this is a long drawn-out process and that most people need time for it. That is the underlying reason back of the college program for many "laboratory" experiences that are distributed over a period of years. These probably started with simpler plans and were gradually stepped up in scope and significance. Through all these direct experiences we can gradually gain insight into the concepts and acquire the competences that teachers need to have. The direct experiences we have will become more complicated and yield more learnings from actual participation as we proceed. We begin by observation, go on to greater participation, and finally take full responsibility in our student teaching experience. Thus, we should be able to discover for ourselves the theory and planning that underlies a teacher education program.

Further on in this program, many will probably conclude that their own growth into competence and toward understanding will continue on after they graduate and enter teaching. And we shall be on sound grounds when and if we do make such a discovery. Our own growth should continue as we teach. Here is the sound justification for what we call "in-service" education programs for teachers. Many other means of personal growth and improvement will be available to us as we take control of our own growth.

Teacher growth is a responsibility for sincere and responsible teachers. It is the matter of professional growth through participation in the affairs and interests of organizations and activities related to education. Among one's own goals of increasing competence and growth should be that of worthy membership in the professional life open to teachers.

We have everything to gain and nothing to lose as we go in for continued growth as a person and as a teacher. The best approach is to take active charge of our own growth in understanding, in skill, and competence.

Prelude to Program Planning

What teachers should learn

One approach to teacher education is obvious in terms of the duties and tasks that teachers must perform and accomplish. It is true that one would find that much of the time of many thousands of teachers is devoted to similar duties, and for many people this is the concept of the teacher's work. It would include the number of classes taught, the number of preparations to be made by the teacher, the assignments to keep study hall, duty in the corridors and playground supervision, the grading or marking of papers, giving tests or examinations, advising student organizations, serving as sponsor and counsellor to home room groups, selecting instructional materials, keeping various records, conferring with parents, reporting pupil achievement or progress, "housekeeping" one's classroom, checking attendance, making health inspections, showings films, and attending teachers' meetings. This is a limited, literal way to describe the teacher's work. This appears to be a mere catalog of items that conveys little of the real meaning and significance of teaching.

Another step could be taken in the shape of a simple analysis or evaluation of what teachers are found to be doing. For example, one popular booklet points out to prospective teachers that teaching involves each week some 25 to 30 hours of actual classroom instruction, some 15 to 20 hours of outside preparation by the teacher, a small average number of hours of duty in lunchroom or playground supervision, and other tasks.

Still another study tried to show the teacher's job in terms of her "relationships" to other persons concerned with the work of the schools. We could make an extensive survey of practices of teachers with average time for each but we might conclude that even this had little significance.

We could make a number of approaches to this but sooner or later, we would surely begin to ask not merely "What do teachers do?", but rather "What should teachers do?" When we try to get sound answers to that last question we shall be better prepared to provide good programs of teacher education. Answers will have to be based upon several kinds of studies and approaches and few will be final or uniform. The work of teachers varies from one age group of children to another, from one subject matter area to another, in different communities, and from school to school. The very personalities of the teacher and of the group of pupils have much to do with it.

There are, however, both general and specific functions of teachers and there are broad common elements or phases in all of these. The teacher must be aware of the broad "competencies" needed for the big common areas of responsibility and look to these in his preparation program. Teacher candidates must simultaneously keep in mind the need to be flexible, varied, and different in details and specifics because of the factors, needs, and circumstances of a given situation.

COMPETENCIES TEACHERS SHOULD DEVELOP

The work of the teacher in the light of her responsibilities in our culture is diversified and varied. Various studies have pointed out this varied role or pattern of "roles." Reports of the National Commission for Teacher Education and Professional Standards have suggested six distinct roles of a teacher as follows: (1) as a director of learning; (2) as a counselor and guide for pupils; (3) as a member of the "school community"; (4) as a mediator of the culture; (5) as a link with community; and (6) as a member of the teaching profession.[1] These relate chiefly to the responsibility of promoting pupil growth. We could possibly identify other responsibilities and functions together with "roles" of the teacher. The important point is that we come to have our own view of the broad competencies the teacher needs.

Competencies and understanding

What we desire in teachers for a free society can hardly be described in limited terms. We need ever so much more than specific and relatively tangible skills and techniques. We do want teachers to have these and more.

There are some critically significant understandings that we (and other teachers) should have before we begin to teach America's boys and girls. We might well start our catalog or list with an understanding of the nature and values of democracy. Democracy is more than political institutions and documents. It is a

[1] See National Commission for Teacher Education and Professional Standards, *Factors in Teaching Competence,* Albany Conference (Washington: NEA, 1954), p. 411.

way of life, a method of thought, a system of values, and a kind of philosophical system. Our democracy is diverse, pluralistic in nature, and versatile. A teacher should appreciate its complex nature and its multifarious institutions. Our society has many educative agencies but the public school is the one peculiarly responsible to the purposes and nature of democracy as a whole. A clear view of the rise and progress of the common school with its current status, issues, and problems belongs in the "big picture" of appreciation of American democracy that all teachers should have. If we lack this kind of understanding of America, we must achieve it while we are working in various scholarly fields of study and as we function as a user of democracy in many groups and relationships.

In this effort we should achieve a deep regard for people—everyone else, big and little, and old and young and middle-aged, everybody—the real ends of living. It is manifestly important that teachers should know what research indicates about people and how they behave and learn to behave better. Our teacher education experiences should teach us more about growing persons and how they learn. One of the best ways we can acquire these major skills and understandings is by actually working with learners and in various kinds of institutions where their problems are tackled.

We should see the relationship of our courses to the responsibilities of teaching. It would be ideal if one could see that many of the courses focus directly upon one or more of the competencies he must have as a teacher. This will be difficult to do, but growth and progress is enhanced by what is done along this line: Real in-

Courtesy St. Charles (Ill.) School District No. 303

A new teacher represents many competencies.

sight into this suggestion will make it possible to derive the most help from courses. It would mean *purpose*—a real motive for taking the course—and would contribute to greater *interest,* especially if one felt this strongly enough to be called a *need.* Once we see the point of this, our own appreciation of the problems of assisting boys and girls to learn will be illuminated. One's own growth and experiences should be, in effect, a "laboratory-in-learning," enabling him to have a clear graphic understanding of the principles and concepts of learning that make a great teacher.

Concepts for competent teachers

Any considered study of basic "concepts and understandings" should certainly include the following major items in a minimum initial list. The good teacher will:

1. Have a clear understanding of the values of democracy, as a set of political institutions, as a way of life, and as a method of thought, and their significance and promise for the American people.

2. Have a lucid understanding of the school as an instrument of society and of the goals of education as derived from those of the culture.

3. Have a discriminating understanding of the development of public education in the United States, of the intimate relationship between the common school and American liberties, and of the background of current organization, problems,

and issues of public schools in our democracy.

4. Have an appreciation of the complex pluralistic culture of the United States, of the interrelated nature of its problems, and of the responsibility of individuals to aid in their solution.

5. Have a good working understanding of the community, its organization, institutions, leadership, ways of getting things done, and its values; also, of the relationships of schools and school people to the community of its problems.

6. Have an up-to-date understanding of the growth and development of children and of the relationship between learning and growth.

7. Have a clear concept of the most valid and scientifically derived principles of learning, and of the practical utilization of learning theory in the work of the teacher.

8. Have sound working knowledge of the recent discoveries and theories of group dynamics and of human relations and of their practical application to educational programs.

9. Have adequate knowledge of the basic philosophical and historical thought that illuminates current educational issues and practices.

10. Have an informed basis for understanding and utilizing findings from research in the improvement of teaching.

A second big category of results desired in teacher education is that of "attitudes and appreciations." The teacher should:

1. Have a scientific attitude toward problems which he faces in school and in life.

2. Be cooperative with his fellow faculty members, pupils, and with members of the community in which he lives.

3. Assume responsibility for his own actions, and be ready to accept the responsibilities of a teacher and of a citizen in a free society.

4. Be honest with himself and in his dealings with his fellow men.

5. Act in a manner commensurate with the highest standards of his profession in his relationships with pupils, faculty members, parents, and other members of the community.

Finally, there should be an adequate development of "skills and abilities." The teacher should have developed skill in:

1. The tools of communication, with particular emphasis on clear, effective speech and writing.

2. The techniques of group problem solving.

3. The use of educational research results, and the ability to interpret and apply these findings to the clarification and solution of educational problems.

4. The organization of an educational program in the planning and preparation of material for instructional purposes, and the establishing and maintaining of the most desirable atmosphere for effective learning.

5. The contriving and carrying out of meaningful educational activities for children, which would include skill in the use of the resources of the community.

6. The use of various instructional materials, teaching devices, and multisensory aids.

7. The arts of working with people.

8. The use of scientific method as a way of problem solving and as a way of learning.

We should be able to think about the desirable competencies of the teacher in terms comparable to those of the foregoing list. It will not be easy but it is worth some effort. Our progress will be clearly evident when we are able to rephrase items like these in our own language and to add others. When this takes place, we can be sure we are taking charge of our own growth toward profound understanding and competence.

GENERAL PRINCIPLES FOR PLANNING

Our concern about teaching and the development of understandings and skills should lead us to make extraordinary use of the facilities, resources, and opportunities for learning that are afforded in our colleges. Some general but useful principles should be clearly applicable in our own guidance and planning activities.

1. All departments and services of the institution share responsibility for teacher education. Teacher candidates should make optimum use of any and all offerings and services that can contribute to their own purposes and needs.

2. A college of teacher education should provide an adequate guidance program. By all means, take advantage of it.

3. General education is the literal foundation of any program of professional education. Each student should make certain that the program of general education is comprehensive and that he understands what general education is and why it is important in order that he may make better progress.

4. Begin work in professional education as early as possible in the college;

make a modest start in the first semester with a gradual increase of emphasis in successive semesters. The purposes of self-study, orientation, and guidance are those for emphasis in one's initial education courses and experiences.

5. Some experiences with children and learning situations should be provided for teacher candidates in each year of the program.

6. Likewise, the prospective teacher should participate in the work of student groups, activities, and campus affairs as practicable and valuable source of learnings. One of your best bets will be the campus S.N.E.A. chapter where all will be welcome, and needed. More important, all need the contacts, the friendships, the skills of working together, the learnings that result from this kind of investment of time.

7. The future teacher should learn much about teaching methods and about learners in the course of his college classes and other experiences. True, some of this may be negative (how not to teach a class in this subject) but if one is intelligently concerned about it, he will gain much.

8. Programs should be flexible and practical so as to provide for the interests and needs of different individuals.

9. Time should be allotted to courses and other experiences for teacher candidates in proportion to need. For example, a large block of time is needed for observation and participation in school programs and even greater provision must be made for a term of student teaching. Perhaps the best way to state this general principle is: The length of time allotted for any part of the program should be determined by the nature of the experi-

ence and by the student's need to learn from it.

10. Future teachers should have plenty of experience in working as groups, in cooperative planning and in analysis of these approaches for purposes of improved learnings.

11. Three specifics of both perennial and current significance deserve consistent emphases even though deliberate provisions have to be made for future teachers to gain such experiences. These include: (a) appreciation of the nature, theories, and potentialities of democracy; (b) knowledge of community and the problems of our society; and (c) understanding of the functional values of Western civilization.

12. Provision should be made for evaluation on a sound and continuing basis.

A program for the education of teachers that exemplified the foregoing general principles would include five major components: guidance, general education, special curriculum areas for teaching purposes, professional education, and individual interests. A closer look at each of these broad areas may prove helpful to each of us as we study our own programs.

Guidance offers opportunity

Two major types of benefits should materialize from the guidance services and program of the college of teacher education. In the first place, all teacher candidates should get the help they need to assess themselves, to explore and study fields and opportunities of interest in terms of their capacities and aptitudes, to identfy their problems, and to begin the constructive effort needed to solve them.

The end result should be that aspirants for teaching who have other interests, or little aptitude, are helped to make another and sounder vocational choice; those well-suited to teaching as determined by aptitude testing, tryout experiences, and other criteria are admitted to the teacher education program. They participate in professional laboratory and study programs to fit aspects of their own educational growth and are helped and encouraged to go on.

The second desired outcome is that the future teachers will gain a good concept of what sound guidance really is while in college and that they will use it in their own teaching. This is but another instance of the influence of a good idea or a sound practice. It is, also, an economical, sound, and effective way for future teachers to learn.

An illustration or two should make this point clear. Let's take two colleges of teacher education and look at their programs of guidance. Take the testing program for instance. In the first school the teacher candidates are given certain tests in a hurried manner with no explanation or discussion of their purpose. Even though the teacher candidate later gets the information about his own performance on the test, there is no enhancement of the understanding about this whole aspect of the teacher's work.

In a second teachers' college, let us assume that the counselor teaches a group of first semester freshmen, or at least that he helps with them during a period of orientation. As one of the valuable and functional experiences for freshmen, the early tests needed would be given during the class meetings. There would also be examination of other forms of the same test and discussion of their use and value.

The observed score of the pupils would be given to them with adequate explanation. Questions would be answered and the group would come to know a good deal about some needs for testing and at least one testing instrument. The students would be beginning to get fuller meanings out of their educative experiences.

You see that your own guidance needs and helps can also be a functional and helpful kind of learning experience—a growth in competence, so to speak, rather than a mere episode of counseling for the moment. The philosophy of a college and faculty concerned with teacher education does make a difference.

A Sound Program of Teacher Education

General education is basic

"General education" is a term that has frequent and varied usage. It should be reserved for that part of higher education that helps different people to meet common needs and to function as versatile and cooperative persons in a wholesome society. In other words, it deals with the components of "the good life." It is the converse of special education and the foundation for professional specialized education at the same time.

A good working definition of general education may be taken from the celebrated Harvard Report:

General education, as education for an informed responsible life in our society, has chiefly to do with . . . the question of common standards and common purposes. Taken as a whole, education seeks to do two things: help young persons fulfill the unique, particular functions in life which it is in them to fulfill, and fit them so far as it can for those common spheres which, as citizens and heirs of a joint culture, they will share with others. Obviously these two ends are not wholly separable even in idea—much less can preparation for them be wholly separate. Who does not recall from school or college some small, seemingly quite minor subject which through a teacher or on reflection took on inclusive meaning? Yet to analyze is inevitably to separate what in fact cling together, and . . . general edu-

cation will perforce deal mainly with preparation for life in the broad sense of completeness as a human being, rather than in the narrower sense of competence in a particular lot.[2]

General education is not necessarily the same as liberal education, having only incidental connection with certain areas of study that have been traditionally implicit in liberal arts college programs. General education is in no sense a rival or opposing force for any college curriculum, however old or new it may be. General education is simply a deliberate kind of effort to provide coherence and communication—some of the indispensable ideas and values that enable people to appreciate and cooperate in a highly disparate and specialized society. Conditions of our times and of our technological society require greater aptitude for cooperation and common understandings as the complement for the vastly increased specialization that makes people less able to communicate. In such a society responsible leadership is even more necessary than in former times and societies. General education tries to insure that highly specialized persons in fields of engineering, medicine, industrial chemistry, law,

[2] Harvard Committee, *General Education in a Free Society* (Cambridge: Harvard University Press, 1944), p. 4. Used by permission.

military science, theology, nuclear science, Egyptology, and educational administration can communicate and act together in matters of community interest and well-being. We can appreciate the need for effective understanding of school programs and problems by the thinking people of our community. The same concern applies to the public health department, the community red-feather services, the various local and state governmental agencies, and to many non-public organizations. Yet how shall we get common understanding and agreement upon any controversial issue or even a difficult problem unless those who can take an effective part in its solution have commonly held values and shared concerns about some basic matters.

General education is not necessarily the same for everyone, since people are not carbon copies of old Adam. Neither should it necessarily be a uniform program among colleges all over. It should represent an active deliberate effort on the part of the college to provide adequate and effective offerings to this end.

Teacher education depends upon the general education program to help future teachers acquire broad scholarship. Teachers should be conversant with major components of Western civilization, able to appreciate the institutions, the ideas and values, the humane tradition and the arts, and the functional sciences that have aided mankind. One report of an important study in teacher education expresses this very well:

The general education program should provide experiences which will enable the prospective teacher to develop broad scholarship, including effectiveness in communication. The student should understand the factors that affect human growth, development, motivation, learning, behavior, and personality. He should become sensitive to beauty and should wish to express ideas and moods through music, art, literature, drama, and dance. He should become a healthy person, both physically and mentally, and should develop a feeling of responsibility for maintaining community health. He should be an attractive, well-adjusted person; he should develop economic competence. He should develop an experimental attitude and a sustaining philosophy of life.[3]

A growing number of outstanding colleges have developed promising programs of general education. You will find many references to the approaches devised at Columbia, Chicago, Minnesota, Wisconsin, Colgate, Harvard, Dartmouth, St. John's (Annapolis), and many others. Moreover, there are numerous developments to this end among the colleges of teacher education. You now have the opportunity to be in on the planning and development of at least *one* general education program in a college.

Teaching specialties are varied

A great deal of explanation of this aspect of teacher education is set forth for students in college catalogs and publications of state departments of education. Usually, certain requirements for teaching credentials, certificates, or licenses are specified by statute or by regulation of state boards of education to define a field of specialization for teaching purposes.

In elementary education this may be a comprehensive pattern setting forth subject matters in a number of areas that

[3] Southern Association's Cooperative Study in Elementary Education, *Education of Elementary School Personnel* (Atlanta: Southern Association of Colleges and Secondary Schools, 1951), p. 20.

contribute to the content of the school curriculum. Appreciation subjects such as art, music, and folk dancing may be stipulated along with functional courses such as first aid, nutrition, and child psychology. In this approach the specialization is not narrow and limiting and gives added opportunity for the teacher to achieve general education. It may well be this feature of the pre-service education of the elementary teacher that often makes them effective teachers for the "core" programs at the junior high school level.

The teaching fields for teachers in the secondary school have been traditionally recognized in terms of specialization in one or more of a number of subjects. These are the subjects so commonly listed in high school study lists with which you are quite familiar: there is English with newly-added speech and journalism and drama; history has been joined by economics, sociology, government, and "problems of American democracy" plus the fused courses labelled "social studies"; the sciences—general science, biology, physics, and chemistry with some physiology, physiography and elementary applied courses; that old bug bear mathematics, has some new modified types of courses—revised mathematics to take the place of algebra and geometry for many pupils; the language studies still include Latin for a smaller proportion of students, French, Spanish, and occasionally Russian and German in larger schools; there are all these and a great many newer departments with various courses in commerce, agriculture, home-making, consumer science, vocations, and shop courses. All of these fields must be taught by persons who have aptitude and good preparation for the task.

Usually, the *teaching field* is expressed in terms of a *major, minor,* or an *area of specialization.* A *major* for the purpose of teaching a given subject is usually set at twenty-four semester hours.[4] The *minor* is normally defined in terms of eighteen semester hours. A *teaching area* or an *area of specialization* may be arranged in a program of forty-eight semester hours. This is popular in the natural sciences area, for example, where it is demonstrably essential for a teacher of any given science to have considerable understanding of other science fields. Teacher candidates for high school work may offer two majors, a major and a minor, a major and two minors, or a teaching area.

This is one part of the program that calls for guidance and help by a counselor. A student may need to learn more about himself—interests, aptitudes, and other qualities—as a preliminary step to electing a given area or field of teaching specialization. Everyone should make the most of the help which the college offers.

Certain problems for the teaching profession are evident in this part of teacher education. One is the paradox of increasing emphasis upon specialized areas for teaching with certification limited to only those areas, while there is an ever-growing development of core programs and unified studies in the junior high schools and even in the senior high

---

[4] A major in the field of English may require thirty semester hours including the six semester hours required of all freshmen in this field. There is a slight trend toward the raising of requirements for majors in certain fields. Obviously, the requirements for teaching specialties in colleges with a quarter system are set in quarter hours, which total normally one-half above the total in semester hours.

schools. To be sure, some states have begun to authorize certification for teachers of core programs. This practice will probably become more general.

It would be helpful for the class group to examine some current state department of education publications that describe the various requirements for certification of teachers. This will give a good idea of the trends and newer approaches in elementary, junior high, and senior high school programs that are recognized.

Professional education is functional

It should be evident that preparation for teaching involves a great deal more than giving an able college graduate (with a good general education and a big chunk of specialized subject matter) the keys to a classroom and a record book. That something "more" is largely what is contributed through the professional education component of teacher education. It is designed to give future teachers the understandings, skills, attitudes, or other "competencies" that will enable them to teach the young of our democratic society effectively and conscientiously. This means teaching so the best interests of both the child and of the *whole* society are respected and served. Every prospective teacher (really every prospective parent) should know human growth and development, the needs-interests-motivations of people, especially children, the best theoretical knowledge of learning, and how all these are inter-related and related to other areas of knowledge. These relationships bring up other indispensable knowledges and appreciations of the teacher and some specific modern skills. Future teachers must understand the environing democratic culture with all its institutions and agencies, the role of the public school therein, and the problems of cooperation with and between community agencies. Our urgent appreciation is that of the development of American democracy and of the wellbeing of our free institutions and values. Teachers need to know the essential nature and values of democracy and the indispensable skills of working with all sorts and conditions of people. Such are the contributions of professional education courses in the so-called "foundations" areas. These understandings are not merely theoretical; they should be truly functional in making education truly related to our democratic society and to the real needs and interests of people. "Functional" means *capable of use,* a practical, relatively indispensable kind of usefulness, and it is only right to expect all parts of teacher education to measure up to this criterion.

In this respect, the intelligent teacher can find needed help in the useful functional contributions from social, historical, philosophical, psychological, and sociological foundations of education. Many practical illustrations could be given by any experienced teacher or professor. For example, it has helped me to recall some of the basic findings about children and youth. Occasional wrangles and arguments between teenagers of opposite sexes were much easier for the professor-father to take when he remembered that such episodes are perfectly normative in the growth and development of children and youth. Truly, these knowledges can and should be *functional* in the work of the teacher and school.

Most people understand the need for courses in "methods" of teaching, tests and measures, and student ("practice") teaching. These or their counterparts are universally found in colleges of teacher education, but trends and changes are clearly discernible. It is more representative of newer findings to consider a great many kinds and means of "laboratory experiences" for the future teacher. Preferably these begin early in the college career, increase in frequency and intensity as the student grows in understanding and readiness to take new steps, culminating in an extended period of student teaching. Some programs provide for a final seminar or study to help the future teacher to clarify and mature a general point-of-view or philosophy of education.

Our experiences in professional education can be some of the high points in our whole career. Most of the teachers will be able, dedicated persons and one will associate with many promising, interesting and attractive young people like himself. Moreover, we will learn to accept, understand, and respect a large number of children. Most important of all, we shall all be joined together in interests and projects, big and little, that are shared and which provide that motive power for learning, *need* and *interest*. We will become excited and vitally concerned; more and more we may begin to give ourselves to this job. And we shall have the rare, significant excitement of a warm "afterglow," of a sense of satisfaction when things go well, and a thrill when we find that we are needed. Our professional education courses will then be seen clearly and definitely to be *functional*.

Individual interests mean enrichment

No program of education approaches any measure of democratic criteria unless it provides for the development and realization of individual interests and potentialities of the person. Our schools have long been committed in some degree to this philosophy, and some of the most promising developments have included provision for choice of curriculums and of activities that mean most to individual pupils in terms of their interests and needs. It is through this general philosophy that our schools discover the need for a comprehensive program of student activities. Many clubs, hobby groups, organizations in music, drama, speech and art, recreational programs, and a host of others are now in the schools. All of these need advisers and sponsors, teachers who like to do or take part in some activity and to work with youth. We come to a good and worthwhile reason for going in for activities in college, those that fit one's own interests and aptitudes. One day the skills and leadership we shall have acquired will go far toward making us acceptable and well-liked teachers in a good school.

There is another and even better reason for following up our individual interests by doing something active and definite to develop them. That reason is, the potential person each one of us can become if he makes the most of what he has to start with. In other words, activities are but a part of the means for facilitating growth into the all-round, versatile and effective person one can become. There are also added benefits that accompany activity and accomplishment in the form of relaxation, fun, the change of experiences, better balance among one's interests, in personality growth and through satisfactions in achievement.

All students should live as fully as possible, developing a variety of interests and gain a sense of accomplishment and satisfaction from a richer and larger pattern of life. Future teachers, in particular, should follow their individual interests and make the resulting activities an effective part of their teacher education. The teachers owe it to themselves to do this as enlightened self-interest. Adequate growth and services to young people are so clearly served by this phase of education that teachers cannot afford to neglect it.

This kind of perspective will enable us and our colleagues to judge sound uses of our time and energy in a number of activities. College youth may enter into a number of organizations, clubs, activities and hobbies that contribute to an all-round versatile sort of personality.

Can we begin with purpose?

The point of this part of our investigation is important, namely that we have clear purposes and incentives to derive the most from your teacher education program. We need to have a real concept of the big kinds of "competencies" that teachers should develop. Then, we should be able to visualize the potentive values and relationships to these competencies that inhere in the offerings of a teacher education institution. Finally, we should keep in mind the ever-present opportunity we have to learn from each and every experience we have in classes, in activities, in social relationships, in reflective thinking, in participation, in accepting responsibility, in appreciation episodes, in recreation, and whatever others we may have. Our competencies as teachers and their consistent development—these represent the important features in our pattern of conscious purposes. We shall find that it pays to take charge of our progress with clear constructive purposes.

Teachers Grow in Service

We have probably long since discarded the notion that our competency will be finished and complete when a diploma is put into our hands at Commencement, and that our subsequent growth will be automatic, painless, and effortless on our part. Our own good experiences of accomplishing or achieving anything should have provided us with the best clue or insight into the major question now before us.

A fundamental observation concerning the life of organisms seems to apply to the career of the teacher. Activity, change, growth, even learning never cease during one's lifetime. The end of growth or cessation of improvement mean stag-nation, decline, and death. The teacher, as an intelligent organism and responsive person, must go on acting, changing, doing, and learning throughout life. Of course, life goes on even if one sits down as long as one wishes, but it hardly deserves to be counted alongside the stirring and challenging performances which the most versatile and generous lives offer by way of inspiration.

One actual episode will illustrate this point. An older teacher, generally known to be extremely reactionary in outlook and methods, prefaced a remark upon school policy with "After all, I've had thirty-six years of experience." Later, when this was mentioned in a small group, someone observed: "Miss .... was wrong. She has not had thirty-six years of experience. She had one year of experience and has repeated it thirty-five times."

Few would question the essential soundness of the oft-quoted "As is the teacher, so is the school," a phrase not literally and invariably true but a good axiom for all practical purposes. It follows that teachers and parents, the adults of the future, are substantially made by the influences and experiences provided by those who are teaching today. If the school is to be a live, pleasant, happy place where young folks grow, it appears that the teacher must be alert to and interested in these outcomes. The key to an improving, interesting school is a teacher who grows and develops in many ways and with several competences. But how do teachers get that way?

An actual experience may provide a graphic impression of this concept. One evening after an educational conference two young men—visiting speakers at the sessions—were entertained in the home of one of the university administrators. After an exciting and interesting evening of discussion it was evident that an older liberal and alert mind had discovered two younger ones of similar stamp. In them he saw representatives of the quality and general type of educator that we need in American schools. Finally, he said, "Now we've exchanged views and ideas all evening. Clearly, you young fellows have got some of the interests, ideas, and standards of judgments that we need in our teachers and leaders. Now what I want to know is 'How did you get that way?'"

The dean's query is that which lies back of the approach implicit in this chapter. Our immediate great task is also our finest opportunity. It is to take command of our own development, to plan and envision widely and soundly, to be a conscious factor in all our own learning experiences to the end that our own understanding is always enhanced and enriched as the result. In other words, by deliberate attention and conscious awareness of what goes on and its meanings one can radically improve and facilitate the learnings that come from experience. The alert purposeful student is no longer an organism (with a high I. Q. but low in purpose) to whom many things happen, among them some of the potentially meaningful and revealing steps or experiences in the way of arriving at teaching. We get into the picture with ideas, plans, and purposes to guide ourselves gradually and experientially on the level of quality of preparation that we should aspire to as a teacher. Then we must keep on growing as we teach. Our skills, the fine positive attitudes toward people and teaching, the wide interests and capacities for growth, a clear grasp of democratic values and purposes of education—all these should be the result. In short, let us take charge of our *growth toward competency*.

IN-SERVICE EDUCATION
OF TEACHERS

No wise teacher expects to stop growth and learning when he leaves college with a diploma and a credential that he is fitted to teach. Learning as we have often noted is a lifelong process and any intelligent person is a testimonial to this fact. This point should be appreciated particularly by teachers. So vital is the fundamental of continued growth that our best school systems and state education authorities have planned to promote in-service educational opportunities and incentives for the teachers. No sounder or more important policy has been undertaken in the school systems of America than this. We will profit from this general practice when we begin to work in the public schools as teachers. We should begin to get ready to understand and to use effectively the opportunity that in-service educational programs can bring to us and to discover insights into ways and means of fostering your own growth and progress by personal effort and planning. Thus, we need never be dependent upon the provisions of others to promote our own personal and professional improvement. We should give attention to some major considerations that relate to this phase of teacher education.

Continuous growth of the professional person is one of the earmarks of the true professional. Teaching can never become the profession it deserves to be unless that kind of professional improvement becomes the rule. It is now well on the way to general acceptance.

Experiences of professional leaders have disclosed some important problems that affect provisions for in-service growth of teachers.[5] Among them are: (1) need for cooperative democratic program development in local school systems; (2) need to utilize the profession in development of in-service teacher education source offerings by colleges; (3) development of practicable workshop programs based on real needs of teachers; (4) the problems

[5] T. M. Stinnett, *The Teacher and Professional Organizations* (Third Edition) (Washington: NEA, 1956), p. 43.

of handling credits and standards while serving needs of teachers in courses; (5) provision of on-the-job equivalents for credit courses; and (6) bottlenecks of time, money, resources, and leadership for in-service programs in local school districts. Doubtless there are others—big and little. Nevertheless, there is no reason for discouragement. The very fact that some groups have encountered these problems means that someone has been trying to do something. A sure sign of vitality in an organism or an organization is the appearance of problems and challenges. We should make it our business to help with the solution of those that interrupt our progress.

Provisions for in-service growth

Responsibility for the continued growth and improvement of teachers is a shared obligation. Obviously, the teacher is responsible always and to the extent that he or she is able to control the factors that enter into the situation. The individual teacher must want to improve and grow, must be willing to put forth effort, and utilize what is pertinent to his personal and professional well being. But others must share this overall responsibility.

The school system which employs a teacher has a major responsibility to foster and promote the continued growth of its teaching faculty and staff. It is not only an obligation of a professional character; it is equally important as an investment in good and improved schools in the future. It has been shown that the school system can approach this responsibility by varied means: by making it possible to have teachers together for conferences, study groups, and committee work (upon planning and curriculum development for example) and visitation; through adequate pay and favorable security benefits that free teachers from apprehension and worry and facilitate the learning of more desirable insights and skills; and the utilization of intelligent approaches to learning in various opportunities for teachers. Clearly these are ways to foster and effect in-service growth of teachers. The responsible authorities and policy-makers of school systems have a moral responsibility to study and plan carefully and soundly to this end. Perhaps the most effective and intelligent means of fostering continued educational growth of teachers through board and administrative policies is that of *recognition*. Teachers cannot live upon approbation and verbal or written statements of appreciation, but these tangible signs of sincere and honest recognition of the worth and effort made by a good teacher go a long way toward an excellent morale and good climate of opinion among those who serve the children. Recognition, even in a tangible sort of way, is hollow and of no more than transitory effect if it is not sincere. Let no one be deluded or kidded; anybody with brains soon discovers that he is being misled whether he is free to react positively or not. Thus, the basic principle for the powers-that-be is clear: almost any sincere expression of recognition for teachers who do try to improve and to do an excellent job of teaching will be conspicuously successful. Sometimes recognition can go so far toward tangibility and concreteness as to become expressed as *incentive pay*.

This type of recognition of in-service growth of teachers is found in various guises in the standard or uniform salary schedules adopted by village, county, and larger city school systems all over the nation. Likewise, this principle is often found in the state finance programs designed to equalize support and to provide a minimally decent program of public education everywhere. Finally, the board and administration policy-makers for our common schools may use the in-service growth of teachers as criterion or index for *promotions*. On the surface this looks like a fair and equitable policy: the more alert and progressive the teacher the more worthy is she for promotion; but there are some problems, too. Sometimes, the best classroom teachers are systematically drained off from the instructional work of the school to become administrators. Many school people have wished for some better way to reward and to recognize the excellent teacher who improves herself by giving recognition to her classroom situation.

Other lesser but specific ways and means to promote the in-service education of teachers can be utilized by the school system. Ideally, the schools should be attractive, hygienic places to live and to work; space to work, relax, and to play should be available; a professional library, labor-saving gadgets, and an adequate instructional materials center would further the growth-improvement of the teaching personnel. Basic factors such as a reasonable workload, intelligent assignments in areas and fields of specialty, and relative freedom from distractions, negative forces, and pressures are likewise important. The school system can provide sympathetic, intelligent, and cooperative supervisory staff; it can divide the labor of curriculum development among all hands through a system of committees and working groups; helpful visiting consultants and resource persons can be furnished to schools whose teachers are trying to do things; and a plan of carefully scheduled inter-visitation can be arranged to help teachers whose needs are readily identifiable. The school system has a great many promising approaches and practices at its command for use in promoting further growth toward competence by the teachers. It has a great stake in this prospect, one matched only by its deep responsibility for a strategic role in this kind of program.

The community has a share

Many, many teachers have had lasting impressions and attitudes built into their personalities by some early experiences in the community in which they first taught. There can be little doubt that the narrow and extreme views of some community leaders have caused needless suffering to a great many teachers and occasioned some negative attitudes and feelings that helped no one, including the children. Fortunately, these conditions have changed materially for the better in the past two decades and teachers can be far more confident of being regarded as human in most communities. Few places now subject teachers to close scrutiny in their personal lives, or try to dictate to them in matters of associates, church attendance, local purchases, recreation, and the like. In the past few years, more communities have tried to do something kind and memorable for the teacher. School authorities, parent-teacher organizations, civic groups and friendly individuals have taken the initiative in this respect. The result is a situation that can make for greater freedom and initiative on the part of the young teacher. More of this time and freedom can be devoted to personal growth and further education.

Individual responsibility for teacher growth

Everything considered, one person has the major role to perform in the continued education and improvement of a given teacher. That is the individual teacher himself. The community can be a wholesome place to live and work; the people can accept teachers as natural human beings; in the school systems the conditions can be conducive to added growth and improvement, but there is no automatic professional advance unless the teacher himself has the initiative and desire to grow and progress toward competence. Conversely, even when there is little community awareness of this responsibility, and when the school system does little to foster teacher growth, there can still be real and effective improvement on the part of an individual teacher. It will not be as easy but it can be done. The goals of added professional competence and of personal improvement are important and feasible for anyone who really wants to achieve them. Hence, the admonition to future teachers to make the most of their opportunities even to the point of making their opportunities when there is no other way.

A great many steps to improve one's competence and skill in teaching can be taken by almost anyone. One is to engage in systematic study of materials related to one's job.[6] Another is the collecting and use of teaching aids. In schools where few instructional materials beyond free

---

[6] A useful guide for self-study by the teacher is one by Darlington and Skudler, *In-Service Education of Elementary Teachers* (Lincoln: D-Swynne Company, 1946). A copy should be in your college library or reference shelf for this course.

texts are available, the teacher can improve the situation materially by use of miscellaneous materials gathered from a variety of sources. Good teachers can use a wide variety of materials bearing upon a number of topics. The clue to a successful collection is imagination; clever teachers can see ideas nearly everywhere. A third imperative is to develop a convenient and useful filing setup. Usually the school librarian can be a great help on this problem. Another important point is to enlist the assistance of pupils. They will help to collect and to use materials for your classes and may even handle much of the arranging and filing of items. Still another consideration is that of caution about the soundness and appropriateness of the materials. It will not do to introduce materials in the classroom which are questionable or offensive. Sometimes teachers are deluged with free materials that are obviously propaganda for some vested interest. Any user of this must surely take note of its nature and primary purpose. It is likewise important to be prudent in the use of advertising matter in schools. Much useful material is available from advertising sources that can be used without violation of professional standards. Material that is offensively commercial and one-sided should not be used. The NEA policy on use of advertising matter in schools is a safe guide for teachers to use.

Much helpful free and inexpensive materials can be procured by the expenditure of a few post cards. Several useful guides to this kind of material are available.[7] Teachers find that there are many uses for a great number of these.

[7] See, for example, the following titles: *Free and Inexpensive Learning Materials,* Division of Surveys and Field Services, George

Developing new ideas

Teachers with initiative and imagination go far beyond the stages of collecting, arranging, and using miscellaneous teaching materials. Soon the resourceful person sees that materials are important for and because of ideas, a purpose, need, or value related to education. The big effort is then that of gaining and using better ideas—new ideas or those already "proved up" in practice. Teachers who have caught up this challenge find new and greater satisfactions in finding, using, and improving plans, approaches, techniques, materials, and evaluative measures. This might be termed the master stage or level of the good teacher's work as compared with the earlier or apprentice phase.

How and where do the best teachers find and develop ideas? A logical question if there is one, but an easy answer is almost impossible. It is almost as easy to describe or explain where and how any great creative artist gets and develops his ideas. It is true to say that the ideas are found almost anywhere and by any of many means, but this is too general to satisfy you. Good teachers do get ideas by talking to other teachers and "helping teachers," by observations, from creative films, from chance contacts and experiences in the community, from friendly critics of the school program, from those

Peabody College for Teachers, Nashville, Tennessee, current edition; *Free and Inexpensive Educational Materials,* The Quarrie Reference Library, 35 East Wacker Drive, Chicago, Illinois, current edition; *Elementary Teachers Guide to Free Curriculum Materials,* Educational Progress Service, Randolph, Wisconsin, current edition; *Bibliography of Free and Inexpensive Materials for Economic Education,* Joint Council on Economic Education, 2 West 46th Street, New York 36, New York, May 1, 1956.

pupils who have problems and from others who can help those who have difficulties, from reading experiences of other teachers, by visits to school exhibits, to museums, and through reflection upon one's problems.

It is a marvelous discovery to find that one can have revealing and exciting new flashes of insight (better understanding and ideas to try out) into the problems of teaching or the problems of life, for that matter. In this respect it is true that we learn from our problems when we are truly free to use all our intelligence to discover, develop or create solutions. Ideas are, in this case, a creative product of the free mind at work upon a problem situation.

The wise teacher will keep some kind of notebook or other practicable means of recording ideas and notes for future reference. The first one hundred ideas are the hardest.

Writing and talking

Good teachers often discover the satisfactions that follow the preparation of an acceptable article or book for either professional or general groups of readers. A sound plan for passing on one's ideas and experience is that of writing for professional journals. Sometimes the very effort to complete an article becomes an aid to thinking through an idea or set of ideas. All sound ideas and discoveries of educators deserve to be shared with other members of the profession and ultimately with the people in whose interest the public education enterprise is carried on.

There is great need for popular articles and accounts of good school practices directed to the parents and to the general reading public. One mounting problem of public schools in this country is the imperative need to interpret and explain good educational practices and needs to the people. The teacher who has ideas and worthwhile experiences to share with parents of her own classroom can be practically sure that other parents will be interested in her findings. The writing for popular journals may be an effective instrument for good public relations and a helpful means of professional growth at the same time.

What has been said about professional writing is applicable to the preparation of addresses and informal talks to both lay and educational groups. In this way the discerning teacher can make contributions to the improvement of the community, the school program, and to her own in-service educational growth.

Experimentation and research

An invaluable means of teacher growth is that of trying out ideas, experimenting to find out what works and how, and the efforts that follow an insatiable desire to know the best possible answer to professional questions. The only answer to many questions connected with teaching must come from experimentation. Here and there imaginative and resourceful teachers try to enlarge the areas of knowledge about some of these questions. These are the true discoverers and forerunners of the educational profession. It is a responsibility of the administration and policy-making authority of the school system and of the teaching profession alike to foster and promote experimentation and all types of research by capable teachers. There is no alternative to continued efforts in research for the improvement of teaching, for the solution of compelling educational problems, for the optimum contribution of education to our democratic society and to our way of life. Incidentally, the accomplishment of research is an important and effective means of teacher growth on the job.

Travel and new experiences

One of man's basic needs is to have varied experiences, or a relief from monotony. Teachers are no different from the typical layman in this respect. Certainly, no one can deny that travel is a particularly effective means of self-improvement for the teacher. First-hand acquaintance with much of the subject matter of social studies, literature, and commerce has an immediate effect upon the teaching done by the traveller. Furthermore, there are the added gains in personality growth and emotional maturity evidenced in poise, self-respect, and new interests. The pupils and associates gain much from the teacher who has had satisfying travel experiences. So generally is this accepted that many school systems give credit for travel alongside summer school attendance in matters of policy on in-service education and salary increment.

Teachers can make their travel experiences yield greater returns by some attention to planning. There can be advance planning and study of the areas to be visited to insure greater appreciation of what is to come. There can be some purposeful collecting of materials from and about the places visited. A record of some sort can be kept during the trip as an aid to recall and added appreciation later on. One valued means is that of the snapshot or movie camera fan whose records of travel experiences often prove to be the best single investment made for the project. Traveling teachers can always be on the lookout for contacts and acquaintances to be kept up in later years. Many personal and professional friendships have been made in this way. One specific benefit to children is that of "pen pals" and other educative experiences. The NEA has a Travel Bureau that provides much help and assistance to teacher groups interested in travel, both foreign and domestic.[8]

One of the finest experiences open to our best teachers is that of an *exchange* arrangement for a year abroad. This type of professional exchange has become more and more common since World War II. Two teachers from similar school positions are simply "exchanged" by the educational authorities of their governments for a year. The United States and Great Britain have exchanged most teachers under this plan, but there have been a good number with France, with most of the Western European nations, Australia, Latin America, and certain oriental countries. In 1956–1957 the total number of exchange teachers exceeded 500; in 1961–1962, 1025 exchange professors and teachers were abroad.[9] The language barrier is the principal handicap for most teachers, a matter in which our teachers do not compare favorably with those of several nations. Other opportunities to attend seminars during the summer and to study abroad are available. Information can be gained about teachers exchange and other programs from the U.S. Office of Education in the Department of Health, Education, and Welfare.

[8] Write to the NEA for information, 1201 16th Street, N.W., Washington 6, D.C.

[9] *Higher Education,* **XVIII,** No. 8 (June 1962), p. 21.

The teacher is the answer

The key person in the matter of continued growth and improvement of the teacher is the teacher himself. The school system that employs teachers, the community in which teachers work, the college of teacher education, and the associates of the teaching profession can and should take an interest in the growth of any and all teachers. The major responsibility is upon the teacher himself to improve, to grow personally and professionally, to become a finer person and better teacher. No one can achieve that for him. For the teacher with ambition and courage, few obstacles can deter and prevent the achievement of this purpose. We remember some. What these teachers have done, we can do. We can use almost any kind of experiences as a means of growth toward competence.

The determined young teacher can use his reading for this purpose. That means a purposeful, balanced program of reading, but this is the only intelligent way to plan one's reading in any case. It means the selection of general reading over a range and variety of subjects and works to give balance, depth, and versatility. Any good librarian will be glad to help a reader with a purpose. It also means that professional reading should have a place in one's interests. A personal library can be gradually accumulated as an aid to one's reading and as a means of added competence in the classroom.

Much of the same discrimination and choice could be used in mass media of communication. Along with these interests, there should be time given to pursuit of personal interests—hobbies and avocations—and recreation. Experiences gained in other kinds of work often are amazingly fruitful and helpful to teachers. Friends and friendships are indispensable ingredients in the life plan of any person. The teacher will want and will value friends and the experiences of friendship from many persons.

There is the over-arching concern of one's philosophy of life, one's values—that which enables a person to become a discriminating, choosing responsible human being—is to be considered. Most teachers are unusually sensitive to these major concerns, being motivated and guided by their feeling for people and for what happens to others. Our purpose here is not to lecture about this central aspect of one's life; it is mentioned to congratulate some upon this kind of sensitivity and to suggest that this is a quality that sets young teacher candidates apart, one that places them in company with those spirits that care about other people. Teachers should not minimize or neglect to keep this part of their "personality for teaching" well up on their list of points to be held in high regard. This should be a mirror in which teachers can be proud to view themselves. In many, many instances, it is that.

Our prospects

What has been set down here will have more meaning for many future teachers as they enter actively upon their work in the schools. Nevertheless, it is not amiss for youth to give some consideration to matters of personal and professional growth even though they are still engaged in the pre-service phase of preparation for teaching. It is true that your present stage of preparation is but a step in that long and continuous growth toward competency. You will not gain competency and acquire the many skills of the teacher quickly or even completely from your experiences in the teachers' college. There will be no single and final step to this end in college or even in one's first year of teaching. This will gradually be achieved and approached as we continue to grow personally and professionally through the years. During our college years we are starting and insuring real progress toward that objective.

Professional Responsibility of Teachers

The responsibilities of the teacher do not end with the discharge of his responsibilities in the classroom and doing his part in PTA work or even when he makes a worthwhile contribution to the community. There remains the matter of professional relationships and responsibilities which are all too often left to be done by a few teachers and administrators. We may recall the figures concerning NEA membership and wonder just why there are not one and a half million members. The answer is simple and short but not sweet: too many teachers are not full participants in their profession. That's the simple unadorned fact. No other important professional group in our nation has so large a part of its membership content to remain in an inactive non-participating role.

The work of the professional organizations go on because a few teachers and administrators have enough initiative and pride to work at the job. Their efforts can never be completely effective until the national, state, and local organizations are fully manned and directed by the force and enthusiasm which the nearly two million teachers can give.

You may wonder just why this problem is laid in your lap so early in the game, even as we are only considering whether to become a teacher. That unspoken question raises a point which needs to be examined. Perhaps the reason why so many teachers do not actively participate in their own professional organizations and activities is because little effort has been made to acquaint them with these opportunities and responsibilities. Professional pride and interest, the sense of responsibility to do one's part in solving problems together are learned just as are many other aspects of teacher education. It seems essential and wise to give our young teacher recruits the chance to know more of these opportunities and responsibilities. Everyone will then have a better chance to make an intelligent decision about the part they will play as a teacher among other teachers.

There are other significant opportunities for professional growth and action by teachers. We can name some right off if we give it some thought. Teachers owe it to themselves and to the youth they serve to keep alert and to grow professionally by study and other means of keeping abreast of developments in their field. Teachers who have ability owe to their colleagues the especial contributions they can make to professional advancement. Research, a good idea which has been tried, suggestions for improved teaching, are examples of the kinds of articles gifted teachers should write. It may be a matter of speaking, or serving on committees. Finally, there is the whole area of professional practices, attitudes and values which we may think of as the "ethics" of our profession. Certainly, the ethically conscious teacher will wish to know and to observe the best standards the professional organizations have formulated.

Four brief phrases seem to sum up these essential responsibilities of teachers: (1) "Take part," (2) "Keep up," (3) "Help out," and (4) "Be professional."

THE PATTERN OF
PROFESSIONAL ORGANIZATIONS

Teachers are coming to recognize the importance of and necessity for more effective organized efforts for promotion of improved educational policy and for the advancement of interests of the profession.[10] The teacher crisis and the need for vastly improved programs of financial support have given great impetus to the growth and strength of professional organizing. The teachers of America may now affiliate with an appropriate professional organization from the local to the international level. There is a local education association which is affiliated with the state and national groups. In many states, there are district or area associations which operate at an intermediate level between the local and state groups. All of the states have active strong education associations, as do the territories

[10] One of the best treatments of this whole topic may be found in T. M. Stinnett, *The Profession of Teaching* (Washington: The Center for Applied Research in Education, Inc., 1962). This is a volume in a new series, *The Library of Education.*

and the District of Columbia. At the national level is the active and alert National Education Association with headquarters in the nation's capital. The NEA was a charter member of the recently-organized international body known as the World Confederation of Organizations of the Teaching Profession with which many of our leading professional organizations are affiliated. Individual teachers, too, may become associate members for a modest annual fee.

The pattern of educational organizations for teachers appears to be complete. In spite of this fact, teachers as a professional group are not well organized. By this we mean that teachers have not participated in their professional organization to the extent that architects, dentists, lawyers, nurses, physicians, or social workers have done. For more than a century the NEA has fought strenuously and ably for professional goals, but its membership has usually represented only a fraction of the potential strength it should have had. Soon after the second World War its membership reached an all-time high both in number and proportion of teachers; it was approximately 51 percent of educational personnel at work in our schools. Since then its growth has continued as has its influence; in 1963 its total membership numbered 860,000 teachers. At the local level, the teaching profession has been inadequately organized for effective action but there is encouragement in the fact that good increases have appeared in the postwar years. At the state level teachers have made the best showing of professional unity and strength. Almost invariably in recent years, the membership of affiliated state education associations has exceeded one and a half million teachers.

*The National Education Association
of the United States*

Our national professional organization of teachers is the largest in the world. Its long and active history of professional activity began in 1857. The NEA dates from an organization formed on August 26 of that year by 43 educators who gathered in Philadelphia in response to a call signed by presidents of ten state teachers associations. In 1870, the National Association of School Superintendents and the American Normal School Association joined with the National Teachers Association to form the NEA. Membership increased considerably after the 1886 meeting. In 1886 the organization was incorporated under the District of Columbia law and in 1905 it was chartered by Congress under the above title. In 1920 it acquired a headquarters in Washington at that famous address, 1201 Sixteenth Street, N.W.

Since then, the NEA has grown greatly both in membership and in the scope of its activities. Its research activities date from the appointment of the famous "Committee of Ten" in 1892. Manifold activities in behalf of teacher welfare have been carried on for over 45 years. Among these were promotion of credit unions and retirement programs in the states and the establishment of a term-life insurance program for members. The popular *NEA Journal* was started in 1921, series of reports and other publications followed. American Education Week was inaugurated that same year.

In 1920, the NEA discontinued its open business sessions and provided for a Representative Assembly to conduct its official business. Delegates are chosen by both local and state organizations in proportion to their membership. In 1946, the NEA entered into a cooperative program with state and local organizations for expansion of membership and development of services.

The NEA has long sponsored and maintained a wide range of projects and services. It publishes the *NEA Journal* and various research publications; it sponsors American Education Week and Teaching Career Month, the Future Teachers of America and Student NEA; it produces professional films such as *Assignment: Tomorrow, Skippy and the Three R's, Freedom to Teach,* and *A Desk for Billie,* and television programs; it holds the Institutes on Organization Leadership and for Professional and Public Relations. Twenty-six important Commissions and Committees have been maintained. Among these were the Educational Policies Commission, and the Commission for the Defense of Democracy Through Education of which you have probably heard. Joint committees are maintained in cooperation with the American Legion, American Library Association, American Medical Association, American Teachers Association, American Textbook Publishers Institute, National Congress of Parents and Teachers, Magazine Publishers Association, and the National School Boards Association. Thirty-three strong departments are maintained to serve the needs of various professional groups, twenty-one of which maintain staffs at NEA headquarters. Prominent among these are the American Association of School Administrators (the old Department of Superintendence), the Association for Supervision and Curriculum Development, the National Association of Secondary School Principals, the

National Council for the Social Studies, and others representing the interests of educational personnel in many fields. Many of these publish journals, yearbooks and other publications. An exhibit of the publications which issue from NEA in a single year would prove an impressive and interesting demonstration.

Perhaps the most important aspect of the work of the NEA is that of providing vigorous leadership in professional matters at the national level. In recent years, the NEA has tackled problems of serious interference with public education policy in a number of communities with encouragingly effective results. The NEA has long given consistent leadership in the fight to secure federal aid legislation by the Congress. Through the years the Association has steadfastly favored the support of the constitutional principles related to education (a state function, and public funds for public education only). In recent years it has participated in many activities in cooperation with other national and international groups in education. In 1961, the NEA adopted a policy for professional negotiations with boards of education upon salary and contractual policy. American teachers have the right to feel a pride in the policy and programs of their national professional group—the NEA.[11]

State education associations

The importance of state education associations is evidenced by the fact that the vast majority of American teachers maintain membership in their respective state organizations. The state responsibility for education and the fact that most

[11] See the *NEA Handbook* for the current year for up-to-date information about NEA.

school legislation is enacted by the state legislatures cause teachers to feel that their organized effort should be made to count at the state level.

There are one or more education associations in each state and the territories. The state education associations are affiliated with the NEA, but each one has its own constitution and bylaws, governing boards and officers. Most maintain a permanent headquarters and staff. Usually there are several standing committees and a representative assembly which transacts business of the Association. Journals are published, some research activities are carried on, annual meetings are held and there are departmental and sectional meetings. Membership is usually open to all persons engaged in school work. Annual dues range from $1 to $10 and usually the state journal is included. The total number of members in the 64 affiliated organizations at the state level reaches above one and one-half million teachers.

Local education associations are growing

Local professional organizations of teachers are older than the state associations in this country. Records show that groups of Boston and New York City teachers were organized as early as the 1790's. Today local organizations are overshadowed by the activities and strength of the state education associations chiefly because it is at the state level that leadership and pressure produce legislative action. Local education associations have larger memberships and there are more of them than at any previous time in our history. In 1962 over 7,500 local education associations were affiliated with the NEA.

Local associations are organized by teachers to serve their needs for a professional organization. The type may vary according to the school system or district in which the teachers work. A group may or may not affiliate with the state or national associations as it wishes, but the vast majority find it desirable to do so. These groups send delegates direct to the Representative Assembly of NEA for the annual meeting held in July.

Teachers who have had experience in their local education associations gain valuable experience and find many opportunities to work for professional goals. The local association often provides the group with which school boards and authorities cooperate in the development of policy on a "democratic" basis. Unity of the profession is fostered by the presence of a strong local association and teachers in some communities have found such groups helpful when schools or teachers are placed under pressure by vested interest groups. Here is where the professional negotiation between teacher's group and the school board on salary and contracts takes place. Most local education associations work closely with their state education associations as well upon matters of professional concern. Often a local group sends one of its officers to the annual leadership training institute sponsored by the NEA. Good sources of information on local education associations are the *NEA Handbook* and the *NEA Manual for Locals*.

Teachers should join professional organizations

Teachers as members of a great profession owe it to themselves to join and actively participate in the work of their local, state, and National Education As-

sociations. Plenty of evidence shows that the partially united profession has made tremendous gains in advancing professional standards and conditions which affect education. A brief account of these achievements may be found in the *NEA Handbook*. The reports indicate what could be accomplished if all teachers took an active part in professional organizations.

From a strictly financial standpoint, membership in the NEA and affiliated groups is a great bargain. Annual membership dues of $5 bring the *NEA Journal* and help support the multifarious activities and services of the NEA. An annual fee of $10 brings the *Journal,* research reports, and other publications issued by NEA departments and committees during the year. Life membership entitles one to all the services and publications of the NEA for the payment of $150 dues, $15 each for ten installments.

The real argument for participation in the professional organization is that a real profession must have its own autonomous body able to control its own affairs in the public interest. If the teaching profession does not do this, it will lose the chance to set its own standards and come to be regulated by other agencies and means.

Other professional organizations

Several other important organizations exist at the national level. None of these approach the size or strength of the NEA but each serves particular needs and interests of its membership.

There is the small but active American Association of University Professors with headquarters and staff in the nation's capital and chapters in most of the larger institutions of higher learning over the land. It publishes a *Journal* and maintains an active program of support for standards and principles vital to higher education. A major concern for academic freedom in higher education and its studies of professorial salaries are outstanding accomplishments of the AAUP as the Association is popularly known.

There are several other national organizations, chiefly research and scholarly groups, that exist outside the NEA pattern. Among them may be mentioned the National Society for the Study of Education which succeeded the old National Herbartian Society that started in the 1890's. The NSSE, as it is called, produces two outstanding "yearbooks" annually, each represents an up-to-date summary or presentation of content upon an important topic or field of education. Educators speak of the "41st Yearbook" to refer to an outstanding symposium of reports on either the philosophies of education or the psychology of learning by a number of leading men in each field.

The National John Dewey Society is a small but active group interested in studies of education in the democratic culture. Its yearbook and special publications have been of uniformly high order and it has cooperated with the Philosophy of Education Society in publishing the journal, *Educational Theory*.

The Philosophy of Education Society, the National Society of College Teachers of Education, and the Comparative Education Society are smaller groups of professors in their respective fields, organized for research and services in activities related to their work. These are illustrative of a great many of this type that serve the higher education fields.

The National Catholic Education Association is a nationwide organization of religious and lay personnel connected with the diocesan and parochial schools and higher education institutions of the Roman Catholic Church in the United States. Its headquarters is at the Catholic University of America in Washington, D.C. It holds annual meetings and publishes the *Proceedings* and a *Bulletin*.

The American Federation of Teachers

There have been several organizations of the "teachers' union" type at various times but only one that has continued to grow to the present. This is the best known of these organizations, the American Federation of Teachers. The AFT, as it is popularly known, was organized in 1916 and immediately became affiliated with the American Federation of Labor. Its membership rose from approximately 3,000 to 12,000 by 1920, fell off to the former figure during the 1920's, and grew again after World War II. During the periods of rivalry among the other labor organizations various groups competed for teacher memberships in certain urban centers but made little inroads upon the "craft union" pattern. The AFT became a part of the merged AFL-CIO in the 1950's.

Membership is open to all educational personnel except those in top administrative positions. The "locals" at the community level are designated by charter numbers. There are federations at the state level. The national headquarters of the AFT is located in Chicago. Dues are somewhat higher than for NEA. Annual conventions are held and the official publication, *The American Teacher,* is published monthly through the school year.

The AFT emphasizes various objectives but principally those related to teacher welfare. Its methods differ radically from those of the NEA as one would expect from its affiliation with the AFL-CIO. The strong influence and backing of the labor unions of the national federation provide the "teachers' union" its most potent weapon. Publicity, parades, protests, meetings and the like are used to secure action to improve conditions affecting teaching. The AFT has adopted a "no-strike" policy but there have been deviations from this policy, notably in New York in 1960 and 1962. Although the total membership of the AFT (70,000) is small compared to the NEA, it is recognized as a potent force in certain city school systems.

Unions vs. professional organizations

You may wish to pursue the study of the "teachers' union" further as you get ready to teach. Certainly you can hardly miss hearing discussions of the propriety or advisability of joining a union among your teacher friends. This is a question which you will have to study and decide for yourself. The advocates stress the strength which AFT has in the backing of organized labor groups of the AFL-CIO. They point out the consistently friendly attitude of organized labor toward education in past years. They also maintain that the interest of teachers is bound up with those of labor groups. The spokesmen often refer to the "craft" of teaching rather than the profession. Union leaders insist upon a union for teachers only, administrators are not eligible to belong, being viewed as "management." One other argument is often advanced, viz. that the profes-

sional organization (NEA) has not accomplished much and that the vigorous action of the union promises greater results.

On the other hand, you hear arguments which maintain that the professional organization (NEA) is the appropriate agency of action for teachers. In this view further progress and improvements will come through vigorous efforts to unite the entire profession, administrators *and* teachers, into an organization as effective as those of the bar and medical groups. The affiliation of the teaching profession with organized labor would involve teachers in the traditional clashes between labor and management. Teachers would then be less free to deal objectively with many public issues and economic problems in their classrooms. These leaders feel that teachers cannot afford to lose their strongest position of impartiality in economic questions. They aver that the NEA and its Department of Classroom Teachers can act decisively and vigorously if teachers participate actively in their programs. They point to recent accomplishments in several school systems where the NEA took vigorous action to improve professional conditions and to the new policy of professional negotiations on salary agreements and contracts as evidence that the professional organization is competent and vigilant. The NEA and its affiliates have undertaken strong efforts to strengthen the professional status of teachers and to effect recognition of the profession. This appears to be an important consideration in the views of teachers as shown by the favorable response in most places. The philosophy of a profession and that of a craft union are too far apart for many teachers to elect a change of affiliation.

Professional growth of teachers

Teachers who find their professional life stimulating and interesting express interest in keeping up with developments. They find that professional meetings are stimulating and helpful just as well-informed doctors find it necessary to attend meetings of their colleagues. Professional minded teachers find attendance at educational meetings and conferences no bore, but rather a privilege. Professional competence is not acquired without effort any more than other worthwhile returns may be expected without some investment on one's part.

Other practicable ways of investing in one's professional growth are regular practices of reading professional books and periodicals. Few teachers can afford to take all the journals they would like or to buy many books, but ways can be found to meet these needs. School systems can be induced to provide modest professional libraries for the use of teachers. Where this is not possible teachers with initiative have effected cooperative arrangements whereby each obtains some journals and books which are shared with their colleagues. There is hardly a teaching situation so desperate and poor that some means of professional improvement and growth cannot be found, that is, if teachers are alert professionally and active.

Teachers contribute ideas and leadership

The best teachers are not content with mere holding of membership in professional organizations and attendance at meetings. Capable, professional-minded teachers become leaders by contributions to the professional activity and literature of our field. Activity and participation appear to be good clues to continued growth and interest on the part of teachers. Many teachers have experiences and ideas which are well worth the attention of others. These teachers should write articles for professional journals and learn to speak before their colleagues in meetings. Opportunities to serve on committees, participate in study groups should be accepted by the teacher who expects to grow in competence and effectiveness. These efforts and activities will result in a gradual upgrading or improvement of our professional work. Teachers lose a good bet when they fail to use every opportunity to participate in professional activities and growth.

Student groups are important

You may have the impression that what has been said is more applicable to teachers in service than to teacher candidates. That is true in a sense but it is certain that we must do a better job to help young persons entering the profession to understand and participate more actively. Such an opportunity is available in the Student National Education Association movement. This organization offers a practicable and effective means of giving teacher candidates actual experiences and participation in professional organizations and activities. Every teacher education institution should have an SNEA chapter as an integral part of its program.

SNEA began as the Future Teachers of America established by the NEA in 1937. The name was changed in 1958.

It is carried on as a special project by the staff of the NCTEPS. Its direction is provided by a national committee consisting of the Executive Secretary of NEA, the editor of the *NEA Journal,* and six other members of the staff. Correspondence and inquires are welcomed by the SNEA, National Commission on Teacher Education and Professional Standards, NEA, 1201 Sixteenth Street, N.W., Washington 6, D.C.

SNEA is looked upon as a laboratory experience in civic and professional action. Out of this kind of active participation and experience should emerge potential leadership for future professional activities and organizations. SNEA is considered an organic part of local, state, and national associations. All members receive the NEA and their state journals, and the National Committee donates books and pamphlets to SNEA chapters for a professional library and each member receives ten *Personal Growth Leaflets.*

Purposes of the SNEA have been officially expressed as follows:

1. To develop among young people who are preparing to be teachers an organization which shall be an integral part of state and national education associations.
2. To acquaint teachers in training with the history, ethics, and program of the organized teaching profession.
3. To give teachers in training practical experience in working together in a democratic way on the problems of the profession and the community.
4. To interest the best young men and women in education as a lifetime career.
5. To encourage careful selection of persons admitted to schools which prepare teachers with emphasis on both character and scholarship.

6. To seek through the dissemination of information and through higher standards of preparation to bring teacher supply and demand into a reasonable balance.

SNEA chapters have latitude to develop objectives for their programs and activities at the campus level. The *Yearbook* for a given year provides numerous illustrations of projects and activities of chapters in various institutions.[12] Outstanding chapters are designated each year on the basis of eight criteria.

The Future Teachers of America movement has been continued in the high schools.[13] Students interested in teaching may form an "FTA Club" and apply for a charter. The National Committee provides some helpful material for clubs and sponsors. The organization of FTA clubs in high schools has been proved an appropriate and valuable activity for FTA chapters in teacher education institutions.

The "code of ethics" for teachers

Teachers belong to a great profession, one dedicated to highest ideals of service. It is imperative that their standards of personal and professional conduct should reflect these ideals in practice. Young teachers have the benefit of the experience of teachers and professional organizations in the form of codes of ethics which have been developed. The NEA revised its "Code of Ethics" which was adopted by the NEA Representative Assembly at the 1963 Convention in Detroit. The new Code of Ethics of the

[12] See *SNEA Yearbook* for current year for latest data and for full information.

[13] Ellis F. Hartford, *A Plan Book for Future Teachers* (Evanston, Illinois: Row, Peterson, 1961).

Education Profession is presented for purposes of information and study:[14]

The Code of Ethics of the Education Profession

PREAMBLE

We, the professional educators of the United States of America, affirm our belief in the worth and dignity of man. We recognize the supreme importance of the pursuit of truth, the encouragement of scholarship, and the promotion of democratic citizenship. We regard as essential to these goals the protection of freedom to learn and to teach and the guarantee of equal educational opportunity for all. We affirm and accept our responsibility to practice our profession according to the highest ethical standards.

We acknowledge the magnitude of the profession we have chosen, and engage ourselves, individually and collectively, to judge our colleagues and to be judged by them in accordance with the applicable provisions of this code.

PRINCIPLE I

Commitment to the Student

We measure success by the progress of each student toward achievement of his maximum potential. We therefore work to stimulate the spirit of inquiry, the acquisition of knowledge and understanding, and the thoughtful formulation of worthy goals. We recognize the importance of cooperative relationships with other community institutions, especially the home.

In fulfilling our obligations to the student, we—

1. Deal justly and considerately with each student.
2. Encourage the student to study varying points of view and respect his right to form his own judgment.

[14] NEA Committee on Professional Ethics, *Code of Ethics of the Education Profession* (adopted by the NEA Representative Assembly, Detroit, Michigan, July 1963) (Washington: NEA, 1963). Used with permission.

3. Withhold confidential information about a student or his home unless we deem that its release serves professional purposes, benefits the student, or is required by law.
4. Make discreet use of available information about the student.
5. Conduct conferences with or concerning students in an appropriate place and manner.
6. Refrain from commenting unprofessionally about a student or his home.
7. Avoid exploiting our professional relationship with any student.
8. Tutor only in accordance with officially approved policies.
9. Inform appropriate individuals and agencies of the student's educational needs and assist in providing an understanding of his educational experiences.
10. Seek constantly to improve learning facilities and opportunities.

PRINCIPLE II

Commitment to the Community

We believe that patriotism in its highest form requires dedication to the principles of our democratic heritage. We share with all other citizens the responsibility for the development of sound public policy. As educators, we are particularly accountable for participating in the development of educational programs and policies and for interpreting them to the public.

In fulfilling our obligation to the community, we—

1. Share the responsibility for improving the educational opportunities for all.
2. Recognize that each educational institution may have a person authorized to interpret its official policies.
3. Acknowledge the right and responsibility of the public to participate in the formulation of educational policy.
4. Evaluate through appropriate professional procedures conditions within a district or institution of learning, make

known serious deficiencies, and take any action deemed necessary and proper.

5. Use educational facilities for intended purposes consistent with applicable policy, law, and regulation.
6. Assume full political and citizenship responsibilities, but refrain from exploiting the institutional privileges of our professional positions to promote political candidates or partisan activities.
7. Protect the educational program against undesirable infringement.

PRINCIPLE III
Commitment to the Profession

We believe that the quality of the services of the education profession directly influences the future of the nation and its citizens. We therefore exert every effort to raise educational standards, to improve our service, to promote a climate in which the exercise of professional judgment is encouraged, and to achieve conditions which attract persons worthy of the trust to careers in education. Aware of the value of united effort, we contribute actively to the support, planning, and programs of our professional organizations.

In fulfilling our obligations to the profession, we—

1. Recognize that a profession must accept responsibility for the conduct of its members and understand that our own conduct may be regarded as representative.
2. Participate and conduct ourselves in a responsible manner in the development and implementation of policies affecting education.
3. Cooperate in the selective recruitment of prospective teachers and in the orientation of student teachers, interns, and those colleagues new to their positions.
4. Accord just and equitable treatment to all members of the profession in the exercise of their professional rights and responsibilities, and support them when unjustly accused or mistreated.
5. Refrain from assigning professional duties to non-professional personnel when such assignment is not in the best interest of the student.
6. Provide, upon request, a statement of specific reason for administrative recommendations that lead to the denial of increments, significant changes in employment, or termination of employment.
7. Refrain from exerting undue influence based on the authority of our positions in the determination of professional decisions by colleagues.
8. Keep the trust under which confidential information is exchanged.
9. Make appropriate use of time granted for professional purposes.
10. Interpret and use the writings of others and the findings of educational research with intellectual honesty.
11. Maintain our integrity when dissenting by basing our public criticism of education on valid assumptions as established by careful evaluation of facts or hypotheses.
12. Represent honestly our professional qualifications, and identify ourselves only with reputable educational institutions.
13. Respond accurately to requests for evaluations of colleagues seeking professional positions.
14. Provide applicants seeking information about a position with an honest description of the assignment, the conditions of work, and related matters.

PRINCIPLE IV
Commitment to Professional Employment Practices

We regard the employment agreement as solemn pledge to be executed both in spirit and in fact in a manner consistent with the highest ideals of professional service. Sound professional personnel relationships with governing boards are built upon personal integrity, dignity, and mutual respect.

In fulfilling our obligations to professional employment practices, we—

1. Apply for or offer a position on the basis of professional and legal qualifications.
2. Apply for a specific position only when it is known to be vacant and refrain from such practices as underbidding or commenting adversely about other candidates.
3. Fill no vacancy except where the terms, conditions, policies, and practices permit the exercise of our professional judgment and skill, and where a climate conducive to professional service exists.
4. Adhere to the conditions of a contract or to the terms of an appointment until either has been terminated legally or by mutual consent.
5. Give prompt notice of any change in availability of service, in status of applications, or in charge in position.
6. Conduct professional business through the recognized educational and professional channels.
7. Accept no gratuities or gifts of significance that might influence our judgment in the exercise of our professional duties.
8. Engage in no outside employment that will impair the effectiveness of our professional service and permit no commercial exploitation of our professional position.

The significance of the new Code of Ethics of the Education Profession can be appreciated by the profession and the general public in the light of needs for better controls over professional practices in recent years. There have been some extreme instances of expulsion of persons from the NEA and state associations for violation of professional ethics. The new code should set standards for the entire profession.

We can be professionals

Young persons who are entering teaching probably need few lectures upon the significance and importance of the profession. Neither do they need to have the importance of the profession pointed out to them again and again. It is unlikely that they need further emphasis upon the importance of continuing their own professional study and growth after graduation. What they may need is more information about the professional opportunities available to them for continued growth and improvement. To sum up, we need only a few phrases:

1. Take a part in professional organizations;
2. Keep up with latest developments in your profession;
3. Help out by making your own contributions; and
4. Be professional in your actions and dealings.

You can become an alert professional in your chosen work of teaching.

Selected Bibliography

Abraham, Willard. *A Handbook for the New Teacher.* New York: Holt, Rinehart & Winston, Inc., 1960.

Armstrong, W. Earl and Stinnett, T. M. *A Manual on Certification Requirements for School Personnel in the United States.* Washington: NEA, 1962. (See latest biennial issue.)

Cottrell, Donald P. (Ed.) *Teacher Education for a Free People.* Oneonta, New York: The American Association of Colleges of Teacher Education, 1956.

CTA Research Bulletin, *Information on Merit Rating of Teachers,* Bulletin No. 98. San Francisco: California Teacher Association, December, 1956.

Filbin, Robert L. and Vogel, Stefan. *So You're Going to be a Teacher.* Great Neck, N.Y.: Barron's Educational Series Inc., 1962.

Ford Foundation, *The New Teacher.* New York: Ford Foundation, 1962.

Fund for the Advancement of Education, *Teachers for Tomorrow.* New York: The Fund, 1955.

Graham, Grace. *The Public School in the American Community.* New York: Harper & Row, 1963, pp. 475–507.

Haskew, Laurence D., *et al.,* "Teacher Education," *NEA Journal,* **XLVIII,** (April 1959), pp. 15–31.

Herrick, Virgil E. "Our Future in Teacher Education," *Teachers College Record,* **LVII,** (February 1956), pp. 323–332.

Hodenfield, G. K. "Nobody Asked Me, But . . . ," *Saturday Review,* **XLV,** (January 1962), pp. 51–52.

——— and Stinnett, T. M. *The Education of Teachers: Conflict and Consensus.* Englewood Cliffs, N.J.: Prentice-Hall, Inc., 1961.

Lindsay, Margaret. "Ask Yourself Some Questions," *NEA Journal,* **XL,** No. 3 (March 1951), pp. 173–175.

Mackie, Romaine P., *et al. Qualifications and Preparation of Teachers of Exceptional Children,* Department of Health, Education and Welfare, Office of Education. Washington: U.S. Government Printing Office, 1954.

Moffitt, John Clifton. *In-Service Education for Teachers.* Washington: The Center for Applied Research in Education, 1963.

National Commission on Teacher Education and Professional Standards, Margaret Lindsay (Ed.) *New Horizons in the Teaching Profession.* Washington: NEA, 1961.

National Education Association, *Handbook for Local, State, and National Associations, 1961–62.* Washington: NEA, 1961, see current edition.

NEA, How to be a Pro, Rev. ed. Washington: NEA, 1961.

NEA, Research Division, *Teachers Supply and Demand in the Public Schools.* Washington: NEA, 1962. See current edition of this report published annually. See chapter 6.

Peters, Herman J., *et al. Introduction to Teaching.* New York: The Macmillan Company, 1963.

Riccio, Anthony C. and Cyphert, Frederick P. *Teaching in America.* Columbus: Charles E. Merrill Books, Inc., 1962, pp. 231–345, 444–467.

Snow, Robert H. "Anxieties and Discontents in Teaching," *Phi Delta Kappan,* **XLIV,** No. 7 (April 1963), pp. 318–321.

Stiles, Lindley J., *et al. Teacher Education in the United States.* New York: The Ronald Press Company, 1960.

Stinnett, T. M. *The Profession of Teaching.* Washington: The Center for Applied Research in Education, Inc., 1962. See chapters V–VII.

Stinnett, T. M. and Huggett, Albert J. *Professional Problems of Teachers,* 2nd ed. New York: The Macmillan Co., 1963.

"Strikes or Sanctions," *Phi Delta Kappan,* **XLIV,** No. 1 (October 1962), pp. 1–9.

Woodring, Paul. *New Directions in Teacher Education.* New York: Fund for the Advancement of Education, 1957.

Wynn, Richard. *Careers in Teaching.* New York: The McGraw-Hill Book Co., Inc. 1960, pp. 242–291.

Aids for Part V

AUDIO-VISUAL MATERIALS

FILMS

Accent on Learning, Ohio State University (30 min., b & w). Illustrates different teaching methods and the work of the teacher. [13]

Adventure in Teaching, Harmon Foundation Films (20 min., color). Presents prospective teachers in metropolitan classrooms. [13]

American Teacher, McGraw-Hill (15 min., b & w). Characteristics of good teachers are reflected in the purposes and the quality of their programs of living with children. [13]

And Gladly Teach, NEA (28 min., color). Satisfactions of and opportunities in teaching. [13]

Appointment With Youth, Crowley Films (26 min., b & w). Presents the work of the teacher, conditions and satisfactions of teaching. [13]

Assignment Tomorrow, NEA (30 min., b & w). Shows teacher shortage after end of World War II. [13]

No Teacher Alone, NEA (20 min., color). Work of professional organization. [14]

Not by Chance, NEA (28 min., color). Programs of teacher education for today. [14]

Our Teacher, Mary Dean. Produced for the teaching profession by Phi Delta Kappa (22 min., color, sound). An excellent study of a likable and effective teaching personality. Shows desirable characteristics and qualities. Request from nearest Phi Delta Kappa or film bureau. [13]

Planning for Personal and Professional Development, McGraw-Hill (18 min., b & w). Case studies of four teachers and their plans. [14]

Preparation of Teachers, United World Films (20 min., b & w). Provides experiences of two future teachers and a view of what teaching is like. [14]

Teachers at Work (22 min., sound). Presents several classroom situations and teacher's work in elementary and secondary schools. [13]

Teachers for Tomorrow, University of Wisconsin (22 min., b & w). Shows a teacher education program in a university. [14]

The Teacher, Encyclopaedia Britannica Film (13 min., b & w). Reasons why a good teacher sticks to her profession. [14]

What Greater Gift, NEA (28 min., color). Shows a teacher as a professional and what is involved in modern teaching. [14]

Who Will Teach Your Child? National Film Board of Canada (24 min., sound). Shows what teaching means to different persons by a number of classroom situations; stresses importance of having good teachers. [13]

FILMSTRIPS

Let's Take a Look at Teaching, Wayne University (50 frames, b & w). An overview of teaching and what it offers. [13]

Teaching as a Career, National Film Board of Canada (47 frames, b & w). Presents the "pros" and "cons" of teaching as a career, information about opportunities, requirements, and preparation of teachers, [13, 14]

RECORDINGS

Characteristics of a Good Teacher, Educational Recording Services (30 min., 33⅓ rpm, microgroove). The characteristics and qualities of good teachers, evaluation of teaching. [13]

QUESTIONS FOR DISCUSSION

1. How do the current demands for teachers and the annual supply available relate to each other? Explain.
2. What is the current status of teaching in terms of prestige? future prospects? How do teachers rate among the professions?
3. What reasons do your former schoolmates and your college classmates give for their dislike of teaching? What use can teachers make of the reasons which students give for their dislike of teaching?
4. Do you believe that teachers should be recruited from the ablest students in the high school population? Why?
5. What can a teacher do to change the community attitudes and customs which prevent her from leading a normal social life?
6. Why do teachers fail in their work? Do the tentative answers you get indicate that the kind of person the teacher is has anything to do with success or failure?
7. Are the *best* teachers also the *best-liked* teachers? Read up and discuss.
8. Are good teachers *born* or *made*? What is personality? How is personality achieved?
9. Is it better to simply be oneself or to try to be like someone else who is popular, capable, and efficient? Explain.
10. How can the teacher keep her work from becoming monotonous, routine, and dull?
11. How much work outside of her classroom and outside of regular school hours should be expected of a teacher?
12. Do parents and pupils approve the same characteristics and qualities in teachers? Why do you answer as you do?
13. What would you like to see in a film designed to portray the work of a good teacher?
14. What has been your observation of the great teachers you have known?
15. In what ways can the importance or significance of teaching be presented? Prepare your own analysis and response to this question.
16. What is the net effect of popular stereotypes for teachers such as the TV stars, "Miss Brooks," "Mr. Novak," and the hero of a book, "Mr. Chips"?
17. Do the motives or purposes for the selection of teaching have any relation to one's success and accomplishments as a teacher? Explain.
18. What about those teachers who dislike their work? Should they continue to teach?
19. What are the indications that the general public is becoming more concerned about the need for capable teachers in our schools?
20. Why is the pay of teachers the most discussed question related to the teacher shortage? What are the trends in teacher pay?
21. What are the current trends with respect to tenure, leave policies, retirement, and other benefits for teachers?
22. What are the two sides to the question of tenure provisions for teachers?
23. What is your evaluation of the various studies that have been made of teaching ability and efficiency?
24. What is your present opinion of the value of tests that are designed to reveal aptitude for teaching?

25. Do you see any significant differences in the desirable personal qualities and/or characteristics among teachers for elementary, secondary, and higher education?

26. Do the requirements for teaching certificates in your state serve to identify the most important qualifications (characteristics) a good teacher should possess?

27. When does a teacher's education come to an end?

28. Are the satisfactions of the good teachers' work the same as those derived from other professional fields of service? Discuss fully. Why do you see it as you do?

29. How would you respond to the statement that teaching offers a good professional outlook for the decade ahead?

30. Should a future teacher take any initiative or part in planning his own program of preparation for teaching?

31. What is general education? Does it apply to teacher education? Why do you take this view? What are the big components of an individual program for growth toward teaching competence?

32. Can future teachers get more out of college experiences by trying to anticipate the outcomes needed or desired from them? What significance does your answer have?

33. How do good teachers keep from becoming complacent and self-satisfied on the job? Whose responsibility is it to provide for in-service teacher education?

34. What is a teacher's responsibility to his profession? to colleagues? Should teachers join unions? Why?

35. What do you think of the NEA "Code of Ethics of the Teaching Profession"?

IDEAS FOR INDIVIDUAL STUDY

1. Prepare a list of the characteristics of the best teachers you have had. Do the same for the poorest teacher you have known from your school experience. Compare and discuss with your classmates.

2. After you study the general lists of characteristics of good teachers in this unit prepare your own tentative list "Desirable Qualities of Teachers." Discuss with successful teachers, your instructor, and classmates.

3. Search the columns of an educational journal for several issues and study the references made by teachers to their work. Make any sound observations you can about the qualities that are indicated in your report.

4. Make a study of the comments and ideas of children about their good teachers by some appropriate means. You might do a brief survey, review the literature, or work out a way to record random remarks of pupils.

5. Prepare and give a book report upon teaching, a great teacher, or teacher's life.

6. Select the most appropriate tributes to good teachers that you can find for your notebook to use in your class discussions.

7. Prepare a revealing appreciative description of the greatest teacher you have known.

8. Make a study of the caricatures of teachers that have appeared in literature, on the stage, and in modern mass media programs. (From Ichabod Crane to Mr. Conklin in "Our Miss Brooks.")

9. On your next trip home for a weekend look up some of your former schoolmates. Mention casually that you are considering a career in teaching. When, and if, they challenge your choice of a vocation give them several good reasons for your selection of teaching. For your notebook, summarize their questions and the points which you make in reply.

10. Arrange interviews with some experienced teachers and inquire about the rewards and satisfactions which they have found in teaching. Write up their replies with your comments.

11. Find some quotations about teaching which reflect your own attitudes toward the profession and its significance.

12. Read at least one study of the characteristics and qualities of good teachers and make notes.

13. After your readings and the groups reports are completed, consolidate your own ideas about "What it takes to be a good teacher" into a master list.

14. Catalog the activities and first-hand experiences that you have had that gave you some insight into teaching. Arrange in some kind of order of priority or value. Discuss.

15. Prepare an inventory of yourself using all the known facts you have from physical examinations, health record, test scores, (mental ability, achievements, personality, etc.). Work experience and the like should be included. You may find that you know more than you thought. You may also discover some points which you need to find more about. You might call this page in your notes "An Interesting Subject" and organize the data in graphic form.

16. Try out yourself on the lists of questions and on rating scale for teachers. Analyze your ratings of yourself constructively and objectively. You might arrange your findings in 3 columns headed: *Strong Points—Undecided Items—Points for Improvement.*

17. Using all the data you have about yourself, work out your own program for self-improvement.

18. After you have read the content materials of this unit, do some careful thinking about your interest in teaching. Then, prepare a list of the *reasons* you decided to teach or not to teach, with pertinent comments.

19. Survey a number of catalogs of teacher education institutions to learn what is recommended for future teachers.

20. Make an outline or chart of desirable learnings and understandings for teachers arranged by semester and teacher education experiences that you would consider ideal.

SUGGESTIONS FOR GROUP WORK

1. Summarize a recent article upon "Teaching" from a popular magazine for a report to the group. Keep your notes upon similar reports by other members of the group.

2. Prepare a list of the "Advantages and Disadvantages of Teaching" for your notes for use in a group discussion.

3. Arrange to interview several high school or college students and formulate a list of the reasons given by them as their objections to teaching as a career. Discuss these in a group meeting noting whether any of these also appear as objections to other professions. Keep your own notes and comments upon this discussion.

4. Participate in a panel discussion on the subject "Is This A Good Time To Enter Teaching?" Keep your notes and comments from this discussion.

5. Do some research to supplement the "facts and figures" included in this unit and write up the result in your notes. Prepare, for example, comparative figures for beginning salaries in teaching and other occupations common to your community, educational requirements for entering various professions, and estimates of the

cost of college preparation for teaching as compared with that for the other professions. Other studies should be suggested to be undertaken by the group.

6. Have some class member write to your own state department and/or your state education association for any helpful publications to use in this Unit. Others should write to other states which have useful booklets. Florida has two, *Teaching As a Career,* and *What Are You Looking For?*, both published in 1953. You should find others by asking the New York State Teachers Association and other sources of this type.

7. Prepare a list of questions about the teacher crisis and the teaching profession to be used in group discussion. Keep the list in your notes together with comments upon the group discussion.

8. Investigate the findings of "Why I Teach" contest sponsored in recent years by the American Legion Auxiliary to get ideas about the motivation that leads some of our best teachers to enter the profession. Address inquiries to the National Headquarters, American Legion Auxiliary, 777 N. Meridian Street, Indianapolis 7, Indiana.

9. Review the various approaches that have been made to the study of teaching efficiency and summarize the findings.

10. Participate in a cooperative study of application forms used in school systems of your state to find what superintendents wish to know about teachers. Write up the findings in your notes.

11. Participate in some appropriate group discussion or "role playing" to identify and bring out some of the observable qualities or characteristics of excellent teachers. Devise with some classmates your own plan for doing this and give the result before your entire class group.

12. Arrange with your instructor to use the *Minnesota Teaching Aptitude Inventory* for self-evaluation purposes.

13. Form a committee to plan and use the NEA films and other visual aids on "Professional Organizations" in your class.

14. Help plan a symposium by faculty members from your college upon "What Constitutes Good Teacher Preparation?" for your class group.

15. Form a committee to view a number of films that depict good teachers at work. Compile a master list of all the ideas this gives you about ways teachers grow and improve.

16. A helpful group project would use the biographical articles and books written by teachers to find the suggestions that are made about ways to learn and grow toward competence.

17. Visit and report upon a meeting of a local PTA, or a local education association.

18. Take part in an interview with the officers of a local teacher's organization to find information about the program.

19. Have a report upon your state education association.

20. Help a group stage a skit about the professional responsibilities and work of teacher groups.

21. Take part in a panel discussion of "An Ideal Personal Improvement Program for Teachers" as a member of a discussion group on "What Good Teachers Recommend as Means of Growth."

22. Ask your instructor to help your group to study various types of teacher organizations open to teachers. Make a study of the membership dues and other professional expenditures by teachers.

23. Prepare an exhibit of current issues of professional journals and materials published by teacher's organizations and departments.
24. Take part in a study of the NEA publication "The Teacher and Professional Organizations" by a division of labor among committees with reports to entire class.
25. Participate in class discussion on questions about professional obligations: Is there any reason why teachers should not work for the improvement of the conditions under which they work? Doctors and lawyers have effective professional organizations which have been instrumental in raising professional standards and the status of their professions. Can teachers expect anyone to be more interested in their profession than they?

VI. PROSPECT

Chapter 15

The Promise of American Education

American education can be as good as the American people want it to be. And no better.

And in striving for excellence, we must never forget that American education has a clear mission to accomplish with every single child who walks into the school. Modern life has pressed some urgent and sharply defined tasks on education, tasks of producing certain specially needed kinds of educated talent. For the sake of our future we had better succeed in these tasks—but they cannot and should not crowd out the great basic goals of our educational system; to foster individual fulfillment and to nurture the free, rational and responsible men and women without whom our kind of society cannot endure. Our schools must prepare *all* young people, whatever their talents, for the serious business of being free men and women.*

Introduction

The prospects of American education are of the greatest significance to each and every one of us; the future prospects of our people and way of life are inextricably bound up in this outcome. The whole point of this relationship could be put even more strongly and simply: our future prospects depend upon the nature and quality of American education. If there is to be any future for Americans in a democratic society, our educational systems and the other agencies must provide the necessary concepts, understandings, skills, loyalties and values that characterize a dynamic constructive free society in a world and an age that faces unprecedented challenges. No one who is aware of the changing society and contemporary world scene needs to be reminded of the drastic changes and innovations that the past twenty-odd years have brought to the attention of both public officials and private citizens. Novel forces of scientific and technological discoveries and devel-

* John W. Gardner, "Goals in Education" in *Goals for Americans,* the Report of the President's Commission on National Goals (Englewood Cliffs, N.J.: Prentice-Hall, 1960), p. 100.

opments are demanding recognition even before the affluent societies have comfortably assimilated former changes and innovations. World scale political machinery and processes must be tested out and perfected at the same time that the nations are coping with domestic changes and problems of regional well-being. Forces of bygone eras flourish in national states without the counter-balancing factors of industrial, economic, and social growth that had paralleled comparable movements in Western history. The long-continued "cold war," with concomitant little shooting wars in various quarters of the globe, alternating pressures and overtures in critical hot spots, and the constant tension demanding vigilance on the part of the free world has further confused any recognizable pattern of post-war adjustment and recovery that Americans may have hoped to experience.

The contemporary social scene in these United States affords no fixed answer to the questions about the prospects of American education. A wide variety of conditions and trends contribute to unprecedented social change and educational developments. The tremendous changes in living patterns of Americans and current trends of our society may be expected to influence the school and college programs of America in a marked fashion. More people voice this view in spite of the fact that schools have always lagged behind the present and potential conditions of life and needs of the people. In the Space-Age Sixties with the increased tempo of change in our ways of living, it is imperative that the educational programs upon which people depend shall make their greatest possible contribution to individual growth and national well-being.

Various Approaches

There are several possible ways to approach the study of the future prospects and place of American education in our time. An analysis of social changes and future trends of American society should yield some helpful ideas about forthcoming educational tasks for schools and colleges. A survey of the opinions and predictions of authoritative scholars and experts would afford other pertinent challenges for the educational enterprise. Some form of a discriminating review of the educational trends, both current and emerging, should be made although it must be remembered that innovations and social changes are becoming more

abrupt and drastic in their effects, a fact that may interrupt or divert the apparent course of a trend. A consideration of some of the persistent educational problems may throw light upon the program and improvements that might be expected in American education if and when these problems are solved and removed. Tomorrow's citizens and teachers should study available experimental research findings for clues to further educational growth and improvement. The contributions of those perceptive persons with imagination and insight who have envisioned schools and colleges of the future should be considered in the light of all the other understandings and insights that we have at our command in thinking ahead to the future.

ANALYSIS OF SOCIAL CHANGE

Our analysis of social trends and changes in American life will be continued in further social science courses and study. The potential content is extensive and an illustrative example or two will have to suffice for the movement.[1] A trend that promises to materially change the living patterns of most Americans and to bring new demands and many implications upon education is the trend toward *automation*.

Automation and education

Nearly every discussion of current social change in American life refers to automation and its implications for leisure, family living patterns, economic trends and education. Anticipation of the far-reaching nature of these has occasioned various studies of the changes and effects that education should take into account. A significant discussion of this challenge sponsored by the NEA stirred a great deal of thought upon certain tentative suggestions.[2] One proposal assumed a revision of the 40-hour

[1] A helpful recent examination of changing America and its educational needs is by Solon T. Kimball and James E. McClellan, *Education and the New America* (New York: Random House, 1962). See also a discussion of educational trends in relation to social changes by Henry J. Perkinson, "American Education: Icons and Images," *The Education Digest*, XXVIII, No. 8 (April 1963), pp. 1–5.

[2] Editors of *Education U.S.A., The Shape of Education for 1962–63* (Washington: National School Public Relations Association, NEA, 1962), pp. 19–20.

week with 36 hours of labor and 4 hours devoted to educational programs. A wide range of academic and vocational courses could be made available for selection by employees. These might be carried on a part-time basis or by full-time study for a period made possible by accumulation of the 4-hour blocks over a period of time.

Details of the many programs that will certainly materialize will have to be developed in terms of the specific conditions, needs, and resources to relate to each situation. Advance discussion is helpful in promoting awareness of the coming educational emphases for factory and office personnel and greater appreciation of some principles that should apply to programs of this type. Education will undoubtedly have a larger and more varied part to play in America as the technological revolution proceeds to the ultimate degree of completion, i.e. optimum automation of plant and office processes.

Among the new and revised concepts and views about education, several should be mentioned for illustrations. Technological change is so vast and complete that old concepts of job preparation and security are outmoded; many youth now in school will work at jobs not now provided; many others will work at three or four different ones during the working years, requiring different knowledges and skills each time. All of these facts of social change suggest characteristics of the education that the working force of America will need in the future. Education will come to be accepted as the lifelong process or activity that perceptive educators have believed it should be.

The reduced work week that will

follow universal automation may cut present working time to nearly half, thus requiring extensive programs of educational preparation for leisure time activities, interests, and living. Some see here a major need for *a second career* of non-economic nature, related to an avocational interest and possible public service contributions. Adult education will need to expand and change in its concept, content, and pattern of organization if the basic educational needs of future decades are to be met.

Vocational education of the limited, relatively fixed type that so frequently lags behind the practices and needs of industry will have to be replaced by programs that place emphasis upon transferable skills and understandings that will be generally useful in any industrial or technological field.

The arts and education

Status symbols are important clues to the values and aspiration of people in any culture. A new status symbol in the United States is seen in increased patronage of the arts according to a Stanford University research study.[3] The Research Institute found that participation in the arts was a concomitant of wealth, good education, high status jobs, and improved social position. Over 50 million Americans were considered to be active participants—500,000 amateur actors, over a million photographers, about 15 million painters and some 32 million who play some musical instrument. It appeared that fishermen are outnumbered by pianists; amateur painters equal the number of hunters; and baseball spectators

[3] *Education U.S.A.* (December 20, 1962), p. 63.

equal only half the number of concert and recital ticket holders. The Museum of Modern Art in New York ranks second only to the Empire State Building in number of visits by servicemen on leave in that city.

Many teachers can remember when interest in the arts was extremely low. They remember frequent criticism of the "fads and frills" in the curriculum by outsiders during recent decades. This is but another index of the rapidity and degree of cultural change. The school led by the teachers of tomorrow may expect equally abrupt changes in American life.

EXPERT OPINIONS AND PREDICTIONS

A number of perceptive thinkers have turned their attention upon the future prospects of and developments in society and shared their visions with the rest of us. One approach to the future of human society is provided by great visionaries who have described ideal societies as the fabulous "Utopias" you have often heard about. These extend from Plato who lived about four hundred years before the Christian era to recent science-fiction paperbacks which are available in many kinds of stores today. Some of these are forbidding forecasts of totalitarian, rigidly controlled societies in which human freedoms are nonexistent and individuals are pawns of those who control the state. Two of these have received much attention in recent years, *Brave New World* by Aldous Huxley and *1984* by the late George Orwell. Although these will chill your blood with apprehension, they may be well worth study to remind us of some of the wonderful aspects of democratic society that we take for granted. The important secondary point is that these clearly show by implication how education is intimately related to the kind of society it serves and which maintains it. The nature and quality and, above all, the purposes of that environing society make all the difference in the world!

This should suggest the significance of the ideas, the dreams, visions, and aspirations of people about our society and its future. When we ask a thinker, a scholar, or some kind of expert about predictions for the future of our nation and its education, we want them to be sincerely committed to democratic institutions and values, and to the purposes of public education.

A statement of goals for the emerging industrial age of American democracy, that followed an analysis of the sociological and technological trends of our times will do for an illustration.[4] These were expressed as thirty needs in education for our future industrial society. The needs comprised seven groups as follows: education for (1) individual excellence, (2) a society of equals, (3) a government of free men, (4) an economy of plenty and security, (5) a civilization of beauty and grandeur, (6) an enduring social order, and (7) a world community.

You can see how intimately the education for such a society will be related to its very nature and quality. A free society, highly industrialized and complex in its economic organization, with international commitments and inescapable relationships, yet flexible and adapt-able, based on democratic concepts of people and institutions, and committed to human rights and pluralistic values, must be supported and served by an education that respects these commitments and goals.

The President's Commission on National Goals, composed of some of the best thinkers and leaders of the nation, reported a challenging list of "Goals for Americans" in 1960. These begin, appropriately, with an affirmation that the well being of the *individual* must continue to be America's primary concern. The institutions of our society—economic, political, social—must contribute to the optimum self-realization of persons and enhance their opportunities to choose and realize individual goals. The list comprises well-stated goals of *equality,* the *democratic process, education* at all levels for both individual and national growth and well-being, *arts and sciences, an economic system* compatible with our political system, economic growth, technological change, agriculture, living conditions, and health and welfare on the domestic scene. Internationally, the commission presented goals that would foster an open and peaceful world (including trade policy and foreign aid), defense of the free world, disarmament, and the future of the United Nations Organization. This report on programs of action for the Sixties offers a good starting point for consideration of the future needs and opportunities of the society in which American education must make its best contribution.[5]

---

[4] George S. Counts, *Education and American Civilization* (New York: Teachers College, Columbia University, 1952).

[5] The President's Commission on National Goals, *Goals for Americans* (New York: The American Assembly, Columbia University, 1960), pp. 1–23.

Another recent statement of comparable significance may be found in the reports of distinguished panels of leading Americans published as The Rockefeller Panel Reports. This provocative series deals with the major demands, problems and needs of the times, along with the opportunities and potential before our society. Reports of the panels concerned with foreign policy, military preparedness, social and economic matters, and education have been published separately and collectively for the use of interested citizens.[6] There are other useful comprehensive works upon this general subject for the discriminatory student who is interested.

There are various reports and studies of single needs or opportunities in our society that have implications for education in the immediate future. A good example may be seen in a recent report of a committee concerned with the national manpower needs. The President's Advisory Committee has recommended that graduate degrees in mathematics, engineering, and science be more than doubled by 1970. The group proposed an annual crop of 7,500 Ph.D.'s by 1970 as compared with 3,400 in 1962 in these fields. Total cost over the seven-year period was estimated at $4.7 million.[7]

REVIEW EXPERIMENTATION AND RESEARCH

Educational experimentation and research represent a modern development and has developed during the past sixty-five years; that is to say, since the so-called scientific study of education began toward the close of the 19th century. Actually some experimenting, and the trying out of new ideas, had taken place in education long before that time.

The rapid rise of the sciences in the last century quickly led to companionate movements in the social sciences, in psychology and in education. Great minds like G. Stanley Hall were studying and developing some of the psychology upon which education was based. Although his theories are now chiefly of historical importance, they were deemed highly significant in the 1890's. Students of the great German educator, Herbart, and his associates returned to America fresh from German universities. Soon the Scientific Study of Education was on its way.

Educational historians often speak of J. M. Rice's studies of spelling errors reported to the NEA in 1897 as a milestone in educational research. E. L. Thorndike's long series of studies began shortly thereafter. The first quarter of the century saw tremendous development of research in many aspects of education; the findings are available in hundreds of reports and volumes.[8]

Obviously it would be impossible to trace the history of research in American education in an introductory textbook. Our present purpose can be served by notice of some illustrative studies which will show the rate of progress, something of the scope of their investigations, and types of research which have been utilized. As you continue your studies in education you will learn to use the literature of the field including the periodicals

[6] The Rockefeller Panel Reports, *Prospect for America* (Garden City, N.Y.: Doubleday & Co., Inc., 1961).

[7] *Education U.S.A.* (December 20, 1962), p. 62.

[8] You should learn to use the available volumes of the *Encyclopedia of Educational Research,* a standard reference work in libraries.

and reports which summarize research studies and findings.

A great group of educational psychologists may be given much of the credit for developing the scientific movement in education. Building upon the work of G. Stanley Hall, William James, and G. McKeen Cattell, the indefatigable E. L. Thorndike took the lead in developing the modern fields of educational psychology and measurement. His studies were so extensive that we can list only a few examples. He began early experimental studies with children, worked on mental testing, studied many aspects of learning, re-examined the older concept of formal discipline, and made studies of adult learning. His work led to the development of a carefully selected word list, the concept of the S-R bond (stimulus-response) and connectionist psychology, the tentative formulation of some laws of learning, and further clarification of the concept of individual differences. Thorndike had able students who carried his work further in various areas of education. While Thorndike pioneered at Columbia, Charles H. Judd did extensive research at Chicago.

Simultaneously, vast strides were being made in the fields of testing and measurement. In this country J. McKeen Cattell and Lewis M. Terman were early experimenters in areas which had been explored by the research of two French scientists, Binet and Simon. Mental measurement instruments and techniques were developed early in this century. The greatest boost for this field came during World War I when millions of young Americans were given group intelligence tests in the armed services. Scales for measuring achievement in most popular subjects appeared. Achievement

tests in the various subject matter fields were soon popularized in American education. A leading exponent of the measurement concept was William M. McCall. You should look up his celebrated statement of the theses of measurement. So many published tests have appeared that a set of huge volumes is required merely to list and briefly describe them.[9]

By the 1920's the researchers were busy in studies affecting numerous aspects or phases of education. A great number of studies of curriculum construction appeared during this period. In another decade the extensive series of state curriculum programs was developed beginning with the famous Virginia course of study early in the 1930's. Meanwhile many experiments and methods of organizing subject matter had appeared. Notable among them were the Dalton Plan, the Winnetka Plan, and H. C. Morrison's unit mastery technique. Extensive experiments with high school curricula were conducted. Research in the administration field has made extensive use of the school survey, developed by Paul Hanus and George D. Strayer, and brought numerous approaches and methods to the study of school problems.

The period between the two world wars brought a flood of studies and researches in all fields of American education. A sampling can hardly suffice to indicate its extent. Kefauver and Hand made a study of guidance in 19 high schools in 10 cities; Harold Spears studied 18 school systems to get a representative picture of outstanding curriculum development; Lehman and Witty's study of

[9] Look for the latest edition of the *Mental Measurements Yearbook* by Oscar K. Buros, another standard reference you will find in the library.

the play activities of children revealed much of interest to educators; and Rulon investigated the effectiveness of visual aids in science teaching. We can find these and many other studies readily and learn to locate reports of research in current periodicals.[10]

Research in fields related to education has provided much of the basis for some of the psychological and sociological foundations of education. Studies by physiologists, psychologists, psychiatrists, researchers in various fields of medicine, and many other specialists have given educators a sounder base for theory and practice. A few illustrative examples should suffice to show their importance: (a) Child's studies of physiological gradients in growth of organisms helped establish the organismic concept,[11] and (b) Coghill's studies which showed the importance of physiological maturation for learning.[12] Important modifications of preschool and elementary programs have followed better understanding of maturation and readiness on the part of the learner; (c) Thorndike's many studies of the effects of certain factors upon learning, and adult learning; (d) Gesell's noteworthy studies of infant and child growth and behavior;[13] and (e) the Harvard

Growth Study by Dearborn and Rothney is another illustration less comprehensive than the former. Further examples of landmarks in research included: (f) the famous Russian psychology professor, Ivan P. Pavlov, whose classic experiments in conditioning of reflexes in animals gave great impetus to further work in educational psychology;[14] (g) the extensive character education studies of Hartshorne and May revealed important implications for education;[15] (h) extensive studies by Lewis M. Terman and others of both bright and retarded children have provided background for educational programs for both groups;[16] and (i) Kurt Lewin and others studied the effects of experimentally controlled social climates upon personality and learning in groups of children.[17] A complete listing of research studies of comparable significance would comprise a lengthy roll. The famous study of social class structure in "Yankee City" by a team of anthropologists and sociologists proved to be a landmark in community study.[18] Many other studies of the class structure and organi-

[10] See for example, the *Journal of Educational Research, Review of Educational Research, NEA Research Bulletins*, and *NEA Research Reports*.

[11] C. M. Child, *Physiological Foundations of Behavior* (New York: Holt, Rinehart & Winston, 1924).

[12] G. E. Coghill, *Anatomy and the Problem of Behavior* (New York: Macmillan, 1929).

[13] Arnold Gesell, *The First Five Years of Life* (New York: Harper & Row, 1940). See also Gesell and Ilg, *The Infant and Child in the Culture of Today* (New York: Harper & Row, 1944).

[14] Brief descriptions may be found in any one of numerous psychology textbooks.

[15] Published in 3 volumes, *Studies in the Nature of Character* (New York: The Macmillan Co., 1928–30).

[16] Many references could be cited for these studies. See for example, Lewis M. Terman and Barbara S. Burks, "The Gifted Child" in Murchison's *A Handbook of Child Psychology* (2nd ed., rev. (Worcester, Massachusetts: Clark University Press, 1933).

[17] Reported in *New York Times Magazine*, December 15, 1940.

[18] W. Lloyd Warner and Paul S. Lunt, *The Status System of a Modern Community* (New Haven: Yale University Press, 1942). See also W. Lloyd Warner, *et al., What You Should Know About Social Class* (Chicago: Science Research Associates, Inc., 1949), for a concise treatment.

zation have appeared. An unusual study of the informal social structure of a high school and its community has been helpful to teachers and parents.[19]

Some of the major influences upon educational development came from extensive experimentation on a larger scale than individual research projects. This approach to the discovery and refinement of new ideas, materials and procedures is chiefly the product of the twentieth century. Much was accomplished by experimental schools here and there: the early days of John Dewey's Laboratory School at the University of Chicago, the school named for Col. Francis W. Parker and his pioneer work in that city, the Fairhope (Alabama) School, and certain laboratory schools attached to university schools of education and some private schools. Many of these developed programs that reflected some of the ideas and theories of John Dewey. By the end of the 1920's the term child-centered school had come into prominence in educational literature.[20] Several experimental schools including the Horace Mann and the Lincoln schools of Teacher's College, the Ethical Culture Schools, and the "Little Red School House," existed in and around New York City. During the period immediately preceding and after World War II many research studies and projects directed attention to certain community schools.[21]

Detailed plans for more individualized instruction were developed by a num-

ber of school systems during the early part of this century. Among these the Dalton Laboratory Plan (Helen Parkhurst and others at Dalton, Massachusetts); the Winnetka Plan (Carleton Washburne and his associates, Winnetka, Illinois); and the Gary Plan, often called the Platoon School which provided work-study-play programs for many children with a minimum plant. About this time there was much use of terms such as the project method and activity program.

Extensive programs of experimentation in education have provided for participation of many schools and schools of different types. The famous Eight Year Study of the Progressive Education Association (1930–38) included 30 high schools and some 200 colleges which cooperated in the development of new curricula and the evaluation of student progress.[22] The 30 high schools included 12 public, 12 private and 6 that were connected with teacher education institutions. The Southern Association of Colleges and Secondary Schools conducted a five year study among 33 public high schools in 11 states beginning in 1938. The most extensive undertaking in a study of elementary education was completed in 1953 by 13 Southern states under sponsorship of the Southern Association of Colleges and Secondary Schools and 6 other regional organizations. The extensive studies of Wrightstone deserve mention—all illustrations of efforts to evaluate newer instructional practices developed in elementary schools.[23] Tentative

[19] A. B. Hollingshead, *Elmtown's Youth* (New York: John Wiley & Sons, 1949).

[20] Harold Rugg and Ann Shumaker, *The Child Centered School* (Yonkers, N.Y.: World Book, 1928).

[21] Edward G. Olson, *School and Community* (Englewood Cliffs, N.J.: Prentice-Hall, 1945).

[22] W. M. Aikin, *The Story of the Eight-Year Study* (New York: Harper & Row, 1942).

[23] J. Wayne Wrightstone, *Appraisal of Newer Elementary School Practices* (New York: Teachers College, Columbia University, 1938).

conclusions indicated that newer practices resulted in equally good progress in subject matter and superior growth of children in social development. A study and its sequel afford students of American education an extraordinary opportunity to assess a school program that exemplified many concepts of progressive education. The senior class of a university high school wrote a report about their own school experiences that received wide attention. After twenty years a longitudinal follow-up study of these graduates reported upon their post-school life and progress.[24] Studies of real significance for our times have been made in the areas of intergroup understanding, emphasis upon moral and spiritual values, and in citizenship education.[25] There are many other examples which we should come to know as we become serious students of education.

One can hardly miss the significance of research in American education today. It would be putting it mildly to say that present day education would be impossible without it. We can also discern much of the developments and probable trends in American education from the research. More research is on the way and the scope of educational research is constantly being broadened. The close relationship of research in education and in other fields continues and grows stronger.

Now we can begin to see one of the problems which must inevitably be encountered. It is simply this, *How can the findings of research be more quickly utilized in our educational program?* Future citizens and teachers must provide part of the answer. One of the promising leads would be to discover what is meant by action research and to note how it is directly related to the problems and situations that are studied.

STUDY DEVELOPMENTS AND TRENDS

Trends show the way

American education has been characterized by amazing growth and change. Education in a dynamic society like ours has to change in order to maintain its essential role in the culture. One kind of indicators of changes in the near future are the trends in education. A trend may be a change just getting underway. We should watch for the trends, at least know where they are going, even better get in and help direct them in the right direction and toward desirable ends. Any interested student can make a personal survey of current educational literature and discover an impressive list of developments and trends in American education. Every aspect or field of education shows trends—administration and finance, curriculum and instruction, evaluation, guidance, student activities, school plants and equipment and even philosophies of education. We can learn a great deal by keeping up with these developments.

In administration the trend toward

[24] Senior Class, Ohio State University High School, *We Were Guinea Pigs* (Columbus: Ohio State University, 1938). See also, Margaret Willis, *The Guinea Pigs Twenty Years After* (Columbus: Ohio State University Press, 1962).

[25] See William H. Kilpatrick and William Van Til (Eds.), *Intercultural Attitudes in the Making* (New York: Harper & Row, 1947); Educational Policies Commission, *Moral and Spiritual Values in the Public School* (Washington: NEA, 1951); Educational Policies Commission, *Learning the Ways of Democracy: A Case Book in Civic Education* (Washington: NEA, 1940).

more state control rather than further local responsibility is observable. This trend is not yet removed from the status of an issue inasmuch as there are strong objections to the relaxation of local control and lack of appreciation of the kind of working partnership between state and local units that should be developed. People should not wish to lose the local sense of responsibility for education, but it is necessary to use the state's power to raise money to help areas which cannot support adequate programs of education. Further consolidation and merging of school districts into larger units with responsibility for both elementary and secondary education continues as a strong trend. The number of school districts has decreased at an annual rate of nearly 2,000 in recent years as many one-teacher schools were united into larger units.

There is a trend toward more federal aid for specific aspects of education notably in communities affected by national defense developments and in certain vocational fields. In 1958 the National Defense Education Act made federal funds available to aid states to provide guidance and counselling services, to procure aids to instruction, to improve the teaching of science, mathematics, and foreign languages, and certain other objectives. The matter of federal aid for education in general is yet in the realm of live issues, bills for that purpose have lodged in every Congress for the past forty years.

Important trends in state school administration may be observed in the tendency to have the chief state school officers selected by a state board of education rather than election by popular vote, and the establishment of the state boards as the policy-making authority in educational matters. All but three states now have such boards, and Illinois is trying to establish one by a constitutional amendment. It is important that the people have the right to designate their policy-makers on boards of education if our public schools are to serve democracy fully and effectively, and a slight trend in that direction has become evident. Ohio, for example, changed its Constitution and elected its board by popular vote in 1955.

Certain trends in elementary education are discernible to the capable observer. Enrichment of the elementary school curriculum is underway in various places. Schools have introduced foreign language study in the intermediate grades (even earlier in a few places), experimented with new mathematics content and improved the teaching of science by use of instructional aids, and direct experiences for children.

Various trends are perceptible in the field of secondary education. These may be observed in most aspects of secondary school programs. Those we may expect to find will include: (1) a continued shift to 6-3-3 plan of organization; (2) increased emphasis upon junior high schools with further study of its functions and curriculums; (3) further growth of experimental and reorganized high school programs (e.g., Melbourne, Florida, High School ungraded plan may be tried and adapted elsewhere); (5) wider use of team teaching in both junior and senior high schools; and (6) emphasis upon phases of secondary education for which NDEA funds are forthcoming (instructional materials and facilities for foreign languages, mathematics, and science; guidance and counselling services).

Evidence of consistent trends in the

improvement of salaries for teachers is unmistakable. The security of teachers improves as definite trends occur in the provision of tenure, retirement benefits, leaves of absence and sick leave. Likewise the use of the single salary schedule is a strong trend, almost an accomplished fact by now. A more recent development is the emergence of plans for merit rating of teachers but these have not been uniformly successful. Many plans have not proved acceptable to teachers' groups and an equitable, and a practicable scheme has yet to be developed and adopted by the profession.

School buildings have undergone a great transformation. No longer does the architect strive for impressive or even ornamental buildings to stand as monuments in the community. More nearly the emphasis is upon utility and flexibility—getting the most in functional use for the dollars and bonds of the taxpayer. Suburban schools feature use of space and the terrain with far-flung, blocklike structures, connected according to their function. In recent years, the pattern of metropolitan schools has begun to reflect the changing megalopolitan community. Skyscraper schools with classrooms and facilities below and apartments for rent above, have come into use. Play space makes use of gymnasiums, tops of lower wings, and the roof. A study of some recent buildings will give you a good idea of new features that make for greater adaptability of space and use for many purposes.[26] Partitions among rooms allow use of large group introduction and quick conversion to small group discussion. Individual study spaces are being provided for each group to facilitate individualized

study. Elaborate carrels with built-in facilities for TV, tape recorders, and other instructional aids are available for installation in education buildings.

New plans for school buildings that meet needs of urban centers are being developed by architects and builders of vision.[27] A new kind of schoolhouse is being planned in New York City. A 38-story skyscraper will house a school on the first eight floors and offices in the 30 upper stories. Office rental will ultimately pay off the cost of the skyscraper and leave a balance. Already, New York, Newark and Chicago have schools in buildings that also house apartments. Pittsburgh has planned convertible buildings in housing developments to be used as schools and adopted into residences when no longer needed as school facilities. Pittsburgh has long been famous for the skyscraper, Cathedral of Learning of the University of Pittsburgh.

Increasing use of instructional devices and aids and the team teaching plan are reflected in new designs for buildings and equipment.[28] Emphasis upon community use of the school plant is increasing, and this is affecting the design of school buildings. An extreme example is a high school which was built entirely below ground level to provide for fallout shelter space for the community. There is a trend toward the provision of ample playing space about school buildings of all kinds, and for use of buildings for community

[26] *Education U.S.A.* (December 20, 1962), p. 61.

[27] J. Lloyd Trump, "Places for Learning," *The Education Digest,* XXVIII, No. 6 (February 1963), pp. 16–18; see also Vern J. Schipper, "How Holland Built Its School," *The Education Digest,* XXVIII, No. 6 (February 1963), pp. 19–21.

[28] Some of this work has been done by the Educational Facilities Laboratories, New York, New York.

functions and activities. Our own study should include examination of the best planned school plants and facilities you can find.

The scope of the public education program also exhibits trends. Already a strong movement to provide junior college opportunity for all youth is under way. There is evidence that the community school and vocational education programs are showing concern for more adequate adult education programs. This bids fair to become a trend as soon as leadership continues to show the way. There is a slight trend at the other end of the educational ladder toward provision of preschool education. Kindergartens are fairly well accepted in the minds of people, but financial support and lack of capable leadership hold many districts back. Nursery schools have come into popular demand partly as a result of federally aided programs of recent years. Chief drawbacks are lack of public funds and trained teachers for schools for young children.

There is room for encouragement in all this, in the sense that an intelligent outlook upon education is growing. Gradually the view that education is a life-long process, that it does not start and stop at five or six years old and at 18 respectively, and that opportunity should be open to all who need to learn, is coming in the thinking of people. When this view is more prevalent, we shall see the community school idea in action; we shall have tomorrow's schools, and the people generally will use them.

In instruction, trends are basically different from earlier emphases on specific methods or techniques of teaching, and systematized programs for curriculum construction. A major trend is the growing use of educational television. What is popularly called team teaching is one of the recent trends that attracts much attention. Another is the growing use of programmed learning in auto-instruction devices, frequently termed teaching machines.

There is evidence of a tendency to regard the instructional program as a unitary organic situation in which teacher and pupils plan, work, learn, and evaluate together. In this process, supervision and curriculum development are not seen as separate programs but are incidental to the continuing effort to improve the educative situation. Teachers are not thought of as being supervisers but are themselves participants in the improvement of instructional programs. There is far less emphasis upon curriculum procedures or specific methods and techniques than was formerly the case. Activities or experiences that are deemed necessary, are used or provided naturally. Likewise the methods and/or techniques are used when intelligent choice indicates their fitness for the job at hand. Creative leadership for the improvement of instruction is a better concept than those that have held sway in supervision for decades.

Many specific new trends in the curriculum may be observed in schools which attempt to keep up with social trends and needs. Most attention has been given to new studies by committees of expert authorities and teachers in the revision of the basic sciences and mathematics fields in the light of new developments. The educational literature today features many accounts of citizenship practice, intercultural education, teaching about the United Nations and UNESCO, study of civil rights, programs of family living, and resource-use-education. These are trends which illustrate newer content for schools that are alert to the needs of modern society.

Those who looked at some recent textbooks used in schools we visited, must have observed something in the way of a trend. For one thing there was less dependence upon textbooks as such; more and varied materials of instruction are being used in our best classrooms. We might conclude that increased use of audio-visual aids was a trend until it is observed that this is only part of a larger one, viz. the increased use of a rich variety of instructional materials. Here and there one will note increased emphases upon hitherto neglected instruction such as driver training for 16-year-olds in high school and other safety education provisions for younger children.

Even the philosophy of education shows some discernible trends. For one thing, there is less emphasis upon *talking philosophy,* and more upon the point-of-view of what the schools do or try to do. All over the nation high schools which belong to great regional accrediting associations have made use of *The Evaluative Criteria.* The first step in that process involves a statement of the school's philosophy and objective—what it is trying to do. The faculty of the school expresses its statement of its function and is evaluated in terms of its accomplishments toward those objectives. Studies looking forward to the revision and improvement of this and other evaluation instruments are already under way. In still other places, groups of school people are developing their own approach to evaluation and the improvement of the instructional program.

We may discover that the philosophy of a school appears in many aspects or phases of its work. The concepts of democratic administration, of pupil-teacher planning, the teacher consultant approach to supervision, and the community school indicate some aspects of an emerging philosophy of education. More and more we are coming to think of a school's philosophy as it shows in action rather than in a statement no matter how plausible or pertinent it may sound. Each aspect of the school program is related to every other part, the whole being one social organism changing and moving in response to needs and opportunities.

One of the most encouraging of all trends is the strong and active interest that citizens groups have taken in studying and improving public schools during the fifties and sixties. The National Citizens Commission for the Public Schools and thousands of local community groups were instrumental in this trend of awakened interest in public education.

SCHOOLS OF THE FUTURE

Educational thinkers and leaders of vision can make something better than an educated guess about the kinds of schools and their characteristics. Some of these are made, now and then, and usually follow an appraisal of the social changes and developments that may be expected. Students of education should investigate this source for added insight and inspiration.[29] The teachers in the public school systems that produced men like John Glenn and Walter Schirra can take their

[29] See for example, *Educational Leadership,* **XVIII** (May 1960) for an excellent series on future schools; see also *Schools for the 60's* (New York: McGraw-Hill, 1963); Arthur D. Morse, *Schools of Tomorrow—Today* (Garden City, N.Y.: Doubleday & Co., 1960), and Alexander J. Stoddard, *Schools for Tomorrow: An Educator's Blueprint* (New York: Fund for the Advancement of Education, 1957).

challenge seriously. Both have pointed to the great responsibility teachers face in preparing youth for roles in the Space Age and the vastly increased knowledge that must mark each step toward the stars. Who can doubt that the school of the future must have an effective instructional program of knowledges, skills, competences, and other learnings far beyond even the best of today?

Elementary schools of the future

One leading authority in elementary education visualizes even greater changes during the next 25 years than has transpired in schools during the past quarter-century.[30] Social and technological changes will probably increase in tempo, and the climate of opinion will become more favorably disposed toward education, thus accelerating the rate still further. The schools will have support in form of interest and funds. Relatively greater amounts will be spent for research on the pressing problems that will be encountered and the findings of research will be accepted and utilized more rapidly.

Elementary school buildings are expected to be one-story structures to accommodate from 500 to 1000 pupils. Specialized facilities will include a health and psychological center, gymnasium (multi-purpose room), cafeteria, library, conference rooms for teachers and parents, and outdoors areas and a swimming pool. Work laboratories would be accessible to all classrooms with equipment for science instruction, experiments, and individual study booths (or carrels). All classrooms will have facilities for television, tape recordings, records, typewriters,

[30] J. Murray Lee, "Elementary Education: 1985," *Educational Leadership,* **XVII** (May 1960), pp. 475–479.

and auto-instruction devices. Undoubtedly, spaces would be adaptable for large-group instruction, small discussion groups, as well as individual study.

The school staff would include a full-time principal who would really work with instruction, a school secretary and secretaries for every five teachers. Teachers would have master's degrees with a specialization in some area of the elementary school program. Each teacher would serve as a resource person in his area of specialization for curriculum work, team teaching, and planning. The school will have child psychologists to work effectively with parents and teachers and individual children. Consultants in art, music, speech, and physical and special education and a school nurse would be at hand. The full-time librarian would have charge of an instructional materials center. A large room should be provided as a center for individualized instruction in foreign languages, speech correction, music, or phonics using latest equipment, tapes, and materials.

The school organization would be flexible and children would remain with a teacher for two years or more. In the intermediate grades, a variety of organizational plans may be expected. Secretarial help and television will free teachers for more strategic tasks in instruction. Science and mathematics will be taught as ideas and principles using discovery through experimentation as the approach. Social studies will profit from use of television programs. Reading programs will be more individualized. Children will have opportunity to learn a foreign language by use of modern facilities. Great emphasis will be placed upon physical and motor development of children with individualized help as needed. Likewise, the early school years, five to twelve, will be considered especially important for emotional and social development, and school experiences designed to that end. Creative experiences for children will be emphasized and teachers will be encouraged to do research on problems and needs.

Teachers and parents will work together in many study groups. The kindergarten teachers will devote part of their time to home visitation and liaison with parents. Teachers will be periodically engaged in in-service education programs to keep abreast of new content and professional developments. The schools of tomorrow will be so far beyond those of today that many features can only be imagined. They will have children and teachers looking out upon the new worlds of challenge.

Secondary schools of the future

The schools for adolescents in the 1980's will seek to help each youth: (1) to develop values that will contribute to improved behavior; (2) to learn skills required for effective participation in his social environment; (3) to achieve economic, political, scientific, and social understandings and (4) to prepare for a contribution to society in keeping with his capabilities.[31] The school curriculum of four phases is designed to foster the attainment of these goals.

Analysis of experience and values is promoted by arrangement of pupils in groups of ten that meet six hours per week. The group is led by a teacher-counsellor and explores ideas, questions, and values that members propose. Groups are relatively homogeneous as to native

[31] See Kimball Wiles, "Education of Adolescents: 1985," *Educational Leadership*, **XVIII** (May 1960), pp. 480–483.

ability but come from different economic and social backgrounds. Groups are relatively stable and membership continues throughout the school experience. Each analysis group teacher meets three groups each week.

Acquisition of fundamental skills is a far larger task in the schools of the future. Children read, spell, and compute before high school having developed these by use of autoinstruction devices in elementary schools. Mathematics, foreign languages, and many scientific fields are taught by machines and by programmed materials supervised by librarians and technicians. Students are instructed to work upon the required skills at their own rate. When ready, the student goes to the library and materials center, schedules a machine, and gets to work. Pupils may finish the skills early, but some work on these until they leave school.

Exploration of cultural heritage occupies about one-third of a student's time in curriculum development, and teachers are continually working to keep teacher materials up-to-date. Large group instruction is often used, often with films, or television to several hundred at one sitting. The school has one subject-matter specialist and an assistant for each area in this phase of the curriculum.

Specialization and creativity is the most flexible elective phase of the youth school program. Most students elect to develop a specialization. Available are laboratories, shops, studios for many special interests. Students may go to a workshop or studio or laboratory to work on an educational program of their own. Seminars of about 15 students are formed when there are enough students to compose a group. Specialized teachers are available, one to some 40 or 50 students.

School requirements and red tape have been largely eliminated. Students continue to work in high school until they have passed their college entrance examinations or get a job. Most students enter some secondary school about the age of 13; some leave early by 15 and a few linger to 20. Students are expected to complete their experiences in cultural heritage, fundamental skills, and their individual programs, based on their purposes.

The school plant exhibits much variety in size and arrangements of rooms. Analysis groups, specialized classrooms, studios, and laboratories, are smaller. Cultural heritage instruction is carried as in large halls, equipped for use of all media and instructional aids. Libraries, certain studios and basic shops are large facilities. Work cubicles (or carrels) are provided for individualized study.

Funds for schools for adolescents are generally provided by the Federal government and educational opportunity for all adolescents is virtually guaranteed no matter his place of residence, class orientation, economic status, or any other factor. The secondary school of the 1980's reflects the comprehensiveness found necessary when the nation recognized that the interests and needs of all youth should be taken seriously.

Unfinished Business in Education

Vantage points for surveying the future prospects of American education may be reached by surveys of the unfinished tasks that are before the schools and people. The successful completion of these needs and tasks would materially affect the future of public education. Illustrative items have been selected for your consideration in three areas: (a) common criticisms of public education, (b) some continuing problems, and (c) selected imperative issues that face public education. A study of three kinds of unfinished business should give you a larger view of some potentialities for change and growth in American education.

COMMON CRITICISMS OF PUBLIC EDUCATION

It is clear that the American people have become vitally concerned about public education since World War II. One index of that concern is the great volume of criticism that has been voiced and printed during the past decade. Much of this criticism is beneficial because it can lead to improvements and to increased efforts to make schools and colleges better. Human institutions, including schools, are capable of improvement and constructive suggestions are helpful to those in positions of policy-making and leadership. In the case of public schools, helpful suggestions and constructive criticism should be accepted in good spirit by the boards of education—the people's representatives —and the school leaders they have selected. The public and the schools are better for the help that comes from friendly critics who are willing to assist in the necessary efforts to improve the situation.

It is equally clear that all criticism of public education cannot be accepted in the same manner. There are, unfortunately, a number of criticisms from sources that can only be viewed as destructive. Some of these appear to emanate from sources that lack information or real understanding of the situation; others have been the result of misinformation. These are not good, may even be destructive in their effects, but they may not be malicious or deliberate attacks upon public education. There are still other criticisms that can only be termed malicious in nature, deliberately designed to impair public confidence in and respect for public schools.

The response of lay and professional friends of public education to the various critics should be clear. The constructive criticisms should be carefully studied, evaluated, and steps taken to effect improvements that are found to be needed and practicable. A good sign is to find that the critic is willing to help in the improvement of the situation that he has criticized.

Criticisms that reflect the lack of information must obviously be met with adequate sound factual data, clearly presented that all may get the facts straight. Lack of understanding on the part of the critic calls for patient explanation and interpretation of school purposes, policies, programs, and procedures. When a common basis of information and effective communication have been established, the whole situation can be improved. There are plenty of instances of vociferous school critics that have been involved in citizens school study groups who became dependable interpreters of the educational programs.

Criticism designed to attack and obstruct the progress of public education must be met with whatever measures are necessary. It is important to make clear the source of the attack that the motivation may be known, and to meet allegations and charges with facts and evidence that are both honest and intelligible. The prelude to any response to criticism is an objective appraisal and analysis to provide a sound and informed position for those who make public schools their cause.

An NEA study of periodical literature over a 3-year period disclosed the ten most frequent criticisms of public education.[32] These are presented in outline form for convenience in planning study of this important area of unfinished business in American public education.

Critics frequently voice and write charges concerning: (1) the control of public education policy-making and those in charge of this vital matter; (2) progressive education; (3) life adjustment education; (4) school practices relating to promotions and reporting to parents; (5) the state and nature of discipline in the public schools; (6) instructional program in ancient and modern languages; (7) mathematics and science in the high school; (8) educational neglect of gifted children; (9) teaching of moral and spiritual values; and (10) the teacher education program and students. Every potential parent and teacher should investigate this type of problem for his own sake and for the confidence it should bring concerning his ability to deal with such concerns in the future.

Charge No. 1—the public schools are dominated or controlled by the professional educationists in the teacher's colleges, and schools of education, by ex-

[32] National Education Association, Research Division, *Ten Criticisms of Public Education, Research Bulletin*, **XXXV**, No. 4 (December 1957).

perts and specialists in state departments of education, the U. S. Office of Education, and the NEA, and by the superintendents of schools.

An investigation of the facts concerning this charge will undoubtedly disclose that each state has legislation to provide for the control of the public schools by boards responsible to the people. School superintendents are elected by the boards and their duties are clearly outlined by school law. The degree of efficiency and effectiveness of the work of boards and of superintendents varies with the community and among the persons who are involved. Studies of this whole matter indicate that people want to participate in the educational programs; that various lay organizations and individuals do seek to influence school policy in terms of their own interests; that most educational administrations, professors and teachers want citizens to actively participate in school studies and efforts to improve education; that school people generally respect a division of responsibility between the board and the professional administrations; and that professors of education do not control educational policy, although some of them do exercise an influence upon educational thought and practice.

Charge No. 2—that progressive education led by John Dewey has taken over public education and that this is the source of the educational crisis.

A study of this allegation should begin with learning just what progressive education *is* or *was,* a step that many who glibly discuss the subject have never taken. One might check this point for himself by asking the next ten persons who mention the term to tell him where to find the principles of progressive education spelled out so he can read them for himself. Continue the investigation of this charge by reading the studies that have been made, noting the chaotic confusion of terms and frequent oversimplifications, and reach your own opinion in the light of information, rather than bias. One of the important points to remember is that the term progressive education has been used so loosely and irresponsibly that it often refers to something someone does not like. If we take the actual principles of the Progressive Education Association as originally formulated in 1924 and restated several years later, we can reach a sound judgment as to the soundness of this charge. Progressive education, on this basis, is far from being in control of American schools. Studies of the views of teachers show they are neither progressive nor traditional but partly both.

Charge No. 3—that education for life adjustment as a movement has replaced intellectual training with a hodgepodge of soft courses and programs dealing with trivia in our public schools.

When we look into this matter we will find that it is frequently alleged that educationists prescribe life-adjustment education for the majority of high school youth deemed incapable of success in programs of intellectual content or vocational training for skilled occupations. It is stated that masses of students receive recreational-social-welfare services and adjustment by learning to conform which has supplanted the fundamental subjects. This emphasis has been responsible for lowered standards, poor performance by college freshmen, and the dilution of the high school curriculum in the opinion of certain critics.

All of this can be looked into if one can take the time to check the references. He will find that life-adjustment is a concept rather than a curriculum, subject, or a course. Only the term itself is recent. The ideal of providing education appropriate to the needs, interests, and future responsibilities of each student is part of the public school tradition. Anyone who needs evidence for this idea should look at the rate of drop outs from our high schools in many communities. Evidently something is lacking in the school experiences of many youth. Charges that academic subjects are watered down and that college freshmen are unprepared are preposterous on any general scale, although one could find some schools, public and private, in which standards might well be improved.

Charge No. 4—the competitive spirit, so necessary as a learning incentive, has been destroyed by the universal promotion of students each year and by the use of an unintelligible type of report cards to parents.

Studies show clearly that the number of schools that practice automatic promotion of all pupils annually is no larger than those that follow extremely rigid promotion standards. The trend appears to be away from either extreme to flexible policy with standards applicable to individual students. The modal practice of reporting to parents is by report card on a five-letter system, which retains some element of competition. Many school systems have experimented with various plans for improving their promotion criteria and their reports to parents. It is in the interest of the children that schools be encouraged to continue research upon policies and practices for both of these matters.

Charge No. 5—that lack of discipline in public schools is partly responsible for increased juvenile delinquency in our nation and communities.

Any study will reveal that juvenile courts have reported increased number of cases since the second world war. Certain reports of school systems indicate evidence to the same effect. On the other hand, the total number of classroom delinquents is under one percent, but they receive more publicity than the ninety and nine. The national level of juvenile delinquency is reportedly under two per cent. Unbased allegations as to single causes of juvenile delinquency such as to lax discipline are ridiculous oversimplifications but they persist. Questions about discipline should be studied carefully and honestly by those who presume to form opinions and to coach teachers and parents. Any serious study by reasonable people will lead to fewer allegations and foolish statements. The clue to an understanding of discipline should follow from an effort to answer these questions: what should we try to accomplish through discipline? and what procedure would be best in view of this pupil's background, needs, and motivation? Actually, the behavior of pupils is largely determined by that of their parents and the standards of the whole community.

Charge No. 6—that instruction in ancient and modern foreign languages is being neglected in public schools, that most public high schools do not offer modern foreign language courses.

Investigation will reveal that this type of charge, once heard quite frequently, had no sound basis in fact, and that the situation has changed materially in recent years. The comparisons of percentages of high school students who studied foreign language in 1900 with the percentage for 1957 was misleading to begin with as the two high school populations were not comparable.

Charge No. 7—that even bright pupils avoid science and mathematics and that enrollments in these courses are lower than they were two or three decades ago.

One will find the same specious comparison of percentages of pupils taking courses in 1900 and now, which we found in another subject. Those who make this allegation do not explain the facts—that only the extremely small high schools failed to offer full programs of mathematics and science courses. Actually, there have been significantly increased enrollments in mathematics and science, and new courses have been developed for use in high schools. It is possible that the criticism in this area and for foreign languages lent some impetus to their inclusion in the National Defense Education Act of 1958.

Charge No. 8—that the education of gifted children has been neglected because the instructional programs have been planned for the average child.

Examination of professional literature reveals no lack of interest in the gifted child.[33] Many public schools have made consistent efforts to produce programs for the development of the potential leaders represented in this group.

There are many that need to make improvements to this end. Our society needs the contribution of the talents and capabilities of all its youth and all schools —public and private—should never cease to work intelligently and diligently to make this possible.

Charge No. 9—that public schools do not teach moral and spiritual values.

This is a complex subject and should be studied carefully before you form your own conclusion. Much is involved here. Definitions and concepts, religious preferences, bias, and commitments enter into the picture. Too many people decide what they want before they understand the implications of this general problem. It comes down to a few questions: should the public schools accept any responsibility for character education of pupils? Most people would agree that this should be done. The next question is—How? The best answer of the public school profession is that by the Educational Policies Commission in 1951.[34] Public schools cannot teach religion; they can and should emphasize moral and spiritual values on a functional basis through choices students learn to make in actual life situations. That this can be done has been proved by a number of sound experimental programs. The usual claim by teachers that they always teach values is hard to accept. No doubt most of them try to do so, but it is all too often by mere admonition

[33] See for example James J. Gallagher, *The Gifted Child in the Elementary School*, No. 17, in *What Research Says to the Teacher Series* (Washington: NEA, 1959), or Southern Region of Education Board, *The Gifted Student*, A Manual for Program Improvement (Atlanta, Georgia: Southern Regional Education Board, 1962).

[34] *Moral and Spiritual Values in the Public Schools* (Washington: The Commission, 1951); see also Ellis F. Hartford, *Moral Values in Public Education* (New York: Harper & Row, 1951), chapters 1–5; William Clayton Bower, *Moral and Spiritual Values in Education* (Lexington: University of Kentucky Press, 1952); and Julia Weber Gordon, "Values in the Classroom," *The Education Digest*, **XXVIII**, No. 8 (April 1963), pp. 14–17.

and it is not enough. Teachers who take this responsibility seriously enough to think through the sound theoretical basis for a program of emphasis in all the experiences of the pupil can expect to make an exciting discovery. A good number of teachers have tried and it works.

Charge No. 10—that schools of education and teachers' colleges have low academic standards, admit the poorest students, and offer too many courses of doubtful value in content.

Criticisms of teacher education institutions continue from various sources, one being the schools of education themselves through efforts to strengthen the preparation programs for teachers at all levels. Teacher education is a late-comer in many universities and like all professional programs has had to struggle for acceptance by the older professional schools that have longer histories in higher education. This fact does not explain away all the charges about teacher education. Many studies have revealed that the actual number of education courses students take is far below the alleged totals. There are weak courses in some institutions of teacher education just as there are in other programs for pre-professional and professional education. It is reported that mass testing of college freshmen on a national scale has formerly yielded average score for freshmen in teacher education that were under the all-freshmen average.

Most colleges of teacher education are sincerely interested in attracting the best students possible in the hope that many will freely choose the great tradition of teaching. Our children deserve the best. Our society needs great teaching. Teacher education institutions should make their programs accordingly. In the best schools of education, students are encouraged to take a challenging course in education as part of their general education (and as a pre-professional course for those who later choose teaching). All of these will probably be parents and taxpayers; some will serve on boards of education, and some will teach. All should know and appreciate public education in this democracy of ours. Teacher education can be interesting, challenging, and mildly exciting.

Current problems and opportunities

In the lengthy catalog of unfinished business of American education, there are some perplexing problems which must be solved if our schools are to make progress. Problems, as used here, refer to questions which remain after the basic issues have been pretty well agreed upon but which still require action, money, or work to become effective. There is not much question but that the American people desire reasonable equality of educational opportunity. The big problem is how it shall be financed, one that involves two or three basic issues. The working out of the details of the problem must depend upon the resolution of these big issues.

Recent public opinion polls indicate that a majority of our people desire federal aid for education *without federal control*. On the other hand, some influential organized groups are strongly opposed to any legislation to this effect. There are other vested interests that oppose any federal aid unless parochial schools share the public funds provided. The basic issue continues unresolved. The big problem of getting the legislation through Congress cannot be solved while certain constitutional issues and realistic political considerations remain.

The problem of the selection of enough capable youth for the teaching profession is another illustration. No one denies that we need teachers nor that we should have capable personnel for our schools. The problems of getting enough of the best talent into our teacher education institutions, of preparing them for today's and tomorrow's schools, and keeping enough of them in the areas of most need in the nation, still require solution.

A problem which plagues many educators and other leaders is how the schools may emphasize character education without becoming involved in sectarian arguments or violating the accepted principle of church-state separation. Various efforts in the form of released time programs, shared time plans, emphasis upon moral and spiritual values represent attempts to solve this problem. Recent decisions of the Supreme Court have clarified certain issues related to religious practices in public schools.

In some communities, schools are making attempts to ameliorate the problems of intolerance, racial bias, and religious prejudice, and discrimination by programs of intercultural education, and teaching about civil rights. The complex of problems in many metropolitan centers that lead to the disadvantaged pupil is one of the most imperative concerns of school leaders. You can find encouraging accounts of progress in this connection. Our own experiences will suggest the work needed before the problems can be solved in many communities.

There are many communities that still have problems related to the desegregation of their school systems. Notable progress has been made in most states since the 1954 decision of the Supreme Court that struck down the separate but equal facilities policy. In a few states there has been little or no effective effort. Certain communities outside the South have experienced various problems related to racial bias and segregation.

There are problems and opportunities for teaching about basic issues and questions of international relations, the United Nations, UNESCO, *the Declaration of Human Rights* and others. It appears that not enough schools are trying to meet this need.

Numerous other problems could be listed at each level of educational responsibility—national, state, and local. Even the individual school in your community has its problems. These may include the development of curricula to meet the needs of the youth of the community, to solve the problem of dropouts, greater participation of teachers in the making of school policy, or providing for wider use of the school plant by the people of the community. In any case, the problems should be on the agenda for solution by the cooperative thinking and planning of school and community leadership. We cannot dodge our share of this problem-solving. Problem-solving is life, we learn by solving problems. Learning and life are practically synonymous.

Live institutions face issues

American education faces important issues, some of general nature, others that relate to one or more level or type of school. We should not be discouraged no matter how disturbing and controversial these become since their occurrence is good evidence of life within these educational institutions. We can be sure that no dead or decadent institution is plagued by live issues and problems such as we have in education in these United States. As long as there are big issues to be settled, there is likely to be interest and effort to effect solutions and improvement.

Much has been written about the big issues of education in our time and a complete list would run to great lengths. A representative list has been compiled for purposes of illustration. As an alert student and future citizen, you will become familiar with other issues and problems in further social science and education courses. Some basic issues may be cited as follows:

1. *Shall we have a minimum program of education for the nation as a whole?* This issue has appeared in various proposals for guaranteeing equality of educational opportunity. It has been advocated in connection with various attempts to get legislation to set up a national department of education with a secretary in the cabinet and to have a national board of education. Proponents have offered many suggestions including plans for equalizing educational opportunity, the need for a coordinating agency at the cabinet level for education (separate from the public health and social security programs) and even proposals for a national body to develop curricula. Support for these proposals has been slight and there is some indication that these have caused some opposition to federal aid bills by those who see serious danger in the threat of federa control of the schools. Proposals for

a national commission on curriculum have received considerable attention. The obvious advantages must be weighted against the possibility that state and local efforts to improve curriculums would decline in view of a national norm. Public schools in the various states have shared many purposes and values, and developed many definite common characteristics, but these have been chosen, not forced, upon the schools.

2. *Shall public education be centrally controlled?* This perennial issue arises in discussions of support for education at both state and federal levels, but principally in the former. The affirmative arguments have usually stressed the possibility of greater efficiency through centralized control, the need for equalizing support among the local districts of a state, the dangers of political influence in local school administration, and the fact that some state controls in matters of certificating teachers and the like appear to be necessary. Arguments against further centralization tend to deny certain of the above claims, to point out the damages to education and to community life when local participation and responsibility is removed, that errors and mistakes in a centralized system are far more costly and dangerous, that state political machines are more dangerous than local politics, and that the removal of local controls is undemocratic.

The same type of debate follows proposals for federal aid to public education viz., whether this would result in loss of control of the states over their public school systems. In other words, can we accept needed help from an outside source, yet keep the controls at home?

We should continue to study such

basic issues as these for ourselves. Right now it would be unwise to attempt to decide on an all-or-none basis. There is much to be said for the idea of a working partnership of the local, state, and federal governments to maintain an adequate system of schools for the children of all citizens.

3. *Shall public education be broadened or lengthened to provide opportunity for people of all age levels?* This basic issue will be involved in proposals about educational programs you will hear more frequently as you continue your studies. While this issue is not always brought out explicitly, it is implied in many attempts to establish preschool programs, to enrich elementary school curricula, to enlarge the exploratory function of the junior high school, and to broaden the offerings of the senior high school, to initiate the community junior college, and to provide adult education opportunities at public expense. Many people give lip service to the idea that education should be a lifelong process and to the accentuated need for re-education in the new age of automation and space. When it comes to the establishment of programs and the financial support of added educational opportunity, the matter appears to be an issue not yet settled.

4. *Shall private and sectarian schools participate in public funds for education?* This basic issue has been a factor in the violent debates over federal aid legislation. A few states have used the child benefit argument to permit the limited use of public funds for a single purpose such as to provide free textbooks or to transport pupils to and from parochial schools. In practically all states it is illegal or unconstitutional to use

public funds for nonpublic schools and institutions. All future parents and teachers should be informed about recent Supreme Court decisions which relate to this issue and study certain federal aid proposals which would leave this problem up to the various states. Some proposals for federal aid bills have been designed to find ways to make either grants or loans or both to church-related and other nonpublic schools and colleges. The whole principle of separation of church and state has become somewhat obscured by the strategic moves and propaganda campaigns of vested interests upon this constitutional issue.

5. *Shall the high school provide for the educational needs of all youth?* This issue exists regardless of statements to the contrary. Legally all normal youth of high school age have the right to attend secondary schools. The fact that offerings of many high schools are so limited as to meet the needs of only a part of the school population prevents the reaching of the goal to which most school people give lip service. Barriers of economic nature, and some social factors, still prevent some youth from completing a high school education. The large number of dropouts shows that we are not yet beginning to meet this issue. An important sub-issue of this is whether we have made an honest effort to meet the needs of our gifted children. Certainly, programs that can be truly called comprehensive are not the general rule despite the findings of notable study groups and leading spokesmen like Dr. James Bryant Conant. Yet there are some excellent high schools fit to be models for others.

6. *Shall we provide a different kind of education for ablest pupils?* This issue keeps bobbing up in various forms in

many of our communities. A frequent proposal is to provide special college preparatory high schools for pupils with "high I.Q.'s". The same viewpoint is reflected in the questions and responses that follow biased descriptions of continental systems of secondary education. Most Americans would reject the idea of class education at both elementary and secondary levels. The very philosophy that bids our schools minister to the needs of all pupils should inspire our high schools and elementary schools to challenge and help our academic-minded and gifted students to realize their potentialities for growth. Right now only a few schools even try; all too often planning for the mediocre (meaning middle) group sets the pace for all classes.

Dr. Conant had much to say on this at the final dinner of the National Citizens Committee for the Public Schools at Cleveland, January, 1956: "Schools are *failing to recognize the talents of their pupils* in the *early years of schooling*," Dr. Conant stated. "Somehow the *talents that exist in the youth of each community must be brought to the surface*." He thought some of the difficulty pupils have with the study of *mathematics* in school stemmed from our neglect to identify *those pupils* with *more than the average aptitude for mathematics* at an early age, and teach them accordingly. If such pupils were identified and stimulated to proceed at top speed with their studies, a large group of the incoming freshmen in our colleges would have the necessary mathematical aptitude to handle *physics and chemistry* courses with both enthusiasm and success according to this view. This is a good illustration of this practical issue.

This is an issue that could be resolved if American teachers could find ways to make good their verbal commitments to the philosophy of helping each pupil to reach his full potential.

7. *Should the schools teach controversial issues?* This can be put in different form: shall teachers have academic freedom? This question brings in another; shall we expect teachers to be objective, to practice intellectual honesty? We probably see little reason why this should be debatable, but there are some groups and individuals who object to teaching controversial issues, even in college and university. Some others would prefer to have only one side or viewpoint of an issue taught. Those who appreciate the freedom to use their intelligence as widely as possible will need to be alert to this issue in the educational institutions and public forums of our society. Citizens must understand that academic freedom for teachers is necessary for students to have full access to all approaches to truth, i.e. full freedom to learn.

8. *Should public schools teach religion or stress moral and spiritual values?* This is one of the significant and pressing issues before the people of many communities. There are various pressures from ethnic and religious groups both *pro* and *con* on the teaching of religion. The school people have long since generally accepted the policy that the secular curriculum should continue to prevail in the school for all children but that the public school should emphasize moral and spiritual values without teaching religion. The report of the Educational Policies Commission represents the policy of the teaching profession but there

are some critics who are not satisfied with this policy. In some communities there are sharp controversies over religious observances and even instruction in schools maintained by public funds.

9. *How shall we achieve quality education?* This sincere concern of many thoughtful citizens has not been answered conclusively. Many efforts have been made to spell out what it would take (and cost) to provide quality education for all boys and girls. The total cost in dollars for adequate facilities, good equipment and capable teachers would reach an impressive figure. This is the kind of information the general public can evaluate and think about. When people see this is necessary, the general climate of public opinion becomes favorable. People say "If money alone will get a quality school we can have it." Unfortunately, this does not get to the full significance of the issue. Some questions about the quality of education raised by individuals and groups are not answered in terms of dollars and cents. This fact tends to keep this general question open as an issue before the American people.

10. *What should be taught to children who will live in an Age of Space?* This perennial issue, briskly debated and argued since the days of Aristotle, continues to demand attention, especially in periods of significant social change and times of national emergency. The successful launching of the first "Sputnik" by the Russians October 4, 1957 touched off a prolonged and violent debate over the *content* and the quality of American education—from kindergarten through graduate study. Positions range all the way from those who maintain that the curriculum should be the same for all

people in any age to those who despair of anticipating what tomorrow's citizens will need and therefore counsel that we teach for adaptability. As we read, we will find advocates of the "Great Books" curriculum, those who would stress essentials or the perennial concerns and materials, revised proposals concerning liberal education, and a host of specific suggestions for practical subjects, vocational education and technical studies for the new ages in which we live. Developments of the Atomic Age and the entrance into the Space Age have led to intensified emphasis upon mathematics and sciences in schools and colleges. Foreign languages, long a weak area in secondary and higher education curriculums, have received unprecedented attention in this country. In midst of these new emphases, there are serious questions and cautions about neglect of the humanities and social sciences. In recent years, these questions have tended to overshadow the time-honored ones about too many frills and too little time on fundamentals.

11. *Shall teachers join labor unions?* This issue has become heightened in the postwar years of the teacher crisis and reached its climax in the 1960 and 1962 teacher strikes in New York City. Efforts to secure better salaries and to ameliorate teaching conditions have led to greater stress upon organized activity by teachers. In a small number of communities, teacher strikes have been called with indifferent results. Some contend that all teachers should enter the American Federation of Teachers and thus affiliate with the American Federation of Labor-Congress of Industrial Organizations complex of labor unions. The argument is that labor

groups have usually been friendy to public education and that the sympathetic support of organized labor would give teachers a better bargaining position. Others believe that the NEA and state education associations can undertake and carry out vigorous efforts to improve the professional status and pay of teachers by means of professional negotiation with school boards. The latter view holds that teachers should retain their strong strategic position by refusing to affiliate with labor pressure groups and continue to work through their own professional bodies. They point to the success of other professional groups as support for their argument. It has been noted that teachers can hardly be free to teach some controversial issues in economics as they would be if they were in an organization affiliated with labor, that they should not favor either side. The 1962 NEA Convention at Denver took vigorous steps to reiterate the strengths of the professional type organization. The issue is still live and unresolved. Certain communities have recently experienced successful negotiations of contracts between school board and local education associations.

12. *Shall the schools follow or lead society?* This is one of the most discussed questions in the philosophy of education. It has been debated for years and the controversy continues. You will encounter it in other places and hear it debated in many circles as you continue your education.

Some Practices of Promise

Practices that offer good results plus the promise of better showings yet-to-come represent an intriguing set of factors in the puzzle presented by our attempt to assess and predict future developments in American education. At best, any approach will include a great deal of educated guesswork, possibly some wishful thinking, and a certain amount of reliance upon tentative evaluations of current practices that are deemed best calculated to grow in use and usefulness. The number and variety of potential practices of promise that might be named, is such that a rigid selection has to be made. The following items have been designated with a view to the selection of representative practices in a number of areas of education which meet the criteria of potential growth and utility.

The promising practices have been grouped under headings of improvement of instruction, curriculum developments, experimentation and research, and the extension of educational opportunity, all of which are considered to be significant in the American educational scene of the Sixties.

ACCENT ON IMPROVED INSTRUCTION

Concern about American education has been evident in many segments of our society. There has been the conscientious concern of school leaders that public education in our time should measure up to its responsibilities and role. The hysterical flareup of irresponsible criticism and the scapegoating that followed the

Sputnik period inspired much honest and realistic appraisal of our schools and colleges. Thousands of citizen's study groups have investigated one or more phases of public education during the past 15 years. Numerous efforts to find adequate school support in communities across the nation and national organizations alike have stressed that Americans must have quality education. This has been voiced at every level of interest and concern from the Pine Grove community center to the Educational Policies Commission; from the Jefferson County Board of Education to the Congress, the President, and the Supreme Court of the United States. Quality education implies improved instruction; some developments and practices show promise.

Use of autoinstruction devices

A spectacular innovation of the Fifties was the introduction of programmed learning following the development of teaching machines by Skinner and others. Programmed learning offered individual instruction by use of a pre-planned program of learning steps, in an appropriate sequence and graduated in terms of difficulty. Ideally, the subject matter was carefully planned in detail by steps, definite and comprehensible, by expert teachers and published in a form that could be presented by a device (machine), one step at a time. The students could read, make a response to a question or test item, and get an immediate reward or correction by merely pushing a button or turning a knob. This principle of reinforcement was calculated by Skinner to provide the motivation needed for continuing work in programmed learning. A wide variety of devices were developed

for the educational market and many publishers embarked upon publication programs of planned courses and subjects. In the course of a few years a large number of offerings in programmed learnings for use in teaching machines have appeared and their use has increased significantly. A more appropriate term for this new instructional approach is that of autoinstruction devices.

Certain advantages have been claimed for this type of learning program. The machines and programmed learnings provide devices for pacing individual instruction to fit the rates of speed and ability of different pupils. It is capable of use in many areas of subject matter and facilitates swift, accurate learning. The planned simplification of content makes it possible for pupils to deal with certain subject matter at an earlier age. This type of program lends itself neatly to new comprehensive approaches to instruction such as team teaching. One phase of team teaching stresses individual study by pupils according to their interests, needs, and abilities. Some of this can be provided by choice of programmed learning materials and use of appropriate teaching machines.

Autoinstruction devices are not free of disadvantages.[35] There are subjects and content that must be oversimplified and limited for purposes of presentation. Certain outcomes of learning, not readily measured and evaluated, are not realized by sole use of autoinstruction devices. There remains some of the problems of

[35] Joachim F. Wohlwill, "The Teaching Machine: Psychology's New Hobbyhorse," *The Education Digest,* **XXVIII,** No. 6 (February 1963), pp. 5–8; see also John F. Feldhusen, "Taps for Teaching Machines," *The Education Digest,* **XXVIII,** No. 9 (May 1963), pp. 11–13.

relatively greater expense and the resulting effort to provide more economical and simpler devices by competitors. Claims of manufacturers and publishers have sometimes been extravagant and some disillusionment has followed. The most important question is the implication for educational policy, namely how shall we guarantee the intellectual honesty and integrity of the programmer. The autoinstruction devices present and teach what is put into the program by the programmer; a propagandist could ask no greater opportunity. This point bears watching by the teaching profession, the parents, the competing publishers of textbooks and autoinstructional devices and educational authorities.

More channels for learning by ETV

Educational television in one form or another is rapidly gaining acceptance in classrooms over the nation. Estimates for 1962–63 indicated that over 6 million pupils received part of instruction by ETV. The National Association of Educational Broadcasters surveys show that an overwhelming majority of school systems intend to use ETV as early as it can be made available. Most colleges and universities contacted also indicated that ETV was or could be the means of solving some of their instructional problems. Principal handicaps now are lack of enough channels, insufficient funds to establish authorized educational television networks, lack of facilities for ETV reception, and need for teacher preparation in use of ETV programs.

Experimentation with ETV utilizes four types of installations and systems of transmission into the classrooms.[36] Larger metropolitan centers either have their own educational television stations, operating on an assigned regular power VHF or UHF channel or they share the use of the community's ETV channel. Six cities (Oklahoma City, Ogden, Utah, Miami, Milwaukee, New York, and Pittsburgh) each have two ETV stations.

At the other extreme small school systems in communities without television stations usually operate on closed-circuit coaxial-cable installations. This kind of installation requires no license from the Federal Communications Commission but it affords no ETV for the community outside the school buildings. Two well-known systems of this type are Hagerstown, Maryland, and Anaheim, California.

The low-power broadcast station with minimum equipment and low cost has proved its usefulness to both schools and the community of Richardson, Texas, for more than three years. This system operates on a UHF channel with FCC license. The open circuit television makes it possible for any home to watch ETV by use of an inexpensive converter. Public interest developed to the point where plans for future adult education and community interests programs are under way.

A new type of on-air closed-circuit (microwave) system has been put into use. This low-powered, low-cost type of transmission, known as a "quari-broadcast" system has been tried out in Plainedge School District on Long Island. This

[36] Harold Wigren, *et al.*, "Which ETV for Your School System?" *NEA Journal*, **LII**, No. 2 (February 1963), pp. 40–42, 62.

involves use of a low-power transmitter (probably 10-watts power), operating in a reserved UHF band (either 1990–2110 or 2500–2690 megacycles), with receiver-converters in each school to take the signal and convert it to any of the conventional channels, and ordinary receivers in each classroom. This system gives some advantages of closed circuit TV, but allows more flexibility at low cost. The Plainedge experiment is being watched and studied by responsible authorities in both education and communications (mass-media) fields.

Spectacular developments in the establishment and operation of the Midwest Program of Airborne Television Instruction and its operation since 1961 have stimulated growth in a six-states area of the Midwest. A large number of states have enacted legislation and appropriated public funds to establish state-wide ETV networks. The school boards, administrators, and faculties must be prepared to make sound decisions and plans concerning this versatile new source of help for our progress of instruction.

Problems of use of ETV have moved principally into the realm of practical considerations—cost, expediency, and feasibility of various installations. Whether ETV is to be used or not has been largely resolved as an issue. There are still the realistic problems of planning, installing, and operating whatever systems best fit the school system and the community's pocketbook.

The educational policy presents another problem. Teachers and citizens must resist the urge to proclaim ETV as the solution to many instructional problems. Actually, the soundest use of ETV

is the selection of it by teachers when it can accomplish a specific teaching job. ETV should be a means to a greater end than the teacher can accomplish without it. Many programs have effectively demonstrated the wisdom and soundness of this approach.

Team teaching is sound strategy

An old definition of strategy is using what you've got. It is in this vein that the struggle of a new approach to teaching becomes clear. Team teaching was originated in a few schools willing to experiment with and try out ideas for making the most effective use of the talents and strengths of the faculty and to provide the best instruction for all the pupils.[37] As the concept has worked out in practice, there are three major phases to the approach: large group instruction, small groups for discussion and other activities, and individual study upon projects related to the pupils' interests and needs. The list of high schools that pioneered in early efforts to develop the idea of a versatile attack upon instructional problems should constitute an honor roll in American education. Extension of this

[37] See Arthur D. Morse, *Schools of Tomorrow—Today* (Garden City, N.Y.: Doubleday & Co., Inc., 1960), pp. 9–25, for an interesting account of this plan that began in the Franklin Public School of Lexington, Mass., in 1957. See also, J. Lloyd Trump and Dorsey Baynham, *Focus on Change, Guide to Better Schools* (Chicago: Rand-McNally, Inc., 1961), for extended explanation of the whole project of the National Association of Secondary School Principals that began in 1956. See also Malcolm P. Douglas, "Team Teaching: Fundamental Change or Passing Fancy," *The Education Digest,* XXVIII, No. 9 (May 1962), pp. 49–52; and Ned Hooper, "Team-Teachers Play a Winning Game," *The PTA Magazine* (March 1961).

general approach into other levels and into large school systems has already begun.

An extensive experiment in team teaching in the Pittsburgh public schools affords further evidence of the usefulness of the idea. A three-year program begun in five elementary schools has been extended into the junior high school and a six-year high school with encouraging results. Each teaching team in Pittsburgh included a team leader, four regular teachers, a teacher intern, and a team mother (or aide for junior high teams). Teachers were assigned according to their interests and capabilities, with the load divided as nearly equally as possible. One teacher may introduce a unit of instruction to all pupils in a large group. Small groups then meet, each with a teacher, to follow up, to do research, carry out projects, or review the material. Individual pupils work upon special problems and projects. The teacher intern assists teachers, participates in planning sessions, and progresses from minor assignments until he is a member of the team. A large number of interns gain this valuable experience and preparation each year, which is an excellent way for a large school system to help prepare some of the teachers it will need. The team mother (or aide) performs many non-instructional duties to relieve teachers for instruction—operate audio-visual aids, handle and distribute supplies, prepare displays and exhibits, and help with properties and construction of instructional materials.

Teams meet weekly or oftener to make plans. Teams are organized on a grade level basis in the primary depart-

ments, and by academic subjects in the intermediate grades and junior high school. Teachers of special subjects—art, music, physical education, etc. work as a group of resource persons for the teams as needed.

Many plans and adaptations have resulted in schools that have attempted to experiment with effective ways to improve instruction. At Evanston Township High School, the large student body and faculty have been organized into major divisions—schools within the school—to facilitate individual attention that had characterized the school when it was smaller, while retaining the advantages of the large high school. There have been a number of other plans and adaptations of interest.

Teachers and parents should know the team teaching concept represents only part of the studies and findings of the study group that sponsored the early experiments. Their purpose was to study the whole complex problem of instruction in high schools of the Fifties and Sixties with a view to finding constructive ways to utilize the faculties and facilities to best advantage.

The Commission on the Experimental Study of the Utilization of the Staff in the Secondary School was appointed by the National Association of Secondary School Principals and its studies were supported by grants from the Ford Foundation and the Fund for the Advancement of Education. American education and Americans should be thankful that their traditional genius for experimentation, the willingness to try to find a better way, and the courage to change are still available in the leadership and school faculties of many institutions. This potential represents one of the most heartening clues to the promise of American education in the future.

The nongraded high school

The concept of providing a flexible, more adaptable plan of school organization has gained ground in many places in recent years, notably in the primary grades of elementary schools which have begun to establish ungraded units. This practice is growing and offers some promise that our schools may become free of the lock-step rigid organization that has come to be viewed as traditional. Actually, there is nothing canonical about the graded school. It was itself an innovation of the 19th century that replaced the traditional ungraded school from colonial days. A principal reason for the change was the view that it was more efficient and economical to provide free public education. American parents and teachers could study our educational history to advantage.

Most of the current innovations of this type are to be found in elementary schools. A novel program calculated to provide students with the opportunity to move at full capacity and speed to achieve their educational goals is the so-called nongraded high school of Melbourne, Florida.[38] Sponsors of this plan view the conventional graded organization as an anachronism of the past, a hand-down from the *gymnasium* of the

[38] B. Frank Brown, "The Non-Graded High School," *Phi Delta Kappan,* **XLIV,** No. 5 (February 1963), pp. 206–209; see also John I. Goodlad, "Inadequacy of Graded Organization," *The Education Digest, ***XXVIII,** No. 9 (May 1963), pp. 8–10.

late middle ages. Some see the possibility that many intellectually respectable high schools will experiment with nongraded programs in the immediate future.

The Melbourne High School reclassifies pupils on the basis of their achievement rather than according to number of years and promotions they have experienced. Nationally recognized standardized testing instruments provide the basis for this classification. The plan for continuous learning provides for youth to be placed temporarily in learning situations called phases from which they can move, any time this is indicated. A phase is defined as a stage of development with a varying time element. Students remain in a phase for varying periods depending upon their progress in achievement.

Most students are placed in phases as follows:

Phase 1. Studies centered around needs for remedial work;

Phase 2. Subjects of study concerned with basic skills;

Phase 3. Subjects typically included in an average education;

Phase 4. Subjects available for students who wish to achieve education in considerable depth;

Phase 5. Subjects open to students who will assume responsibility for their own educational progress and who plan to exceed course boundaries.

There is another phase—"Q"—to which only those students with creative talents are admitted. The "Quest" phase of the curriculum, which encourages individual fulfillment, fosters curiosity, stresses research, and creative efforts. The student may spend from one to three hours daily in "Quest." Certain non-academic subjects that do not relate to student progress are placed in another category—phase X—e.g. physical education and typing.

Students are phased in various subject fields according to their performance in achievement measures. A typical schedule might show that a given pupil attends courses in English (Phase 1), mathematics (Phase 3), world history (Phase 2), biology (Phase 3), physical education (X), and typing (X). Another might be in phases 4 or 5 in English, mathematics, a science, social studies, and a foreign language *plus* a special interest advanced course in Phase "Q."

Implementation of the nongraded organization and grouping of students into classes by phases has brought some departures from traditional practices. There is no standard class size. Typing classes have been enlarged to fit the largest available space; phase 1 courses in English and mathematics are each given double periods daily until pupils progress in achievement to a higher standard; and the whole schedule is characterized by flexibility. One of the chief values is that a greater degree of versatility is made possible in the school's instructional program. Another is the rewards that derive from seeing pupils progress at a rate more clearly geared to their abilities, needs, and interests. This plan came from within the school and has occasioned no larger budget than for the conventional organization.

A versatile approach to reading

Among the cacophony of charges and criticisms of American education in the postwar era was that pupils were not being taught to read, that the wrong method was used, and that the return to the use of phonics was the answer. An extended acrimonious conflict has received much attention during the past decade or so. Proponents and opponents of the various approaches have held forth. Many books and still more articles have appeared. Textbooks have been blamed for many shortcomings, shallow content, limited vocabularies, class bias and other faults. The whole-word recognition approach, popularly called the look-say method has been denounced and defended with equal intensity. Reading clinics have flourished and more centers of this type have been established by teacher education institutions. After several years the controversy has not ended.

As a contribution to the improvement of the situation, the Carnegie Corporation sponsored a conference of the leading reading specialists to seek a consensus upon the problem and to recommend constructive action. Twenty-eight of the nation's authorities met with Dr. James Bryant Conant as chairman, for this purpose early in 1962. The group included many authors of popular textbooks, reading consultants, and other experts. After deliberation they agreed, with one partial dissenter, on a report, published under title, *Learning to Read.*[39]

The report focused upon the prin-

[39] *Learning to Read: A Report of a Conference of Reading Experts* (Princeton, N.J.: Educational Testing Service, 1962).

cipal charge made by attacks upon modern reading instruction in our schools, namely that phonics are neglected for the look-say method. The conference denied that schools primarily use the sight-word approach, also that most schools do not teach phonics. The principal finding of the group was that good reading instruction involves a composite procedure, using the best methods that are available from experimental research, theory, and sound good sense of experienced teachers.

The experts agreed there was no single best way for people to learn to read nor a single best method to teach them to read. The best teacher wisely makes use of all the techniques available and selects from all available tools in adapting procedure to the needs of the different learners. As pupils are individuals, with many individual differences, so are their interests and needs in learning, and this applies to their learning to read.

The conference report approved the readiness concept but noted that reading activities had most value for those children who are immature, slow in perception, limited by handicaps or meager backgrounds, no reading program should be rigidly maintained at cost of delay for those pupils who have started to read on their own, or for those who are ready to start. A challenging section of the report urged teachers to remember that pupils come to school with desire and expectation of learning to read. Teachers should capitalize upon this desire immediately— by simple reading if necessary, but reading in any event.

The experts believed that reading could not be taught entirely by exclusive use of the look-say method. They also considered phonics (phonetic analysis) one of the essential skills that children need to identify unknown printed words. This is necessary for children to become discriminating, efficient, and self-reliant readers.

The conference had some unusual significance. It should tend to clarify and terminate the long drawn-out battle of reading matter about the teaching of reading. Certainly, it was encouraging to find so many of the nation's top reading experts ready to formulate a comprehensive philosophy about the methodology of reading instruction. The strategy of the sponsoring foundation appears to have been timely and appropriate.

A study reported by an outstanding authority bears out the view that superior achievement in reading depends upon highly differentiated and enriched instruction.[40] The report compares reading instruction in Lynnfield, Massachusetts, with a nearby school system in "Town X," both of which used the same basal reading system. Factors in the instructional programs of the two school systems were comparable.

The only important difference was the approach to the teaching of reading. Teachers in Lynnfield began with a variety of activities and testing and started actual reading instruction at once. In "Town X" the early weeks were devoted to the reading readiness program and more dependence was placed in teaching sight words. Teaching was in large groups and the same instruction for all. The difference in teaching philosophy was

[40] Editors of *Education, U.S.A.,* "Reading in Lynnfield—and in 'Town X'," *The Shape of Education for 1963,* pp. 25–29.

evident. At Lynnfield supervisors believed that every child could learn to read the first year if the instruction was appropriate, with suitable materials, and procedures selected according to needs. The viewpoint in "Town X" stressed the lack of readiness of many children, counselled waiting, casual learning, and time. Reading failure was explained as due to immaturity and emotional problems. Lynnfield teachers counted strongly upon the desire of children to learn to read and their enjoyment of successful learning. Success proved to be effective therapy for emotional problems.

Reading performance proved convincing. At the end of the first year, 51% of the Lynnfield pupils read above the third level but only 5% of those in "Town X" reached this point. No Lynnfield pupil ranked below 1.5 (primer) but 28% of "Town X" pupils did. The average achievement in reading was 3.2 and 1.9 for Lynnfield and "Town X" respectively. Experiments such as this have attracted much attention to the possible greater use of public school programs in teacher education.

DEVELOPMENTS IN CURRICULUM CONTENT

The postwar period has been characterized by a strong accent upon research and development of new content and revised curriculums at various levels. A sampling of the views of elementary and secondary school principals has disclosed their belief that the new emphasis upon content of the curriculum represents the most important development in our schools in recent years. The new content in science and mathematics was especially

noted, also the renewed emphases in the fundamentals—reading, writing, and arithmetic. The other changes of the past five years that were deemed important were emphasis on subject matter, shifting of subjects into earlier years of the school program (such as foreign languages into intermediate grades), grouping for more purposes and types of instruction, team teaching, educational television, also of other technological devices for instruction and communication, and the use of teacher aides and other means to conserve teacher's time for instruction.

Most principals believed the aroused public interest (and alarm) after the Sputnik episode had the major influence in making the changes. Other important influences upon the instructional programs were: stricter college admissions standards, criticisms by individuals and lay groups, stronger popular demands for certain changes and emphases, constructive criticism within the teaching profession, findings from testing programs, influence of citizen's study groups, and pressures from influential persons.

Changes anticipated in the Sixties included continued emphasis upon the curriculum trends now in progress, more efforts to teach American democracy (civil rights, etc.) renewed efforts to develop broad fields curriculum on problems-of-living approach, especially for non-academic pupil groups, more experimentation with subject-matter shifted to elementary years, much extended use of ETV, audio-visual aids, tape recorders, and other gadgets, and increased pressure for more work by students. The demands upon schools in future years will tend to increase the tempo or pace of their work and also of the changes therein.

One of the heartening current developments of American education is the continuing efforts and studies that are effective revision and reconstruction of the science and mathematics curriculums of the schools—elementary and secondary. The major work on this has been contributed by several working committees composed of scientists and/or mathematicians and teachers. The committees have made studies, revised course content, written new school texts and other teaching materials, pioneered in the production of teaching films and programmed materials for autoinstruction, and reconstructed these in the light of tryout and experimentation. A number of alert teachers in good school systems have provided the necessary facilities and programs of instruction for the tryouts. As a result, the schools of the Sixties and Seventies will have the option of electing new science courses with content that reflects the revolutionary concepts and theory of the past 20-odd years. The new mathematics programs offer appropriate content related to current needs and concerns all the way from the primary levels through the high school.

New content for mathematics courses

New mathematics programs have paved the way for comprehensive changes and reconstruction of courses and offerings of the secondary schools—junior and senior. Indeed, much new mathematics content has been successfully introduced into various elementary school curriculums on an experimental basis. More than half a dozen national institutional committees—groups of mathematicians

and teachers—have worked on new and revised content for courses in the secondary schools.[41] Emphasis on teaching for the basic concepts involved in mathematics and for insight into the structure of the various subjects is central to the new approaches and plans.

New approaches to science instruction

There has been a growing concern of informed persons about the widening gap between discoveries and developments in science and the contents of science courses in the schools. The postwar period has brought encouraging efforts and means that promise to fill that gap. This progress is the result of an intelligent interest on the part of some leading scientists, timely financial support from forward-looking private foundations and the National Science Foundation and an awakened public demand for constructive action. The result is a comprehensive pattern of study committees with research and development projects in all major fields of the science curriculum. Their experimental materials and reorganized content have proved their usefulness in a variety of tryout situations. It is significant to find that these projects reflect cooperative effort of scientists and teachers. Emphasis has been placed on the

[41] These include the (1) Committee on Mathematics of the College Entrance Examinations Board; (2) Secondary School Curriculum Committee of the National Council of Teachers of Mathematics; (3) The University of Illinois Committee on School Mathematics; (4) The School Mathematics Study Group, Stanford University (popularly called "SMSG"); (5) The University of Maryland Mathematics Project (junior high); (6) The Bell State Teachers College Mathematics Program; and (7) the Boston College Series (4 year program, grades 8–12).

concepts and principles that should characterize science and science instruction such as encouragement of curiosity, creative inquiry, and learning by discovery.

A variety of science courses are available that were developed by different approaches in each subject field. Biology may be approached by choice among three plans of organization developed by groups working with the Biological Sciences Curriculum Study.[42] This group of scientists and classroom teachers was set up by the American Institute of Biological Sciences, with headquarters at the University of Colorado. Biology has advanced so rapidly that the significant knowledge in this field has doubled since the end of World War II. Traditional biology courses in schools may be as much as 20 years behind the latest developments in the field.

The BSCS sponsors three teams to work on new approaches, prepare experimental texts and guides, and to arrange tryouts in selected schools. Nearly a thousand teachers are teaching some 85,000 pupils using new materials. The "green" approach to biology stresses ecological principles—living organisms and their environments; the "blue" emphasizes the origin and evolutionary development of life forms and the nature of scientific inquiry; while the "yellow" gives most attention to cells and biochemistry. About 70% of the three versions is common. All of them emphasize learning by discovery —as does the scientist. A block of time for laboratory work offers this opportunity for all. Gifted students are challenged to work on some unsolved riddles of science.

Chemistry, the traditional nemesis of generations of students, may be studied from either of two approaches. The "chemical bonds" approach was developed by the Chemical Bond Group working at Earlham College, another by the Chemical Materials Study of the American Chemical Society, and from a center in Claremont, California. Each of these has its own logical justification and its advantages.

The new approach to physics came from early work by the Physical Science Study Committee with headquarters at the Massachusetts Institute of Technology. New courses and materials developed by this approach have been used in a growing number of schools. It has been reported that at least 20% of all high school students in physics classes are now using these materials.[43]

Sponsors of the various committees and projects include the National Science Foundation, the Ford Foundation, and the Carnegie Fund. Implementation of the findings of the project committees and of the use of the new instructional materials has been chiefly by means of institutes during summer vacation periods and scholarships for a year's study (on leave arrangement) for experienced teachers. The National Defense Education Act has provided funds to enable the states to help school districts to acquire modern equipment and materials for science teaching, a feature that has made a considerable showing since 1958. There is interest in a 12-year science curriculum for the elementary and secondary schools and the National Science Teachers Association has begun work toward this objective.

[42] Editors of *Education, U.S.A., The Shape of Education for 1963*, pp. 39–41.

[42] *Education, U.S.A.,* January 24, 1963, p. 83.

In all of this variety there are some common features and characteristics. All were developed by working committees of top-rank scientists and capable teachers; all reflect a cooperative process that integrated theoretical content and teachable material. All proceed upon the conviction that science should be learned through creative inquiry rather than static rules and principles to be mastered. This is needed to produce future scientists which we shall need in ever-increasing numbers and to prepare future citizens to make better decisions about questions and concerns that involve more new scientific knowledge and implications. In other words, all of these new science programs are designed to be functional, to make a difference in the manner and level of people's living.

Teaching about communism

Teachers who have been in service only a few years can recall some marked shifts in public opinion toward the schools and the curriculum. A good illustration is the changed attitude toward teaching about communism in the schools. For some years after the war there was a strong reactionary influence in public sentiments that included opposition to teaching about communism. Recently, there has been almost a complete reversal upon this matter, and all manner of groups are calling upon the schools to teach about communism with effective programs calculated to acquaint future citizens with the real nature of the threat to the free world. Indeed there is a mild trend to provide formal instruction about communism in secondary schools.

A joint publication of the NEA and the American Legion has provided a general outline of a comprehensive course upon this general subject.[44] The report proposes use of:

(1) The long historical heritage of the rise of human liberties under law contrasted with the struggles of men under tyranny in its various forms;

(2) The philosophy and terminology of communism and analysis of key concepts—historical and dialectical materialism, and class struggle;

(3) Careful study of the constitutions, the governmental and the actual power structure in communist countries with special attention to the operation of courts and the administration of justice;

(4) Comparative studies of the economic systems and social institutions of communistic and non-communistic nations;

(5) Available documents and other evidences of the long-time communist goal of world domination, the strategy and tactics designed to that end, including operations of communists in the U.S.A.

Teachers with adequate general education background should be able to develop useful teaching units by use of the materials afforded by this set of guidelines. The report charged teachers with the responsibility for challenging youth to develop loyalty to American democratic institutions by careful examination of their freedoms, their nature, origin and significance, and of their competing ideologies. Thoughtful Americans know that democracy and our way of life can be compared with all other systems and that

[44] Editors of *Education, U.S.A., The Shape of Education for 1962–63* (Washington: National School Public Relations Association, NEA, 1962), pp. 13–14.

accurate and complete knowledge for more people is the surest foundation for deep and abiding loyalty to democracy and its institutions and values. Here, in the last half of the 20th century, is a valid use of one of Mr. Jefferson's views, namely his faith that error abroad in the land was not dangerous as long as the minds of men were free to deal with it.

EMPHASIS UPON EXPERIMENTATION AND RESEARCH

An old cliche puts the lag between a new idea or research finding and acceptance into common practice at from 20 to 50 years. Another popular impression is that teachers and school administrators have been unduly conservative folk, reluctant to accept innovations and changes. Experimentation has come and gone in many school systems without substantial improvements and modifications of the curriculum and school practices. The general public, alert to new body changes and styling in automobiles, sleek cabin cruisers, color TV sets, high-fidelity reproduction of music, and other status symbols, has been generally unimpressed and unconcerned about educational innovations if not actually antipathetic toward new developments in schools. Criticism of new school programs and of curriculum changes has mounted in recent decades to the great discomfiture of many school leaders.

The returns from educational experimentation and research have been disappointingly meager and slow until very recent times.[45] Extensive research pro-

grams were completed, and the findings published without making lasting impression upon the contemporary educational scene. American education, by and large, experienced little of the vast transformations that took place in the suburbs, industrial developments, and transportation systems of metropolitan American communities until very recent years. There appeared to be few developments comparable to the epoch-making discoveries and perfection of new techniques from research laboratories, clinics, medical research centers, and in industry during the post-war period. This was the background for and the context of a new activity and interest in certain fields of research and experimentation in American education.

A new instrument for experimentation

One reason for the greater effectiveness and acceptance of current developments and findings in public education has been the invention of new social machinery for their try-out, adaptation, and promotion. An outstanding example of this is a new setup designed to assist school people to become familiar with new research, techniques, gadgets, and ideas and to promote further tryout and improvement of same by actual school use.[46] This new program has a formidable title but it is reasonably descriptive and capable of abbreviation—the School and University Program for Research and Development, SUPRAD for short.

SUPRAD was developed by the faculty of the Graduate School of Education at Harvard in the mid 1950's to afford a

[45] A useful summary of educational research during a quarter-century may be found in "Twenty-Five Years of Educational Research," *Review of Educational Research*, **XXVI**, No. 3 (June 1956).

[46] Paul A. Perry (Editor), *SUPRAD, An Interim Report on the School and University Program for Research and Development, 1957–62 (Cambridge*: SUPRAD 1962).

practicable means of cooperation among the school system and a professional school of education in making optimum use of new ideas, research findings, and techniques. Various foundations provided initial support and the faculty arranged cooperative programs with the Concord, Lexington, and Newton school systems in the area of Greater Boston.

Research and tryout projects of schools in SUPRAD exemplified close cooperation of university and school faculties, the translation of theory into practice and patient, unhurried efforts. Noteworthy efforts to adapt and utilize new ideas and proposals were made in team teaching, use of teacher aides and lay readers, development of curriculums on contemporary affairs, and experimental use of new mathematics and science content prepared by study committees composed of top rank authorities and teachers. Experimentation with team teaching disclosed successful efforts to adapt instruction to individual differences among pupils, resulted in more effective utilization of the talents and aptitudes of the teachers themselves, gave greater recognition to superior teachers in the elementary schools (who are often enticed away to other positions), produced more work on curriculum than teachers had ever done before, and aroused pupil interest. One finding of practical significance was that team teaching could be successfully done in an older conventional school building.

Experimental use of lay readers to assist teachers of English with themes and written work brought about increased and improved writing among students and more time for other activities by regular teachers at an economical cost (four readers and supplies cost about $2,400 a year). A series of experimental tryouts of the new programmed materials in junior high mathematics showed that students learned as much mathematics as did students in conventional classroom programs, but in one-quarter of the usual time!

There were other experiments and projects that are worth learning about. One of the principal professional advantages of this program has been the advancement of the professional concept of teaching. Teachers have become more competent, they have employed the assistance of appropriate helping personnel, and public school faculties have worked side by side with university professors upon projects of great challenge and satisfaction to all. Programs like SUPRAD reinforce findings of other strong studies concerning patience, time, and dollars. These do pay off in professional dividends. This is a pattern that might well be utilized in a good number of areas within reach of an appropriate institution of teacher education.

Historians who treat of cultural changes in, and the social significance of the post-war period will have a good deal to say about education. They will have to pay some attention to the challenges and pressures that American education experienced and met in some fashion. These included continuing debate and controversy about many phases of education in the domestic scene and unprecedented number and variety of contacts and relationships on an international scale. Among the many outcomes of this involved situation were two that promised to become indispensable features of American schools of the future. One of these brought attention to the needs and potential of the gifted child with effort to provide differentiated programs to meet this challenge. The second was the emergence of experiments and programs designed to study creativity and devise ways to foster, promote, and realize this invaluable quality or what-ever-it-actually-is in individuals.

Research on creativity

Significant research has been conducted in several centers during the past decade on creativity. Reports of various studies have lent considerable encouragement to those who would have educational programs emphasize the creative potentialities of individuals. Research in creativeness in the arts at Pennsylvania State and in the sciences at Southern California has disclosed common attributes of creative persons that are distinctive as follows: sensitivity to problems, fluency of ideas, flexibility, originality, redefinition, and ability to rearrange, ability to abstract, ability to synthesize, and coherent organization.[47] Other research at Ohio State tends to substantiate findings that creativity cuts across disciplines. Substantial reports of researches on this general subject have been made from projects at Michigan, Minnesota, Chicago and by the National Merit Scholarship Corporation. Many of these separate researches tend to substantiate their respective findings.

Among the reports from various research centers and projects concerned with studies of creativity is an emerging profile of the creative mind. Tentative findings of the six-year study of the Institute of Personality Assessment and Research at the University of California describe the creative person after analysis

of several hundred architects, artists, mathematicians, scientists, writers, and others—all rated as highly creative in their respective fields.[48]

Creative persons are intelligent (but not necessarily those who score highest on intelligence tests), curious, skeptical, deeply involved in and committed to their work, independent, introverted (usually), nonconformist, may appear egotistical, usually express a "sense of destiny," and may be more interested in meanings and implications than with details. Interests of the creative persons are most likely to be common to those of other artistic, esthetic and creative fields. There is relatively little in common with people in commercial, financial, production, and service occupations.

Creative persons do not tend to be what are termed well-rounded personalities, often exhibit strong facets and interests early in life that indicate their future careers. For example, architects and mathematicians usually display talent in their fields as children even though they may not develop their careers until later. Usually they are strongly motivated and committed to what is deemed important. Esthetic and theoretical values are generally held by all creative persons, but mathematicians and artists tend to hold both in equal regard. It is believed that creative persons have the capacity to hold conflicting values or to resolve them into some larger pattern. Creative persons seem better able to express opposite sides of their nature than most people. They clearly have more tolerance for complexity, even disorder, than do people generally. Creative persons choose more

---

[47] Viktor Lowenfeld, "Current Research on Creativity," *NEA Journal,* **XLVII,** No. 8 (November 1958), pp. 538–540.

[48] Frank Barron, "Creativity—What Research Says About It," *NEA Journal,* **L,** No. 3 (March 1961), pp. 17–19.

abstract art, employ more colors and are able to achieve a higher level of order among the elements of a chaotic situation.

It is obvious that schools have often failed to discover the creative student who does not show up on intelligence tests or by consistent work. Often, they have been viewed as unsatisfactory students, not interested in group work, individualistic in preferences and goals, not concerned about conformity or grades. Some creative persons have been advised to leave conventional school programs for lack of talent. Some have not been admitted to graduate schools for lack of good grades. Yet these individuals held to the purposes and interests of most significance to them and became recognized as richly creative persons. Schools of the Sixties must learn to use more knowledge about more people with more kinds of talent with greater skill and understanding and to develop curriculums that meet their needs and interests.

The quickening interest in creativity and concern about identification of this quality in pupils have led to interesting efforts to develop ways to foster or realize this potential. Several research projects in recent years have yielded findings that help recognize the creative mind, and some means that promise to help develop "creativity." Tests designed to identify creativity showed superior performance by an experimental group after a course in creative problem solving. Two tests of qualitative nature of ideas and certain measures of personality characteristics such as dominance, self-control and the need to achieve, were included in evaluation of the study at the University of Buffalo.[49]

[49] "Developing Creativity," *Education, U.S.A.*, January 10, 1963, p. 73.

An effective technique for creative problem-solving is the principle of deferred judgment, a deliberate effort to separate idea-production from evaluation. Pupils listed every idea or fact related to the problem under study, then culled out the most important facts, set up the most important questions and sources of data and criteria for evaluating tentative solutions. The final step was the exercise of rigorous judgment, applying their own criteria, to each possible tentative solution, redoing those that best endured the testing and evaluation process.

Creative thinkers tend to produce more and better ideas. The typical student tends to accept the first plausible solution that occurs to him; the creative pupil is not satisfied with the first idea, has found by experiment that best ideas may come later. An illustration may be found in the common experience of many speakers who have been chagrined to find that excellent ideas have occurred to them hours after the speech was over.

Experimental programs and research studies on the subject of creativity and means of developing this quality in pupils should receive more attention and support in schools and colleges of the nation. The nation needs the creative talents as well as those of its gifted pupils in academic and scientific fields. These examples of current programs hold promise.

EXTENSION OF EDUCATIONAL OPPORTUNITY

The community junior college movement

The fastest-growing segment of American education is the junior college (often termed community college, or, even, the people's college) with nearly 700 units (including 250 under private control) with an enrollment of 800,000. More than four-fifths of the states (41) now have public two-year colleges and all are expected to establish one or more in the near future. About 25 new junior colleges are established each year. Students of higher education see the junior college as the most practicable answer to the impending increased college enrollment. Some estimate that ½ of all college students will be in junior colleges by 1975.

Growth problems of the junior college have complicated the role and functions of this type of institution. Four functions have been defined for junior colleges as follows:

1. transfer—two years of college work for students who will transfer to a senior college. This was the original function and some authorities stress this role as a means of freeing state institutions from need to accept all who wish to try out their aptitude for college study.

2. terminal—up to two years of college work as terminal general education for those who can profit from post-high school study in a type of program related to vocational preparation and improvement.

3. technical—technical, semi-professional programs to prepare technicians and professional assistants in various new fields; programs that require use of science and mathematic content of college grade.

4. community—serve educational needs of groups and individual adult education of the community. This may be a miscellaneous group of program offerings depending on needs and offerings as a continuing education experience.

Currently, more and more junior colleges are entering upon the community function; technical education programs are in demand and some are being established in private institutions.[50] Expansion has been rapid especially in those states that have made great strides in technological and educational growth since World War II.[51] California has approximately 70 tuition free junior colleges, the 3rd part of a comprehensive state pattern of higher education, with an enrollment of nearly 100,000. More than 20 new institutions are planned. Florida has planned to have public junior colleges within commuting distance of all high school graduates, with 25 already in operation. New York added 19 units with 40,000 students to its state university system in the past ten years or so.

The major emphases in community-type junior colleges are instruction and community service. The need for faculty personnel has been the most pressing problem. Recently, the W. K. Kellogg Fund has granted the American Association of Junior Colleges funds to support ten centers for preparing junior college administrators. Various studies of the success of junior college graduates who enter senior colleges have been made and others are in progress. Many educational groups and leaders have pointed to the junior college as the type of program most appropriate to help solve the impending college enrollments problem.

[50] T. R. McConnell, *A General Pattern for American Public Higher Education* (New York: McGraw-Hill, 1962).

[51] *Education, U.S.A.,* January 24, 1963, p. 81.

Our Commitment Is What Counts

Our thinking and planning for the future must take increasing stock of education, both from the standpoint of our democratic society and in terms of individual wellbeing. In this case, these two interests are compatible, as democracy is the social system that places greatest premium upon the individual. It is more than a neat phrase when we speak of the *uniqueness* and the *worth* of an individual; it is *the central concept of democracy*. Parents and teachers who really understand this and accept it represent the strongest and firmest support of free institutions, including the common schools, that we can expect to have. This is the note on which we should close our study of education in these United States.

In this study we have considered many important concepts and understandings, much valuable information, and developed or modified certain attitudes and appreciations. Most of these will make a difference in your future—as a good citizen, friend of public education. Certain of these may prove helpful in a possible career in teaching. If those goals have been accomplished through this study as a part of our general education, then it has been eminently well worthwhile to us, and for the state that provided most of the financial support that made college study available to you. It is our responsibility to remind each one to make the most of this phase of his general education and to follow this up by active, informed, and courageous participation in public affairs—and especially in public education—in the years ahead.

In this active informal participation, each one will exemplify the one factor that will mean the most, will be the kind of *commitment* he has made in his thinking, accepting, and acting process. We are talking about whatever it is that one has come to believe, to stand for, to be willing to protect and extend, what is most significant and worthy of one's loyalty. This is what we mean by our commitment.

As a citizen, parent, taxpayer, voter, or teacher, our most important commitment should be to the concepts and values of democracy. Our commitment to this ideal will make a difference throughout a lifetime of participation. Beside this consideration, other matters related to education and teaching shrink to lesser proportions. One might well be convinced of the value of a new approach to teaching, a better formula for planning, school support, or an improved testing instrument, all of which are good, but these will grow out-of-date, or they could be used in a social order that placed low value on people as persons. As conditions and needs change, your views of these matters must necessarily shift and vary. These are not the considerations and factors that spell the difference in the future of our way of life and of the public school as the cornerstone of a pluralistic free society.

It is to those concepts, institutions, and values that are uniquely the substance and the support of democracy (and people) that our commitment is imperatively needed. We can make it and live with it in the knowledge that we are making our optimum contribution to the best interests and the wellbeing of people, for whom democracy and all its institutions exist. As long as we are a nation and a people that believe and support a way of life that represents fullest self-realization, our commitment will be important and significant. It is imperative that we have citizens and teachers with that understanding and commitment as the support for education in these United States.

Selected Bibliography

A Parents' Guide to Teaching Machines and Programmed Instruction. New York: Center for Programmed Instruction, 1962.

American Association for the Advancement of Science, "Report on Broad Improvement in Science Education," *Science Education News* (December 1961).

American Association of School Administrators, *The High School in a Changing World, 1958,* Yearbook. Washington: NEA, 1958.

American Educational Research Association, "Twenty-five Years of Educational Research," *Review of Educational Research,* **XXVI,** No. 3 (June 1956).

Anderson, Harold H. "Creativity and Education," *College and University Bulletin,* **XIII,** No. 14 (May 1, 1961).

Association for Supervision and Curriculum Development, "Science in the School," *Educational Leadership,* **XIX** (January 1962), pp. 209–280.

Barron, Frank. "Creativity—What Research Says About it," *NEA Journal,* **L,** No. 3 (March 1961), pp. 17–19. See also pp. 20–27.

Boutwell, William D. (Ed.) *Using Mass Media in the Schools.* New York: Appleton-Century-Crofts, 1962.

Broudy, Harry S. "Teaching Machines: Threats and Promise," *Education Digest,* **XXVIII,** No. 3 (November 1962), pp. 1–4.

Brown, B. Frank. "The Non-Graded High School," *Phi Delta Kappan,* **XLIV,** No. 5 (February 1963), pp. 206–209. Description of the 7-phase program of Melbourne, Florida, High School by the principal.

Cook, Desmond L. "The Hawthorne Effect in Educational Research," *Phi Delta Kappan,* **XIV,** No. 3 (December 1962), pp. 116–122.

Current Curriculum Studies in Academic Subjects. Washington: NEA, 1962.

Department of Elementary School Principals, *The Flexible School—a Guide to School Planning.* Washington: NEA, 1957.

Drought, James. "The Friendly Teaching Machines," *Kiwanis Magazine,* **XLVII,** (December 1961–January 1962).

Editorial Feature, "Collective Bargaining and Strikes on Professional Negotiations and Sanctions," *Phi Delta Kappan,* **XLIV,** No. 1, (October 1962), pp. 1–12.

Editors of *Education, U.S.A., The Shape of Education for 1962–63.* Washington: National School Public Relations Association, National Education Association, 1962.

Editors of *Education, U.S.A., The Shape of Education for 1963,* National School Public Relations Association, National Education Association, 1963.

Editors of *Education, U.S.A., The Shape of Education for 1963–64,* National School Public Relations Association, NEA, 1963.

Finn, James D. and Perrin, Donald G. *Teaching Machines and Programmed Learning, 1962*; a survey of the Industry. Washington: NEA, 1962.

Gallagher, James J. *The Gifted Child in the Elementary School,* No. 17, What Research Says to the Teacher series. Washington: NEA, 1959.

Graham, Grace. *The Public School in the American Community.* New York: Harper & Row, 1963, chapters 2–7, 15.

Guthridge, Beatrice M. "New Trends in Today's Teaching," *Parents' Magazine,* **XXXVII** (February 1962), pp. 64, 78, 80, 82.

Leonard, George B., Jr. "Big Trouble in Our City Schools," *Look,* **XXV** (September 26, 1961), pp. 28–38.

Leonard, George B., Jr., "It's Practical to be Intellectual," *NEA Journal,* **LII,** No. 5 (May 1963), p. 31.

McConnell, T. R. *A General Pattern for American Public Higher Education.* New York: McGraw-Hill Book Co., Inc., 1962.

Mayer, Martin. "The Trouble with Textbooks," *Harper Magazine,* **CCXXV,** No. 1346, (July 1962), pp. 65–71.

New York State Education Department, *Report of Regents Conference on the Improvement of Reading.* Albany: The Department, 1962.

Overstreet, Harry and Bonaro, "The Angle of Approach," *PTA Magazine,* **LVI,** (February, 1962), pp. 4–7.

Perkinson, Henry J. "American Education: Icons and Images," *The Education Digest,* **XXVIII,** No. 8, (April 1963), pp. 1–5.

Peters, Herman J., *et al., Introduction to Teaching.* New York: The Macmillan Company, 1963, pp. 339–363.

"Reading," Special Journal Feature, *NEA Journal,* **XLVIII,** No. 3, (March 1958), pp. 159–169.

Schrawn, Wilbur. *Programmed Instruction.* New York: Fund for the Advancement of Education, 1962.

Schwab, Joseph J. and Brandwein, Paul F. *The Teaching of Science,* Cambridge, Mass.: Harvard University Press, 1962.

Stanford University, Institute for Communication Research, *Educational Television: The Next Ten Years.* Stanford, California: the Institute.

Stein, Jay W. "Matching Teachers for Your Schools," *Rotarian,* **IC** (September 1961), pp. 36–39.

Stocker, Joseph. "The Rise of the Junior College," *Kiwanis Magazine,* **XLVII,** (December 1961–January 1962), pp. 75–77, 88–91.

"Team-Teachers Play a Winning Game," *PTA Magazine,* (March 1961).

"Team Teaching," *Good Housekeeping,* **CLIII,** (October 1961), pp. 144–145.

"The Truth About Those Teaching Machines," *Changing Times,* **XVI,** (February 1962), pp. 15–18.

Tobin, Richard L. "Can Educational TV Turn the Corner?" *Saturday Review,* **XLV,** (January 13, 1962), pp. 69–70.

"Today and Tomorrow in Elementary and Secondary Education," Special Journal Feature, *NEA Journal,* **XLVII,** No. 1, (January 1958), pp. 43–113.

Torrance, E. Paul. *Creativity,* No. 28, in What Research Says to the Teacher series. Washington: NEA, 1963.

Travers, Robert M. W. *Essentials of Learning.* New York: The Macmillan Co., 1963, see chapter 15.

Warner, Ruby H. *Elementary School Teaching Practices.* Washington: The Center for Applied Research in Education, Inc., 1962, pp. 43–113.

"Worldwide Renaissance in Education," *The Education Digest,* **XXVIII,** No. 9, (May 1963), pp. 5–7.

Aids for Part VI

AUDIO-VISUAL MATERIALS

FILMS

And No Bells Ring, Part I and II (28 min. each, b & w). Presents and explains the "team teaching" approach as developed in a number of schools. [15]

Born Equal, Library Films (10 min., b & w). Interpretation of UN declaration of human rights and implications. [15]

Challenge of the Gifted, McGraw-Hill (13 min., b & w). Work of teachers who specialized in programs for the academically gifted pupils. [15]

Dilemma of Thomas Jefferson, University of Michigan (29 min., b & w). Vision that helped establish our common school system. [15]

Education for Democracy, Missouri State Teacher's Association (22 min., color). Sets forth purposes and practices of schools in democratic education. [15]

How Good Are Our Schools? CBS (28 min., b & w). Documentary produced to present findings of Dr. Conant's study of high schools. (Distributed by NEA.) [15]

I Want to Go to School, British Film Institute (32 minutes). A day in an English primary school. [15]

Learning Democracy Through School-Community Projects, Educational Film Service (21 min., color). How schools teach democratic procedures by variety of means. [15].

Meet Comrade Student, McGraw-Hill (54 min.). This is a study of schools of the U.S.S.R. based on an ABC special projects presentation. [15]

The Influential Americans, Carousel Films (45 min.). Emphasizes good teaching, new ideas, modern practices, and technological developments in our schools.

We Plan Together, Columbia University (20 min., b & w). A core program in 11th grade group. [15]

Who's Delinquent? This is America Film, distributed by McGraw-Hill (17 min., b & w). Deals with one of most serious problems of urban school systems. [15]

FILMSTRIPS

Focus on Change, NEA (28 min.). Brief presentation of team teaching approach. [15]

Focus on Quality Instruction, NEA (28 min.). Highlights from a major conference on this topic. [15]

QUESTIONS FOR DISCUSSION

1. Is there any extraordinary reason for concern about the future prospect of American education today? Explain your view.
2. What social change(s) do you envision that will have most significance for American education? Why?
3. How do you account for the increased popular interest in the arts in American life in recent decades?
4. How would you classify the various books and other futuristic writings about our society-of-the-future? Give examples of each type or class that you identify.
5. What is your estimate of any one of the fictional or analytical works that forecasts future society?

6. What fields of research have been most closely linked with educational research and experimentation?
7. What are some of the notable contributions of research in other disciplines to the field of education? Explain the significance of each.
8. Do you see evidence of any major trends, changes in types, or in the nature of research in American education over the past six decades? Explain.
9. What is meant by the term *action research?* Give examples.
10. What do you think about trends as indices and indicators of the future? Explain.
11. What are the most significant trends in education in the state of_____?
12. How much significance do you ascribe to the descriptions of schools-of-the-future? Explain your answer.
13. What are the major items of "unfinished business" of education in the state of _____?
14. How can you find reliable information about the contemporary criticisms of American public education?
15. Do you find much published criticism of nonpublic schools and colleges?
16. How should educators react to criticisms of public education?
17. What can America's educational and lay leaders of school support learn from criticisms of education?
18. What do you consider the most imperative issue(s) relating to American education? Explain.
19. Can important educational issues be settled intelligently by referendum at the polls? Discuss.
20. What is the most significant educational issue in the state of_____?
21. What practices of promise can you add to the selected examples in this chapter? Describe each.
22. What implications for education policy and in our educational philosophy do you see in the use of ETV? Programmed instruction? Team teaching? Ungraded schools?
23. What significance do you attach to the number and variety of new curriculum developments in American education?
24. Why are the new curriculum developments to be found chiefly in 3 or 4 fields of study and not in other subjects?
25. How do you account for the shift in public opinion concerning the need for teaching about Communism in American schools?
26. What current research programs appear to have most significance for future curriculums?
27. Can teachers learn to teach creativity? Discuss.
28. What are the hallmarks of the community college?
29. What are some major developments in higher education in the U.S.A.? In the state of_____?
30. What is meant by commitment? What commitments should college students make?

IDEAS FOR INDIVIDUAL STUDY

1. Read and report upon one study of the changing American culture and the implications for education.
2. Make an investigation of one area of the arts in a major city or in the state and prepare a report on the trends and future prospects.

3. Prepare a critical analysis of one of the futuristic novels about the society-of-the-future.

4. Investigate and write a paper about research in a subject field or specific phase of American education of particular interest.

5. Prepare a chronological table or chart to show the major research accomplishments in American education since 1920.

6. Write a digest of an article upon recent developments and trends in one phase of education for your notes.

7. Search the file of one educational journal for the past 5 years and make notes upon the unfinished business that you can identify from the content.

8. Choose one field of study or one type of criticism and make a thorough study of the literature on the subject. Write up your findings.

9. Make a special study and a report upon "Education of the Gifted," or "Teaching for Creativity" in American schools.

10. Write a book report upon one of the significant publications of the Educational Policies Commission (i.e. dealing with moral and spiritual values, central purpose of American education, the contemporary challenge, and the like).

11. Make a thorough study of recent Supreme Court decisions that relate to religion and public education. Prepare a special paper to be read to the class.

12. Prepare a digest of recent articles on some new development in instruction or school organization.

13. Write to manufacturers of auto-instruction devices for informational materials about the machines available.

14. Do some research upon new curriculum content in a selected subject field and prepare an exhibit to illustrate its nature and scope (i.e. what it is like and how it should be used).

15. Devote some time and study to a personal evaluation of progress and changes that have been experienced in this course. List the major understandings that can be identified.

SUGGESTIONS FOR GROUP WORK

1. Arrange for a visit to an industrial plant or other installation to observe automation that has replaced many workers. Get information about the changes and innovations that have followed.

2. Participate in a symposium on "the changing society and our future" (with several persons taking different aspects of social change and their implications for education) before the class. Keep notes.

3. Take part in a committee study to investigate the future prospects of major occupations in the light of current and anticipated social change and report the findings to the class by means of graphic exhibits.

4. Make a comparative study of the major studies and reports by official and other authoritative bodies upon the future prospects and purposes of American society and present the findings to the class by some means selected to fit the materials to be presented.

5. Arrange a series of brief reports on important research in American education since 1900 and follow with a discussion of some leaders whose contributions have been outstanding.

6. Invite some specialists to take part in a panel discussion of "current trends in American Education" before the class.

7. Participate in a group discussion on "What Features of Today's Schools Should be Preserved in Schools of the Future."
8. Arrange for a committee to study the major criticisms of American schools to get full information about each and prepare some form of presentation to bring findings to the entire class.
9. Arrange for a discussion of practicable plans for public schools to teach moral and spiritual values without giving sectarian instruction in religion.
10. Conduct a series of interviews with education and social science professors to get information upon issues in American life and education.
11. Arrange committees to collect information about the professional and other organizations of teachers for exhibit to the class.
12. Arrange to view a film on one of the newer practices of promise and follow with class discussion.
13. Participate in a committee project to investigate and report on Team Teaching, "Teaching Machines," and ETV. Prepare an exhibit of pictures and explanatory material for the class.
14. Arrange for visits to schools that have some outstanding new type program of instruction (for the gifted, teaching reading, team teaching, language laboratories, etc.).
15. Participate in arranging to visit an exhibit of instructional materials (textbooks, new curriculum materials on mathematics, science, foreign languages, etc., audio-visual aids, programmed materials and auto-instruction devices, and the like).
16. Participate in a group discussion of "What Are Our Commitments to American Education?" Keep notes.

Index